ECONOMIC DISTURBANCES AND EQUILIBRIUM IN AN INTEGRATED GLOBAL ECONOMY

ECONOMIC DISTURBANCES AND EQUILIBRIUM IN AN INTEGRATED GLOBAL ECONOMY

INVESTMENT INSIGHTS AND POLICY ANALYSIS

VICTOR A. CANTO

ANDY WIESE

ELSEVIER

ACADEMIC PRESS

An imprint of Elsevier

Academic Press is an imprint of Elsevier
125 London Wall, London EC2Y 5AS, United Kingdom
525 B Street, Suite 1800, San Diego, CA 92101-4495, United States
50 Hampshire Street, 5th Floor, Cambridge, MA 02139, United States
The Boulevard, Langford Lane, Kidlington, Oxford OX5 1GB, United Kingdom

NOTICES

Knowledge and best practice in this field are constantly changing. As new research and experience broaden our understanding, changes in research methods, professional practices, or medical treatment may become necessary.
Practitioners and researchers must always rely on their own experience and knowledge in evaluating and using any information, methods, compounds, or experiments described herein. In using such information or methods they should be mindful of their own safety and the safety of others, including parties for whom they have a professional responsibility.

To the fullest extent of the law, neither the Publisher nor the authors, contributors, or editors, assume any liability for any injury and/or damage to persons or property as a matter of products liability, negligence or otherwise, or from any use or operation of any methods, products, instructions, or ideas contained in the material herein.

Library of Congress Cataloging-in-Publication Data
A catalog record for this book is available from the Library of Congress

British Library Cataloguing-in-Publication Data
A catalogue record for this book is available from the British Library

ISBN: 978-0-12-813993-6

For information on all Academic Press publications visit our
website at https://www.elsevier.com/books-and-journals

Working together
to grow libraries in
developing countries

www.elsevier.com • www.bookaid.org

Publisher: Joe Hayton
Acquisition Editor: J. Scott Bentley
Editorial Project Manager: Katerina Zaliva
Production Project Manager: Priya Kumaraguruparan
Designer: Miles Hitchen

Typeset by Thomson Digital

Table of Contents

V

THE FINANCIAL CRISIS—A CASE STUDY

32. The Financial Crisis: Inflection Point or Black Swan?

33. The Financial Crisis: Could We Have Avoided It or At Least Minimize Its Impact?

34. The Roadmap to a Backcast

VI

CHINA—A CASE STUDY

Preface

The writing of this book is the culmination of a long journey that began in the south side of Chicago several decades ago. In retrospect, attending the University of Chicago was a great professional decision. There was no better place to be if you were an economist than Hyde Park during the early 1970's. The stars were properly aligned. The economics department and business school were full of luminaries, not only with future Nobel Prize winners but also many professors who, even though they did not win a Nobel Prize, were or would later become giants in their field. The economics and finance workshops were amazing. Anybody who was somebody in the profession either presented at the workshops or at least tried to do so. I feel fortunate to have been there. It was an amazing time.

The University of Chicago Economics department played a major role in shaping the way I view the world and interpret unfolding and past events. Although many people deserve credit, a few had a disproportionate influence in my economic education. Early on, one of the professors teaching the introductory price theory sequence made an incredible impression on me. It was none other than Gary Becker. From time to time I re-read his textbook, Becker (1971). It still amazes me how brilliant and insightful he was.

After the Becker price theory sequence, I began to focus on preparing for the core exams. As I had not majored in economics, I decided I needed to shore up my international economics. I figured that an MBA course on the subject would be what I needed to be reasonably prepared for the core. It was a decision that led me to meet Arthur Laffer, with whom I would develop a friendship that lasted many years. Laffer's lectures introduced me to the general equilibrium framework used in international economics. It piqued my interest on the subject and I followed up with Harry G. Johnson's lectures. Harry G's lectures helped me become an expert on the two-sector model.

The international economics sequence turned out to be a good and important decision for my professional career. I was introduced to the teachings of Robert Mundell, which helped me to further expand my economics portfolio in a systematic and coherent way. But that was not enough. My interest in policy led me to Al Harberger's lectures on public finance, project evaluation, and economic development. Alito, as we affectionately called him, embodied all of the characteristics that I value in an economist: great intellect combined with an ability to apply his insights and knowledge to real life problems faced by different economies. Two of his published papers had a great deal of influence in my career path. One was *The Incidence of the Corporation Income Tax* (1962). That opened my eyes to the fact that a tax on one factor of production could have a devastating impact on a completely different factor. The other paper had to do with Alito's famous welfare triangles (1964). The article illustrated what H. Gregg Lewis called a practical general equilibrium analysis. Alito's so-called "reaction coefficients" were nothing more than reduced form coefficients of the general equilibrium's response to the changes in distortions. One insightful point made in this paper was that all the properties of the traditional demand and supply curves applied to this general equilibrium-derived demand and supply curves. The Harberger approach opened my eyes to the possibility of a practical general equilibrium analysis, going well beyond the ability of analyzing the impact of tax rates and other policy shocks to an economy's equilibrium conditions. Alito had the biggest impact on my economic profession. I am really proud to be one of his boys, as his wife Anita fondly called us.

During my time in Hyde Park, the Efficient Market Hypothesis (EMH) was all the rage, so I decided to take Gene Fama's course to find out what it was all about. While exciting and interesting, the finance literature created a bit of a problem for me. Most of the presentations assumed that the individual investor was a price taker and that meant to me a partial equilibrium analysis, not a general equilibrium one. The second problem was that the finance literature did not provide a simple way in which one could link the effects of policy changes to some of the coefficients, as traditional economic analysis does. In part, that was due to the fact that EMH in its strong form assumed that all the relevant information is included in the asset prices. Therefore EMH was not amenable to establishing a relationship or link between the policy variables and the reduced form coefficients. Robert Barro's teachings and the Rational Expectations Hypothesis (REH) literature solved that problem. It showed me that one could develop a structural model, decompose the policy variables into their expected and unexpected components, and solve for the reduced form coefficients measuring the impact of anticipated and unanticipated policy shocks [1]. The introduction of adjustment costs generated some interesting dynamics that were quite different than those produced by an instantaneous adjustments to a new equilibrium. The efficient market and rational expectations hypothesis added a new dimension to my views of the world. This was a promising approach, but it created another problem. The average investor may not have the sufficient math and statistics skills to deal with such an approach. All of this brought me full circle. To borrow an H. Gregg Lewis phrase, the issue at hand was how to develop a practical general equilibrium analysis that the average investor could use, that would also be consistent with the profit maximization efficient markets/rational expectations hypothesis, while also allowing the investor to incorporate policy changes into the prospective analysis. For me, the starting point was the Harberger triangle combined with the Mundell-Johnson-Laffer monetary approach to the balance of payments was the way to go and that gave rise to our current undertaking.

The idea behind the new project was to outline a framework that combined elements of finance and international economics in a general equilibrium setting. One benefit of the practical general equilibrium analysis approach is that it allows one to weed out inconsistencies in an economic analysis, as well as identifying the inconsistencies in the policy recommendation derived from the different points of views. This insight was seared in my mind when I was a graduate student and took a summer job with the finance minister of the Dominican Republic. At the time, the finance minister assembled a group of ten economists and each one was charged with leading a different project or policy initiative. The list of projects included a group studying export promotion policies, while another group focused on import substitution policies. At a meeting with the minister, I pointed out that these two projects were inconsistent with each other. If the export promotion was successful, a general equilibrium budget constraint would suggest that imports would also rise. Think of the extreme case where everything the country produced was exported, then everything the country consumed would have to be imported. The import substitution would have the opposite effect. If in the extreme the country could produce domestically everything it previously imported, all the resources that were previously devoted to the export sector would now be employed there, and hence exports would fall. The lessons learned during my real world experience were quite powerful. I understood the importance of a general equilibrium framework. At least it helped identify inconsistencies in policy recommendations. Generalizing this insight takes us to the interesting proposition that, at the very least, general equilibrium

modeling forces one to develop a consistent view. While this does not assure that one has the correct view of the world, the process weeds out models where the explanations for the different components contradict each other or do not add up to a consistent framework. The general equilibrium approach only includes logically consistent explanations. As such, it reduces the number of possible solutions and increases the odds that one is on the correct path. It may also allow for a quick approximation of the new equilibriums that a policy shock may cause.

We hope to outline a parsimonious, yet realistic, representation of the global equilibrium conditions that could be used to derive practical insights. We begin the journey by attempting to show that many of the terms and insights developed using the modern finance literature, such as the efficient market hypothesis, are easily derived using the simple concept of demand and supply elasticities. We contend that the economic approach offers the opportunity to anticipate changes in the parameters or reaction coefficients, this in the context of the finance literature means that the macroeconomic analysis may allow us to anticipate the changes in the betas and other parameters used in the modern portfolio theory. That, in turn, may allow us to make better investment decisions. The remainder of the book contains six parts, each focusing on a different topic. The approach is a simple one; we begin with the broadest concepts such as mobility and arbitrage and as the sections progress we add additional considerations such as changes in terms of trade, the trade balance, and the balance of payments.

The organization of the different sections posed a major challenge for us. We had to choose between placing the building block chapters at the beginning or the end of the different sections. The reason for placing the building block chapters at the end of the sections is that the building block chapters describe in algebraic form many of the relationships developed in earlier chapters. The algebra and formal derivation of the different concepts may intimidate some of the readers. While the building block chapters are not necessary to illustrate the concepts formalized in the chapters of each of the sections, ignoring the building block chapters could deprive the reader from some of the additional insights generated from a formal derivation of framework building blocks. In the end, we concluded that the formal derivation of the different propositions merits placing the building blocks up front and thereby risk alienating the readers intimidated by the algebraic formulation. In each section, we label a chapter as a building block that formally develops the theoretical foundation for the component of the general equilibrium approach that we hoped to outline in the book. Collectively, the different building blocks add up to the general framework that we develop in the book. The remaining chapters in each of the sections apply the basic concept developed in the first chapter of that section to actual policy or investment issues. The hope is that these examples illustrate the applicability of the concepts in the context of the framework being developed. The last two sections of the book apply the different concepts developed in the building blocks to two different case studies: the financial crisis and Chinese economic miracle. The hope is that these two case studies show the flexibility and robustness of the basic framework outlined in the different building blocks.

Simplicity in the outline of our framework would be a virtue; the simpler the framework, the easier it is for the average investor to incorporate the basic framework into their decision-making process. We also look for a robustness and flexibility that allows the individual investor to modify the basic framework to suit their needs, as well as to allow the investor or analyst incorporating additional features that further expand the framework's capabilities. Simplicity and elegance do not matter if the model does not produce sensible outcomes. Hence, we should also add the explanatory power of the framework as a criterion of paramount importance. Next, we need to discuss the difference between the explanatory power and causality. We do not claim, nor do we represent, that the statistics and data presented in this book provide proof of a causal relationship. In many cases the relationship is assumed and all we show is that the evidence is consistent with our framework. Recall that our objective is to develop a framework that helps us make consistent choices. A framework that helps us weed out bad ideas and theories. It was our objective that the approach outlined in this book makes it easier for an investor or policymaker to analyze the impact of policy changes and other economic shocks on the overall equilibrium conditions for global and different national economies.

We foresee several possible applications of the framework. The policymakers could focus on the impact of the different policy combinations on the equilibrium values for the variables of interests such as real GDP growth, inflation, the trade balance, the balance of payments, and capital flows, among others. In turn, the investors would also add the impact on the rates of returns of the different factors across different localities. If adjustment costs are positive, the long run equilibrium will not be reached instantaneously. Knowledge of the long run and the adjustment process could be very useful to investors and the information gained from this analysis could easily be incorporated in the development of a successful investment or portfolio strategy. In short, this book summarizes much of the progress we have made over the last several decades. We do not claim to have reached the end of the road. Hopefully the user may feel, to the extent that we succeed or get closer to our goals and objectives, that we have made progress toward our final goal.

During the last decade, I have been fortunate to run into Andy Wiese. We have worked side-by-side conducting research and gathering data. We have coauthored many articles. For others that he did not coauthor, Andy was quite instrumental in their publication, preparation, and data gathering. Without him many of the publications under my authorship—including this project—would not have been possible. For that reason I consider him a coauthor.

Jaime Olmos selflessly devoted a great deal of time proofreading many of the chapters and for that we are indebted to him. We have benefited from discussion and conversations with many colleagues and friends, who in one way or another have had a major impact on how we see the world. To all of them, our sincere gratitude for allowing us to benefit from their wisdom.

Victor A. Canto
La Jolla, CA

Reference

[1] I tried this approach early on in my career, see Canto, Joines and Webb (1984). But even in a very simple model, the math gets difficult in a hurry, creating a major obstacle for most of the general population.

Introduction: Asset Allocation: Indexing, Smart Beta, and ValueTiming

According to a common saying originated with a Chinese proverb, the journey of a thousand miles begins with a single step. We have taken many steps in our quest to develop a framework broad enough to analyze the effects of global shocks to the global economy, as well as on the equilibrium relationships among the different nations of the world. With every additional step we get a bit closer to our goal. This is one more step on that quest. Our goal is to combine the best of the developments in finance literature with a general equilibrium macroeconomic framework into what we have called a ValueTiming strategy.

It has been our experience that, in general, many people trained in finance and/or economics have a compartmentalized view of the two. They behave as if the two are totally independent and there is no direct linkage between the two. Yet we know that economics is much more general and that it encompasses finance as one of its specialties. But there is more to this. In fact, we can show that many of the key concepts of modern finance as embodied in the Capital Asset Pricing Model (CAPM) [1] have a counterpart in the traditional textbook economic framework. In most cases, there is a one-to-one correspondence between the CAPM terms and some textbook economics concepts. At the risk of mixing metaphors, we are going to argue that finance and economics are two sides of the same coin. This is very important to us. What some may view as very esoteric and abstract concepts in finance literature, they may have a simple explanation in the context of traditional economic analysis. More importantly, one can develop a link between the economic shocks caused by policy changes, natural events, or innovations and the parameters used in finance literature. This allows us to relate every day issues and concepts used in the finance literature. In effect, we view this exercise as a translation of many ideas of modern finance literature into traditional, everyday economic concepts. In what follows, we use the CAPM as our version of the finance literature to illustrate the mapping or correspondence between the CAPM components and the simple textbook economic concepts.

FINANCE: ONE SIDE OF THE COIN

It is striking how little most people understood about risk as recently as three decades ago. Fortunately, developments in modern portfolio theory provide a framework for addressing the way risk can affect expected returns. We now have the CAPM, which looks at the relationship between an investment's risk and its expected market return [2]. One major insight of the CAPM is that not all risks should affect asset prices. For example, if two assets are negatively correlated and move in opposite directions, the volatility of a portfolio consisting of these two assets would be much lower than that of a portfolio consisting of only one of the assets. The latter represents an example of a risk that can be diversified away by combining it with other assets in the portfolio. If the asset does not add to the volatility of the portfolio, it should not be priced for risk, or more plainly, investors would not demand additional return or a premium over and above the current expected return.

In the context of the CAPM, the valuation of a risky asset has two components. One is the time value of money represented by the risk-free rate, R_f. It compensates the investors for placing money in any investment over a period of time. The second component calculates the amount of compensation the investor needs for taking on additional risk. This is calculated by taking a risk measure, beta (β), of the nondiversifiable risk as related to the covariance of the asset with the market, and scaling the returns of the market, R_m, by the beta measure. That is:

$$R_i = R_f + \beta^* (R_m - R_f) \qquad (I.1)$$

Hence, investors are compensated in two ways: the time value of money and their risk taking. The CAPM says that the expected return of a security or a portfolio equals the rate on a risk-free instrument plus a risk premium. Using the previous equation, one can calculate the security market line, which describes the possible combinations of risky investments that maximize the expected returns for a given level of risk, or betas, relative to the market returns. Once the security market line is calculated, investors are free to choose the risk return combinations that maximize their preferences.

The CAPM says nothing about what determines the risk-free rate (R_f), the market volatility (σ_m), or market returns (R_m). And to us, knowledge of the risk-free rate, market returns, and volatility are of vital importance to an investment strategy. Hence, to determine what drives the risk-free rate and market volatility, we need an additional theory to supplement the CAPM framework. We believe that a top-down macroeconomic approach fills the void identified in this paragraph.

In the process, as the macroeconomic views are incorporated, one may be able to find a simple explanation as to why the alpha and beta of the different asset classes may change in response to policy changes, as well as to the changing economic conditions that result from these policy changes or other economic shocks. Viewed from this vantage point, finance turns out to be a branch of the much broader economic framework. Hence, borrowing a line from a famous movie, finance should say to economics, "you complete me."

THE ECONOMIC SIDE OF THE COIN: ELASTICITIES

In the next few paragraphs, we provide a simple explanation for the links between the concepts of a beta in finance literature and an industry or firm's supply elasticities, or flexibilities to respond to different demand shocks.

In the traditional textbook presentation, inelastic industries that are unable to alter production plans easily (i.e., industries with inelastic supply) change their prices to accommodate fluctuations in demand. A classic example of an inelastic industry was the airline industry before it was deregulated in 1978. Largely because of government restrictions, airlines were unable to easily expand their supply in times of increased demand. As a consequence, when more people wanted to travel, ticket prices rose. In contrast, during tough times when people did not travel as much, ticket prices fell. For inelastic industries, profitability and share prices primarily reflect changes in demand.

Industries whose elasticities are of a smaller magnitude than the economy as a whole will not be able to adjust their supply as fast as the rest of the economy. Therefore during periods of aggregate demand increases, in relation to the overall economy, they will have to ration the increased demand through above average price increases. During periods of declining aggregate demand, the inelastic industries will experience a larger than average decline in prices. The inelastic industries will experience above average profit increases during periods of rising aggregate demand and above average declines in profitability during periods of declining aggregate demand. That is the inelastic industries will experience an above average beta.

In contrast, elastic industries will adjust their production levels to accommodate the shifts in demand with little or no impact on their relative profitability. Hence, elastic industries will have a beta similar to that of the overall market.

The economic analysis also explains negative beta stocks. All one has to think is in terms of the so-called inferior goods. These goods have a negative income elasticity of demand. That is, when the economy-wide income rises, the demand for inferior goods decline, producing a negative beta. The magnitude of the beta is directly related to the price inelasticity of supply. When all is said and done, the combination of income elasticities and price elasticities can be used to explain positive and negative betas of different magnitudes. This relationship between profits and the economy closely matches the high beta concept, a beta in excess of 1, of the CAPM that dominates much of modern finance.

These insights lead to a possible investment strategy: forecasting changes in the level of economic activity, in general economic conditions; and in aggregate demand is of critical importance for the cyclical investor. For inelastic industries, profitability oscillates with the vibrancy of the economy. Profits will rise and fall faster than the economic activity for the inelastic industries.

The knowledge of the elasticities offers the possibility of two types of investment strategies for investors. Combining the investments in industries with different elasticities will reduce the volatility of the cash flows generated by the investment. In the context of the CAPM, it reduces the riskiness of cash flows. A second strategy would be for those who can anticipate the shifts in aggregate demand. They can pursue an active investment strategy that focuses on buying the high beta during upswings and selling them during downswings, and perhaps buying the lower beta or none at all. The counterpart within the context of the CAPM is an active beta strategy. It requires knowledge or a forecast of the changes in returns of the overall market.

So far we have established a one-to-one correspondence between the CAPM and the elasticity concept. That is why we believe that they are two sides of the same coin.

ARE BETAS OR ELASTICITIES EXOGENOUS?

The empirical data shows that industry responsiveness to economic shocks is not invariant to economic regulations. Our analysis also suggests that the beta does not have to be constant over time. It can change.

The Oil and Airline Deregulation Experience: The oil price controls in the 1970s reduced the ability of the domestic industries to respond to increases in demand and we inadvertently shifted demand to the Organization of Petroleum Exporting Countries (OPEC) cartel. The increased demand for foreign oil and reduced supply elasticity at home increased OPEC's monopoly power. President Reagan decontrolled the price of oil and the beta of the oil industry declined dramatically [3].

A close look at the airline industry demonstrates this. Deregulation, by way of the US Airline Deregulation Act of 1978, changed the shape of the airline industry's supply curve. The entry of new carriers almost instantly increased competition and industry prices became more elastic. Demand, in short, was largely met with the arrival of new airlines. Once the scheduled flight was operational, independent of which airline was flying it, empty seats drove the market. With an occupancy rate below 100%, the marginal cost of filling the extra seat was very low. So competition for the marginal, "elastic" passenger pushed the marginal price of coach tickets down. The industry lost most—if not all—of its pricing power in the mass market. Fluctuations in demand following deregulation were satisfied primarily by altering production levels without the industry experiencing significant changes in profitability. In other words, there is very little correlation between the rates of returns and the level of economic activity. Though profit per unit (profitability) will remain similar, profits will rise and fall in proportion to the level of economic activity. In the context of the CAPM model, the elastic industries will have a beta close to 1. Their profits will move in line with the pace of economic activity.

The Technology Story: The absence of substitutes (i.e., inelasticity of supply or high beta and alpha) can be used to explain some of the effects of the technological revolution of the last three decades. The changes are nothing short of a miracle comparable to the industrial revolution. It is hard to imagine a world without a personal computer, the internet, or a cell phone. These technological innovations have transformed the world in which we live. They have made our lives better and for that we should be grateful to the pioneers of industry.

Most news stories about the death of Steve Jobs described him as a visionary who created products we did not know that we needed. In economic terms, this means that initially he was the sole supplier, that is, the supply was inelastic, and if we realized we needed the product, then the demand for these gadgets would explode. The innovations made Steve Jobs right; they were creating products that the market did not know they really needed, like iPads. The innovations and lack of alternatives also generated an alpha effect. Demand did explode and the gadgets made Steve Jobs iconic, as well as a very wealthy man. Looking through other segments of the industry, we have Larry Ellison at Oracle, Irwin Jacobs at Qualcomm, and Bill Gates at Microsoft. They all led companies that produced attractive and unique products, that is, inelastically supplied with positive alpha. As the demand for and use of these inelastically supplied products surged, these companies' market capitalization rose and made some of their original investors billionaires.

Once again, the supply elasticity combined with a surge in aggregate demand easily explains the success of these companies, as well as the vast amount of wealth created for their investors. While to some these increases in wealth may be excessive, people fail to take into account the improvement these products make in our lives. If one were to add the increased well-being to all the users, we would venture to say that the sum of the benefits would far exceed the net worth or increase in wealth of the creators of these products. The world is better off with these products than without them.

LINKING THE ELASTICITY CONCEPT TO CAPM AND THE BETA CONCEPT

The airline and oil industries examples show how government regulation may significantly alter the response functions of an industry to changing demand conditions. But in the same way, technological innovations and other variables can affect the supply and/or aggregate demand functions of an industry. Technological innovations can also be used to explain the measured alpha of the different industries, countries, or sectors. An increase in aggregate demand will result in an above average performance of the inelastic factors and during economic downdrafts, it would produce a below average returns for the same factors. That is, the behavior is qualitatively the same as the one generated by an above average beta.

Positive alpha industries can be characterized as both inelastic and experiencing an increase secular aggregate demand, which may come as the result of technological innovation, government regulation, or a number of other factors. Additionally, due to supply constraints, the industry will not be able to accommodate all of the increase in demand. Hence, prices will ration the available output. All of this suggests that the beta in the CAPM can be replicated by the elasticity of supply of different factors.

GLOBAL EQUILIBRIUM: THE OVERALL MARKET

In the context of the CAPM, once one knows the risk-free rate, alpha, and the beta, one has all the information needed regarding the assets and the construction of an investment portfolio. Yet the approach has some potential weaknesses.

One obvious concern with regards to the CAPM is that it provides a valuation relative to the market and risk-free rate. In fact, we know that a weighted average of all assets will add up to the market, which means that a weighted average of all the alphas is zero and a weighted average of all betas is 1. Hence, we can infer from this that any asset with a positive alpha has to have a counterpart with a negative alpha. Furthermore, a positive or negative alpha has to be temporary; otherwise investors could flock to these stocks to generate persistent returns in excess of the ones prescribed by the CAPM. The increase in aggregate demand would result in a change in the pricing of the asset class and the capitalized value of the alpha will be incorporated in the valuation of the asset class. Simply put, the argument suggests that any alpha effects will be temporary.

There is a parallel in the context of the supply and demand analysis presented here. Beta is the measure of a portfolio systematic risk in relation to the overall market, and the alpha, the measure of excess returns. Inelastic industries generate above average returns during periods of aggregate demand increases and below average return during periods of declining demand. However, we contend that competition, new entrants, capacity expansions intended to capture high and/or rising profits will have the effect of eroding or reducing the alpha, as well as the inelasticity or high betas. Put another way, competition will tend to erode the excess rates of return. Therefore, over time we expect the alphas to dissipate and the long run elasticities converge to the economy's. That is as new entrants compete in the market place, the alphas and betas will converge to the economy's long run value of a zero alpha. Any excess return will decay over time. Understanding the rate of decay may improve a portfolio's long run performance.

Another void within the CAPM is that it says nothing about what determines the risk-free rate and the overall market volatility and rates of return. We believe that this is a void that economic analysis can fill. And this belief leads us to the next point: anticipating the changes in the market rates of return and volatility, as well as the changes in the risk-free rate will impact the choices suggested by the CAPM. As such, it would impact the portfolio strategies based on the CAPM. If that is the case, then economic analysis could add a great deal of value to a CAPM-based investment strategy.

FINANCIAL ECONOMICS: THE MARRIAGE OF FINANCE AND ECONOMICS

We have shown that there is a clear correspondence between finance and economic literature and that the CAPM alpha and beta concepts can be easily explained in simple economic terms. The elasticity concept is directly related to the beta concept. Inelastic factors tend to outperform during periods of rising demand and to underperform during periods of falling demand. The alpha effect can be explained in terms of unique characteristics, that individuals can do the job of other factors of lesser skills and ability. We also argued that government regulations and taxes may also affect the elasticity of supply/the beta, and quite possibly the alpha of the different factors.

The examples previously mentioned suggest that a beta or elasticity is dependent on the economic environment. Government regulations can significantly impact the rates of returns of businesses located within their tax and regulatory jurisdiction. We have shown elsewhere that the burden of these regulations fall disproportionately on the immobile factors of production within the jurisdiction. Similarly, the decline in regulatory burden results in a disproportionate benefit on the immobile factors of production. In short, there is a location beta/elasticity that is the result of the regulatory/tax jurisdiction. There is a link between the changing environments to the policy shocks. Supply and demand elasticities, whether it is for a country, industry, or a factor of production, are determined by government regulations and economic policy.

In a world economy, the "demand" for a country or an asset class is determined in part by the sum of the monetary and fiscal policies of the world's countries. Trade policy also determines the mobility of goods and services along with factors of production across national borders. In short, regulatory, trade, and tax policies all have a part in determining the elasticity of responses to changing economic conditions.

These insights provide us with a clue as to the reaction function or how different variables respond to economic shocks, whether they are caused by government policies, innovations, or other economic shocks. The changes in the ability to respond to these shocks alter the alpha and beta of the different asset classes. This approach also suggests that explicit policy changes may alter the reaction coefficient and, as a result, the government may be able to achieve certain policy objectives. An investor who pays attention to government regulations and technological innovations may be able to anticipate industry responses to aggregate demand shocks. In doing so, he may be able to anticipate changes in the alpha and beta coefficients of the different countries, industries and from there implement a successful industry-selection strategy. By anticipating and understanding the impact of these policy changes an astute investor will be able to position their portfolio to take advantage of the impact of the policy changes in the economy.

THE CAPM: PORTFOLIO CONSTRUCTION

The attraction of the CAPM is that it offers a powerful and intuitive prediction about how to measure risk and the relation between expected returns and risk. No wonder that the CAPM has become the dominant paradigm in the asset allocation business. However, many of the implications of the CAPM are dependent on the simplifying assumptions made in the derivation. Despite its mixed empirical performance, some of which we will discuss later on, we now think differently about the relationship between expected returns and risks and how investors should allocate their investment portfolios.

According to the CAPM, the only risk that should be priced is the risk that cannot be diversified away, the residual risk or systematic risk. The CAPM is firm on this point. What should matter to the investor, therefore, is the incremental volatility on the overall portfolio volatility—not the individual investment volatility. When considering adding an asset to a portfolio, focus on two different variables is needed. The asset may impact both the portfolio return as well as the overall volatility. Hence the investor has to determine whether the incremental investment adds to the risk or volatility as well as the return of the overall portfolio. In turn, the investor then has to decide whether the incremental return is sufficient to compensate the investor for any added risk to the overall portfolio. Another way of putting the investor choices is that they must decide whether they are more concerned about their portfolio relative risk, measured as the tracking error relative to a benchmark or whether they are more concerned about their portfolio total risk, measured as the standard deviation of returns.

Nobel Prize winner Bill Sharpe has come to the rescue of investors who must perform this task. Because of him, we now have the Sharpe Ratio at our disposal [4]. This well-known formula is useful for evaluating potential investments and determining when to add additional assets to a portfolio. If a potential addition to a portfolio improves the Sharpe Ratio, the asset in question adds to the return of the portfolio over and above the return required to compensate for the increased volatility of the new portfolio. Thus, adding the asset should improve the overall portfolio performance. Needless to say, from an economic perspective, investors and market participants would prefer policies that produce an improving economy with little or no volatility; most often that is not the case. Investors must decide whether a macroeconomic policy shock's impact on total returns is sufficiently large to compensate the economy for the uncertainty and/or volatility the economy must experience as it approaches the new equilibrium. The Sharpe Ratio is tailor made to address this issue.

THE CAPM: ACTIVE VERSUS PASSIVE INVESTING

An efficient portfolio is defined as a portfolio that contains returns that have been maximized in relation to the risk levels that individual investor's desire. In a market that is in equilibrium, where the number of winners and losers must balance out, adding one additional asset class or stock does not increase the portfolio's risk return ratio. This means the portfolio containing risky assets with the highest Sharpe Ratio must be the market portfolio. In other words the market portfolio is an efficient portfolio and as such denotes a great starting point in any portfolio strategy.

The Case for Passive Investing: For those who believe that markets are in continuous equilibrium, the insight that holding the market portfolio at all times yields the highest Sharpe Ratio is an important one. Investing suddenly seems very simple; the market portfolio is an efficient portfolio. If we add to this, the assumptions of market efficiency as well as the common argument that there is not much one can do about economic shocks as one cannot anticipate most shocks and we end up with the conclusion that one cannot beat the market. We can see the argument that we are much better off as a result of the insights on risk developed by modern finance. For example, we have a very clear risk return trade-off mechanism. It is summarized in the efficient frontier. In this context the CAPM may very well be an appropriate technique to optimize investment strategy.

In the context of a traditional economic approach, the problem faced by investors is to find a mix of investments for which the weighted average elasticity maximizes the returns while at the same time minimizes the volatility of the returns for each level of returns. The various combinations describe the efficient frontier. And the investors based on their risk return preferences choose a point in the efficient frontier.

A low cost index portfolio will over the long term minimize management costs without significantly impacting long run performance. As one can see from the previous lines, the case for passive indexing is very compelling. Once one buys into the passive strategy, it follows that the market portfolio may be the way to go. It is an efficient way to achieve the broadest diversification possible. As we will show next, this insight is very important even for those of us who believe in implementing active strategies from time to time.

ASSET ALLOCATION AS A BETA STRATEGY

When one assumes an unrestricted risk-free borrowing and lending, the expected return on assets that are uncorrelated with the market (which is the asset's expected return less the beta, times the expected market returns less the risk-free rate) must equal the risk-free rate. For those who keep score this is the Sharpe-Lintner version of the CAPM. With unlimited risk-free borrowing and lending, there is no alpha or risk adjusted excess return. In other words, managers do not have superior information.

All an investor can choose is the appropriate beta mix that is the appropriate elasticity mix. Hence, the asset allocation process becomes one of estimating the betas and or elasticities of the different asset classes to finding the combination of funds that produces the ratio of volatility to expected returns consistent with the investors' preferences or risk tolerance. Once this is done, buying the cheapest funds with a given beta exposure will maximize the investors returns, hence the case for Exchange Traded Funds (ETFs).

SMART BETA

The marketing of the Smart Beta strategies is very interesting. The proponents of these strategies argue that in the past, investors had two choices. Those who believed markets were largely efficient or doubted their ability to select skillful managers would choose low-cost, capitalization-weighted index funds. On the other hand, those who believed markets were inefficient and had confidence in their manager selection process would choose active management approach. In contrast, the Smart Beta proponents argue that both types of strategies have their drawbacks. They point that cap-weighted equity index funds automatically increase their exposure to stocks whose prices appreciate and reduce their exposure to stocks whose prices fall. As a result, the proponents of the Smart Beta argue that cap-weighting tends to overweigh overvalued securities and underweight undervalued ones.

Instead of accessing this market exposure via traditional cap-weighting, Smart Beta strategies advocate the use of alternative-weighting schemes to increase the portfolio exposure toward certain factors. In theory, Smart Beta strategies preserve the typical benefits of traditional capitalization-based strategies, such as broad market exposure, diversification, and liquidity. It also offers the benefits of passive approaches such as transparency, consistency, predictability, and low cost, while providing the presumptive benefits of active investing styles. As such, the Smart Beta strategy offers investors either a third choice or a better and improved second generation of index investing. Smart Beta offers the promise of delivering the best of both active and passive investment strategies [5].

The Objective: Smart Beta strategies are designed to add value by systematically selecting, weighting, and rebalancing portfolio holdings on the basis of characteristics other than market capitalization. The Smart Beta approach aims to develop a transparent, consistent investment process to explicitly capture a desired factor (or multi-factor) exposure relative to the cap-weighted market portfolio; the strategy offers the possibility for customization. It provides a way for investors to gain exposure to the market. It allows managers to design investment solutions based on the client's risk and return objectives. If successful, the strategy offers the potential for a better portfolio with lower costs.

The process should be investible and scalable. It can be employed across asset classes where evidence suggests that durable factor premium exist and strategy implementation can be repeated at relatively low cost with scale. The excess returns associated with Smart Beta portfolios should not be viewed as skill-based alpha, as they reflect a systematic source of return that can be captured predictably at relatively low cost. The question is what are these factors? If they are empirically determined, they suffer from many of the deficiencies that we have already mentioned, which brings us to the issue of whether or not the durability of the factors are a result of economic policy. We have argued and will continue to argue that the durability of the factors is in fact the result of economic adjustments to a new equilibrium.

The Construction of Smart Beta Portfolios: Traditionally the Smart Beta strategies have two major components: one is to consider the effect of a factor. An exposure or attribute that is relevant in explaining the return and/or risk of an asset over time. Academic and practitioners have over the years identified a series of commonly known compensated factors, that is, those expected to generate a premium. The list includes, among others, factors such as value, momentum, size, volatility and quality of the portfolio returns.

The second component of the portfolio construction is a rules-based process to tilt toward value, momentum, volatility, and quality factors. There are two approaches for construction of Smart Beta Portfolios.

- One is to build optimization-based weighting methods, minimum variance, and/or risk efficient portfolios.
- The other alternative is to use heuristic weighting methods, using simple and sensible rules. Equal-weighting schemes and fundamental weighting are two such examples of the heuristic weighting.

IMPLEMENTATION OF THE CAPM AND SMART BETA: THE ESTIMATION OF THE COEFFICIENTS

A major step in the applicability of the CAPM and Smart Beta frameworks is the ability to obtain information on two parameters, alpha and beta, for the respective asset classes. Traditionally, the estimates for these coefficients are estimated empirically and that leads to a number of implementation issues. One issue is the way the parameters are estimated. Many practitioners use alternative optimization and portfolio construction processes when estimating the relevant parameters. For some of the asset allocation and minimum variance Smart Beta strategies, the parameters have to be estimated using optimization-based weighting methods, which are complex and subject to errors in estimating expected returns and covariance.

Another issue in the way the parameters are estimated is that many practitioners use an optimization and portfolio construction process to estimate the relevant parameters using a 60-month running window. If our cycle theory is correct, these estimation procedures will lead to some significant problems. For example, during the first month of a new cycle, the optimization procedure will be using 59 months of data from the previous cycle and only 1 month of data from the new and relevant cycle. Obviously as time goes on, the sample of the current cycle used in the estimation procedure will increase. However, this means that during the first 5 years of a cycle, the optimization procedure will be using biased estimates of the true alpha and true beta. This is a major problem for the traditional optimization and portfolio construction software. One simple way to eliminate the estimation bias is to eliminate the data from the previous beta cycle. However, that raises the issue of what to do early on when the sample size is too small or identifying when a cycle has changed. Even this raises a couple of issues. The first one is an estimation one, as one must determine what to do when the sample size is too small after a turning point. The second one is how to correctly identify the turning points.

The identification of a changing alpha and/or beta could be a useful tool in a portfolio strategy. One could alter the portfolio in response to the changing alpha or beta as soon as the information becomes available. Our approach offers potential answers or solutions to the two concerns raised in the previous paragraphs. We contend that a top-down macroeconomic view is the way to identify the turning points that lead to the different cycles. We also believe that similarity of the environment is more important than temporal precedence. Hence, using estimates from a period where past economic policies produced a similar environment to the one we foresee, it may provide more accurate estimates of the parameters than those using the previous 60 months.

Looking at previous shocks of a similar nature can give us a sense of the likely response of the different sectors and even the economy. While one may not be able to precisely estimate the response elasticity of the different sectors, the previous shocks may give a qualitative information that may allow for a faster response to the shock. The initial portfolio in response to the qualitative information can be adjusted as data becomes available and better estimates of the elasticities are obtained. We contend an economic analysis that focuses on what determines beta and/or alpha would enhance the usefulness and the returns generated by a CAPM or Smart Beta model-based portfolio strategy.

MACROECONOMICS TO THE RESCUE

An economic approach could easily fill the empirical holes of the estimation process outlined in the previous section. An important insight is that by applying standard macroeconomic analysis, one can then assess the impact of the economic variables on the economy's aggregate level of economic activity, that is, the risk-free rate, the market volatility, and absolute rate of return. We have also argued that simple textbook economics concepts, such as the elasticity of demand and supply, could easily explain the beta concept of the CAPM. By focusing on their ability to react to economic shocks (technological advances, regulatory changes, etc.), we have witnessed how changes in elasticity have generally been gradual and predictable. We have also seen, almost without exception, that similar shocks cause similar economic responses, while stock price performance varies with the asset class elasticity.

As we mentioned, inelastic industries initially adjust to demand shifts by varying prices while keeping output levels roughly constant. Consequently, the profits of inelastic industries are very sensitive to demand shifts in the short run. Investors and portfolio managers would obviously prefer to hold inelastic industries that face rising demand and elastic industries that are experiencing declining market conditions. In short, the one-to-one mapping of the finance terms to the economic terms allows us to replicate the results of the CAPM in the framework of textbook economics and go even beyond, to deal with variables that the CAPM does not address.

More importantly, to the extent that economics explains the CAPM parameters, we have found a way to intuitively present variables that may impact the industry's, sector's, or factor of production's ability to respond to economic shocks, that is beta changes. The variables in question include: policy changes, tax rate changes, regulatory changes, as well as technological innovations. Using changes in these variables, we may be able to anticipate and predict changes in the alpha and beta parameters and adjust the portfolio strategy accordingly to produce positive risk-adjusted excess returns.

The moral of the story, at least for investors who want to identify industries, countries, and asset classes likely to outperform the market, is that they must decide whether demand for that industry, country, and/or asset class product will rise or fall, and then decide whether or not an industry, country, or asset class has pricing power, be it on the demand or supply side. The airline industry tells us that elasticity depends partly on government regulation and partly on industry-specific innovation. One insight produced by this approach is that the output response, that is, the elasticities, will not be invariant to the shocks. This means not only that the betas would not be invariant to the nature of the shocks, but it also means that they may be predictable and identifiable. Once the nature of the shocks is identified, so would the appropriate beta. If that is the case, it may be a mistake to use historically estimated betas, as opposed to economic shock-based historical betas.

WHAT CAUSES THE ECONOMIC CYCLES?

We believe that the economic cycles are nothing more than temporary deviations from long rates of return. We can rationalize these deviations as part of the process of adjustment to a new equilibrium brought about by economic shocks. In some cases, these shocks are predictable and policy driven, while at other times they appear to be random (as in the case of some natural disasters). Whether predictable or not, once the shock occurs, the prices will change to clear the market. Whether the long run equilibrium is restored instantaneously or not depends on the existence of adjustment costs. Hence the adjustment costs will affect the speed of adjustment to the new equilibrium and that in turn will generate a path to a new equilibrium.

Over time, prices and output will change and the economy will eventually reach its new long run equilibrium. We contend that with the aid of a top-down macroeconomic approach, once the current equilibrium disturbance is identified and the new long run equilibrium is identified, one may be able to surmise the adjustment process.

This discussion brings us to express some dissatisfaction with the concept of risk as the CAPM is commonly applied. In particular, we refer to the use of beta as a measure of risk as it relates to the market, as well as the concept of residual risk or undiversified risk. An important insight provided by the approach is that different shocks will elicit different responses from different industries. This suggests to us that different shocks will then generate different betas or covariance with the markets.

Another insight provided by our analysis is one that that the ValueTiming active strategy we outline later on seeks to exploit: the temporary cyclical deviation from the long run returns. This is a very important insight for the estimation of the betas as well as the implementation of Smart Beta strategies. If the beta changes over time, the Smart Beta will underperform during some portion of the cycle.

THE EVIDENCE

The approach outlined by our top-down view of the world also suggests simple adjustments to industry specific shocks or a changing beta for individual industry groups. Take the case of the health care sector. Before its implementation, we argued that the ObamaCare mandate would result in an increase in the number of people enrolled in the program [6]. Hence it would be safe to assume that the demand for the services would increase. We contended that the inelastic factors would be the main beneficiaries. We also knew that government regulations would affect the supply elasticities of the different industry groups within health care. Finally, we also knew that the price controls would have a significant impact on the overall supply. So the task of a portfolio manager is to find out which sectors will experience the increase in aggregate demand without being offset by price controls and/or regulations. Health care distributors, life science tools and services, and managed healthcare providers outperformed. In contrast, health care equipment, health care services, and health care supplies underperformed during the period surrounding the implementation.

The relative performance of these groups is easily explained. The price controls significantly affect the suppliers and it is clear that the government wants to steer people into managed care; that is the closest thing to universal health care. Hence it is not surprising to see that health care distributors and managed care seem like winners; they benefit from the increased volume. The one industry that requires additional explanation is that of the life science tools. We believe that the research being conducted and advances being made, with all the patents, as well as potential benefits these industries may produce, clearly makes it an inelastic factor that should benefit from an increase in demand generated by a recovering economy and the ObamaCare mandate.

Our framework also suggests that the factors used in Smart Beta will vary in response to shocks and policy changes. Again if the adjustment is costly, it will take time for the long run equilibrium to be restored, which may give rise to a mean reverting cycle for changes in the betas and the factors used in the construction of the Smart Beta portfolios.

There may be many reasons cited for the superior performance of small capitalization stocks over the years, but we contend economic policy—particularly fiscal policy—plays a leading role. The explanations for the existence of this "size effect" range from the fair pricing of risks to arguing that size is a distinct factor. But these explanations aren't entirely satisfactory in explaining the observed empirical facts. Looking back to the 1926 through the mid-1980s time period, the data points to the potential existence of systematic patterns in the relative performance of different size stocks. The large-cap stocks consistently outperformed during the first half of the 1940s, the first half of the 1960s, and the first half of the 1980s. An empiricist might argue that large caps are more likely to outperform in the first half of the decade. But then, what of the '50s? An economic explanation is that, during these periods, there was a major change in the economy's incentive structure. In the '40s the United States had World War II, in the '60s we had the Kennedy fiscal moves, and in the '80s we had the Reagan tax rate cuts. The three episodes suggest a plausible economic explanation for the size effect.

We contend that in the long run corporations have the ability to alter the way they deliver returns to investors, that is, the capital structure, to minimize the taxes and other regulatory costs imposed by the Federal and state and local government. This insight leads us to a simple theory regarding the size factor or size effect [7]. Congress and tax collectors like to go after big game. As a consequence, our tax codes and regulations are aimed primarily at large corporations. In fact, many laws are written in such a way as to exempt smaller companies from compliance. This means that smaller companies are able to "morph" themselves to take advantage of the tax code and government regulations. In an unindexed tax code, inflation generates illusory profits that will increase the effective tax rates of businesses and corporations. Those who are nimble will be able to reduce the impact of the inflation tax and therefore outperform its less nimble peers. All of this suggests a very simple theory of the size factor. Small-cap companies have an advantage over the larger-caps when it comes to inflation hedging, tax sheltering, and regulatory skirting during turning points in economic policy. Thus periods of

tax rate changes, rising inflation, or rising regulations will all favor the smaller-cap stocks.

The 1970s and 1980s is a clear and simple illustration of the dramatic effect that the economic environment can have on the size factor. During the late 1970s when inflation, bracket creep, and regulations were rampant, the small-caps outperformed. In fact many small-cap managers would boast that small-caps had not underperformed more than two years in a row in more than a decade. Yet as the mid-1980s rolled around, the large capitalization stocks began a cycle of consistent outperformance over the smaller capitalization stocks. What changed? Well Paul Volcker changed the Fed's operating procedures and the double digit inflation rate converged to a low single digit number. President Reagan administration lowered the personal income tax rates from a high of 70% to a top rate of 28%. In addition, regulations as measured by the numbers of pages in the federal register declined significantly. These policy changes wiped out the small-cap advantages.

The Reagan policies also made the United States a much more attractive place to invest as the dollar went through the roof. In fact, the tax rate changes do match the dollar appreciations. Initially President Reagan lowered the marginal tax rates to 50% from 70%. On an after tax basis this means that a dollar at the highest marginal tax rate delivered 30 cents on the dollar after taxes. After the reduction in marginal tax rates, a dollar delivered 50 cents after taxes. That is a 66% increase in after-tax rates of return. A profitable company, even without changing anything would deliver an after-tax increase of 66% to its investors. Hence the after-tax cash flow would increase in value by 66%. On top of this, companies and people will now have a higher increase in incentives to work and produce at the lower tax rates. The increase would also attract foreign investors. Capital would flow into the country. The inflow would continue until the after tax return was equalized across countries. Again if there are positive adjustment costs, the equilibrating process would take some time. The dollar, on a GDP weighted basis, increased 66% by 1985 and gave it all back in the next two years [8]. Notice that the increase is exactly what the tax rate cuts suggested and the gradual increase fits our description of positive adjustment costs delaying the equilibrium process. It is no wonder the market valuation increased.

The Republican victory of 1994 also coincides with another exchange rate market cycle. The Republican victory made gridlock a popular term and believed that it was good for the markets. While it is true that the Republicans derailed much of the original Clinton agenda, such as health care and thereby derailed a major expansion of the public sector, President Clinton deserves much credit for what he did. He shifted gears and played ball with the Republicans. President Clinton pivoted and led the charge for the free trade deals and the reduction of the capital gains tax rate. He cooperated with the Republicans and passed welfare reform. It is fair to say that these measures were not high on the priority list of the early years for the Clinton administration, yet he followed through and delivered. Viewed this way, the 1994 victory simply forced the president to cooperate and adopt policies that effectively continued the previous policy mix that resulted in a continuation of a rising real exchange rate. In fact, looking at the data, the election was a turning point that resulted in a visible surge in the real exchange rate from 1994 to 2001.

The cyclical fluctuations, the exchange rate cycles of the early 1980s and mid-1990s, were real exchange rate cycles driven by real rate of return differentials. In the case of President Reagan, the tax rate reduction increased the after tax rate of returns in the United States relative to the world. That led to a surge in the dollar and over time, as capital flew in, the excess rate of returns was arbitraged away and the world economy returned to its long run equilibrium path and Purchasing Power Parity (PPP), hence the inverted V cycle. The investment implications are straightforward. In the country with the appreciating real exchange rate, the rate of return of the nontraded good outperforms that of the traded good. The higher rate of return will attract foreign and domestic capital. In contrast, in the country with the depreciating real exchange rate, the nontraded good will underperform the traded good sectors. Put another way, we expect the nontraded goods in the country with the appreciating currency to deliver the highest rate of return and the nontraded goods in the country with the depreciating real exchange rate to deliver the lowest rate of returns. The nontraded sector returns will span the traded sector returns. The relationship between the real exchange rate and the relative performance of the United States and rest of the world stock market returns is as predicted by our framework.

The episodes already mentioned provide some illustration of the capability of the elasticities to explain much of what a Smart Beta would have done had the concept of a Smart Beta been operational around the time. Yet as we also show with our writings, the elasticity approach did explain much of what happened at the time in a contemporaneous manner. The size and exchange rate cycles as well as the secular bull market. The elasticity approach is even more versatile than that. It is capable of providing a straightforward explanation for the changes in the distribution of income during the last two or three decades, it is also capable of explaining the distribution of salaries among professional athletes and even the CEO compensation relative to their workers [9].

ECONOMIC POLICY AND INVESTMENT STRATEGIES: VALUETIMING

We have just shown how economic policy could affect the economy's growth rate, its volatility, and the risk-free rate, parameters that are taken as given and exogenous by the CAPM. The important point is that we believe and have shown some evidence that economic policy impacts the CAPM parameters in predictable ways. Hence, by taking into consideration the impact of government policy on these parameters, one may be able to alter its portfolio allocation in anticipation of these macro changes to the economy.

We have also documented that rising inflation, rising regulations, and rising tax rates tend to create an environment that favors the smaller-cap stocks over the larger-cap stocks. Differences in policies such as changes in the tax rate differential across countries will impact the relative response of the different economies, giving rise to a differential or relative country effects. Finally, we have also shown how specific government actions such as oil or airline deregulation have impacted and altered the supply elasticity and thus profitability/beta of these specific industries. In short, by linking policy changes to the economic environment and the size, location, and industry effects, we can determine how the alphas, betas, and Smart Betas of different asset classes will change.

From that point, an optimized allocation that differs from the static allocation produced by the CAPM model or Smart Beta can be determined. These examples suggest that there is a one-to-one correspondence between these finance and economic concepts. We believe that an economic approach can help us obtain better estimates of the CAPM parameters. At the very least, such an approach would allow the empiricists to eliminate the data prior to the policy changes that altered the alpha/beta generation process from the estimation sample. Hence, we could use policy changes to identify different alpha and beta regimes and, in doing so, the better and more reliable estimates of the alpha and beta parameters would generate returns superior to those of the empirical estimates based to the fixed 60 months estimation rule. In principle, the framework could be extended to incorporate likely changes in policy and thereby anticipate possible changes in the individual assets alpha and beta parameters. That would be a great improvement over the traditional CAPM.

However, there is more to this story of delivering alpha through beta. The strategy we have in mind differs from that of a straightforward market timing strategy. We believe that economic shocks disturb the economic equilibrium and thus elicit an adjustment to a new equilibrium. We also believe that adjustment to economic shocks is costly and does not occur instantaneously.

Hence, economic shocks generate persistent return differential cycles where one asset class will outperform the other asset classes. To generalize, we believe that different shocks generate different cycles of relative performance patterns. As during these cycles the sectors that outperform exhibit returns that are well above their historical averages, one may say that these sectors experience a temporary increase in their beta. Recall that, to us, beta is the result of the demand and supply elasticity response to the economic shock. By cataloguing the different economic shocks, we can identify the adjustment process to the new equilibrium and the pattern of relative performance. We believe that we can anticipate these responses and the changes in the beta for the different sectors during the various shocks.

What we have in mind here is a strategy that takes advantage of the changing response of the different sectors to different economic shocks and those are reflected as temporarily different beta for the different sectors. However, as we look at our strategy, in so far as we have identified the economic shocks, we will be delivering above average excess returns, over and above the market and the historical risk adjustment (i.e., delivering alpha). That is the essence of the ValueTiming strategy [10].

So far we have presented evidence that suggests the possible value added of a top-down investment strategy. We have linked the relative performance of large and small-cap stocks, domestic versus international, and industry selection choices to the economic environment created by changing economic policy. To the extent that these changes in the economic environment can be anticipated by the portfolio managers, there is the potential additional value added of a top-down, relative to index passive strategy. To the extent that there are adjustment costs to reach a new equilibrium, the changing rates of return divergences from the long run will be temporary and mean reverting. To the extent our approach identifies these cycles correctly, the elements outlined here will deliver returns superior not only to a passive index strategy, but also relative to the Smart Beta strategies.

Understanding how the global economy reestablishes equilibrium once the shock has taken place is a very important insight for both policymakers and investors. The former will be able to understand the political pressures that their government will be facing during the adjustment process and hopefully will take steps to ameliorate them in the process of bringing the economy to new and (hopefully) improved economic conditions. For the investors, the path to the new equilibrium allows them to identify short-term deviations from the long run equilibrium conditions. Armed with these insights, they can develop strategies aimed at taking advantage of these temporary excess returns. While the investors know that the excess profits will eventually dissipated, earning an excess returns for a short period of time is nothing to sneeze at. The accumulation of short-term excess returns could lead to a large increase in the wealth, something that most investors strive to achieve.

The one-to-one mapping between the parameters in the CAPM/Smart Beta and the elasticity concepts suggests an equivalence between the financial economics approach to investments and the top-down macroeconomic approach. Under these conditions and up to this point, both will be equivalent. However, to us, the tie-breaker is the fact that the top-down approach allows us to incorporate the effects of policy changes in the analysis in a way that the other quantitative approaches may not. Also, the top-down macroeconomic approach allows for a faster update of the estimates of the reaction coefficients, that is, betas or elasticities, to the different economic shocks.

Our next step in the journey is to develop a framework general enough to be able to analyze shocks to specific industries, the local economy, and the global economy. Our approach will be based on an economic analysis that focuses on the economy's general equilibrium reaction coefficients to different shocks. From this point forward, we will not focus on the traditional CAPM parameters. The reason for that is, as we have stated, there is an equivalence between the economic and the CAPM parameters. If we are correct on this view, the equivalence suggests that only one of the two is sufficient and the other may be redundant. We chose the economics approach for the simple reason that we will be able to incorporate policy changes in the analysis, something that would not feasible using the alternative approach.

Parsimony is one of the guiding principles that we follow in the development of the framework. To that end, we attempt to make the least number of assumptions necessary to develop a framework that provides us with the simplest and most logical explanations for the economy's response and adjustments to different shocks, whether they are caused by nature (such as natural disasters) or man-made. If they are man-made, they are the result of economic and political changes in the global or local economies. Such a framework will strive to make consistent choices based on the information at hand and on the analysis developed by our framework. Understanding that disturbances have a shelf life and having an idea of how long these temporary deviations from the long run equilibrium will last is another important insight that an investor who understands the framework will be able to take advantage of. Investors who pursue our approach will have to be comfortable understanding that they will not fit into a narrow investment strategy category. Sometimes the disturbance will favor large-cap stocks, while at other times it may favor small-caps, value or growth stocks, or different regions of the world.

References

[1] A very nice and complete half century financial economic development survey can be found in Fama and French (2004) and Perold (2004). Fama EF, French KR. The capital asset pricing model: theory and evidence. J Econ Persp Summer 2004; 18(3): 25–46. Perold AF. The capital asset pricing model. J Econ Persp Summer 2004; 18(3): 3–24.

[2] The CAPM can be traced to Lintner (1965), Mossin (1966), Sharpe (1964), and Treynor (1962). Lintner J. Security prices, risk and maximal gains form diversification. J Fin December 1965; 20: 578–615. Mossin J. Equilibrium in a capital asset market. Econometrica 34 (1966): 768–83. Sharpe WF. Capital asset prices: a theory of market equilibrium under conditions of risk. J Fin 1964; 19: 425–42. Treynor JL. Toward a theory of market value of risky assets. Unpublished Manuscript (1962). Final Version in Korajczyk RA, ed. Asset Pricing and Portfolio Performance, London: Risk Books, 1999: 15–22.

[3] A more detailed analysis of the regulations, deregulation of the energy sector can be found in Canto, Bollman, Melich, and Canto and Melich (1982). Canto VA, Bollman G, Melich K. Oil decontrol: the power of incentives could reduce OPEC's power to boost oil prices. Oil Gas J 1982, Vol. 8.

[4] See Sharpe (1994). Sharpe WF. The Sharpe Ratio. J Port Manage Fall 1994; 49–58.

[5] For the traditional investors, information and a nice description of Smart Beta can be found on different websites such as www.iShares.com, www.ssga.com, and www.researchaffiliates.com.

[6] See Canto (2013a, b). Canto VA. ObamaCare, La Jolla Economics, October 29, 2013. Canto VA. ObamaCare: a portfolio strategy, La Jolla Economics, November 4, 2013.

[7] A more detailed analysis of the size, value, location cycles can be found in Canto (2006). Canto VA. Understanding asset allocation, Pearson Education, New Jersey, 2006.

[8] See Canto (1988, 1987). Canto VA. Tax rates move currencies, and there's no easy fix. Wall Street Journal, September 22, 1988, p. 36. Canto VA. Competitiveness and real exchange rates. Wall Street Journal, March 18, 1987, p. 30.

[9] See Canto (2008, 2011a, b). Canto VA. The economics of superstardom: are CEOs overpaid? Harvard College Econ Rev Spring 2008; II(2): 33–35. Canto VA. Income inequality, aggregate demand, and factor supply elasticity. La Jolla Economics, November 10, 2011. Canto VA. Prosperity and elasticity explain the disparity between the compensation of executives and the average worker. La Jolla Economics, May 17, 2011.

[10] See Canto (2007). Canto VA. Cocktail Economics Pearson Education, New Jersey, 2007.

ARBITRAGE AND MOBILITY

1

Arbitrage, Mobility, and Equilibrium Prices

Social scientists and money managers value parsimony, forecasting accuracy, and explanatory power. As a result, these scientists aim to develop the simplest models and theories possible with the maximum predictive and/or explanatory power possible. The idea behind the modeling assumption is to eliminate and/or remove superfluous details and focus on the issues that are truly important to the topic at hand. They try to maximize their bang for the buck. Given the forecasting accuracy and explanatory power, the simplest theories are considered the most elegant. They are also easier to articulate and in general make the most sense. They are also the easier sale; they make a good story and may even deliver performance.

The simplification of the modeling is not without risk. In some cases once the simplifying assumptions regarding the world are made, the die is cast. In these cases, the policy implications are a direct result of the assumptions made by the model builder. Viewed this way, one can consider economic modeling an art, the art of choosing the relevant set of simplifying assumptions. One example we have frequently used is the combined assumptions of profit maximization and free mobility of goods and services/factors of production. These apparently innocuous assumptions lead to a very strong implication: Differences in prices across national borders will be arbitraged away and so will the differences in rates of returns across countries.

The equalization of factor returns across national borders is insured by the mobility of factors of production. However, Nobel Prize winner Paul Samuelson also showed that if there are enough goods and services traded across national boundaries, the returns to the factors of production could be equalized, even when the factors of production do not move across national borders [1]. This is an important point, for it suggests that a combination of goods and factor mobility insures the equalization of returns to factors that are immobile across national borders [2]. An example will clear this point. If labor and land are used to produce rice, which is freely traded, we know that the price of rice will be equalized across national borders, say $100 per bushel. If labor is free to move, the wages will also be equalized across borders. If both countries use the same techniques, then the labor costs will be the same across the economies, say $40. Given the total coast and labor costs, it follows

Economic Disturbances and Equilibrium in an Integrated Global Economy. http://dx.doi.org/10.1016/B978-0-12-813993-6.00001-5

that, with the same technology, the land intensity will be the same and so will the land returns, $60 in this example. The assumption of free trade, zero transportation costs, and the same technology lead to the result that the production labor costs are the same across the national borders. Under these conditions the returns to the land-owners will be the same across the two economies.

In the area of international finance these key simplifying assumptions yield the result commonly known as purchasing power parity (PPP). Put another way, profit maximization and free mobility insure that the dollar price of any commodity will be the same across the world. The origin of this literature can be traced to Swedish Economist Gustav Cassel believed that, if an exchange rate was not at parity, it was in disequilibrium—either prices or the exchange rate would adjust until parity was again achieved. Parity would be ensured by arbitrage [3].

The remaining chapters develop a simple approach with a dual purpose: one is to identify the economy's adjustment process to shocks or economic disturbances and the other purpose is to analyze and suggest policies that will address some of the problems faced by the domestic and global economies.

We begin by making the simplest set of assumptions and see how far we can take these assumptions. After exploring and developing the insights derived, we introduce additional assumptions and examine how the additional add to the ability of our framework to explain and analyze additional economic events of greater complexity. As we acquire new insights, we become better equipped to develop policies aimed at addressing the economic problems at hand.

The astute investor will be able to use the framework developed here to anticipate the adjustment process needed to achieve national and global equilibrium resulting from policy changes and/or unexpected economic shocks. In some cases, these insights may be translated into new portfolio and/or investment strategies, which we have called the value timing approach [4]. The approach is similar to that of the peeling an onion: at each successive layer, the richness and intricacies of the framework will be revealed. Let's begin by exploring the implications generated by the assumptions of perfect mobility and profit maximization.

A 2X2X2X2 WORLD

Initially we assume that there the world consists of:

1. Two countries: Westland and Lakeland.
2. Two goods: Westland produces mostly wine and Lakeland produces mostly cheese. P_{wn} and P_{cn} denote the price in Westland of wine and cheese in notes currency. P_{wp} and P_{cp} denote the price in Lakeland of wine and cheese in pesos currency.

3. Two factors of production: Labor and land.
4. Two currencies: Westland uses notes as its currency and Lakeland uses the peso as its currency.

The rationale for the 2X2X2X2 assumptions is due to the fact that we live in a three dimensional world. And one can draw two variables in a page or blackboard and analyze the effect of two variables, say labor and land on the level of production of one or two particular goods. Prior to the advent of high powered mathematics, economists were quite fond of graphical analysis and intuitive solutions. Intricate knowledge of the two-sector model was a must for those economists aspiring to understand international trade and its general equilibrium conditions. Harry Johnson's used the two-sector model not only in his lectures, but also in many of his most brilliant pieces is a testimony to the versatility of the two-sector model and its applicability to many economic problems and policy issues [5].

EQUILIBRIUM UNDER AUTARKY

Initially we assume that Lakeland and Westland do not trade with each other. Under this assumption the local price of cheese and wine is determined solely by local demand and supply conditions. Fig. 1.1A depicts the autarkic equilibrium for the cheese market in Lakeland. The market clearing conditions are determined solely by the intersection of the demand for cheese, D_L, and supply of cheese, S_L, in Lakeland.

The point of intersection of the demand and supply curves (D_L and S_L) is the market "clearing" equilibrium price for cheese, P_{cp}^*, and quantity of cheese, Q_{cl}^*, produced in Lakeland absent in the international trade.

Similarly, Fig. 1.1B shows the demand (D_w) and supply (S_w) conditions for cheese in the Westland economy. The intersection of the two curves denotes the market clearing price, P_{cn}^*, and quantity of cheese produced, Q_{cw}^*, in Westland under the autarkic conditions.

GLOBAL AND NATIONAL EQUILIBRIUM

Next, we explore the implications of opening trade between the two nations under the following assumptions regarding profit maximization and mobility:

1. We assume that the economic agents maximize profits.
2. We assume that there are no transaction costs or any frictions restricting the mobility of goods and services across the two economies.

These two assumptions are sufficient to ensure that the profit maximizing agents "arbitrage" any differences in prices across national borders. More than likely the

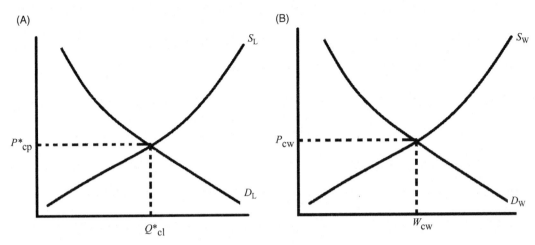

FIGURE 1.1 (A) Lakeland autarkic equilibrium for the cheese market. (B) Westland autarkic equilibrium for the cheese market.

autarky cheese price, the market clearing price that would prevail in the absence of trade will be different in the two localities. In the example depicted in Fig. 1.1, they are, here is how the arbitrage process would work: in the absence of trade between the two countries, P_{cp}^* and P_{cn}^* denote the autarky market clearing price of cheese in Lakeland and in Westland.

The autarky (no trade) price in Lakeland is given in pesos, while the corresponding price in Westland is quoted in notes (the Westland currency). Fig. 1.2 shows the autarky prices of cheese for both countries in pesos, the Lakeland currency. In order to compare the two prices it is necessary to convert the two prices to a common currency.

Initially, in the absence of trade the price is higher in Westland than it is in Lakeland. That creates a profit opportunity that can be arbitraged away by profit maximizing agents

That is,

$$E \times P_{cn}^* > P_{cp}^* \qquad (1.1)$$

The difference in price may be attributable to several factors. One possibility is differences in tastes. Other possibilities are the differences in technology or production function and or relative factor endowments. In what follows we will assume that the two economies have similar tastes as well as similar technologies. As trade opens between the two economies, cheese will be exported from the locality with the lower price of cheese, Lakeland, into the higher price locality, Westland in this case. Initially, the arbitrageurs will make a profit equal to the difference in the two prices:

$$\text{Arbitrage profits per unit} = E \times P_{cn}^* - P_{cp}^* \qquad (1.2)$$

As a result of the arbitrage process, there will be a smaller supply of cheese in the exporting locality, which will, all else being the same, drive the price up. At the

same time there will be a higher supply of cheese in the importing country, which will, all else being the same, reduce the price of the cheese in the importing country.

Notice that we appear to be quite fond of using and numbering equations. There is a rationale behind it. We use the equations to memorialize the different relationships and assumptions, as well as a filing system for these relationships so that we can refer to it later on when we expend and or modify the relationships describing our basic framework.

The combined effect of these arbitrage driven price changes ultimately leads to the following responses:

1. After the opening of trade, the higher price per pound of cheese in Westland produce a profit opportunity for the people of Lakeland. In order to take advantage of the higher price in Westland, Lakeland's producers increase their production in order to export to Westland and take advantage of the higher prices. This is depicted in Fig. 1.2 as an upward movement along Lakeland's supply curve. The production of cheese will rise from Q_{cl}^* to S_{cl}.
2. The higher price of cheese in Westland will also affect the Lakeland cheese consumers. As the market price will rise their consumption of cheese will decline. This is depicted in Fig. 1.2 as an upward movement along the demand curve. The local consumption of cheese in Lakeland will fall to Q_{cl} from Q_{cl}^*.
3. The increased production less the reduced consumption in Lakeland leads to a surplus of cheese that is now exported to Westland. Lakeland exports are denoted by X_{cl}.
4. The lower price for a pound of cheese in Lakeland will produce a profit opportunity for the people of Westland too. In order to take advantage of the lower price, arbitrageurs will import cheese from Lakeland and sell in Westland at a price higher than Lakeland but lower than Westland. The lower price will result in an increase in the quantity demanded of cheese.

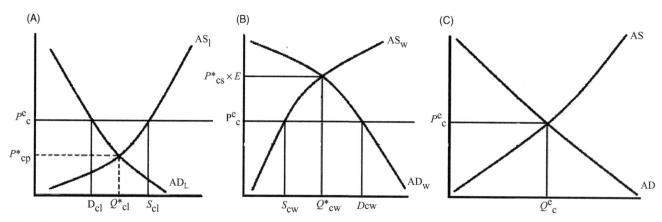

FIGURE 1.2   Arbitrage (A) country 1: Lakeland (peso), (B) country 2: Westland (in Pesos), (C) world equilibrium.

This is depicted in Fig. 1.2 as a downward movement along Westland's demand curve for cheese. Westland demand for cheese will increase from Q^*_{cw} to Q_{cw}. The import competition also puts downward pressure on the price of and production of cheese in Westland. This is depicted in Fig. 1.2 as a downward movement along the supply curve, the production of cheese in Westland will fall to S_{cw} from Q^*_{cw}.

5. Westland cheese imports, M_{cw}, will be the difference between the domestic consumption of cheese and the domestic production of cheese in Westland, that is, $S_{cw} - Q_{cw}$.

The arbitrage process continues as long as there is a cheese price differential between the two countries. The process stops when cheese prices are equalized across the two localities. At that point there is no longer an arbitrage profit opportunity.

Global equilibrium is depicted in Fig. 1.2 as the intersection of the world demand and supply curve for cheese. The global demand is nothing more than the sum of the two countries demand curves while the global supply is the sum of the two countries supply curves for cheese. The global market clearing prices and quantities of cheese produced can be depicted as P^e_c and Q^e_c.

Once the global market clearing conditions are established, that is, the world prices are determined, then it is possible to use the global price combined with the local demand for and supply of a commodity such as cheese in each economy, and determine the consumption and production of cheese and thus the net exports in each country.

Namely:

$$X_{cl} = S_{cl} - Q_{cl} \tag{1.3}$$

$$M_{cw} = Q_{cw} - S_{cw} \tag{1.4}$$

Where S_{cl} and S_{cw} denote the production of cheese in Lakeland and Westland, respectively, and Q_{cl} and Q_{cw}

denote the consumption of Cheese in Lakeland and Westland, respectively. The two-country world model is fairly general. When focusing on one particular country, it may be possible to lump or aggregate all other countries into "the rest of the world" or country 2.

The Law of One Price: The insight gained here is that profit maximization combined with absence of transaction costs ensures that economic agents will cause the cheese prices in notes in Westland multiplied by the exchange rate, $P_{cn}*E$, to be the same as the peso price of cheese in Lakeland. X_{cl}

Formally:

$$P_{cp} = P_{cn} \times E \tag{1.5}$$

Similarly, arbitrage ensures that the peso price of wine in Westland, $P_{wn} \times E$, is the same as the peso price of wine in Lakeland, P_{wp}. That is,

$$P_{wp} = P_{wn} \times E \tag{1.6}$$

E is the exchange rate between the two currencies. As we have shown earlier it allows converting the prices in terms of one country's currency into prices expressed in another country's currency. That is, how many pesos versus how many notes are needed to purchase a bottle of wine or a pound of cheese. The exchange rate is defined as the ratio of the price of a commodity; say cheese, in the two currencies. Eqs. (1.5) and (1.6) show that arbitrage insures that the price of any commodity expressed in one currency is the same all over the world.

Eqs. (1.5) and (1.6) show that PPP holds across commodities, this implies that there is a single global price for each of the commodities. Fig. 1.2 illustrates graphically the global equilibrium. The world demand for and supply curves are nothing more than the sum of the demand for and supply of cheese for each of the countries in the world.

If the relative price remains unchanged, then wine and cheese tend to be consumed in fixed proportions. If that is generally the case for all goods consumed, then one can make a composite good comprising all the goods and services consumed by each economy, and call it the economy's consumer price index (CPI) [6].

Under the assumption that the terms of trade remain unchanged, assuming similar consumer baskets among the economies, arbitrage will ensure that the "LAW OF ONE PRICE" prevails. That is, the peso price of the consumer basket will be the same in each locality.

In a formal equation, the law of one price or PPP relationship can be expressed as:

$$CPI_p = CPI_n \times E \qquad (1.7)$$

The dynamic version of this equation can be expressed in terms of the rate of change of each CPI, that is, the domestic inflation rate in local currency, and the rate of change of the exchange rate:

$$\pi_p = \pi_n + \mathcal{E} \qquad (1.8)$$

Where π_p, denotes the Lakeland inflation rate in pesos; π_n, the Westland inflation rate in notes; and , is the exchange rate appreciation of notes in terms of pesos.

Eq. (1.8) is nothing more than the dynamic version of the PPP equation also known as the law of one price. It is easily derived by differentiating logarithmically Eq. (1.7). It shows that when relative prices are constant, the inflation rate of the country with the appreciating currency is lower than the other currency by the amount of the exchange rate appreciation. Put another way, differences between the inflation rates of the two countries are directly and exactly reflected on the rate of change in the currency exchange rate.

GLOBAL EQUILIBRIUM AND THE TRADE ACCOUNTS

The assumption of a two-country world allows us to establish several identities and equalities. For example, since there are only two countries in this world, Fig. 1.2 shows that equilibrium requires that the global demand equal global supply. Therefore one country's cheese imports have to match the other country's cheese exports.

That is,

$$X_{cl} = M_{cw} \qquad (1.9)$$

Where X_{cl} denotes Lakeland's cheese exports and M_{cw} denotes Westland's cheese imports.

The same logic applies to the wine. The one difference being that Westland is the low cost producer under autarky and hence the exporter.

$$X_{ww} = M_{wl} \qquad (1.10)$$

X_{ww} denotes Westland wine exports and M_{wl} denotes Lakeland wine imports.

But that is not all. In this world there is only one time period, profit and utility maximization implies that there will be no net lending among the parties. The reason is simple: in a one period model, the lending never gets repaid; hence the consumers would be better off not lending and increasing their consumption and thus their utility or well-being. Lending or borrowing requires multiperiod modeling. Lending affords the lender the opportunity to transfer resources into future time periods, presumably to finance future consumption. For now we will ignore the multiperiod issues.

So far we have established that in a single period model, utility maximization yields the following budget constraint: income will equal expenditures at all times. That is,

$$Y_i = P_{ci} \times S_{ci} + P_{wi} \times S_{wi} \qquad (1.11)$$

Where Yi denotes the income of country i measured in its local currency.

$$C_i = P_{ci} \times C_{ci} + P_{wi} \times C_{wi} \qquad (1.12)$$

Where C_i denotes the i country's overall consumption of wine and cheese measured in local currency.

Subtracting the domestic consumption from both the income and expenditures yields the result that for each country the value of the imports must equal the value of the exports. After some manipulations we can easily show that if one country imports a commodity it must finance the imports of each country yields the result that the world trade balance in the trade balance for each country, TB, will always be zero. That is,

$$TB_l = P_{wp} \times M_{wl} - P_{cp} \times X_{cl} = 0 \qquad (1.13)$$

Where P_{wp}, denotes the price of wine in pesos (Lakeland's currency); M_{wl}, Lakeland wine imports; P_{cp}, the price of cheese in pesos; and X_{cl}, is Lakeland's exports of cheese.

$$TB_w = P_{cn} \times M_{cw} - P_{wn} \times X_{ww} = 0 \qquad (1.14)$$

Where P_{wn}, denotes the price of wine in notes (Westland's currency); X_{ww}, is Westland's wine exports; P_{cn}, is the price of cheese in notes; and M_{cw}, is Westland's exports of cheese.

Irrespective of which currency is used, the value of Lakeland cheese exports will equal the value of Lakeland wine imports. The budget constraint also means that the value of Westland exports equals the value of Westland imports.

$$P_{wp} \times M_{wl} = P_{cp} \times X_{cl} = P_{cn} \times E \times M_{cw} = P_{wn} \times E \times X_{ww}$$

$$(1.15)$$

THE TERMS OF TRADE OR REAL EXCHANGE RATE

Arbitrage also ensures that the relative price, terms of trade, or real exchange rate is the same across the two markets. That is, one pound of cheese gets the same amount of wine in Lakeland or Westland, otherwise an arbitrage profit opportunity would continue to exist. And this brings us to the second term we need to define. The terms of trade T, between the two economies. It is a measure of the relative price of wine in terms of cheese. T, measures how many units of one of the goods are needed to acquire a unit of the other good. That is, how many pounds of cheese are needed to acquire a bottle of wine Therefore the arbitrage process also ensures that the relative price of the two goods in question are equalized across economies:

$$T = P_{wn}/P_{cn} = P_{wp}/P_{cp}$$

$$(1.16)$$

INTEREST RATE PARITY

Nominal interest rates, i_w and i_l, denote the opportunity costs of holding noninterest bearing money in terms of bonds in Westland and Lakeland currencies, respectively. Borrowers and lenders have the choice of either borrowing or lending in either of the two currencies (notes or pesos).

Let's take the perspective of the people of Lakeland.

- If they save 1 peso at home at the end of the year, they receive $1 + i_p$, or 1 peso plus the Lakeland/peso interest rate.
- Alternatively, the investor could have converted the peso into notes at the current spot exchange rate, invested in notes in Westland's market and earn $1 + i_n$ at the end of the year, while simultaneously buying a futures contract on the currency that locks in the conversion or exchange rate. Investors would then arbitrage any difference between the two strategies, investing in the home market or foreign market. The end result of the arbitrage is what is called the interest rate parity theorem [7]:

$$i_p - i_n = \mathcal{E}$$

$$(1.17)$$

Next, we need to add one more relationship, the Fisher equation, relating the nominal and real interest rates (ρ) and the inflation rates (π) [8]

$$i_p = \pi_p + \rho_p$$

$$(1.18)$$

$$i_n = \pi_n + \rho_n$$

$$(1.19)$$

The interpretation of the equation is straight forward: the inflation rate denotes the opportunity costs of holding cash in terms of goods and services in each of the economies. That is, those who hold commodities experience a nominal capital gain equal to the inflation rate. The real rate of return is nothing more than the interest rate charged for lending and borrowing in terms of the commodity in question. For example, if one borrows 100 bottles of wine to repay them a year later and the borrower has to repay 103 bottles, the real interest rate in terms of wine, ρ_n, is 3%. Similarly, if one borrows 100 pounds of cheese and has to repay 104 pounds of cheese a year later, the real interest rate in terms of cheese, ρ_p, is 4%.

The Fisher equation is now easily described. If a person borrows 100 pounds of cheese, in order to break even, they have to produce 104 pounds of cheese. If the inflation rate is 3%, then at the end of the year the lender receives 4% more cheese, as well as a 3% appreciation of the value of the cheese in peso prices, for a nominal rate of return in pesos of 7%.

If one subtracts Eq. (1.18) from Eq. (1.19), one ends up with

$$i_p - i_n = \pi_p - \pi_n + \left(\rho_p - \rho_n\right)$$

$$(1.20)$$

Now if one substitutes Eq. (1.17) in Eq. (1.20), we get the following conclusion:

$$\rho_l = \rho_w$$

$$(1.21)$$

The intuitive explanation for this result is straightforward. If the relative prices between wine and cheese remain unchanged, the borrowers and lenders will be indifferent as to how individuals transfer resources to the future from the present. This is a very important result for it shows that the conditions under which interest rate parity and PPP hold result in the complete equalization of real rate of returns across economies.

One implication of this analysis is that whether you invest abroad or at home, the real rate of return is the same. There is no need to go anywhere else in the world. Another insight is that the adoption of free trade and the elimination of trade barriers leads to a convergence of rates of returns. The implementation and adoption of the Euro is a good case study of the convergence proposition [9].

WHAT HAPPENS WHEN THE TERMS OF TRADE CHANGE IN PREDICTABLE DIRECTIONS?

The terms of trade, T, is defined as the price of one country's exports in terms of the other (say the price of wine in terms of cheese). A change in the terms of trade means that for the economy with the more favorable terms of trade, say Lakeland, a pound of cheese is now able to get a larger quantity of wine. This means that the rate of return earned by producing cheese increases relative to the rate of return earned in the production of wine. As a result Eq. (1.21) has to be modified to account for the change in terms of trade. In dynamic form the terms of trade equation now becomes:

$$\rho_1 = \rho_w + \tau \tag{1.22}$$

Where τ denotes the change in terms of trade between the two economies.

The combining of Eqs. (1.17) and (1.20), yields the following relationships:

$$i_1 - i_w = \text{\textEuro} = \pi_1 - \pi_w + (\rho_1 - \rho_w)$$

Substituting Eq. (1.22) into the previous equation yields:

$$i_1 - i_w = \text{\textEuro} = \pi_1 - \pi_w + \tau$$

Rearranging the terms we get an expression for the changes in terms of trade:

$$\tau = \text{\textEuro} - \left(\pi_1 - \pi_w\right) \tag{1.23}$$

This equation provides an interesting insight: violations of PPP reflect changes in the terms of trade of an economy.

The change in the terms of trade is measured as an appreciation of the exchange rate over and above the inflation rate differential between the two currencies. It reflects an increase in the real rate of return of an economy relative to the real rate of return of the other economy.

The Real Exchange Rate or Terms of Trade Appreciation has a Secondary Effect on the Economy: The higher real rate of return means that one pound of cheese in the earlier example can now buy more bottles of wine. This induces people in Lakeland to devote more resources to cheese production at the expense of wine production. These forces will also be at work in Westland, where resources will now be diverted from wine production to the production of the import substitution good: domestic cheese. Therefore, cheese production worldwide increases, while wine production unambiguously declines.

The higher rate of return also means that the resources that are intensive in the production of the appreciating good, say pasture land, experiences an increase in valuation, while the factors intensive in the production of wine decline in value [10]. Cheese land appreciates relative to wine land. Given the assumption that Lakeland is intensive in cheese land relative to Westland, we expect to see the Lakeland stock market outperform the Westland stock market.

The Terms of Trade Analysis is Simple and Straightforward: When a commodity's relative prices remain unchanged, for example, when the price of cheese in terms of wine remains unchanged, so do the terms of trade. In that case, arbitrage ensures that PPP, holds and real rates of return are equalized across countries. Under PPP, the exchange rate changes only reflect inflation rate differentials across countries.

Now if PPP does not hold, then the deviations from PPP reflect relative price changes. For example, when the price of cheese in terms of wine increases, that is, terms of trade changes, the country which experiences currency appreciation over and above the inflation rate differential, Lakeland, will also experience a stock market appreciation relative to its trading partner, Westland.

The increase in real rate of return diverts capital from wine production to cheese production in both countries, Lakeland and Westland. Therefore global production and employment in the cheese industry will increase, while wine production and employment in the wine industry decreases.

ADDING THE FINAL X2

Recall that we have assumed a 2X2X2X2, so far we have introduced the two countries, two goods, and two currencies. However we are still short of a 2. We now address this deficiency by introducing two factors of production.

In what follows, both factors are considered in the production of the two goods, wine and cheese, in both countries. However they are used in different proportions, we will call one factor "wine intensive" while the other will be called "cheese intensive."

Assuming that both countries have the same technology and tastes across the two economies, it is easy to show and/or argue that the relative abundance of the factors of production is a major determinant of the relative production of wine and cheese. In that case it is easy to conclude that in Westland the wine intensive factor will be relatively abundant while the cheese intensive factor will be relatively abundant in Lakeland.

Under some general conditions one can show that there is a one to one correspondence between the relative prices of the final product, that is, wine and cheese, and the returns from the two factors in question [11].

In order to show this lets specify the general model and then show what assumptions are required to make the conclusions that we are referring to in the previous paragraphs:

$$P_{wl} = \alpha_1 \times W_{wl} + (1 - \alpha_1) \times R_{wl} \qquad (1.24)$$

P_{wl}, denotes the cost of producing a bottle of wine in Lakeland in pesos; α_1, represents the labor share of the costs; W_{wl}, the prevailing wage in Lakeland wine sector; R_{wl}, is the rental cost of wine land in Lakeland.

$$P_{cl} = \beta_1 \times W_{cl} + (1 - \beta_1) \times R_{cl} \qquad (1.25)$$

P_{cl}, denotes the cost of producing a pound of cheese in Lakeland in pesos; β_1, represents the labor share of the costs; W_{cl}, the prevailing wage in Lakeland cheese sector, R_{wl}, is the rental cost of cheese/dairy land in Lakeland.

$$P_{ww} = \alpha_w \times W_{ww} + (1 - \alpha_w) \times R_{ww} \qquad (1.26)$$

P_{ww}, denotes the cost of producing a bottle of wine in Westland in notes; α_1, represents the labor share of the costs; W_{ww}, the prevailing wage in Westland wine sector; R_{wl}, is the rental cost of wine land in Westland.

$$P_{cw} = \beta_w \times W_{cw} + (1 - \beta_w) \times R_{cw} \qquad (1.27)$$

P_{cw}, denotes the cost of producing a pound of cheese in Westland in notes; β_1, represents the labor share of the costs; W_{cw}, the prevailing wage in Westland cheese sector; R_{ww}, is the rental cost of cheese/dairy land in Westland.

The previous four equations contain four different prices, four wage rates, and four rental rates for the land. That is, 12 unknown in 4 equations. Assuming that the equations are independent, we will need to remove eight degrees of freedom in order to obtain a unique solution to the system of equations. There are some reasonable assumptions that we can make and depending on these assumptions we will get different answers regarding the impact of demand and supply shocks on the different prices and or factor returns.

Scenario 1: Free trade in goods and services.

So far we have been assuming that there is free trade between the two economies, Lakeland and Westland, and that there are no transportation costs. These two assumptions combined with arbitrage yield the result that the peso price of cheese is the same anywhere in the world and that the peso price of wine is also the same everywhere in the world. That is,

$$P_{wl} = E \times P_{ww} \qquad (1.28)$$

and

$$P_{cl} = E \times P_{cw} \qquad (1.29)$$

Our analysis also has been assuming that there is no migration across national borders. That is, the factors of production are immobile across borders. However we have implicitly assumed that they are mobile within national borders. That is labor and land production can shift costless from cheese production to wine production and vice versa. These assumptions mean that arbitrage leads to the equalization of wage rates across sectors within each of the economies and of the rental price of land. Under these assumptions the following relationships must hold at all times:

$$W_{wl} = W_{cl} \qquad (1.30)$$

$$W_{ww} = W_{cw} \qquad (1.31)$$

$$R_{wl} = R_{cl} \qquad (1.32)$$

and

$$R_{ww} = R_{cw} \qquad (1.33)$$

Assuming that both countries have the same technology, substituting Eqs. (1.28) through (1.33) into Eqs. (1.24) to (1.27) yields:

$$P_{wl} = \alpha \times W_1 + (1 - \alpha) \times R_1 \qquad (1.34)$$

$$P_{cl} = \beta \times W_1 + (1 - \beta) \times R_1 \qquad (1.35)$$

and the difference between the two prices

$$P_{cl} - P_{wl} = (\beta - \alpha) \times (W_1 - R_1) \qquad (1.36)$$

or

$$W_1 - R_1 = (P_{cl} - P_{wl})/(\beta - \alpha) \qquad (1.37)$$

If one takes the price of the finished products as given, the previous two equations has two unknowns and can be solved for the prevailing wage rate and rental rate in Lakeland, that is, in pesos:

$$R_1 = (\beta \times P_{wl} - \alpha \times P_{cl})/(\alpha - \beta) \qquad (1.38)$$

and

$$W_1 = ((1 - \beta) \times P_{wl} - (1 - \alpha) {}^* P_{cl})/(\alpha - \beta) \qquad (1.39)$$

The information presented in the previous section shows that under the free trade assumption and no transportation costs prior to the opening of trade, a pound of cheese was relatively cheaper in Lakeland than in Westland (Fig. 1.2). From Lakeland's perspective, the opening of trade resulted in an increase in the price of cheese in Lakeland and a decline in the price of cheese in Westland. It is therefore safe to conclude that:

- The returns to the cheese intensive factors in the production of cheese in Lakeland rises, while those in Westland declines. If Cheese is the relatively labor intensive factor, then $\beta > \alpha$ holds at all times and we can safely conclude that in Lakeland, the return to the cheese intensive factor, labor, rises both in absolute terms, Eq. (1.36), as well a rising relative to the Wine intensive factor, see Eq. (1.37). In Westland, the cheese intensive factor experience an absolute and relative decline.
- The same information also suggests that the returns to the factor intensive in the production of wine rises in absolute and relative terms in Westland while declining in both absolute and relative terms in Lakeland.

This analysis is very important because it allows us to identify the changes in factor returns due to changes in the terms of trade. As we will show later on, this is key component of the protectionist pressures and the politics of the special interest groups.

A different scenario: All factors of production are free to move across borders but the goods are not permitted to move.

Under these assumptions we know that if labor is free to move across sectors, the wage rate differential is arbitraged. We know that land is not mobile. For the purposes of this section we will assume that capital is the second factor used in the production of both wine and cheese.

The mobility of the factors of production combined with profit maximization yields the following equilibrium conditions:

$$W_{cl} = W_{wl} = E \times W_{cw} = E \times W_{ww} = W \quad (1.40)$$

and

$$R_{cl} = R_{wl} = E \times R_{cw} = E \times R_{ww} = R \quad (1.41)$$

In an integrated world, measured in a common currency, the wage rate or rental rate of a factor return is the same everywhere in the world. Hence

$$P_{cl} = E \times P_{cw} \quad (1.42)$$

and

$$P_{wl} = E \times P_{ww} \quad (1.43)$$

Profit maximization insures that migration and movement would continue until the factor returns were equalized across countries. If the technologies are the same across the economies, the equalization of factor returns implies that the price of the final products will also be equalized across the two economies. The conclusion being that as far as the product and factor price is concerned migration is a substitute for trade, a very important insight that we can use later on.

A Third Scenario: Not all goods and or factors are mobile. The profit maximization assumption means that, absent transportation costs, arbitrage can be affected through either trade in goods, production factor migration, and or a combination of the two. In practice the arbitrage is also shaped by transaction and/or transportation costs incurred by the products in addition to the factors of production.

The profit maximization assumption ensures that the arbitrage process will be one that minimizes the transaction and/or transportation costs, as broadly defined. In general it may make sense to argue that some of the factors of production face higher transportation costs than the goods in question. Land is one such example; it is virtually impossible to move land from one country to another. People may be attached to their family and localities and may not choose to migrate in spite of a salary differential. Hence some factors of production and some goods may face higher "transportation costs" than the cost of shipping wine and/or cheese. Given that we know:

- Free trade in the two finished goods leads to equalizations of the two factor returns even if the factors of production do not move across national borders.
- Free mobility of the two factors of production leads to equalization of the two factor returns as well as the equalization of the price of the two finished goods even if the finished goods do not move across national borders.

However, we have yet to address the issue of what happens when only some goods and some factors are free to move across national borders. What is a necessary condition for the equalization of factor and product prices across the national borders? We hope to answer the question in the next few paragraphs.

Let's assume that one of the goods faces no transportation or any other costs when moving across national borders. In that case arbitrage insures that the price of a bottle of wine is the same in the two countries. That is,

$$P_{wl} = E \times P_{ww} \quad (1.44)$$

We also assume that one of the factors of production is able to move freely across national borders as well as within the country. The mobile labor arbitrages any differences in wages in the different sector and countries by moving from the low wage areas to the higher wage areas until there is no gain from moving.

$$W_{cl} = W_{wl} = E \times W_{cw} = E \times W_{ww} = W \quad (1.45)$$

Although the other factor, land, cannot move across national borders, it can be used to produce either wine or cheese. This means that the rates of returns of the immobile factor will be equalized across sectors within the countries.

$$R_{cl} = R_{wl} \quad (1.46)$$

and

$$E \times R_{cw} = E \times R_{ww} \quad (1.47)$$

Arbitrage requires that

$$P_{wl} = E \times P_{ww}$$

Substituting these equations into (1.24) and (1.26), we get:

$$\alpha \times W + (1-\alpha) \times R_{wl} = \alpha^* W + (1-\alpha) \times R_{ww} \times E \quad (1.48)$$

The previous equation yields the following result:

$$R_{wl} = R_{ww} \times E \quad (1.49)$$

Which, in turn, yields:

$$R_{cl} = R_{wl} = E \times R_{cw} = E \times R_{ww} = R \quad (1.50)$$

The mobility of one product and one factor of production lead to the equalization of the immobile factor, as well as the return of the immobile factor across national borders.

MOBILITY, TRADE, AND THE EQUALIZATION OF PRICE AND FACTOR RETURNS ACROSS BORDERS

Each of the three scenarios presented leads to the equalization of factor returns and product prices across national borders. By combining these three scenarios it leads to a generalization of the conditions that lead to the equalization of factor prices and factor returns across national borders. It suggests that a necessary condition is that the sum of mobile goods and or factors has to equal or be greater than the number of immobile goods and factors within the country.

Several implications are easily derived from our framework and lead to a few interesting insights. Under the assumptions made, arbitrage ensures that there is a single price for each of the commodities in the global economy. This is the so-called "Law of One Price."

A related insight is that the global economy is an integrated economy with a single global market for each of the commodities. This is very important, for it suggests that changes in global prices elicit the same qualitative response across the global economy.

Higher prices either reduce the consumption levels in a country and/or increase the production of the commodity whose relative price has increased. The magnitude of the changes in each country will depend on demand and supply elasticities of the commodities in question (Fig. 1.2). The flatter the demand and supply curves, the more elastic they are and the larger will be the quantity response and the lower the price change needed to clear the market.

The factor price equalization theorem has additional interesting implications.

Any tax or other restrictions on a particular good or factor of production will not affect the equalization of gross tax prices and or returns as long as the number of goods plus factors of productions free to move across national borders *exceeds* the numbers of factors of production. Factor returns will also be equalized across countries. However, what the restrictions do is, it alters the composition of products and or factors of production across national borders.

Again, the incidence of any tax or economic shock is influenced and determined by the mobility of the different factors of production and/or goods and services. In the example of this section any tax ultimately fall on the immobile factors, the local land.

This framework yields some other interesting insights regarding the implications of a policy of free trade and immigration restrictions, as well as implications of a policy of trade restrictions and free immigration with amnesty. The policy of free trade and immigration restrictions suggests that arbitrage in factor returns will take place through trade in goods. That is, goods will move across national borders while factors of production will remain in their native countries. In contrast, the factor return equilibrating process of a policy that restricts trade and allows free immigration will then take place through migrations of the factors of production. Clearly these two policies have different implications for population growth and the makeup of a country's future population.

One final insight generated by this framework is an obvious one. If a country experiences either a man-made or natural disaster and the infrastructure is not rebuilt, it may not be possible to rearrange the productive machinery to absorb all the forces and equalize factor returns.

In that case, the abundant factor experiences a decline in its rate of return. One way to eliminate and arbitrage the differences is through the migration of the factor return to the area with a higher return. This is particularly applicable to the regions devastated by war and other political events. The failures of the developed world to help and implement a successful reconstruction effect have generated an out migration from the devastated areas into the more prosperous areas. The migration does not necessarily occur to super wealthy and developed economies. All that is needed is that the destination country has a higher standard of living or a better safety net than the country of origin.

TRANSPORTATION COSTS AND OVERALL EQUILIBRIUM

Next we explore some additional insights derived through modifications to the basic framework by introducing transportation costs and other manmade artificial trade barriers, such as taxes and other restrictions. The broadly defined transportation costs may prevent the full equalization of prices and or factor returns across borders.

Example: the prevailing market clearing prices for a pound of cheese in Lakeland is 1 peso and the price in Westland is 2.50 pesos and it costs 1 peso to ship a pound of cheese from Lakeland to Westland and vice versa. How will the equilibrium including transportation costs differ from the one we have just discussed in the previous paragraphs?

Direct Arbitrage: Arbitrage and profit maximization will take care of the differences in prices less the "transportation or transaction costs" associated with moving the commodity, that is, cheese, across the national border. Profit maximization dictates that cheese will be exported from the low price locality, Lakeland, to the high price locality, Westland.

Initially, the transaction nets a gross profit of 1.50 per pound of cheese, which reduces the transportation costs and amounts to a net gain of 0.5 pesos.

As more cheese is exported from Lakeland the increased scarcity creates upward pressure on the local price. Conversely, the increased supply of cheese in Westland creates an incipient downward pressure on the local price. The net effect of all this being a decline in the price differential between the two localities, that is, a decline in the profits generated by the arbitrage.

The arbitrage, profit maximization generates an equilibrium process similar to the one described in the previous sections, depicted in Fig. 1.2.

The one difference being that a difference in prices less than or equal to the transportation costs are not profitable and hence these differences will not be arbitraged away. Simply put, the transportation costs produce equilibrium short of the unfettered equilibrium described in Fig. 1.2.

In the numerical example presented here, the process continues until the price differential falls to 1 peso, the transportation costs. At this point all the profit from shipping a pound of cheese has been arbitraged away.

Equilibrium requires that the global demand match global supply. A second necessary equilibrium condition is that the transportation costs introduce a wedge between the price paid by the importing country and the price received by the exporting country. The wedge or difference in national prices is nothing more than the "transportation costs." The new equilibrium inclusive of transportation costs is shown graphically in Fig. 1.3. Notice that the two equilibrium conditions previously mentioned are satisfied in the graph:

- The wedge or difference between the price paid by the importers in pesos, $P_{cn}^t * E$ and the price received by the exporters, P_{cp}^t, is nothing more than the transportation costs, TC. In equation form, the wedge or price difference can be written as: $TC = P_{cn}^t * E - P_{cp}^t$
- The global quantity demanded consumed, Q_c^t, will match the global quantity supplied or produced, Q_c^t.

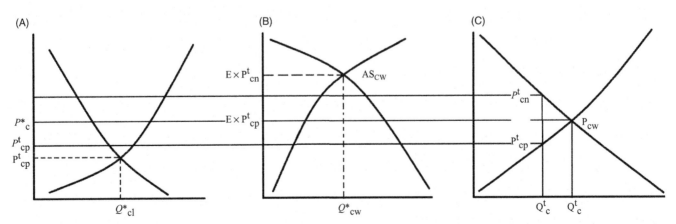

FIGURE 1.3 Transportation cost and worldwide equilibrium. (A) Country 1: Lakeland (peso), (B) country 2: Westland (in pesos), (C) world equilibrium.

A similar argument can be made that differences in excess of the transportation costs for a bottle of wine, 5 pesos, will also be arbitraged by exporting the wine from the locality where wine is lower priced, Westland, to the locality where wine is higher priced, Lakeland.

Arbitrage combined with transportation costs suggests that the differences in the price of a pound of cheese across national borders will not be higher than 1 peso and that of a bottle of wine not higher than 5 pesos. Any differences in price between the two localities that exceeds the transportation costs will be arbitraged away.

What else can we say? In order to further extend our analysis, we need to specify the prices of a bottle of wine and a pound of cheese. Let's consider a scenario where the price of a pound of cheese in Lakeland is 10 pesos, while the price of a bottle of wine in Lakeland is 20 pesos. Since cheese is exported to Westland, the price of cheese in pesos in Westland will be the Lakeland price plus the transportation costs that is, 11 pesos. On the other hand, since wine is exported from Westland, the price of a bottle of wine in Westland will be Lakeland's price less the transportation costs, that is, 15 pesos.

Notice that in this example, the transportation costs for the two commodities are not the same. The information presented in this paragraph can be used to show the following:

- The transportation costs for the export of cheese account for 10% of the price of a pound of cheese in Westland.
- The transportation costs for the import of a bottle of wine account for 25% of the price of a bottle of wine in Lakeland.
- The ratio of the price of a pound of cheese and a bottle of wine show that in Lakeland it takes 100 bottles of wine to get 200 pounds of cheese.
- However, in Westland it takes 100 bottles of wine to acquire 136 pounds of cheese.

In spite of the differences in prices in each economy, the numbers show that the transportation costs prevent any additional arbitrage of these differences in price across borders. A successful arbitrage process will ship the products from the relatively low price area to the relatively high price area. The calculations in the example given in the previous paragraph present some important information:

- The rate of exchange in the two localities shows that cheese is relatively more expensive in Westland than in Lakeland.
- The direct arbitrage opportunities have been exhausted; the peso prices of a pound of cheese and a bottle of wine in the two economies differ by exactly the transportation costs.

Another way of illustrating the arbitrage opportunities is as follows:

The data shows that wine is relatively more expensive in Lakeland than in Westland. Hence the arbitrage would need to find a means to: "effectively" ship cheese from Lakeland to Westland (i.e., as inexpensively as possible) and "effectively" ship wine from Westland to Lakeland. Think of the profit opportunity this way, removal of the transportation costs would generate an arbitrage opportunity. Since:

- 100 bottles of wine in Westland fetches 136 pounds of cheese.
- 100 bottles of Westland wine will fetch 200 pounds of cheese in Lakeland.
- There therefore is a potential arbitrage gain of 74 pounds of cheese.

Unfortunately, this arbitrage opportunity is wiped out by the transportation costs, which for a bottle of wine is 25% of the price. Hence transporting 100 bottles to Lakeland yield a net profit of 75 bottles, which will only fetch 150 pounds of cheese. However the transportation costs for cheese is 10% and that means a net of 135 pounds of cheese will arrive at Westland after the transportation costs are deducted.

All the "low hanging fruit" or direct arbitrage has been taken and all that may be left is the "high hanging fruit," indirect arbitrage.

Indirect Arbitrage: The issue for the arbitrageurs is how to get to the high hanging fruit? Direct arbitrage on the commodities market has eliminated any price difference other than the 25% transportation cost barrier.

In contrast for the cheese industry (the export sector) the producer is indifferent for selling at a 10% discount to the domestic consumers or charging full price inclusive of the transportation costs to the people of Westland.

Absent any mobility from one industry to another the factor returns in Lakeland's wine industry has a 25% edge or protection from foreign competition, that is, the 25% transportation cost of a bottle of wine. At the margin the Lakeland industry can afford to pay 25% more and make the same profit as in the case when transportation costs are nonexistent. It will also make the same amount of revenues as any importer. On the other hand if it did not pay premium salaries, its profitability would include an additional 25% of the price per unit since Lakeland wine makers do not incur these transportation costs when they sell their wine locally. This situation however, would not stand for long, "competition" will attract new entrant into the local Lakeland wine-producing sector, thus increasing the domestic wine production.

In the latter case at the margin, the Lakeland wine industry would want to hire additional factors of production (i.e., additional skilled labor, etc.) this would result in an increase in the production of wine in Lakeland wine and that in turn would produce lower prices of wine in Lakeland. In order to attract the factors into wine production the Lakeland wine industry has to pay slightly higher salaries. And as more and more people are hired, the increased salaries result in an increase in marginal costs, the process continues until the marginal cost rise by 25%. At that point there will be no additional incentives to hire more workers and increase production.

The net effect of these changes will be a higher domestic wine production and a lower cheese production. That is, Lakeland's imports of wine fall and so does Lakeland's exports of cheese. The returns for the factors intensive in the production of wine rise relative to the factors intensive in the production of cheese. As the price of wine rises relative to the price of cheese, Lakeland's relative prices converge to those of Westland.

In Westland the change in the market equilibrium is a mirror image of what happened in Lakeland. The cheese industry expands and so does the relative return of the factor intensive in the production of cheese. In turn the wine industry output declines. Again, cheese imports decline and so does the wine exports. Notice that in this scenario, the two countries react to minimize the relatively high transportation cost of wine, that is, the 25% transportation costs. On the other hand cheese, the product with the lower transportation costs of 10%, is the commodity that continues crossing borders in order to bring about a new equilibrium.

The conclusion here is that arbitrage, in a roundabout way, reduces and in some circumstances *eliminates* trade of the commodity with the highest transportation costs as a percent of the product price, in this example wine. If this process is successful, at equilibrium the price of cheese will differ across the two economies by 10%. In addition the price of wine will also differ by 10% across the two economies and will NOT differ by the 25% transportation costs of a bottle of wine (transportation of wine will no longer occur at the new equilibrium). Since the difference in prices across national borders is 10%, it follows that the relative prices of the two economies are the same. The indirect arbitrage ensures the equality of relative national borders irrespective of the transportation costs.

What the transportation costs and profit maximization do is to ensure the difference in absolute price differences across national borders matches the lowest transportation cost in the range of products traded internationally.

MOBILITY AND THE INCIDENCE OF TAXES AND OTHER ECONOMIC SHOCKS

It is now time to expand the analysis to include mobility of factors of production across national boundaries. The assumption of profit maximization can be used to show that in the case of perfect mobility the differences in factor returns are arbitraged away.

Until now we have assumed fixed costs of moving across borders. This is analogous to buying a ticket on an airplane or paying a fixed cost to mail a package. The transportation costs considered range from zero to prohibitive, in the former case the factors and or products are free to move without any costs and in the latter the costs of moving are infinite. We have shown that if there are zero transportation costs, the differences in prices for similar products will be arbitraged away. And price disturbances will be transmitted across all economies and as a result will have a common qualitative effect across borders. The difference in the magnitude of the response will depend on the countries demand for and supply elasticities with respect to the price changes [12].

Arbitrage and mobility ensure that capital is rearranged in such a way that the after-tax rate of return is the same across industries, as well as across borders. The mobility assumptions yield some insights into the potential incidence and burden of different shocks and or economic policies.

Let's take the case of an open economy that is very small in relation to the world economy. So small that it has no impact on world prices no matter what this economy does. In economic parlance, the small open economy is a "price taker." This means that the unit cost for wine and cheese and the cost of capital are determined by the world market, that is the intersection of the world global demand and supply for the commodity in question and there is nothing the small country can do to alter the global price of these traded good and factors of production.

Now let's consider the impact of a 10% tax on the price of the exported products, say cheese, in the small economy, and call it Lakeland for the time being. Since the country is a price taker, any export tax means that the net price received by the domestic producers will fall by 10% below the world price. That is,

$$P_c^* \times (1-t)$$

where P_c^* is the worldwide equilibrium price for cheese and t is the export tax rate. A 10% tax in a product is equivalent to a tax on each for the factors of production. Labor is assumed to be free to move across national borders, this means that labor or any other mobile factor has to earn the same after tax rate of return as anywhere else in the world, W_e^*, otherwise it will leave the country in search of the higher rate of return. Therefore the salaries paid in Lakeland to the mobile factor have to be grossed by the tax.

Substituting these relationships into the costs of producing a pound of cheese in Lakeland, Eq. (1.25) we get:

$$P_c^* \times (1-t) = [\beta^* W_1 + (1-b) \times R/(1-t)] \times (1-t)$$

Solving for the equilibrium wage rate $\qquad (1.51)$

$$W_1 = [P_c^* \times (1-t) - (1-b) \times R]/[b \times (1-t)]$$
$$= (P_c^*/b) + \{(1-b) \times R/[b^*(1-t)]\} \qquad (1.52)$$

Since P_c^* and W are determined in the world economy and we have assumed that the small economy, Lakeland, has no global market power. The only variable Lakeland can affect is the export tax rate. The previous equation shows that the increases in the tax rate lower the equilibrium wage rate. The incidence of the tax rate increase depends in the intensity of the immobile factor in the production of cheese. The lower the intensity of the immobile factor the greater the impact of the tax rate on the equilibrium rate of return of the immobile factor.

If, as we have assumed, capital is the perfectly mobile factor, the incidence of any tax on capital falls on the fixed factor of the country. This is the direct result that arbitrage ensures that the after-tax income remains the same across industries and countries. Given the unit labor costs, it means that as a result of the tax increase, there is less money available to be paid for the fixed factor. Hence a tax on the mobile factor lowers the rate of return of the fixed factor. The one insight derived from this is that the export tax falls completely on the domestic immobile tax, such as land or any other factor that is not able to move across the national border, that is, is unable to leave the country.

Given that the immobile factor of production is a fraction of the unit costs, it follows that the fluctuations in rates of return to the fixed factor is a magnified version of the fluctuations in the price of wine and cheese. The magnification factor is the inverse of the fraction of the fixed factor as share of unit costs, $(1-\beta)/\beta$.

The point that we want to make here is that the degree of mobility both across domestic industries and across the border has a significant impact on the incidence of different taxes and or economic shocks on the immobile or less mobile factor returns. The lack of mobility reduces the ability of these factors to shift the burden of the shock to other factors of production. Hence one should take into account the mobility of the factors of production and or the goods and services when analyzing the economic shocks on an economy's overall equilibrium and its factor returns.

An investment insight is that one should want to increase exposure to the economy whose exchange rate is appreciating over and above the PPP relationship. In fact, an even better excess return is obtained by increasing exposure to the factors intensive in the production of the country's exports.

THE SPEED OF ADJUSTMENT TO A NEW EQUILIBRIUM

Up to this point we have implicitly assumed that there is no adjustment costs in reaching a new equilibrium in the aftermath of an economic shocks such an increase in aggregate demand and or aggregate supply. If that is the case, the adjustment is instantaneous. Any profit opportunity that arises as the global economy moves from its preshock equilibrium to the new equilibrium is immediately arbitraged, as a result the new equilibrium is reached instantaneously.

However, in real life there may be adjustment costs. For example, it takes time to convert a field from pasture to winegrowing. It may take time to train people to acquire new skills etc., all of this suggests that the longer the time horizon the larger the long run elasticities of supply. Put another way there are costs associated with the speed of adjustment to a new equilibrium.

As long as the costs are positive the adjustment will not be instantaneous. This is a very important insight for investors with a global view. First it means that there will be a window of opportunity for investors who guess the new equilibrium. These investors will be able to earn an above average or excess return during the adjustment process to a new equilibrium.

If investors can anticipate the new equilibrium they may be able to approximate the adjustment path. This is where our framework comes into play, it may help us anticipate the new equilibrium. One final point is that the excess return or the will be a temporary one, once the new equilibrium is reached the excess returns disappear. Put another way, any edge that once can get from an approach as we have outlined here, will be a temporary one.

References

[1] Samuelson Paul A. International trade and the equalization of Factor Prices. Economic Journal 1948;58:163–84. June. Samuelson Paul A. International Factor Price Equalization Once Again. Economic Journal 1949;59:181–97. June.

[2] Mundell RA. International trade and factor mobility. Am Econ Rev 1957;47(3):321–35.

[3] Cassel KG. Abnormal deviations in international exchanges. Econ J 1918;413–5.

[4] Canto VA. Cocktail economics. New Jersey: Pearson Education; 2007.

[5] Johnson HG. Two-sector model of general equilibrium. New York: Aldine-Atherton; 1971.

[6] Hicks JR. Value and capital. 2nd ed. 1939. Oxford: Oxford University Press; 1946.

[7] Frenkel JA, Levich RM. Covered interest arbitrage: unexploited profits? J Political Econ 1975;83(2):325–38.

[8] Fisher I. The theory of interest. Philadelphia: Porcupine Press; 1977. [1930].

[9] Agmon T. The relations among equity markets: a study of stock price co-movements in the United states, United Kingdom, Germany and Japan. J Finance 1972;27:839–55.

[10] On this issue, see Stolper and Samuelson (1941). There is an extensive literature on the topic, find references to the Stolper-Samuelson theorem on the relationship between relative prices and relative actor returns. While the Factor Price Equalization Theorem, Samuelson (1948) relates the product prices to the factor absolute returns.

[11] Early on there were studies that challenged the validity of the Law of One Price such as Isard (1977) and Richardson (1978). There are several sources that give rise to these temporary deviations in some cases one may argue that they are the result of index measurements associated with changes in relative price changes. Another possibility is that the deviations are due to non-traded factors or goods specific to individual countries. These studies emphasize that measured prices can deviate for a sustained period. This fits our views of adjustment costs associated with terms of trade changes. Once the adjustment occurs, the relative prices remain unchanged and the composite good conditions applies once again.

[12] On this Issue see Canto and Webb (1987), Canto, Laffer, and Webb (1992).

I. ARBITRAGE AND MOBILITY

2

Practical Applications: The Investment and Policy Insights and Implications Derived From Arbitrage and Mobility

Purchasing Power Parity (PPP) and Interest Rate Parity (IRP) are our starting point of most of the international economic analysis and countries' comparisons [1]. As we showed in the previous chapter, both concepts are easily derived once profit maximization, and the absence of transaction costs are assumed. Combined, the two assumptions lead to the conclusion that the price of any commodity, say a ton of steel, be it the Dollar, Euro, or any other currency unit, and has to be the same all over the world. If it was not, the difference in price and the absence of transportation or transaction costs would create a profit opportunity that arbitrageurs would exploit and eventually eliminate.

We made liberal use of equations to illustrate the relationships implied by our assumptions. In addition, we made very explicit and somewhat restrictive assumptions during the specification of the relationships in the equations; this was done to arrive at clear and precise conclusions. Relaxing these assumptions allows us to examine how the model implications would change. The reader is free to do so. Our next step is to assess how robust are the conclusions reached in the previous section. If they are, they provide us with a framework from which one may be able to analyze policy changes and anticipate the new equilibrium conditions.

This is what we affectionately call the Wayne Gretzky approach. When Gretzky was asked why he was such a good player even though he was not a fast skater, his answer was that most people skate to where the puck is. He did not. He said that he skated to where the puck was *going* to be. That is the investment approach that we hope to derive from the use of the framework outlined in the previous paragraphs. But that is not all. If we know where the puck is going to be, we may also know what drove it there. The analogy here being that our framework may help us understand the impact of the different Policies, and that in turn could be quite useful in designing Policies that will drive the puck where we want it to be. In the process, we may be able to identify and discard the policies that will not drive the puck to the goal.

We also want to make a very important point. It is our belief that the framework is the key to understanding the policies that impact the world. How the global economy reaches a new equilibrium from which one can develop investment and policy insights? How the average person does conduct this analysis? Does it require an advanced

Economic Disturbances and Equilibrium in an Integrated Global Economy. http://dx.doi.org/10.1016/B978-0-12-813993-6.00002-7

knowledge of econometrics and statistics? We contend that these tools are useful but not required. As opposed to a precise and delayed answer provided by such rigorous approach, we believe that what is important is the intuition and the understanding that allows a person to get a good approximation of the correct answer as quickly as possible. To do so we need to have a very good understanding of the framework, and to speed up the process we also need to be able to do back-of-the-envelope calculations that point us in the direction of the precise answer.

With this in mind, we try to avoid regression analysis and other econometric techniques, and attempt to illustrate the relationships graphically and perform a simple qualitative analysis that point us in the right direction in very little time without requiring an advanced degree in statistics and/or econometrics. Common sense and a bit of logic as outlined in the equations presented in the previous chapter can take us a long way.

IS THE LAW OF ONE PRICE A USEFUL CONCEPT?

There is a simple and direct way to answer the question. Let's put the theory to the test, then look at the data and see if the implications yielded by the framework hold water.

Our first case study is the state economies within the United States. The different states in the union are as large as or larger than many countries in the world. In fact, the state of California often brags that if it was a country it would be the 7th largest economy in the world. We are going to look at the United States as a global economy where member states maintain a fixed exchange rate system, the dollar. Also because of the interstate commerce clause, there are no trade restrictions among the states.

Factors are free to move about both within the state as well as across the states. We concede that within the US economy some factors face high transportation costs, with land being the textbook example. Other factors may face some immobility for other reasons such as family ties and so on. Hence in what follows, we assume there is true free trade in goods and services across state lines and partial, if not full, mobility of factors of production.

The Hypothesis: We have shown in the previous chapter that under some general conditions, the free trade in goods combined with mobility leads to the equalization of factor returns across state lines. We also showed that differences in transportation costs lead to nonarbitrageable differences in prices across state lines equal to or smaller than the transportation costs. Also as the states' economies have a single currency, in effect they have a fixed exchange rate system; therefore arbitrage insures the equality of the prices net of transportation costs as well as of the inflation rates across the different states.

The Data: The US Department of Commerce provides free of charge and easily downloadable data on the states' gross state product (GSP). The ratio of the constant dollar and current dollar data provided us with an estimate of the states' deflators, a proxy for the price index. Using the individual states' data, we calculated several other variables such as each of the states' real GSP growth rates, the state's share of the US GSP, the states' terms of trade, and each state's inflation rate for each calendar year.

The Inflation Results: Next, we ranked the inflation rate during each of the years from high to low to get a sense of the dispersion among the states' inflation rates. We then divided each year ranking into quartiles and calculated the average inflation rate for each of the quartiles.

Fig. 2.1 presents information on the average inflation rate for each of the quartiles as well the average inflation

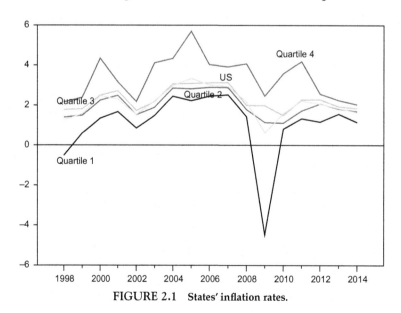

FIGURE 2.1   States' inflation rates.

rates for all the states, that is the US inflation rate. It uncovers several interesting pieces of information. The first one being that the second and third quartiles are fairly close to the US inflation rate. In fact, visually it is hard to separate one of the series from the other. The first quartile, the lowest inflation quartile, is close to the average with the noticeable exception, the big recession, where it takes a big dip relative to the other series. While not perfect, the data suggests that for at least three of the quartiles, the inflation rate is not that much different than that of the states' averages. This is precisely the result one would expect under the profit maximization arbitrage conditions we have derived, the Law of One Price or PPP holds. The data suggests that more often than not, it holds. Thus this is a good starting point.

The data presented in Fig. 2.1, in particular quartile 4 shows that some states experience an above-average inflation rate that visually is clearly different from the average of the other quartiles and the US average inflation rate. This result may be interpreted as either a blemish on the Law of One Price or as evidence that we need to expand the framework.

Something we have done in the previous chapter is that we showed that changes in relative prices would lead to deviations in the underlying inflation rate across the state economies' consumer price index (CPIs). These deviations would accord our view and reflect changes in terms of trade across the different economies. Reversing the process, we are now going to assume that the differences in the inflation rates across states are the result of terms of trade changes that will be discussed later on.

The States' Growth Rates: According to our framework, mobile factors arbitrage differences in salaries by simply moving to the state with the higher salaries. We also showed that if the number of mobile factors plus traded goods exceeds the total number of factors of production, prices and factor returns would be equalized across state lines. If the states also have a similar mix of factors, one can then stretch the analysis and argue that there will be a tendency for the equalization of the income derived by similar factors in the different localities. There will be a tendency for a state's GSP, as well as its growth rate to converge to the national average.

Again as before, to test our hypothesis, we ranked the growth rates of the states from high to low each of the years and separated them into four quartiles. The times series generated by these quartiles as well as the US growth rate are reported in Fig. 2.2. Notice that the different series tend to move together. The second and third quartiles appear to be undistinguishable from the average.

Our interpretation of the data and explanation of the results is quite simple; we contend that the differences in growth rates are due to a combination of factor immobility and region-specific shocks. The latter could be natural causes and or man-made such as fiscal policy chocks [2]. The common movement is easy explained in terms of an integrated global/US economy. Under a global economy with free trade and no transportation costs, prices are determined by the global demand and supply of the different commodities. Changes in these prices induce a common response across the different countries' demand and supply curves, thereby introducing a common effect across the different economies. However, for the factors facing prohibitive moving costs, the market-clearing conditions are determined by the local demand and supply conditions.

A rising local price for a nontraded factor or product results in a higher factor return and a higher output in that locality relative to the rest of the world. The price and output response in each locality will have two different components: the contributions of the mobile factor, which will be common among the localities and the contributions of the local or nontraded factors, which

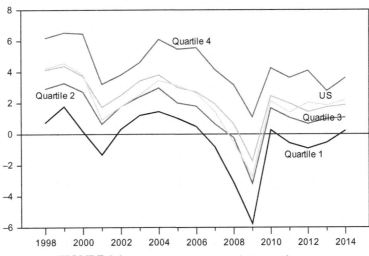

FIGURE 2.2 States' gross state product growth rate.

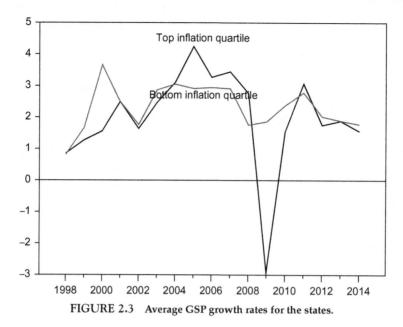

FIGURE 2.3   Average GSP growth rates for the states.

will be specific to the localities. All of this suggests that in the faster growing economies, the immobile factors and product will experience a faster price appreciation, that is a faster inflation rate. The excess inflation and faster growth rates are nothing more than a reflection of the improving terms of trade effect in the locality.

Real GSP Growth and the Terms of Trade: To further test our hypothesis regarding the relationship between the real GSP growth rates, the terms of trade, and the states' inflation rates, we compared the US growth rate to the average GSP growth rate of the states in the top and bottom inflation quartile (Fig. 2.3). The data shows that the states in the top inflation quartile experience an above-average real GDP growth during periods of economic

expansion, while the states in the bottom quartile show a below average growth during these same periods.

To test the robustness of these results, we reversed the process. Fig. 2.4 reports the average inflation rate for states in the top and bottom quartiles of growth respectively. The data presented in Fig. 2.4 shows that the states in the top real GDP growth experience an above-average inflation rate during periods of economic expansion and a below average inflation rate during periods of economic expansion.

No matter how the data is sliced, it uncovers a positive relationship between the local growth rate and the inflation rate. This we have attributed to the terms of trade effect. While the data suggests that is the case, there is a

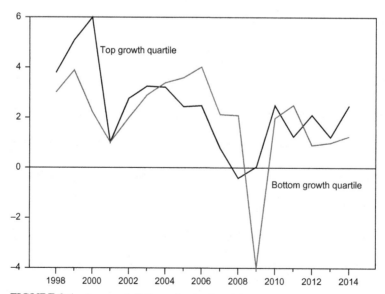

FIGURE 2.4   Average inflation rates for the states.

simple way to test this point of view: looking at the data directly. Fig. 2.5A–F shows the relationship between the terms of trade and the states' share of the US GSP for the following states—Alaska, Indiana, New York, North Dakota, Ohio, and Texas. The results, while not perfect, point to a clear positive correlation between the state's share of the US GSP and its terms of trade relative to the US economy. Adding more states would not add to the qualitative information, but it would clearly take more space.

The Investment and Policy Implications: One often hears that certain areas have become very expensive to live, that the affordability index is very low. More often than not, these expensive areas are prosperous areas where there is some fixed or inelastic factor, the quintessential one being real estate. As the mobile factors are attracted to the area, the demand for the inelastic or fixed factor rises, as do prices. The area prices go through the roof and some of the more dilapidated areas get gentrified. That is how the market works. It is no different than investing in the stock market. People want to buy stocks that are undervalued and likely to appreciate. Nobody wants to buy a stock that will become more affordable. The same holds for real estate: as the affordability declines due to a higher demand, price increases. The latter attracts suppliers, be it through new construction or gentrification.

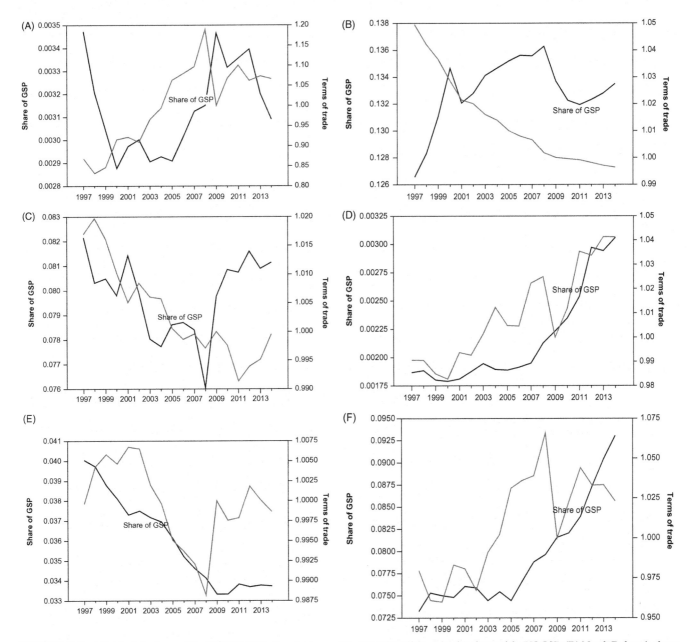

FIGURE 2.5 (A) Alaska's share of the US GSP; (B) Indiana's share of the US GSP; (C) New York's share of the US GSP; (D) North Dakota's share of the US GSP; (E) Ohio's share of the US GSP; (F) Texas' share of the US GSP.

To implement a successful real estate investment strategy, all one needs to do is identify areas that are likely to grow and prosper. In those areas, the fixed factor will appreciate, while areas where the economy is likely to slowdown, the prices and returns to the fixed factor are likely to decline. Good policy that attracts businesses does a lot for the returns of the fixed factor and that reduces the affordability index. But that is not a bad thing. A rising tide lifts all boats. While people complain about the lack of affordability, the jobs will be plentiful in these areas. Think of the Silicon Valley, Manhattan, and Austin in recent years. The easiest way to increase the affordability is to destroy the local economy. Detroit and South Central Los Angeles during the last few decades comes to mind. The investment and policy implications could not be clearer. The same goes for the economic policy recommendations for a state politician: adopt pro-growth policies. These policies attract skilled workers and jobs, as well as producing higher asset prices and higher income, thereby expanding the state tax base.

CONVERGENCE: THE IMPLEMENTATION OF THE EURO

The events leading to the implementation of the Euro meant that within the Eurozone all prices would be quoted in the local currency, the Euro. Hence, the price comparison is fairly straightforward. As economies within the Eurozone use the same currency, the exchange rate is by definition fixed. This means that absent transportation costs, arbitrage requires that the underlying inflation rate in each of the Eurozone economies converges to a common underlying inflation rate, presumably set by the European Central Bank (ECB) [3]. That is, the arbitrage process when applied to commodities, leads to the PPP conditions outlined. And when applied to securities, such as bonds, it leads to the IRP. The concept is the same, except that a time span is now involved. Again, if the yield comparisons occur between two countries within the Eurozone, there is no exchange rate fluctuation. Then IRP and arbitrage suggest that, absent transaction and/or transportation costs, the yields of countries in the Eurozone have to converge.

The simple framework shows that profit maximization, perfect mobility, and foresight require the inflation rate to be the same in each of the economies within the Eurozone, that is PPP holds. Now these same assumptions and the fact that PPP holds also tell us that the real rate of return has to be the same in each economy in the region, that is IRP holds. The latter is easy to show. If the real rate of return differs across countries, capital will move to arbitrage these differences. The process will end and equilibrium will be achieved when the rates of return are equalized across national borders.

The framework is relatively simple and its implications are quite insightful. We have used the PPP–IRP approach quite frequently in the past and found the implications derived to be easily implemented in a way that produces above-average returns.

What We Said at the Time: Leading up to the implementation of the euro, we were quite emphatic about who the early winners and losers of the creation of the euro would be. At the time, many pundits argued that Germany would be the big winner. However, we did not share that opinion—at least not in the short run. We argued that the adoption of the euro would result in a convergence of bond yields across the member countries. The investment implication was that the worst countries, that is those with the highest yields, would do well and that the best countries, those with the lowest yields, would underperform. Here is what we said in March of 1998:

> The run up to the European Economic and Monetary Union, its electronic start in 1999, and its impact on monetary and fiscal policy afterwards, have important investment implications. To better understand these implications it is useful to draw a parallel between the EMU and our own United States.

Convergence

The proposed monetary union in Europe closely resembles the system already in place in the United States. The union of the states under a federal central bank in 1913 led to the convergence of interest rates across states, which resulted in virtual equality of rates across the nation. But, despite this near equality, growth rates do differ among states. These growth differentials are largely explained by variations in state fiscal policies.

For portfolio managers, this interest-rate convergence and growth-differential paradigm is useful when applied to the European landscape. European Union member nations, like our states, employ various fiscal and monetary policy instruments to meet the Maastricht Treaty convergence criteria. The interest-rate provision of the treaty says that, to be eligible for entrance into EMU, a nation must have an average nominal interest rate on long-term government bonds over the past year of no more than two percentage points above that of the three best-performing member states in terms of price stability. Thus far, the eleven nations vying for admittance - Austria, Belgium, Finland, France, Ireland, Italy, Luxembourg, Netherlands, Germany, Spain and Portugal - have fared relatively well in meeting this provision...As the EMU approaches and interest rates converge, and as they fluctuate within a narrow range after January 1, 1999, **the policies employed to meet the Maastricht criteria will dictate growth differentials among the nations**. The investment implications are easy to see. We have said previously that the best portfolio strategy for the transition is to buy shares of companies in those countries whose interest rates are higher and most distant from German rates. This convergence insight has served portfolio managers well so far in the transition. The Maastricht Treaty also includes a price stability provision. It states that, for a nation to be admitted, it must have an average rate of consumer price inflation during the year before the examination (this year) that does not exceed by more than 1.5 percentage points that of, at most, the three best performing member states. This provision also has been met with some success...The data shows that Spain's convergence accelerated late in 1996. The Maastricht conditions have forced a change in policies for aspiring members of the currency union. They have all converged to the German rates, effectively making Germany's central bank the precursor of the European Central Bank [4].

THE CONVERGENCE AND POSTCONVERGENCE EURO ENVIRONMENTS

The IRP- and PPP-driven insight proved quite useful. As we were arguing that the adoption of the euro would result in a convergence, it meant that the largest risk premium reduction would occur in the weaker countries, mostly the portugal, ireland, italy and greece (PIIGS). One does not need to be a rocket scientist to know that if the highest yields decline the most, the highest yield bonds would produce the largest appreciation. Fig. 2.6A shows that our yield forecast and anticipated convergence did come to pass. Also, a fact that is difficult to discern from the data is that Germany, the strongest economy with sound policies, became the benchmark as far as bond yields is concerned (as we had anticipated). The euro yields are no different than those of the German bond yields.

After the initial convergence in bond yields across the Eurozone, IRP was essentially achieved. But, as we have already mentioned, despite the near equality, shortly after the adoption of the euro, growth rates did differ among states. We argued then (and still do) that these growth differentials are largely explained by variations in state fiscal policies. After the transition to the euro,

when interest rates and inflation rates convergences were achieved, the relative performances of the economies would be explained by the real exchange rate or terms of trade changes, much like we showed previously with the states' situation. Again, to reiterate, these terms of trade changes could be explained in terms of fiscal policy changes and other real shocks to the economies in the region, but more on this later.

The convergence produced by the announcement and the measures leading up to the adoption of the euro is clearly visible in Fig. 2.6A. The left portion of Fig. 2.6B provides evidence of the convergence in the context of a longer time period.

The middle of the graph illustrates what we called the pure IRP and PPP, the time period when interest rates and inflation rates had converged, and the differences in return were attributable to the differences in fiscal policies.

DIVERGENCE: THE DISMANTLING OF BRETTON WOODS

The Bretton Woods Agreement was developed at the United Nations Monetary and Financial Conference held in Bretton Woods, New Hampshire, from July 1 to July 22, 1944. The landmark system for monetary and exchange rate management was based on a gold exchange rate standard where member countries would fix their exchange rate to that of the US dollar and, in turn, the United States would fix the value of the dollar to the price of an ounce of gold (in a later chapter we discuss in greater detail how this system operated. For now, we will focus on the events surrounding the dismantling of the system).

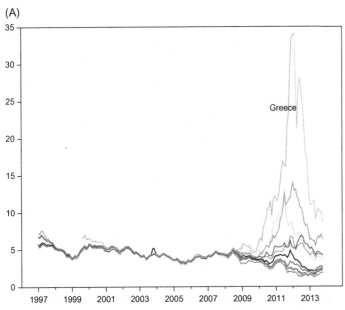
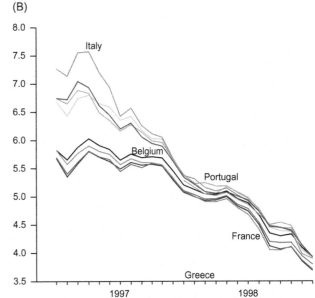

FIGURE 2.6 (A–B) Selected Eurozone countries bond yields.

We contend that during the mid-1960s the United States got increasingly involved in the Vietnam War, the increased involvement contributed to an increase in military spending. Domestically, the Johnson administration was implementing the "Great Society" programs. Both the domestic and defense spending put enormous pressure on the overall spending of the federal government. The President of the United States, Lyndon B. Johnson, used the phrase "guns versus butter" to catch the attention of the national media while reporting on the state of national defense and the economy. Indeed the Johnson administration faced a choice. Given limited resources, it had to decide where to spend the same. The financing choices were also limited. Taxes could not be raised. Doing so would reverse the famous Kennedy-Johnson tax rate cuts. The Vietnam War was unpopular making the issuance of public debt difficult. The one option available to the administration that could be done without any Congressional approval was to print money. In fact, the easy money policy had an added attraction. To the extent that the rest of the world used the dollar as its international reserve, the United States was effectively forcing the rest of the world to share the money financing costs.

As the United States printed money to finance the Vietnam War, the excess money was exported to the rest of the world as a balance of payment deficit. By 1965, the rest of the world began accumulating dollars and some complained. The leader of this group was none other than Charles de Gaulle. He forced the US hand when, in accordance with the Bretton Woods Agreement, he threatened to bring US dollars to the Fed and demanded gold at the official exchange rate. Initially the United States honored the gold exchange commitment. Unfortunately, it also continued printing money, which meant

that the US gold reserves would suffer a steady decline. At some point something had to give. Either the United States would run out of gold or the excess money printing would have to stop. Yet the Nixon administration chose neither. Instead, in 1970 and 1971, it took a series of steps in its attempt to defend the dollar and control inflation. It enacted wage and price controls, devalued the dollar and allowed it to float. Milton Friedman had made the case earlier in 1950, but many economists picked up on the theme around that time [5].

President Nixon accepted the now-conventional view that favored a freely floating exchange rate and ultimately the Nixon administration accepted these arguments and the dollar were allowed to float freely in the open market.

THE LOCAL INFLATION RESULTS

One of the major arguments in favor of the flexible exchange rate was that it would insulate the countries from external monetary/inflationary shocks. The allure was that it would stop inflation and seigniorage tax the United States was imposing on the rest of the world. The implication was that by adopting the flexible exchange rate, the non-US inflation rate would decline. Sadly, as shown in Fig. 2.7, the forecast did not materialize. Contrary to expectations, the inflation rate surged all over the world. It was a disappointment to the proponents of the flexible exchange rate who had promised or forecasted an insulation from external shocks as well as a lower inflation rate. The rise in inflation was not an isolated phenomenon. Not only had the inflation rates increased across the globe, the near double digit inflation continued throughout the decade and didn't peak until late in

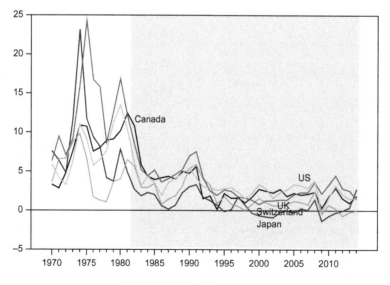

FIGURE 2.7   Inflation rate.

1979 and early 1980, when Paul Volcker changed the operating procedures of the Fed and eventually tamed the inflation beast.

The unhinging of the Bretton Woods system produced some interesting results. Not only did all the countries inflation rates surge (Fig. 2.7), but when converted to dollars (Fig. 2.8) the inflation rates hovered around that of the United States. The differences in inflation rates we attribute to terms of trade effects.

The information presented in Figs. 2.9 and 2.10 are quite interesting, and produce qualitatively similar results to those presented in Figs. 2.7 and 2.8. Yet there are significant differences regarding the series. In Figs. 2.9 and 2.10, the time series were constructed as follows: using the full sample of the 189 countries in IMF data base, for each year we ranked the information from high to low, irrespective of the country. We constructed 189 time series, where the first one consisted of the highest inflation rate each year. The 189 series consisted the lowest inflation rate in the world during that year. The series were grouped in quartiles and we calculated the average inflation in each quartile.

The selection process is such that, on average, we would expect to see the second quartile be above-average, and the data shows that is the case. That logic would also lead us to expect the average inflation rate to

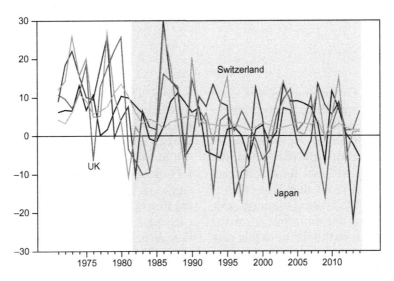

FIGURE 2.8   Local inflation rate in US dollars.

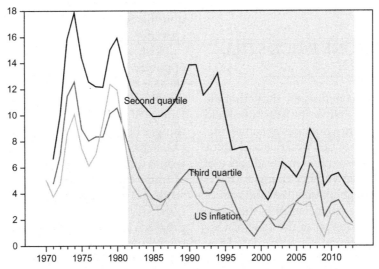

FIGURE 2.9   Worldwide inflation statistics in local currencies.

I. ARBITRAGE AND MOBILITY

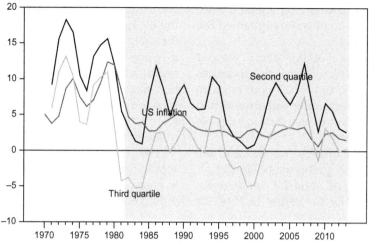

FIGURE 2.10   **Worldwide inflation statistics in US dollars terms.**

be below the median, and it is. However, whether the average inflation rate in the third quartile is below or above the US inflation cannot be determined a priori. In theory, the US inflation could rank anywhere. Nevertheless, as a point of reference, the second quartile shows that the countries' average inflation is not that much different from the US inflation. Taken at face value, these results suggests that the adoption of the floating exchange rate was not successful in isolating the countries form the supposedly undesired inflation of the 1970s, in this case the United States. The data suggests that at best the inflation rate was similar to the United States and, at worst, the local inflation rate deteriorated in both absolute and relative terms (see third quartile information presented in Fig. 2.9). The conclusion is that the floating exchange rate did not deliver the results promised by the people who advocated for the floating exchange rate system.

DOES THE LAW OF ONE PRICE STILL HOLD?

Although Figs. 2.7 and 2.9 conclusively show that the floating exchange rate did not deliver the inflation shield that the countries expected from a floating exchange rate, the issue as to whether the Law of One Price still holds is another matter. We have shown that in the absence of transportation costs and of relative price changes, that is terms of trade effects, arbitrage insures that the rate of change of each country's consumer basket is the same across countries. This is the version of the Law of One Price or PPP that we now examine using the data from the 189 countries. Our first step was to convert the rate of change of the consumer basket in local currency into

dollars. That is, we calculated the inflation rate in domestic currencies and subtracted from it the local currency exchange rate depreciation vis-a-vis the US dollar. We call this the countries' dollar inflation rates.

Our next step was to rank each of the countries' dollar inflation rates, from high to low for each of the years. Again as before, we constructed 189 time series where the first one consisted of the highest dollar inflation rate each year. The 189 series is made up of the dollar inflation rates for countries with the lowest dollar inflation rate in the world during that year. The series were then grouped into quartiles, and then we calculated the average inflation in each quartile. Fig. 2.10 plots the two quartile series as well as the US inflation rate. There are several interesting features of the two series. The turning points appear to coincide. In effect, the two series appear to be parallel to each other. Needless to say, the second quartile is the higher of the two series. The two series span the US inflation rate.

Next, as we look at Figs. 2.8 and 2.10, it becomes apparent that the exchange rate adjusted inflation series are much closer to the US inflation series. The fact that the difference between the second quartile and the United States has narrowed significantly suggests a few things. First, the exchange rate adjustment brings the two series much closer, just like the Law of One Price would predict. We attribute the divergences to terms of trade effects. Nevertheless, we can safely argue that while not perfect, the Law of One Price framework is a good starting point. A broader and comprehensive approach would incorporate changes in the terms of trade to enhance the explanatory power of our framework. The third observation is the fact that the dollar inflation is lower than the inflation in local currency means that,

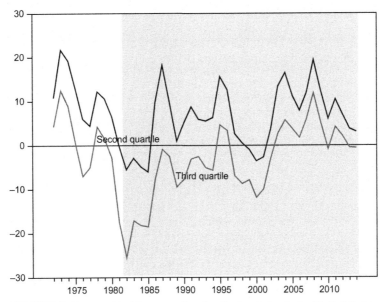

FIGURE 2.11   **Worldwide terms of trade effects relative to the United States.**

on average, the rest of the world's exchange rate depreciated. Hence the unhinging from the dollar with the adoption of a floating exchange rate may have brought about a higher global inflation rate in local currencies. This is nothing more than the so-called divergence effect.

ARE THE TERMS OF TRADE CONSTANT?

Using worldwide data, we calculated the terms of trade or relative price changes as the local inflation rate less the local exchange rate depreciation against the US dollar, as well as the US inflation rate. A positive number means an improvement in the foreign economy's terms of trade relative to the United States. That is, it takes more US goods to acquire one unit of the foreign good. A negative number means an improvement in the US terms of trade or a deterioration of the foreign economy's terms of trade.

We applied the same methodology as before. We ranked the terms of trade changes for each year, constructed 189 series and split them into quartiles. We then calculated the average terms of trade changes for the second and third quartile. The results are reported in Fig. 2.11. The data shows that for most of the turning points, peaks and trough for the two series coincide.

One interpretation of these results is that the series identify the terms of trade changes. The fact that second quartile series is consistently higher than the third quartile has not escaped us. This result is not unrelated to the fact that the dollar inflation for the third quartile

(Fig. 2.9) is lower than that of the third quartile. One possible explanation is measurement errors. If that is the case, then when the measurement errors are corrected, we would observe second and third quartile series converge to each other. And that will bring it all together. The relative price changes or terms of trade impact the different countries' CPI differently. This suggests that these differences between the inflation rate series may be capturing the terms of trade changes. Once these relative prices are accounted for, the Law of One Price holds.

References

[1] Cassel KG. Abnormal deviations in international exchanges. Econ J 1918;28:413–5. Frenkel J, Levich R. Covered interest arbitrage: unexploited profits? J Polit Econ 1975;83(2):325–38.

[2] Canto VA, Webb RI. The effect of state fiscal policy on state relative economic performance. S Econ J 1987;54(1):186–202. Canto VA, Laffer AB, Webb RI. Investment strategy and state and local economic policy. Connecticut: Quorum Books; 1992.

[3] Canto VA. Everything you always wanted to know about the European Monetary System, the ECU, and ERM, but didn't know who to ask. Financ Anal J 1991;47:22–5. Mundell RA. Uncommon arguments for a common currency. In: Johnson HG, Swoboda AK, editors. The economics of common currencies. London: George Allen and Unwin; 1973.

[4] Canto VA, Carrillo CJ. The European Economic and Monetary Union: convergence parallels with the U.S., investment implications and lessons for Asia. La Jolla Economics; 1998.

[5] Friedman M. The case for flexible exchange rates. Essays in positive economics Chicago. University of Chicago Press; 1953. Johnson HG. The case for flexible exchange rates 1969. In: Baldwin RE, Richardson JD, editors. International trade and finance: readings. Boston: Little Brown; 1974.

3

Are Commodity Price Increases Equivalent to Tax Increases?

During the first half of 2004, the price of a barrel of oil shot up more than 5%, setting repeated record highs. Early in June of that year, a barrel of oil shattered the $42 per barrel mark prompting concerns that the high and rising oil prices could jeopardize the economic recovery. The reasoning went as follows: if consumers and companies pay more for energy, they buy less of something else. Oil price increases are like a tax on business. In the aggregate, the higher price of oil reduces the economy's aggregate demand and that, in turn, produces lower GDP. Yet, as it turned out, the tax analogy could not have been more wrong.

The causes and consequences of the rise in commodity prices have been thoroughly discussed by the pundits, as well as by the editorial pages of most newspapers. The theories and explanations are limited only by the imagination of the analysts. In what follows, we focus on three distinct and popular interpretations of the causes and consequences of rising commodity prices. One view argues that the rising prices are a harbinger of inflation to come. Another view argues that a commodity price increase is equivalent to a tax increase. The third view is quite different. It argues that the rising prices are equivalent to tax rate increases under certain conditions and a bullish sign under other conditions. If the latter is correct, as we believe, then investors have a signal extraction problem. As we show later on, the solution to the

signal extraction problem is simple and straightforward. It is obvious that the rising prices means different things to different people. The question is why? Given our focus on the investment implications, we are going to focus on the conditions that give rise to each of the possible signals generated by the rising commodity prices.

ARE COMMODITY PRICE INCREASES A HARBINGER OF FUTURE INFLATION?

Price appreciation is the sole return generating mechanism for commodities. Therefore it is important that the commodity investors correctly anticipate the nature and cause of a price appreciation. The commodity prices can rise for two different reasons. One source of the return may be that the commodity price rises, while all other prices remain unchanged. The commodity in question can be exchanged for a higher amount of other goods and services. The price appreciation captures the real rate of return generated by the commodity. We define this as a relative price or terms of trade change. The second source of commodity returns can be a generalized price increase and by that we mean that all commodities rise at the same rate on average. In the case of a generalized price increase, there is no relative price change between commodities and the generalized consumer

Economic Disturbances and Equilibrium in an Integrated Global Economy. http://dx.doi.org/10.1016/B978-0-12-813993-6.00003-9

basket. The only change is the decline in the purchasing power of money and we call that inflation.

There are two possible reasons for commodity price increases: a relative price change is one reason and inflation is the other. That is the signal extraction problem that we alluded to earlier. Investors need to find a way to determine whether the price hikes are signaling a relative price change or are signaling a higher inflation rate as they have different implications regarding the future path of the economy and, in turn, different investment strategies.

SOLVING THE SIGNAL EXTRACTION PROBLEM

The price rule provides a simple solution to the signal extraction problem. Under a domestic price rule, the Fed targets the rate of change of the CPI and as long as the Fed adheres to the rule, changes in commodity prices reflect relative price change. Looking back in time, the absence of a surge in the inflation rate leads one to conclude that either the signal extracted from the commodity price/

price rule combination was either right on target or else we must have had a very long lag. We believe that the inflation data clearly supports the price rule interpretation. If the Fed abandons the price rule, going forward the signal extraction problem will become a bit more difficult. However, even if the Fed abandons the price rule, there is still room for relative price changes in the rest of the world economy and that leads to a related signal extraction problem. That is, the investor has to determine whether relative price changes are a bearish signal equivalent to a tax rate increase, or a bullish signal.

SEARCHING FOR THE EQUIVALENCE BETWEEN PRICE AND TAX INCREASES

A tax increase drives a wedge between the price paid by consumers and the price received by suppliers. Graphically the effect of the tax may be depicted as an upward or inward shift of the supply curve where the vertical distance between the two curves is the amount of the tax (Fig. 3.1A–B). Consumers facing a higher price

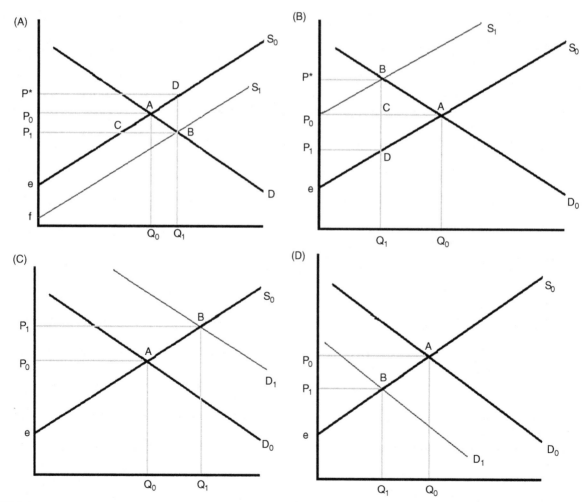

FIGURE 3.1 (A) Effects of an outward shift in the supply curve. (B) Effects of an inward shift in the supply curve. (C) Effects of an outward shift in the demand curve. (D) Effects of an inward shift in the demand curve.

(i.e., P*) move up along the demand curve and cut back on their, Figure 3.1B. Consumption of the taxed commodity falls to Q_1 from Q_0. Suppliers facing a lower price (i.e., P_1) reduce the quantity supplied to the market place. As consumers want to buy a lower quantity and suppliers want to sell a lower quantity too, the new equilibrium requires that a lower quantity is transacted. The difference between the price paid by consumers (P*) and the price received by the suppliers (P_1) denotes the marginal tax rate, while the new quantity transacted denotes the tax base. The product of the two denotes the tax revenues collected (i.e., the rectangle P*-D-B-P_1). Finally, the triangle e-C-P_1 denotes the profits generated by the suppliers.

Fig. 3.1B shows that a leftward shift of the supply curve is in effect equivalent to a tax increase. In both cases the price paid by consumers increases and the output decreases. A monopolist or a cartel, exploits its market power by curtailing the quantity supplied. Graphically, the monopolist gets to collect the tax revenues (the rectangle P*-B-D-P_1 and the production profits, the triangle e-D-P_1). One can see from Fig. 3.1B the monopolist's incentive. By curtailing output it gets to collect a higher profit. Presumably this is what OPEC did during its heyday. At the time oil price hike that the effects described and the analogy was quite apt. The US economy went into recession in the aftermath of the oil price hike [1].

Graphically, one can easily show that a price decline resulting from a supply shift is analogous to a subsidy (Fig. 3.1A). The new equilibrium produces a higher quantity transacted (Q1) with consumers paying a lower price (P1). The triangle f-B-P1 denotes the profits generated by the suppliers and the rectangle P*-D-B-P1 denotes the cost of the subsidy.

The discussion in this section shows the precise conditions under which a price increase is analogous to a tax and/or subsidy. First, the price of the commodity must rise relative to all other commodities, that is the price index. Put another way, the terms of trade must increase. The second condition is that the relative price or terms of trade changes must be the result of a shift in the supply curve.

DOES THE PRICE/TAX EQUIVALENCE ALWAYS HOLD?

Price hikes generated by supply shifts are analogous to tax increases and they result in a lower output and lower overall profits (Fig. 3.1A–B). Those who argue that a price hike relative to the CPI is like a tax are implicitly assuming that the disturbance that caused the new equilibrium was a supply shift. However, supply shifts are not the only disturbances in a market. Demand shifts may be equally important. Fig. 3.1C and D show that the demand shifts produce a positive relationship between the change in the equilibrium price

and quantity. More importantly, under a demand shift (Fig. 3.1C) one can show that the higher relative price leads to higher output (Q1) and higher profits. The trapezoid P_0-A-B-P_1 denotes the increment in profits produced by the new equilibrium.

CONSIDERING THE DIFFERENT POSSIBILITIES

So far the moral of the story presented is that price changes alone are not sufficient to determine the equivalence between price and tax changes. We have shown that the nature of the shift is an important piece of information. If the price change is generated by demand shifts, one gets a very different outlook than when the price changes are generated by supply shifts. In some cases the demand/supply shifts are quite bullish and in others they are quite bearish. For example, the increase in the relative price of oil and other commodities early in the new millennium had a bearish slant if interpreted as a supply shift and quite a bullish if interpreted as a demand shift. On the other hand, price declines such as tech prices are quite bullish when interpreted as supply shifts and the example of Japan's falling prices are quite bearish when they are the result of demand shifts.

Therefore it behooves the investors or policymakers to make sure that they identify not only the relative price change, but also the source of the price change. As already discussed there are four different possibilities:

1. A relative price increase caused by an inward shift in supply for the goods in question. This is the case where the new equilibrium is analogous to a tax increase (Fig. 3.1A–B).
2. A relative price increase caused by an outward shift in the aggregate demand. In this case the tax analogy does not hold (Fig. 3.1C).
3. A relative price decline caused by an outward shift in the supply curve (Fig. 3.1A–B). In this situation the new equilibrium is analogous to a subsidy when compared to the old equilibrium.
4. A relative price decline caused by an inward shift in the demand curves (Fig. 3.1D). Again in this case the analogy to a tax/subsidy breaks down.

Relative price changes alone are not enough to determine whether society is better off or worse off. Our analysis illustrates that there are good price increases (i.e., demand-led) and good price decreases (i.e., supply-led). Symmetrically, there are bad price increases (i.e. supply-led) and bad price decreases (i.e. demand-led). Therefore, to make inferences about the state of the economy, we need two pieces of information. We need to determine the direction of the price change and the nature or source of the change; was it a demand shift or a supply shift?

The four possibilities outlined indicate that the tax/subsidy analogy holds when the sources of the disturbances to a market equilibrium are the result of supply shifts. Therefore those who equate the relative price increase to a tax implicitly assume that the reason for the relative price change was due mostly to a shock to the supply side. However, we know that is not always the case. In fact one can argue that as a result of the prevalence of Keynesian economics, most governments are more likely to attempt to stimulate aggregate demand, hence we contend that more often than not the policy shocks would tend to be of an aggregate demand nature.

INTERPRETING RELATIVE PRICE SWINGS

The next few paragraphs illustrate the importance of the framework in identifying the relevant economic environment. We need to know when the relative price changes are analogous to a tax and when the relative price changes are bullish or bearish. The next four cases help us illustrate what we have in mind.

Case I: The rising relative price, supply shift scenario. The quintessential example used to make this point is the 1970s oil price increases. The parallel between a tax rate hike and the oil price increase is quite exact. During the 1970s, the OPEC oil cartel curtailed the supply of oil and the lower supply resulted in higher oil prices. Higher oil prices reduced the supply of goods and services as well as lowered profit levels. As a result, GDP, corporate profits, and the stock market declined, hence the tax analogy [2].

One question remains: why did the inflation rate increase? The answer is quite simple; as the economy slowed, the demand for money declined [3]. The Fed, bent on maintaining constant growth of the quantity of money, inadvertently created an excess money supply condition when it did not accommodate the money demand decline associated with the economic slowdown. The excess money resulted in higher inflation.

Under this scenario a higher oil price is equivalent to a tax increase when the higher prices are caused by a supply curtailment. It is quite a bearish scenario. The experiences of the decade of the 1970s tells the whole story: double digit inflation, a severe bout of stagflation, and a stock market that in nominal terms remained flat for a decade. In real terms, the stock market lost about two thirds of its value during the decade. As we have also outlined, whether such an oil price hike is inflationary or not depends on the organization of the monetary system. Under a price rule, the relative price increase will have no significant impact on the domestic inflation rate.

Case II: The rising relative price, demand shift scenario. This totally different interpretation of the events is produced by the belief that the high energy prices were due to a demand shift.

The essence of our insight is simple. We contend that as the global economy expanded, in particular China, it increased the demand for agricultural commodities and minerals used in the production of goods and services. The US ethanol mandate also added to the demand for agricultural commodities. Adding the fact that the emerging economies' technologies are less efficient than those of the developed countries, it is easy to see why they incrementally used a higher amount of BTU per unit of GDP than the developed economies. The increase in global demand led to an excess demand for goods at the original prices. The excess demand required a new equilibrium. There are two mechanisms to eliminate excess demand (Fig. 3.1C). One is price increases and the other is higher output. How much of each takes place depends on the aggregate demand and supply elasticity of the commodities in question. The lower the supply elasticity, the higher the price increase will be. The higher the supply elasticity, the greater the output response will be. The higher price would result in additional profits for the producers and the higher output would produce higher employment.

According to the demand shift view, the high price of oil is a demand-driven phenomena. The price will remain high as long as the world economy is growing. The commodity price increase also has a clear macro effect. An increase in the commodity prices means that every unit of nontraded goods now acquires more internationally traded goods than before. This implies that the real rate of return of domestically located assets increases relative to the rest of the world, and so will domestic asset values. In an attempt to arbitrage the higher rates, investors will flock to the local economy. The country will experience an inflow of capital as a result of the increased rate of return. A decline in commodity prices will have the opposite effect. It will result in a lower rate of return for domestic assets. The relationship between the commodity prices and the performance of the domestic stock market relative to the global economy will be a positive one.

The high commodity prices in this case are a bullish scenario. The investment implications are obvious: buy the commodity-producing companies and invest in the countries producing the commodities. The countries producing these commodities could now get many more goods per unit of the commodity sold. Simply put, the terms of trade shifted greatly in favor of the commodity producers.

Although some people argued that the price increases were a harbinger of future inflation, our reply was that the global price rule was doing a pretty good job of containing inflation to the target range set by the different monetary authorities. Finally, for those who believed in the power of the OPEC cartel, we had a simple question: why in 2004 was the price of oil in constant dollars about a third of what it was during the heyday of the cartel? And why had the price remained there for the last 20 years?

Case III: The falling relative prices supply shift scenario. We have already shown that price increases induced by supply shifts generate effects that are similar to a tax increase. Symmetry suggests that a supply side-induced price reduction should produce effects similar to a tax rate cut. It does, and as we have shown under these conditions, the total profits of the suppliers increases, while the price paid by consumers declines (Fig. 3.1A–B). It is a win-win situation where everyone benefits, a quite bullish scenario. The outward shift is a result of the technological innovations and the huge increase in productivity we have experienced during the last few years. The computer sectors are the prime example as computing power has increased enormously while the price of such computing power has declined. Price declines induced by supply shifts are quite bullish for the world economy.

In a free market, prices provide a signal as to where resources should go. The high prices also motivate people to find a way to deal with the shortages or to take advantage of these high prices, and eventually the market will. That is exactly what happened with the commodity boom. Fracking in the United States is one example. The Chinese had a lot of inferior ore, but there was no available technology to turn that ore into steel. Eventually they developed the technology and began to produce steel in large quantities and that led to a lower price of the commodity. Brazil was able to alter the acidity of the savannahs or *corrados*, and the country was able to use these lands in the production of grain and other agricultural products. The United States was undergoing a fracking revolution in spite of the regulatory obstacles faced by the industry. These technological innovations can be modeled as an outward shift in the aggregate supply curve. In turn, the increased supply lead to a price decline. How large of a price decline? Again, the new and lower price will depend on the nature of the supply and demand elasticities. Technological innovations also impact the profitability of old and new suppliers. The price decline results in a decline in the profits of the existing suppliers who were displaced by the lower costs technologically advanced producers.

Also, consumers now have more abundant and cheaper commodities. More importantly, notice that the producers' loss, that is the terms of trade effect, is now part of the consumer surplus. Hence the producers' loss is not a loss to society; it merely represents a transfer to the consumers. In this case, the old producers' loss is the consumer's gain. Overall, society is better off since the consumers' gain is greater than the old producers' loss. Once you add the increased profits by the new producers, the world is well ahead.

The implication is that users of these commodities have cheaper inputs and that could translate to higher volume and higher profits. Invest in the users of the commodities and the innovators who now produce the incremental commodities. For the economies with the old production processes who did not innovate, we see the adverse terms of trade effect having a negative impact on the economy. These economies are to be underweighted.

Case IV: The falling relative price demand shift scenario. The commodity super-cycle (both mineral and agricultural) greatly benefited the commodity-producing countries, many of which were emerging economies. With the commodity super-cycle coming to an end, the fortunes reversed for those who benefited from rising commodity prices. Price declines induced by demand shifts are quite bearish for the world economy (Fig. 3.1D). The lack of demand induces a doubly negative effect on profits. Not only do producers collect less money per unit sold, they sell fewer units too. To us the quintessential example is Japan during its deflation years. Japan got trapped in a vicious cycle, the bubble bursting of the early 1990s reduced the net worth of individuals and corporations alike. In turn that reduced their credit worthiness forcing banks to curtail their loans to corporations and banks. But that was not all; the decline in asset prices also reduced the net capital and capital adequacy of the banks, forcing them to further curtail their loan operations. These conditions created what some called a liquidity trap. As the central bank printed money to stimulate the economy, the commercial banks did not lend the extra money, instead the money was held as excess reserves at the banks. The abundance of bank reserves reduced short-term interest rates while the stagnation lowered the long-term interest rates. Worse, the yield curve flattened and fell to near zero levels, hence the liquidity trap. The Japanese economy remained stagnant for several years.

IS A COMMODITY RELATIVE PRICE INCREASE BULLISH OR BEARISH?

The answer is that it could be either one. If the increase is due to a demand shift the increase is bullish. If on the other hand, the increase is due to a shift in the supply curve, it is a bearish sign. As simple as this insight is, it is not always obvious to the pundits and analysts. In some cases some of the pundits do not bother to determine the nature of the shift. Obviously if people assume the wrong shift, they will also get the wrong implications.

A clear example of this was the relative price hike of oil early in the new millennium when commodity prices began a steady ascent. Many of those who remember and may have been traumatized by the 1970s, a rise in oil prices evoked very unpleasant memories when output declined and the inflation rate increased just like the tax rate increase analogy suggested. All in all, a pretty grim outcome suggesting that the oil price increase was a really bad tax. Given the 1970s experience, it is not surprising that early on during the commodity super-cycle many analysts believed that that supply shifts were the source of the increase in the price of oil. Some offered a cyclical or short-term fluctuations, like Venezuela and Iraq's shortfall in production. Others believed that it was also based on more permanent factors such as Hubert's theory [4] and the belief that OPEC is an effective cartel/monopoly. Proponents of the shortage view believed that all of these factors contributed to an inward shift in the world supply of oil, and, all else the same, produce higher prices (Fig. 3.1A–B).

While one can argue that in the future it made sense to assume that Venezuela and Iraq would get back to normal conditions, if one buys into Hubert's theory the global outlook was very grim. The secular trend was for the supplies to decline and the supply curve to become less elastic, increasing OPEC's monopoly power. At the margin, OPEC's incentive will always be to curtail output. This is quite a bearish outlook. So it not surprising that these people would be quite worried when oil prices began to rise a few years back. Those with vivid memories of the 1970s began to forecast a surge in the US inflation rate as well as a weakening of the economy's performance. Well these people were wrong on both counts. The surge in the inflation rate or slowdown in the economy, if they materialized at all, was well after several years of commodity price increases. That is why we say that if in this case there is any connection between relative price change and inflation, then the lag between cause and effect is quite long.

This episode is a perfect example as to why it behooves investors and analysts to focus on the causes of the price increase. To look for data that documents and/or refutes their assumption. As oil prices began to increase, we argued that they were the result of global growth, a demand shift. Using this insight we reasoned that the price hike would be a bullish sign and therefore an increase in exposure to equities was warranted. The insight was quite rewarding for those who took the advice.

But the saga continues. We have said several times in a free market, prices are an equilibrating mechanism and this situation is no exception. The worldwide increase in demand resulted in an excess demand for oil and movement along the supply curve. To bring equilibrium, prices had to increase to clear the market. The higher price produced a movement along the demand curve. Thus, the higher prices in effect crowded out the less elastic demanders of energy. The question is who may that be? We have hinted at one group already. If we believe that the price of oil is linked to world growth, it follows that the slower growing countries would be squeezed out of the market by the price increase. In our view, the income increase more than made up for the adverse effect of the commodity price hike.

The higher relative price made it attractive for suppliers to attempt new and innovative drilling and extraction methods that had been unprofitable heretofore. The higher prices created an environment favorable to the new technology, and as a result "Fracking" took off. Not only were some of these new well cheaper to build and produce, they were also easier to turn on and off. Although each individual well may have faced an upward slopping marginal curve, collectively their overall supply was very elastic. The frackers were nimble and could adjust production much more easily than other production. That combined with the ease of entry made the industry fairly competitive at the margin. All of this suggests that the assumption of a monopolist setting the price, that is OPEC, was the wrong paradigm. A more appropriate one would be that of a demand-driven competitive market. This insight is useful for a number of reasons. First, as the innovation took effect, it explains how the price of oil declined while production still increased, that is the supply shift shown in Fig. 3.1A–B. It also helps explain what happened to the overall equilibrium as China slowed down and the increased global supply led to a commodity glut. The financial crisis and subsequent weak recovery further weakened the demand relative to the supply Fig. 3.1D. Under these conditions equilibrium requires that the price declines. The lower price would drive some suppliers out of the market and if, as we have argued, the market is fairly competitive, the decline in oil prices was demand-driven and, as a result, a very bearish indicator. The lower price of other commodities signals an even weaker demand and thus an even weaker economy.

This is a very different outlook than the one implied by the tax analogy, which assumes that lower prices are bullish because they are analogous to a tax cut. Again, the key distinction between these two outcomes is that the tax analogy assumes that the price decline is due to a shift in the supply curve, while our analysis argues that in this case the price decline is due to weak demand.

The moral of our story is that price alone is not enough to make economic inferences about changes in the equilibrium quantities, that is changes in the level of output. Knowledge of the nature of the shifts, whether in aggregate demand or supply, is also a must.

References

[1] Canto et al. (1982) present a simple graphical analysis of how US policies of price controls and environmental regulations on the domestic supply of oil and other fuels enhanced OPEC's monopoly power and how the deregulation weakened it. Canto (1982) and Canto and Kadlec (1986) also show that adjustment is costly. That in addition to the initial disturbance the markets may take a long while to completely adjust to a new long run equilibrium. Understanding this can lead to developing portfolio strategies aimed at capturing some of the non-instantaneous adjustments in the economy and the markets.Canto VA, Bollman GW, Melich K. Oil decontrol: the power of incentives could reduce OPEC's power to boost oil prices. Oil Gas J 1982;80(2):92–101. Canto VA, Kadlec C. The shape of energy markets to come. Public Utilities Fortn 1986;117:21–8.

[2] Canto et al. (1982) present a simple graphical analysis of how US policies of price controls and environmental regulations on the domestic supply of oil and other fuels enhanced OPEC's monopoly power and how the deregulation weakened it. Canto (1982) and Canto and Kadlec (1986) also show that adjustment is costly. That in addition to the initial disturbance the markets may take a long while to completely adjust to a new long run equilibrium. Understanding this can lead to developing portfolio strategies aimed at capturing some of the non-instantaneous adjustments in the economy and the markets.Canto VA, Bollman GW, Melich K. Oil decontrol: the power of incentives could reduce OPEC's power to boost oil prices. Oil Gas J 1982;80(2):92–101. Canto VA, Kadlec C. The shape of energy markets to come. Public Utilities Fortn 1986;117:21–8.

[3] Canto and Webb (1987) and Canto, Nickelsburg, and Rizos (1987) provide a plausible theoretical and empirical explanation for stagflation in the United States.Canto VA, Webb RI. The effect of state fiscal policy on state relative economic performance. S Econ J 1987;54(1):186–202. Canto VA, Nickelsburg G, Rizos P. The effect of fiscal policy on the short-run relation between nominal interest rates and inflation. Econ Inquiry 1987;25(1):27–43.

[4] Geologist M. King Hubbert, in a 1956 presentation to the American Petroleum Institute, delivered his now famous Hubbert Peak Theory which essentially argues that for any given geographical area, the rate of petroleum production tends to follow a bell-shaped curve. Early in the curve (pre-peak), the production rate increases because of the discovery rate and the addition of infrastructure. Late in the curve (post-peak), production declines because of resource depletion. The Hubbert Peak Theory is based on the observation that the amount of oil under the ground in any region is finite, therefore the rate of discovery which initially increases quickly must reach a maximum and decline.

4

The Terms of Trade

In a frictionless world where factors and products are free to move, we would expect to find that the price of each commodity would be arbitraged across localities. That is, the law of one price or purchasing power parity (PPP) will hold at the individual level. Under these conditions, if the tastes are the same across different localities, one can then show that the consumer basket will be the same across the world. In such a case, the CPI in local currency converted into a common currency will also be the same across the world. The law of one price or PPP can be extended to the broad consumer basket.

Relaxing some of these assumptions or allowing for different tastes, some of the immobile factors and/or differences in technology will insure that the consumer baskets will not be the same across localities, even though PPP holds at the individual commodity level. The terms of trade measure how much of a consumer basket in one country, say the United States, will buy of another country consumer basket, say Germany. On a practical level, these are not foreign concepts. Recall a few years back when *The Economist* reported in the back of its issues the price of a Big Mac in local currency converted back into US dollars and compared it to the US price of a Big Mac. *The Economist* was giving the reader a quick and dirty way to determine whether PPP held across the world economies. And if PPP did not hold, the Big Mac prices gave people an idea of how large was the deviation from PPP across the various economies, that is, the terms of trade.

A BROADER ESTIMATE

The Big Mac is just a single commodity, and as it may be representative of an economy, a more precise estimation of the deviations from PPP is needed. Fortunately, the IMF estimates the member countries' GDP based on current prices, current dollars, and a PPP-adjusted basis. In our case, we take a more US-centric view of the world by taking a weighted average of the terms of trade of major trading partners of the United States to construct a broader and more ready measure of the terms of trade or real exchange rate index. Fortunately, the Federal Reserve Bank of Saint Louis' economic database, FRED, publishes a series consisting of the trade-weighted foreign exchange value of the dollar. In order to convert the series into the US terms of trade, we have to account by the changes in each of the countries domestic price levels. Fig. 4.1A shows our estimate of the US terms of trade. The data presented in Fig. 4.1A identifies three major exchange-rate cycles—both the first two complete cycles denote an inverted V. We can also see that troughs in the index return to a value along a flat line. So, the data clearly does not show a secular long-term trend. The real exchange rate cycles measure identifies major changes in the US terms of trade during the 1980s, the 1990s, and more recently in the aftermath of the financial crisis.

The FRED-based data is not the only estimate we use for the terms of trade, the OECD also does that job for us. It publishes a dollar-based PPP adjusted GDP,

Economic Disturbances and Equilibrium in an Integrated Global Economy. http://dx.doi.org/10.1016/B978-0-12-813993-6.00004-0

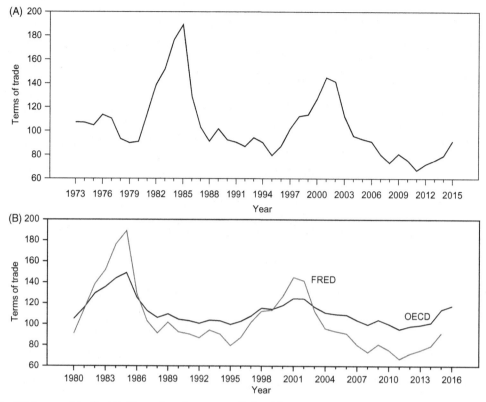

FIGURE 4.1 **The US terms of trade.** (A) The real exchange rate, Federal Reserve Bank of Saint Louis' economic database (FRED) data. (B) Organisation for Economic Co-operation and Development (OECD) versus FRED data.

which is divided by the country's GDP in dollars yields the real exchange rate or terms of trade relative to the United States, unfortunately the data is only available for a smaller sample period (Fig. 4.1B). Comparing the two series, both identify the same inflection points; the one major difference between the two is the magnitude of the upswing in the US terms of trade since the financial crisis. The most important differences between the two series is that the FRED data is based on the trade weighted index among the United States major trading partners while the OECD data is based on a GDP weighted index that includes all nations. These differences in weighting schemes that can in principle provide us with potential explanations for the differences in the index.

POLICY LINKS

Fig. 4.1A shows three major real exchange rate cycles. One begins in 1980, peaks in 1985, and troughs somewhere around 1988. The second cycle begins in 1995, peaks around 2001, and troughs in 2008. The third cycle begins around 2008. In between the first two cycles the real exchange rate moves sideways, although one could argue that there is a slight downward trend.

The timing of the cycles may be coincidence, yet they are highly correlated to major policy changes. During the 1980s, the United States adopted a very different policy mix than the one that had prevailed during the previous decade. Recall that Paul Volcker changed the Fed operating procedures and, according to our interpretation of the data, the Fed moved to a domestic price rule. This was important for a number of reasons, not the least being that under a domestic price rule with the inflation within a target range; fluctuations in the nominal exchange rate would solely reflect fluctuations in the real exchange rate. But more on this in a later Part IV, Chapter 3. On the fiscal side, President Reagan enacted a tax rate cut that lowered the top personal income tax rate of the US taxpayers to 50% from 70%. Recall that the tax rate cut was phased in over 3 years.

During President Bush the elder, the top tax rate was raised to 31% and then President Clinton raised it some more to 39.6%; and, as shown in Fig. 4.1A, the dollar drifted downward. It was not until 1995 that the dollar surged. What happened then? Three things occurred. The first one was the Contract With America, when the Republicans took over Congress and that led to gridlock. The Gingrich victory meant a slowdown or derailing of the Clinton's healthcare agenda and other programs. Second, whether it was luck, we had the productivity surge, which we believe was the result of previous policies. More importantly, President Clinton changed strategies. He adopted his famous triangulation policy and enacted some interesting reforms and even lowered the capital gains tax rate. Finally, some critics also argued that the period's easy credit fueled a couple of bubbles (the tech bubble and ultimately the real estate bubble). Perhaps it is a coincidence, but the top of the real exchange rate occurred right around Y2K, when the Maestro flooded the market with cash and after nothing happened, he quickly withdrew it. It is possible that the rapid expansion and withdrawal of cash may have had an impact on the real exchange rate. If the Maestro made a monetary mistake, as we claim, his mistake may have marked the end of the cycle and accelerated the reversal.

Needless to say, the United States was not alone in the world. We have highlighted the US policy actions, however, it is clear that the rest of the world was also reacting to our policy changes. During the 1980s, the developed world and much of the emerging markets lowered their tax rates too and adopted price rule-like monetary policies. These policy changes partially reversed or offset the impact of the US policies on the real exchange rate. However, these are not the only reasons for the round trip on the real exchange rate. The markets equilibrating process has something to do with it.

THE ADJUSTMENT PROCESS: INVESTMENT IMPLICATIONS

In the absence of adjustment costs, the adjustment to a new equilibrium would be instantaneous. In turn, the presence of adjustment costs will slow the economy's speed of adjustment to a new equilibrium. This is an important feature for portfolio managers; the costly adjustment gives rise to differential return cycles that an astute investor may take advantage to deliver an above average performance. One striking feature of Fig. 4.1 is that the exchange rate cycles are fairly long. The dollar appreciation cycles and corresponding depreciation cycles each lasts several years. One justification for the duration of the cycles is that adjustment is costly.

The presence of adjustment costs leads to a simple conclusion: if disturbances take several years to dissipate before the economy reaches a new long-run equilibrium, trends will develop. Simple momentum-based investment models will be able to exploit these trends. No knowledge of the causes or consequences is needed for the momentum investor during this trend period. However, if the evidence in Fig. 4.1A–B is correct, the momentum models invariably fail around the turning point until a new trend is established. However, our framework offers the possibility of not only taking advantage of the trend, but it may also allow us to anticipate the turning points in the real

exchange rate and relative rates of returns. Let's consider an example based on the Reagan tax rate cuts.

The Disturbance: When President Reagan got elected, the top personal income tax rate was lowered from 70% to 50%. Let's look at the impact of the tax rate reduction in the after-tax cash flows of US-based entities. Before President Reagan, a $100 worth of pretax income, after paying the 70% tax rate, would yield only $30 worth of after-tax income. Immediately after the Regan tax rate cuts were passed, the same $100 worth of pretax income would now be subject to only a 50% tax rate, thereby delivering an after-tax income of $50. Put another way, the Reagan tax rate cuts would increase the after tax cash flow by 66%, that is, $50/$30.

The Economy and Market Adjustments: Let's generalize the results to US-based activities. If their after-tax cash flows increased by 66%, what would we expect to see happening to the foreign exchange value of the dollar and the market value of US-based assets? It would not be too difficult to argue that the asset values should rise by 66%. Will the adjustment be instantaneous? We would argue that it would not for two different reasons that we have already alluded to. One reason is that the adjustment is costly. The second reason is that the tax rate cut was phased in over 3 years. Looking at Fig. 4.1A, we can see that the real exchange rate cycles associated with lower tax rates are best described as an inverted V. This is also an important fact that leads to some interesting economic and investment insights. As we have already mentioned, the Reagan tax rates resulted in a 66% increase in the keep rate. By the simple stroke of a pen, President Reagan increased the after-tax cash flows of US-based economic activity by 66%. Investors who see the potential of realizing a higher after-tax cash flow would bid up the value of these cash flows. How much? We would argue that a 66% increase in a valuation would not be out of the question. But that is not all. Foreigners see the higher after-tax cash flows too, and they would like to take advantage of them. Their investment will generate a capital inflow into the United States. In order to buy the US assets, they need to acquire US dollars. The demand for dollars will rise relative to other currencies. How much? Again the 66% appreciation is a pretty good number. As we have a floating exchange rate system, the balance of payments is always zero. That means that the capital inflows will be the mirror image of the trade deficit. As capital flows in, the differential rate of returns between the US assets and the rest of the world will diminish. The adjustment costs will prevent the instantaneous adjustment. However, over time capital flows will completely eliminate the excess returns and PPP will be reestablished. In other words, the deviation from PPP will be temporary and mean reverting. The PPP deviation will look like an inverted V for the country with the real exchange rate appreciation.

Putting it all together, our framework suggests that lower tax rates would lead to higher asset values, higher levels of economic activity, a trade deficit, and positive capital inflows. For the investors, the important point is that the tax rate cuts would lead to higher asset values and equity returns, while the real exchange rate appreciation means that the United States will outperform the rest of the world. The investment implication is straightforward: increase exposure to equities, in particular, US equities.

DOES OUR THEORY HOLD WATER?

When we look at Fig. 4.1A–B, we find support for the adjustment cost theory. The peak in the US dollar was in 1985, 2 years after the tax rate cuts were fully enacted. However, looking at the peak, we find that the real exchange rate only appreciated about 35%. Why? Our answer is simple. As the rest of the world saw the US success, the rest of the world began to adopt similar policies and, as a result, lowered their top income tax rate. The rest of the world tax rate reductions eroded some of the US relative returns advantages. However, we should not be too upset with this. The competition from the rest of the world increased the after tax returns of their assets. We could argue that the Reagan policies fueled a global bull market.

The data also shows that, as expected, the real exchange rate reflected a temporary deviation from PPP and in due course PPP was restored (the inverted V). This also means that during the time between the Reagan and Contract With America cycles, the United States was around the PPP trend line.

So far, so good. Now we need to focus on the relationship between the real exchange rate and relative stock returns. The latter is calculated as the ratio of the United States and the World ex-US MSCI stock indices. As shown in Fig. 4.2A–B, the relative stock returns follow a path similar to that of the real exchange rate. The relationship also holds when applied to the share of US GDP relative to the world economy's GDP (Fig. 4.3A–B). The rising terms of trade increases the relative price of US goods. That is a unit of the US consumer basket buys more of the foreign goods consumer basket. The higher relative price increases not only the profitability, but also the incentives to work and produce in the US. The positive correlation between the terms of trade and the relative stock market valuation, as well as the relative share of GDP are quite robust as shown in Fig. 4.2A–B, as well as Fig. 4.3A–B.

According to our interpretation of the data, and the information presented in Fig. 4.1A we have identified two distinct full cycle real exchange rate episodes: the Reagan cycle (1980–88) and the beginning of Contract with America (1994). In between, we observe the real exchange rate drifting slightly lower, but, in the big scheme of things, we characterize that period as one of approximate PPP. The figures show that the FRED and OECD base terms of trade produce a good fit for the

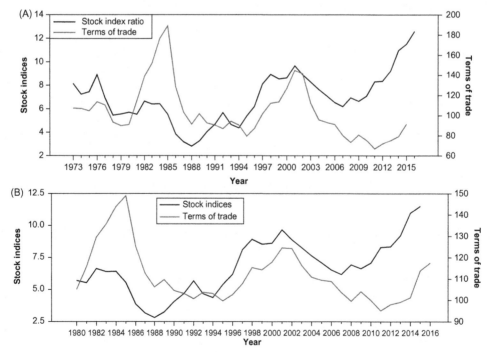

FIGURE 4.2 (A) The US terms of trade, FRED data, versus the ratio of the United States to the MSCI Ex-US World Stock Index. (B) The US terms of trade, World Bank data, versus the ratio of the United States to the MSCI Ex-US World Stock Index.

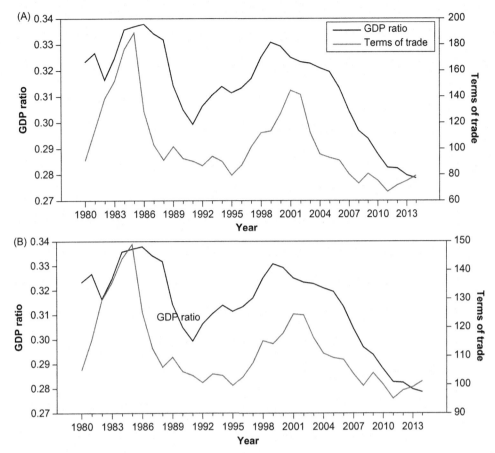

FIGURE 4.3 (A) The US terms of trade versus the ratio of the United States to the World Ex-US GDP. (B) The US terms of trade, OECD data, versus the ratio of the United States to the World EX-US GDP.

relative stock market performance and the relative GDP performance (Fig. 4.1A–B). The data suggests that either of the two terms of trade measures have a pretty good explanatory power. Therefore, although we lean to the Fred-based terms of trade series, either of the two series is acceptable for the analysis at hand.

DOES THE RELATIONSHIP HOLD FOR OTHER COUNTRIES?

The IMF database contains information on the stock market and real exchange rate for 189 countries in the world. As already mentioned the real exchange rate or terms of trade is a bilateral relationship that measures how much of one country's goods, say Australia's consumer basket, buys of another country's goods, that is, the other country's consumer basket. As there are 189 countries, it follows that there will be 188 terms of trade or relative prices. One versus each of the other 188 countries. This hold true for all countries. However, as we move to the next country, say Afghanistan, we do not need to calculate 188 terms of trade. The terms of trade between Afghanistan and Australia are the inverse of Australia–

Afghanistan terms of trade. Hence, we only need to calculate 187 relationships. The next round means that we only have to calculate 186 independent relationships. The sequence can be expressed in algebraic form as:

The number of independent pairwise terms of trade is =

$$\sum_{1}^{188}(188-i) = 17766.$$

Obviously, 17766 is a large number of time series requiring significant amount of space and difficult to present in a succinct way. For that reason we have chosen to illustrate the process using a small subsample, thus focusing on a handful of countries. The way we envision using the framework and the relationships developed here is taking a narrow focus, on the countries that interest us for the particular issue at hand. In the process, we illustrate how easily it would be to extend the analysis to any other individual and or group of countries.

Let's assume that for some reason we are focused on five individual countries—the United States, Australia, Germany, the United Kingdom, and Mexico. The previous formula suggests that we will have 4, 3, 2, and 1 for a total of 10 independent relationships describing all the interactions among the 5 economies. The first step in the process is to calculate the ratio of the MSCI Stock Indices of each country relative to the US Index, as well as calculating the terms of trade for each country in terms of the US goods. The process yields four different graphs, one for each country relative to the United States (Fig. 4.4A–D). However, this is only a start. It does not provide us with the complete set of relationships among the different countries.

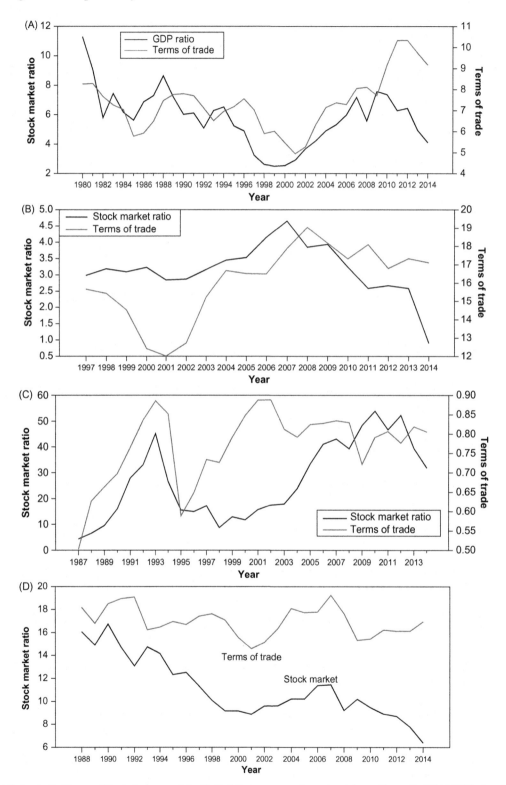

FIGURE 4.4   (A) Australia Terms of Trade in terms of the United States versus the ratio of Australia to the US MSCI Index. (B) EMU Terms of Trade in terms of the United States versus the ratio of EMU to the US MSCI Index. (C) Mexico Terms of Trade in terms of the United States versus the ratio of Mexico to the US MSCI Index. (D) UK terms of trade in terms of the United States versus the ratio of United Kingdom to the US MSCI Index.

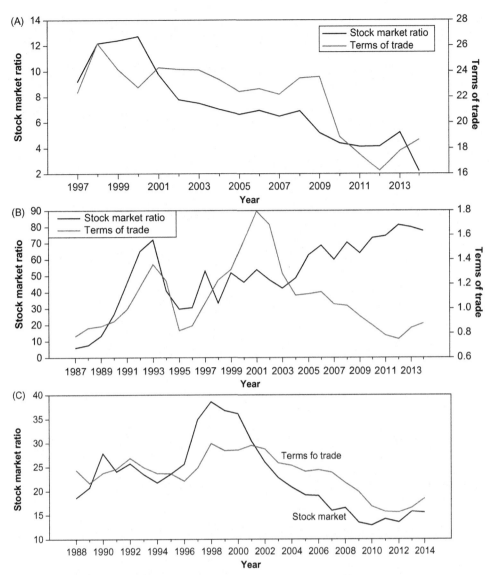

FIGURE 4.5 (A) EMU terms of trade in terms of Australia versus the ratio of EMU to the Australia MSCI Index. (B) Mexico terms of trade in terms of Australia versus the ratio of Mexico to the Australia MSCI Index. (C) UK terms of trade in terms of Australia versus the ratio of United Kingdom to the US MSCI Index.

Next we calculate the same information with respect to the Australian economy. We have already noted that the Australia terms of trade with respect to the US economy is the inverse of the US terms of trade with respect to the Australian good and services; however, we can skip this calculation. That leaves us three different relationships to calculate. The terms of trade and stock market ratio between EMU, Mexico, the United Kingdom, and Australia (Fig. 4.5A–C). Next as we continue the process, we focus on the EMU and we now only have to estimate two independent relationships between the German economy and those of the United Kingdom (Fig. 4.6B) and Mexico (Fig. 4.6A). Finally the last round leaves us to calculate

the relationship between the United Kingdom and Mexico (Fig. 4.7).

Once the 10 graphs are calculated we have identified all the possible relationships between the 5 economies in question. As one looks at the 10 graphs, it is clear that a relationship exists between the terms of trade and the ratio of the GDP between the 2 countries in question. The closeness of the relationship varies across the different economies, but the nature and direction of the relationship is undeniable. A rising terms of trade is associated with an improvement in the relative performance. This empirical regularity is very important in a number of ways and illustrates the value of the terms of trade as both a policy and investment indicator.

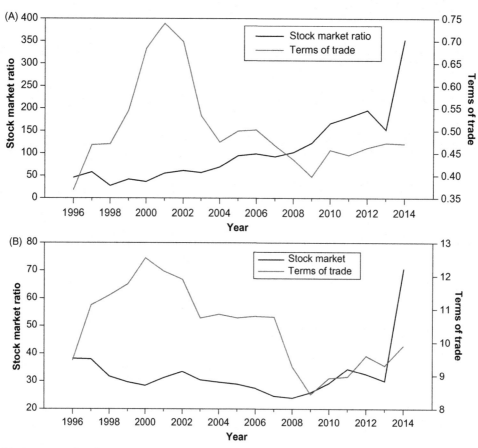

FIGURE 4.6   (A) Mexico terms of trade in terms of the EMU versus the ratio of Mexico to the Australia MSCI Index. (B) UK terms of trade in terms of the EMU versus the ratio of the United Kingdom to the EMU MSCI Index.

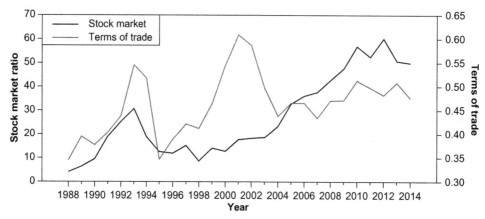

FIGURE 4.7   Mexico terms of trade in terms of the United Kingdom versus the ratio of Mexico to the UK MSCI Index.

5

Yields, Risk Premium, and Terms of Trade

In a frictionless world where factors and products are free to move, we would expect to find that the price of each commodity will be arbitraged across localities. That is, the Law of One Price or Purchasing Power Parity (PPP) will hold at the individual level. Under these conditions, if the tastes are the same across the different localities, one can then show that the consumer basket will be the same across the world. In such a case, the consumer price index (CPI) in local currency converted into a common currency will also be the same across the world. The Law of One Price or PPP can be extended to the broad consumer basket.

Profit maximization, and an absence of transaction costs are the starting point of our economic analysis. With these two assumptions, the arbitrage process applied to commodities leads to the PPP conditions outlined earlier [1]. And when the arbitrage is applied to securities, such as bonds, the arbitrage process leads to the Interest Rate Parity (IRP) [2]. The concept is the same, except that a time span is now involved. The arbitrage comparison is as follows: to compare the yields on, say one year bond/ deposit in local currency or euros to those of a foreign security, investors first have to convert the euros into foreign currency; hence the spot exchange rate is needed. Then one has to invest in the foreign deposits and, at the end of the time period, repatriate the investment; thus a future exchange rate is needed to convert the foreign deposit back into local currency. The IRP requires that the euro yield matches the foreign yield plus any exchange rate change fluctuations. Again, if the yield comparisons occur between two countries within the Eurozone, there is no exchange rate fluctuation. Then IRP and arbitrage

suggest that, absent transaction and/or transportation costs, the yields of countries in the Eurozone have to converge.

Next we introduce a modified version of the Fisher equation:

Yield = **inflation rate** + the real rate of return + risk premium

At this point, we can show that when both the PPP and IRP conditions hold, the real rates of return plus the risk premium are also equalized across these economies. Therefore the deviations from PPP and IRP may be interpreted as differences in either real rates of return or risk premium across the economies. We have already discussed and established the impacts of the terms of trade changes in the economy and financial markets. Up to this point we have ignored the effect of a changing risk premium, a deficiency that we intend to remedy next.

In addition to impacting the interest rate differential across national economies, the risk premium will also have an impact on valuation. The impact is easily established: the higher premium effectively increases the discount rate, and thus reduces the value of an income stream. If the two assets across national borders now have different risks, then it is safe to assume that the IRP condition will be "violated," reflecting the gross of risk premium. If we are willing to assume that, in the long run, these violations of IRP will be corrected, then we have a mean-reverting process. During the risk increasing part, valuation will rise slower than expected and may even decline. In turn, during the period of declining risk premiums, then valuation will improve and may even appreciate.

Economic Disturbances and Equilibrium in an Integrated Global Economy. http://dx.doi.org/10.1016/B978-0-12-813993-6.00005-2

THE DIFFERENT STATES OF THE WORLD

The impact from risk premium increases on an asset valuation is analogous to a decline in the real rates of returns. In some cases the changing risk premium (i.e., the violations from IRP) will reinforce the effects of the real return and/or inflation differentials (i.e., the violations from PPP). However, in other cases these two effects will work to cancel each other out. Under some circumstances investors could face a signal extraction problem. For example, is a rising interest rate differential the result of an increase in risk premium (bearish scenario) or is it the result of an increase in the economy's relative rate of return (bullish scenario)?

We contend that there is a way to deal with the signal extraction problem. A top-down approach helps a great deal. The nature of the different economic disturbances may help identify the source of the deviation from PPP and/or IRP and armed with that, one may be able to ascertain the net effect of the violations of PPP and IRP on the markets.

To simplify any possible signal extraction problems and to disentangle the impact of the different shocks, we begin by identifying the different states of the world that the IRP and PPP violations may generate.

The IRP condition holds while the PPP does not: This means that the interest rate differential across countries will be zero, while the inflation rate differential will not be so. In the special case, where there is no risk premium, the idealized situation of no transaction costs and perfect foresight, the equation shows that the real rate of return has to equalize across countries. This is a very important insight that allows us to simplify the framework. Under these circumstances, the real return differential across countries is the mirror image of the inflation differential across countries. This will give rise to two different states of the world:

1. Countries that have a below average and/or falling inflation will tend to have an above-average and rising rate of returns and thus should have an appreciating bourse relative to the EU index.
2. Countries that have an above average and or rising inflation will tend to have a below average and falling rate of returns and thus should have a depreciating bourse relative to the EU index.

The PPP condition holds while the IRP does not. If PPP holds then it follows that the differences in yields between a country and the EU yield reflects that country's risk premium relative to the EU.

3. Given most valuation models, positive risk premiums will, all else the same, result in a lower valuation. A rising risk premium results in a declining valuation in absolute terms and relative to the EU.

4. In contrast, negative risk premiums will, all else the same, result in a higher valuation in both absolute terms and relative to the EU. In addition, a decline in the risk premium results in a valuation over and above that implied by either the PPP or a rising relative rate of return in the economy in question. The previous paragraphs suggest that it is extremely important to identify the nature of the disturbances to determine whether the bourses' relative performance will be below or above the relationship suggested by the PPP or IRP relationships. The discussion also suggests that it is extremely important to identify the beginning, peak, and end of the risk premium and/or inflation/real rate of return cycles, since they allow us to anticipate markets' accelerations or decelerations, a key ingredient to a successful international investment strategy.

The IRP and PPP violations reinforce each other: That gives rise to two different scenarios.

5. A rising risk premium and deteriorating terms of trade will reinforce each other to reduce a country's competitiveness. The rising risk premium will reduce the discount rate, while the declining terms of trade reduces the real rates of return. Either of these two variables is sufficient to reduce asset valuations. The two combined will reinforce each other and produce what would appear to be turbocharged valuation results, both in absolute terms and relative to the EU. The asset decline will be larger than what would normally by implied by the PPP and/or real rate of return relationships.

6. A falling risk premium and improving terms of trade will each have a positive impact on valuation, both in absolute terms and relative to the EU. Hence the combined effect will reinforce each other, turbocharge the valuation, and create the impression of overshooting when compared to the historical relationships when the two effects are not jointly present.

The IRP and PPP violations work to cancel each other out. These are the most difficult situations for investors. They will have to make a determination as to which of the two opposing forces will dominate, and then invest accordingly. Depending on the situation, we could get one of these different outcomes.

7. If the bullish factor dominates, that is improving terms of trade or a declining risk premium, then we expect valuations to rise in both absolute and relative terms, and thus an increased exposure to that economy may be warranted.

8. If the bearish factor dominates, that is a deteriorating terms of trade or a rising risk premium, then we expect valuations to decline, both in absolute and relative terms. Thus, a reduced exposure to that economy may be warranted.

IDENTIFYING THE DIFFERENT ENVIRONMENTS

The creation of the euro is a good example to attempt to identify some of the environments outlined in the previous paragraphs. Since we argue that Germany is the anchor country, it follows that the other countries converged to Germany's inflation rate during the transition to the euro. Again, if Germany is the anchor country, then it is the benchmark against whom the risk premium is measured.

The first part of the information presented in Fig. 5.1A shows the convergence effect. Fig. 5.1B denotes the PPP or IRP world. Fig. 5.1C illustrates the divergence of bond yield caused by the financial crisis.

The three episodes/sections in the graphs can be used to illustrate the usefulness of the PPP and IRP approach. One aspect that we have already discussed is the investment implication of the convergence effect. We anticipated it then, and looking back we can explain the context of the risk premium. The adoption of the The Euro resulted in a convergence that eliminated the relative risk premium of the member countries. Since the country with the best inflation track record became the anchor of the

monetary union, the inflation rate of the whole region converged to that of the country with the superior monetary policy. Viewed this way, Germany's inflation did not deteriorate, that is Germany did not lose, while the inflation outlook improved for the rest of the Eurozone. The risk premium of the Eurozone members fell and, as a result, valuation rose. The gains were the largest for those countries, which experienced the largest decline in risk premium.

However, the financial crisis reversed many of the gains or reduction in risk premium experienced by the EU countries with the weaker financial conditions. While we could enumerate the differences in fiscal policies across the countries in the Eurozone, ex-post there is a very simple way to identify the different groups: separate them by changes in the risk premium in the aftermath of the financial crisis.

Fig. 5.2A and B separate the countries into those who experienced the largest increase in the risk premium and the rest of the Euro countries. Upon inspection of the figures, it is visually apparent that the countries with the largest increase in risk premium are none other than the Portugal, Ireland, Italy, Greece, and Spain (PIIGS). Within the second group, it is apparent that Belgium

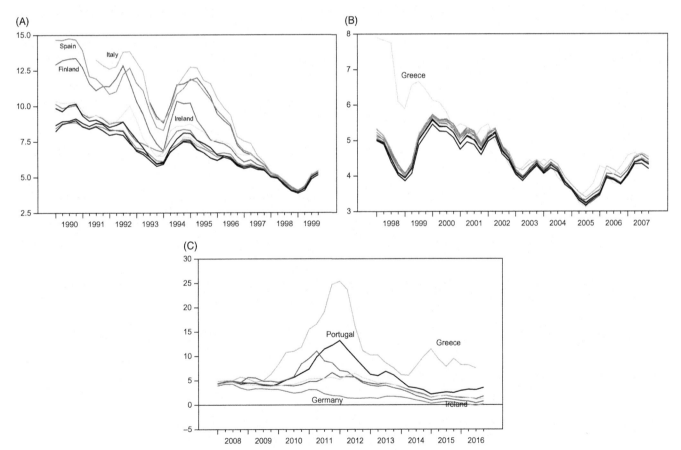

FIGURE 5.1 Eurozone bond yields.

(A)

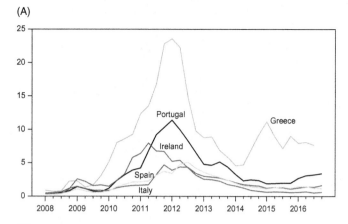

(B)

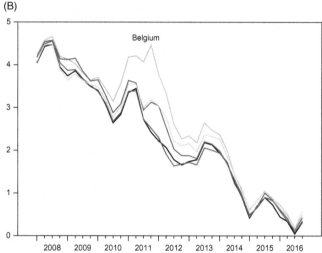

FIGURE 5.2 Selected Eurozone countries risk premium.

SUMMARY

The theoretical framework, PPP, and IRP have very clear implications. Under such idealized conditions, we expect that in an unfettered free market, real rates of returns will be equalized. Add tax rates, regulations, and/or transportation costs, and we can easily explain how economic disturbances give rise to deviation from PPP and IRP, which are correlated to the stock market relative performance. The framework also shows that increases in risk premiums may sometimes reinforce or offset the terms of trade deviations. When the risk premium reinforces the terms of trade effect, the former will add an additional impetus to the market and the relative performance could very well be interpreted as an overshooting. However, as we have argued, the relationship is completely justified and explained by the two explanatory variables. More importantly, some of the arguments presented here suggest that fiscal policy differences and other economic shocks will give rise to the changes in terms of trade, as well as impacting the risk premium as we have defined here. To the extent that we can establish the connection between the shocks/policy changes and the terms of trade and risk premium, one can easily develop a country-based portfolio strategy. For large enough economic shocks, the disturbance could last several months or years, creating a long wave that an astute portfolio manager with the appropriate framework may ride to the top of the charts.

is the country with the largest risk premium increase. However, the increase is smaller than any of the PIIGS. The disparity in risk premium increases could be easily explained in terms of the fiscal policies adopted by these countries, that is the tax and spending rates, as well as their debt levels.

References

[1] Richardson JD. Some empirical evidence on commodity arbitrage and the law of one price. J Int Econ 1978;8(2):341–51.
[2] Agmon T. The relations among equity markets: a study of stock price co-movements in the United States, United Kingdom, Germany and Japan. J Financ 1972;27:839–56. Frenkel J, Levich R. Covered interest arbitrage: unexploited profits? J Polit Econ 1975;83(2):325–38.

6

The Competitive Economic Environment: Lessons From the States

Much has been written about the impact of tax rates on the aggregate economy, as well as the states' relative performance. While political campaigns in the United States are focused on federal tax policy and whether the top personal income tax rate should be increased or not, we believe that the states' experiences have much to teach us about what happens when tax rates are changed. The parallel between the United States and the world economy is an obvious one. The United States consists of 50 separate state economies and factors of production, and as a result of the interstate commerce clause, the states enjoy free trade of goods and services and the factors of production enjoy freedom of movement. Thus, businesses and people can relocate anywhere within and across the states. The choice of location may be based on a multitude of factors, such as climate or other endowments. We contend that a state's fiscal policies can also alter these conditions and make relocation to their jurisdiction more or less attractive. Hence, the state and local fiscal policies can become a key driver of the economic well-being of a state, a significant driver of the state revenue coffers, as well as an important determinant of the internal migration patterns within the United States.

At the national level, the political debate regarding the impact of increases in tax rates is focused on the aggregate labor supply elasticities. We contend that the relevant elasticities are larger than the ones cited in the academic literature. One of the reasons for this conclusion is the fact that most people acknowledge and are aware that earners can move taxable income between different years, as well as change the timing of charitable contributions and capital gains realization. In addition, some taxpayers are able to convert earned income into capital gains, that is, the carried interest in private equity.

Interestingly, these measures, without affecting the aggregate labor supply, either reduce the tax base or the marginal tax rate to which income is subjected. Another effect is simply relocation or moving away from the tax jurisdiction. Outsourcing and outright migration are just two examples of how the tax base of a particular tax jurisdiction can change, even though the supply per worker remains the same. Migration and outsourcing reduces the number of workers and factories and thus the tax base of the tax jurisdiction where companies were previously located, while it increases the tax base of the jurisdiction where they relocate.

Higher tax rates collect more per dollar taxed. However, the base reduction due to avoidance, migration, or simply lower aggregate supply per unit worker means that there will be fewer dollars to be taxed. So whether tax revenues increase or decrease depends on whether the reduction in the tax base is large enough to offset the tax rate increase.

Economic Disturbances and Equilibrium in an Integrated Global Economy. http://dx.doi.org/10.1016/B978-0-12-813993-6.00006-4

The anecdotal evidence suggests that the sensitivity of the states' revenue collection to tax rate changes is much greater than the proponents of tax rate increases claim or believe. In Oklahoma, Republican Governor Frank Keating and then-Democrat Brad Henry cut the income tax rates to 5.25% from 7%, and revenues kept rising. Maryland's Governor Martin O'Malley raised taxes in 2007, saying that he could balance the budget by taxing high-income people. His strategy did not work very well. The number of millionaires in the state fell sharply. Some of this was due to the recession, but some of it was also due to migration out of the state. Then, to close the budget gap, the governor proposed more taxes, this time on the middle class.

In general, states with some of the highest income tax rates—Maryland and Illinois—have had the toughest time staying out of the red. In contrast, states with no personal income tax—New Hampshire, Tennessee, and Florida—manage to balance their budgets.

THE STATES' COMPETITIVE ENVIRONMENT

The relative performance and the changing fortunes of the high-tax and low-tax states does not bode well for the supporters of tax increases. The issue is how significant the impact of tax rate changes is on the tax base (labor supply per worker), tax minimization and avoidance (by altering the timing of income realization), conversion (from one form of income into another), and relocation of factors (out of the tax jurisdiction) or businesses to lower tax states (domestic corporate inversions). The sensitivity of the tax base to tax rate changes may be greater than estimates made by simply using the labor supply elasticities or some other narrowly defined measure. Those estimates are ignoring the outsourcing and evasion effects on the tax base.

Time and distance also enter into the relocation decision. Take the case of a potential migrant. The larger the migration gains, the more likely the factors of production will migrate. The longer the factors' horizon, the easier it will be to amortize the cost of migration. This argument suggests that the supply elasticities increase with time. The further the factors have to move, all else the same, the higher the transportation costs, the less likely a factor is to move to that location. The insight here is that while most people consider neighboring states to be their direct competitors, the fact remains that all other locations across the world are alternatives that any mobile factor may or should consider when contemplating a move out of state. It is a mistake to focus on the local economy as if it were a closed economy. Hence we need to develop a framework that considers all these possibilities where all localities are in competition.

One important implication of this is that the immobile factor bears the full burden of economic policy, both the good and the bad. When good things happen in a state and transportation costs are reduced, the after-tax returns of land, the fixed or immobile factor increase disproportionately. Similarly, when the transportation costs increase, land will also bear a disproportionate impact.

THE STATES' INCOME TAX RATES AS A PROXY FOR THEIR COMPETITIVE ENVIRONMENT

We argue that trade and factor mobility result in the equalization of the gross of tax factor returns across state boundaries. Hence a tax increase in one state results in a lower after-tax rate of return in that state. However, that alone is not enough to determine whether the factor will move across state borders. Our framework suggests a simple answer: as the gross of tax returns are the same, all one needs to know is the differences in tax rates between the state in question and the rest of the world. Therefore, by understanding and anticipating changes of the transportation costs, that is, the differences in tax rates across state boundaries, one may be able to anticipate the changes in the differences in expected returns and correlation between the rates of return of the immobile factors across the different state borders. It is these differences in correlation and expected returns that give rise to the states' relative economic performance.

Using the top personal income tax rates for each of the states in 2017 and 2008, we separated the states into one of four groups: no state income tax rates, high state income tax rates, rising state income tax rates, and other or "average" tax rates. Using the data for each of the states reported in Table 6.1, we grouped the net migration information into one of the several groups.

The listing for each of the tax groups is as follows:

- States with no state income tax rates: Alaska, Florida, Nevada, South Dakota, Texas, Washington, and Wyoming.
- States with high state personal income tax rates: California and Connecticut, the District of Columbia, Hawaii, Illinois, Idaho, Iowa, Maine, Minnesota, New Jersey, New York, Oregon, South Carolina, and Vermont.
- States with the low personal income tax rates: Alabama, Arizona, Mississippi, New Hampshire, New Mexico, North Dakota, Oklahoma, Pennsylvania, Tennessee, and Utah.
- States with increase in the top tax rates: California, Connecticut, Delaware, District of Columbia, Illinois, Maine, Minnesota, New York, Oregon, and Wisconsin.

TABLE 6.1 Top Personal Income Tax Rates 2017 and 2008, and Right-to-Work Designation

State	2017 Top income tax rates	2008 Top income tax rates	Right to Work
Alabama	5.00%	5.00%	1953
Alaska	0.00%	0.00%	
Arizona	4.54%	4.54%	1946
Arkansas	6.90%	7.00%	1944
California	13.30%	10.30%	
Colorado	4.63% of federal	4.63% of federal	
Connecticut	6.99%	5.00%	
Delaware	6.60%	5.95%	
District of Columbia	8.95%	8.50%	
Florida	0	0	1944
Georgia	6.00%	6.00%	1947
Hawaii	8.25%	8.25%	
Idaho	7.40%	7.80%	1985
Illinois	3.75% of federal	3% of federal	
Indiana	3.23% of federal	3.4% of federal	2012
Iowa	8.98%	8.98%	1947
Kansas	4.60%	6.45%	1958
Kentucky	6.00%	6.00%	2017
Louisiana	6.00%	6.00%	1976
Maine	10.15%	8.50%	
Maryland	5.75%	5.75%	
Massachusetts	5.60%	12.00%	
Michigan	4.25% of federal AGI	4.35% of federal AGI	2013
Minnesota	9.85%	7.85%	
Missouri	6.00%	6.00%	
Mississippi	5.00%	5.00%	1954
Montana	6.90%	6.90%	
Nebraska	6.84%	6.84%	1946
Nevada	0	0	1952
New Hampshire	5.00%	5.00%	
New Jersey	8.97%	8.97%	
New Mexico	4.90%	5.30%	
New York	8.82%	6.85%	
North Carolina	5.499%	8.000%	1947
North Dakota	2.90%	5.54%	1948
Ohio	4.997%	6.555%	
Oklahoma	5.00%	5.65%	2001
Oregon	9.90%	9.00%	

(Continued)

I. ARBITRAGE AND MOBILITY

TABLE 6.1 Top Personal Income Tax Rates 2017 and 2008, and Right-to-Work Designation (*cont.*)

State	2017 Top income tax rates	2008 Top income tax rates	Right to Work
Pennsylvania	3.07%	3.07%	
Rhode Island	5.99%	9.90%	
South Carolina	7.00%	7.00%	1954
South Dakota	0.00%	0.00%	
Tennessee	5.00%	6.00%	1947
Texas	0.00%	0.00%	
Utah	5.00%	5.00%	1955
Vermont	8.95%	9.50%	1947
Virginia	5.75%	5.75%	
Washington	0.00%	0.00%	
West Virginia	6.50%	6.50%	2016
Wisconsin	7.65%	6.75%	2015
Wyoming	0.00%	0.00%	1963

Source: Tax Foundation and the National Right-to-Work Committee.

- States with a decrease in the top personal income tax rates: Idaho, Kansas, New Mexico, North Carolina, North Dakota, Ohio, Oklahoma, Rhode Island, Tennessee, and Vermont.
- The other or "average" states: Arkansas, Colorado, Georgia, Indiana, Kansas, Kentucky, Louisiana, Maryland, Massachusetts, Michigan, Missouri, Montana, Nebraska, North Carolina, Ohio, Oklahoma, Rhode Island, Virginia, and West Virginia.

There are a couple of points that need to be made regarding our classification. First, notice the overlap between the high tax rate states and the states with rising rates during the period. Second, the grouping is based on events from 2008 through 2017. Thus, it includes the aftermath of the financial crisis.

THE EVIDENCE: THE CHANGING COMPETITIVE ENVIRONMENT

Fortunately, there is a way that allows us to test the basic hypothesis that tax rates do matter and that migration is one way to arbitrage the differences in the after-tax rates of return. The Internal Revenue Service (IRS) publishes information on annual state-to-state migration. Although the data is readily available, it is presented in a cumbersome way and it requires a bit of work to manipulate the information. Then there is the issue that the migration is based on returns filed and, as such, it

may not capture some of the migration at the lower end of the income scale or people who do not file a return. Using the IRS data, we have summarized the migration inflows, outflows, and nonmigration statistics of the states grouped by the previously mentioned tax level classification. As we are looking at the total inflow and outflow by state, the grouping will include some double counting. That is there may be some migration from one state to another in the same grouping and while technically we should remove it, which is not possible, using the broad data used to construct Table 6.2.

The level of state income tax rates: the information presented in Table 6.2 is quite intriguing and supportive of our underlying assumption. The last row of the table reports the aggregate data for the United States. Notice that the average adjusted gross income (AGI) per return is $51,755.73 for the inflows and $51676.9 for the outflows from the states. The net difference between the two is $78.83, an insignificant amount. This information may lead some to suggest that in the aggregate there is no net gain from migration from one place to another. Yet as one looks to the different groups, the story is quite different. The first thing to notice is the relationship between the net inflows and the tax classification. The data shows the largest outflows for the states with the highest tax rates. The outflow is larger in both absolute terms, as well as a percent of the nonmigrant population. As we move down the tax groups from the highest toward the average and low tax states, the outflow diminishes and turns into a net inflow for the states with no income tax rates. The highest tax rate states are losing population at

TABLE 6.2 2008–2015 US Migration Across States

States income tax rates classification	Nonmigrants			Inflows			Outflows			Net Inflows		
	Returns	Households	AGI per return	Returns	Households	AGI per return	Returns	Households	AGI per return	Returns	Households	AGI per return
High tax rates states	265,047,198	575,732,909	69,016.09	5,883,209	10,335,157	54,279.59	6,583,482	11,881,296	59,266.39	−700,273	−1,546,139	−4986.80
Middle tax rates states	266,478,783	575,681,282	60,301.08	7,356,005	13,917,055	47,936.07	7,695,438	14,464,480	49,849.83	−339,433	−547,425	−1,913.76
Low tax rates states	107,793,819	236,636,834	57,032.06	3,010,989	5,852,434	47,849.31	3,170,276	6,109,980	46,197.62	−159,287	−257,546	1651.69
No income tax states	129,052,291	280,378,754	60,006.63	4,306,928	8,220,598	57,562.94	3,879,809	7,294,044	46,899.77	427,119	926,554	10,663.17
All states	768,372,091	1,668,429,779	62,799.23	20,557,131	38,325,244	51,755.73	21,329,005	39,749,800	51,676.90	−771,874	−1,424,556	78.83

I. ARBITRAGE AND MOBILITY

the fastest rate, while the no income tax states are gaining. The data suggests a clear correlation between the states tax rates and the net migration across state lines.

Another interesting piece of information is presented in the last column of Table 6.2. It shows the difference between the average AGI per return between the inflows to that of the outflows experienced by the groups of states. For the states with the highest tax rates, the difference is −$4986.80. Yet as one moves down the column toward the states with lower tax rates, the negative differential narrows and turns positive for the group of lower tax rates, as well as those with no income tax. These results show that for the higher tax rate states the income of the inflows or immigrants is lower than that of the outflow or the people leaving the state, while the reverse is true for the lower tax rate states.

Given the progressivity of the tax code, combined with a progressive taxation in some states, it follows that the higher income taxpayers will be the ones with the largest potential gains from leaving the high tax area. Under a highly progressive structure, there may not be a meaningful tax arbitrage opportunity for the lower income taxpayers. More important, if the high tax rates are the result of profligate spending, whether in large benefits to public employees or expansive, and in some cases mean-tested, social programs, these policies may attract lower income taxpayers who could take advantage of these mean-tested programs. The end result may be an outflow of taxpayers with a high taxable income combined with an inflow of taxpayers of lower taxable income. Some may call that a tax-driven "brain drain."

The changes in state income tax rates reported in Table 6.3 tell the same qualitative story. The outflow is greater in both absolute, as well as in percentage term of the state's populations for those states experiencing an increase in the state income tax rates. Again, as before, the income of those leaving the rising tax rate states is higher than those coming into the state. In contrast, for those the states with declining tax rates, the income is approximately the same, while the net flow is very close to a wash. This data suggests that the outflow from the rising rate states is more than likely to go not necessarily to the states with declining tax rates, but to those with the lowest tax rates.

The Right to Work principle affirms the right of every American to work for a living without being compelled to belong to a union. A Right to Work law guarantees that no person can be compelled, as a condition of employment, to join or not to join, nor to pay dues to a labor union. Section 14(b) of the Taft-Hartley Act affirms the right of states to enact Right to Work laws. Some studies have documented the fact that Right to Work states have greater economic vitality; official Department of Labor statistics show, with faster growth in manufacturing and nonagricultural jobs, lower unemployment rates

and fewer work stoppages. Under these conditions, one would expect a net inflow of workers into the Right to Work states. The net migration patterns into the states with and without Right to Work legislation can be found in Table 6.4. The results reported in the last three columns tell a familiar story. The Right to Work states are gaining populations while the non-Right to Work states are losing population. While the income of the inflows into the non-Right to Work is a bit smaller than that of the outflow, that differential reverses sign and is much more pronounced for the Right to Work states. The inflows have a higher income to the tune of $2395.378. Hence not only are the Right to Work states gaining taxpayers, the ones they are gaining have a higher income than the ones they are losing. Brain drain anyone?

If one takes the Right to Work laws as a proxy for government intervention, regulations, and other rigidities, the data show that states that are less regulated and more sympathetic to free enterprise (i.e., the Right to Work states), gained population and increased their tax base. The opposite holds true for the states with no Right to Work laws. The one issue that we have yet to focus is whether there is any interaction between the states' tax rate policies and the Right to Work in determining and affecting a state economic environment.

THE INTERACTION AMONG STATES' MIGRATION, STATE INCOME TAX RATES, AND RIGHT TO WORK

Information regarding the interaction between the migration patterns, the state's income tax rates, and whether a state is a Right to Work state is reported in Table 6.5. The top panel reports information on the states classified as high tax rate states. Notice that this group is then subdivided into Right to Work, rising tax rates, average tax rates, and falling tax rates. The relevant information for purposes of the current discussion is reported in the last column of the table. Upon inspection of the data a clear pattern emerges. Within the high tax rate states, the following groups of states for whom the net inflows or net immigration show a positive number. That is the incoming people as a group experience a net gain and thus show a positive number; see the last column of Table 6.5. The states with population and income gains are either states located in: Right to Work states or states with falling tax rates and/or "average" tax rates. Notice also that the high tax rates states lost population to all the groups except for the Right to Work states with "average" income tax rates.

The second panel reports the data for the "average" tax rate states. Again, a pattern emerges. The states with no significant tax rates and/or falling tax rates that also happen to be Right to Work are the only group of

TABLE 6.3 Migration in States With Rising and Falling Income Tax Rates

	Nonmigrants			Inflows			Outflows			Net inflows		
	Returns	Households	AGI per return	Returns	Households	AGI per return	Returns	Households	AGI per return	Returns	Households	AGI per return
States with rising tax rates	232,581,084	504,458,452	68,888.14	4,731,844	8,135,998	54,183.53	5,397,210	9,655,252	60,119.28	−665,366	−1,519,254	−5,935.75
States with falling tax rates	99,993,695	234,352,149	55,758.72	2,884,756	6,075,056	46,712.25	2,946,227	6,163,984	46,350.94	−61,471	−88,928	361.30

I. ARBITRAGE AND MOBILITY

TABLE 6.4 Migration and Right-to-Work States

	Nonmigrants			Inflows			Outflows			Net inflows		
	Returns	Households	AGI per return	Returns	Households	AGI per return	Returns	Households	AGI per return	Returns	Households	AGI Per Return
Not right-to-Work	588,176,827	1,264,383,357	65,211.4	14,458,987	26,260,381	54,221.4	15,420,868	28,048,500	54,804.3	−961,881	−1,788,119	−582.86
Right-to-Work	180,195,264	404,046,422	54,925.8	6,098,144	12,064,863	45,909.5	5,908,137	11,701,300	43,514.1	190,007	363,563	2,395.38

TABLE 6.5 Interaction between State Migration Patterns, State Income Tax Rates, and Right-to-Work Laws

	No. of States	Nonmigrants			Inflows			Outflows		
		Returns	Households	AGI per return	Returns	Households	AGI per return	Returns	Households	AGI per return
High tax rates	14	296,786,958	649,000,562	67,560.93	5,883,209	10,335,157	54,279.59	6,583,482	11,881,296	59,266.39
Right to Work	4	94,594,361	200,955,394	67,799.43	1,475,563	2,455,806	57,718.52	1,813,595	3,160,480	65,018.83
Right to Work and falling tax rates	2	33,764,781	76,625,251	54,914.28	207,292	407,182	46,288.48	214,422	409,392	42,334.82
Rising tax rates	8	214,627,195	466,277,767	69,661.37	4,401,268	7,528,618	54,530.78	4,983,411	8,915,958	60,853.46
"Average" tax rates	4	48,394,982	106,097,544	67,069.12	1,274,649	2,399,357	54,711.81	1,385,649	2,555,946	56,178.63
"Average" tax rates and Right-to-Work	2	21,430,655	48,223,724	54,271.01	636,710	1,240,945	48,911.01	542,811	1,028,586	41,974.15
"Average" tax rates and Not Right to Work	2	26,964,327	57,873,820	77,240.78	637,939	1,158,412	60,501.43	842,838	1,527,360	65,326.71
Falling tax rates	2	33,764,781	76,625,251	54,914.28	207,292	407,182	46,288.48	214,422	409,392	42,334.82
Falling rates and Right to Work	2	33,764,781	76,625,251	54,914.28	207,292	407,182	46,288.48	214,422	409,392	42,334.82
"Average" tax rates	20	249,507,691	538,075,925	60,525.45	7,519,605	14,178,602	48,363.80	7,828,425	14,694,047	49,734.62
Rising tax rates	2	17,953,889	38,180,685	59,644.70	330,576	607,380	49,560.19	413,799	739,294	51,277.42
No tax rate change	13	176,704,206	385,778,036	59,395.20	4,910,694	9,386,687	46,889.42	5,089,826	9,692,682	49,094.16
No tax rate change and Right to Work	4	64,379,032	145,280,565	54,703.45	1,917,459	3,743,967	44,397.42	1,850,417	3,645,737	43,863.70
No tax rate change and not Right to Work	9	112,325,174	241,957,405	62,264.68	3,156,835	5,904,267	49,476.14	3,372,396	6,276,512	51,726.47
Falling tax rates	5	54,849,596	112,657,270	64,085.50	2,114,735	3,922,988	50,112.65	2,191,813	4,032,504	51,335.11
Falling tax rates and Right to Work	2	3,640,114	7,368,183	62,206.17	1,080,154	2,132,873	47,915.90	999,989	1,989,715	45,394.29
Falling tax rates and Not Right to Work	3	51,209,482	105,289,087	64,219.09	1,034,581	1,790,115	52,406.17	1,191,824	2,042,789	56,319.70

(Continued)

TABLE 6.5 Interaction between State Migration Patterns, State Income Tax Rates, and Right-to-Work Laws (*cont.*)

	No. of States	Nonmigrants			Inflows			Outflows		
		Returns	Households	AGI per return	Returns	Households	AGI per return	Returns	Households	AGI per return
Low tax rates	10	93,025,151	200,974,538	57,580.30	3,010,989	5,852,434	47,849.31	3,170,276	6,109,980	46,197.62
Falling tax rates	4	32,609,537	72,240,314	51,229.55	998,345	1,994,291	44,145.77	954,565	1,837,614	45,046.61
Falling tax rates and Right to Work	3	20,916,843	46,179,472	53,379.88	375,509	760,740	41,570.15	336,915	668,426	44,050.70
Falling tax rates and Not Right to Work	1	4,768,505	10,577,202	60,461.77	176,584	386,278	49,298.55	202,823	454,708	44,573.24
No tax rate change	6	60,415,614	128,734,224	61,008.13	2,012,644	3,858,143	49,686.40	2,215,711	4,272,366	46,693.49
Right to Work	7	50,152,112	11,1750,942	54,698.91	2,053,073	4,120,876	45,823.85	2,097,464	4,216,023	43,105.85
Right to Work and No tax rate change	3	27,661,560	61,536,498	51,534.79	835,954	1,670,399	44161.64	812,470	16,07,044	43,493.13
Right to Work and Falling tax rates	4	22,490,552	50,214,444	58,590.53	1,217,119	2,450,477	46,965.51	1,284,994	2,608,979	42,860.98
No income tax	7	129,052,291	280,378,754	60,006.63	4,143,328	7,959,051	57,166.79	3,746,822	7,064,477	47,035.77
Right to Work	2	8,612,255	18,558,577	59,358.10	312,518	629,715	40,829.11	318,809	643,795	43,590.14
Not Right to Work	5	120,440,036	261,820,177	60,053.00	3,830,810	7,329,336	58,499.62	3,428,013	6,420,682	47,356.21

I. ARBITRAGE AND MOBILITY

states showing a net gain from migration as well as a positive or net inflow of people. Notice also that on average the magnitude of the migration gains is smaller for the "average" income tax rate states than for the high income tax rate states.

The third panel shows that for the low tax rate states the groups experiencing a net outflow also experience an income gain. This fits our view that the people will migrate to improve their income levels even if they are in a low tax rate state. The biggest income gains is experienced by the groups of states that have a falling tax rate and are Right to Work states.

The fourth panel shows the states with no income tax rates; again the data shows that these groups of states show a net inflow of people and these groups of states also show the largest gains in income. The one anomaly here is that the Right to Work states show an unexpected result: a net outflow and a net income loss. But this makes some sense. People will move to areas where there are more opportunities. You would expect the lower income people the ones likely to gain an increase in income. One possibility that we have not discussed up to this point is how the social safety net may affect the migration level of the lower income groups. The differential in social safety net benefits may be an important factor for the lower income groups.

The data in the panels show that the income difference between the inflows and outflows are the largest for the most extreme tax rate changes. The gains are the largest for the no income tax rate states while the losses are the largest for the high-income tax rate states. Another result suggested by the data is that the interaction between the Right to Work and tax rates seems to break down for states with no income tax rate states. If as we argue that the Right to Work may be a proxy for the regulatory and overall environment, one can also argue that the no income tax rate state may also reflect similar environments. Hence, we would expect the Right to Work to be more important the higher the tax rates.

BRAIN DRAIN?

The findings reported in the previous section and the overall migration away from the high tax states to the other states is in line with the competitive environment framework that we have outlined. One concern is that the migration patterns are such that the people leaving the high tax states tend to have higher income than the people moving into the state thereby raising the possibility of a brain drain effect taking place in these high tax rate states economies.

To investigate this possibility, we chose a high tax state that is dear to our hearts, California, and examined the emigration and immigration patterns to and from

high and low tax rate states and Right to Work states. Once we show that the patterns are consistent with the results already reported, we focus on the migration patterns with the neighboring/bordering states.

The results reported in Table 6.6 shows that California is only gaining people from states with high and rising or average tax rates, as well as from states with average and rising tax rates. More importantly, the people moving in from those states have a higher income than those moving out to those states. In this case, the brain drain is working in California's favor. But sadly there are not that many states that have as high or higher tax rates than the state of California. For the remaining group of states, California is losing population to these states, in particular the Right to Work states or states with no income tax rates. The data shows that the people moving to these states have a higher income than those coming in from these states, a result that supports the brain drain hypothesis.

The data on the migration patterns with the neighboring states is also quite interesting and consistent with the results already reported. But one result stands out; the gains from moving to Arizona and/or Oregon are roughly the same, slightly better than $6000. However, the gains from moving to Nevada at $22,534.27 are almost four times larger than those of moving to Oregon and or Arizona. Recall that Oregon and Arizona were both designated as high tax rate states while Nevada has no state income tax rate. It is important to note that the people incoming from Nevada have an average income of $38,387.15 while those moving out have an income of $60,921.42. This number raises the issue as to why are these lower income people coming here from Nevada.

Notice that there is a net outflow to each of the neighboring states. It seems that California is like an exploding supernova sending jobs all over the United States' universe and, in particular, its neighbors. If this is true, the neighboring states should erect statues to the governors of California. The state's bad fiscal policies have caused a net emigration out of California to the benefit of the neighboring states.

The differences in taxation across the states explain the patterns of emigration as well as the AGI of the migrants to its neighboring states. Our basic hypothesis is simple: in the absence of any tax effect or any other impediment, we would expect that the migration out of California into neighboring states to be distributed in direct proportion to the relative sizes of the neighboring economies. For example, as Arizona accounts for 48.69% of the nonmigrant population of the region during the time period, all else the same, we would expect the state to capture 45.82% of the migration. Yet Arizona only accounts for 19.41% of the net flows. In contrast, Nevada with only 21.66% of the nonmigrant population accounts for 41.34% of the net migration flows.

TABLE 6.6 California Migration by States' Economic Environment Classified by Top State Income Tax Rates and Right to Work

	Immigration			Outmigration			Net inflows		
	Returns	Households	AGI per household	Returns	Household	AGI per household	Returns	Households	AGI per households
Immigration	1,581,844	2,805,818	54,791.58	1,657,989	3,101,575	57,616.64	−76,145	−295,757	−2,825.06
High tax rates									
Rising rates	108,493	176,931	67,798.04	83,341	140,770	58,227.81	25,152	36,161	9,570.23
Average rates	126,278	212,389	65,352.16	107,113	186,144	64,477.59	19,165	26,245	874.57
Falling rates	52,989	99,146	48,817.10	53,800	105,017	49,269.50	−811	−5,871	−452.41
Average tax rates									
Rising rates	146,937	221,325	77,207.59	117,136	177,176	71,613.10	29,801	44,149	5,594.49
Average rates	312,070	563,603	51,714.69	323,549	621,294	55,148.54	−11,479	−57,691	−3,433.85
Falling rates	44,621	72,807	50,911.64	37,564	67,068	51,076.91	7,057	5,739	−165.27
Low tax rates									
Rising rates									
Average rates	94,055	16,2078	51,383.73	93,920	179,836	54,668.72	135	−17,758	−3,284.99
Falling rates	49,648	89,958	43,906.95	52,958	99,806	41,771.28	−3,310	−9,848	2,135.67
No income tax	378,267	703,309	53,884.39	450,248	885,974	60,309.37	−71,981	−182,665	−6,424.98
Right to Work	234,342	443,764	43,789.42	266,724	534,098	48,316.32	−32,382	−90,334	−4,526.89
Other states	1,079,016	1,857,782	60,317.62	1,052,905	1,928,987	60,949.37	26,111	−71,205	−631.74
Arizona	111,731	215,104	44,370.59	126,098	241,154	51,178.21	−12,353	−26,050	−6,807.62
Nevada	96849	183,937	38,387.15	88,178	239,428	60,921.42	−29,249	−55,491	−22,534.27
Oregon	59,906	105,231	44,252.83	83,341	157,908	50,287.85	−28,272	−52,677	−6,035.01

TABLE 6.7 Tax Brackets for California and its Neighbors

Income bracket	California	Arizona	Nevada	Oregon
$0	1.00%	2.59%	0.00%	5%
$6,700	1.00%	2.59%	0.00%	7%
$16,030	2.00%	2.50%	0.00%	7%
$16,900	2.00%	2.50%	0.00%	9%
$20,357	2.00%	2.88%	0.00%	9%
$38,002	4.00%	2.88%	0.00%	9%
$50,890	4.00%	3.36%	0.00%	9%
$59,978	6.00%	3.36%	0.00%	9%
$83,258	8.00%	3.36%	0.00%	9%
$101,779	8.00%	4.24%	0.00%	9%
$105,224	9.30%	4.24%	0.00%	9%
$250,000	9.30%	4.24%	0.00%	9.90%
$305,336	9.30%	4.54%	0.00%	9.90%
$537,500	10.30%	4.54%	0.00%	9.90%
$644,998	11.30%	4.54%	0.00%	9.90%
$1,074,996	12.30%	4.54%	0.00%	9.90%
$1,074,996	13.30%	4.54%	0.00%	9.90%

Now tax differences and other transportation costs would affect the emigration pattern out of California. As Nevada is classified as a no income tax state, Arizona and Oregon as high rate states, the tax arbitrage hypothesis suggests that Nevada should gain a more than proportionate share of the emigration out of California. Nevada accounts for 21.66% of the neighbors' nonmigrant population and yet it captures 41.34% of the net outflows from California to its neighbors.

So far we have been able to provide a tax-based explanation for the emigration out of California. However, the converse does not hold water. Looking at the tax rate data presented in Table 6.7, it is apparent that, on average, people would not move to California from Nevada for tax reasons. They may move from Oregon, the high tax state. The tax story would suggest that as far as immigration into California goes, Oregon should be an outperformer and Nevada, the no tax state, should be an underperformer. Yet as we look at the bottom half of Table 6.6, we find that this is not the case.

We have already hinted at the rationale for the possible migration patterns. The reason why many of these states have high tax rates is that they have a government that has enacted a multitude of social and other public spending programs. However, one of the requirements for enjoyment of the benefits is need. Hence to the extent that the public services are means tested, they will attract migrants from states with no such programs. Hence if

the tax rate is a proxy for the spending levels, the progressivity of the state tax code and strict means testing is all we need to add to the mix. Then we can easily argue that the migration from lowest tax neighbor, Nevada, to California will be in excess of the states' share, while the opposite will hold for the highest neighboring state, Oregon. The income data for the people coming into California at the bottom of Table 6.6 shows that this is the case.

The data clearly support our views that the high tax rates will induce the higher income taxpayers to emigrate and the provision of means tested public services will induce the immigration of lower income taxpayers. The net effect of these policies is a net outflow, as well as a "brain drain" that results in a net reduction in tax revenues per dollar worth of income. In addition, the expansion of public services not only attracts the taxpayers that will pass the means test (i.e., lower income taxpayers), but it will also result in an increase in public spending. The progressivity reduces the base for two reasons: there will be fewer people and they will have a lower income. Under a progressive tax code this will have a disproportionate effect on revenues. The end result is higher tax rates, lower revenues per capita, and higher spending per capita. The combination leads to a brain drain and that is not a good thing for the state's finances. However, if our views are correct, the problem is reversible and its solution is an obvious one.

SUMMARY

The states' experiences enhance the supply-siders' arguments as to why tax rate changes can have a significant impact on the tax base. Proponents of tax rate increases concede, in principle, the qualitative arguments that we are making. They just do not agree with the magnitude of the effects in question. Essentially what these economists are saying is that they don't believe that these people will respond to the disincentives. If they do, the government should be ready to step up its enforcement to make sure it collects. But the one area that enforcement cannot help is to force people to work, hire workers, or invest.

On the issue of personal and corporate income taxation, there is a considerable disagreement as to what the impact of the tax rates on the economy and the tax base will be. Needless to say, proponents of the tax increases argue that the substitution effects are small or negligible, and will have no significant effect on the economy's growth rate and/or tax revenues in the short or long run. We disagree. Our view is that to the extent these moves make the capital markets more efficient, the economy will benefit and so will the long run growth rate. The higher after-tax rates of return will increase the overall supply of labor and capital to the economy, thereby increasing the level of output and quite possibly the growth rate. What happens to tax revenue collections depends on the overall response. However, the story here suggests that the longer the horizon, the greater the flexibility of the economy to adjust and thus the larger the impact of the tax rate changes will be on the tax base.

The one major criticism that we have regarding the supply-side effects of the tax rates is that the critics focus mainly on the aggregate supply from a closed economy perspective. As we have already mentioned, this debate is about the magnitude of the response of the factors within the economy. We have made our views known in the previous paragraph. The critics believe that the supply response will be modest at best, where as we think it is much larger. We also think they are ignoring one very important effect that significantly underestimates the supply response. They have much to learn from the states' experiences.

So, the big issue is whether the tax increase will slow down the pace of economic activity and thus, in the long run, reduce the tax base. To this they conclude that to reduce tax avoidance opportunities, tax rates on capital gains and dividends should be increased along with the basic rate. Closing loopholes and stepping up enforcement would further limit tax avoidance and evasion. However, that will not produce the desired results in the long run and quite possibly the short run too.

To make our point we need to make a parallel. Imagine equilibrium in an integrated economy, say the United States, consisting of a union of 50 states. Each of the states can be thought of an open economy where factors of production are free to move. The data shows that states with rising tax rates tend to suffer outmigration of both people and capital, and, as a result, a reduction in the tax base, while states with lower tax rates gain population, as well as experiencing a capital inflow and a tax base increase.

7

Economic Policy and Performance: The Small-Cap and Country Effect

The assumption of mobility and profit maximization yields many interesting insights. In the previous chapter, we showed how differences in the states and local fiscal policy differences as well as differences in the social safety net may help explain some of the migration patterns in the United States. The study is the natural progression and follows in the footsteps of earlier landmark studies such as the Sjaastad migration model and the famous Tiebout Hypothesis [1]. The former treats migration as an investment flow while the latter believes that the local governments have a more precise and detailed knowledge of the needs of the local population; thus as a result, municipalities within a region or states across the United States in our case will offer different baskets of government services at a variety of prices (tax rates).

Given that individuals have differing personal tastes, depending on the adjustment costs, the utility maximizing individuals will move to the locality that maximizes their well-being. Through the choice process of individuals, jurisdictions and residents determine the provision of local public goods in accordance with the tastes of residents, thereby sorting the population into optimum communities. Needless to say, transaction costs will, according to our framework, affect how close the individual can and the communities get to the ideal distribution.

Interestingly, Tiebout foresaw many of the issues that related to the impact of mobility and consumer choice on government policies. He argued that the local economies have two roads that they can go about in trying to acquire more persons in their economies. One route is for the municipalities to act as a cartel, enforcing a singular tax rate among the various communities. In modern times, we call this tax harmonization. The best example of this was the pressure that the EC put on Ireland to harmonize its tax rate. The EC was hoping that the Irish would raise its bottom tax rates to match the top rates and align itself more closely with the EC tax rates. Instead, in a rebuke to the EC, Ireland dropped its top rate and chose what Tiebout considered the second option: tax competition. In his paper, Tiebout claims that harmonization would shrink the right of voice and exit to the individual. If the economies are similar in endowment and tastes, competition would force the economies' tax structures to converge around an average rate. If that is the case, then the differences in tax structures may reflect differences in endowments or tastes across the different economies. An important point to make here, and one that disagrees with the Tiebout Hypothesis, is that while competition leads to some form of harmonization, the outcome need not be the same as that of a harmonization that forces all economies to have the same tax structure.

Economic Disturbances and Equilibrium in an Integrated Global Economy. http://dx.doi.org/10.1016/B978-0-12-813993-6.00007-6

A FRAMEWORK FOR REGIONAL ECONOMIC PERFORMANCE

We argue that tax competition has an impact on a state's performance. States with an improving economic environment tend to have an above-average improvement in their personal income as well as in the returns of the stocks of small companies located within their jurisdiction.

Policymakers should note that good economic policy, defined as restrained spending and an improving tax burden relative to the national economy, creates jobs and income at a rate faster than the national average. Investors should also note that small-cap stocks located within states with an improving economic environment tend to outperform the market.

Our argument is as follows: in a frictionless world, Purchasing Power Parity (PPP) would hold. To see this, consider a perfectly mobile factor located in region A. If rates of return are higher in location B, the factor in A will move to arbitrage the difference.

Generalizing this mechanism, we conclude that, for mobile factors, after-tax returns will be equalized across countries. That's what we mean when we say that the factor is priced in the national economy–local returns for a factor will be the world's after-tax return grossed up by local taxes. Changes in factor returns/prices send a common signal to the state's economies, which, all else the same, induce a common economic response across states. This is an important insight for predicting regional economic performance. So, in the absence of any PPP violation, to forecast a state's economic performance, all we need to do is forecast the national economy. As part of our economic analysis, we forecast the US real GDP growth on a regular basis; thus we already have the forecast for the impact of PPP on a state's economic performance. All we lack is a forecast for the impact of the dispersion in state and local fiscal policy actions on the states' relative performance.

The calculus for immobile factors of production is a little different. By definition, the factor cannot move across state boundaries; therefore that factor cannot escape local taxes. The point here is that for the immobile factor, the after-tax return or valuation need not be the same across states. Thus, if mobility is not perfect across countries or factors of production, the level and type of government expenditure and the manner in which revenues are raised across states produces systematic deviations from PPP. The burden of taxation will fall disproportionately among the least mobile factors across states and this will result in systematic differences in the pattern of returns across states. Differences in fiscal policies across states go a long way in explaining the dispersion among the state's economic performances.

THE RANKING OF THE STATES

The ranking of the states has kept economists interested for some time. The most common way to rank states is to calculate the changes in state fiscal policy as projected in their budgets. The National Conference of State Legislatures (NCSL) publishes the revenue impact of state and local actions enacted each fiscal year. These estimates, with a little manipulation, are easily converted into proxies describing changes in the dispersion of state and local fiscal policies across states.

APPLICATION: THE STATES' GDP RELATIVE PERFORMANCE

The ranking is then used as a ranking of expected economic performance. While this is a proper first step, the ranking of the state's changes in fiscal policy is not enough. First, there is no reason to expect that states will have the same response coefficient. The history of previous tax actions may affect the state's economic responses. Similarly, it is possible that the state's current pace of economic activity may be in part affected by the recent past. In other words, a state's momentum may matter.

Our methodology attempts to correct some of these deficiencies. We then estimate historical relationships between state economic performance in terms of US economic performance and the dispersion of fiscal policy changes across states. The estimates of state actions for the coming fiscal year are generated by the NCSL and the equations estimated using historical relationships are then used to calculate each state's forecast as well as the likelihood that the state will grow faster than the United States. The evidence produced by our research shows that a state's competitive environment is directly related to its tax actions [2].

APPLICATION: THE STATES' RELATIVE STOCK RETURN PERFORMANCE AND THE SIZE EFFECT

The regional framework is easily adapted to understand and perhaps even anticipate the relative stock returns across different localities. The larger companies are more likely to have miltiplant facilities some located outside the local taxing and regulatory jurisdiction. This means that to conduct a proper analysis, one would have to apportion the business to the different localities and then focus on the impact of the local policies on the local component of the business. For that reason, we tend to focus on the smaller capitalization stocks in the localities. These are the companies more likely to have all their facilities within a single taxing and regulatory jurisdiction.

For this reason we believe that these are the companies that are most likely to suffer the full burden of the local policies. Therefore we contend that our framework is much more relevant for the smaller-cap stocks. The relationship between the regional stock return differentials and the state competitive environment is well documented [3].

There are other reasons that lead us to focus on the smaller capitalization stocks. We believe that increases in the regulatory burden due to the changing tax laws have tilted the economic environment in favor of smaller-cap stocks. The smaller caps are more nimble and thus can react much more quickly to a changing economic environment. Since the smaller caps can move more quickly to take advantage of the changing regulations, it is easy to see why the changing environment favors the smaller caps in the short run. Nevertheless, as time goes on, many of the scheduled changes do take effect and the need to be nimble to take advantage of the changing regulatory burden disappears.

In addition, one can argue that during the last 35 years we have never gone more than one presidential term without changing the tax code in a significant way. Reagan lowered tax rates twice. Bush senior raised them once and Clinton raised the personal income tax rate and lowered the capital gains tax rate. George W. Bush lowered the top tax rates and the dividend and capital gains tax rates. President Obama raised the top personal income tax rates. Viewed this way, the uncertainty associated with the temporary nature of the tax code may be overstated. There is no reason to expect the rates to remain unchanged. Therefore we believe that a changing tax rate environment favors the smaller more nimble stocks.

However, if the tax code and regulatory environments were to become more predictable, our analysis would point to a market where the larger caps dominate the economic landscape. Again the rationale for this conclusion is straightforward. As uncertainty regarding the tax code is reduced, its impact on the regulatory burden becomes smaller and more predictable. The larger caps have the resources to hire the best lawyers and accountants, and thus they have the ability to chip away at the regulatory burden.

To the extent that one views the regulatory burden as a fixed cost, the larger corporations have an advantage over the smaller ones. The regulatory fixed costs amount to a lower increase in the per unit cost for the larger corporations. One example that immediately comes to mind is the effect of the regulatory burden and the mandated use of catalytic converters in automobiles a couple of decades ago. Because of antitrust provisions (i.e., another regulatory burden), the big three domestic automakers were forced to develop their own catalytic converters. In the absence of the antitrust provision, the three

automakers could have joined forces and developed a single converter that they could have shared. Needless to say, the antitrust provision forced the development of two catalytic converters too many. The higher costs reduced the attractiveness of domestic cars relative to foreign cars not subject to the antitrust provision.

The extra costs associated with the development of the catalytic converters were borne in part by the shareholders in the form of lower profits and by the domestic workers in the form of lower employment. But that is not all. The regulation had a disproportionate impact on domestic producers. If the costs of developing the converter were roughly the same for the three automakers, the amortization of the development costs increased the unit costs of the smallest company the most. This means that the regulation put the smallest company at a competitive disadvantage over the larger ones.

The catalytic converter example provides us with a powerful insight that has clear investment implications. Once the environment becomes predictable, the regulatory burden becomes a "fixed" cost and it tends to favor the larger-cap stocks because they can amortize the costs over a larger base. One simple way to reduce the effect of the regulatory burden is to get bigger. Thus, companies have an incentive to get larger. Whether or not it is through direct investments or acquisitions is irrelevant to our argument. As long as they get larger, they will minimize the impact of the regulatory burden. By the way, one can make a similar argument regarding technology. If the gains related to productivity are large, then the larger is the ensuing volume of output. The cost amortization argument points toward a consolidation of business where a few large companies will dominate their industries.

The international trends are also inadvertently pushing the world toward consolidation. The removal of trade barriers is making the world markets approach a single market. To see this, consider the extreme case of two identical countries with trade restrictions so high that they do not trade at all with each other. In this case two identical economies will develop. The world will have two of everything. However, what if the two economies decide to merge in a union and eliminate any barriers among them? The answer depends on whether there are economies of scale or not. If they are, it will behoove the companies to grow. The one who grows first will have a cost advantage and thus will eventually dominate the market. In real life, we do not start with countries or companies being of equal size. Freer trade will give an advantage to those that are more efficient and could dominate the combined markets.

The move toward freer trade may in fact cause some consolidation to take advantage of economies of scale in the production process. Yet, the consolidation argument that we are advancing goes beyond the traditional economies of scale. The economies of scale we are focusing on are a direct result of the regulatory burden and how to amortize its costs. The quest for consolidation is that the larger the volume, the lower the per unit regulatory cost/burden. As, in general, regulations tend to be national in scope, it follows that a prudent company will tend to have a well-diversified portfolio of production facilities. The advantages of diversification to a local shock are significant. One example that comes to mind is the California energy crisis. It had a disproportionate impact on the companies located in California. This is understandable as energy costs surged mostly in California; only those who produced in California would be affected. Our research found that even within California companies, the smallest cap suffered the most. Again this is understandable; the larger-cap stocks tend to have multiplant facilities, with some outside the state. As energy costs soared in California, the multiplant companies shifted their production to facilities outside the state thereby minimizing the impact of the energy prices. In contrast, the smallest-cap companies, many of which were single plant or had the bulk of their production facilities in California, were not able to shift as much of their production outside the state. The higher energy costs had a direct and disproportionate impact on their cost, profits, and production levels. We made a similar argument during the California crisis. To test our theory we looked at the companies in the S&P 1500 headquartered in California. We also excluded the tech companies to exclude the tech debacle. The results of the remaining companies were enlightening. The large-cap companies headquartered in California lagged the non-Californian large-cap by 20 basis points. In the mid-cap universe, the Californian companies lagged the non-Californian companies by 300 basis points. For the small-cap comparison, the gap grew to 700 basis points. The results are fairly conclusive; the larger caps are able to insure against localized shocks. The corollary of that is that the larger caps will not be able to fully capture the impact of beneficial shocks. The only way to do so will be to shift all their production to the locality. If they cannot do that, then the smaller caps located in the region will outperform. The small-cap effect is the way to take advantage of location/country effects. In the world we foresee the larger caps are trying to become location-independent concerns.

INVESTMENT IMPLICATIONS

The various markets will consolidate and will be dominated by a few global companies. Thus for large-cap managers, company location will become irrelevant. Large caps will become truly global concerns.

To some extent they will become location/country independent and the concept of international/global investment will become meaningless at the large company level. The relevant framework of analysis for company selection will be the sectoral/industry analysis.

We have made a compelling case for the larger-cap stocks in the long run. Does this mean that the small caps have no future? Nothing could be further from the truth; the case for the small caps is a bit different. The fact that a few global companies will dominate the markets does not rule out a role for the little guy. Although the concept of an integrated economy with a single global market is a great theoretical construct in real life, it is a chimera. The local or country effects are here to stay. There will always be the special interest groups that will create artificial barriers that will partially segment some markets (i.e., trade barriers etc.). In other cases, the local effect may be due to immobile natural resources (i.e., tourism) or due to explicit economic policy (i.e., the California energy crisis). The regional/country effects may create market segmentation that represents too small a market share for the larger global companies. Given the size of the market in relation to that of the company, it may not be worth it for the larger companies to alter their overall plans to capture such a small market. The larger companies may very well decide to bypass or ignore that market altogether. The larger companies will cede that market to other players.

One example that comes to mind is in my own native Dominican Republic (D.R.). With the opening of trade, it has become clear that many of the Dominican agricultural operations will not be able to compete with the United States. The D.R. is much better off importing rice and many other staples. The question is what would the Dominican farmers produce? Some smart producers have recognized that and instead of going toe to toe with the US producers in the regular staples, they would be better off specializing in niche markets. They have discovered that the developed countries are quite interested in organically grown products. More importantly, the organically grown products sell at a premium. The organic market is a great opportunity; it allows the local grower to use less of a very expensive product (i.e., fertilizers and other chemicals), which is too expensive for them to use. Converting to the organic reduces the use of the expensive inputs; however the decline in production would be much less than that of the US farmers who switch to organic methods because, to begin with, the D.R. farmers employ a less intensive use of the chemicals. In other words, the D.R. farmers have a clear comparative advantage in the production of the organic products.

Natural endowments, government regulations, and many other factors combine to create pockets of market segmentation/product differentiation. It is in those markets where the smaller-cap stocks have the greatest advantage. They are nimble and can adjust faster to the changing market conditions. It is at the small-cap level where the democratic capitalism will flourish and give an opportunity to compete with the emerging nations. Local entrepreneurs will develop products for the niche markets. As they become successful overtime, they will expand their scale of operations and move into the more conventional markets. In the process, these companies may join the larger-cap universe. It is at the niche level that investors have to isolate regional differences due to government regulations and other country-specific locations. Alternatively stated, it is at the small-cap level that the country effect will be most pronounced.

References

[1] Sjaastad LA. Costs and returns of human migration. J Polit Econ 1962;70(5):80–93. Tiebout C. A pure theory of local expenditures. J Polit Econ 1956;64(5):416–24.

[2] See Canto and Webb (1987) for a formal description of the framework and the empirical evidence on the effects of the state's fiscal policies on the states relative economic performance. Canto VA, Webb RI. The effect of state fiscal policy on state relative economic performance. S Econ J 1987;54(1):186–202. Also Canto, Laffer and Webb (1992) present a wider range of applications of the basic framework. They analyze the impact of states and local relative fiscal policy on a variety of activities, such as General Obligations, GO, bond rating and yields, the relative performances of real state, migration patterns and the relative stock returns. Canto VA, Laffer AB, Webb RI. Investment strategy and state and local economic policy. Connecticut: Quorum Books; 1992.

[3] Cantov VA, Laffer AB. A not-so-odd couple: small-cap stocks and the state competitive environment. Financ Anal J 1989;45(2):75–8.

8

Migration: A Political Problem, an Economic Problem, or Both?

We believe that market forces are such that resources are allocated to the highest return for the investor. Hence, in case of absence of any restrictions, resources are allocated to the highest rate of return globally. What happens when a country faces foreign competition in a product and the competitor is more efficient in the production process? The answer is that they will be able to produce the goods cheaper. Competition will displace some local production; the domestic producer will cutback and free resources that will now be able to go to other industries where the country has a comparative advantage and thus can generate a higher rate of return. The process continues until the rates of return are equalized across industries and across nations. A new equilibrium will be reached when domestic production is displaced by the imports, as the resources move to the export sector and the country will export more. The opposite results happen in the rest of the world.

Trade in goods is not the only way through which factor returns and prices are equalized across national borders. If a country can produce a good cheaper than other countries, it can increase its profitability by increasing its production of goods and services. Put another way, this industry can afford to pay higher salaries or higher rates of returns, and it will attract factors of production from either other local industries or from other countries as a result. The movements within the country from one industry to another or from another country to the local economy will continue until the rates of return are arbitraged [1].

The point of this discussion is that trade in goods, migration, or factor movements are alternative mechanisms by which profit maximization results in the equalization of factor returns and/or product prices. Trade in goods is a substitute for factor mobility, as far as profit maximization is concerned. The question is to determine which of the global market clearing mechanisms the profit maximizing process will choose. The answer depends on the transaction costs. The profit maximizing agents will always choose the least costly way, and that depends on true transportation costs, trade barriers, and any other obstacles that a national

Economic Disturbances and Equilibrium in an Integrated Global Economy. http://dx.doi.org/10.1016/B978-0-12-813993-6.00008-8

government, trade union, or any other national group may impose on the flow of goods, migration, and mobility across the domestic economy, as well as across national borders.

In the next few sections, we will show how political decisions have a real and significant economic impact on the economy. More importantly, we show how disturbances in one part of the world could have a significant impact on other parts of the world.

MIGRATION: EUROPE AND THE MIDDLE EAST

As a general rule, we believe that the "transportation costs" faced by capital and goods tend to be lower than those faced by labor. The goods or capital have no particular attachment to any locality. In contrast, labor faces family ties and perhaps traditions that make the physical and psychological costs of moving higher than those faced by capital or goods produced in different countries. Any disparity in prices or returns is arbitraged away through trade in goods or capital flows or both. Again, whether it is the goods or capital depends on the "transportation costs." However, that is not always so. Take the case of a region devastated by war, terrorism, or political uncertainty. Under these circumstances, local production and international trade may not be viable in that situation. The factors of production not destroyed by war will be relatively abundant and in the absence of international trade, their rates of return will decline both in absolute terms and relative to the returns they could earn outside the country. The return differential will increase the benefits to migration; as a result, these factors of production may choose to leave even in the face of very high transportation costs. Put another way, when society and the rule of law disintegrate, the only way to avoid being subjected to the uncertainty or overall costs is to leave. In that case, the "transportation costs" are significantly lower than the costs of staying put. People will migrate. That is one way to describe what is going on in the Middle East.

But that is not all. The migration has a significant impact on the host countries too. Expenditures in social safety net programs increase. If the incoming factors find employment, their inflow will unambiguously alter the mix of the different factors of production and to achieve full employment and overall equilibrium; the production mix, patterns of trade, and factor returns will likely change in predictable directions. The relative returns are likely to change too. Wages are likely to experience downward pressures while the returns to the immobile factors will likely rise in Euroland. In particular, the European factors, analogous to the factors destroyed or rendered unusable in the Middle East where the events are taking place.

To the investor who understands what the new equilibrium will look like, opportunities for making profits will be readily available. For the policymakers who understand and anticipate what is likely to be the new equilibrium, they may take steps and adopt new policies that aim to reduce the negative effects with the adjustment costs associated with a new equilibrium. Now a little bit of political economy shall be focused. Many of the decisions the Euroland nations take will have long-term consequences in the economy. When analyzing these decisions, one has to keep in mind the difference between making a bad decision and a sound decision.

One should also keep in mind the nature of the outcome. Sometimes a good decision-making process produces bad outcomes. Some argue that the Bush administration made a big mistake invading Iraq. That may very well be the case, and the Bush administration should bear some of the blame if that is so. For the time being, let's assume that is the case. But sunk costs are sunk costs and bygones are bygones. There is nothing one can do about the event. All one can do is to learn from the previous mistakes to avoid repeating them and to figure out how to recover as best we can learn from these mistakes. It seems that the Bush administration did learn from its mistakes and took steps to correct some of its previous mistakes. The surge is one such example. When President Bush left office, Iraq was relatively stable and President Obama had a decision to make: to continue the Bush policy or to get out. Recall that President Obama ran on a platform of getting the United States out of the unjust war, and that is what he did. One can argue that President Obama was trying to correct President Bush's mistake. However, the president was unable to secure a status of force with the Iraqi government and the US troops left Iraq. Since then, the country appears to have gone on a downward spiral. Whether that was a bad decision or a bad outcome is for historians to decide. It is irrelevant to our analysis. The fact is that Iraq was disintegrating.

Another important decision in the region was Libya, where the Obama administration endorsed the ousting of Gaddafi and yet chose to lead from behind. Add to this the famous "red line" on Syria's Assad, which Mr. Assad crossed and the United States did nothing. The lack of forceful response by the United States and its NATO allies left a void that was quickly filled by terrorists such as ISIS.

The disintegration of the legal structure in these economies quickly degenerated into a political and economic chaos with a significant increase in overall uncertainty for the physical well-being of the region's residents, and especially for those who did not share the views of the new occupying forces, ISIS, which by all accounts encompassed the majority of the population in the region. The Europeans and other NATO members did not engage Assad militarily or take stronger action in Libya. The inaction created a political void in the region. Iran took advantage of it and so did ISIS. Jointly, all of these political decisions resulted in the disintegration of much of the legal and political infrastructure of these countries. One can debate whether one decision or another would have changed the course of events. But as we already said, sunk costs are sunk costs. The point we want to stress here is that these political actions have some economic consequences and will impact the overall economic equilibrium in other parts of the world.

The destruction and barbaric tactics of ISIS signaled to the people in the region that these groups do not put much value on the lives of the people who did not submit to their views. Those who submitted to their views also suffered significant loss of freedom and income, which increased the gains of migration. The fact that people are willing to die traveling to Europe tells us what they think of what life would be like under ISIS. We will come back to the human tragedy later on. Now we want to focus on the impact on the economies in the EU. Assuming profit maximization and flexible markets, the increased labor force will reduce the EU capital/labor ratio.

WHERE WILL THE MIGRANTS GO AND WHAT WILL BE THEIR ECONOMIC IMPACT ON THESE ECONOMIES?

Will the EU economy be able to absorb the increased labor force? The easiest way to absorb the influx of immigrants is by expanding the production of the labor-intensive product. The increased labor force will result in an increase in the overall supply of labor-intensive products in the EU. All else the same, the price of the labor-intensive products will decline relative to the price of the capital-intensive products. Also, the inflows of labor will, all else the same, result in a lower wage rate in the EU. That tends to create an antiimmigrant sentiment among the groups most directly affected by the migration. They will contend that the immigrants are not only taking jobs away from them, but also lowering their wages. The protectionist pressures unambiguously rise [2].

Another question of interest is, how will the market distribute the inflow of immigrants? Profit maximization offers an answer along the lines described in the previous paragraphs. Labor will be distributed in such a way that the wages and rates of return will be equalized across regions. However, what if there is some rigidity that is different across national boundaries? These rigidities may be the result of the technologies employed in the different economies, the natural endowment, and—more to the point we want to focus on—they may be due to rigidities in the economy that result from regulations,

such as labor restrictions on the hiring and firing of employees (common among European economies). There are also differences in the social safety nets across the different countries.

Immigrants, like most other people, are looking out for their welfare. They will sort themselves out by countries. They have to evaluate where they will get the most income, whether it be through work or through the social safety net. Immigrants with employable skills and language knowledge will go to the areas where it may be easier for them to get jobs. Those less employable have to look at the social safety net options.

A recent study by Michael Tanner and Charles Hughes of the CATO institute calculated the welfare benefits provided by different EU countries [3].

They found out that:

- The welfare benefits in 9 EU countries—Denmark, UK, Finland, Austria, Netherlands, Ireland, Belgium, Germany, and Sweden—exceed $18,200 per year.
- In 6 of the countries—Denmark, UK, Finland, Austria, Netherlands, and Ireland—the welfare benefits exceed $24,300. At $38,558, Denmark offers the most generous package.

Looking over recent newspaper clips at the beginning of the surge of immigrants to Europe is instructive. The articles suggested that, once most of the immigrants reached the EU, they headed to the Nordic Countries, Germany, and the UK. Notice that these are the countries with the highest welfare benefits. If the causal relationship is as we expect, it reassures our faith in markets and incentives. More importantly, the fact that migrants from regions such as Eritrea, Libya, and Syria are well aware of the difference in social safety net benefits across EU countries suggests that the markets are fairly efficient in the transmission of information. Additional proof of the efficiency of information and the desire to reduce the broadly defined "transportation costs" can be found in the stories reported in the press, where some of the migrants went through Russia and bicycled across to the Nordic countries. In an interview, one of the migrants argued that the Russian route was faster and quite possibly cheaper than going through Greece.

POLITICS OR ECONOMICS?

The argument that there is a major noneconomic component in the migration flows used by many migrants is that they are fleeing repression and seeking freedom. But many of these people make it to Turkey, yet they choose not to stay. In fact, some go back to Iraq, to gather the necessary resources or funds to make it to Europe. One very important point that we want to make is that we are not making a normative conclusion; rather we are making a positive statement. We are trying to understand and anticipate economic changes and the impact of the immigration. Once these are known, people can make investment decisions. Others can make their judgments as to whether this inflow of migrants is good or bad.

It is undeniable that the inflow of immigrants will increase the social expenditures in the continent and if our analysis is correct, the location choice may further reinforce the increase in expenditures, for many will choose to go where the benefits are the highest. Any obstruction on the part of the border or entry point's countries will only increase the entry costs. However, once they are in the EU, the issue is whether they can gain access to the social benefits in their preferred localities. This is where the registration of the immigrants at their point of entry comes into play. If applied literally, the entry point's economies will suffer a disproportionate share of the costs.

The story does not end here. If incentives matters (as we believe) and the benefits are mean or income tested, then people leaving the social safety net will face an effective marginal tax rate made up of the decline in benefits, as well as the tax rate generated by the income earned by those leaving the welfare rolls. The previously mentioned CATO institute study shows that

- Austria, Croatia, and Denmark face an effective marginal tax rate of nearly 100% for those leaving welfare for work.
- Slovenia and Belgium face an effective marginal tax rate in the 80% range.
- Ten other countries—Czech Republic, Germany, Finland, Estonia, Lithuania, UK, Netherlands, Latvia, Sweden, and France—all face an effective marginal tax rate in the 60%–80% range.

IS EUROPE UNIQUE OR ARE THESE EFFECTS UNIVERSAL?

In our analysis of the effects of fiscal policies on the states of the Union competitive environment, we identified a clear link between the relative tax rates changes, our proxy for the economic environment and migration among the 48 contiguous states [4]. The analysis showed that the people with the most to gain, those with the higher income at the higher tax states had the most to gain by migrating to a lower tax state. We also identified a direct link between social safety net and the migration patterns. The households with the lowest income levels in the states with the lower safety net benefits had the most to gain by migrating to the higher benefit states. Also to the extent that the social safety net benefits need to be financed by public funds such as tax rates, we can

safely argue that the higher the benefits of the social safety net, the higher the average tax rates are likely to be in the state in question.

These results suggest that the policy mix combination of tax rates and social safety net would be a key driver of the composition of migrants across state lines. The European data presented here suggests a similar type of effect, leading us conclude that these experiences are not unique. The choice of work and/or welfare migrants, whether is internal migration and/or foreign migration, depends on the migrants' skill level, the level and way the benefits are distributed and on impact of the regulatory and tax system on the incentive structure. Ironically, the combination of high tax rate and high public spending discourages high income earners from staying, and encourages the lower income people who benefit from the social programs to migrate to this country. In effect, a policy of tax and spend can be thought of a policy encouraging a brain drain within the sates. The two components or drivers of the internal immigration, tax rates, and social safety net benefits, have clear implications for internal migration among the states in the United States as well as countries in the EU. The framework is robust enough to allow us to also make inferences regarding international migration.

THE RECENT US EXPERIENCE

Anyone who watches television has seen the images during the summer of 2014 of the surge in border crossings byunaccompanied minors. The children have entered the United States. illegally. The Obama administration tried to insist Central Americans not to send their children on the perilous journey north, but the fact remains that with the current US law and backlog in the immigration courts, the consensus among experts was that these children will be allowed to stay for years or perhaps permanently.

The migration outburst can be explained in simple economic terms. Most people agree that the trip is dangerous and expensive for the children and families. The fact that they are willing to take the risk and bear the costs means that they perceive the benefits of coming to the United States to exceed the costs. If that is the case, as the Neil Diamond song says, "They're coming to America."

Immigration is once again on the front pages and whether we like it or not, the United States will have to deal with the issue in the near future. What is clear is that the migrant children will in the short-run tap into the social safety net. If the latter is successful in provide them with an education, in the long run they will benefit themselves and the rest of the United States with the benefit on an education.

IMMIGRATION AS AN ECONOMIC PROBLEM

We have argued that the final distribution of migrants will be impacted by the countries' social safety nets programs. The entry points are determined by geography. It seems reasonable to assume that the Europe entry-point countries and in the United Statesthe entry point states as well as the localities with the higher social safety net will shoulder the bulk of the burden of the costs associated with the inflow of immigrants. Social spending is a national/state choice while the entry point is not. The entry point countries/states/counties have a legitimate argument for getting help from the rest of the countries/states/counties as the case may be. They also have the leverage, in that if they do not get the help, they will let them through.

We believe that people are not lazy, nor are they stupid. The combination of high welfare benefits and a high effective marginal tax rate may prove to be a very expensive proposition for the EU. These economies will attract migrants and, in turn, those migrants will face strong disincentives to work. That is a recipe for increased expenditures and for pressure for further tax increases to finance these additional expenditures.

Europe faces an additional hurdle that the US economy has not quite reached yet. If the European countries do not increase the flexibility of the labor markets or reform the disincentive structure implicit in the social safety net programs, the Euroland economies will face increased spending and tax pressures, which will perpetuate the Euroesclerosis that has affected the region for many years. Other alternatives available to the EU governments are attempting to reduce the immigration flows in a number of ways. The roadblocks enacted and their effects on the migrants can be analyzed in the context of transportation costs. The barriers only raise the transportation costs and only those whose benefits exceed the costs and have the resources to pay for the transportation costs will get to Euroland. However, enforcement and regulations are costly. Just like tax rates increases, they will slow down the economy.

This discussion brings us back to the issue of whether (after acknowledging that the Bush administration made a mistake) the West and, in particular, Europe should have thought that sunk costs were sunk costs and that the best course of action for the Europeans was to restore order in the region. Looking back, one has to wonder, whether it would have been cheaper and better in the long run to get involved with a commitment in taking steps to stabilize the economies of the Middle East and Latin America? Europe and the United States are going to pay for the lack of action and/or bad policies toward the rest of the world with the costs associated with a massive inflow of people.

WHO SHOULD BE COMING INTO THE COUNTRY?

Under the current circumstances, it is the migrants and other countries who decide who to come here first. It is only natural that we, as a sovereign country, should be the ones deciding who comes here and who does not. Viewed from this perspective, it makes sense to secure the border to insure that only the people we want to immigrate are the ones who actually immigrate. If that is the case, we need to revisit the criteria for immigration.

Are we going to continue the preference system where the relatives of current citizens/residents get a higher priority with the intent of keeping families together or are we going to change the selection criteria and add some skill-based categories? If it is the latter, we will accept and facilitate the migration of skill that is in short supply in the country. The latter criteria will increase the likelihood that those who come here will come to work and improve their standard of living by working. In the process of making themselves better off, they will also make us better off through their contribution to our society [5]. The preference system does not guarantee that the migrants are high-skilled workers or what the economy is lacking. In some cases, it is possible that their economic well-being will improve by simply enjoying the benefits of the social safety net. That will be the case if our programs offer a better quality of life than they would enjoy in their home country.

The appropriate migration criteria must also take into account the interaction of the migration policies with current market or economic conditions, as well as the interaction with other domestic policy initiatives. Once the feedback among the different policy objectives are taken into consideration, some interesting modifications to our current immigration policies become apparent. At that point one can design a policy mix that will effectively regulate or determine the compositions of the immigration flows.

HOW WOULD WE MODIFY IMMIGRATION: WHAT TO LOOK FOR AND HOW TO TAKE INTO ACCOUNT THE POLICY INTERACTIONS?

Immigration is a hot political issue and we do not claim to have the answer. However, we do know the features that we would like to see in a comprehensive immigration reform. Up to this point, we have tried to provide an economic explanation as to how different components could be affected by economic policies without ascribing any value judgment to the merits of the different options. Next, we add some value judgments, which hopefully would help us narrow the policy options that we may adopt as a country. For example, under current conditions, the United States and the EU are passive participants to the immigration problems that these economies face. This interpretation lends support to the view that the Central American countries and Mexico are dictating US immigration policy and that the Middle East is dictating the EU immigration policies.

To see the US passivity and the potential suboptimality of the current policies, one needs to ask a couple of questions. First, if we were going to let in 12 million people into the United States, would the United States have chosen the current 12 million illegals? If we were designing an immigration policy from scratch, would we end up where we currently are? Most people's answers are likely to be negative. Asking the same question about legal immigration would probably get a negative answer too. If that is the case, then our immigration policy is due for an overhaul.

Family Affiliation Immigration System: The foundation of the current immigration policy is based on the preference system that attempts to keep families together, among other things. That is a noble goal, but in some circumstances it may have undesirable consequences. The preference system does not say anything about the skill level, the health of the prospective immigrant, nor does it address the issue as to whether that immigrant will become a contributing member of society or an economic burden. All we know is that the closer the person is to the sponsoring relative, the higher the preference level. Whether that candidate skill level is in excess supply or not is irrelevant to the process. For these reasons, we believe that the preference system could also have undesirable composition effects. It is possible that the skill level of the immigrants is such that they will qualify for our safety net programs immediately and that these people never truly join the labor force. The questions are whether the system traps them, and can they escape the poverty trap implicit in the social safety net programs. We could argue that these immigrants will become a burden to society without ever having contributed to the social safety net, and now they will draw from it. They will cause an increase in expenditures in social programs. This line of reasoning suggests that the preference system should be modified to incorporate skill levels as one of the path to migration.

A skill-based immigration program would be a net contributor to the economy. If the skills are in demand, the immigrants will be able to find employment right away and become taxpaying, contributing members of society. Critics of this approach would argue that if the demand were temporary, we would be giving permanent residency to people whose skills we will not need in the long run. Our answer to that is that the immigration program could be combined with a guest worker type of program. That way we could let in anybody that is needed in the economy even for a short-term basis.

Guest Worker Programs: There are some added benefits to a guest worker program. Many of the would be guest workers are some of the current illegal immigrants. But why are they here permanently? The answer has to do with the toll tax they have to pay every time they enter the country. We understand that the going price for a "coyote" smuggling a person is about $5000, which is a heavy toll for a migrant worker. If they go and visit their family once a year, a big chunk of their income is spent on the trip. A more sensible strategy from an economic point of view is for them to roundup enough money to bring their family and never go back. That way they only pay the toll once.

Contrast this outcome with one where the guest-worker permit is easy and cheap to get. In that case, the guest worker would leave his or her family at home. They will save their money to send it back home. The reason for this is that the cost of living is likely to be much lower back home. The guest worker would cross the border several times a year to go visit their family. In the meantime, there would be less illegal immigrants taxing the social services programs.

One insight derived from this analysis is that as we secure the border and make it more difficult to cross, the coyote smuggling prices will increase and that will result in increase in the proportion of "permanent" illegal residents. In contrast, a loose border will ease the burden of keeping their families at home. One has to look at legal residents and US citizens who live in Tijuana and commute to San Diego for work.

The US situation is much different than some European countries. In Italy and Germany, the birth of the children of a foreign national does not automatically confer citizenship from the country of their birth. In Germany, there is a large population of "Turkish" citizens who have never been to Turkey. Their parents were legal residents/workers. They were born in Germany but are not entitled to German citizenship. This brings another set of problems like alienation. The point of all this is to illustrate some of the complexities and interaction of immigration policies with the rest of the US's legislative and social safety net structure.

The guest worker program fits our free trade and immigration view. People should be allowed to work anywhere in the world, as long as they are not a burden to that economy. Viewed in isolation, this conclusion is easy to reach. Unfortunately, we do not live in an isolated world and there will be interaction with other policies in the economy or national laws. For example, we have the issue of birth. Children born in the United States, with some minor exceptions, are automatically US citizens. Given the US's desire to keep families together, this confers their parents a higher preference in case they choose to become legal. The children are entitled to all the social services, irrespective of the parents' legal status. One simple way to solve this problem is for the guest worker to come by themselves without their partners, which reduces the likelihood of children of illegal aliens, assuming that one of the two parents does not have a valid work permit.

By choosing to do a guest worker program, one must take into account other variables that affect immigration and vice versa. Hence, we must take into account the feedback effect among macroeconomic variables.

THE ECONOMIC DETERMINANTS OF MIGRATION

The reason for migration can largely be explained in economic terms. As one compares the change in economic well-being gained by moving from one locality to the United States, it is easy to determine that the likely candidates to migrate are those for whom their income and well-being (net of the "transportation costs") increases as a result of the migration. Hence, we can separate the benefits/costs of migrating into three different components: the income to be realized at home, the income to be realized in the United States, as well as the "transportation costs" associated with traveling from the home country to the United States. There are three potential variables that impact the decision to migrate: economic policies in the destination country, the countries of origin, and the conduit countries.

Income in the Destination Country: Economic analysis suggests that the one sure way to eliminate the migration is to reduce the benefits of migrating. For those who doubt the efficacy or usefulness of this approach, we only need to remind them that migration flows declined significantly during the recession. Our explanation for this is quite simple. The US recession reduced, and quite possibly eliminated, the economic rationale for migrating to America. The lack of jobs and reduction in pay created a situation where the potential income gains, net of transportation costs, were no longer positive for many potential migrants. The recession experience shows one way to reduce the migration: reduce the potential income gains associated with a migration to the United States.

Unfortunately, that is not an acceptable way to reduce migration. On average, the US recession made all of us worse off. It does not make sense to slowdown the US growth to stop immigration. We do not want to shoot ourselves in the foot. This is an important point, as it shows how the interaction with other policy objectives may limit or constrain the likely course of action that we as a country may take to deal with immigration. Most people would argue that they want faster growth, and that would increase the incentives for legal and illegal immigration. Most people would argue that is a nice

problem to have and we must deal with immigration in some other nonrecessionary way.

Income and Security in the Country of Origin: As we believe that the source of immigration can be posed as potential economic gains, and given that we want to have as high an income as possible in the United States, one way to reduce the income differential between the source and destination country is to increase the income and individual security of the country of origin. Good policies in the home country may do that. The other country can help in many different ways, for example in the case of Mexico, the United States, and Canada, one can argue that NAFTA was one such measure. The free trade agreement allowed for the expansion of the export sector in Mexico. That in turn increased wages and salaries of the workers in these sectors. As the standard of living rose, so did imports and the volume of trade among the different trading partners [6].

In addition to adopting progrowth policy, there are other steps the local countries can take to reduce the migration. As many migrants cite crime as one of the reasons for migration, attempting to establish law and order in the source region may increase the benefits of staying and thus reduce the migrant flow. Essentially they need a law and order campaign, where the governments combat crime and guarantee the safety of their citizens. The United States can help with economic aid and military support against the war on drugs and crime. Colombia, under the Alvaro Uribe presidency, was quite successful in pacifying the country. But the Uribe administration appears to be the exception rather than the rule.

Law and order and the protection of human life and property rights would go a long way to keep the people at home. If people do not feel secure, there is no reason to stay. The drug trade and related violence is a major cause for the migration north in Latin America.

Transportation Costs: The possible contribution of a prosperous country like the United States is that it can prod its poorer trading partners into adopting progrowth policies that increase the standard of living of its partners. Unfortunately, the United States as a country does not control all the necessary levers to induce these countries to adopt the progrowth policies. Nor is it clear that the US recommended policies would deliver the results either. One only needs to look at the United States where the growth rate has been well below the average of the last three decades during the last 5 years. It is up to each individual country to find its way.

One policy option to arrest the immigration without hopefully creating a negative impact on the well-being of the local residents is to raise the "transportation costs" faced by the migrants. If sufficiently high, the transportation costs may stop the migration. Visa restrictions and other border controls do raise the transportation costs. The question is how effective those measures are and whether they stop people who are truly desperate and have nothing to lose. Under these conditions, the host country will have to deal with an unending and steady inflow of immigrants. One problem with such measures is the impact it may have on the composition of the migrants. It is possible that the people who are successful in circumventing the restrictions may not be the ones that fill the country's needs.

THE ANCHOR BABIES

In the United States, the anchor babies are nothing more than a loophole created by the preference system. The economics of the anchor babies is simple and straightforward. After the child turns 21, relatives of a children born in the United States who apply for residence to the United States will, under the preference system, be able to jump the line ahead of others who do not have relatives. The closer the blood relationship, the higher will be the preference status and thus the shorter the wait for a green card [7].

Next let's take an economic approach to the anchor babies issue and ask what the profile of the people is most likely to take advantage of this loophole. Ironically, the answer is that the some of the poorest and the some of the wealthiest people are the likely candidates. Let's take each group separately.

Consider a person living near the US border. For them, crossing over to have the baby may be relatively inexpensive. Once they are here, the hospital care will be free and the child by virtue of being a US citizen will be entitled to attend public school and receive many other social services benefits. In theory, the kids could live in Tijuana and go to school in the United States. However, if the poor family makes it to the United States, the whole family may be able to stay even though the rest of the family is comprised of "illegal" immigrants. They will have access to many of the social services and may be able to work. For many of the poorest, living under these "dismal conditions" may be better than living under the extreme poverty in their homeland. An obvious question that arises from all this, is how come we do not have all the poor people of the world here? The answer is the broadly defined transportation costs. It takes resources to make it here, there is interdiction, and other risk and costs. Even then, not all the ones who try succeed. All these factors limit the inflow naturally. Again we get back to basics: the lower the transaction or transportation costs, the lower the cost of migrating, and the greater the income differential inclusive of social safety benefits in the two localities. Low bars for the poorest means the greater likelihood of migration.

While the economic argument is the same for the wealthiest, their horizon may be a bit different. It will not be as immediate as the poorer people. For the wealthy in a hurry, there is a different entry process. Under the program known as EB-5, they can effectively buy a green card by making a minimum $500,000 in certain investments that create at least 10 jobs per investor.

For those who are not in a hurry, the birth tourism offers an interesting option. If they are wealthy enough they can come to the United States, have the best medical care that they pay for and the hospital are more than happy to have them as clients. They stay here and spend money, so far so good. Put in the economic context, these expenditures are a good proxy for the transportation or transaction cost. But why do they do it? Their benefit is that their child will be a US citizen and when the child is old enough that child will be able to attend high school and college in the United States. Is that all? Not quite. While they may be very successful and happy in their home country, in many parts of the world, changes in the political winds tend to affect the economic well-being and freedom of people who benefit from the current system. One way to buy insurance against the adverse changes is too keep money outside the country, something that while it is possible is getting much more difficult to hide. The other problem is the ability to live the country and relocate in another. The anchor baby is an insurance policy that may allow these people to get a foothold in the United States. While the circumstances of the wealthy may be different than the poor people, their motivations are the same: safety, security, and well-being.

The anchor baby topic is of great interest especially during an election cycle. Some politicians offer solutions such as altering their countries constitution to deny citizenship to the children born to nonlegal residents. Luckily for some, in the United States a constitutional change requires that two thirds of the states approve the amendment, a daunting task. However, the bar is not that high in other countries. The Dominican Republic in a move that has caused a great deal of international turmoil recently changed its laws regarding the children of people who were not legal residents of the country. The detractors of such measures argue that the law is being applied retroactively and that is unconstitutional, though the Dominican Republic's Supreme Court has ruled the law constitutional. Yet in spite of all this, the international pressure has not subsided. The question is whether this is a defense of the rule of law or an expedient way to deal with a Haitian immigration problem, where the Dominican Republic will be forced by the international community to shoulder the burden all by itself.

THE POLITICS OF IMMIGRATION

Critics of the US and EU administrations argue that the laws are not being enforced and that encourages the immigrants to come even if the methods are not deemed legal. Hence they argue that the first step in immigration reform is to secure the border. Once the border is secure and the current laws enforced, one can talk about immigration reform. Opponents of this view argue that the advocates of the previous positions are antiimmigrant.

As these positions are so prevalent all over the world, one must ask whether these apparent inconsistencies can be reconciled in terms of the policy of the politics of special interest group. The differences amongst groups regarding immigration policies can be ascribed in the context of the potential impact of migrants as a voting block and on the potential effect that migrants would have on public spending. If one party believes that they can garner the larger share of the immigrant vote, political self-interest dictates that they will be amenable to immigration.

A large inflow of immigrants could change the makeup of the population. Let's deal with the potential negative aspects first. Immigration could have an adverse effect on overall expenditures related to the social safety net. This may especially be the case if the immigrants consist mostly of a low skill force. The low skill workers' wages would not be much different than the equivalent wage provided by the social safety net programs. Worse yet, the social safety net has a built-in poverty trap. As the beneficiaries of the social safety net income rises, the benefits will decline. The means testing of the benefits will produce a decline in benefits due to a rise in income rise thereby partially or in some cases totally offsetting increases in income earned. That is, at the poverty level, the income increase may incur a built-in increase in the effective tax rate additional to the regular income tax rates. The combiined tax increase may even approach a 100% effective tax rate. In the case where the effective tax rate approaches 100%, it will never pay for these people to join the labor force.

The social safety net could create a permanent unemployed class. It is not that they are lazy; in fact these people are quite laborious. Their actions are the result of the perverse incentives built into the social safety net programs. These people could be trapped at a permanent poverty level by the social safety net. So the big issue here is whether the immigrants come here to work or are they going to fall into the poverty trap? If they fall into the poverty trap, they will become dependent on government services and assistance, this will put upward pressures on the social safety net related spending. The party willing to increase the safety net may be able to gain favor with immigrants once they gain voting privileges. However, the taxpayers and those whose position are taken by the immigrants or feel their wages have been reduced as a result may oppose the immigration. The politics of special interests will play out in full in this case. We should observe an increase in nativist proposals and outright antiimmigrant measures and sentiment. In

contrast, those who hope to woo them, may impugn the motives of the opposition and brand them as racists.

It does not have to come to this. As already mentioned, there is a simple way to alter the composition of the migrants, as well as reducing the incentives for the social safety net programs. A high growth rate will attract all kind of immigrants, especially those who want to work regardless of their skill levels. Secondly, a reduction in the social benefits will reduce the incentives for the migrants to choose the social safety net over work. The latter action may be favored by those who want to reduce the size and scope of the safety net and while those in favor of an expansion of the latter will clearly oppose. The political battle lines are fairly clear.

Now let's focus on the positive aspects of immigration. If the immigrants come here in search of opportunities, they are less likely to fall into the social safety net. Instead they will look for work and move up the ladder. They will also understand that taxes have to be increased to finance the social safety net and that the lower the tax rates, the higher their take home pay. These groups are likely to lean away from the party espousing redistribution of income and an expansion of the social safety net.

The previous paragraphs suggest that the answer regarding the political impact of immigrants is an ambiguous one. We have outlined the conditions consistent with each of the two alternative views. Looking at the data, one may be able to surmise which of the tow views is the one with the most relevance to a society. A recent study by the National Academy of Sciences and Medicine reported in a recent review and outlook section of the *Wall Street Journal* sheds some light on this issue and provides us with interesting information. Here is a key sentence of the report:

> ...Across all measurable outcomes, integration increases over time, with immigrants becoming more like the native-born with more time in the country, and with the second and third generations becoming more like other native–born Americans than their parents were...[8]

This conclusion suggests that over the long-term immigrants become more like the native-born. Hence policies aimed and/or favoring the immigrants, if they are resented by the general population, they will be eventually resented by descendants of the immigrants as well. Therefore the long-term effects of policies favoring the immigrants are ambiguous at best.

Another concern expressed by many analysts is in reference to the potential political impact of the mass migration on the European and US economies. When looking at the situation, one has to keep in mind the significant difference that exists between the United States and the EU. Most countries in the EU are a *jus sanguinis* states, as opposed to *jus soli* state, meaning that it attributes citizenship by blood, not by location of birth. Hence, unlike the situation in the United States, the children of these immigrants born in the EU will not acquire citizenship automatically. They will not become a voting block that will be able to influence politics; for that, they have to become citizens. Hence, any power they acquire will have to be by means other than the voting booth. Nevertheless, the mass migration will have significant impact on EU politics. They may demand accommodations in education and other public policy areas. In the United States, the path to citizenship may be easier. While these people are potential future voters, one should not be too worried about it if in fact in the long run the immigrants become more like us.

However, with respect to the immigration policy, it seems reasonable that the United States should be the country dictating its own immigration policies. The country should take a proactive approach rather than a passive one where the actions of the other countries and their nationals effectively determine US immigration. With this in mind, we believe that one of the top priorities of immigration reform is to take control of the borders. This would have several potential benefits to the US economy. It would reduce the likelihood of terrorists coming into the country posing as illegal immigrants. It would also allow the United States to determine the composition of the immigrants coming into the country. The one possible downside of a secure border is that it will increase the price coyotes charge to cross the border. The higher the price, the more likely that the illegal immigrants will stay permanently, bring their family to the United States, and increase the burden of the productive segment of society who pay for the social safety net through their taxes.

Fortunately, as we have already argued, this problem could be significantly reduced through a guest worker program. Depending on how it is implemented, the guest worker program could make it easy for the workers to come and go. If that is the case, experience suggests that they will leave their family in their home country. If it works as we suggest, the guest worker program will reduce the number of illegals residing in the United States and that will reduce the pressure on the social safety net.

Tilting away from a preference system based on family relationships to a skill-based system could have several beneficial effects on the economy. First, giving preferences to relatives does not insure that skilled workers will be allowed in the country. Nor does this policy insure that the new immigrants will not become a burden to society and tax the social safety net programs. In contrast, a skill-based migration will allow for the migration of people who will be gainfully employed and they will become taxpayers. Hence, skill-based immigrants are not likely candidates to use the social safety net in their early working years. If they are young enough, the will have a long working life ahead of them, and they will

spend a lifetime making social security contributions. They will help shore up the unfunded liabilities of the social safety net and retirement programs. We do not expect the all the skill-based migrants to be scientists, inventors, or entrepreneurs. Society also needs nail filers, factory workers, doctors, etc. Immigration policy should focus on satisfying the needs of the economy. If it does, then we expect the economy to run more efficiently and grow faster. Any innovation produced by the new immigrants is a bonus and, if the past is any guide, the highly skilled immigrants will more than pay for themselves.

THE BURDEN OF ADJUSTMENT

One area where politics and economics intersect is on the issue of immigration. The best way to illustrate the issues is to consider extreme situations, cases where the immigration reaches the level of a humanitarian crisis. Examples of large migration from failed states and war zones include the recent European experience, the child migration from Central America into the United States and to show that this is not necessarily a wealthy country problem. That all that is needed is that one of the countries is a bit better and the transportation costs low, the mass migration from Haiti to the Dominican Republic is another example.

All three cases have been designated humanitarian crisis by the international press. The pressure is for the host countries to accept the immigrants in light of the crisis. Even Pope Francis has chimed in on this issue. During his visit to the United States, he talked about the migration from south to the north, without mentioning countries. But the reference was clear. The Pope argued that these people were migrating to improve their economic life and his tone suggests that they should be allowed to migrate. At least the Pope is consistent on this issue whether it is migration to the United States, EU, and even tiny Dominican Republic. Yet many countries pubic positions and policies toward the migrants into their borders do not square with their foreign policy views.

Let's take the humanitarian argument; it is a very compassionate argument. However there are costs associated with the migration and accepting the immigrants, who will pay for these costs? The entry points, such as Greece and Italy among others in the EU, The US Border States and the Dominican Republic who shares the island with Haiti will have to shoulder a disproportionate share of the costs of protecting the border and managing the inflow. The Pope views ignores an important point. Most of these economic migrants' remittances are very important to their local economies. This suggests that without the remittances the local economy would be much worse. Also, it also suggests that if economic opportunities were plentiful, these people would not migrate. Viewed from this perspective, the problem seems to be bad-economic policies in the countries of origin. Why should the other countries be held accountable and forced to solve and/or pay for the culprits' mistakes? Where was the international community outrage when these countries were making the wrong policy choices that have impoverished their nations?

The Haitian case is an interesting one. In the context of the arguments presented earlier, the United States has tried to improve the country's economic conditions with its reconstruction and aid program in the aftermath of the hurricane. The hope was that these "Investments" would get the economy on a path toward a higher standard of living and faster economic growth. The United States spent billions and billions of dollar rebuilding Haiti, sadly little or no progress has been made. The country would have been better off, if the United States took that money and set IRA types of accounts for each resident. The United States tried and failed to improve the lot of the Haitian people by reactivating its economy.

After failing on the rebuilding of the economy, the one option left for the Haitian people was migration, the question was where? The largest income gains resulting from migration would be relocation to the United States. The question is whether the gains exceed the transportation costs? The common way for people to attempt the trip would be by boat. But that is dangerous and the US coast guard is fairly effective at stopping this flow. Put in the context of our framework, the risk involved and the Coast Guard raise the transportation costs, if the increase is large enough it will not pay to take that option. The low-transportation cost area is the Dominican Republic (DR) and while the income differential gains are smaller than the migration to the United States, net of the transportation costs the DR is a viable option for the Haitians. It seems that the international community is content with letting the DR be the solution to the problem. The DR has no leverage against the rest of the region or the world. As a result it gets little or no help from the international community, it must shoulder the migration costs from a failed state that has a larger population than its own.

In the EU case, the situation is a bit different. The entry point countries do have leverage. The reason for this is that the migrants do not plan to stay in these countries; they want to migrate to countries with better social safety net or better employment opportunities. If these EU countries do not get help the entry point countries, they can increase the inflow of immigrants which in turn will increase the budgetary and social pressures in these economies. The border countries can in effect force the other EU member countries to shoulder much of the costs. However this is a myopic view. One question that we will never get the answer to is whether the "Coalition of the willing" could have prevented the debacle in the region. Is it possibly that if the coalition had stayed longer in the region, the nation building a peace keeping process could have been successful. There are differences of opinion about this, however one cannot rule out this possibility.

The one issue that no one seems to discuss is related to what some may call a policy myopia that ignores the dynamic effects of these policy actions. Allowing the migration will foster and encourage people in other regions of the world. A longer term view is needed to reach a long term and sensible solution to the problem where the well-being of the would be migrant is improved, thereby reducing their need to migrate. However the solution is not pouring money into the problem, Haiti is one clear example where this type of policy failed. What is needed is to help the country build an infrastructure where property rights and the rule of law are observed. That combined with an incentive structure conducive to inducing people to work save and invest is what is needed. The British did this with Hong Kong, when it adopted a fixed exchange rate currency board and a low tax rate structure. Hong Kong became a beacon of economic success not only for the region but also for the world. Let's hope that China affords Hong Kong the opportunity to continue on this path. NAFTA provided a somewhat different solution, the free trade with the United States and Canada made Mexico better off and reduced the illegal immigration flow from Mexico to the US NAFTA and Hong Kong are two examples illustrating the range of what is possible to arrest an outflow of people and capital and improve the standard of living of a country's nationals.

References

[1] Sjaastad LA. Costs and returns of human migration. J Polit Econ 1962;70(5):80–93.

[2] Troianovski A. Europe's populist politicians tap into deep-seated frustration. Wall St J 2015;A1.

[3] Hughes C, Tanner MD. The work versus welfare trade-off: Europe. Policy Anal 2015;. Cato Institute, August 24, No. 779.

[4] See Chapter 6 of this part.

[5] Canto VA, Udwadia FE. The effect of immigration quotas on the average quality of migrating labor and income distribution. S Econ J 1986;52(3):785–93.

[6] IMF working paper, how has NAFTA affected the Mexican economy? Review and evidence; April, 2004.

[7] Jordan, M. Federal agents raid alleged 'maternity tourism' businesses catering to Chinese. Wall St J 2015:A.3.

[8] Those assimilating immigrants. Wall St J 2015:A.16.

SECTION II

THE TRADE BALANCE

9

Global Investing: The Macro Prospective Building Blocks

In our previous installment, we raised the issue that recent events in the financial markets have reminded investors that it is important to have a framework to analyze events in the global economy. A casual reading of the financial press, as well as some of the commentaries made by pundits, politicians, and policymakers, point to a narrow focus on individual issues that are not consistent with a narrow view held by the same parties on other issues.

One such example was why some people favor trade in goods, yet not on all factors of production and vice versa? We wondered if these points of view were inconsistent. If so, how can one reconcile the inconsistencies? We believe that the economic and ideological inconsistencies would be avoided if the parties had taken the time to develop a broader and more general framework capable of incorporating all the different issues. Under a general framework, politicians, investors, and pundits would be forced to weed out some of the assumptions that, while convenient simplifications for one particular problem, would contradict and complicate the analysis of other problems. Identifying these inconsistencies and contradictions leads to the development of a framework where the analysts would at least make consistent choices in a logical context.

Our previous installment outlined the price adjustment process needed to clear the global and national markets. This next installment focuses on the quantity adjustments and the impact on the National Income and Product Accounts generated by different policies. We build on our previous outline of a simple framework describing the global economy.

THE FRAMEWORK

We assume that there are two countries: Westland and Lakeland. Westland produces mostly wine and its currency is called notes. Lakeland produces mostly cheese and it uses the peso as its currency. P_{wn} and P_{cn} denote the price of wine and cheese in notes, while P_{wp} and P_{cp} denote the price of wine and cheese in pesos. The exchange rate between the two currencies, E, is easily calculated as the ratio of the price of a commodity, say cheese, in the two currencies. In practice, the exchange rate can be measured as the ratio of the price of wine in the two countries, P_{wn}/P_{wp}, or the ratio of the price of cheese in the two countries in local currencies, P_{cn}/P_{cp}. The terms of trade, T, between the two economies is measured as the relative price of wine in terms of cheese in either of the two economies. The terms of trade can be measured as P_{wn}/P_{cn} or P_{wp}/P_{cp}.

If the relative price remains unchanged, then wine and cheese tend to be consumed in fixed proportions. If that is the case, one can make a composite good of all the goods and services consumed in each economy [1] Each

Economic Disturbances and Equilibrium in an Integrated Global Economy. http://dx.doi.org/10.1016/B978-0-12-813993-6.00009-X

economy's consumer price index (CPI) is now denoted as P_n and P_p, where P_n denotes the CPI in Westland and is denominated in notes, and P_p denotes the CPI in Lakeland and is measured in pesos. One point we need to make here is that the assumption that relative prices remain unchanged means that all prices will increase at the same rate. Hence by simply focusing on the price of a single commodity, we can generalize it to the economy's underlying inflation rate.

Next we assume that economic agents maximize profits and that there are no transaction costs or any frictions restricting the mobility of goods and services across the two economies. These two assumptions are sufficient to insure that the profit maximizing agents arbitrage any differences in prices across national borders. Economic agents make sure that the cheese price in Westland in notes multiplied by the exchange rate is the same as the peso price of cheese in Lakeland.

$$P_{cp} = P_{cn} * E \qquad (9.1)$$

Eq. (9.1) shows that purchasing power parity (PPP) holds across commodities and the economies. This implies that there is a single global price for each of the commodities. The previous equation suggests that all else the same, whenever prices in Lakeland rise faster than the prices in Westland, Lakeland will experience an exchange rate depreciation. Later on, we will relax these assumptions. However, for now we see how far the model can take us.

THE MONETARY SYSTEM

Next we make the assumption that inflation is a monetary phenomenon, in which case monetary equilibrium can be described as:

$$(B*m)*v = P*Y \qquad (9.2)$$

where B denotes the monetary base in the economy, m is the money multiplier, v is the velocity of circulation of money, P the price level in local currency, and Y is real GDP in the economy in question. The information in the equation can be rearranged to solve for the price level:

$$P = \left((B*m)*v\right)/Y \qquad (9.2')$$

The equation is fairly general and can accommodate different monetary views and variations. For example, the product of the monetary base, B, times the money multiplier, m, denotes the quantity of money circulating in the economy, money zero maturity (MZM). All else the same, increases in the quantity of money lead to a higher price level. Also, increases in the real GDP, Y, lead to a decline in the price level. We do not

necessarily assume that the velocity of money is constant; we have to allow for shifts in the demand for money or changes in the velocity of money, but more on this later on.

The dynamic version of the previous equation can be written as:

$$\pi = \beta + \mu - \eta \qquad (9.2'')$$

where π denotes the rate of change of the price level or inflation rate, β denotes the growth of the monetary base, η the real GDP growth rate, and μ is a term capturing the changes in the money multiplier and the velocity of money, that is, shifts net shifts in money demand.

THE EXCHANGE RATE AND THE ORGANIZATION OF THE MONETARY SYSTEM

Over the years we have argued that the organization of the monetary system determines an economy's inflation potential, the impact of capital flows on money supply, as well as an economy's balance of payments (BoP). In what follows, we will consider two alternative organizations, a floating exchange rate system and a fixed exchange rate system. We then argue that most other arrangements can be expressed as combination of these two components.

Floating Exchange Rate System: Initially we assume that people in Lakeland only use pesos in their everyday transactions, while the people of Westland only use notes as their currency. If that is the case, then the demand for each currency is solely based on the domestic demand for the currency in question, while the supply is presumably controlled by the central bank.

We have already shown that under the assumptions of free mobility and profit maximization, arbitrage insures that the peso price of each commodity will be the same across localities. The same can be said about the notes price of each commodity. Simply put, PPP holds across each and every commodity in question. Now, if we assume that there are no relative price changes, that is, changes in the terms of trade, then we can show that the PPP relationship will hold even when we apply it to each of the economies' CPI. In its dynamic version, the exchange rate equation can be written as:

$$\pi_p = \pi_n + \mathcal{E} \qquad (9.1')$$

where π_p is the rate of change in domestic prices, that is, Lakeland's inflation rate in pesos, π_n is the inflation rate in Westland notes, and $\mathcal{E}$ is the rate of change in the exchange rate that allows the conversion of notes into pesos, that is, the exchange rate depreciation rate.

Eq. (9.1') shows that the country with the higher inflation rate will experience currency depreciation equal to the inflation rate differential. Substituting Eq. (9.2'') into Eq. (9.1') and rearranging terms, one can solve for an expression denoting the determinants of the changes in the nominal exchange rate.

$$\mathcal{E} = (\beta_1 - \beta_w) - (\eta_1 - \eta_w) + (\mu_1 - \mu_w) \qquad (9.3)$$

The first term in parenthesis shows that all else the same, whenever the Lakeland money growth exceeds the Westland money growth, the peso depreciates. The second term shows that if Lakeland grows faster than Westland, the peso will tend to appreciate. The third term captures the effects of changes in the demand for money and/or the money multiplier in the various economies, which up to this point we have assumed to be exogenous.

The next topic of discussion is the international accounts under a floating exchange rate system. Recall that we have assumed that locals only use the local currency in domestic transactions. Under these assumptions, there will be no net money flow between the countries. This means that the BoP will be zero at all times. And as the BoP has two components [the trade balance (TB) and the capital account (KA)], it follows that the TBs will be the mirror image of the KA. Formally we can express these relationships as:

$$BoP = TB + KA \equiv 0 \qquad (9.4)$$

This is a very important point which leads to a very interesting insight. Eq. (9.4) shows that there are two undetermined variables. Given that there is only one equation, there is only one degree of freedom. Once you know one of the variables in the equation, the other one is known. Alternatively stated, the previous equation can be written as:

$$TB = KA \qquad (9.4')$$

The insight derived from Eq. (9.4') is that one cannot develop two independent theories (say one theory for the TB and a different theory for the KA). The correct theory has to be able to explain both at the same time. This means that views that develop two separate theories for the two accounts will, at the very least, have one of the theories wrong and quite possibly both.

THE TRADE BALANCE AND CAPITAL FLOWS

The terms of trade, T, is defined as the price of one country's exports in terms of the other (say the price of wine in terms of cheese). In our earlier installment of the global perspective, we showed that when the terms of trade do not change, the interest rate parity (IRP) and PPP hold at all times and the real rate of returns is equalized across countries. Under this scenario, there is no need for global investing. One can get the same rate of return at home as one can get elsewhere. A more interesting case is one where the terms of trade are changing.

A favorable term of trade change to Lakeland means that a pound of cheese is now able to get a larger quantity of wine. Another way of saying the same thing is that the rate of return earned by producing cheese increases relative to the rate of return earned in the production of wine. The question is how we modify our analysis to account for the change in terms of trade. We do so in the below equation:

$$\rho_1 = \rho_w + \tau \qquad (9.5)$$

where τ denotes the change in terms of trade between the two economies.

Combining the two versions of IRP developed in our earlier installment of the global framework, we obtain the following relationships:

$$i_1 - i_w = \mathcal{E} = \pi_1 - \pi_w - (\rho_1 - \rho_w)$$

Substituting Eq. (9.5) into the previous equation yields:

$$i_1 - i_w = \mathcal{E} = \pi_1 - \pi_w + \tau \qquad (9.5')$$

Rearranging the terms, we get an expression for the changes in terms of trade:

$$\tau = \mathcal{E} - (\pi_1 - \pi_w) \qquad (9.6)$$

This equation provides the following insight: violations of PPP reflect changes in the terms of trade of an economy. A terms of trade appreciation over and above the nominal exchange rate appreciation. Or the real exchange rate reflects an increase in the real rate of return of the exported and exportable products relative to the other economies' exported products, as well as the import competing products at home.

To summarize, it is the deviations from PPP that reflect the terms of trade changes and the corresponding rates of return differentials across countries. Therefore if devaluation is to have a real effect on the economy, that is alter the price of imports in terms of exports, it must generate deviations from PPP. We contend that only real variables or variables that affect the real economy, such as tax rates or technological changes, can cause changes in the exchange rate over and above the PPP fluctuations. Thus netting the inflation rate differential from the exchange rate changes gives us an estimate of the countries' terms of trade changes

WHAT HAPPENS WHEN THE TERMS OF TRADE CHANGE IN PREDICTABLE DIRECTIONS?

When relative commodity prices remain unchanged (the price of cheese in terms of wine for example), so do the terms of trade. In that case, arbitrage insures that PPP holds and real rates of return are equalized across countries. Under PPP, the exchange rate changes reflect inflation rate differentials across countries. Now if PPP does not hold, then the deviations from PPP reflect relative price changes. For example, when the price of cheese in terms of wine increases (terms of trade changes) and the country with an appreciating currency (Lakeland) over and above the inflation rate differential, we should observe the following:

- The real exchange rate appreciation has a secondary effect on the economy. The higher real rate of return means that one pound of cheese now buys more bottles of wine. This induces people in Lakeland to devote more resources to cheese production at the expense of wine production.
- These forces are also at work in Westland, where resources will now be diverted from wine production to the production of the import substitution goods, domestic cheese. Therefore cheese production worldwide increases, while wine production unambiguously declines.
- But we can say much more than this. As cheese is now more valuable and resources are being attracted from the domestic wine production (as well as from the foreign wine production) and attracting previously idle or unemployed domestic resources, we can easily show that the increase in the value of cheese production in Lakeland will exceed the value of the decline in wine production, hence real GDP will also increase in Lakeland. The opposite result will hold for Westland. The real GDP growth rate in Lakeland will increase relative to Westland.
- Also, to the extent that resources flow from Westland to Lakeland, the latter will experience a capital inflow, while the former will experience a capital outflow.

- The end result is that when the real rate of return for cheese making increases relative to winemaking, Lakeland's GDP growth rate accelerates relative to Westland's GDP growth rate. If the initial disturbance is demand-driven, the TB will worsen. On the other hand, if the initial disturbance is supply-driven, the TB will improve.
- The higher rate of return also means that the resources intensive in the production of the appreciating product, say pasture land, experiences an increase in valuation, while the factors intensive in the production of wine decline in value. Cheese land appreciates relative to wine land. Given the assumption that Lakeland is relatively intensive in cheese land compared to Westland, we expect to see the Lakeland stock market to outperform the Westland stock market.

Our analysis is simple and straightforward. We have developed a framework that links the relative rates of returns to relative economic performance, that is, relative GDP growth, changes in the TB, and capital flows, as well as the relative stock market performance. It is quite a mouthful. The equation below summarizes the TB drivers:

$$KA = TB = \alpha\left(\eta_l - \eta_w\right) = \alpha\sigma\left(\rho_l - \rho_w\right) \qquad (9.7)$$

The seven equations outlined in here describe a simple framework. The complete system can be now used to analyze policy changes and other disturbances. Under a floating exchange rate system, once the shock is identified, the system of equations or the model framework can be used to identify and analyze how economic and policy disturbances are propagated through the real economy. One way to test the model is by examining the correlations between the different variables induced by the different disturbances or economic shocks derived from the system of equations outlined in here.

Reference

[1] Hicks John R. Value and capital. Oxford: Oxford University Press; 1939. (2nd ed. 1946).

CHAPTER

10

Diversity and Harmonization

In economics, a voluntary exchange between two parties, at worst, makes no parties worse off. In fact, it is quite possible that both parties will be made better off. This, in turn, leads us to ask what gives rise to the potential gains in trade that make people engage in free exchanges. Differences in taste and/or endowments are two of the most common reasons cited by the economists. Here we focus on differences in endowments. For the sake of argument, let's consider two isolated economies with identical tastes. To see these principles in action, let's also assume that one economy has an abundance of agricultural land and the other an abundance of oceanfront.

AUTARKIC EQUILIBRIUM

In the case of "absent trade" between the two economies, in each of the economies, consumers will have to eat what they produce and produce what they eat. Given the similarity in tastes combined with the differences in endowments, we can easily show that the economy with a relative abundance of agricultural land will produce a higher proportion of agricultural products than the economy with a relative abundance of oceanfront. But there is more. The assumption that the two economies have the same tastes and the differences in endowments also allows us to establish that there will be a difference in the relative prices of the two commodities across the two economies. As the agricultural goods are relatively

abundant in the economy with a relative abundance of agricultural land, the agricultural goods will fetch a lower number of marine products. The opposite is true for the economy abundant in oceanfront.

FREE TRADE EQUILIBRIUM

The opening up of trade between the two economies gives rise to a new equilibrium. Absent transportation costs, arbitrage insures that the differences in relative prices are eliminated. A single price prevails in the world economy and it is determined by the interaction of the global demand and supply curves. To achieve a global market-clearing price, arbitrage insures that the goods flow from the areas where they are relatively cheap into areas where they are relatively expensive.

Given the tastes and relative endowments of the two economies, we know that the relative price of agricultural goods will be lower in the economy with a relative abundance of agricultural land. Hence, that economy will export the agricultural goods and, in the process, domestic supply will shrink. If so, it will lead to an increase in the domestic prices of agricultural goods in the exporting country. The opposite happens in the economy with a relative abundance of oceanfront. It will necessitate importing of the agricultural goods, and the increased supply leads to a decline in the relative price of agricultural goods. The process continues until the relative price of the agricultural goods is equalized in the two economies.

Economic Disturbances and Equilibrium in an Integrated Global Economy. http://dx.doi.org/10.1016/B978-0-12-813993-6.00010-6

At that point, there will be no arbitrage or profit opportunity. The world market will be in equilibrium [1].

SOME GENERALIZATIONS

The countries' endowments allow us to make inferences about trade patterns. The economy with an abundance of agricultural land exports agricultural goods and imports marine goods from the economy with an abundance of oceanfront. As we have assumed an absence of transportation costs, arbitrage insures that the relative prices are the same across the economies. The assumption of similar tastes in the two economies insures that in equilibrium, the proportion in which the two goods are consumed is identical across the two economies. Here we end up with a very important insight: irrespective of the differences in endowments, the opening of trade leads to a convergence or harmonization of the consumption bundles across the two economies (i.e., the proportion of the goods consumed is the same across the two economies).

On the production side, the effect is completely different. In the economy with an abundance of agricultural land, the opening of trade allows the producers of the agricultural goods to sell their product at a higher price in the world/foreign markets. As a result, they are now able to pay higher wages to workers in the agricultural production. Resources will be diverted away from the marine sector and into the agricultural sector. A similar argument leads us to conclude that the oceanfront abundant economy will now produce more marine products at the expense of agricultural products. By virtue of the differences in endowments, the two economies concentrate their production in the goods and services in which they have an endowment comparative advantage and import the goods in which they do not have a comparative advantage. Here we end up with another important insight. Ironically, in this example, the opening of trade leads to a divergence between production and consumption in both countries [2].

THE LINK BETWEEN CONSUMPTION HARMONIZATION AND PRODUCTION DIVERGENCE

The opening up of trade leads to a convergence of consumption patterns and a divergence of production patterns. Free trade together with the resulting specialization of production leads to greater diversity across the economies on the production side. Yet at the same time, we find that the similarity in tastes will lead to a convergence or harmonization of the consumption patterns across the two economies.

The diversity on the production side and harmonization on the consumption side is to be celebrated; every country is made better off. They get more of what they want at a lower price and they sell more of what they produce at a higher price. It does not matter where the goods are being produced, what matters is their availability.

We have illustrated one simple example where harmonization and diversity are being simultaneously celebrated. The key point here is that the diversity and harmonization are not necessarily independent of each other and attempting to control one may adversely affect the other and make society worse off. Attempts to increase the domestic production of one good result in inefficiencies and a decline in the production of other goods. This is a point that is commonly missed by policymakers, especially when they discuss international trade and outsourcing. Politicians tend to ignore the other side of the coin.

THE POLITICS OF JOB PROTECTION POLICIES

Many political pundits and some economists argue that a trade balance deficit and outsourcing amounts to the net export of jobs. Largely as a result of these beliefs, they advocate protectionist policies aimed at improving the trade balance and reducing or eliminating the practice of outsourcing. Some economies do not see any problem with their attempts to manipulate their currency with the hope of improving their trade balance, yet these same countries complain bitterly when other countries adopt similar policies.

One can gain insights as to why outsourcing has become such a major political issue by focusing on the incentives and the impact of the costs and benefits of outsourcing, currency manipulation, and the trade balance on the well-being of special interest groups. The benefits of outsourcing—lower prices and higher profits—are spread out among shareholders and consumers. Consumers see lower prices and shareholders see higher profits. The rising stock market, if strong enough, offsets any protectionist pressure generated by the fear of job losses due to an increase in imports or job outsourcing. The investor class understands that a rising tide lifts all boats. The politics of the special interest groups explains why it is that during good times when the economy is expanding that free trade forces prevail.

In contrast to the diffused benefits of outsourcing, the costs are concentrated on a particular special interest group (i.e., the displaced employees). The dispersion of benefits and the cost concentration affect the politics of outsourcing. Our own research shows that protectionist pressures are directly related to a loss of jobs. Import penetration is usually equated with job losses that could be avoided if goods were produced domestically. The politics of special interest groups explains why outsourcing concerns may give rise to an increase in protectionist pressure and why these pressures are higher during tough economic times.

In addition, the pressure is not uniform among different companies. For example, larger companies are more likely to have multiplant facilities all over the world and, thus, may be the ones taking advantage of outsourcing. In turn, smaller companies are likely to be single plant facilities that are threatened by the outsourcing. Not surprisingly, multinational companies and small manufacturing companies would tend to be on opposite sides of this issue. It should not be surprising that politicians catering to the union vote are likely to be the sponsors of protectionist legislation. Dozens of bills to protect US jobs have been introduced in state legislatures and in Congress. Some are a variant of the traditionally protectionist local content laws. Finally, there are also bills that would restrict companies from bringing foreign workers to the United States on guest visas to do jobs previously done by Americans. This is an ironic piece of legislation, for it is these same employees who we do not let immigrate permanently who came here to get training and then go back and work in the outsourced industries. The question is whether these people, if allowed to stay, would start their businesses here and thus provide employment opportunities locally. Some point to Silicon Valley as the test case. Yahoo, eBay, and Google among others were started by immigrants. Some 40% of patents in the United States are awarded to immigrants [3].

DIVERSITY AND HARMONIZATION

During the 2008 presidential campaign, then candidate Obama had pledged to renegotiate NAFTA and labeled China a currency manipulator. Does this remind us of another presidential candidate who was also elected president? However, once elected, President Obama and apparently, President Trump eased their stance. The Obama Treasury did not label China a currency manipulator, NAFTA was not renegotiated, and the free trade agreement with Panama was allowed to proceed. More importantly, the United States was a signatory of the Trans-Pacific Partnership (TPP), which is quite a change from the campaign rhetoric common among politicians running for office. In contrast, The Trump Administration withdrew from the TPP and has threatened to renegotiate NAFTA but like the Obama Administration, it has yet to designate China a currency manipulator.

Nevertheless, trade skepticism and populist sentiments run high on Capitol Hill and there are other strains of protectionism that show up. Even President Obama, who signed the previously mentioned deals, has chimed in. On the issue of taxation on foreign earnings of US corporations, President Obama argued that deferral encourages US corporations to build facilities and create jobs overseas rather than here at home. In other words, it results in an outsourcing of jobs. In fact, during the presidential campaign, then candidate Obama raised that issue. As president, during his joint session of Congress, he made it clear where he stands. He pledged to "restore a sense of fairness and balance to our tax code by finally ending the tax breaks for corporations that ship our jobs overseas." whether policies aimed at improving the trade balance, saving jobs in particular industries, or whether increasing the domestic diversity of the production base does in fact result in higher domestic employment and "reduce economic dependency" is an empirical issue. There are also some solid theoretical arguments as to why these policies will not deliver the goods.

Before we get into the theory, let's look at some of the evidence that is readily available. One implication of the protectionist view is that as the trade balance worsens, imports would increase relative to exports and that, in turn, would result in a net export of jobs. Hence protectionist logic would call for a negative correlation between the trade deficit and the unemployment rate. A worsening of the trade deficit should be associated with a rising unemployment rate. Yet, as we look at the data reported in Fig. 10.1, we find that the protectionist hypothesis does not hold water. When the trade balance worsens, the unemployment rate declines. Put another way, an improving trade balance is associated with a rising unemployment rate.

Presumably, outsourcing accelerates as we sign free trade agreements and open our economy to international trade. Yet, as we look at the data in Fig. 10.1, we can see a downwards-secular trend for the unemployment rate. The decline in the unemployment rate accelerated after the signing of North America Free Trade Agreement (NAFTA). A casual look at the data suggests that rather than causing more unemployment, the opening of trade reduced the unemployment rate. This is a clear contradiction of the protectionist view of the world.

Our explanation for the result is a simple one. Protectionists focus solely on the narrow, direct effect of policies in a particular industry, rather than the economy as a whole. Outsourcing does in fact reduce domestic employment in the particular industry where outsourcing is occurring. The outsourcing also opens up the opportunity for outsourced workers to move to other industries where they may produce higher valued products. This latter effect counteracts the outsourcing. We showed earlier that the opening of trade leads to a divergence of production and a convergence of consumption. The divergence of production may be inadvertently interpreted as a loss of jobs. Yet as we

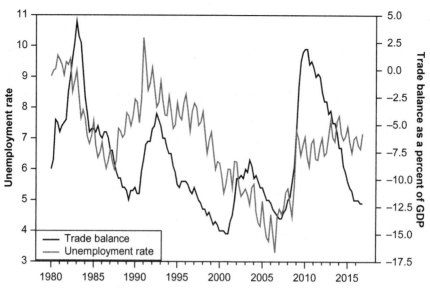

FIGURE 10.1   The trade balance as a percent of GDP versus the unemployment rate.

show, the decline in one industry is more than made up by an increase in the employment and output of other industries. Protectionist policies, by harmonizing the production and consumption of an economy, clearly reduce trade flows and could very well end up reducing the divergence in consumption choices which would, in turn, reduce the overall well-being of the global economy as well as market valuation. This is an important point. The Obama administration's focus was on fairness issues and was determined to address certain apparent disparity issues by enacting policies that attempt to harmonize the distribution of income. Whether these polices succeeded in doing so remains to be seen. Our bet is that these policies will have negative consequences for economic efficiency and market valuation. The question is whether the electorate is willing to accept the implicit trade-off in policies.

References

[1] On a formal basis, the analysis presented here flows directly from three different theorems in international trade, the Factor Price Equalization Theorem, the Stolper-Samuelson Theorem and the Rybczynski Theorem. These three theorems provide information about the effects of opening trade. Free trade tends to equilibrate relative goods and factor prices between countries, benefiting the factor used relatively intensively in the good in which the country has a comparative advantage, at the expense of the other factorSamuelson PA. International trade and the equalization of factors prices. Econ. J. 1948;58:163–84. Stolper WF, Samuelson PA. Protection and real wages. Rev. Econ. Stud. 1941;9:58–73. Rybczynski TM. Factor endowment and relative commodity prices. Economica 1955;22:336–41.

[2] The description in this section is nothing more than a description of the opening of trade under a simple exactly what the Heckscher-Ohlin Model of international trade suggests.Heckscher E. The effect of foreign trade on the distribution of income. Ekon. Tidshrift 1919;21:497–512. Ohlin B. Interregional and international trade. Cambridge Mass: Harvard University Press; 1933. Meade JE. A geometry of international trade. London: Allen & Unwin; 1952. Jones R. Factor proportions and the Heckscher–Ohlin theorem. Rev. Econ. Stud. 1956;24:1–10.

[3] There is an extensive literature on the politics of special interest groups, rent seeking and revenue seeking.Buchanan J, Tullock G. The calculus of consent: logical foundations of a constitutional democracy. Ann Arbor: University of Michigan Press; 1962. Buchanan J. Public finance in democratic process: fiscal institutions and individual choice. UNC Press; 1967. Buchanan J. The demand and supply of public goods. Rand McNally; 1968. Bhagwati JN, Srinivasan TN. Revenue seeking: a generalization of the theory of tariffs. J. Political Econ. 1980;88(6):1069–87. Becker G. Economic theory, Alfred Knopf books in economics; 1971.

11

The State Competitive Environment: Integration and Convergence

Although economists agree that an improvement in overall economic well being is a desirable objective, there is considerable disagreement as to how to best achieve this objective. Again, most people agree that some government services are essential, but two issues arise regarding the government: how large and how best to pay for it.

Supply-siders argue that a broad tax base is desirable, because the greater the base, the lower the rate and, thus, the lower the distortions or disincentives to save, work, and produce. They also argue that the greater the tax differential between activities, the greater the after-tax income gains from switching incomes from one tax treatment to another will be, and the greater the incentives the taxpayers will have to convert from one form of income to another. Similarly, the narrower the tax base, the greater the number of tax schemes. Thus the broader the tax base and the smaller the differences in tax rates among different activities, the smaller the incentives taxpayers will have to alter their tax status.

The one clear conclusion coming out of this analysis is that uniformity reduces avoidance. Is uniformity in taxation a desirable objective? Within the country, should all income be treated the same? How about the taxation of income across borders? The answers to these questions are important issues that have clear implications for national, state, and international economies.

We believe that market forces lead to a convergence of tax rates here defined as a broader base and lower tax rate. However, that is not the only way tax rates may converge. The alternative is for all the governments to collude and unilaterally impose common high tax rates, although they do not call it collusion—that is too ugly a word in the economic lingo. Instead, these governments call it "harmonization." No matter what they call it, the outcome is the same: a collusion to raise tax rates at the expense of the taxpayers. Politicians have self-interest. Their well being depends on the resources they control and the power they exercise.

Examples of the collusion effect are abundant. A few years back, Ireland had a two-tiered tax system, and the high tax rate countries pressured Ireland into adopting a single tax rate under the guise of harmonization. The EMU countries were betting that Ireland would harmonize at the higher rate. To their surprise and with the approval of the financial markets, Ireland chose the lower tax rate. The economic success of Ireland is well documented. Supply-siders attribute in great part the Irish success to the tax policy the country adopted. Not everyone agrees with this view of the world.

Economic Disturbances and Equilibrium in an Integrated Global Economy. http://dx.doi.org/10.1016/B978-0-12-813993-6.00011-8

The opposition to the lower tax rate in effect acknowledges that lower tax rates alter economic behavior and that impacts a country's tax revenues, growth rates, and economic well-being [1]. The argument against the reduction in tax rates and tax competition is that they create a loss of revenues to the competing governments. In effect, they are implying that the tax competition involves a dead weight loss. This is not necessarily the case. Ireland is the clear counter example to the dead weight loss argument. Having said this, we concede that some measures are a waste. Examples would include tax credits and abatements that do not affect the producers and/or workers marginal tax rate. If there is no marginal tax rate reduction, there is no incentive effect and no positive feedback to the economy.

In short, we are not necessarily for tax competition. What we are all about is "tax rate" competition. Low tax rates are good for economic activity. The competition keeps politicians in check. If tax rates get out of hand, the high tax rate economies will lose business to neighboring economies.

This argument hold true in Euroland, as well as in the United States, where the competition among states is quite intense. Yet, the anticompetitive forces are alive and well. Recently, the Supreme Court heard a case regarding the right of states to use tax policy to attract business. In Cuno v. DaimlerChrysler, the taxpayers challenging the law cleverly used the anti-commerce clause in the Constitution to argue in favor of a "harmonized tax rate." Fortunately, the Supreme Court turned them down, and tax competition lived to fight another day.

The empirical evidence presented earlier in Chapter 6, as well as some of the empirical evidence presented here, shows that tax competition has an impact on a state's performance. States with an improving economic environment tend to have an above-average improvement in their personal income, as well as an improvement in the returns of the stocks of small companies located within their jurisdiction.

Policymakers should note that good economic policy defined as restrained spending and an improving tax burden, improving relative to the national economy, creates jobs and income at a rate faster than the national average. Investors should also take note that small-cap stocks located within the states with an improving economic environment tend to outperform the market.

A FRAMEWORK FOR REGIONAL ECONOMIC PERFORMANCE

Arbitrage and factor mobility are two key assumptions used in the development of our global framework. Within the US economy, there is free mobility and free trade among the different states. There is a clear parallel between the United States and the global economy. The latter is made up of the sum of the individual nations, while the US economy is the sum of the individual states. For that reason, the United States and the different states' economies provide us with a nice case study to test and analyze the implications developed by our global integrated economy framework.

There are some significant differences regarding the parallels between the United States and the global economy. The interstate commerce clause prohibits trade restriction among the individual states. As a result, in the United States, there is free mobility of people, goods, and services. The same cannot be said for the rest of the world. Another major difference is that the dollar is the currency that circulates among the states' economy, that is, the different states have a fixed exchange rate and a common central bank. These differences allow us to, for the time being, ignore issues such as exchange rate changes and trade restriction on the overall equilibrium and their impact on the individual economies.

THE DEGREE OF ECONOMIC INTEGRATION

Next, we examine the impact of mobility and arbitrage on the United States and individual states' equilibrium conditions. We then explore how different variables may impact these equilibrium conditions. To begin, we can say that in a frictionless world, purchasing power parity (PPP) will hold. To see this, consider a perfectly mobile factor and/or good located in State A. If rates of return for the factor of production or the price of the good in question are higher in State B, the factor in A will move to arbitrage the difference. Generalizing this mechanism, we conclude that for mobile factors, after-tax returns and the price of goods and services will be equalized across state lines. That is what we mean when we say that factors and goods are priced in the national economy—local returns for a factor will be the world's after-tax return grossed up by local taxes.

Another implication of this insight is that as factor returns equalize, there will be a convergence of income across states. In the absence of trade barriers, the convergence will be such that the income levels for each of the factors will be equalized. Mobility and price arbitrage will be the mechanism that results in a fully integrated economy, wherein the state's growth rates converge to a common average. Changes in factor returns/prices send a common signal to the state's economies, which, all else the same, induce a common economic response across states. This is an important insight for predicting regional economic performance. So in the absence of any PPP violation, to forecast a state's economic performance, all we need to do is forecast the national economy. As part of our economic analysis, we forecast the US real GDP growth on a regular basis; thus we already have the forecast for the impact of PPP on a state's economic performance. Another way of saying the same thing is that when PPP holds, the different economies are fully integrated, and they will move in unisons fully synchronized [2].

Broadly defined transportation costs will prevent the full integration of the different economies. Take the case of an orange. If it costs 5 cents to move the orange from one state to another, then differences in prices of less than 5 cents will not be worth arbitraging. As a result, these differences in the price will persist. The divergences or differences in prices can be interpreted as deviations from full integration. As the trade barriers increase, so does the degree of disintegration, and the correlation between the states' growth rates will decline; in the extreme, a zero correlation implies an autarkic economy with no interaction with the rest of the economy. A measurement of the degree of integration is simple and straightforward. All we have to do is estimate the correlation among the states' economies or each individual state and the overall US economy.

SOME EVIDENCE

Table 11.1 provides us with an estimate of the degree of integration. Our proxy is simple, a state with a fully integrated national economy will exhibit a strong contemporaneous correlation between the state's economy and the US economy; in fact, we can say more than that: in a fully integrated economy, the coefficient for the regression between the two incomes will not be statistically different from 1, that is, the growth rates between the integrated state and the US economy should not be statistically different. In addition, we would expect the constant term not to be statistically significantly different from zero. Looking at the results reported in Table 11.1, we find 28 states fitting the full integration requirement. The list includes the following: Alabama, Arkansas, Colorado, Delaware, Hawaii, Iowa, Kansas, Kentucky, Louisiana, Maine, Massachusetts, Minnesota, Mississippi, Montana, New Hampshire, New Jersey, New Mexico, New York, North Carolina, Oregon, Rhode Island, South Carolina, Tennessee, Utah, Vermont, Virginia, Washington, and Wisconsin.

Two states (Texas and South Dakota) also exhibit a coefficient for the US growth that is not significantly different from 1. However, for these two states, the constant term is positive and statistically significantly different from zero at the usual significance levels suggesting an above-average performance. For this reason, we have classified these two states as integrated and above-average performers. It is interesting to note that the two states are energy-producing states and have no state income tax.

In contrast to the case of the two previous states, the estimated equation for five states—Connecticut, Illinois, Indiana, Michigan, and Ohio—meet the integration criteria of having a US growth rate coefficient that is not significantly different from 1. However, for these states, the estimated constant term is negative and significantly different from zero, hence the classification of integrated and below-average performers. All of these states would fall into the high state tax rate categories during much of the sample in question. However, it is worthwhile noting that since 2012, the tax increase tide appears to have begun to recede in Ohio, Michigan, and Indiana. In 2012, Indiana became a Right to Work State; Michigan did the same in 2013, while Ohio reduced its top personal income tax rate.

Sixteen states failed to meet the full integration classification. For these states, the coefficient for the US growth rate, while positive and significantly different from zero, is also significantly different from 1. Within this group, the estimated equation for four different states produced a constant coefficient that was negative and significantly different from zero. These four states (Nevada, Arizona, Florida, and Georgia) were classified as partially integrated and below-average performers. Nevada and Florida have no state income tax, while Arizona and Georgia are Right to Work states.

The estimated equation for seven states (the District of Columbia, Maryland, Oklahoma, Alaska, Nebraska, North Dakota, and Wyoming) produced a constant coefficient that was positive and significantly different from zero, while the coefficient for the US growth rate was significantly different from zero and also from 1. These states were classified as partially integrated above-average performers. With the exception of District of Columbia and Maryland, the remaining states are either Right to Work states—Nebraska, North Dakota, Oklahoma, and Wyoming—and/or have no state income tax—Alaska and Wyoming.

The remaining six states (California, Idaho, Missouri, West Virginia, and Pennsylvania) posted a constant coefficient that was not statistically different from zero and a US growth rate coefficient that was positive and less than 1. These six states were simply classified as partially integrated to the US economy. Yet, only California and Idaho fall into the high state income tax classification.

The estimated R-squared for the individual states' regression result show that the US growth rate explains a significant portion of the variation in the individual states' growth rates. However, the fact that the explanatory power of the equations is not 100% suggests that there is room for other variables, such as the broadly defined transportation costs, to contribute to the explanation. Depending on the impact of these variables on the states' performance, they could contribute to an above-average

TABLE 11.1   The States' Economies Degree of Integration

Classification	State	R^2	P-value	Coefficients		T-stat	
				Constant	US	Constant	US
INTEGRATED							
	Alabama	0.72	0.31	−0.28	0.95	−0.67	6.14
	Arkansas	0.53	0.17	0.30	0.81	0.57	4.13
	Colorado	0.57	0.03	0.48	1.10	0.73	4.44
	Delaware	0.27	0.26	−0.39	0.97	−0.35	2.33
	Hawaii	**0.18**	**0.01**	**0.37**	**0.61**	**0.42**	**1.84**
	Iowa	0.34	0.45	0.40	0.80	0.52	2.76
	Kansas	0.48	0.62	0.09	0.81	0.16	3.70
	Kentucky	**0.33**	**0.05**	**−0.25**	**0.71**	**−0.35**	**2.70**
	Louisiana	0.01	0.10	0.77	0.16	0.68	0.37
	Maine	**0.58**	**0.08**	**−0.37**	**0.78**	**−0.81**	**4.58**
	Massachusetts	0.65	0.28	0.10	1.01	0.20	5.31
	Minnesota	0.68	0.33	−0.21	1.11	−0.40	5.65
	Mississippi	0.41	0.49	−0.34	0.69	−0.60	3.20
	Montana	0.48	0.41	0.77	0.73	1.47	3.72
	New Hampshire	0.63	0.11	0.12	0.95	0.25	5.07
	New Jersey	0.70	0.41	−0.57	0.88	−1.43	5.96
	New Mexico	0.22	0.28	0.47	0.51	0.71	2.06
	New York	0.25	0.50	0.85	0.55	1.27	2.21
	North Carolina	0.61	0.10	0.46	0.85	0.97	4.80
	Oregon	0.19	0.31	1.85	0.80	1.63	1.89
	Rhode Island	0.50	0.11	−0.23	0.88	−0.39	3.91
	South Carolina	0.74	0.30	−0.22	0.91	−0.59	6.57
	Tennessee	0.56	0.24	−0.02	0.89	−0.04	4.34
	Utah	0.56	0.11	0.88	1.09	1.32	4.33
	Vermont	**0.50**	**0.03**	**0.22**	**0.84**	**0.38**	**3.87**
	Virginia	0.50	0.20	0.65	0.75	1.25	3.86
	Washington	0.46	0.27	0.32	1.00	0.43	3.58
	Wisconsin	0.84	0.05	−0.12	0.85	−0.47	8.79
INTEGRATED ABOVE-AVERAGE PERFORMER							
	South Dakota	0.04	0.70	2.60	0.32	2.41	0.80
	Texas	0.37	0.33	1.97	0.72	3.01	2.96
INTEGRATED BELOW-AVERAGE PERFORMER							
	Connecticut	0.67	0.29	−1.31	1.32	−2.05	5.52
	Illinois	0.89	0.34	−0.68	0.91	−3.07	11.01

TABLE 11.1   The States' Economies Degree of Integration (cont.)

Classification	State	R^2	P-value	Coefficients		T-stat	
				Constant	US	Constant	US
	Indiana	**0.63**	**0.01**	**−1.23**	**1.35**	**−1.72**	**5.06**
	Michigan	**0.61**	**0.02**	**−2.72**	**1.56**	**−3.20**	**4.88**
	Ohio	**0.70**	**0.02**	**−1.06**	**1.02**	**−2.26**	**5.86**
PARTIAL INTEGRATION BELOW-AVERAGE PERFORMER							
	Nevada	0.78	0.02	−2.61	2.31	−3.07	7.25
	Arizona	0.87	0.15	−1.73	2.19	−3.02	10.20
	Florida	**0.79**	**0.02**	**−1.41**	**1.70**	**−2.31**	**7.44**
	Georgia	0.85	0.07	−0.79	1.29	−2.07	9.08
PARTIAL INTEGRATION							
	California	0.90	0.18	−0.49	1.54	−1.38	11.50
	Idaho	0.70	0.19	−0.92	1.83	−1.10	5.85
	Missouri	0.62	0.29	−0.16	0.58	−0.52	4.93
	West Virginia	0.06	0.32	0.65	0.27	0.88	0.99
	Pennsylvania	0.82	0.69	0.24	0.59	1.25	8.31
PARTIAL INTEGRATION ABOVE-AVERAGE PERFORMER							
	District of Columbia	0.10	0.35	1.38	0.30	2.24	1.29
	Maryland	**0.48**	**0.02**	**1.09**	**0.60**	**2.50**	**3.71**
	Oklahoma	0.32	0.11	1.29	0.52	2.51	2.68
	Alaska	0.21	0.17	3.18	−0.88	2.67	−1.98
	Nebraska	0.12	0.10	1.76	0.29	3.34	1.46
	North Dakota	0.02	0.25	5.60	−0.32	3.41	−0.51
	Wyoming	**0.01**	**0.02**	**2.53**	**0.22**	**1.71**	**0.39**

The numbers in bold reflect a P-value below the 10% threshold suggesting an absence of serial correlation for the equation residuals.

or below-average performance, that is, these other variables could add or subtract to the state growth rate over and above the average or US growth rate.

For the states in the bottom half of the table, states from whom the magnitude of the US growth rate coefficient was estimated to be positive and less than one, the magnitude of the coefficient suggests that the degree of integration declines as the magnitude the coefficient declines. We attribute the lack of integration to either natural or manmade barriers to trade or mobility, what we broadly define as "transportation costs."

For purposes of illustration, let us consider alternative transportation costs, with the simplest one being a constant price per unit. Examples of this may be an airline ticket, the UPS or USPS fixed charge per boxes of a certain size, etc. In this example, differences in prices less than the transportation costs will not be arbitraged away. Only when the price differences exceed the transportation costs, the difference in excess of the transportation

costs will be arbitraged away, and the prices will rise at the same rate in the two localities. We contend that only when the transportation costs exceed the price differences between localities, the correlation between the individual state and the overall US economy will weaken, and the full effect of the state and local fiscal policies be felt only on the local economy.

STATES' FISCAL POLICIES COULD POTENTIALLY IMPACT THE DEGREE OF INTEGRATION

The calculus for immobile factors of production is a little different. By definition, the factor cannot move across state boundaries; therefore that factor cannot escape local taxes. The point here is that for the immobile factor, the after-tax return or valuation need not be the same across states. Thus if mobility is not perfect across countries or factors of production, the level and type of government expenditure and the manner in which revenues are raised across states produce systematic deviations from PPP. The burden of taxation will fall disproportionately among the least mobile factors across states, and this will result in systematic differences in the pattern of returns across states.

Differences in fiscal policies across states go a long way in explaining the dispersion among the states' economic performances, as well as the returns of the immobile factors located within the state boundaries. The latter is the essence of our investment strategy that chooses small-cap stocks located in the states with an improving economic environment. The conclusion of this discussion is that only the differences in state and local fiscal policies relative to the US average will have an impact on the state performance relative to the US average, as long as transportation costs are large enough to isolate the local economy from the national economy, that is, as long as transportation costs are large enough to prevent the complete arbitrage of these differences in prices across localities.

We contend that state and federal fiscal and regulatory policies are the basis for much of what we consider to be manmade "transportation costs." We also believe that as the transportation costs rise, the degree of integration declines, giving rise to differences in growth rates relative to the US average. So far, what we lack is a forecast for the impact of the dispersion in state and local fiscal policy actions on the states' relative performance.

THE MEASUREMENT OF THE DIFFERENCES IN POLICIES ACROSS THE STATES

The measurement of the states' policy changes relative to the national average has interested economists for some time. That interest has generated alternative ways to measure the differences across state lines. The most common way to measure the differences is to calculate the state and local expenditures or taxes as a percent of the State Gross Product and compare it to the national average.

The expenditures as a percent of the gross product measure the amount of resources under the control of the authorities. The impact of these expenditures on the local economy will depend in part on the value of the government services or the nature of the expenditures. In what follows, we assume a balanced budget, a requirement for many of the states. If the bulk of the expenditures is in the form of transfer payments, we contend that there will be little or no aggregate effect. One group's gain, that is, the transfer recipient, is

another group's loss, that is, the taxpayers. When the two groups are combined together, there is no net gain or loss. If their marginal propensity to spend is approximately the same, there will be no net aggregate demand effect.

Conversely, if the resources are spent in public services, whether there is a net increase in aggregate demand or not depends on whether the value of the services exceeds the taxes collected. Therefore the impact of an increase in public expenditures relative to the national average on the states' relative performance will be an empirical issue that will depend critically on the value of the services provided relative to the cost of services / taxes collected.

The states' relative average and marginal tax burdens. If distorting tax rates are used to collect the needed resources for the public eservices, the distorting tax rates reduce incentives to work, save, and invest. The magnitude of the disincentive depends on the nature of the distortion created by the tax collection mechanism. Here, we need a word of caution. Some people tend to use the average tax burden as a proxy for the marginal tax rate. However, that is quite possibly a mistake for there is not necessarily a one-to-one relationship between the average and marginal tax rate. There are multiple tax structures with different marginal tax rates capable of producing the same average tax rate. Therefore one cannot make clear inferences about the marginal tax rates simply by calculating the average tax rate or tax burden.

THE STATES' RELATIVE MARGINAL TAX RATES

The previous paragraphs argue that one cannot make differences about competitiveness by looking at the states' relative tax burdens. In order to do so, a measure of the states' marginal tax rates relative to the national averages is what is needed. Elsewhere, we have dealt with this issue in great detail. We have mentioned numerous times that we are quite grateful to The National Conference of State Legislatures (NCSL), who publishes the revenue impact of state and local actions enacted each fiscal year. These estimates, with little manipulation, are easily converted into proxies describing changes in the dispersion of state and local fiscal policies across states [3].

The ranking is then used by some as a ranking of states' expected economic performance. Although this is a proper first step, the ranking of the states' changes in fiscal policy is not enough. First, there is no reason to expect that the states will have the same response coefficient. The history of previous tax actions may affect the state's economic responses. Similarly, it is possible that the state's current pace of economic activity may be in part affected by the recent past. In other words, the state's momentum may matter.

We have developed a methodology that attempts to correct some of these deficiencies. We estimate historical relationships between state's economic performance in terms of US economic performance and the dispersion of fiscal policy changes across states. The estimates of the state's actions for the coming fiscal year generated by NCSL and the equations estimated using the historical relationships are then used to calculate each state's forecast, as well as the likelihood that the state will grow faster than the United States.

INVESTMENT STRATEGY

The states' tax and regulatory policies have the potential to impact a state's relative and absolute economic performance, be it in terms of output produced in the states and/or in terms of the valuation of assets located within the states. While policymakers and job seekers are much more focused on the former, investors may be more interested in the latter.

The fact that small companies have production and sales concentrated in a state suggests that the fiscal policy changes in that state in relation to the rest of the region are a major determinant of their relative performance. The larger companies are either global or national companies. These companies are so large and are located in so many places that the impact of one state's policy is relatively unimportant. This is a powerful insight for it suggests that for these companies, state issues are less significant at the margin—they are impacted by global and/or national shifts. Thus the state factor could be useful in enhancing a small/micro-cap portfolio strategy. Size is simply a useful screen in the identification of the companies most likely to be impacted by the state factor.

Data on the specific location and production facilities is readily available. One can then use a short cut to identify the location of individual companies: the headquarters' location. While this is at best a first-order approximation, it provides a clue as to the usefulness of the state selector as a portfolio strategy. Using companies in the S&P 600, one can then construct cap-weighted state portfolios based on the location of individual companies. Not all states have stocks in the index. The stocks remaining are classified into two distinct groups. The group likely to outperform includes the stocks located in the states at the top of the rankings of the states. The group likely to underperform includes the stocks located in the states in the bottom of the rankings. The historical performance of the two portfolios was pretty much as expected [4].

LIMITATIONS OF THE STATE COMPETITIVE ENVIRONMENT AS AN INVESTMENT STRATEGY

The results reported are robust enough to suggest that paying attention to location and focusing on state and local policies may enhance the performance of a small-cap strategy. Through careful analysis, one can identify the proper regions or states that will outperform.

With few exceptions, state economies are not very well diversified, and a portfolio of the small caps in a state will produce a concentrated portfolio in some sectors of the economy. The concentration relates to the state's comparative advantage. Adverse shocks to these industries will have a devastating impact on a state even if that state tax policy or competitive environment is improving. In the past, we have talked about the California blackouts that occurred a few years ago, which negatively impacted the state without really harming neighboring states. Other effects that may have a broad-based impact on a state economy are natural disasters. Clearly, these unanticipated shocks may render our forecast obsolete.

COMPETITIVENESS, INTEGRATION, AND CONVERGENCE

In the absence of any friction, arbitrage and the mobility of goods and services will insure the equalization of factor returns across state lines. As long as the factors are mobile across state borders, the state will have no power to tax them at a rate higher than the lowest tax state. If it does, the factor will emigrate in search of higher after-tax returns. Those with higher tax rates will experience an outflow to those with attractive tax structures. The mobile factors are priced in the global economy. Overall, equilibrium will be determined by the intersection of the global demand and supply curves. That is what we mean when we say that in an integrated economy the prices are determined in the national economy. In the case of the United States, it is the individual states. In the global economy, it is the individual nations.

Under these conditions, the relative prices will be the same across state lines. Therefore the changes in relative prices will send the same signal across the different sates' economies. The output response will be qualitatively the same, and the economic fluctuations and growth rates will be synchronized across the economy. This does not mean that states have no impact on the mobile factor. Just keep in mind that the global demand is the sum of the individual states' aggregate demand and supply conditions. Hence, global fluctuations will be a weighted average of the fluctuations in the individual states. Thus the impact of a state in the overly equilibrium is determined by its size and the magnitude of the demand or supply changes in the state economy.

Factor mobility limits the power of taxation of the individual states. It induces tax competition across states, or in case where the governments are able to collude, it results in a "harmonization of tax rates," a euphemism for higher tax rates in a region.

The pricing of the immobile factor is a totally different story. The pricing of a factor that is not able to cross state boundaries will be limited to local demand and supply condition. In addition, the state and local government, through its fiscal policy, may have the power and/or tools to affect the local demand and supply conditions and thus the factor returns. This, in turn, suggests that the power of the state and local government to affect its relative economic performance in relation to its neighbors' rests on its ability to affect the local market conditions for the immobile factors located within the state. The immobile factor cannot leave the state to arbitrage differences in rates of returns in toner localities. Hence, it is the differences in the immobile factor returns that will generate the differences in real GDP growth rates across state lines.

The discussion presented here suggests two types of equilibrium conditions. One is the overall equilibrium for the mobile factors. While determined by the sum of the demand and supply in each of the individual localities, the mobility insures that the price is the same in each and every locality, and thus has the same qualitative output response. The disturbances to the mobile factor equilibrium conditions induce a common effect across the different economies. This is truly a case analogous to the rising tide lifting all boats and an ebb tide lowering them. Hence, the collective actions of the individual economies matter a great deal as far as the mobile factor goes. In contrast, the local effects are specifically related to the immobile factors of production. Increases in local demand and supply conditions will determine the pricing of the immobile factor and thus the income of the immobile factor in each area. Those areas for which the

demand exceeds the supply, the price and income will rise, and these economies will outperform their counterpart that did not experience an increase in demand for the immobile factor.

When all is said and done, we know that mobility insures the convergence of the income and factor return of the mobile factor. The astute investor needs to keep track of the sum of the individual states' actions for they make up the global demand and supply conditions that determine the equilibriums price of the mobile factor. So it behooves the investor to correctly identify the global trend if they are to anticipate the global rates of return and global output.

When it comes to the individual economies, in addition to recognizing the global trends, one must be aware of the effect of local demand and supply conditions on factors that cannot move across state lines, for it is the returns to these factors that determine the differential rates of returns across the different states' economies. We contend that focusing on the differences in fiscal policies is a good start. Some of the evidence presented here and referenced support this contention.

References

[1] See Canto and Joines (1983) where they develop a simple general equilibrium model that illustrates the relationship between the constellation of tax rates, output and economic well-being. Canto V, Joines D. Taxation, revenue, and welfare. Econ Inquiry 1983;21(3):431–8.

[2] A formal derivation of the model can be found in Canto and Webb (1987).Canto V, Webb R. The effect of state fiscal policy on state relative economic performance. South Econ J 1987;54(1):186–202.

[3] Earlier we mentioned that our previous research has used the state's tax actions as a proxy for the estimates of the changing tax burden across the states. Canto, V., 2003. The State Selector. La Jolla Economics. Canto, V., Canata, Al., 2003. The State Selector. La Jolla Economics. Canto, V., 2007. The 2007 State Selector. La Jolla Economics. Canto, V., 2008. The 2008 State Selector. La Jolla Economics.

[4] Canto V, Laffer A. A not-so-odd couple: small-cap stocks and the state competitive environment. Financ Anal J 1989;45(2):75–8.

CHAPTER

12

The Degree of Global Integration and National Economies' Policy Options and Limitations

There is a great deal of uncertainty regarding the outlook for the financial markets, the global economy, and individual economies around the world. One issue of concern among the emerging markets is the potential impact of the debt burden in some of the developing nations. Then there is the turmoil in the Middle East and the related inflow of migrants into Euroland, as well as President Trump's views about immigration, both legal and illegal. In addition, there are the traditional trade-related issues regarding the attractiveness and desirability of trade agreements, whether certain countries are currency manipulators who are using the exchange rate policies to gain an unfair advantage over its trading partners, and so forth. This is quite a change, for people are now questioning the benefits of globalization and some are even talking about reversing the globalization trend.

Collectively, the globalization and deglobalization events have an impact on the global economy as well as the national economies. More often than not, the impact of changes to the global equilibrium is not uniform across the board. There are clear winners and losers. And in some special cases, everyone wins, while in others, everyone loses. The Smoot–Hawley Tariffs which either ushered, or where major contributors to the Great Depression is commonly used as the poster child for those who want to lustrate the effects of a policy that makes everyone worst off.

Some, nevertheless, in spite of these possible events and their effects, point to an interdependent global economy where shocks in one economy may spillover and impact another economy or the rest of the world. There is also the issue as to whether an economy can insulate itself from these adverse shocks and how to go about doing it. That quest has led to a resurgence in nationalist and nativist policies across the world economies.

In recent years, the frequent example used to show concerns about economic interdependency has been the preoccupation in the financial press regarding the slowdown in China's rate of economic expansion. The Chinese authorities put their best possible interpretation regarding the slowdown by arguing that we were witnessing the transition from industry toward services. However, the overcapacity and high-debt burden in

Economic Disturbances and Equilibrium in an Integrated Global Economy. http://dx.doi.org/10.1016/B978-0-12-813993-6.00012-X

101

some sectors suggested that the shift was not going to be an easy one. A related question to the travails of the Chinese economy is the potential effect of the Chinese slowdown on the global economy. All of this suggests that there are significant potential spillover effects from one economy to another.

Another way to say the same thing is that domestic policy action may leak into other economies which then becomes a question of how to keep track of these policy leakages to determine the impact on the rest of the world, as well as how the rest of the world leakages impact our economy. One issue that brings home the point is the question as to whether China's economic instability would lead to a slowdown or recession in the United States. We live in an interdependent global economy and thus we are not alone, and the actions of other countries could have a significant impact on individual local economies.

It is widely accepted in the financial press that the commodity supercycle early in the millennium was largely due to China's economic expansion. We will focus on China and the commodity supercycle as a way to illustrate the integrated global economy approach. In the process, we develop some insights regarding the effectiveness and limitation of certain policy actions.

THE INTEGRATED ECONOMY

Arbitrage and mobility determine the global market-clearing price, as well as the prevailing price in the individual economies. In the absence of any transportation costs, steel moves from low steel price countries to high steel price countries. In doing so, the exporter/importer arbitrages the differences in prices and pockets the profit. The arbitrage process continues until the differences in net prices of the transportation costs, whether natural or man-made costs such as tariffs and taxes, are eliminated. That is, differences in prices across localities in excess of the broadly defined "transportation costs" will be arbitraged away. In contrast, differences in prices smaller than the "transportation costs" will not be profitable and thus will not be worth arbitraging. In equilibrium, the price differences across localities will be equal to or less than the "transportation costs."

The global equilibrium prices are determined by the intersection of the global demand and supply curves. In turn, the global demand and supply curves are nothing more than the sum of the individual countries' demand for and supply curves of the different commodities. These conditions define an integrated global market for the economy in question. In the special case where the transportation costs are negligible, the equilibrium price for the commodity will be the same everywhere in the world.

A question that immediately comes to mind is what effect does an individual producer or an individual country has on the price of the global commodity in question. The answer is simple; it depends on two variables:

- One is the share of the world demand for and supply of the commodity in question. The second Variables is the country's demand for and supply elasticity of the commodity. The country share of the world determines the impact the country has on the global demand and supply curves. For example, if the country is 20% of the global economy, a 10% increase in the demand for the commodity will result in a 2% increase in the global demand for the commodity. If the global economy was in equilibrium, then the country increase in demand results in a 2% global excess demand for the commodity in question. On the other hand, if an economy is 80% of the world, then the 10% increase in aggregate demand produces an 8% worldwide excess demand for the commodity.
- But the country's share of the world is not enough to determine the change in global prices, as well as the demand and supply elasticities matter. The greater the magnitude of the elasticity effects, the greater the output response per unit of price increase and thus the smaller the price increase needed to clear the market.

THE PRICE AND OUTPUT ADJUSTMENT TO A NEW EQUILIBRIUM

An increase in one country's aggregate demand in excess of the aggregate supply results in a net increase in the global demand along the lines described in the previous section. The smaller the economy, the smaller the impact on the world price of the commodity in question. In the extreme, there will be no impact and the increase in excess demand will be satisfied through the net importation of the goods and services in question. Another way to view this equilibrating process is that there will be leakages to the policy-induced increases in net aggregate demand. The smaller the economy, the lower will be the impact of the domestic policy on the local economy level of economic activity. Put another way, in a truly open economy with little or no "transportation costs," the domestic policies are not very effective in stimulating the local economy. In such an integrated economy, the only mechanism available to the local authorities through which the local policy affect output is through its effect on the overall elasticity of demand for and supply of goods and services. But this only increases the output response to change in global prices, and as we already established, the prices are not under the control of the small economies.

The adjustment process for the larger economy is a bit different, in addition to the net importation of goods, there is also a price adjustment. We know that the world is a closed economy and thus net imports for the world as a whole are always zero. Therefore as the country grows in size and it approaches the world, the net imports will decline and prices will become the dominant market-clearing equilibrating process for the country in question.

The previous discussion leads to a very important conclusion regarding the market-clearing process: the division between price and quantity adjustment is inversely related to a country's size. The larger the country, the larger the impact on global prices.

THE DEMAND AND SUPPLY RESPONSE

A global increase in the demand for a commodity results in a global excess demand and that requires an increase in the global price of the commodity in question to restore global equilibrium and clear the global market excess demand.

The higher price generates two distinct ways of satisfying the global excess demand. On the demand side, the higher price induces a movement along the demand curve and the quantity demand declines. Some consumers are squeezed or crowded out of the global consumption. On the supply side, the higher price produces a movement along the supply curve. The quantity supplied unambiguously increases. If excess returns are earned by the suppliers, new entrants will come into the market and global supply or global capacity will unambiguously increase.

If adjustment is costly and the excess demand persists, as the supply increases over time, investments lead to an increase in the global production capacity. As the supply increases, the excess returns are reduced and eventually the commodity prices and the rates of returns generated in the production of these commodities approach their long-run equilibrium dissipating the initial global shortage as well as the excess return generated by the global shortage. This analysis suggests that the initial shock results in an overshooting of the long-run commodity price and that the cycle will "mean revert." How large the deviation is from the long-run equilibrium price and how long before restoring the long-run equilibrium depend on the adjustments costs or more formally on the differences between the short-run and long-run elasticities.

The equilibrium process also works in reverse. As the economy slows down, so does the global demand. The price of the commodities in question declines. Again, the market-clearing process produces a movement along the demand that increases the demand for the commodity in question. On the supply side, the effect may be impacted by the ability to adjust the production of the commodity in question. It may be very difficult for certain types of production facilities to adjust their production or output level.

For those businesses that cannot easily adjust their production levels, the major decision is whether to continue producing or shutting down altogether. If the revenue generated by keeping the operations going is enough to cover the variable costs, the businesses will not shut down, and production will continue even thought their profits and stock prices will take a big hit. This means that the equilibrium will have to be accomplished on the demand side; the price has to fall low enough to induce the consumers to purchase the quantities produced. If that is the case, in the short run, the price will overshoot the long-run equilibrium and it will not be until the demand rises secularly or the plants are taken out of production because of deterioration or other reasons. As the supply shifts inward and production declines, the prices firm up and eventually return to their long-run equilibrium.

TRANSPORTATION COSTS AND THE DEGREE OF INTEGRATION

Transportation costs, whether natural or man-made, introduce a band within which it is not worthwhile or profitable to arbitrage the differences in prices across localities. If it costs $100 to ship a ton of steel from one country to another, it does not matter to the buyers and sellers whether the $100 is due to true transportation costs or a man-made transportation costs such as a $100 tax on the importation or export of a ton of steel. If the difference in prices between the two localities is $150 and the transportation costs are $100, there is $50 of arbitrage profits. The point is that only differences in excess of $100 will be arbitraged away. In contrast, differences in prices less than $100 between the two localities will not be worth arbitraging away.

The "transportation costs" as we have defined are also very important for the small economies. Recall that we argued that in an integrated economy, the global price is determined by the sum of the individual countries' demand for and supply of goods and services. In the absence of transportation costs, the price will be the same in each and every locality. We also showed that a country's impact on the global rice would be inversely related to its size. Hence the small economies will have little or no impact on the global price. Given the demand and supply elasticities, it follows that any induced increase in aggregate demand will have no impact on the global prices. As the price does not change as a result of the increase in the small country's excess demand, production will not change in a meaningful way in any of the localities and there will be no price response. This means that the local excess demand will be satisfied through a net importation of the commodity in question. Therefore when all is said and done, the policy-induced excess demand results in a deterioration of the trade balance, no change in domestic production, and no effect on global prices or rates of return. The local policies will have little or no effect on the integrated, small open economy. The impact of the local policies will be felt on the small, open economy's international accounts.

The previous paragraph shows how zero transportation costs are associated with a fully integrated economy. This suggests that as the transportation costs increase, the nonarbitrageable, that is, nonprofitable, differences in prices widen. As the band widens, the degree of integration declines, and now the local government will have some wiggle room to affect the local economy's production and equilibrium prices. As long as any policy-induced changes in aggregate demand do not induce differences in prices over the transportation costs band, these differences will not be arbitraged away. They will have no impact on the rest of the world (recall that we have assumed a small economy). But the policy changes will have an impact on the local prices and that, in turn, will affect the local equilibrium conditions. The local demand and supply will respond to the local price change in proportion to the price change and the elasticities of demand and supply for the goods and services in the local economy. The greater the trade barriers, that is, the transportation costs, the greater the range of disconnection from the global economy and the greater the impact or effect of local policy changes on the local economy. This is one clear reason why politicians may want to widen their countries "transportation costs bands." They want to increase their ability to affect the local economy, even if it is at the expense of the "gains of trade."

Self-interest is a very powerful predictor of behavior. The wider the transportation costs, the greater the ability of local politicians to influence and control the local economy and the smaller the influence of external effects. Viewed this way, it is easy to see why politicians in some countries will choose to go down the protectionist path. But they will not be alone on that quest. In the example as discussed earlier, the local equilibrium price will be $100 higher than in the global economy. This means higher profits and higher employment for those in the local, protected domestic sectors. They will join and, in many cases, pressure the politicians to adopt the protectionist policies. However, the country as a whole loses if the higher marginal costs in the incremental production of the protected goods are higher. Other losers are the consumers who end up paying $100 more per unit of the product.

A final point is related to the politics of special interest groups. In this example, it is quite likely that the benefits of the protectionism will be concentrated in some sector or industry while the benefits of the free trade will be diffuse and spread across the consumers. This means that each consumer has a small gain/loss in relation to the protected sectors. The costs associated with assembling a coalition of the pro-free trade groups are likely to be higher than those of the protectionist groups. If that is the case, the odds are that the protectionists may have a good chance to prevail. The case for free trade requires that politicians and voters mobilize and join forces in favor of reducing the broadly defined transportation costs to maximize gains of trade both in production and consumption.

CHINA AND THE COMMODITY SUPERCYCLE IN THE CONTEXT OF AN INTEGRATED GLOBAL ECONOMY

The integrated economy view of the world goes a long way to explain the commodity supercycle early in the millennium. As the Chinese economy grew rapidly, so did its demand for raw materials used in infrastructure construction. If the global economy was in equilibrium prior to the Chinese expansion, one can then argue that the Chinese expansion added to the global demand for raw materials. All else the same, this created an excess demand for the raw materials which, in turn, resulted in an increase in the global price of the commodities.

It is our position that China played a major role in the millennium's commodity supercycle. China's ascent and strong economic growth fueled a global demand for commodities that resulted in an increase in commodity prices relative to other goods and services. The rising prices led to an expansion of the overall supplies of these commodities. However, to the extent that the Chinese and the remaining of the world's demand for the commodities exceeded the supplies, the commodity prices continued to rise or remained strong. The commodities' suppliers enjoyed a major bonanza. Eventually the party came to an end and it appears to have coincided with China's economic slowdown.

If this interpretation of the events is correct, the slowdown resulted in a decline in the global demand for the basic commodities, resulting in a weakening of the commodity prices. The increased capacity/supply added during the boom years and China's slowdown resulted in a commodities global glut. Some argue that the excess capacity would result in weak prices for several years unless the world economic growth, that is, the global demand, accelerates and absorbs the excess supply.

There are several assumptions embodied in this rendition of the events:

- The first one is that we live in an integrated world economy and the price of these commodities is determined in the global economy.
- One country can have an outsized influence in the global economic equilibrium for a particular commodity, depending on its size in relation to the commodity in question or to the global economy depending on its share of world output.
- We are in an interdependent global economy and disturbances in one region will impact global prices. Through its effect on the world prices, these disturbances will also impact the other regions of the world.

THE COMMODITY SUPERCYCLE

The fully integrated economy approach, where commodity prices are determined in the global economy, provides a straightforward and cogent explanation of the commodity supercycle in which China plays a major if not the key dominant role.

The interpretation is as follows: when China began to open up and engage in a major economic transformation, the increases in productivity and overall economic gains were easy, considered as the low-hanging fruit. China simply appropriated much of the existing technology in legal and other ways. The new technology allowed to absorb or employ some of the abundant labor force. The new technology increased the productivity of the existing labor force, and with an expanding economic pie, there were goodies for everyone. Workers income rose, profits increased, and there was still plenty left over for the party politicians and even for waste and corruption.

During this phase of the development, China's outstanding growth rate was the envy of the world and the command performance was attributed to the Chinese economic model. As China continued its torrid expansion, the economy began to need increased resources and even more technology. In effect, the success forced the authorities to increase the economic openness of the economy. Even on the monetary front, the Chinese made quite a move when they adopted a fixed exchange rate system. At the time, we argued that such a move would increase the economic transparency and confidence in the economy. As long as the renminbi remained tied to the US dollar, investors (whether Chinese or foreigners) knew what a renminbi or yuan would buy in the future. As expected, in the aftermath of the adoption of the fixed exchange rate, the Chinese inflation rate collapsed and approached the US inflation rate. The economic expansion and increased transparency was extended to many of the sectors of the economy. In turn,

that generated a derived demand for the raw materials used in the production of the goods and services, which initially produced an excess global demand for the items in question.

A new equilibrium could be restored in one of the following ways: a price increase, an increase in global output, or a combination of the two. Assuming a normally sloped demand and supply function for the raw materials, the new equilibrium would result in an increase in the price and production of the raw materials. But we can say more than that. Over the short run, the supply curves are less elastic than the long-run supply curves. The reason simply being that if adjustment is costly, it will take time to expand the supply of raw materials. It takes time to build steel mills, it also takes time to prepare more land to produce soy beans, etc. With this in mind, it is easy to see how the derived demand for raw material would lead to a surge in the price of the raw material. As the high growth rate in China persisted, so did the increased demand for the raw materials. Times were good for the suppliers of the raw materials. Production, employment, and profits increased significantly in the countries exporting the raw materials. The emerging markets fared quite well.

As long as the price and global demand expectations remained high for an extended period of time, capacity began to expand to satisfy the increased demand. Also as long as the increased capacity did not keep up with the increased demand, the upward price pressure would remain and so would the commodity supercycle. Once the capacity caught up with supply, the upward price pressure will dissipate and so would the commodities' prices.

Now if the capacity expands beyond the increased supply or the demand for raw material slows, there will be an incipient excess supply of raw material. The excess supply produces downward pressures which, all else the same, produces a movement along the demand curve and the quantity demanded rises as a result of the lower prices, partially eliminating some of the excess demand. On the supply side, the lower price reduces the profitability and that reduces incentives to produce. If the speed of adjustment is costly, it follows that the magnitude of the long-run supply elasticity will be larger than the short-run supply elasticity. The price mechanism will shoulder the burden of clearing the markets. In the short run, the prices will decline the most. Over time as supply is reduced, the commodity prices will climb back to its long-run equilibrium.

Governments, in this case the Chinese government, may also attempt to prevent the end to the commodity supercycle by attempting to increase the demand for the commodities. The standard prescription for stimulating aggregate demand being an economic stimulus package. It is safe to say that China unsuccessfully tried this policy option as the economy continued to decelerate even after the stimulus packages were adopted and implemented.

POLICY DIFFERENCES AND THE DEGREE OF INTEGRATION IN AN ECONOMY OUTPUT LEVEL

The degree of integration leads to two extreme country descriptions. One we call the fully integrated economy, where there are no broadly defined transportation costs. Second, at the other end of the spectrum, we have the autarkic economy with no international trade whatsoever. These two extreme cases lead to vastly scenarios regarding the effect of a country's economic policy. Let's consider each of the two types of economies separately.

The autarkic economy is an economy where transportation costs are so high that no matter what the price differences are between locations, these differences in prices will not and cannot be arbitraged away. The conclusion here is obvious: this economy is a closed economy that will not trade with the rest of the world. As there is no economic contact with the rest of the world, it follows that changing conditions in the rest of the world will have no impact on the local economy. The only policy changes that impact the domestic equilibriums conditions are domestic policy changes. Hence it is under the autarkic conditions that the local policy changes have the largest impact on the local economy, while the foreign policy shocks have the least impact whatsoever.

While some may feel that maximizing the impact of local policies maybe a good thing, this is not without costs. Isolation means that the economy does not enjoy the gains of trade in both production and consumption. But then again, if there is no information about the opportunity costs, that is, the gains of trade, then the local residents do not know what they are missing. Local governments face a tradeoff between the impacts of local policies and the gains of trade, increased availability of goods, and services of better quality and at lower costs.

One obvious question is why would people accept this choice? The answer is that they will not. It is no wonder that these autarkic societies tend to be ones where an autocratic government controls the information flows and keeps is local residents isolated from the rest of the world. Think of North Korea, Cuba, Iran, etc. An opening of trade and information flows may have the people demanding more openings economically and politically. However, those in control may have a lot to lose and thus may want to preserve the status quo and may even resort to force to preserve the status quo. The question is whether the people in power can manage a transition to an open economy while preserving power. That remains to be seen and is one choice that China faces.

An integrated economy facing no transportation costs represents the other end of the spectrum. The global integration is one insight that is not fully appreciated by many analysts. One way to appreciate what integration does for the global and individual economies is through the following exercise. If the countries in the world got together and coordinated their economic policies such that each and every country adopted a policy that increased the aggregate demands in their economy by the same amount across the world, what would happen to world output? Assuming that the countries have similar demand and supply elasticities, the average response to a price change will be similar across each of the economies.

In this example, the aggregate demand in each country increases by the same amount, which we will call the average amount. Since there are no deviations from the average, there is nothing more to explore. A more interesting question is what happens when the countries do not coordinate their policies? The answer depends on the degree of integration.

Arbitrage and the perfect mobility of goods and services and as well as factors of production insures that the price of a commodity is the same anywhere in the world. The market-clearing price for each commodity is determined by the world demand for and supply of the commodity in question. In turn, the global demand and supply functions are nothing more than the sum of the individual countries demand and supply function. Hence the percentage changes in the world demand and supply for the commodities is determined by the weighted averages of the individual countries percent changes in the demand for and supply of goods and factors of production. As we are now explicitly assuming no coordination in policy across the economies, we would expect to find that in some countries the policies adopted result in an above-average increase in the aggregate demand, that is, an increase larger than the world. The answer for the autarkic economy is straightforward. As there is no international trade whatsoever and all economies have similar demand and supply elasticities, the countries with the most expansive economic policies will experience an above-average response that will result in an above-average percentage increase in output as well as the price of the commodity. Similarly, the countries experiencing below-average expansive policies will experience a below-average percentage increase in economic activity and prices.

Now think of the following exercise. What would have been the difference if the countries were open to trade and faced no transportation costs? The areas experiencing above-average performance would also experience above-average price increases, while the below-average performers would experience a below-average price increase. Arbitrage will induce a movement of goods from the cheaper areas to the more expensive areas. This means that the demand for goods from the below-average performers would rise and so would the local price and production levels for these products. The arbitrage would disappear when the prices in these localities rise to those of the market-clearing world prices. As the goods are imported and they become more available in the faster growing areas, the local prices and local production will fall in the areas. This process will continue until the price and output increases converge to the market-clearing percentage increases in world price and output. The price changes induce a common response across the different economies, with the magnitude of the responses depending on the demand for and supply elasticities.

The point of all this is that once the price changes are determined, there is nothing that the individual countries can do to alter the equilibrium conditions in any of the localities and/or the world as a whole. In the context of the traditional macro model that views the demand for imports as a leakage in an economy's aggregate demand, as the degree of openness or integration increase, so do the leakages. In the extreme case of perfect mobility and no transportation costs, the leakages are 100%. This is a very powerful insight. In an integrated economy, the only effect a country has on the local price level and output level is through its impact on the world prices. Nothing else matters. This is a hard pill to swallow for local politicians who make promises to the voters.

We know that free trade maximizes the global efficiency and thus the world's potential output. However, the cost of that is the loss of local control and political power, as well as the loss of rent for the protected sectors.

CHINA'S IMPACT ON THE GLOBAL ECONOMY'S EQUILIBRIUM OUTPUT

So far, we have shown that the integrated approach is capable of explaining the commodity supercycle that the world economy experienced during this millennium. Our interpretation puts China at the center of the explanation. In fact, it is our position that China's economic expansion and its derived demand for raw materials was the key driver of the commodity supercycle. The logic is quite seductive and many in the popular press use this type of reasoning to argue that a Chinese economic slowdown could have qualitatively a similar impact on the world economy. Some pundits go as far as to argue that the Chinese slowdown could push a weak global economy into recession. While we do not disagree with the argument qualitatively, we do have some issue on the magnitude of the potential impact of a Chinese slowdown on the global economy.

Our case against the global recession is based on the magnitude of the impact on the global demand induced by a Chinese slowdown. To do so, we will compare the differences between the impact of the Chinese economy on the commodity supercycle and the current global economic conditions.

According to the *World Steel Association*, in 2004, China's share of the world's steel consumption was 28%. By 2014, the share of the world's steel consumption had grown to 46%. During that same time, world steel consumption had grown by 60%. With a bit of manipulation, one can show that China's steel consumption grew by 160% during the same time period and the rest of the world grew a solid 20%. More importantly, we can also show that China accounted for about 75% of the increase in the global demand for steel. These numbers clearly show that China was the true driver in the commodity supercycle. It accounted for 45% points of the 60% point increase in steel consumption.

Let's compute similar numbers for the world demand for goods and services as measured by GDP. According to IMF data, the US accounts for approximately 25% of the world's GDP, while China only accounts for approximately 10%. Next, we need to make some assumptions regarding a potential China slowdown. Currently China is supposed to be growing at a 6% real GDP growth rate. That is China's demand for goods and services are growing at a 6% rate. These numbers would put China's contribution to the increase in world demand for goods and services at 0.6%. Even if one is willing to assume that China's growth rate is going to zero, the slowdown would only reduce the global growth rate by 60 basis points. Only if the rest of the world was declining at a rate in excess of 0.6% will the world economy post a negative growth rate? Also since the United States is (according to these numbers) 2.5 times larger than the Chinese economy, a one-quarter of 1% US real GDP growth rate would offset the presumed Chinese slowdown.

If one is more charitable and uses the Purchasing Power Parity adjusted GDP, then China's share of the world GDP rises to 16% from 10%, while the US share of the world income declines to 16% from 25%. The conclusion remains the same: China's impact on the commodity supercycle was much larger than any possible impact that a Chinese slowdown may have on the global economy.

The degree of integration is another variable that impacts the effect of disturbances in an economy on the global economy's equilibrium conditions. Our analysis shows that broadly defined transportation costs introduce a divergence between the local price and overall global market-clearing prices. Differences in prices less than the transportation costs will not be arbitraged away. Thus the transportation costs offer a window of price differential within which the local government's may be able to affect local prices and thereby impact local output that will be independent of economic fluctuations induced by the global prices. Under these circumstances, the growth rate will differ from that of the common trend induced by the chaining global market-clearing prices.

Put another way, an increase in the transportation costs reduce the amount of aggregate demand that leaks into the demand for goods produced in foreign markets.

Transportation costs can take many forms. One could literally be transportation costs and other costs associated with bottlenecks. Other costs take the form of regulations and taxation. Restrictions on ownership and the "borrowing" of foreign technology, restriction on capital repatriation and the amount of capital that residents can take out of China every year, as well as the degree of political freedom all impact the "transportation costs." All of this also suggests that the transportation costs are not necessarily uniform across commodities or factors of production. The regulations and government restrictions will impact the different factors differently.

Hence to the extent that China is not a truly open economy, its impact on the world aggregate demand will be smaller than its size in relation to the world economy. The greater the transportation costs, the less effect of changes in local aggregate demand on the global economy market-clearing prices.

IMPLICATIONS AND INSIGHTS

The analysis presented here suggests that China's growth rate is well above the world average and is a positive contribution to the world's real GDP growth rate. However, the magnitude of the contribution to the global growth rate is not large enough for a Chinese economic slowdown to cause a worldwide recession. Recall that the impact of an economy on the world's GDP growth rate or aggregate demand depends on the product of three different variables:

1. The magnitude of the real GDP growth rate. So far, the consensus is that China is slowing down, but there is considerable disagreement as to how much. Not many people are calling for a recession where the Chinese economy contracted by 4%. Under this scenario, that would be a reduction in the economy's growth rate of 10% points.
2. The size of the Chinese economy in relation to the global economy. As the world growth rate is a weighted average of the individual countries growth rate, the size of China's economy determines the potential contribution of a 1% increase in magnitude of the real GDP growth rate to the world growth rate. We have presented data that suggests that China's share of the world's GDP ranges between 10% and 16% of the world GDP.
3. The third factor affecting the potential impact on the world economy has to do with the degree of integration. It measures how much of the Chinese economy is fully integrated to the world economy.

For it is the latter that would impact the traded goods or integrated economy equilibrium conditions.

The data and arguments presented here suggest that China is nowhere near being a fully integrated economy. There are too many restrictions and transportation costs that prevent a full integration of the economy. Although looking at the trend over the last two or three decades, it is obvious that China is a much more open economy. One can argue that the country's desires to be a major player in the world economy, such as being Reserve Currency Country or a full member of the World Trade Organization and other international entities, have nudged China in the direction of freer markets, greater political freedom, and better property rights. If you add to this the increase in well-being of the Chinese people and the aspirations that a higher income will bring about economic well-being, the overall political and economic freedom will continue pushing China in the direction of greater integration to the world economy.

However, the path to greater integration is not necessarily a clear path. Let's consider the possible downside to the current Chinese authorities and let's also consider what a full integration means. First, in a fully integrated economy, there will be significant policy leakages. Recall that our analysis shows that in a fully integrated economy, the local authorizes have no impact on the local economy other than the impact they have on the world equilibrium. In China's case, it represents 10%–16% of the world's income or aggregate demand. This means that the rest of the world will control 84%–90% of the shifts in aggregate demands that cause global prices to change. In turn, the price change will then induce a common movement along the various economies of the world. Simply put, China's growth rate would converge to that of the world's growth rate. China would slow down as its degree of integration has risen. Worse yet, from a control and command economy point of view, the local authorities only control 10%–16% of the global aggregate demand shifts. In contrast under a closed economy, the authorities control 100% of the aggregate demand changes produced by the policy shifts. The choice is clear for the Chinese authorities and the beneficiaries of the status quo. They will never voluntarily adopt full integration.

On the other hand, the people of China will, in the aggregate, push for full integration. Only then will they maximize the gains of trade. These are opposing forces, and depending on which one prevails, it will determine whether China moves to full integration or not. Some may argue that the economic trends are clear. Yet there is evidence that also points to the reaction by current power structures. Witness the way the Hong Kong protests and elections have been handled, as well as how dissident mainland bloggers have been treated. It is not clear to us that the market forces and democracy is winning in China.

Our view is that the Chinese authorities will be tempted to attempt to stimulate its economy through local measures. The only way these measures can have an impact on the domestic policy without leaking into the rest of the world is if the transportation costs rise. Under this scenario, the Chinese policy will have little or no impact on the rest of the world's economy. On the other hand, if the economy's openness continues to increase, the Chinese stimulus will "leak" to the rest of the world. Yet the numbers reported as discussed earlier suggest the impact will not be as large as many of the pundits indicate. The question that remains is the following: if the Chinese authorities, as a result of their actions, see little or no stimulus domestically, will they double down? Given their recent experiences, we doubt it.

In conclusion, while we believe that China is a major player in the world economy, we believe that those who are questioning whether a Chinese slowdown would cause a global recession are overestimating the impact of China's economy on the world economy. We do not share that view and suggest that we should focus on finding a different culprit to blame for the global economy's travails. Interestingly, the integrated economy framework offers us a culprit.

Let's consider once again the differences between a fully integrated economy open to trade and facing no transportation costs and an autarkic economy that faces prohibitive transportation costs. In the case of the autarkic or closed economy, there will be no international leakages or interaction. The local prices are determined by local demand and supply considerations and they will be totally devoid of foreign influence. In the context of the traditional macro model who view the demand for imports as a leakage in an economy's aggregate demand, as the degree of openness and integration increase, so do the leakages, and a greater portion of the goods and services of the local economy will be priced in the global economy. In the extreme case of perfect mobility and no transportation costs, the leakages are 100%. This is a very powerful insight. In an integrated economy, the only effect a country has on the local price level and output level is through its impact on the world prices. The price changes induce a common response across the different economies, with the magnitude of the responses depending on the demand for and supply elasticities. The point of all this is that once the price changes are determined, there is nothing that the individual countries can do to alter the equilibrium conditions in any of the localities or the world as a whole. Nothing else matters. This is a hard pill to swallow for local politicians who make promises to the voters.

If this framework is correct, we have found our culprit for the slow growth experienced by the global economy during the last few years. In our view, it is the policy mix the different governments have adopted. In the developed world, most governments adopted some sort of stimulus program and their central banks adopted a low interest rates policy. While there were some stylistic differences and some variation on the magnitude of the different components of the policy mix adopted across the world, the common elements are undeniable. The fact that the global economy has not responded is an indictment of the policy mix adopted by the various countries. But it is not uncommon among politicians to blame someone else for their policy failures and to claim credit for the economic success. A global solution requires a major change in the global policy mix being adopted by the different economies. If that does not change, then the individual economies searching for their own solution will have to reduce the leakages to maximize the impacts of their policy initiatives on the local economy. Translation: if the global economy does not alter its policy mix in a pro-growth direction, the countries attempting to find their own individual solution to their economic problems will have to reduce the leakages. The degree of integration will decline as the countries adopt a protectionist and isolationist stance. The question is what choices will the different economies take? Will the leaders lead? If not, protectionism will be on the rise.

13

A Unified Theory: Terms of Trade, Real GDP Growth Rate Differentials, the Trade Balance, Capital Flows, and the Relative Stock Market Performance

Earlier, we have shown that mobility plays a major and important role in the degree of integration and thus the correlation among the different variables describing the performance of different economies in the world. We made two extreme assumptions to illustrate these differences.

THE TWO POSSIBILITIES

At one end of the spectrum, we assume that perhaps as a result of natural barriers or perhaps as a result of a deliberate policy of the powers that be, there is no contact with the outside world. Under this assumption, autarky will rule the day. Since there is no international trade and no other contact with the rest of the world, it follows that the local prices will be determined solely by local demand and supply conditions. There will be little or no outside interaction, and thus no outside influence with the exception of common factors such as weather. For example, a global drought will have a common and negative effect across the economies of the world, even if they are isolated and do not trade with each other. However, other than that, there is no reason to expect any correlation among the local prices and output levels with their counterparts in the rest of the world. Simply put, the local prices and output levels will be uncorrelated between the isolated economies and prevailing prices and output in the rest of the world.

At the other end of the mobility spectrum, we have a perfect mobility where the products and factors of production face little or no transportation costs. Under this assumption, arbitrage insures that there are no price differences across localities. For each commodity, there will be a single price in the world economy. That price is determined by the global demand for and supply of the individual commodity. Once the demand and supply elasticities are determined, the increase in the global demand, that is, the excess demand, is the only piece of information needed to determine the change in the price for the individual commodities. The conclusion is that a country's effect on the price of the individual commodities is directly related to its size and the magnitude of the local increase in demand, nothing else matters about

Economic Disturbances and Equilibrium in an Integrated Global Economy. http://dx.doi.org/10.1016/B978-0-12-813993-6.00013-1

the local economy. The changing global prices induce a common effect across all the economies of the world. The individual country output increases for the particular commodity is determined solely by two factors: the magnitude of the price increase, which is common to all the economies, and the magnitude of the supply elasticities. In general, this result suggests that there will be a positive and very high correlation among the individual economies increase in output, that is, real GDP.

The two extreme assumptions regarding the degree of economic integration yield vastly different implications regarding the way economic disturbances are transmitted and propagated throughout the world economy. At one end of the spectrum, there is little or no correlation across national borders. For these commodities, the prices are determined solely by the local demand for and supply conditions. In contrast, when goods and services face no transportation costs, the local conditions are irrelevant once the global prices are determined. All that matters are the global demands for and supply conditions. The country's impact on the global prices depends on its impact on the global demand for and supply of the commodities in question. Within the perfect mobility scenario, size matters. As an economy's relative size declines, so does its impact on the world prices. In the limit, the smaller economies will have no impact what so ever on the prices of any good and or service. This yields a very important policy insight. Once the demand and supply elasticities are determined, there is little local policies can do to alter the path of this economy. Therefore if the local policies are to have any effect on the economy, their focus should be on the demand for and supply elasticities of the economy in question. At the other end of the spectrum, because the economy size increases, it will approach that of the world economy. Hence in the limit, the larger the economy, the greater the economy's impact on the prices needed to clear the markets.

THE TERMS OF TRADE

The two extreme assumptions regarding the mobility of goods and services or factors of production are book ends to a whole continuum regarding the degree of mobility. Combining the two extreme assumptions into a single model could very well yield a more general and robust framework capable of explaining a much more complicated relationship among an economy's prices, output, and net flows of goods and services across its national borders. The first step in our analysis is to focus on the country's terms of trade to make inferences about the degree of integration and the interaction or correlation among the economic indicators.

We have already established that in a perfect mobility world, the price of each individual commodity will be the same in every locality; otherwise a profit opportunity

and arbitrage opportunity would arise. In a world where people maximize profits, the arbitrage opportunity will not persist. Next, if the tastes are similar across countries, it follows that the consumer baskets will tend to be fairly similar too. In the extreme case of identical tastes, we would expect the consumption baskets to be identical. In such a world, the terms of trade will be constant at all times. That is, one unit of the consumer basket in one area will trade for an identical unit in the rest of the world. More importantly, in such a world, Purchasing Power Parity (PPP) will hold at all times.

Now let's incorporate some nontraded goods, or goods and services that are immobile across national borders into the equation. Incorporating the nontraded goods into the consumer price index (CPI), the index would have two components. One consists of the traded commodities whose prices in a common currency will be the same across the different economies. The second component will consist of the price index of the nontraded commodities.

As already mentioned, the equilibrium conditions for the purely nontraded goods are those of the autarkic equilibrium where the prevailing equilibrium price is determined solely by the local demand for and supply conditions. The nontraded good prices are determined by the local conditions and have nothing to do with the rest of the world economic conditions. Hence the relative price of the nontraded goods need not be the same across national borders. In fact, short of common policies or explicit policy coordination across nations, there is no reason to expect the nontraded prices to be correlated across national borders. If that is the case, one should not expect the relative price between the traded goods and nontraded goods to be the same across localities. This means that the broad-based CPI inclusive of traded and nontraded goods will differ across borders. As the traded components is the same across countries, it follows that the differences in CPI or the ratio of the countries CPI's would reflect the differences in nontraded goods relative prices. The latter is commonly called the terms of trade. While the latter is easily calculated, all one needs to do is obtain the CPI's in a common currency; there is no need to perform these calculations. The terms of trade are readily available and calculated by international organizations such as the International Monetary Fund (IMF). All one needs to look for is the PPP conversion rate.

THE GLOBAL ECONOMY'S ADJUSTMENTS TO ECONOMIC DISTURBANCES AND THE CORRELATION AMONG THE KEY ECONOMIC VARIABLES

Economists and investors are quite fond of stressing the importance of freely determined market prices in providing the appropriate signals that brings about a market clearing equilibrium. The terms of trade are no different. Understanding the equilibrium process can allow one to make inferences as to how overall prices will change, as well as deriving the possible correlations among the different variables or key indicators of interest to policymakers and analysts.

Next, we illustrate the correlations by analyzing the effect of a shock in the aggregate demand for goods and services in one of the large economies, let's call it country L. In theory, the excess demand or excess supply shocks could be the result of policy changes adopted in the economy in question. For the time being, we will not focus on the source of the aggregate demand shifts. We are just interested in illustrating the impact of an aggregate demand shock in country L on the relationship among the different economic variables.

An increase in aggregate demand results in a corresponding excess demand for both the traded goods and the locally produced nontraded goods in country L. Keep in mind that the nontraded good must be produced and consumed locally and cannot be imported. Equilibrium requires the intersection of the local demand for and supply function. However, that is not the case for the traded good. Equilibrium requires the intersection of the global demand for and supply of the traded goods. As country L is a fraction of the world economy, the percentage increase in global aggregate demand will be smaller than country L's percentage increase in aggregate demand, while the percentage increase in demand for the nontraded goods in country L will be 100% of the increase in aggregate demand in country L. As there is no initial impact on the excess demand for nontraded good in the rest of the world, it follows that in the rest of the world there will be an excess demand for traded goods relative to nontraded goods suggesting that the nontraded goods relative prices will fall relative to the rest of the world.

All in all, the analysis suggests that the terms of trade shift in favor of country L. That is the CPI in country L will rise more than the rest of the world. That is, one unit of CPI in country L will buy more than one unit of the consumer basket in the rest of the world.

The rising relative price of nontraded goods in country L means that the rate of return and valuation in the nontraded sector rises. In turn, that attracts capital from the traded sector both at home, as well as the rest of the world. For the rest of the world, the lower relative rates of return result in an outflow of capital from the nontraded sector into the traded sectors in their economies, as well as the others in the rest of the world. All of these point to a capital inflow into country L and an outflow from the rest of the world. Also, as the rates of returns in the traded sectors are equalized across all economies, the nontraded sector will be the only source of differential rates of return across the different economies. As we have already established that the rates of return in the nontraded sector of country L outperform the nontraded sector in the rest of the world, we can then conclude that country L's stock market will outperform the rest of the world.

The global excess demand for the traded goods results in an increase in price, but which price? Our answer is that the global excess demand results in an increase in the price of current production relative to future consumption. But what if the real rate of return or real interest rate rises? The higher real interest rate induces a substitution effect away from current consumption into future consumption. Since the rate at which people can transfer resources from the present into the future improves, the savings rate will rise and people will postpone consumption. The desire to transfer resources into the future also increases incentives to work and produce to save more. As a result, global production will rise. Higher production and lower consumption leads to an excess supply of goods.

This is precisely what is needed to satisfy the initial excess demand. We know that the rest of the world produces more and consume less; therefore, the rest of the world will experience an improvement in the rest of the world trade balance (TB). Since the world is a closed-economy equilibrium, it requires that the world TB be zero. This means the rest of the world TB will be the mirror image of country L's TB.

Whether the countries' real GDP growth rates differ depends on the performance of the nontraded sector. Each of the countries' real GDP is a weighted average of the traded and nontraded sectors. The rising real interest rate points to an increase in the global production of traded goods in the world economy. Assuming similar supply functions, the increase will be quite similar across national borders. Since we have already shown that country L's traded sector will outperform the rest of the world's nontraded sectors, it follows that country L's real GDP growth will outperform the rest of the world.

The effect of a supply side disturbance is quite different. It results in a corresponding excess supply for both the traded goods and the locally produced nontraded goods in country L. It leads to a proportionate increase in the supply for the traded and nontraded goods. Since country L is a fraction of the world economy, the percentage increase in global aggregate supply will be smaller than country L's percentage increase. In turn, the percentage increase in supply of the nontraded goods in country L will be 100% of the world's initial increase in aggregate supply of the nontraded goods. Equilibrium in country L requires that the price of the nontraded goods fall relative to that of the traded goods. Since there is no initial impact on the excess supply for nontraded goods in the rest of the world, it follows that in the rest of the world there will be an excess supply for traded goods relative to nontraded goods. This suggests that the nontraded goods relative prices will fall relative to the rest of the world. All in all, the analysis suggests that the terms of trade shift in favor of the rest of the world.

The global excess supply for the traded goods results in a decrease in the global real rates of return in the rest of the world. The lower interest rates reduce the desire to transfer resources into the future, as well as reduce the incentive to save more. As a result, the rest of the world production declines and consumption increases. This is precisely what is needed to satisfy the initial excess supply caused by the original shock in country L. Since the rest of the world produces less and consumes more, it will experience a deterioration in the rest of the world's TB. This means an improvement in country L's TB.

Whether the countries' real GDP growth rates differ depends on the performance of the nontraded sector. Each of the countries real GDP growth is a weighted average of the traded and nontraded sectors. The falling real interest rate points to a decrease in the rest of the world's production of traded goods, which leads us to conclude that the country L's real GDP growth will outperform the rest of the world. The effect on the countries' stock market is a bit different. Lower production and lower prices point to a decline in the rest of the world's real rates of return. Now the story in country L is a bit different. If the initial increase in aggregate supply is the result of a technological innovation or some other shift in the supply function, the lower prices will not necessarily produce lower profits. Once the cost reduction associated with the supply shift is taken into account, one can show that overall profits increase in country L. Therefore the stock market in country L will outperform the rest of the world.

WHAT DOES THE GLOBAL DATA TELL US?

One of the problems presented by a general equilibrium framework as we have described is that every variable depends on every other variable. That is, everything depends on everything else. A simple regression analysis may be quite useful in identifying the deferent correlations among the variables in question—real GDP growth differentials between the countries and the world, changes in the TB as a percent of GDP, the percent changes in the terms of trade, and the relative stock market returns. To obtain the empirical results relating the different variables, we estimated a generic equation that included a constant term, a one lag of the dependent variables, contemporaneous estimates for the explanatory variables, and a one lag value of the remaining three variables. The information produced by such an analysis can be quite useful in identifying the correlation patterns

and possible channels of contemporaneous interaction among these variables. A point that is important to make is that any correlation identified by the empirical analysis should not be interpreted as evidence of a causal relationship.

The global data needed to identify the correlations is readily available [1]. To estimate the correlations implied in the previous section, we have combined two distinct databases. The World Economic Forum database provides us with information on the countries' TB, real GDP growth rates, and the terms of trade. The second data set was obtained from the Morgan Stanley Capital Index (MSCI) and it contains stock market returns for a number of countries. We combined the two databases and used only the countries for which we had a complete set. Next, we focused on identifying and estimating significant correlations among the different variables and whether these correlations or empirical relationships validate or contradict the correlations surmised in the previous section.

The real GDP growth rate differential between the individual countries and the United States and the estimated relationship between the real GDP growth differential, GDP, and the current (ToT) and one year lag (ToT (-1)) terms of trade, relative stock returns and the previous year's stock return differential (Stocks and Stocks (-1)), and the changes in the TB as a percent of GDP (Trade and Trade (-1)) can be found in Table 13.1. Additional results are reported in the appendix.

The first two columns of Table A13.1 shows the estimated R^2 and the P-value for the autocorrelation of the residuals of the estimated equations for each of the countries. The remaining columns provide estimates for the t-statistics for the different coefficients produced by the different countries equations. Based on the usual significance level, the first-row columns suggest that the estimated equations are fairly well-behaved. The explanatory power as measured by the R^2 is pleasantly surprising. Very few equations have a P-value lower than 0.1, suggesting that autocorrelation of residuals is not a major problem.

The results reported in the appendix Table A13.1 are quite interesting in particular as one focuses on the statistical significance of the different coefficient. Table A13.1 shows only in 6 of 43 the country equations is the constant term statistically significantly different from zero. Next, 15 of the changes in the TB as a percent of GDP post statistically significant coefficients for either the current and/or lagged value of the explanatory variable. More importantly, on average, the magnitude of the sum of the TB coefficient is negative in most of the countries. This result is consistent with the demand shock interpretation discussed in the previous section. Twenty of the current and or lagged terms of trade coefficient were significantly different from zero and the coefficients are

TABLE 13.1 Countries GDP Growth Less the US GDP Growth

Country	Constant	GDP (−1)	ToT	ToT (−1)	Stocks	Stocks (−1)	Trade	Trade (−1)
Australia	0.9796	0.1455	0.5427	−0.0518	0.1319	0.2716	−1.8763	−1.4298
Austria	1.3379	0.1402	0.9570	0.4528	−0.0458	0.2617	−0.5359	0.4017
Belgium	1.3120	0.2101	1.3866	1.5076	0.0839	0.2605	−1.8124	−0.7050
Brazil	1.5228	0.1975	−0.0886	0.0648	0.1078	0.3444	−0.2274	−1.7006
Canada	0.4183	0.4733	3.3531	−2.4262	0.1241	0.0888	−0.7015	−0.0536
Chile	0.8533	0.4840	0.4466	−0.3917	−0.0363	0.2608	0.7376	0.5558
China	0.5814	0.7364	1.7687	−0.8746	−0.0151	−0.0325	0.1949	1.0967
Colombia	0.2491	0.3647	1.5810	−1.2284	0.1000	0.0292	−2.1635	0.6196
Czech Republic	1.8119	−0.1745	0.6763	−0.7670	0.1814	0.1707	1.4000	−0.9330
Denmark	3.0223	0.2142	−3.7265	2.1371	0.0363	0.1816	−1.0268	−4.9375
Egypt	−0.6143	0.8234	0.1953	−0.0841	0.0528	0.0853	−1.3982	0.5130
Finland	0.8990	0.2278	1.7242	−1.7408	0.0479	0.0303	−1.2868	0.1247
France	0.3356	0.2414	2.7836	−2.7268	0.0691	0.3064	−0.3913	−0.5388
Germany	0.0461	0.2119	1.8823	0.2534	−0.0053	0.3410	0.5808	0.7987
Hong Kong	1.2052	0.2069	1.2720	−0.6370	0.0554	0.0957	−0.2675	−0.0477
Hungary	5.8381	0.0549	−0.1945	−0.4497	0.0650	0.0457	−3.7807	−0.0322
India	−3.3469	0.1795	0.4416	1.4285	0.1813	0.0998	−0.6431	0.4083
Indonesia	10.5798	0.0741	−1.7202	0.9960	−0.1054	0.3553	−0.3757	−0.9649
Ireland	3.5085	0.0383	0.2299	0.6824	−0.0081	0.1675	0.4030	−0.8095
Israel	4.4721	−0.0422	−1.3087	1.1369	−0.0165	0.0660	−3.1695	−0.3376
Italy	0.5818	0.1849	1.1883	−0.5112	0.0245	0.2605	−1.2107	−1.2974
Japan	8.4815	0.1875	1.6549	1.4846	0.2586	0.0552	−0.1099	−0.2670
Korea	2.7329	−0.0145	−0.6506	1.5589	0.0271	0.1564	−1.6492	−0.4258
Malaysia	3.0819	−0.1837	1.6193	0.4473	0.1152	0.1233	−0.8143	−0.3651
Mexico	0.7199	−0.1529	0.0552	0.0565	0.1079	0.0700	−3.8256	0.4291
Netherlands	1.0727	0.1365	−1.3272	2.3727	−0.0764	0.4578	−0.7302	0.3611
New Zealand	1.4443	0.4405	0.7782	−0.4872	0.0996	0.1335	−0.7404	1.3500
Norway	1.4147	0.3420	0.1262	−0.1971	−0.0067	0.1646	0.1582	−0.5566
Peru	0.3567	0.3190	1.1125	−0.3021	0.0941	0.0608	−1.4930	0.6679
Philippines	0.8137	0.2620	0.1158	0.1463	0.0258	0.1516	−0.1684	1.2885
Poland	2.7846	0.1387	0.6653	−0.4668	−0.0512	0.0714	−2.0151	1.6357
Portugal	−1.1320	0.3992	2.5750	−0.7890	−0.0886	0.2703	0.7375	0.5463
Russia	3.9171	0.4477	−0.7534	0.2627	0.1587	0.1883	3.2729	−0.3938
Singapore	4.9590	0.1500	1.4189	0.3448	0.0974	0.1567	0.0866	0.4305
South Africa	−0.2457	0.2115	−2.1847	2.1544	0.1466	0.1355	−0.3797	0.3626
Spain	1.5700	0.2009	3.1436	−2.8434	0.1955	0.1160	−2.9525	0.6016
Sweden	−2.3703	0.2845	−0.7246	1.9467	0.0342	0.1645	1.3487	−0.6128
Switzerland	1.4040	0.2045	1.6762	0.1595	0.1101	0.4119	−0.5316	0.3258
Taiwan	1.9158	0.2364	−1.0511	1.2741	0.0037	0.0675	−0.6360	−0.4487
Thailand	0.8540	0.1112	0.3880	1.4128	0.0757	0.1177	−0.8187	−0.0808
Turkey	4.3113	0.0080	−0.0958	0.0113	0.0310	0.0234	−4.1535	0.3270
UK	0.6365	0.2824	0.3760	0.1401	0.1421	0.4103	−0.7399	0.9036

positive more often than not. Again, the result is consistent with the demand shock interpretation. Lastly, but not least, 42 of the stock return coefficients for the current and lagged value of the stock return differential are significantly different form zero. As with the other coefficients, the results are consistent with the relationship suggested by the demand shock adjustment to a new equilibrium.

One interesting interpretation has to do with the relative magnitude of the number of statistically significant coefficients. The relative stock returns have either twice or three times as many of the coefficients of the two other variables, the terms of trade and TBs, respectively. However, the terms of trade and TB combined produce a similar amount of statistically significant coefficients. These two variables may be much more closely related and could very well be equivalent proxies.

The changes in the TB as a percent of GDP are reported in Table 13.2 and the relevant statistics are reported in Table A13.2. As with the previous equations for the real GDP growth rate differential, the R^2 are reasonable suggesting a more than adequate explanatory power and the P-value for almost the totality of the estimated trade equations the residual are fairly well-behaved. While on average, the magnitude of the stock return coefficients tends to be positive, however only 10 of the coefficients for the stock return are statistically significant. The coefficients for the real GDP growth rate differential are more often than not negative with only 15 of the coefficients are statistically significantly different from zero. The terms of trade variable with 20 statistically significant coefficients constitute one variable with the largest number of statistically significant coefficients.

Collectively, the estimated coefficients for the three explanatory variables are consistent with the demand shock dynamic. If one is willing to use the number of significant coefficients as a way to determine the relative importance or influence of the different variables on the TB, the terms of trade lead the way.

Changes in the terms of trade and its relationship to the other variables are reported in Table 13.3. As before, the goodness of fit statistics is reported in the appendix (Table A13.3). In many ways, the results are not different from those reported in the other tables in the appendix. The estimated equations are fairly well-behaved. The R^2 or explanatory power of the equations is quite reasonable and the P-values indicate that there is no evidence of autocorrelation of residuals. The 42 set of equations on average identifies a negative relationship with the TB, a view that is consistent with the orthodox theory, a deterioration of the terms of trade leads to an improvement in the TB. The data also reveals no systematic pattern regarding the long-run effects with respect to the impact of the real GDP or relative stock returns on the terms of trade. This is not saying that the results are

not statistically significant. What the data shows is that approximately half the sample has a positive sign, while the other half has a negative sign. This is a result that is consistent with the view that the aggregate demand and aggregate supply shocks are equally prevalent. Looking at the results, it is clear that the relative stock returns are the one variable with the least number of statistically significant coefficients, while the past values of the terms of trade changes are the one variable with the most statistically significant coefficients. The small number of significant coefficients for the relative stock returns suggests that the effect of the relative stock returns on the terms of trade may be a weak one. In contrast, the one important result is that the lagged values of the terms of trade changes have a statistically significant impact on the current changes, suggesting that terms of trade disturbances may persist and impact the rest of the economy for longer than one period.

The relative stock returns yield the smallest number of statistically significant coefficients (see Tables 13.4 and A5.4 in the appendix). One possible explanation for this is that the stock returns are forward-looking and the returns may be a better predictor or expectations of things to come, such as the future path of the variables in question which in effect determine the current valuation. Viewed from this perspective, we would expect the relative stock return to be a better predictor of the other variables instead of the other way around. Also the fact that the relative GDP growth rate has the largest number of statistically significant coefficient followed by the terms of trade fits the relative valuation results. Countries with the fastest growth rates and improving terms of trade will tend to have their earnings increase in both absolute terms, as well as relative to the rest of the world.

A UNIFIED THEORY

The analysis presented here outlines a broad-based global framework with multiple uses both in the understanding of the interrelationship among macroeconomic variables in a global economy. Among the many applications of the framework is one that focuses on the impact of policy changes on the overall equilibrium values of the different variables.How the different shocks have a differential impact on the relative performance of the different variables? Once the shocks are identified and their impact on the relative magnitude of the changes in the equilibrium conditions is established, the policymakers may be able to design a policy mix aimed at achieving a particular impact on the relative performance of the variables in question.

The Theory: One way to illustrate the usefulness of our approach is to trace how economic disturbances originating in one country are propagated throughout

TABLE 13.2   Changes in the Trade Balance as a Percent of GDP

Country	Constant	Trade balance	ToT	ToT (−1)	Stocks	Stocks (−1)	GDP	GDP (−1)
Australia	−0.0046	2.7858	0.2541	−0.2093	0.0016	−0.0028	−0.0633	−0.0046
Austria	0.2616	−24.1144	−0.6198	−0.8488	0.0123	0.0095	−0.0165	−0.0357
Belgium	0.5258	−20.3119	0.5712	0.2854	0.0142	0.0479	−0.0375	−0.0296
Brazil	0.1511	62.8094	0.0122	−0.0075	−0.0041	−0.0136	−0.0035	−0.0146
Canada	0.1592	14.2495	1.4212	−0.8452	0.0141	0.0219	−0.2465	0.0964
Chile	0.0130	1.8612	0.2566	−0.1983	0.0157	−0.0608	0.1375	−0.0980
China	4.2542	−42.6961	−0.4565	0.8692	0.0420	0.0523	0.2709	−0.6385
Colombia	−0.1522	27.5492	0.2883	−0.2015	0.0023	0.0031	−0.0830	−0.0040
Czech Republic	0.0046	13.2861	−0.0161	0.1915	−0.0220	−0.0111	0.0768	0.0020
Denmark	0.6450	−43.9131	−0.0609	0.1975	0.0022	0.0033	−0.0346	0.0153
Egypt	1.1635	−31.8700	0.0290	−0.1078	0.0046	0.0146	−0.1290	−0.0298
Finland	0.4524	−0.2663	0.0136	−0.2672	0.0188	0.0150	−0.0384	−0.0571
France	0.0991	5.2433	−0.2898	0.4074	0.0067	−0.0061	−0.0052	−0.0284
Germany	0.4658	15.1948	−0.4334	0.2574	0.0048	0.0164	0.0124	−0.0313
Hong Kong	1.1560	5.8015	0.6455	−0.2677	0.0235	0.0181	−0.3292	−0.1636
Hungary	1.2932	−5.7108	−0.1376	−0.0222	0.0177	−0.0093	−0.1023	−0.0411
India	2.2861	−30.5952	−0.2687	−0.0981	−0.0164	0.0136	−0.0253	−0.1373
Indonesia	−1.5208	3.4357	0.1340	0.0641	0.0145	−0.0212	−0.0084	0.0160
Ireland	0.3078	−1.8592	0.0053	−0.0414	0.0119	−0.0335	0.0142	−0.0563
Israel	0.9487	14.9206	−0.1310	0.1006	−0.0039	0.0100	−0.1134	−0.0571
Italy	0.0692	24.3914	0.1470	−0.0371	0.0141	−0.0094	−0.0310	−0.0048
Japan	0.8163	26.9430	−0.0340	0.2399	0.0141	0.0017	−0.0021	−0.0390
Korea	1.1907	−17.0730	−0.3021	0.3315	0.0172	−0.0033	−0.2026	−0.0356
Malaysia	−0.6201	−22.5143	1.2911	0.5907	0.0359	−0.0404	−0.1844	−0.0972
Mexico	0.1090	−9.1599	0.0896	−0.0483	0.0016	−0.0053	−0.0906	−0.0256
Netherlands	0.5439	18.0740	−0.5301	0.5674	−0.0112	0.0209	−0.0182	−0.0194
New Zealand	−0.1459	−30.6200	0.2408	−0.0411	0.0077	−0.0227	−0.0254	−0.0252
Norway	−0.2167	34.6733	0.9335	−0.4388	0.0294	−0.0157	0.0208	−0.0329
Peru	0.3650	16.9518	0.4804	−0.2049	0.0322	−0.0091	−0.2424	0.0492
Philippines	2.4175	−46.8525	−0.2877	−0.0760	0.0156	−0.0324	−0.0282	−0.0861
Poland	0.3583	15.9402	0.1964	−0.1411	−0.0104	0.0180	−0.0889	−0.0155
Portugal	−0.1255	4.9571	−0.2634	0.0951	−0.0036	−0.0594	0.0400	−0.1026
Russia	−2.3561	17.9323	0.3594	−0.1040	−0.0127	0.0025	0.0547	−0.0485
Singapore	2.9660	−14.9876	0.1614	0.4707	−0.0097	−0.0050	0.1200	−0.1110
South Africa	−0.7743	26.0603	0.0662	0.0538	0.0046	−0.0175	−0.0055	−0.0067
Spain	0.0120	39.4893	0.1550	−0.0745	0.0202	−0.0281	−0.0614	0.0109
Sweden	0.4810	19.8760	−0.1693	−0.0081	0.0131	0.0175	0.0367	−0.0583
Switzerland	0.5863	1.2238	0.1266	−0.2442	0.0443	0.0235	−0.0638	0.0297
Taiwan	0.5670	1.4307	0.0804	−0.2491	0.0165	−0.0078	−0.0410	−0.0704
Thailand	0.1437	−2.9591	0.3569	0.5696	0.0273	−0.0005	−0.3295	0.0094
Turkey	−0.2156	−26.8894	−0.0069	0.0175	−0.0022	−0.0026	−0.1135	−0.0055
UK	−0.1269	15.6550	−0.1365	0.1685	0.0260	−0.0070	−0.0173	−0.0260

TABLE 13.3 Percent Changes in the Terms of Trade

Country	Constant	Trade balance	ToT	ToT (−1)	Stocks	Stocks (−1)	GDP	GDP (−1)
Australia	−0.0046	2.7858	0.2541	−0.2093	0.0016	−0.0028	−0.0633	−0.0046
Austria	0.2616	−24.1144	−0.6198	−0.8488	0.0123	0.0095	−0.0165	−0.0357
Belgium	0.5258	−20.3119	0.5712	0.2854	0.0142	0.0479	−0.0375	−0.0296
Brazil	0.1511	62.8094	0.0122	−0.0075	−0.0041	−0.0136	−0.0035	−0.0146
Canada	0.1592	14.2495	1.4212	−0.8452	0.0141	0.0219	−0.2465	0.0964
Chile	0.0130	1.8612	0.2566	−0.1983	0.0157	−0.0608	0.1375	−0.0980
China	4.2542	−42.6961	−0.4565	0.8692	0.0420	0.0523	0.2709	−0.6385
Colombia	−0.1522	27.5492	0.2883	−0.2015	0.0023	0.0031	−0.0830	−0.0040
Czech Republic	0.0046	13.2861	−0.0161	0.1915	−0.0220	−0.0111	0.0768	0.0020
Denmark	0.6450	−43.9131	−0.0609	0.1975	0.0022	0.0033	−0.0346	0.0153
Egypt	1.1635	−31.8700	0.0290	−0.1078	0.0046	0.0146	−0.1290	−0.0298
Finland	0.4524	−0.2663	0.0136	−0.2672	0.0188	0.0150	−0.0384	−0.0571
France	0.0991	5.2433	−0.2898	0.4074	0.0067	−0.0061	−0.0052	−0.0284
Germany	0.4658	15.1948	−0.4334	0.2574	0.0048	0.0164	0.0124	−0.0313
Hong Kong	1.1560	5.8015	0.6455	−0.2677	0.0235	0.0181	−0.3292	−0.1636
Hungary	1.2932	−5.7108	−0.1376	−0.0222	0.0177	−0.0093	−0.1023	−0.0411
India	2.2861	−30.5952	−0.2687	−0.0981	−0.0164	0.0136	−0.0253	−0.1373
Indonesia	−1.5208	3.4357	0.1340	0.0641	0.0145	−0.0212	−0.0084	0.0160
Ireland	0.3078	−1.8592	0.0053	−0.0414	0.0119	−0.0335	0.0142	−0.0563
Israel	0.9487	14.9206	−0.1310	0.1006	−0.0039	0.0100	−0.1134	−0.0571
Italy	0.0692	24.3914	0.1470	−0.0371	0.0141	−0.0094	−0.0310	−0.0048
Japan	0.8163	26.9430	−0.0340	0.2399	0.0141	0.0017	−0.0021	−0.0390
Korea	1.1907	−17.0730	−0.3021	0.3315	0.0172	−0.0033	−0.2026	−0.0356
Malaysia	−0.6201	−22.5143	1.2911	0.5907	0.0359	−0.0404	−0.1844	−0.0972
Mexico	0.1090	−9.1599	0.0896	−0.0483	0.0016	−0.0053	−0.0906	−0.0256
Netherlands	0.5439	18.0740	−0.5301	0.5674	−0.0112	0.0209	−0.0182	−0.0194
New Zealand	−0.1459	−30.6200	0.2408	−0.0411	0.0077	−0.0227	−0.0254	−0.0252
Norway	−0.2167	34.6733	0.9335	−0.4388	0.0294	−0.0157	0.0208	−0.0329
Peru	0.3650	16.9518	0.4804	−0.2049	0.0322	−0.0091	−0.2424	0.0492
Philippines	2.4175	−46.8525	−0.2877	−0.0760	0.0156	−0.0324	−0.0282	−0.0861
Poland	0.3583	15.9402	0.1964	−0.1411	−0.0104	0.0180	−0.0889	−0.0155
Portugal	−0.1255	4.9571	−0.2634	0.0951	−0.0036	−0.0594	0.0400	−0.1026
Russia	−2.3561	17.9323	0.3594	−0.1040	−0.0127	0.0025	0.0547	−0.0485
Singapore	2.9660	−14.9876	0.1614	0.4707	−0.0097	−0.0050	0.1200	−0.1110
South Africa	−0.7743	26.0603	0.0662	0.0538	0.0046	−0.0175	−0.0055	−0.0067
Spain	0.0120	39.4893	0.1550	−0.0745	0.0202	−0.0281	−0.0614	0.0109
Sweden	0.4810	19.8760	−0.1693	−0.0081	0.0131	0.0175	0.0367	−0.0583
Switzerland	0.5863	1.2238	0.1266	−0.2442	0.0443	0.0235	−0.0638	0.0297
Taiwan	0.5670	1.4307	0.0804	−0.2491	0.0165	−0.0078	−0.0410	−0.0704
Thailand	0.1437	−2.9591	0.3569	0.5696	0.0273	−0.0005	−0.3295	0.0094
Turkey	−0.2156	−26.8894	−0.0069	0.0175	−0.0022	−0.0026	−0.1135	−0.0055
UK	−0.1269	15.6550	−0.1365	0.1685	0.0260	−0.0070	−0.0173	−0.0260

TABLE 13.4 Stock Market Returns

Country	Constant	Stocks (−1)	Trade	Trade (−1)	ToT	ToT (−1)	GDP	GDP (−1)
Australia	−4.6981	−0.1713	0.3672	4.8000	−1.3196	2.6291	1.0038	−0.4084
Austria	−1.9143	0.3510	5.5999	4.7146	1.0861	19.4515	−0.6402	0.0743
Belgium	−2.6313	−0.2473	3.3274	0.6797	1.1723	1.6780	0.4060	0.1191
Brazil	−6.5163	−0.6305	−2.8865	15.3326	0.5383	−0.3303	1.1811	0.5628
Canada	−2.2902	−0.2249	0.9062	2.0795	−7.4844	4.5685	2.8010	−1.1052
Chile	−6.6917	0.5159	1.8768	−0.4707	2.4796	−0.3205	−0.8104	−0.0348
China	−35.9164	−0.2322	5.8619	7.6419	2.4678	−10.0212	−2.9346	6.6923
Colombia	10.7221	0.2813	1.2384	−3.2547	−4.1151	2.1592	2.1021	−1.7708
Czech Republic	−2.0986	0.0368	−3.6197	3.6988	−0.4261	−0.2213	1.6357	0.5055
Denmark	0.5438	−0.3329	0.3732	4.0056	3.0637	−1.2937	0.2106	0.3311
Egypt	2.5208	−0.3255	3.6838	−8.8488	0.2318	2.6687	3.8858	−6.5548
Finland	−3.0021	0.1237	5.7600	2.7311	0.0004	2.7467	0.4372	0.1363
France	−0.9142	0.1559	1.3349	5.3486	4.3796	−2.2685	0.1819	0.2471
Germany	−3.7412	−0.1050	0.9326	5.3728	0.6485	1.3460	−0.0218	−0.4177
Hong Kong	−6.7711	−0.4019	1.6530	0.4561	−6.2154	3.2428	4.7991	−1.2011
Hungary	−24.7874	0.1070	8.1229	3.3371	6.1505	−2.1537	0.8075	1.9946
India	44.2352	−0.1925	−6.5532	−6.2353	−5.8134	−6.0405	2.8446	−2.2786
Indonesia	37.3446	0.3896	5.9899	0.8812	−2.8656	−0.7222	−0.9677	−0.5470
Ireland	−9.2035	−0.0055	2.3718	3.9482	2.6261	1.2925	−0.0567	0.1613
Israel	0.6781	−0.0368	−1.8342	1.2376	−4.5879	2.0687	−0.2752	0.1330
Italy	−4.9816	0.2504	4.1504	−0.5691	−3.6487	3.2502	0.1840	−0.3649
Japan	−10.8465	0.1371	3.1589	4.0723	−2.3717	0.0548	1.1235	−0.2191
Korea	−9.7271	0.0519	5.2321	7.5832	9.8048	−10.3173	1.0142	−0.3221
Malaysia	−1.6462	−0.0732	3.4771	2.3306	−8.6132	−3.1946	2.5254	0.2939
Mexico	0.4306	0.0064	0.8959	−4.2334	0.3836	−0.0533	1.3901	−0.4011
Netherlands	−1.8982	0.1010	−0.6176	2.4378	−2.6637	1.3172	−0.1044	−0.0556
New Zealand	−4.5493	0.0120	2.3610	−1.1154	−0.7312	1.3115	1.0525	−1.0105
Norway	−2.9624	0.0110	3.6867	−1.0287	−3.3516	2.5142	−0.1100	0.4612
Peru	1.3962	0.0226	9.4962	−3.3007	−7.8408	2.9161	4.5140	−1.7887
Philippines	−19.0808	−0.0399	4.3869	4.3690	0.4582	1.2398	1.2190	0.8392
Poland	−1.2851	0.0069	−1.8418	3.1829	−2.2609	0.5075	−0.3980	0.8983
Portugal	−7.4482	0.1748	−0.5565	−2.2428	0.0622	0.2053	−0.7441	0.1867
Russia	−34.3854	−0.5836	−9.7182	3.2026	3.2725	−0.4615	2.0269	−0.5878
Singapore	−8.2997	−0.4760	−0.2201	−0.9453	−0.2947	0.2947	3.0627	−1.6656
South Africa	1.2630	0.1829	2.1033	3.8191	4.5047	−4.6574	0.9733	−0.1221
Spain	−6.1706	0.0643	6.1790	−0.0421	−3.2820	4.0823	1.2448	0.1737
Sweden	3.2649	−0.1532	1.7085	−1.0075	1.9391	−2.4238	0.1210	0.1220
Switzerland	2.3135	−0.1241	0.9968	−0.7355	−2.7354	3.8524	0.2970	−0.4870
Taiwan	−13.6185	−0.1099	7.7141	−6.3933	−4.4678	1.5213	0.1119	−0.3807
Thailand	−2.9151	−0.3048	4.0493	0.3914	−4.5286	−5.0154	4.5166	−0.9414
Turkey	−1.6945	−0.4918	−1.6976	0.5275	−0.3454	0.1541	0.6692	1.0089
UK	−3.7662	−0.1143	2.2571	3.5571	5.4006	−3.2718	0.2875	−0.0267

the global economy and ultimately leads to a new equilibrium level. Our framework suggests that as a result of an aggregate demand shock, the country where the disturbance originates will experience an excess demand for goods and services. That results in an excess demand for the global goods and services. The increase in global excess demand for traded goods will be equal to the product of the increase in local excess demand times the size of the country in relation to the global economy. In contrast, the demand for nontraded goods has to be satisfied domestically; hence the excess demand increase will be a larger percentage of the nontraded good that that of the traded goods. The relative excess demand means that the relative price of the nontraded goods will increase unambiguously, that is, the terms of trade will improve. The global excess demand means that the price of current consumptions will rise relative to future consumption, the end result being an increase in the real interest rate.

The rising real rates of return will induce an increase in the production of the traded goods and services. The traded goods will increase by the same percentage amount across the different countries. This will induce a positive correlation of the local country's real GDP growth relative to the rest of the world. In the absence of nontraded goods, the correlation would be perfect. Also since the nontraded good price, in the local country where the shock originated, increases, it follows that the nontraded good production increases by a larger percent than the rest of the world. Since the real GDP is a weighted average of the traded and nontraded goods, and the traded component rises by the same percentage amount while the nontraded rises by a larger amount, it follows that the country where the disturbance originated will experience an improvement in both the absolute and relative real GDP growth rate, as well as an improving terms of trade.

The improving terms of trade means that the rate of return in producing nontraded goods rises relative to that of the traded goods. To the extent that is the case, it will attract capital from both the domestically traded, as well as the rest of the world traded sectors. The capital attracted from the rest of the world results in a capital account improvement.

The worldwide excess demand results in an increase the equilibrium real rate of return worldwide. In turn, the higher rate of return will induce an upward movement along the global aggregate supply curve resulting in an increase in the world's real GDP. The higher real interest rates also lead to an upward movement along the world aggregate demand curve, thereby reducing the rest of the world's consumption. The reduction in the rest of the world's consumption combined with the increase in the rest of the world's production leads to an excess supply of the traded goods that, in equilibrium, will be large enough to meet the excess demand for traded goods in the country where the disturbance originally occurred. In short, the country's TB deteriorates simultaneously with the improvement in the country's terms of trade, relative growth rate, and capital account improvement.

The rising real rate means that the valuation of the industries producing the traded good will rise globally. As the rate of return in the local nontraded sector rises relative to the traded sector, we can argue that the increased valuation in the local nontraded sector will be higher than the increased valuation in the traded sector industries. In contrast, for the rest of the world, the traded sector industries' appreciation exceeds that of the nontraded sector. As the local market is a weighted average of the traded and nontraded sector and the traded goods returns are common to all areas, it follows that the relative rates of return will be a function of the rates of return differential in the nontraded sector in the United States and the rest of the world. The local stock market returns will exceed those of the rest of the world rates of return. The rising relative stock returns will coincide with the terms of trade and capital account improvements, TB deterioration, and an improved real GDP relative performance in the country where the initial disturbance occurred.

The Evidence: The empirical relationships estimated and reported in Tables 13.1–13.4 provides us with a system of equations that estimates the magnitude of the various interrelationships among the real GDP relative growth rate, the percent changes in the terms of trade, the changes in the TB as a percent of GDP, and the relative stock market returns. Table 13.5 provides us with a summary of the empirical results. The top of the table

TABLE 13.5   Summary of the Number of Significant Coefficients Generated by the Different Equations

	Explanatory variables				
Dependent variable	Constant	GDP	Trade balance	ToT	Stocks
GDP	6	**9**	15	20	42
Trade balance	13	15	**4**	20	10
Terms of trade	13	23	27	**35**	15
Stocks	3	19	9	12	**4**

The Number in bold indicate the number of equations for which past values of the dependent variable have a statistically significant coefficient lists the number of coefficients that are statistically significantly different from zero. For example, the first row of Table 13.5 shows that the one year lagged coefficient of the relative real GDP growth rate is statistically significant in 9 of the 42 countries, while the TB coefficient for the current and one year lag for the changes in the TB as a percent of GDP is statistically significant in 15 of the 84 estimated coefficients, 20 of the coefficients for the percent change in the terms of trade lagged one year are statistically significant, and so are 42 of the stock market relative returns.

These results suggests that the variable with the broadest measured impact on real GDP growth is that of the real stock returns, followed by the terms of trade, and then lastly by the TB as a percent of GDP. But that is not all. As one reads on the GDP column in Table 13.5, it shows that the interaction is a two-way interaction. In addition to the terms of trade, changes in the TB as a percent of GDP and the relative stock returns explain some of the variation in the relative real GDP growth rate, yet the converse is also true. The second row of column 2, the one labeled GDP, shows that 15 of the coefficients on the TB equations, the relative GDP growth rate have a significant coefficient. For the terms of trade set of equations, the relative GDP growth rate posts 23 significant coefficients and for the set of relative stock returns, the relative GDP growth rates produced 19 coefficients that are statistically significantly different from zero.

The numbers of coefficients make the collective interpretation of the system of equations for each of the countries difficult to interpret and comprehend. We thought about how to present the information in a parsimonious way that captures the essence of the interaction among the system of equations. To do so, we calculated the likelihood of obtaining each set of coefficients that could be generated by a random process. We calculated the likelihood that a binomial distribution with 84 draws with a 10% chance of success would generate the number of significant coefficients reported in Table 13.5. The estimated likelihood of the outcomes being random is reported in Table 13.6. We use a 10% cutoff to determine whether the outcome is statistically significantly different from the one generated by a random draw. The result reported in Table 13.6 suggests a feedback or two-way relationship between:

- The relative GDP growth rate and the changes in the TB as a percent of GDP
- The relative GDP growth rate and the percent changes in the terms of trade
- The relative GDP growth rate and the relative stock performance
- The percent change in the terms of trade and the changes in the TB as a percent of GDP
- The percent change in the terms of trade and the relative stock performance

Empirically, the one exception to the empirically estimated two-way relationship appears to be between the relative stock returns and the TB. For them, the P-value exceeds the 10% threshold but is less than 15%.

Potential pitfalls: The system of equations as we estimated is, at first blush, a complicated one. The estimated coefficients of the individual equations provide us with the short term or initial impact of a disturbance on the explanatory variables—say the changes in the terms of trade—will have on the real GDP growth rate. However, the system of equations also suggests that the initial impact will not necessarily be the same as the final one. The reason is that the terms of trade will also impact other variables and that, in turn, affects the relative real GDP growth rate and vice versa. If the system is stable, eventually the disturbance will die out and the magnitude of the final change will be quite different from the initial one. This is interesting to the investors, as it suggests that, as a result of adjustment costs, the initial disturbances will generate relative return cycles that an astute investor may be able to exploit.

Users of single equation estimates should be aware of the interaction just mentioned. We do not have any problem with that, but the use of single equation could lead to a major potential pitfall. To get the best possible fit, one may develop theories and estimates that are inconsistent with each other.

A simple example will suffice. Let's take the case of a floating exchange rate system. Under the normal assumptions of a floating exchange rate system, it is commonly assumed that there are no currency flows between the two countries. That is, under a floating exchange rate, the balance of payments (BOP) is always zero.

TABLE 13.6 Likelihood That the Set of Equations Generate the Previously Mentioned Significant Coefficients

	GDP	Trade balance	Terms of trade	Stocks
GDP		0.0103	0.0001	0.0000
Trade balance	0.0103		0.0001	0.1135
Terms of trade	0.0000	0.0000		0.0103
Stocks	0.0004	0.1362	0.0573	

Since there is no net money flowing across national borders, it follows that the net flows of goods and services, that is, the TB must be offset by capital flows (KA). Hence, double-entry bookkeeping means that:

$$BOP = TB + KA = 0 \qquad (13.1)$$

Rearranging terms, we get the following relationship:

$$TB = - KA \qquad (13.2)$$

Eq. (13.1) shows a relationship between two variables. This means that there is only one degree of freedom. This is a very important point, as Eq. (13.2) shows that once you specify one of the two variables, the other one is already determined. This is significant because it shows that under a floating exchange rate as we have described, one cannot have a theory for the TB and a separate theory for the KA. Doing so, would violate the budget constraint, Eq. (13.1). Hence the proper theory should be able to simultaneously explain the capital flows and TB with a single theory. The framework developed here satisfies the budget constraint and degrees of freedom condition. Developers of individual theories for single macro variables should be aware of the constraints and degrees of freedom while providing coherent parsimonious explanations.

Reference

[1] The IMF, OECD and even the Federal Reserve Bank of Saint Louis (FRED) have easily accessible data on many of the world economies.

TABLE A13.1   Countries GDP Growth Less the US GDP Growth

Country	R^2	P-value	Constant	GDP (−1)	ToT	ToT (−1)	Stocks	Stocks (−1)	Trade	Trade (−1)
						Coefficient t-statistics				
Australia	0.6748	0.4698	0.6559	0.9516	0.6868	−0.0616	1.9529	3.8918	−1.83632	−1.26051
Austria	0.5738	0.1011	0.9190	1.0465	0.4849	0.2101	−0.8689	5.3780	−0.47182	0.40361
Belgium	0.3529	0.2152	0.6877	1.1765	0.6085	0.9082	0.9387	2.4839	−1.35111	−0.62265
Brazil	0.7744	0.1901	0.5994	1.1281	−1.2909	1.3009	1.3769	4.7273	−0.10213	−0.71672
Canada	0.8505	0.4970	0.8266	3.8611	6.6614	−3.8564	3.6501	2.3088	−2.28611	−0.17412
Chile	0.7779	0.4900	0.4715	3.3880	1.0597	−1.0269	−0.7384	4.9532	1.425075	1.212593
China	0.9659	0.4492	0.2906	3.5255	5.6599	−2.0646	−0.6098	−1.0567	0.667838	4.273439
Colombia	0.6269	0.4177	0.0760	1.4934	1.3934	−1.1908	1.8598	0.4875	−1.68714	0.425547
Czech Republic	0.6199	0.4375	0.7756	−0.6744	0.6286	−0.8813	2.0540	1.4905	1.097811	−0.7897
Denmark	0.5113	0.0899	1.8012	1.5484	−2.7779	1.6415	0.4388	2.3105	−0.9596	−4.1088
Egypt	0.8618	0.0778	−0.2355	3.2449	0.4802	−0.1804	1.6855	3.2218	−1.55551	0.532793
Finland	0.2187	0.1986	0.4414	1.0755	1.6357	−1.7083	0.7162	0.4315	−1.11747	0.117527
France	0.3096	0.2052	0.1977	1.2102	1.1720	−1.2254	0.5640	2.5204	−0.22578	−0.29744
Germany	0.5119	0.3456	0.0259	1.2913	1.9491	0.2541	−0.0536	3.5049	0.426204	0.542167
Hong Kong	0.8520	0.6720	2.1419	1.6677	5.5650	−2.5864	3.0080	4.6306	−1.55381	−0.27297
Hungary	0.5573	0.7957	1.6042	0.1803	−0.1353	−0.3952	0.7806	0.6286	−2.63395	−0.02652
India	0.7078	0.4151	−0.6888	0.6479	0.4946	1.9156	3.7217	2.3098	−0.46343	0.331058
Indonesia	0.8496	0.8610	1.8735	0.4220	−5.5364	2.2134	−1.4296	1.8685	−0.23812	−0.59853
Ireland	0.3197	0.0268	1.6616	0.1763	0.2718	0.7504	−0.0906	1.8151	0.32237	−0.71499
Israel	0.5133	0.0491	2.0999	−0.1711	−1.6818	1.7741	−0.2435	1.0120	−2.70032	−0.2668
Italy	0.4819	0.1330	0.2967	1.1920	1.0936	−0.4848	0.3361	3.4482	−0.98721	−1.01684
Japan	0.5170	0.8094	1.9252	0.9168	0.9377	0.8221	3.2001	0.5803	−0.07654	−0.17278
Korea	0.8192	0.4627	1.4632	−0.0928	−0.6104	1.6511	0.7133	3.5482	−3.00508	−0.53416
Malaysia	0.6701	0.6801	1.4771	−0.8146	1.9695	0.4890	2.7174	2.0108	−1.78361	−0.79632
Mexico	0.6648	0.6222	0.2540	−0.6864	0.1527	0.2624	1.7820	0.9501	−3.08936	0.338487
Netherlands	0.3149	0.4721	0.5100	0.8146	−0.6490	1.2872	−0.4481	2.8375	−0.57982	0.289018
New Zealand	0.5386	0.3351	0.7852	2.2775	0.9137	−0.5723	1.6762	1.8914	−0.67788	1.246488
Norway	0.4464	0.2356	0.9097	2.2549	0.1978	−0.3061	−0.1355	3.2054	0.287115	−1.00654
Peru	0.8406	0.1300	0.2530	2.0191	2.0206	−0.9697	3.0995	1.5118	−2.71541	1.21644
Philippines	0.6955	0.7568	0.2514	1.3961	0.1875	0.2710	0.7644	3.8223	−0.2932	1.958065
Poland	0.3318	0.0082	1.0064	0.5197	0.7496	−0.6196	−0.5198	1.2442	−1.6841	1.454384
Portugal	0.5045	0.3367	−0.5302	1.7251	1.6759	−0.5210	−1.1272	2.6315	0.739549	0.638657
Russia	0.6316	0.6965	0.3545	1.6125	−0.7342	0.7307	2.2844	2.3071	1.548025	−0.37374
Singapore	0.8334	0.6393	2.9992	0.9640	2.9195	0.6950	3.2594	5.3016	0.512489	2.545045
South Africa	0.5597	0.4830	−0.0229	0.8677	−1.3522	1.4517	1.4707	1.2243	−0.16457	0.163868
Spain	0.6119	0.8345	0.7932	1.0645	1.9310	−1.7003	2.8355	1.2859	−2.35275	0.427789

(Continued)

II. THE TRADE BALANCE

TABLE A13.1 Countries GDP Growth Less the US GDP Growth (*Cont.*)

Country	R^2	P-value	Constant	GDP (−1)	ToT	ToT (−1)	Stocks	Stocks (−1)	Trade	Trade (−1)
					Coefficient *t*-statistics					
Sweden	0.2922	0.2016	−0.9819	1.5555	−0.5748	1.6558	0.3223	1.5432	1.14045	−0.55741
Switzerland	0.4456	0.2368	0.6107	1.2356	0.9795	0.0954	0.9192	3.5231	−0.93651	0.532219
Taiwan	0.4075	0.2808	1.1894	1.0321	−1.4858	1.7496	0.0865	1.9278	−0.69421	−0.6856
Thailand	0.8275	0.6476	0.5556	0.6497	0.6130	2.3360	3.0581	3.2069	−2.57857	−0.23052
Turkey	0.6462	0.7847	1.0524	0.0314	−0.6392	0.0698	0.6005	0.5087	−3.89468	0.211905
UK	0.4883	0.6832	0.3585	1.8495	0.2262	0.0978	1.0319	3.1024	−0.56857	0.581848

TABLE A13.2 Changes in the Trade Balance as a Percent of GDP

Country	R^2	P-value	Constant	Trade balance	ToT	ToT (−1)	Stocks	Stocks	GDP (−1)	GDP (−1)
					Coefficient *t*-statistics					
Australia	0.3520	0.3969	−0.0167	0.1297	1.8487	−1.4082	0.1223	−0.1751	−1.83632	−0.16039
Austria	0.4675	0.4995	1.0294	−1.4328	−1.9083	−2.5109	1.3606	0.7668	−0.47182	−1.55812
Belgium	0.4769	0.7588	2.0500	−1.2766	1.8427	1.2091	1.1150	3.4558	−1.35111	−1.15117
Brazil	0.6127	0.5747	0.4752	2.5557	1.4447	−1.2047	−0.3938	−0.9401	−0.10213	−0.64884
Canada	0.3769	0.3236	0.5264	0.7899	3.4851	−1.9226	0.5691	0.8877	−2.28611	1.074221
Chile	0.4356	0.0202	0.0166	0.0905	1.4456	−1.2180	0.7382	−1.9083	1.425075	−1.29813
China	0.6238	0.0236	2.3223	−0.8103	−0.5650	1.6206	1.6166	1.5421	0.667838	−1.98136
Colombia	0.4243	0.8008	−0.2375	0.9950	1.2844	−0.9811	0.1910	0.2634	−1.68714	−0.07705
Czech Republic	0.2538	0.4286	0.0081	0.4709	−0.0625	0.9443	−0.9308	−0.3785	1.097811	0.031841
Denmark	0.1351	0.7532	2.1436	−1.6164	−0.2163	0.7951	0.1422	0.2099	−0.9596	0.57915
Egypt	0.6556	0.3327	1.6336	−1.1377	0.2330	−0.7811	0.4363	1.4133	−1.55551	−0.27703
Finland	0.3871	0.3613	1.3261	−0.0145	0.0710	−1.4983	1.7088	1.2735	−1.11747	−1.60354
France	0.2265	0.5641	0.5085	0.2510	−1.0530	1.6218	0.4763	−0.3909	−0.22578	−1.23579
Germany	0.5043	0.7900	1.9147	0.7083	−3.4859	1.8844	0.3360	0.9614	0.426204	−1.30694
Hong Kong	0.2972	0.9297	1.8106	0.2992	1.8093	−0.8839	1.0045	0.5826	−1.55381	−1.15775
Hungary	0.6062	0.7106	2.4007	−0.2871	−0.5903	−0.1177	1.3587	−0.7813	−2.63395	−0.84545
India	0.6275	0.4302	3.0562	−1.3282	−1.6555	−0.5938	−1.2518	1.4417	−0.46343	−3.3637
Indonesia	0.6421	0.6819	−1.7931	0.1415	1.9316	0.8643	1.3091	−0.6940	−0.23812	0.614816
Ireland	0.3263	0.4720	0.7326	−0.0862	0.0332	−0.2387	0.7234	−1.9552	0.32237	−1.4574
Israel	0.5847	0.1123	2.4659	0.6312	−0.8277	0.7608	−0.3075	0.7972	−2.70032	−1.30071
Italy	0.2883	0.6487	0.2204	1.2044	0.8374	−0.2192	1.2475	−0.6485	−0.98721	−0.18645
Japan	0.2842	0.6063	1.2818	1.2924	−0.1360	0.9586	1.0797	0.1270	−0.07654	−1.4004
Korea	0.6838	0.5796	1.8811	−0.6126	−0.8149	0.9571	1.3331	−0.1657	−3.00508	−0.65855
Malaysia	0.7087	0.5989	−0.5955	−1.0443	4.2231	1.4214	1.6028	−1.3092	−1.78361	−0.90938
Mexico	0.6705	0.4873	0.2499	−0.4710	1.7407	−1.5467	0.1631	−0.4618	−3.08936	−0.74827
Netherlands	0.1761	0.1988	1.7250	0.9310	−1.7235	2.0410	−0.4182	0.7212	−0.57982	−0.73083

Country										
New Zealand	0.4463	0.7289	−0.4247	−1.5525	1.5772	−0.2591	0.6647	−1.7137	−0.67788	−0.64502
Norway	0.6872	0.6356	−0.3794	1.8034	6.8328	−2.0251	1.7429	−0.7164	0.287115	−0.54947
Peru	0.6376	0.6728	0.6514	0.7412	2.2179	−1.7530	2.3905	−0.5213	−2.71541	0.686309
Philippines	0.4459	0.5752	2.0162	−1.7010	−1.1795	−0.3444	1.1484	−1.5814	−0.2932	−1.10027
Poland	0.4829	0.1725	0.6021	0.6355	1.0769	−0.9067	−0.5049	1.5372	−1.6841	−0.27488
Portugal	0.3828	0.1401	−0.2509	0.2465	−0.6937	0.2683	−0.1899	−2.4329	0.739549	−1.93884
Russia	0.8610	0.6124	−1.8879	1.4242	4.3887	−2.9060	−1.2451	0.1981	1.548025	−1.30711
Singapore	0.0744	0.6297	1.3536	−0.6768	0.2439	0.8086	−0.2313	−0.0988	0.512489	−0.59929
South Africa	0.3104	0.3120	−0.6088	1.0179	0.3206	0.2810	0.3551	−1.3309	−0.16457	−0.22225
Spain	0.6192	0.7113	0.0417	2.1051	0.6207	−0.2929	1.8872	−2.3001	−2.35275	0.393787
Sweden	0.2795	0.1088	1.2205	1.1166	−0.8201	−0.0395	0.7571	0.9717	1.14045	−1.98623
Switzerland	0.0701	0.9360	0.7390	0.0574	0.2098	−0.4233	1.0747	0.4769	−0.93651	0.505735
Taiwan	0.4133	0.5014	1.4066	0.0850	0.4245	−1.3032	1.6213	−0.8142	−0.69421	−1.22347
Thailand	0.5944	0.5381	0.1462	−0.1329	0.8991	1.3663	1.4961	−0.0172	−2.57857	0.085243
Turkey	0.6576	0.4667	−0.3093	−1.0885	−0.2755	0.6637	−0.2497	−0.3434	−3.89468	−0.13178
UK	0.2303	0.3688	−0.4689	0.6614	−0.5403	0.7791	1.2488	−0.2942	−0.56857	−1.06871

TABLE A13.3 Percent Changes in the Terms of Trade

Country	R^2	P-value	Constant	ToT (−1)	Trade	Trade (−1)	Stocks	Stocks (−1)	GDP	GDP (−1)
Australia	0.5374	0.5474	1.1532	4.4314	1.8487	−1.8914	−0.6040	1.4183	0.686826	−1.66448
Austria	0.2379	0.6000	−0.4733	−0.5133	−1.9083	−1.0925	0.1466	−0.4984	0.484925	0.10777
Belgium	0.3695	0.2431	−0.3336	0.0186	1.8427	0.9681	0.2323	−1.4732	0.608524	−1.84693
Brazil	0.7887	0.0203	0.6157	5.3891	1.4447	−2.6056	2.8372	1.9865	−1.29091	−0.53498
Canada	0.7533	0.8713	−0.0225	3.7426	3.4851	−0.4929	−2.0275	−0.8583	6.661387	−3.28516
Chile	0.7222	0.1847	1.4466	4.3777	1.4456	−1.4124	1.2600	−0.0801	1.059746	−1.28795
China	0.9523	0.3778	0.0960	2.2332	−0.5650	−4.0455	0.2545	2.2338	5.659916	−2.89563
Colombia	0.9261	0.0535	0.1906	10.7470	1.2844	−2.0417	−0.7537	0.2300	1.393368	−1.0548
Czech Republic	0.5488	0.4938	0.0986	2.2106	−0.0625	−0.9271	−0.1295	−1.7243	0.628593	0.743598
Denmark	0.5122	0.2223	1.7547	3.3091	−0.2163	−3.5267	0.8403	1.7607	−2.77794	0.118109
Egypt	0.4923	0.7394	0.9678	2.1699	0.2330	0.1118	0.0658	−0.0512	0.480177	−0.08501
Finland	0.3890	0.4600	0.8466	2.7753	0.0710	−1.3829	0.0001	1.1482	1.635707	−1.84638
France	0.8460	0.1755	−0.3293	9.6814	−1.0530	−1.7440	1.1345	−2.4528	1.172023	−3.4163
Germany	0.5859	0.4364	1.1536	0.8987	−3.4859	−1.0657	0.3082	−0.1174	1.949116	−0.10066
Hong Kong	0.8797	0.9397	−1.1400	6.0936	1.8093	−1.0125	−2.1203	−1.9545	5.565005	−1.02549
Hungary	0.9270	0.6053	0.9106	8.1328	−0.5903	−0.1527	1.3030	−1.1778	−0.13532	−1.18939
India	0.7013	0.1095	3.0045	0.8765	−1.6555	−2.6778	−1.8260	0.9901	0.494643	−1.79825

(Continued)

II. THE TRADE BALANCE

TABLE A13.3   Percent Changes in the Terms of Trade (*Cont.*)

Country	R^2	*P*-value	Constant	ToT (−1)	Trade	Trade (−1)	Stocks	Stocks (−1)	GDP	GDP (−1)
Indonesia	0.8614	0.8619	3.8918	0.9137	1.9316	−0.1419	−2.0573	1.6396	−5.53639	−0.33733
Ireland	0.4234	0.1306	0.2658	2.4330	0.0332	0.3581	1.2144	−0.2436	0.271762	−0.39742
Israel	0.8199	0.2844	1.1247	4.8248	−0.8277	−1.2858	−1.4043	−0.1425	−1.68176	0.565881
Italy	0.7905	0.0529	0.1571	8.7438	0.8374	−0.9758	−1.2316	0.1625	1.093607	−1.97255
Japan	0.5121	0.5330	−1.7152	3.5368	−0.1360	−1.4329	−0.6389	0.0871	0.937704	−1.37408
Korea	0.7951	0.5531	1.7016	6.1357	−0.8149	−3.4513	1.5894	−0.5375	−0.61035	−0.70096
Malaysia	0.7136	0.6883	1.7121	−3.2278	4.2231	2.1789	−2.3110	−0.0787	1.969509	1.715429
Mexico	0.6209	0.0014	2.4355	4.9476	1.7407	0.2599	0.2964	−0.6804	0.15269	−0.06572
Nether-lands	0.6269	0.3112	−0.1531	5.4276	−1.7235	−0.0108	−1.1330	0.0578	−0.64903	−2.29427
New Zea-land	nd0.7543	0.2364	0.8213	6.7839	1.5772	−1.4890	−0.2600	1.9272	0.913726	−2.2066
Norway	0.6880	0.5402	1.2956	2.0392	6.8328	−1.9493	−1.3390	1.0070	0.197829	0.473263
Peru	0.9085	0.1569	0.8092	7.8852	2.2179	−1.2687	−2.0684	0.6635	2.020574	−1.59973
Philip-pines	0.5282	0.8163	2.7581	2.2140	−1.1795	−2.1359	0.1078	−1.0564	0.187484	−1.50802
Poland	0.9200	0.0588	−0.5415	8.9243	1.0769	0.1228	−0.9229	0.8792	0.749628	0.153211
Portugal	0.8635	0.4614	0.1816	7.7314	−0.6937	−0.6730	0.0130	−0.3315	1.67589	−2.58158
Russia	0.9033	0.4362	4.5763	4.2748	4.3887	−1.0582	0.9030	−1.1929	−0.73417	−0.36536
Singapore	0.6625	0.7074	−5.4942	−2.7287	0.2439	−1.9167	−0.0934	−1.1590	2.919511	2.623502
South Africa	0.4060	0.0370	2.5145	1.3327	0.3206	−0.4796	1.0556	0.3503	−1.3522	−0.9858
Spain	0.8952	0.1162	−0.3633	13.5348	0.6207	−2.8280	−0.7537	−1.2758	1.931003	−3.35395
Sweden	0.4953	0.4497	0.9511	4.4098	−0.8201	−0.1596	0.8230	0.9691	−0.57481	−1.38201
Switzer-land	0.2575	0.0167	−1.8468	1.9144	0.2098	−1.3685	−0.9729	0.5596	0.979532	−1.51129
Taiwan	0.5298	0.1875	−1.1229	3.4247	0.4245	−0.7691	−1.1239	0.5196	−1.48577	1.651323
Thailand	0.2663	0.3627	1.5387	−0.5688	0.8991	0.4292	−0.9389	−1.2873	0.613006	1.210849
Turkey	0.6391	0.0922	0.8832	4.4204	−0.2755	0.2823	−0.4942	−0.4400	−0.63922	1.016176
UK	0.6881	0.9044	1.8069	5.4051	−0.5403	−3.3317	2.5646	0.0333	0.226244	−0.45704

TABLE A13.4   Stock Market Returns

Country	R^2	*P*-value	Constant	Stocks (−1)	Trade	Trade (−1)	ToT	ToT (−1)	GDP	GDP (−1)
Australia	0.3386	0.2591	−1.1605	−0.7093	0.1223	1.5578	−0.6040	1.1645	1.952878	−0.96856
Austria	0.3078	0.1294	−0.3467	1.3616	1.3606	1.3050	0.1466	2.7522	−0.86888	0.14525
Belgium	0.1188	0.7444	−0.6258	−0.9778	1.1150	0.2711	0.2323	0.4538	0.938731	0.295484
Brazil	0.5153	0.9032	−0.7821	−1.7648	−0.3938	2.2592	2.8372	−2.2096	1.376865	0.95908
Canada	0.4387	0.8922	−0.9570	−1.1467	0.5691	1.4818	−2.0275	1.2475	3.650083	−1.5749
Chile	0.3849	0.2333	−0.7909	1.4226	0.7382	−0.2092	1.2600	−0.1729	−0.7384	−0.04024
China	0.5475	0.3294	−1.4392	−0.5170	1.6166	1.2987	0.2545	−1.5693	−0.60976	1.672745
Colombia	0.4459	0.6248	0.7280	1.0565	0.1910	−0.4885	−0.7537	0.4366	1.859844	−1.59839

Czech Republic	0.5579	0.7421	−0.2918	0.0967	−0.9308	1.0676	−0.1295	−0.0816	2.05403	0.649446
Denmark	0.1918	0.1694	0.1266	−1.6834	0.1422	1.0943	0.8403	−0.3931	0.438775	0.966688
Egypt	0.4971	0.4959	0.1125	−1.0811	0.4363	−1.1163	0.0658	0.6801	1.685471	−2.82961
Finland	0.2394	0.2220	−0.4881	0.5850	1.7088	0.8648	0.0001	0.8548	0.71619	0.208139
France	0.2403	0.0821	−0.3323	0.7127	0.4763	1.9496	1.1345	−0.6148	0.564026	0.750158
Germany	0.2134	0.6130	−1.0552	−0.4362	0.3360	1.9081	0.3082	0.6687	−0.05357	−1.24878
Hong Kong	0.2774	0.3993	−1.2232	−1.6111	1.0045	0.2802	−2.1203	1.2979	3.007969	−1.00631
Hungary	0.4854	0.0668	−2.0432	0.4136	1.3587	0.8024	1.3030	−0.5402	0.78064	2.236971
India	0.8059	0.1184	2.8957	−0.9821	−1.2518	−1.3584	−1.8260	−2.0869	3.721685	−2.48043
Indonesia	0.2649	0.3436	2.2625	0.6255	1.3091	0.1788	−2.0573	−0.4725	−1.42963	−1.05423
Ireland	0.2803	0.5227	−1.6400	−0.0206	0.7234	1.3613	1.2144	0.5316	−0.09065	0.28033
Israel	0.2495	0.7439	0.0674	−0.1334	−0.3075	0.2394	−1.4043	0.7236	−0.24353	0.131968
Italy	0.1761	0.3056	−0.9409	1.0150	1.2475	−0.1594	−1.2316	1.1475	0.336117	−0.84584
Japan	0.5340	0.5289	−1.1302	0.6932	1.0797	1.3061	−0.6389	0.0144	3.200134	−0.50819
Korea	0.3945	0.7125	−0.8197	0.1477	1.3331	1.6563	1.5894	−1.8100	0.713271	−0.33799
Malaysia	0.4379	0.6141	−0.1592	−0.2307	1.6028	1.1023	−2.3110	−0.7524	2.717369	0.27392
Mexico	0.3045	0.8607	0.0422	0.0235	0.1631	−0.9503	0.2964	−0.0688	1.782039	−0.49852
Netherlands	0.1889	0.6779	−0.7772	0.4677	−0.4182	1.7669	−1.1330	0.5961	−0.44812	−0.2806
New Zealand	0.1961	0.5094	−0.7601	0.0489	0.6647	−0.3076	−0.2600	0.4728	1.676154	−1.52635
Norway	0.1549	0.8159	−0.4638	0.0443	1.7429	−0.4512	−1.3390	0.9784	−0.13552	0.689425
Peru	0.5291	0.8463	0.1428	0.0749	2.3905	−0.8449	−2.0684	1.4005	3.099516	−1.55311
Philippines	0.1667	0.7738	−0.8740	−0.1086	1.1484	0.8962	0.1078	0.3345	0.764398	0.624566
Poland	0.4643	0.3722	−0.1605	0.0406	−0.5049	0.9747	−0.9229	0.2386	−0.51979	1.265474
Portugal	0.1522	0.4173	−1.2450	0.5026	−0.1899	−0.9152	0.0130	0.0464	−1.1272	0.258383
Russia	0.5342	0.1405	−0.8971	−1.8914	−1.2451	0.8741	0.9030	−0.3528	2.284404	−0.53993
Singapore	0.4226	0.5070	−0.7767	−2.1434	−0.2313	−0.9024	−0.0934	0.1049	3.259367	−2.02128
South Africa	0.3109	0.2600	0.0456	0.6163	0.3551	0.6808	1.0556	−1.1895	1.470718	−0.18914
Spain	0.3823	0.1233	−1.2583	0.2738	1.8872	−0.0118	−0.7537	0.9317	2.835541	0.357732
Sweden	0.0753	0.7190	0.7125	−0.7378	0.7571	−0.4863	0.8230	−1.0634	0.322311	0.339271
Switzerland	0.1910	0.8773	0.6127	−0.5310	1.0747	−0.7353	−0.9729	1.4617	0.919172	−1.85528
Taiwan	0.3679	0.5140	−1.5839	−0.5245	1.6213	−1.9315	−1.1239	0.3532	0.086514	−0.29502
Thailand	0.4381	0.6723	−0.2438	−0.8753	1.4961	0.1444	−0.9389	−0.9644	3.058069	−0.71342
Turkey	0.3498	0.0241	−0.0863	−2.7536	−0.2497	0.0735	−0.4942	0.2058	0.600532	0.878639
UK	0.3142	0.8103	−1.5581	−0.5189	1.2488	1.6880	2.5646	−1.6946	1.031882	−0.11535

II. THE TRADE BALANCE

SECTION III

EXCHANGE RATE AND THE TERMS OF TRADE

14

Protectionism, Devaluation, and the Terms of Trade

The exchange rate and terms of trade are two variables that are intertwined and quite often are used as a proxy for one another. While under some circumstances the interchangeability may be appropriate, that is not always the case.

An exchange rate, E, measures the price of one currency in terms of another. It is the unit of the foreign currency that the local currency buys. In turn, the terms of trade, T, measure how many units of the foreign goods one unit of the domestic good can acquire. It is the ratio of the two countries Consumer Price Index (CPIs) in a common currency, that is, (US CPI in $)/(Foreign CPI in $). In turn, the CPI in each country measures how many units of the local currency are required to buy a unit of the local good. The terms of trade, T, definition can be used to illustrate interrelationship among the variables:

$$T = (\text{US CPI in \$})/(\text{Foreign CPI in \$}) = (\text{US CPI in \$}) \\ /(\text{Foreign CPI in Local Currency}/\text{Exchange Rate}) \tag{14.1}$$

Hence, the previous equation can be expressed as:

$$T = \text{Exchange Rate} \\ *(\text{US CPI in \$}/\text{Foreign CPI in Local Currency}) \tag{14.1'}$$

Rearranging terms, we get

$$\text{Exchange Rate} = T*\left(\frac{\text{Foreign CPI in Local}}{\text{Currency}/\text{US CPI in \$}}\right) \tag{14.1''}$$

The previous equation shows that, as long as the ratio of the CPIs in local currencies remains unchanged, the terms of trade and exchange rates will move in the same proportion. That is the precise conditions under which the nominal exchange rate and the terms of trade are equivalent and thus interchangeable. But there is no reason to expect the ratio of the CPI's to be constant, in which case the nominal exchange rate and real exchange rates will no longer be interchangeable or equivalent.

If, as we believe, inflation is a monetary phenomenon, to analyze the impact of a devaluation on the terms of trade, the trade balance, employment, and real GDP growth, we need to introduce money into the framework that we have been developing. The determinants of the underlying inflation rate drive the nominal exchange rate, the price of one currency in terms of another, while the real variables determine the terms of trade, the number of foreign goods that a unit of the domestic good fetches.

To simplify the analysis, we shall make a couple of strong and simplifying assumptions regarding the role of money. The first assumption is that inflation is purely a monetary phenomenon. With that in mind, we then specify the money demand, Md, function as:

$$\text{Md} = (1/v)*P*Y \tag{14.2}$$

where v denotes the velocity of money, P is the price level measured by the consumer basket, and Y the economy's real GDP.

Economic Disturbances and Equilibrium in an Integrated Global Economy. http://dx.doi.org/10.1016/B978-0-12-813993-6.00014-3

And we specify the money supply, Ms, function as:

$$Ms = B^* m \qquad (14.3)$$

where B denotes the monetary base and m is the banking system's money multiplier.

Combining the two previous equations, the monetary equilibrium can be described as:

$$(B^* m)^* v = P^* Y \qquad (14.4)$$

The information in the equation can be rearranged to solve for the price level:

$$P = ((B^* m)^* v) / Y \qquad (14.5)$$

The previous equation is fairly general and can accommodate different points of views regarding the causes and effects of changes in the underlying inflation rate. For example, the product of the monetary base, B, times the money multiplier, m, denotes the quantity of money circulating in the economy, Money of Zero Maturity (MZM). The equation also shows that, all else the same, increases in the quantity of money lead to a higher price level. That increases in the real GDP, Y, lead to a decline in the price level. The formulation need not assume that the velocity of money is constant; we have to allow for shifts in the demand for money or changes in the velocity of money, but more on this later on.

The dynamic version of the previous equation can be written as:

$$\pi = \beta + \mu - \eta \qquad (14.6)$$

where π denotes the rate of change of the price level or inflation rate, β denotes the growth of the monetary base, η the real GDP growth rate, and μ is a term capturing the changes in the money multiplier and the velocity of money, that is, net shifts in money demand.

THE NOMINAL EXCHANGE RATE

The exchange rate measures the relative value of two currencies. As the value of each currency is reflected by its purchasing power, it follows that the rate of change of an exchange rate reflects the differences purchasing power or changes in the nominal rates of returns across different economies. In turn, the nominal rates of returns are the sum of two different components—inflation and the real rates of returns.

Depending on the organization of the monetary system, as we will show later on, the nominal exchange rate may reflect changes in the terms of trade (T), see Eq. (14.1'). This is certainly the case under a floating exchange rate system, where the exchange rate is determined by the relative demand for the currencies. So according to our framework (as we showed in Part II, Chapter 9), a favorable change in the terms of trade is associated with a higher rate of return in the country relative to the rest of the world, a capital inflow, and an increase in the real GDP relative to the rest of the world. In turn, the other country experiences a capital outflow, a slower growth rate, and a slower stock market appreciation. All of these effects point to an increase in the demand for the currency experiencing an improvement in the terms of trade vis-a-vis the rest of the world. In short, all else the same, the nominal exchange rate appreciates to reflect the terms of trade.

Exchange rate changes jointly reflect changes in the differential inflation and/or real rate of return across the different economies. Viewed this way, there are two possible pure drivers of the exchange rate:

- A rising/falling inflation differential, that is, changes in (Foreign CPI in Local Currency/US CPI in $)
- A rising/falling real return differential, that is, changes in T

The fluctuations in the exchange rates are a weighted average of these two effects. As the inflation rate and/or the real rate of returns differential have a different effect on the relative valuations of fixed income and equity instruments, it behooves investors to determine the source and nature of the exchange rate fluctuations. Put another way, the investor has what is commonly known as a signal extraction problem.

We contend that an analysis of the economic policy response to the shocks, as well as knowledge of the organization of the monetary system, can be useful in solving the signal extraction problem. Also, as the signal extraction problem consists of assigning weights to the two alternative sources of exchange rate fluctuations, once the signal extraction problem is solved, we can then move on to assigning relative weights or importance to the inflation and real return to develop an exchange rate-based investment strategy.

FLOATING EXCHANGE RATES, PURCHASING POWER PARITY, AND THE TERMS OF TRADE

Let's return to our $2 \times 2 \times 2$ world of Lakeland and Westland. Initially we assume that people in Lakeland only use pesos in their everyday transactions, while the people of Westland only use notes as their currency. In formal and technical terms, initially we assume that there is no currency substitution across the two economies. Initially, we assume that this is the result of legal tender restrictions strictly enforced in each of the economies. Here we are making explicit what is basically an implicit assumption in many economics books dealing with international relations and the balance of payments.

The assumption of zero substitutability or lack of use of other countries' currencies in domestic transaction means that the demand for each currency is solely based on the demand of local residents, that is, domestic demand for the currency, while the supply, the ability to print and increase the quantity of money, is at least for the time being presumed to be controlled by the central bank.

We have already shown that under the assumptions of free mobility and profit maximization, arbitrage insures that the peso price of each commodity will be the same across localities. The same can be said about the notes price of each commodity. Simply put, purchasing power parity (PPP) will hold across each and every commodity in question. Next, if we assume, as we have so far, that there are no relative price changes, that is, changes in the terms of trade, then we can show that the PPP relationship will hold even when we apply it to each of the economies' CPI.

In its dynamic version, the PPP equation can be written as:

$$\pi_p = \pi_n + \mathcal{E} \tag{14.7}$$

where π_p is the rate of change in domestic prices, that is, Lakeland's inflation rate in pesos, π_n is the inflation rate in Westland notes, and $\mathcal{E}$ is the rate of change in the exchange rate that allows the conversion of notes into pesos, that is, the exchange rate depreciation rate. Eq. (14.7) shows that the country with the higher inflation rate will experience currency depreciation equal to the inflation rate differential.

Substituting Eq. (14.6) into Eq. (14.7) and rearranging terms, one can solve for an expression denoting the determinants of the changes in the nominal exchange rate.

$$\mathcal{E} = (\beta_1 - \beta_w) - (\eta_1 - \eta_w) + (\mu_1 - \mu_w) \tag{14.8}$$

The first term in parenthesis shows that all else the same, whenever the Lakeland money growth exceeds the Westland money growth, the peso depreciates. The second term shows that, if Lakeland GDP grows faster than Westland, the peso will tend to appreciate. The third term captures the effects of changes in the velocity of money and/or the money multiplier in the various economies, which up to this point we have assumed to be exogenous.

The terms of trade, T, is defined as the price of one country's exports in terms of the other, say the price of wine in terms of cheese. In our earlier installment of the global perspective, we showed that when the terms of trade do not change, the interest rate parity (IRP) and PPP hold at all times and the real rate of returns is equalized across countries. Under this scenario, there is no need for global investing. One can get the same rate of return at home as one can get elsewhere.

A more interesting case is one where the terms of trade are changing. Let's consider the following scenario: A

favorable term of trade change to Lakeland means that a pound of cheese is now able to get a larger quantity of wine. Another way of saying the same thing is that the rate of return earned by producing cheese increases relative to the rate of return earned in the production of wine. The question is how to modify our analysis to account for the change in terms of trade. We do so in the below equation:

$$\rho_1 = \rho_w + \tau \tag{14.9}$$

The equation can be written as:

$$\tau = (\rho_1 - \rho_w) \tag{14.10}$$

where τ denotes the change in terms of trade between the two economies and $\Delta\rho$ the differences in real rates of returns, the rate of change in the relative price between wine and cheese.

Combining the two versions of IRP developed in our earlier installment of the global framework, we obtain the following relationships:

$$i_1 - i_w = \mathcal{E} = \pi_1 - \pi_w + (\rho_1 - \rho_w) = \pi_1 - \pi_w + \Delta\rho$$

Substituting Eq. (14.9) into the previous equation yields:

$$i_1 - i_w = \mathcal{E} = \pi_1 - \pi_w + \tau \tag{14.11}$$

Rearranging the terms, we get an expression for the changes in terms of trade:

$$\tau = \mathcal{E} - (\pi_1 - \pi_w) \tag{14.12}$$

Eq. (14.12) provides the following insight: violations of PPP reflect changes in the terms of trade of an economy, τ. An appreciation over and above the nominal exchange rate appreciation, or the real exchange rate, reflects an increase in τ. The real rate of return of the exports relative to import and import competing products at home.

To summarize, it is the deviations from PPP that reflect the terms of trade changes and the corresponding rates of return differentials across countries. Therefore if devaluation is to have a real effect on the economy, it must be associated with deviations in the PPP. We contend that only real variables or variables that affect the real economy, such as tax rates or technological changes, can cause changes in the exchange rate over and above the PPP fluctuations. Thus netting the inflation rate differential from the exchange rate changes gives us an estimate of the countries' terms of trade changes

CURRENCY MANIPULATION

Let's now consider the effect of a deliberate monetary devaluation by a country's central bank. Our favorite illustration is to assume that the central bank declares that from a certain point forward a quarter will be called a "new dollar." Obviously, the net effect of the action is that people will quadruple the prices of goods and services quoted in the new dollars and will carry on as if nothing happened. The price of haircuts in terms of corn (i.e., the terms of trade) will remain unchanged, so will the production of haircuts and corn, and the volume of corn imported. The only thing changing as a result of the new dollar is that the domestic inflation will rise by the amount of the devaluation, prices will quadruple, and PPP will hold.

Yet in spite of the previous argument, according to street lore, devaluation gives the devaluing country an advantage over its competitors. The logic goes as follows: let's say that Lakeland devalues the peso. Presumably the devaluation of the peso makes the price of the Lakeland exports, that is, cheese, less expensive to the residents of Westland and the imports from Westland, that is, wine, more expensive to the residents of Lakeland [1].

Let's follow the logic of this analysis to show that, in most cases, it is an incomplete analysis. The same logic used before suggests that wine has become also relatively more expensive for the Westland residents and cheese has become relatively cheaper for Lakeland's residents.

Now let's evaluate what happens to the global demand for wine and cheese. As the relative price of cheese declines in both markets, it follows that the demand for cheese will increase in both markets; hence the global demand for cheese will rise. On the other hand, the relative price of wine has increased in both markets; hence the demand for wine will decline in each of the two markets. Therefore the global demand for wine will fall.

Facing a global glut for wine and a global shortage for cheese, what should happen to the prices? The answer is that the price of cheese rises, while the price of wine declines, until both markets clear and once again reach equilibrium. Where will that be?

If the devaluation has no impact on the production process, technology dictates the way and extent to which resources will be transferred from one activity to another, generating a tradeoff between wine and cheese.

The marginal rate of transformation simply is the equilibrium terms of trade. If the terms of trade remain unchanged, then there is no change in the global equilibrium and the devaluation only results in an inflation differential between the two economies. That is what Eq. (14.7) tells us.

A devaluation that solely alters the relative inflation rate will have no real effect on the economy. This yields some interesting insight for those who advocate currency manipulation and evaluation as a mean to alter the terms of trade. If as we assumed at the beginning, money is only a veil, then devaluation will be futile. It will not have a real effect and all the devaluing country will be left is a rising inflation rate in both absolute and relative terms.

TERMS OF TRADE CHANGES, THE WEALTH EFFECT, AND THE TRANSFER PROBLEM

Given the equilibrium conditions, we proceed to consider the components of the global equilibrium, the national trade balances of Lakeland and Westland.

We focus on the income effect of the changes in the terms of trade. We know that Lakeland's output is relatively intensive in the production of cheese while Westland is relatively intensive in the production of wine. Hence, a terms of trade change that increases the price of cheese in terms of wine mean that a unit of cheese will get more wine than before.

A switch in the terms of trade in favor of Lakeland has a positive income or wealth effect not captured in the equilibrium conditions previously described. The reason for this is that the wealth effect washes out. Lakeland's gain represents Westland's loss. The best way to think about it is that the relative price change affects a transfer of wealth from Westland to Lakeland [2]. This is a zero-sum game in the aggregate as one country's increase in demand for goods and services is offset by the other country's decrease in demand. The transfer however matters a great deal for the individual countries and their international accounts.

As Lakeland overall production is by assumption cheese intensive, we have established that Lakeland will be a net exporter of cheese and an importer of wine. The terms of trade effect will lead to an increase in the consumption of goods, cheese, and wine, as well as an increase in the demand for "leisure." The supply of factors of production for market-related activities will decrease. Lakeland's consumption of both cheese and wine will increase while the production of both cheese and wine will tend to decline. In other words, Lakeland's exports of cheese will decline while its imports of wine will increase. In short, the trade balance will deteriorate.

The terms of trade effects mean that the relative price of cheese and the returns of the factors intensive in the production of cheese will rise. As Lakeland's factor endowments are the factors intensive in the production of cheese, Lakeland's income will increase by a larger percent than the income from Westland. Also, as the equilibrium conditions point to an overall increase in the relative price and quantity of cheese produced, it is not difficult to establish that global GDP measured in cheese units has increased. Although cheese production rises in both economies, the relative intensity of the factors across the two economies suggests that Lakeland's income rises by a larger percentage amount than Westland's.

The increase in the relative price of cheese means that the factor intensive in the production of cheese will experience a magnified increase in its returns [3]. The returns of the factor intensive in cheese production will increase in percentage terms more than increase in the relative price of cheese. The market capitalization of the factor intensive in the production of cheese will increase relative to the market capitalization intensive in the production of wine. The stock market of the country intensive in the production of cheese will rise relative to that of the country intensive in wine production.

The previous analysis suggests that politicians who spend their time worrying about currency manipulations are barking up the wrong tree. Currency manipulation does not affect the trade balance; it only affects the inflation rate differential. Hence, currency manipulators, those who weaken their currencies in an attempt to gain a trade advantage, are rewarded with a higher inflation rate.

The country initiating a currency devaluation counter measure will, in the long run, reduce domestic output, reduce market valuations, as well as reduce access to cheaper and perhaps superior goods. All of this lowers their constituency's well-being. Getting into a trade war in response to a currency manipulation only makes everyone worse off.

A SIGNAL EXTRACTION PROBLEM

One point that many people misunderstand and confuse on this topic is that an inflation rate differential as well as a terms of trade change can both cause and exchange rate fluctuation. However, the reverse is not necessarily true. A monetary devaluation has no impact on the technology and/or on profit maximization; these two dictate the way in which resources are allocated in an economy, and as such a society's choice of technology and the economic desire for profit maximization will determine the relative price among the different goods which is the terms of trade. Hence, devaluation will (in the long run) have no real impact on the economy. Therefore making inferences from nominal exchange rate fluctuations are analogous to reversing the deduction process to identify the changes.

Reversing the deduction process will result in the inference of one of two possible outcomes. The first possible outcome will be to infer a change in the terms of trade with real implications for the economy. The second possibility is to infer that a pure inflation rate differential has taken place.

Yet a casual reading of the financial press and according to many politicians' statements, exchange rate fluctuations seem to always be attributed to a change in the terms of trade or a change in competitiveness. That is, however, not always the case [4].

The source of the confusion is that at times changes in the exchange rate do measure changes in the terms of trade (i.e., real exchange rate changes). At other times, the exchange rate changes only reflect relative inflation rates. This is the classic signal extraction problem. The investor needs to know how to distinguish between these two types of shocks. Knowledge of the nature of the shock goes a long way to help understand the impact of the exchange rate change on the economy.

Additional help in the identification process is provided by Eq. (14.11):

$$i_1 - i_w = \epsilon = \pi_1 - \pi_w + \tau$$

The equation allows us to decompose the exchange rate fluctuations into its real exchange rate or terms of trade components and its nominal exchange rate component. The latter provides with information regarding the inflation rate differential while the former provides us with information regarding the real rates of return differentials.

The decomposition into these two components is quite useful and can become the basis for a global or international investment strategy that focuses on nominal returns as well as on real rates of return differentials across regions. The investment implications for the nominal exchange rate fluctuations are straightforward. A country with a depreciating currency will have the higher inflation rate. Fixed income obligations that are not indexed for inflation will underperform those of the countries with the appreciating currencies; the longer the maturity of the instruments, the worse the performance.

The implications for the relationship between the fluctuations in the nominal exchange rate and the relative stock returns are a bit different than the one we just described for the relative performance of fixed income instruments.

In the absence of an unindexed tax system, equities are likely to be an inflation hedge. As a result of a nominal shock, stocks will rise in proportion to the inflation rate. However, under a progressive tax system, the profits of corporations will be overstated and, as a result, the effective corporate tax rates will rise. Hence under an unindexed tax code, stocks in the countries with the depreciating currency may underperform those of the countries with the relative appreciation.

References

[1] Alexander (1952) provides an interesting review of the elasticities and absorption approach. Notice that in either model if the devaluation is to improve the trade balance, it must have a real effect.Alexander S. Effects of a devaluation on a trade balance. Staff Papers – Int. Monetary Fund 1952;2(2):263–78.

[2] Originally it was the result of war reparations, but it can be the results on wealth transfer or redistribution form one nation to another. The issue focuses on a financial transfer of wealth between countries that necessitates adjustments in expenditures, production, and relative prices that collectively comprise the transfer problem. See Bhagwati JN, Brecher RA, Hatta T. The generalized theory of transfers and welfare. Am Econ Rev 1983;73:606–18.

[3] Stolper WF, Samuelson PA. Protection and real wages. Rev Econ Stud 1941;9:58–73.

[4] Steil B, Smith E. The Trump-Sanders China syndrome. Wall Street J 2016;A13.

15

Exchange Rates, Devaluations, and the Terms of Trade

The CBO said that it expects net exports to contribute to US economic growth over the next two years. That's because growth, on average, will be stronger abroad and because "the exchange value of the dollar… will remain low, keeping the relative prices of imports high for US households and businesses and the relative prices of US exports low for foreign buyers." [1]

The earlier quote, from a *Wall Street Journal* article, represents both the conventional wisdom and a large fraction of mainstream economists' views regarding the effects of the foreign exchange value of the US dollar. Taken at face value, the quote can be used to derive some empirically testable implications regarding the trade balance. According to the quote, a weaker dollar keeps the relative price of imports high, which results in lower imports. Similarly, a weaker dollar keeps the relative price of exports low for foreign buyers, resulting in higher exports. These results allow us to conclude that a weaker dollar results in an improvement in the trade balance. This is an empirically testable implication.

The logic is impeccable if one buys into the explicit and implicit assumptions in the quote. The key assumption made in the earlier quote is that the weaker dollar makes the price of imports high and the price of exports low. We will agree with the earlier quote, if in fact the weaker dollar makes the price of imports high and of exports low. This is nothing more than the so-called beggar-thy-neighbor policies under which one country attempts to remedy its economic problems by means that tend to worsen the economic problems of other countries.

Under the beggar-thy-neighbor policy scenario there is the belief that a decline in the foreign exchange value of the dollar will more than likely argue will improve the competitive position of the country with the depreciating currency [2]. Hence it is not surprising that trading partners of a country with a weakening currency may become suspicious of the country's policies and may take actions to offset any perceived advantage gained by the country with the depreciating currency.

There are many policies at the disposal of the countries experiencing a currency appreciation that they may adopt to arrest the perceived loss and thus the perceived loss of competitiveness due to another country deliberated weakening of its currency. One possible course of action may be to take action to reverse the exchange rate change by affecting its own devaluation. However, this strategy could easily degenerate into a currency war of competitive devaluations. Another possible course of action may be to designate a country a "currency manipulator" and impose countervailing duties equivalent to the amount that the currency manipulator is undervalued by.

In theory, the countervailing duties will offset the advantages gained by the offending country currency manipulation. Again, this strategy is not free of dangers. It could degenerate into a trade war that hurts commerce. That would eliminate the gains of trade both in production and consumption for the different economies of the world. The economic well-being of the world economy unambiguously declines and in some cases it may have dire consequences. The Smoot–Hawley Tariffs are commonly cited as the classic example of how rising trade restrictions and the corresponding retaliatory actions can contribute to a global depression [3].

THE EQUIVALENCE BETWEEN CURRENCY MANIPULATION AND COUNTERVAILING DUTIES

The designation of a country as a currency manipulator is a serious matter. Once the country is designated a currency manipulator, the injured country will take steps to remedy the injury. Hence in many cases, it requires domestic legislation and then cooperation of international organizations such as the World Trade Organization (WTO) and its member countries.

A general outline of the US process is as follows: the US Treasury Department, in consultation with the International Monetary Fund, analyzes the exchange rate policies of foreign countries. Semiannual reports are due April 15 and October 15. The reports examine whether countries are manipulating their currency's exchange rate with the US dollar for purposes of gaining unfair competitive advantage in international trade. If manipulation is found, the Treasury Secretary initiates negotiations with such foreign countries on an expedited basis, in the International Monetary Fund or bilaterally, for the purpose of ensuring that such countries regularly and promptly adjust the rate of exchange between their currencies and the United States dollar. In cases where such negotiations would have a serious detrimental impact on vital national economic and security interests, the Treasury Secretary must notify leaders of the Senate Banking Committee and the House of Representatives' Financial Services Committee of his decision.

The currency manipulator designation triggers a priority investigation from the US Commerce Department as to whether the undervaluation is an unfair subsidy for that country's exports at the expense of US industry. It must then impose import duties to counteract the subsidy. Treasury is required to immediately consult with

all countries with misaligned currencies and engage the International Monetary Fund in priority cases. After 90 days of the designated country's failure to make appropriate policies, the United States must incorporate the currency undervaluation into its dumping calculations for products from that country. Federal purchases of goods and services from the country would be prohibited unless the country is a member of the World Trade Organization's Government Procurement Agreement. The US President could put the process on hold after the initial 90 days of inaction if he determined that it would harm national security or the economic interests of the United States, but this must be explained and could be overridden by a congressional disapproval resolution.

After 360 days of failure to adopt appropriate policies, the US Trade Representative must request WTO dispute settlement consultations with the designated country. The US Treasury would be required to consult with the Federal Reserve and other central banks to consider remedial intervention in currency markets.

WHY TARIFFS MAY FAIL

A declaration in favor of imposing countervailing tariffs against countries that "unfairly" keep their exchange rate artificially low is not only a complicated and lengthy process as discussed earlier, but it is also an economically flawed view of trade policy. A key assumption in the analysis is that currency devaluation is equivalent to a country enacting an export subsidy. Later on, we will argue that such reasoning is fallacious, but for now let's see where that assumption takes us. Let's be blunt and focus on the main target of most recent a declaration against unfair exchange rate management, the country is none other than mainland China.

The facts are that China has a large positive trade balance with the United States and if one takes a mercantilist view of the world, the trade balance represents exports of jobs to China. The mercantilists would argue that if the United States found a way to restrict the inflow of goods and services from China, perhaps these goods would be manufactured here. Singling out all the goods from a particular country may cause some problems with the WTO. Also, the enactment of the restriction could allow other country to impose retaliatory trade actions. However, we contend that even if the countervailing duties were allowed by the WTO and the imposition of duties without retaliatory actions by the counterparty, we believe the countervailing duties would fail.

Let's see why even if the United States was successful in eliminating the flow of Chinese goods into the US markets, the policy may still fail. If there were other regions in the world manufacturing the same goods, say other emerging nations, as well as other regions of the world consuming those goods, say Europe, the taxes on Chinese imports would only serve to alter the patterns of trade. Here is how it would work, China would now export to Europe and the other emerging markets who previously exported to Europe would now export their goods to the United States. No change in employment would take place and the only impact of the policy would be to increase the transaction/transportation costs of shipping the goods and services to the new markets.

The only way the tariff would be completely effective is if the rest of the world went along with the United States and imposed similar trade restrictions against Chinese goods. One can argue that some of these worldwide measures have had some degree of political success. Two examples commonly used are South Africa during its apartheid days and the Iran embargo. However, the latter is a chapter that has yet to be written completely. Time will tell whether the recent Iran deal was a good one that made the world economy safer and more prosperous.

If the world successfully enacts broad global tariffs against the Chinese goods, then and only then, would the flow of Chinese goods stop? If one country did not go along, that country could become the conduit for the transshipping. Again, this evokes memories of some countries facing global embargoes partially circumventing the restrictions. When there is a profit to be made, some people or countries may be tempted to play along and evade the embargo. Incentives do matter. In this case, the patterns of trade would be more complicated but to the extent that trade is still fungible nothing would change. Thus, the tariff policy requires the complete cooperation of the rest of the world, which is an unlikely outcome. Even then, it isn't clear that the US production of the goods being affected by the trade action would increase. Who is to say that the next lowest cost producer, another emerging nation, would not fill the gap? In that case, the world would end up paying a slightly higher cost, for a lower quality product. Everyone would be worse off.

THE PROTECTIONIST CASE FOR EXCHANGE RATE MANAGEMENT

The direct trade action is full of perils and that is why the exchange rate appears to offer a better alternative. The theory being that all else being equal, a higher exchange rate will make the price of the Chinese goods more expensive and as a result they would be exporting less to the rest of the world. There would be no leakage or fungibility to deal with. All the United States has to make sure of is that the emerging markets do not pick up the slack. Once again, the exchange rate comes to the rescue; the solution would be to force each and every nation with a trade surplus with the United States to revalue

its currency. In this case, the United States would just be pursuing the traditional beggar-thy-neighbor policies of the past. The difference being that, if the US Treasury has its way, rather than devalue the US dollar, the US Treasury would force every other country to revalue their currencies and thus, according to the mercantilist views, accomplish the same objective.

The equivalence between the trade restriction and currency appreciation is a very seductive equivalence. If the domestic prices in China do not change, and this is a big if, a currency appreciation will have the effect of increasing the price of Chinese goods in the world market. In other words, the effect will be identical to a tariff increase by the rest of the world. This is a much more elegant solution to the problem as it is easier to monitor. All one has to look is at the exchange rate to determine whether China or any other country is "protecting" against the rest of the world. The only disadvantage of this approach is that it is the foreign government who will collect the "tariff" revenues.

There are several other problems with this view of the world. If the exporting nations could arbitrarily raise their exchange rate/terms of trade in their favor, it would mean they have some monopoly power. Then one would question why didn't they use it before? Another equally important question is what is the revenue-maximizing tariff/exchange rate? The classic example of this was Organization of Petroleum Producing Countries (OPEC); it did exercise its monopoly power when it could. However, as Ronald Reagan showed, deregulation and market forces produced a lot of oil in the non-OPEC countries and allowed for the creation of substitutes in the process weakening OPEC monopoly power. OPEC has not been the same since the Gipper deregulated oil prices [4]. Reagan showed us that good economics makes good politics.

THE CASE AGAINST DEVALUATION OR REVALUATION

Another problem with the protectionist view is that as we have a trade deficit, it follows that in the end if the United States has its way, the rest of the world will be forced to reevaluate their currencies against the United States. The big question is what will the reevaluation of the foreign currencies bring? Well, the history of the 1970s tells us that a devaluation does not have any impact on the trade balance, the only effect of a devaluation is an increase in the differential inflation rate between the area with the depreciating currency vis-a-vis the rest of the world.

A simple exercise that we have already discussed will show our point. If all of a sudden the United States decided to call each quarter a dollar, what would happen to the prices of different goods? The answer is that prices would quadruple. Unless the change fools someone in currency, production and consumption will not change.

The reason a currency devaluation/revaluation has no effect on the trade balance is because it has no impact on the real economy. All we know is that as a result of revaluation of the rest of the world's currencies, the US inflation rate will increase relative to the rest of the world. Whether the rest of the world experiences deflation or the United States experiences a rise in the inflation rate depends on the adjustment process determined by the organization of the monetary system.

The one thing we are certain of is that the trade balance will not change, and that means that the protectionist pressures remain. At that point, the mercantilists will argue that since the devaluation did not work, we will have to affect the policies through the US commercial policy. The pressure to enact direct trade restrictions will be enormous. This scenario is not too farfetched if we follow the protectionist path to its logical conclusion. The United States will then proceed to enact tariff increases much like it did with steel to capture the electoral votes of a couple of states [5]. The static thinking may lead to an interesting political calculus, however the dynamic thinking should point out that the consumer, as well as downstream and upstream users of the protected items, will also suffer. the employment in those industries will also suffer. This is one case where good economics also makes good politics. The free market policies have served the United States well. All we need is a clear voice articulating the economic message.

MORE ON THE CASE AGAINST THE NOMINAL EXCHANGE RATE

During the last thirty-five years, with the exception of a couple of visible cycles, the foreign exchange value of the dollar published by the Saint Louis Fed has trended downward and prior to the Financial Crisis it lost about 25% (Fig. 15.1) [6]. Based on the theory outlined in the previous paragraph, the following forecast is easily derived: the decline in the dollar would lead to an improvement in the US trade balance.

Anyone making decisions on these two insights would have been dead wrong. The US trade balance worsened during this time period (Fig. 15.2). The data clearly suggest that something is wrong. Either the theory or the indicator is wrong. Which of these two is the culprit? That is the subject of the next few paragraphs.

EXPANDING THE VIEW

A declining exchange rate leads to an increase in the domestic price of imported products and that in turn leads to an increase in the domestic inflation rate. The devaluationists who ignore this effect argue that while that may be true, imports make a small fraction of the domestic price index and thus have a minimal impact on the Consumer Price Index (CPI)-based domestic inflation. Yet the critics of deliberate monetary devaluation argue that, at the margin, the higher price of imports lead to an increase in the price of import competing goods. The higher price increases incentives to produce more of the import competing goods, and that is good since it improves the trade balance.

Unfortunately, that is not all. To produce more, it has to attract factors of production. The industry does so by paying higher wages and earning a higher rate of return. As it attracts factors of production, fewer factors will be available to produce the exported goods. Exports will decline. The competition for factors of production from the import competing sector will force the export sector to also pay higher wages and salaries. This will increase the production costs and reduce the export sector's profitability and competitiveness.

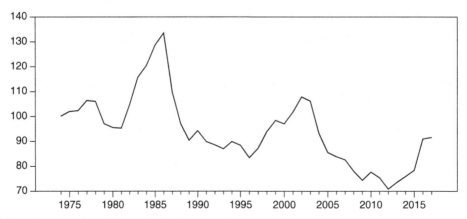

FIGURE 15.1   Foreign exchange value of the dollar (major currencies).

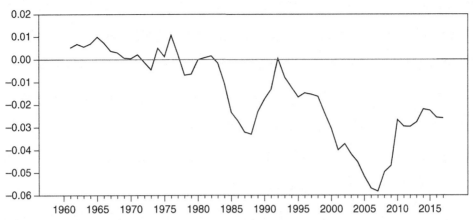

FIGURE 15.2   **US trade balance as a percent of GDP.**

The logic of the argument suggests that as long as the price of the imported products are out of line with their domestic substitutes, resources will be moved to the import competing sector, reducing the country's exports. And to attract the necessary resources to produce the import competing goods, wages and salaries will also increase. The end process is one where no change in the trade balance takes place and the only effect of the declining exchange rate is a higher domestic inflation rate.

THE BIG MAC STANDARD

The critical point made in the previous paragraphs is that the domestic inflation rate can and will offset the competitive advantage of a depreciating currency. Hence whether currency depreciation alters a country's competitive position depends on whether the country's inflation rate adjusts to offset any competitive gain produced by the currency depreciation. The true measure of changes in competitive position is the real exchange rate or terms of trade.

Using the nominal exchange rate as a proxy for the terms of trade/real exchange rate carries with it the implicit assumption that the inflation rate or domestic prices have not offset the exchange rate fluctuations. That may be true some of the times and not true at other times. While we concede that adjusting the exchange rate for the cost of living may be additional work, we have to question the use of a proxy that may or may not give the correct answer at all times.

The methodology for adjusting for the cost of living has been popularized by *The Economist* in its famous Big Mac standard. The magazine reported in the back of its issues the price of a Big Mac in local currency converted back into US dollars and compared it to the US price of a Big Mac. Essentially the Big Mac index is nothing more than an application of the terms of trade equation re-

ported in earlier reports. In performing the calculations, *The Economist* was giving the reader a quick and dirty way to determine relative costs in US dollars across the world's economies and thus a measure of the economies' competitiveness.

The Big Mac is just a single commodity, and while it may be representative of an economy, a more precise estimation of the relative costs is needed. Fortunately we were able to obtain a price index for the rest of the world going back to the early 1970s, call this variable P_f. We also know that the Federal Reserve Bank of Saint Louis publishes a broad-based index measuring the foreign exchange value of the dollar, E, as well as a measure of US prices, P_{us}. The rest of the world's CPI is readily available at the Organization for Economic Co-operation and Development (OECD) website where a measure of the terms of trade or purchasing power parity index is also readily available Plugging these variables in the terms of trade equation, we obtain a measure of the US real exchange rate. An easier way may to use the real exchange rate calculations readily available on the Federal reserve Economic Data, St. Louis Fed (FRED) and OECD websites. The data reported in Fig. 15.3A and B show the real exchange rate based on the FRED and OECD data. While there are some minor differences between the real and nominal exchange rate series, they clearly provide different set of information than the nominal exchange rate. The FRED dollar index, Fig. 15.1, has trended down while the FRED real exchange rate shows no secular trend, Fig. 15.3A.

One of our concern regarding the use of the FRED real foreign exchange value of the dollar is that the values are calculated on a trade weighted index. Such an index would give bigger weight to the traded commodities vis-a-vis the nontraded ones. To capture the impact of the nontraded commodities on the terms of trade, the OECD calculates the real exchange rate using the countries share of the world GDP as their weight. The results of OECD calculations are reported in Fig. 15.3B.

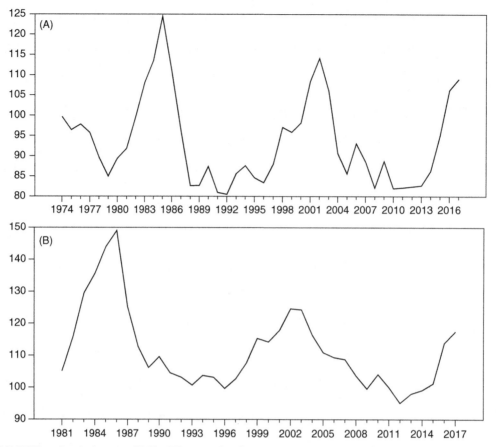

FIGURE 15.3   (A) FRED real exchange rate. (B) The US terms of trade.

THE REAL EXCHANGE RATE OR TERMS OF TRADE AS AN INDICATOR

The Big Mac theory is straight forward. An increase in the Big Mac, or real exchange rate, means a loss of competitiveness. Based on the theory outlined in the previous paragraphs, two forecasts immediately come to mind: an increase in the Big Mac index or terms of trade would lead to a deterioration of the US competitive position and a deterioration of the US trade balance.

Anyone making decisions on these two insights would have been right on the money. First, we know that the US trade balance has worsened during this time period. The data clearly suggest that the terms of trade or real exchange rate provides the correct forecast. All of this suggests that the nominal foreign exchange value of the dollar is not the best proxy for the changes in competitive position. The real exchange rate takes into account differences in the domestic CPI and thus provides a much more accurate measure, as is apparent from the data presented in Figs. 15.4 and 15.5A and B. The foreign exchange value of the dollar (Fig. 15.4), the real exchange rate (Fig. 15.5A), and the terms of trade (Fig. 15.5B) to a different degree capture the cyclical fluctuations in the

terms of trade and/or exchange rate. This suggests that foreign exchange value of the dollar may be a reasonable proxy for the cyclical changes in an economy's competitive position. One way to justify the use of the nominal exchange rate is that it is much easier to calculate and it is readily available. The question is how much do we sacrifice in accuracy? And then if we do the calculations, should we use the readily available trade figures or the more tedious GDP of the countries to calculate the real exchange rates? Put another way, the choice between the indicators is one of expedience versus accuracy. The only way to determine whether it is worthwhile to do the extra work is by calculating the opportunity cost of using the inferior and easier to obtain indicators.

THE BETTER AND BROADER MEASURE

The nominal exchange rate is the appropriate measure of the real exchange rate or terms of trade when the CPI remains unchanged. The nominal exchange rate and real exchange rate provide the same signal only if the CPI changes do not offset the nominal exchange rates. Our theory suggests a simple testable implication.

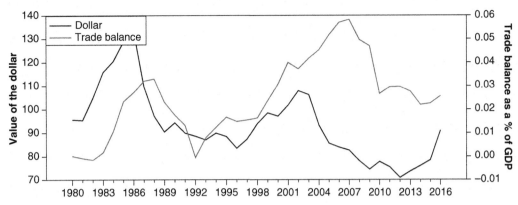

FIGURE 15.4　The foreign exchange value of the dollar versus the negative of the trade balance as a percent of GDP.

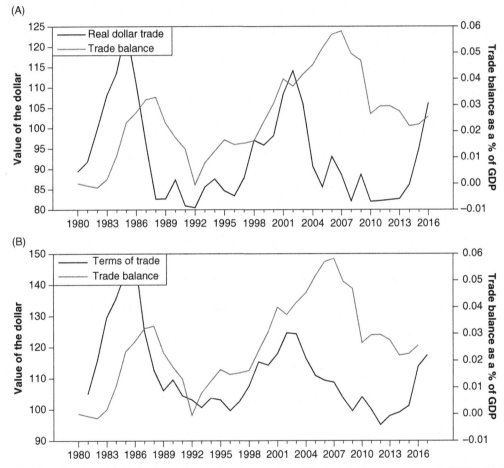

FIGURE 15.5　(A) The real exchange value of the dollar versus the negative of the trade balance as a percent of GDP. (B) The terms of trade versus the negative of the trade balance as a percent of GDP.

When the real and nominal exchange rates diverge, the terms of trade or real exchange rate provides the correct signal.

The data presented in Fig. 15.1 identify two major exchange rate cycles—both are an inverted V. We can also see that in 1979, the index is higher than it is at the end of 2014. So, the data clearly show a slight downward secular trend. In contrast, the Real Exchange Rate Index as calculated by FRED and based on trade flows, Fig. 15.3A, shows the same two exchange rate cycles. In this regard, both the real and nominal exchange rate cycles coincide in identifying major changes in the US terms of trade during the 1980s and the 1990s. However there is one big difference, the FRED real exchange rate computation removed the downward trend that the nominal exchange rate exhibited, now there is no secular trend regarding,

Fig. 15.3A. As the countries GDP's share of the world is used as the weights to calculate the terms of trade, we notice that the new series also identifies the cycles previously mentioned with one major difference.

A major difference between the two series has to do with their secular trend. Notice that Fig. 15.1 shows a downward trend while Fig. 15.3A and B shows a sideways movement consistent with the mean reverting hypothesis. Our view is that if adjustment is costly, the initial adjustment will be reflected as a rate of return differential that will elicit capital flows. Overtime the rates of return will adjust to accommodate the capital flows, and in the long run, the economy will return to is long run equilibrium, that is, the initial terms of trade.

These trends generated by the different series are vastly different implications regarding the United States competitiveness. The data also identify some differences regarding the exact timing of the cycles. The Real and Nominal Foreign Exchange Value of the Dollar trend in different direction during part of the time. These differences imply testable implications that we will use to discriminate and assess which of the two measures, the nominal and or the real exchange rate, is the better proxy for the terms of trade.

Figs. 15.4 and 15.5A and B provide additional information as to which of the variables is a better proxy for the terms of trade. Figs. 15.4 and 15.5B clearly show a much tighter relationship between the negative of the trade balance and the real exchange rate dollar index. Now a comparison between the nominal exchange rate and the terms of trade as we have calculated them shows a much tighter relationship between the terms of trade and the trade balance than the nominal exchange rate.

More importantly, the data also show that the correlation is as predicted by the theory. When the terms of trade improve, that is, the real exchange rate increases, the US trade balance as a percent of GDP worsens, that is, the negative of the trade balance rises. The same cannot be said about the dollar index, in which the relationship is not as tight (Fig. 15.4). The data clearly point to our estimates as the appropriate proxy for the terms of trade.

References

[1] CBO: Dollar's Value to Decline Moderately Over the Next Decade, Wall St J, August 24, 2011.
[2] The term coined during the Great Depression. Currency devaluations are considered beggar-thy-neighbor if they are conducted solely for the purpose of boosting the country's exports by making them cheaper for foreigners to buy and therefore increasing the country's global market share. The trading partners may retaliate by devaluing their currency as well. Such a phenomenon, known as competitive devaluation, is an example. It has also been analyzed as an instance of game theory the prisoner's dilemma, each country individually has an incentive to follow such a policy, thereby making everyone worse off.
[3] Canto Victor A. U.S. Trade Policy: history and evidence. CATO J, Winter 1983/1984; 3(3): 679–98.Canto Victor A. The Determinants and Consequences of Trade Restrictions in the U.S. Economy. New York: Praeger Publishing; 1986.
[4] Canto Victor A, Bollman Gerald, Melich Kevin. Oil decontrol: the power of incentives could reduce OPEC's power to boost oil prices. Oil Gas J 1982;80(2):92–101. Canto Victor A, Melich Kevin. Natural gas decontrol: the road to lower energy prices. Public Util Fortnightly 1982;100(9):31–9. Canto Victor A. Fuel use patterns in the United States: the outlook for the 1980s. Oil Gas J 1982;80(34):125–43.
[5] Canto Victor, Laffer Arthur, Eastin Richard. Failure of protectionism: a study of the steel industry. Columbia J World Bus 1982;XVII(4 Winter).
[6] The data is readily available and published by the Federal Reserve Bank of Saint Louis.

16

The Nominal Exchange Rate, the Terms of Trade, and the Economy

Arbitrage tends to insure that the dollar price of any commodity, say a ton of steel, will converge to the local dollar price in the United States. Arbitrageurs compare the price of a ton of steel in local currency and with the use of the exchange rate they convert it to dollar prices and in turn compare to the local dollar price. Absent any transportation costs and any other transaction costs arbitrage insures that any differences in dollar prices are arbitraged away for each and every commodity. If there are no relative price changes among the different commodities, one can invoke the composite goods theorem and treat the CPI as a single commodity. Next, if one is willing to assume that all countries have similar tastes, the local consumer baskets will be similar across countries.

Under these conditions, we can then conclude that arbitrage insures that the dollar price of the CPI will be the same across the different economies. This is nothing more than the Purchasing power parity (PPP), relationship. The dynamic version of this equation shows that the rate of change or the exchange rate reflects the inflation rate differential across any two economies. That is:

$$\epsilon = \pi f - \pi_{us} \quad (16.1)$$

where ϵ denotes the dollar rate of appreciation vis-a-vis the rest of the world and π_f denotes the foreign or rest of the world inflation rate and π_{us} the US inflation rate.

The nominal exchange rate measures the price of one currency in terms of another. That is how many units of the foreign currency will the domestic currency fetch. In the previous example, the exchange rate is used to convert and compare the consumer basket across different countries in a common currency. Then there are the terms of trade. It measures how much of the consumer foreign consumer basket can be purchased with one unit of the local consumer basket. The terms of trade are defined as:

$$T = (\text{Exchange rate} * \text{Foreign CPI} / \text{Domestic CPI}) \quad (16.2)$$

Notice that in the special case where there no transportation costs and the tastes are the same, the consumer baskets tend to be the same and so will the CPI. In that special case notice that the previous equation simplifies to:

$$T = 1 \quad (16.2')$$

Under the perfect mobility assumption, the terms of trade are always constant. The answer is obvious, under the conditions outlined here the traded components

Economic Disturbances and Equilibrium in an Integrated Global Economy. http://dx.doi.org/10.1016/B978-0-12-813993-6.00016-7

are identical baskets; therefore, the terms of trade will always be constant and will never change.

One insight that is commonly overlooked and that may shed some light regarding the terms of trade is what the absence transportation and transaction costs means to the world economy. If the economy is fully integrated, prices are determined by the world demand and supply for the commodity in question. This means that global price changes will induce a common movement along the world economies. The full integration also means that a country's impact on the price of a commodity is directly proportional to the country size in relation to the commodity. While insightful and parsimonious, there are other alternatives. For example, there is no reason to assume that transaction costs and/or transportation costs do exist.

EXPANDING THE FRAMEWORK TO INCLUDE TRANSPORTATION COSTS

In the extreme case where the transportation costs are excessive, it may be unprofitable to arbitrage the differences in prices across localities. The textbook example for such a nontraded goods is haircut services. Under the assumption of large transportation costs and absence of mobility, the local prices of nontraded goods such as haircuts will be determined solely by the intersection of the local or national demand and supply conditions. The rest of the world demand and supply condition and prices will have no direct impact on the local price of the truly nontraded product. The CPI will then consist of goods and services are international traded, that is, goods that face no transportation costs, as well as goods that face prohibitive transportation costs. In that case, the rate of change in the CPI, that is, the domestic inflation rate, is a weighted average of internationally traded goods composite and the nontraded goods composite:

$$\pi = \alpha * \rho + (1-\alpha) * \rho n \qquad (16.3)$$

where α is the share of internationally traded goods in the CPI, ρ is the rate of change of the traded goods prices, ρn is the rate of change of the of nontraded goods relative to the traded goods.

Substituting Eq. (16.3) the augmented inflation into a dynamic version of the terms of trade Eq. (16.2):

$$\tau = (\varepsilon + \pi_{us}) - \pi_f \qquad (16.1')$$

$$\tau = (\varepsilon + \alpha * \rho_{us} + (1-\alpha) * \rho n_{us}) - (\alpha * \rho_f + (1-\alpha) * \rho n_f) \quad (16.4)$$

But we also know that Eq. (16.1) also holds. Substituting that equation into the previous equation we obtain:

$$\tau = (1-\alpha) * (\rho n_{us} - \rho n_f) \qquad (16.4')$$

The terms of trade, Eq. (16.4'), measure the relative price changes among nontraded products in different localities.

Rearranging the terms in Eq. (16.4) yields another interesting way of interpreting the different relationships among the variables. It yields a broader equation for the nominal exchange rate:

$$\varepsilon = \tau - (\pi_{us} - \pi_f) \qquad (16.5)$$

WHAT DRIVES THE NOMINAL EXCHANGE RATE?

The previous equation identifies two distinct sources regarding what drives the nominal exchange rate: The terms of trade and inflation rate differential between the two countries.

How the inflation rate differential affects the nominal exchange rate has already been discussed. In a world where there are no transportation costs and goods and factors are perfectly mobile, arbitrage will insure that there are no profits opportunities. That will only be the case if the dollar price of every commodity is the same across the world. That is the PPP proposition.

The terms of trade effects are somewhat different. An improvement in the terms of trade in one country means that the nontraded good can now buy more of the traded commodity. The terms of trade have two distinct effects in the country. One is a net wealth effect that leads to an increase in the aggregate demand for goods and services. The other, terms of trade effect, are that an improving terms of trade means that the rate of return of producing the nontraded commodity rises.

As a result of the increased rates of return, capital and other factors will be attracted from the traded sectors both at home, as well as the rest of the world. As factors of production move from the traded sector, the global traded goods production both at home and abroad tends to decline. The increased domestic demand and decline in domestic production of the traded good means that the country's trade balance will decline. The increased domestic demand for the traded good combined with the increase in demand from the rest of the world means an increase in the world's aggregate demand, and the world price for the current consumption of traded goods vis-a-vis the future will unambiguously increase. That will induce a common effect on output across the different economies. World income and the various national productions of the traded goods will tend to rise by the same proportion.

The increase in the global demand for the traded goods will attract resources form the nontraded sectors in the rest of the world. The end result being that the rising price of the traded goods will induce a common effect on all the countries' GDPs. However, the story with the nontraded sector is a bit different. The rates of return in the nontraded sector will rise above that of the traded goods. In the other country, the opposite will happen; the rate of return will rise by less than that of the traded sector.

Notice that, we have assumed here an initial aggregate demand shock that increases local demand. If instead, we had assumed an aggregate supply shock that increases local supply, effect on the trade balance would be different. Yet even under these circumstances, we would expect the country with the aggregate supply shift to improve its growth rate and profitability relative to the rest of the world. Hence, we would expect the stock market to improve its relative performance.

In conclusion, the terms of trade effect result in:

- A deterioration of the trade balance of the country where the aggregate demand shock produces a favorable terms of trade effect.
- An increase in the global output with the country with the favorable terms of trade effect, experiencing an above-average percentage increase, while the country experiencing the adverse terms of trade effect posting a below-average percentage increase.
- The country with the favorable terms of trade experiences an above-average rate of return, while the country with the adverse terms of trade experiences a below-average rate of return.

DEVALUATION AND TERMS OF TRADE EFFECTS

The relationships described by the nominal exchange rate equation pose some interesting questions and also a simple explanation that contradicts some statements made in the press by pundits and even economists who argue that currency manipulation is a way to alter the trade balance. Once they make the argument, they follow up by suggesting monetary action. For the sake of argument, let's take the case of a deliberate monetary devaluation.

The argument commonly made by the pundits and some policymakers is that a weaker currency will make the country's imports more expensive, while making their exports cheaper. If that is the case, it means that the country will import less and export more; thereby the currency devaluation will result in an improvement in the trade balance.

Implicitly, this argument assumes that a monetary devaluation alters the terms of trade in an adverse manner. Unfortunately, the logic of the argument is incorrect. Let's go back and concede that devaluation may initially make the devaluing country's imports more expensive and its exports cheaper. Let's call the devaluing country's imports M, and the devaluing country's exports X. This way we may be able to keep track of the rest of the world's demand for the two goods.

As the devaluation made the price of M more expensive, the rest of the world will now consume less of the more expensive commodity and more of the now less expensive commodity, X.

The sum of the devaluing country's demand and the rest of the world's demand gives us the worldwide demand for both X and M. The demand for M will decline in both the devaluing country, as well as in the rest of the world. In contrast, the demand for good X will increase in both the devaluing country and the rest of the world. The decline in the global excess demand will result in a lower price for M, while the global excess supply will result in a higher price of X.

Recall that M is nothing more than the devaluing country's imports (our proxy for the rest of the world's price), while X is the price of exports (our proxy for the devaluing country's price level). Simply put, the devaluing country's inflation rate will rise relative to the rest of the world. We contend that if money is a veil, the inflation rate differential will completely offset the impact of the devaluation on the terms of trade. Therefore, a monetary devaluation will have no lasting real effect on the economy. The only lasting effect will be a higher price level.

A SIGNAL EXTRACTION OR A CONCEPTUAL PROBLEM?

If the belief that monetary devaluation leads to an improvement in the terms of trade is a pervasive one, it can lead to the wrong decision making process in policymaking, business, and investment decisions. While, we believe that terms of trade effects cause changes in the nominal exchange rate, the converse is not necessarily true. As we have shown, there is another source of exchange rate changes: differential inflation. Once the investor, policymakers, and business people are aware that there are two possible sources that can cause fluctuations in nominal exchange rate, one can argue that these people have a signal extraction problem. However, we have a much simpler explanation.

As discussed in Eq. (16.5), there are two drivers of the foreign exchange value of the dollar. The first one is the inflation rate differential. The higher the foreign inflation rate relative to the United States, the stronger the

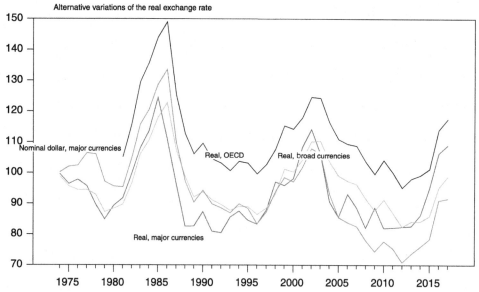

FIGURE 16.1   Value of the dollar against an index of major currencies.

US dollar will be. The second one is the terms of trade. The more a US consumer basket buys of the foreign consumer basket, the stronger the US dollar will be. The rate of change in the foreign exchange value of the dollar consists of the net of these two effects, the real (i.e., changes in the terms of trade) and the monetary (i.e., inflation rate differential).

Now we will discuss how to apportion each of these sources of nominal exchange rate fluctuations. Fortunately, the solution to the problem is readily available. The Federal Reserve Bank of Saint Louis publishes an index of the foreign exchange value of the dollar against major trading partners. In turn international organizations such as the IMF, World Bank, and the OECD publish estimate of the country's economic statistics. Currently we chose to use the OECD data. Most of the data also published the GDP deflator in domestic currency for each of the countries. The ratio of the price deflators' measure the monetary effects and combined with the foreign exchange value of the currency once can calculate the terms of trade or real exchange rate.

Fig. 16.1 provides us a visual representation of the nominal exchange rate and alternative measures of the Real exchange value of the dollar. A casual inspection of Fig. 16.1 shows that the two series are different. Also, the various relationships implied here provide us with some interesting insight. The first one is that if each country's central bank adopted a domestic price rule that kept the local inflation at zero, then the inflation rates in each country would remain at zero at all times. If the inflation rates are the same across countries, then the inflation rate differential would be zero at all times. Eq. (16.5) shows that when the inflation rates are the same across countries, the fluctuations in the terms of trade and exchange

rates will match each other. In contract, when the terms of trade remain unchanged, the only source of exchange rate fluctuations would be the inflation rate differential. Again Eq. (16.5) shows that is the case.

Using this result one can then argue that the differences between the terms of trade and the foreign exchange value of the dollar in Fig. 16.1 would be the cumulative result of the inflation rate differential across the countries ex-the terms of trade. We contend that this differential is in fact the result of monetary policy. Hence, this may provide us with a solution to the signal extraction signal regarding the fluctuations in the nominal exchange rate. We can now decompose the fluctuations in to those caused by the terms of trade and those caused by the monetary rate induced inflation rate differentials. Fig. 16.1 shows the two components of the nominal exchange rate: the two sources of nominal exchange rate fluctuations.

WHAT MOVES THE EXCHANGE RATES AND TERMS OF TRADE?

The information presented in Fig. 16.1 shows that except for the 1970's time period, the terms of trade and nominal exchange rate tend to move together. However, this result may be specific to the sample. Recall that Paul Volcker changed the operating procedures of the Fed a focused on a domestic price rule, presumably targeting a 2% US inflation rate. Since then other countries have also pursued domestic price rules with varying degrees of success eventually their inflation rate converged to the target rate. If the price rule is the prevailing monetary policy, to the extent that these central banks are successful, the inflation rate differential will be relatively constant. This means that the inflation rate differential will not be the source of the exchange rate fluctuations. By process of elimination, we are left with the terms of trade as the main source.

Under the price rule, the bulk of the exchange rate fluctuations will be real or fiscal policy shocks, which are the same variables that impact the terms of trade. Hence, under a domestic price rule scenario, we expect the two variables (the nominal exchange rate and the terms of trade) to move together. That is effectively what we find in the data. This we interpret as a validation of this insight or hypothesis derived for our framework. The price rule makes the signal extraction problem a trivial one. However, under alternative monetary arrangements, the distinction between the terms of trade and monetary shocks will not be an easy one to disentangle.

An important insight derived from all this is that, we can rule out monetary shocks as the source of the exchange rate fluctuations under a price rule. The two real exchange rates inverted versus shown in Fig. 16.1 are intended to capture the full exchange rate cycle caused by the different policy shocks. We can then focus our attention on the real shocks that may impact the terms of trade. Taking a US-centric view of the world, we know that President Reagan lowered US tax rates to 50% from 70%, leaving the after-tax income of a dollar taxed at the highest rate yielding 30 cents on the dollar prior to the tax rate cuts and 50 cents on the dollar after the tax rate cuts. That is a 66% increase in the after-tax income. Not surprisingly, the rate cut produced an increase in asset valuation and a capital inflow. Both contributed to a dollar appreciation over and above the inflation rate differential, that is, terms of trade effect. The fact that it took several years for the dollar to peak even though the tax rate cuts were fully preannounced is consistent with our views that there are significant adjustment costs faced by the economy and the markets. During 1995–2001 time period, the dollar and terms of trade appreciated. That period coincided with the Republicans taking over Congress, the Clinton triangulation, and the Maestro's finest performance. The 1986–88 and 2002–04 time periods coincided with the transition to new tax rates.

THE ECONOMIC PERFORMANCE DURING THE CYCLES

The previous section suggests that by paying attention to the policy changes, one many be able to anticipate the changes in the real exchange rate that drive the real economy relative performance. If one is able to do so, then one can derive a portfolio strategy to take advantage of the impact of the policy changes on the economy and the financial markets. One way to identify the likely changes during the exchange rate and terms of trade cycles is to examine the performance of the different indicators during some of the cycles already identified. Once the data is obtained, we then determine whether the actual performance comports with our framework. If the answer is in the affirmative, then potentially we have the makings of a successful way of analyzing the impact of different policies on the exchange rate and the rest of the economy.

Using the information presented in Fig. 16.1, we identified cycles where the exchange rate and or terms of trade, rose, fell, or stayed flat. The dates for the exchange rate cycles are reported in Table 16.1, while the dates for the terms of trade cycles are reported in Table 16.2.

As already mentioned, it is our view that under a domestic price rule, the nominal exchange rate and the terms of trade will move together. However, when the price rule is not strictly adhered to, then monetary disturbances, according to our framework, will have an impact on the nominal exchange rate and no impact on the terms of trade. Thus, we contend that a failure of the two variables to move together is the result of monetary actions. Looking at the data reported in Tables 16.1 and 16.2, it appears that during the years 1990, 1996, and 2011–13 the two variables did not move in unison.

TABLE 16.1 Dollar Cycles

Period	Cycle
1981–84	Rising
1985–89	Falling
1990–96	Flat
1997–2001	Rising
2002–12	Falling
2013–14	Rising

TABLE 16.2 Terms of Trade Cycles

Period	Cycle
1981–84	Rising
1985–90	Falling
1991–95	Flat
1996–2001	Rising
2001–10	Falling
2011–13	Flat
2014	Rising

In 1990, President Bush went back on his pledge not to raise taxes. 1996 was when triangulation was in full swing and Alan Greenspan is credited with identifying the surge in productivity that began around that time. During both years, the Fed was led by Alan Greenspan, whose Fed attempted to anticipate and accommodate aggregated demand shocks. The Bush administration argued that leading up to the election, the Greenspan Fed was too tight and that may have delayed the economic recovery and cost President Bush his reelection. Mr. Greenspan was clearly correct on the productivity surge and as a result his accommodation was the appropriate one. However, he was certainly wrong on Y2K. Yet looking back, adding the Fed's response in the aftermath of 1987, Greenspan's accommodations were more often right than wrong. In 2010, in part because of the weakness of the recovery, the Bernanke Fed announced a second round of quantitative easing.

The possibilities: The previous discussion suggests that there are four different possibilities about the joint performance of the nominal exchange rate and terms of trade. Two cases involve the nominal exchange rate and terms of trade moving in the same direction (both variables appreciate or depreciate. Then there is the outcome when the two variables move in the opposite direction. In one case, the exchange rate appreciates, while the terms of trade depreciate. The other case is when the exchange rate depreciates, while the terms of trade depreciate.

We have calculated the performance of several macroeconomic indicators during the rising and falling cycles for the nominal exchange rate and terms of trade, as well as the four-possible combination for the joint outcomes of terms of trade and exchange rate fluctuations. As mentioned under a domestic price rule, the real effects will be the only potential disturbances to the overall equilibrium. The real shocks will induce a common movement between the nominal exchange rate and the terms of trade.

The more interesting case is one where the two variables move in opposite directions. These latter cases may allow us to separate and get a sense of the relative impact the monetary effects and or the real effects on the terms of trade and nominal exchange rate.

Table 16.3 summarizes the impact of the monetary and real disturbances on the relative growth rates, stock returns, inflation rate differential, as well as the changes in the terms of trade as a percent of GDP. As we assume that money is a veil, we expect monetary policy to be neutral and thus have no effect on the real variables of the economy. In contrast, those who believe that a devaluation can alter the terms of trade should ignore the first two columns in Table 16.3 and focus solely on the last two columns, irrespective of whether the economic disturbance in question is a monetary or real one.

Table 16.4 reports the performance the developed economies ex-the EMU and the emerging economies relative to the US economy [1]. Notice that we only report the nominal exchange rate cycles and the combined cycles. The terms of trade cycles are not reported because that information is mostly redundant. One can infer or derive most of the results of the terms of trade cycles form the information at hand. For that reason as well as an easier visual representation we decided not to directly report the terms of trade information in Table 16.4.

Looking at the information presented, we find that as one moves from the column reporting the average performance during periods when the foreign currencies depreciate relative to the dollar, column 1, and compare them to the results produced by the periods during which the foreign currencies appreciate relative to the dollar, for both the developed and emerging countries the results point to:

1. A deterioration of the trade balance, for example from to −0.08% form 0.46% for the developed countries in the sample.
2. An improvement in the relative GDP growth rate.
3. An improvement in the PPP adjusted relative GDP growth rate.
4. An improvement in the relative stock returns.

TABLE 16.3   Nominal Exchange Rate and the Terms of Trade Effects

| | Summary of the effects | | | |
| | Exchange rate | | Terms of trade | |
	Depreciation	Appreciation	Depreciation	Appreciation
Trade balance	No change	No change	Improvement	Deterioration
Relative GDP growth	No change	No change	Deterioration	Improvement
Relative GDP growth PPP adjusted	No change	No change	Deterioration	Improvement
Relative stock returns	No change	No change	Deterioration	Improvement
Relative inflation	Higher	Lower	Lower	Higher

TABLE 16.4 Performance of the Developed and Emerging Economies Relative to the United States During Different Exchange Rate and Terms of Trade Cycles

	Foreign exchange rate		Foreign exchange rate and terms of trade both falling both rising	
	Falling	Rising	Falling	Rising
DEVELOPED MARKETS EX-EMU				
Trade balance changes	0.46	−0.08	0.48	−0.12
Relative GDP growth	−3.73	5.65	−4.01	8.36
Relative growth PPP adjusted	−4.01	5.34	−3.43	7.25
Relative stock returns	−6.36	4.81	−6.32	1.17
Relative inflation	0.30	0.34	−0.66	1.25
EMERGING MARKETS				
Trade balance changes	0.52	−0.33	0.94	−0.79
Relative GDP growth	−0.90	5.04	−2.19	5.68
Relative growth PPP adjusted	−10.62	−5.41	−8.17	−7.08
Relative stock returns	−2.30	3.96	−5.71	−4.20
Relative inflation	12.03	10.92	7.18	13.58

All of these results are consistent with the terms of trade effect on these variables as reported in Table 16.3. The results are reassuring to both the terms of trade view of the world as well as to those who believe that a devaluation alters the, that is, improves, the terms of trade.

One interesting result reported in the first two columns of Table 16.4 is the differences in relative inflation; these do not follow the same pattern as the other variables. Later on, we will discuss these results in greater detail.

Moving on to the right side of the table, columns 3 and 4 report the average performance of the different variables when both the nominal exchange rate and terms of trade provide the same signal. Column 3 reports the results for when both variables decline, while column 4 the results when both variables appreciate. As one compares the results in the two columns, we find the outcome consistent with those reported previously. The variables behave as predicted by the terms of trade effect, see Table 16.3, columns 3 and 4.

In some ways, the two periods when the exchange rate and terms of trade produce different signals should be the most interesting. Periods when the two variables move in opposite direction and thus could yield some interesting information that may allow us to disentangle the effects of the terms of trade and those of a monetary devaluation. Unfortunately there are only three episodes that encompass only 4 years. We feel that the number of cycles are too few and their duration too short. Simply put the sample is too small and the events are

not sustained enough to allow us to identify significant differences that may help identify the differential effect of the terms of trade and exchange rate fluctuations on the economy. For that reason we will exclude these observations from the sample and compare them to the complete sample. However, in so far as we exclude these observations, the issue as to whether there are significant differences between the terms of trade and the nominal exchange rates will be left for another day.

Now, on to an interpretation of the inflation rate differentials results, we have argued and shown that under a domestic price rule, the inflation rate differential will not change unless there is a change in the price rule inflation target. We also know and can argue that most of the developed world during this time moved toward a domestic price rule around a 2% domestic inflation target range. If every country was on the price rule and was successful, there will be no inflation rate differential. If, in contrast, the inflation targets were different across countries, but fixed and did not change, then the inflation rate differential would also be constant. In that case, we have shown that the domestic inflation will rise and the differential would reflect a terms of trade effect. That is the case as we compare columns 1 and 2 and columns 3 and 4 for the developed economies relative inflation rate. This result provides a clear signal.

It is the emerging markets inflation rate differential during the different periods that produces a conflicting signal. Notice during the cycles in which both the nominal exchange rate and terms of trade move in the same direction, that is, both appreciate or both depreciate at the same time, the inflation rate differential rises as nominal exchange rate and terms of trade appreciate. Again, it is a result consistent with the terms of trade effect. Yet during period in which the nominal exchange rate appreciates and the fluctuations in the terms of trade are not accounted, columns 1 and 2, the inflation rate differential decreases as the exchange rate appreciates. This result is consistent with the view that the nominal exchange rate fluctuations are the result of monetary disturbances, in which case we should expect the PPP results.

In many ways this result is quite intriguing. One can argue that the PPP type scenario for the nominal exchange rate is much more representative of the relative performance of the inflation rate differential between the emerging markets and the United States. First, the emerging markets have not adopted a domestic price rule. Earlier in the period they adopted an international price rule or, simply put, a fixed exchange rate system. Yet we know that these systems were abandoned by most emerging markets as a result of several financial crises. The first one that comes to mind is that of the Latin Pumas, initiated by Mexico's devaluation in December of 1994. Then we had the Asian Tigers crisis with the Thai Blood Baht in 1997 and capped by the Russian crisis in 1998. In short, all regions of the emerging markets experienced a financial crisis followed by large and abrupt devaluations that decoupled their exchange rates after which they were allowed to float freely.

The large devaluations may be quite useful in providing information that may allow us to disentangle the terms of trade and exchange rate effects. The numbers are consistent with the PPP interpretation. As we compare columns 1 and 2, we find that the average inflation rate declines as the nominal exchange rate appreciates. These results provide support for a terms of trade effect and a monetary effect on the relative inflation. The issue is how can we separate the two sets of results and link them to the country's monetary policy? We sort of did that already when we argued that the developed world followed a domestic price rule and the emerging market did not. This is very useful for it allows an investor or portfolio strategist to take a short cut in interpreting the whole data set and this way get a quicker sense of the market and economic developments, a useful piece of information in the design of a successful portfolio strategy. But can we say more than that? Can we support our views empirically?

While the numbers are consistent with this interpretation, we have to keep in mind that the sample where the nominal exchange rate and terms of trade move in the opposite direction was deemed to be too small. Hence, we have to take the results with a grain of salt.

Nevertheless, they are encouraging in so far as they hold the promise that focusing on periods when these two variables move in different direction is the path to finding a way to separate these two effects.

THE EVENTS

In this section, we focus on different economic disturbances hoping that the differences in experiences across disturbances may allow to further test the applicability and implications of the framework being developed. The first three episodes focus on financial crises in the emerging markets. These large monetary disturbances had quite an impact in the region, as well as other emerging economies. We begin with the Mexican devaluation of December 12, 1994, then move on to the Thai Baht devaluation on July 2nd of 1997, and end up with the August 17th of 1998 Russian devaluation. After these events we move on in time and focus on what one may characterize as a major disturbance to the terms of trade, the commodity super cycle. Although the precise timing of the beginning and end points in the cycle, there is no major disagreement about the cycle. We have settled on the 1999–2011 as the relevant time period for the commodity supercycle. The final event we focus on in an interesting one, for it involves a time period where a country, China, adopts and then gradually begins to abandon a fixed exchange rate system.

MEXICO AND THE TEQUILA EFFECT

Mexico's experience and performance relative to the United States before, during, and after the Mexican devaluation are summarized in Table 16.5. A comparison of the different columns allows one to determine the changes in several of the economic variables that we have previously discussed. The first row denotes the Mexican nominal exchange rate *vis-à-vis* the US dollar. Notice that the Mexican rate of depreciating was approximately 1% per year during the 2 years prior to the devaluation. Then in 1994, it surges to 14%, denoting the devaluation. The data also points that the aftershock was even worst. The peso depreciated by an even larger amount during the 1995–96 time periods. Several factors may account for this. One may be the financial crisis in other parts of the world. But for now, our focus is on the behavior of the different variables.

The Mexican trade balance as a percent of GDP did improve in the aftermath of the devaluation, just as the proponents of devaluation argue. Yet we also find that the real GDP growth rate declined, the inflation rate accelerated and the stock market continued to underperform.

TABLE 16.5 The Latin Pumas and the Mexican Devaluation Relative to the Corresponding Data for the United States

		1992–93	1994	1995–96
Mexico	Exchange rate	−0.94	−14.03	−42.67
	Trade balance changes	−5.27	−5.63	−3.04
	GDP	−0.50	2.01	−3.77
	Inflation	15.94	7.91	17.68
	Stock returns	29.54	−53.62	−38.95
Emerging Latin America	Exchange rate	−68.43	−49.01	−35.19
	Trade balance changes	−3.06	−3.72	−3.62
	GDP	2.41	1.63	0.95
	Inflation	72.69	76.38	51.52
	Stock returns	23.97	16.88	1.73
Emerging Pacific/Far East	Exchange rate	−2.58	−2.78	−2.54
	Trade balance changes	−1.62	−2.31	−2.85
	GDP	4.52	5.47	4.62
	Inflation	6.30	7.90	7.47
	Stock returns	27.12	−7.35	−10.31
Emerging Europe, Middle East and Africa	Exchange rate	−36.69	−37.50	−27.41
	Trade balance changes	−2.50	−2.61	−3.01
	GDP	−3.05	0.48	0.06
	Inflation	35.95	39.92	36.53
	Stock returns	28.49	−42.95	−25.93

Not a pretty picture and perhaps too high a price for Trade balance improving devaluation.

The economic situation clearly deteriorated. The proponents of devaluations have a tough time with the event. If the devaluation does in fact makes the local country products cheaper, the increased exports should have a multiplier effect and thereby result in higher output. Also with the economy contracting, why did the domestic prices rise? Arguing that things would have been much worse had not the currency been devaluated is not an acceptable defense. Instead, we have a very simple interpretation of the events. A monetary devaluation should have no impact on real variables, yet the PPP framework suggests that the devaluation results in a higher inflation rate. It does.

Normally a devaluation is not an isolated policy. Usually it is accompanied by capital controls, other restrictions, as well as austerity measures that have a real impact on the economy. As a result of the companion policies, incentives to produce decline, the economy contracts, and the terms of trade weaken, thereby resulting in an improvement in the balance of trade. Finally, the contraction also means that the

rates of returns to producing nontraded goods decline and that produces a decline in the country rates of return relative its trading partners. The stock market underperforms and capital flows out as a result. This is a nice parsimonious explanation consistent with the view that terms of trade effects mostly impacting the real economy and the devaluations mostly impact the nominal variables.

The data reported in bottom of Table 16.5 is also consistent with a regional contagion. The reason for the contagion may differ. Some may argue that because the economies in the region pursue similar policies, similar behavior is also expected. Another way to say the same thing is that they may be considered near substitutes of each other and as investors sour on the policies in one country, it is more than likely that they will do so for similar economies.

Although not reflected in this data, there is an important point we want to make here is. The volatility in the exchange rate ended in 1996, when the Mexican authorities adopted a new monetary operating procedure that guaranteed the convertibility of the pesos at the margin. Under the new procedure, the Mexican central bank only printed new money to match increases in the central bank's international reserves. The new Mexican policy effectively insured the central bank would only create the money necessary for the economy to function. Any excess creation resulted in a loss of international reserves and a reduction in the domestic monetary base. Similarly, any liquidity shortage created a capital inflow that resulted in a corresponding increase in international reserves and an equal amount of domestic money being created. To enable investors to keep tabs on how the bank is meeting these restrictions, the bank published its international reserve holdings on a weekly basis. These steps helped Mexico weather the Thai devaluation reasonably well. Its stock market outperformed, the economy recovered and Mexico was able to repay the United States emergency assistance loan ahead of schedule.

THE THAI BLOOD BAHT AND THE ASIAN FLU

After 2 years of relative calm, Thailand delivered the foreign exchange markets a wake-up call. The country's battle defending its currency ended July 2 when it freed the baht from its peg with the dollar. The Thai currency promptly fell 15%. The currency depreciation went well beyond this point. Table 16.6 provides a summary of the behavior of the key variables in the events leading up to the devaluation, as well during and after the event. The data produce some surprises. The trade balance, while still positive, did not improve. In fact, it deteriorated in the aftermath of the devaluation. The economy contracted during the devaluation and while the real GDP growth relative to the United States recovered somewhat after the devaluation, it was not a full recovery. Not

TABLE 16.6 The Thai Blood Baht Relative to the Corresponding Data from the United States

		1995–96	1997	1997–98
Thailand	Exchange rate	−8.82	−135.98	24.51
	Trade balance changes	5.07	4.33	2.57
	GDP	−3.02	−7.20	−5.92
	Inflation	2.99	2.63	1.28
	Stock returns	13.63	−19.78	−8.51
Emerging Pacific/Far East	Exchange rate	−2.54	−26.42	−5.89
	Trade balance changes	−2.85	−1.34	4.82
	GDP	−2.98	−6.44	1.80
	Inflation	7.47	4.96	7.03
	Stock returns	−10.31	−59.18	18.89
Emerging Latin America	Exchange rate	−35.19	−8.24	−16.06
	Trade balance changes	−3.62	−3.95	−3.07
	GDP	−0.93	−2.75	−2.44
	Inflation	51.52	10.12	8.21
	Stock returns	1.73	22.60	−12.12
Emerging Europe, Middle East and Africa	Exchange rate	−27.41	−19.48	−25.92
	Trade balance changes	−3.01	−5.35	−2.65
	GDP	0.73	−1.21	0.12
	Inflation	36.53	15.28	14.62
	Stock returns	−25.93	24.65	3.13
Hong Kong	Exchange rate	−0.04	−0.04	−0.21
	Trade balance changes	−3.55	−4.36	3.96
	GDP	0.21	0.65	−6.08
	Inflation	5.09	5.60	−1.48
	Stock returns	−10.19	−29.86	17.91

surprisingly, amid all this negative data, the Thai stock returns underperformed the US stock returns.

The emerging market nations in the Southeast Asia region suffered currency pressures of their own. Contagion was the order of the day. Looking at the bottom of Table 16.6, there is clear evidence of contagion. On average, the other countries in the region also felt the ill effects of the devaluation more so than the other emerging countries, and regions such as Latin America, Emerging Europe, Middle East, and Africa. Shortly after the Thai action, the Philippine peso was forced to float, Indonesia widened its trading band, the Malaysian Ringgit suffered a small devaluation, and even the Singapore dollar, considered the region's strongest currency, was shaken. The degree to which each of these emerging nation's felt the Thai currency shock was largely dependent on the organization of its monetary system.

The predictable comparisons to the Mexican peso crisis in 1994 surfaced immediately in the press. And since the float, analysis has shown some interesting comparisons. Analysts at the International Monetary Fund and the World Bank concluded that Thailand's problems, while the most severe in the region, were not as likely to be as long lasting as Mexico's—primarily because of the region's above average growth. That growth, however, had been largely the result of the region's commitment to strong currencies.

The press has said the Thai correction was inevitable. The product of an overly strong currency was choking net exports. And advocates of the move have said that by floating (devaluing) the baht, Thailand's competitiveness in the global economy improved. At the time, we argued that while this may be the case when applied strictly to the terms of trade, when speaking of the nominal rate, this model is flawed [2].

Failing to differentiate between nominal and real exchange rates produces faulty economic analysis, and has been at the center of numerous currency troubles for decades. Following a set of policy recommendations which fail to distinguish the two can lead to deepening economic hardship. A change in a country's real exchange rate or terms of trade has real impact on other nation's economies. In fact, the relationship between the real exchange rate and the trade balance and capital flows is exactly as described in the press. An appreciating real exchange rate is associated with a deteriorating trade balance and improving capital flows. Quite simply, the terms of trade reflect the real economy, while the nominal rate reflects relative inflation rates across countries. While a currency devaluation may give a brief boost to competitiveness, its impact on a nation's real economy is considerably less certain. Generally, a nation's competitiveness is not enhanced by the devaluation itself, but by the growth-oriented, sound monetary policies that emerge in response to devaluation's most painful product: inflation.

The anatomy of the crisis is worth reviewing. The region has been beset by speculative currency attacks that have transpired for a number of reasons. But basically under a peg or fixed exchange rate system, such attacks are one-sided bets, a kind of "heads I win, tails I don't lose" proposition. Speculators bet against the currency. If the currency folded, they would win big. If the currency withstands the assault, speculators lose only transaction costs. If they have sufficient resources, they might even force the country's currency to fold. True, speculators may inflict considerable damage to emerging nations' economies. But speculators don't deserve all the blame. They didn't set up the game. Central banks set it up and all that the speculators did was play to win.

To understand the Thai crisis, many analysts were drawing a parallel with the 1994 Mexican peso crisis. Such a perspective offers useful insights. The most important of which is that, just as was the case in Asia, Mexico didn't have an independent central bank guaranteeing the convertibility of its currency at the time of its devaluation. By all accounts, the Mexican government used some of its international reserves during the capital-inflow phase to finance government spending. This left the central bank inadequately prepared to defend the peso against a speculative attack. The same mistake was made by the Asian Tigers' central banks. The exception in the region was Hong Kong and its currency board.

Our view then, and still is, was that the Southeast Asia crisis was unnecessary and could have been avoided. We base our arguments on the experiences of Hong Kong in the aftermath of these crisis. Around the time, there was an attack on the Hong Kong dollar that underscored a number of issues in international finance and monetary policy. Foreign exchange speculators sensed that Hong Kong may have been ripe for an attack that would result in an unhinging of Hong Kong's currency from the US dollar. The assault tested the will of the Hong Kong monetary authorities. The peg or fixed exchange rate system had been under siege ever since the Asian Tigers unhinged their currencies from the dollar. The question at the time was whether Hong would Kong prevail.

Repeating ourselves, we have argued that a fixed-exchange rate system sets up a one-sided bet for speculators in the currency game. These currency "gamblers" have much to win if they bet correctly against a currency, and have little to lose (transaction costs) if they guess wrong. This cost-benefit asymmetry encourages speculative attacks. We have further argued that the success of the speculative game depends on the nature of the exchange rate arrangement. If the central bank fixes the exchange rate by employing a currency band, it could, under certain conditions, end up guaranteeing the convertibility of its entire money supply. In contrast, if a nation uses a currency board to direct policy, as Hong Kong does, only the monetary base is guaranteed (the currency board alters the base in direct relation to international reserve holdings). It's easily seen that the currency band system is guaranteed to fail a large speculative attack. The amount of international reserves held by the domestic central bank would never be enough to insure the full convertibility of its money supply (M1, M2, etc.). Therefore, if the attack is large enough, the country will fold, as Argentina did.

However, under a currency board that has stuck to its 100% international reserve backing of the monetary base, authorities will always have enough reserves to survive the attack. This is not to say that the currency board country doesn't pay a price. The capital outflow occasioned by the speculative attack produces a massive credit crunch that affects the nation's real economy. Viewed this way, it's easy to see that speculators can inflict pain on an economy that uses a currency board.

This produces the second component of the speculative attack: to short the local stock market. This way the speculators set up what they believed was a win-win speculative position or a free lunch. The way the saw it, it the country did not devalue, the credit crunch and capital outflow would produce a stock market decline, and they win. In contrast, if the country devalued, they also win. What is the central bank of monetary authorities to do? Again, Hong Kong is the poster child for the proper response. They used their reserves to counter the speculative attack. They bought stocks and prevented the market decline that speculators were looking for. Eventually the carrying costs of the short became too high, the speculators gave up, closed their position, and the Hong Kong monetary authorities won. Once the crisis was over, the HK monetary authorities reversed their stock holding and returned to a normal backing of the HK dollar. The Hong Kong experiences demonstrate to us that the Latin Pumas and Asian Tigers crisis were unnecessary. It's important to note, however, that argument also explains why currency board nations see their economies rebound more quickly after a speculative attack than noncurrency board nations.

In the case of the emerging markets, the data reported in Tables 16.5 and 16.6 show that it is unfortunate that the global markets tend not to distinguish between the good emerging markets and all the others. In effect, international investors punish the sinners and the virtuous equally. The good countries suffer unnecessarily. The investment implications are quite clear: watch the region's capital flows. If the capital flow is positive for the nation in question and the real exchange rate or terms of trade appreciates, investors need not worry about the organization of the nation's monetary system. In these countries, the stock markets—particularly in the nontraded and interest-sensitive sectors—will perform quite nicely. However, the instant the capital flow reverses, even if the economic fundamentals

appear sound, the organization of the monetary system matters a great deal. In these nations, look at the international reserve coverage of the monetary base. If it is inadequate, that is, less than 100%, make sure your investment is partially hedged or predominately in the traded sector, where goods are generally "dollarized." If a currency run materializes, the traded sector will be the least affected.

THE RUSSIAN CRISIS

The problems faced by the devaluing countries such as Mexico during the Tequila Effect period, or Indonesia and others during the Asian Flu, and Russia during their crisis, are a little bit different. The financial institutions got into trouble for making bad loans that were in part encouraged by the cronyism, corruption, or just plain inept management. While this part was similar to other countries, in Russia it was magnified. Most of these economies had an additional complication: the exchange rate. Largely because of mismanagement of monetary policy, these countries were forced to devalue their currencies.

The devaluation was supposed to free these countries from the burden of a fixed-exchange rate system and, according to street lore, would also improve their competitive position. What the devaluation produced was higher inflation, and Russia was no exception (Table 16.7). Prior to the devaluation, these countries had private borrowing in the international markets, the currency depreciation—to the extent it was not accompanied by a corresponding domestic asset appreciation—resulted in additional capital-adequacy problems for the banks. Problem loans proliferated, and to meet the capital ratios either new capital had to be found (an unlikely possibility) or loan activity had to be curtailed. These countries were in the unenviable position of facing a credit crunch and high inflation caused in large part by the devaluation. For example, in Indonesia the interest rate for one-month paper was about 70%.

Again, the experience of the Latin American countries during the Tequila Effect is quite instructive. The Mexican experience is closer to that of the Asian countries. For almost a year, Mexican inflation kept rising despite a contracting money supply. The devaluation had reduced demand for pesos so much that the government could not arrest the peso expansion fast enough to halt the currency slide. It was not until the operating procedures at the central banks were changed—prohibiting creation of additional pesos without the backing of international reserves—that things started to improve. The policy served Mexico well, the exchange rate stabilized at around 7.6 pesos to the dollar, the inflation rate declined to single-digit rates, and the Mexican stock market recovered.

TABLE 16.7 The Russian Crisis Relative to the Corresponding Data from the United States

		1996–97	1998	1999–2000
Russia	Exchange rate	−13.03	−113.49	−5.75
	Trade balance changes	1.37	0.08	18.04
	GDP	−5.58	−10.03	9.07
	Inflation	25.88	17.06	31.94
	Stock returns	83.49	−178.13	−36.22
Emerging Europe, Middle East and Africa	Exchange rate	−20.97	−30.50	−14.50
	Trade balance changes	−5.05	−4.61	0.42
	GDP	0.73	−1.57	1.22
	Inflation	17.78	12.15	16.44
	Stock returns	32.11	−49.50	−31.09
Emerging Pacific/Far East	Exchange rate	−14.20	−13.59	−8.16
	Trade balance changes	−2.14	5.56	2.90
	GDP	−2.98	1.40	2.40
	Inflation	5.20	12.06	3.65
	Stock returns	−28.54	−0.75	−46.04
Emerging Latin America	Exchange rate	−6.95	−14.23	−3.26
	Trade balance changes	−3.78	−4.42	−1.95
	GDP	−0.93	−4.74	0.29
	Inflation	11.90	8.11	6.98
	Stock returns	14.63	−50.25	−28.46

Clearly, Mexico fared much better than the Asian Tigers during their flu-Contagion episode. But, across the board, fixed-exchange rate countries did not experience the same difficulties as those countries that floated or to the same degree. The Mexican experience should have been the blueprint for countries that have devalued or let their exchange rate rise. As they have obligations in foreign currencies, the depreciation causes capital adequacy problems. This, in turn, leads to a credit crunch. The currency depreciation leads to higher inflation. In short, a financial collapse will invariably occur. Recovery did not begin until the inflation rate was controlled and the capital adequacy issue was addressed.

Given the experiences of Mexico, it is clear now that the Asian countries and Russia were as far along as Mexico was in the aftermath of the Tequila Effect. The Russian story was even worse. Russia started from a much weaker economic situation, having never really found its footing with a sustained period of growth under free-market economics. Furthermore, the Russian banks bought everything they could—as long as it was on margin. Influence peddling and cronyism also

abounded. Not surprisingly, as the country's economic policies failed and asset values declined, the banks were unable to meet their obligations.

The capital outflow occasioned by the confidence crisis in the region leads to a reduction in international reserves. As the reserves make up the country's monetary base, the outflow will lead to a reduction in the domestic money supply. Given the magnitude of the money multiplier, there will be a magnified reduction in both the quantity of money circulating in the economy and in domestic credit creation. If the financial markets are not well developed (and they were not in those countries), the banking system was the major source of credit. (The other sources would be the emerging stock market and foreign borrowing). The credit reduction led to a credit crunch, the severity of which depended on the ability of the other two sources of credit to fill the void. In a time of crisis, the stock market was not the vehicle to fill the void—there were few IPO's or nongovernment foreign borrowing. Thus, skyrocketing interest rates would be the order of the day. All of this would result in a rising inflation, slower real GDP growth, a declining stock market in absolute and relative rates of return. Table 16.7 indicates that is precisely what happened to Russia. Again, going back to the basic framework, the performance of the Russian economy during the crisis and its aftermath, it fits our views that the devaluations mostly influences nominal variables with the terms of trade impact the real sectors of the economy. Finally, if there is a lesson for the emerging economies is that Hong Kong was a clear example to emulate.

THE COMMODITY SUPER CYCLE

The commodity super cycle (both mineral and agricultural) greatly benefited the commodity-producing countries, many of which were emerging economies. Now, with the commodity super cycle coming to an end, the fortunes are reversing for those who benefited from rising commodity prices.

The essence of our insight is simple. We contend that as the global economy expanded, in particular China, it increased the demand for agricultural commodities and minerals used in the production of goods and services. There are two mechanisms to eliminate excess demand. One is price increases and the other is higher output. How much of each takes place depends on the aggregate demand and supply elasticity of the commodities in question. The lower the supply elasticity, the higher the price increase will be. The higher the supply elasticity, the greater the output response will be. The higher price would result in additional profits for the producers and the higher output would produce higher employment.

The commodity price increase also has a clear macro effect. An increase in the commodity prices means that every unit of nontraded goods now acquires more internationally traded goods than before. This implies that the real rate of return of domestically located assets increases relative to the rest of the world, and so will domestic asset values. In an attempt to arbitrage the higher rates, investors will flock to the local economy. The country will experience an inflow of capital as a result of the increased rate of return. A decline in commodity prices will have the opposite effect. It will result in a lower rate of return for domestic assets. The relationship between the commodity prices and the performance of the domestic stock market relative to the global economy will be a positive one.

Table 16.8 reports the performance of selected variables for three commodities producing and exporting countries relative to the corresponding performance of these variables in our universe of developed economies. Table 16.9 reports a similar table, but this time the countries selected are all emerging economies and their performance is measured relative to the emerging economies in our universe. A careful analysis of the two tables yields some empirical regularities. For the commodity-producing developed countries, the trade balance worsens while the stock returns performance improves. The inflation rate also rises and the real GDP improves more often than not. The end of the commodity super cycle

TABLE 16.8   Relative Performance of Developed, Commodity-Producing Economies During the Commodity Super Cycle of 1999–2011

Country	Variable	1997–98	1999–2011	2012–13
Australia	Exchange rate	6.66	1.44	1.61
	Trade balance changes	0.08	−0.36	−0.97
	GDP	−8.99	8.27	−0.79
	Inflation	−0.11	2.01	−0.75
	Stock returns	−4.77	2.85	−6.46
Canada	Exchange rate	1.13	0.03	−6.83
	Trade balance changes	0.59	−0.35	−1.33
	GDP	−3.39	−3.77	−6.27
	Inflation	−0.62	0.79	0.26
	Stock returns	1.52	4.63	−9.03
Norway	Exchange rate	2.08	2.92	4.30
	Trade balance changes	0.03	−2.43	−8.72
	GDP	0.92	8.70	8.08
	Inflation	−0.06	3.41	1.82
	Stock returns	−16.30	3.92	−4.87

TABLE 16.9   Relative Performance of Emerging, Commodity-Producing Economies During the Commodity Super Cycle of 1999–2011

Country	Variable	1997–98	1999–2011	2012–13
Brazil	Exchange rate	−10.25	13.80	14.12
	Trade balance changes	4.55	3.90	2.77
	GDP	−1.58	−2.96	−4.66
	Inflation	−4.52	1.58	2.60
	Stock returns	1.24	3.31	−17.38
Chile	Exchange rate	−12.35	−1.72	−1.04
	Trade balance changes	7.51	7.78	5.40
	GDP	−2.47	−1.01	−4.65
	Inflation	−7.51	−1.07	−2.08
	Stock returns	2.49	1.85	−15.64
Mexico	Exchange rate	−5.33	−5.69	−12.50
	Trade balance changes	−4.58	−4.96	−3.99
	GDP	−0.30	−3.09	−2.90
	Inflation	4.59	0.31	−0.95
	Stock returns	19.45	3.63	5.71
Indonesia	Exchange rate	42.87	15.68	−1.72
	Trade balance changes	−23.34	−24.48	−1.36
	GDP	3.10	0.52	−3.93
	Inflation	23.34	3.48	0.74
	Stock returns	44.73	−10.85	14.13
Russia	Exchange rate	42.86	61.24	11.14
	Trade balance changes	−4.91	−25.58	−33.95
	GDP	2.12	7.18	1.58
	Inflation	4.91	12.05	2.66
	Stock returns	−31.80	9.47	−1.97
South Africa	Exchange rate	−6.68	−1.46	3.88
	Trade balance changes	3.08	3.04	1.62
	GDP	0.50	−3.76	−6.37
	Inflation	−3.08	0.94	2.18
	Stock returns	−3.53	1.31	−2.99

also points to a reversal of the relative performance. The one exception has been the trade balance, which continued to deteriorate.

Some of the same cyclical effects are also evident for the emerging economies. The relative inflation rate and relative stock returns tend to rise in relative terms as during the super cycle and then either decline or reduce the rate of appreciation as the cycle ended. For the other variables, it is hard to discern which one dominates, the cyclical relative performance or an apparent secular trend. However, excluding the secular trend, the relative performance during the cycles is in line with the developed market.

We have argued that during a price rule period, the inflation rate measures the terms of trade effects. We have also argued that monetary variables will have little or no impact on the real variables. We do not expect to find a systematic relationship between the nominal exchange rate and the real variables, which appears to be the case. In contrast, most of the counters results are in line with the terms of trade effects identified by our framework.

CHINA

In a short article on the *Wall Street Journal's* editorial page, John Taylor, a former Under Secretary of the Treasury for International Affairs, makes a very interesting point [3]. Mr. Taylor argues that:

> The recent policy shift in China from a pegged to a flexible exchange rate regime starts a new chapter in international finance, comparable to the dramatic end of the Bretton Woods system of pegged exchange rates in 1971. Economists had dubbed the decade-long Chinese peg "Bretton Woods II," because many other countries in Asia kept their currencies close to the Yuan and effectively tied to the dollar. Bretton Woods II is now over, but what is next?

We loved the parallel and agree with the earlier mentioned statement, but where we part company with Professor Taylor is in the conclusion that he makes. We do not believe that the floating of the yuan is such a bullish event. On the contrary, we believe that it will have effects similar to those of the Bretton Woods demise. Among other things, the unhinging of the dollar from gold produced a loss of confidence in the US currency and economy and in a very short order experienced double-digit inflation. We believe that China could follow a similar path.

Before we make our arguments let's review China's experience. Table 16.10 summarizes the performance of different economic indicators prior to the fixing of the exchange, during the peg and the first 2 years of the so-called floating period. The first row illustrates what we already knew. Prior to the peg, China's exchange rate was depreciating relative to the US dollar at a double-digit rate. The peg produced a result similar to the experience of other countries and economic unions that have adopted a fixed exchange rate, the peg induced a convergence of the underlying Chinese inflation rate to that of the country it was pegging its currency to (the US dollar). Since the abandonment of the peg, the managed

float has resulted in a slightly higher depreciation rate. It takes more yuan to acquire a US dollar.

The second row shows that contrary to expectation of policy makers, the unhinging did not result in a deterioration of the trade balance. In fact, the trade balance as a percent of GDP improved. The data shows that relative real GDP growth rate was lower during the peg than during the floating periods. The same is true for the underlying inflation rate. Not much can be surmised about the relative stock returns, all we can say is that over time the relative performance had been steadily improving.

Table 16.11 shows the performance of the Chinese economy relative to the developed world, the emerging markets and the Asian Pacific emerging market region. The patters are basically the same. The trade balance improves as the peg is removed; the relative GDP growth and inflation rates are lower during the peg while the relative performance of the stock market trends up over time.

Now we focus on the effect of unhinging from the US dollar. Let's see and determine what is being lost as China dismantles the system. First, by fixing the exchange rate to the US dollar, the Chinese central bank effectively is importing US monetary policy. Under a fixed exchange rate, absent changes in the terms of trade, arbitrage insures that the price of traded goods converges across countries. The underlying inflation rate in the countries fixing the exchange rate converges to that of the Unites States, the reserve currency country, but there is more to this story. The beginning quote also states that the other Asian countries are quasi fixed to the Yuan. It follows that we have a series of exchange rate/inflation linkages: the Asian countries to China and China to the United States. In the end, the United States is the sole determinant of the underlying inflation rate. Looking back over the past decade, the Chinese and Asia could not have chosen a better anchor than the United States and Sir Alan.

The Yuan had been pegged to the dollar for more than 10 years. Critics complain that it was artificially weak, which gave Chinese exports an unfair advantage. Presumably, the move to float the exchange rate

TABLE 16.10 China's Fixed Exchange Rate Experience

	1993–94	1995–2004	2005–06
Exchange rate	−20.49	0.28	2.57
Trade balance changes		2.56	7.16
Real GDP growth rate	13.49	9.15	11.99
Inflation rate	16.46	3.24	3.84
Nominal stock returns	−17.42	−10.30	36.26

TABLE 16.11 China's Fixed Exchange Rate Experience Relative to Different Regions

	1993–94	1995–2004	2005–06
DEVELOPED COUNTRIES EX-EMU			
Exchange rate	21.85	0.11	−2.77
Trade balance changes		−0.44	1.96
GDP	10.75	6.06	8.69
Inflation	14.29	1.93	1.47
Stock returns	−31.81	−6.85	27.38

will appease the United States and will stop the move to impose a 27.5% tariff on Chinese goods.

The exchange rate manipulation argument is a flawed one. It assumes domestic price rigidities, which leaves the exchange rate as the only mechanism for affecting the terms of trade (i.e., the price of imports in terms of exports). Under this assumption, it is easy to see why some people advocate a currency revaluation. A currency appreciation will make the Chinese goods more expensive in terms of the US goods. But what if prices in the aggregate are reasonably flexible? Then attempts to maintain an artificially low or fixed exchange rate will be offset by the changes in the domestic price levels. A differential inflation will be observed and the country for which the terms of trade are appreciating will exhibit a lower inflation rate. That is precisely what happened in China. Prior to the fixing of the exchange rate, China's inflation rate was much higher than that of the United States. In the aftermath of the fixing of the exchange rate, the Chinese inflation converged to that of the United States and in the years prior to the unhinging it had been slightly lower than the US inflation. This is exactly what the price flexibility hypothesis predicted. Also, if the price level adjusts to reflect the terms of trade, exchange rate manipulations will not affect the terms of trade; they will only affect the country's differential inflation rate.

A very important point is that when the exchange rate system is fixed, the domestic prices adjust to reflect the changes in the terms of trade. Deliberate changes in the exchange rate are not needed to bring about changes in the terms of trade. The impact of deliberate changes in the exchange rate will only produce an increase in the inflation rate differential. The reverse is also true as China showed. A peg will produce a convergence of the inflation rate to that of the reserve currency country.

The Chinese central bank engineered a sharp drop in Yuan market interest rates by flooding the banking system with cash. The move is seen by some as aimed at reducing the demand for the Yuan and to keep it from strengthening. Yet we know what the long-term impact of excess domestic money creation is, either a balance of payment deficit and/or domestic inflation. Neither of

these two outcomes bodes well for China. It was quite recently that people used to talk about China having such a large amount of international reserves, close to 4 trillion dollars, that it could pursue an independent monetary policy. The United States thought the same thing during the Bretton Woods years. Both countries have learned a lesson. The United States had to close the gold window because it was losing reserves at too rapid a pace. The same thing recently happened to China when it lost close to 700 billion dollars in a short span of time.

The move by the Chinese to a managed float of its currency was hailed as one that will allow China to modernize its financial system. The liberalization would allow for the development of currency derivative products, or so the advocates of the float say. However, once one thinks about it, it is a silly argument. The derivatives, such as forwards and swaps, are designed to protect companies from adverse swings in currency exchange rates. Isn't that precisely what the fixed rate delivered? The need for these derivative products exists now because of the uncertainty introduced by the floating exchange rate system. To make matters worse, we know that the derivatives are tough to regulate. We also know that the Chinese government will not give up its right to regulate and manipulate the market as it wishes. We believe that the new exchange rate system has resulted in a more distorted Chinese economy where the true market signals will be more difficult to discern.

The unhinging of the Yuan allows the inflation rate to diverge across countries for reason other than the terms of trade. The inflation rate differentials become a major source of exchange rate movements. But more than that, the expectations of the spikes in the underlying inflation rate leads investors to attempt to avoid the inflation spikes either through derivative product or through pure and direct currency substitutions (i.e., domestic money holders' shift out of the local currency into the foreign currencies). In short, the currency substitution adds another source of demand shifts that if managed incorrectly by the central bank could lead to explosive inflationary bouts with little or no apparent domestic money growth or in a command and control economy it will result in additional regulations, capital controls etc. The central bank response is not known for certain in the economy and its actions may trigger a different response in the demand for money, which if not anticipated will lead to fluctuations in the underlying inflation rate. It is even worse in the case of a nonreserve currency; there will be substitutions on the demand side. The unhinging of the exchange rates leads to more instability of the demand for money and greater volatility in the exchange rate. Also, people do not know with precision the intervention rule with regards to the reference basket of currencies. The forecasting errors on the part of the private sector or the central bank may, under some circumstances, lead to perverse responses that inevitably lead to runs on the currency and spikes on the underlying inflation.

The lack of a fixed exchange rate discipline will now free the central bank to pursue goals other than fixing the exchange rate (i.e., importing the US inflation rate).

Although we think Sir Alan was the best central banker of his generation, we would be remiss if we don't mention that many of the US financial crises have coincided with Sir Alan departing from the price rule. If the Chinese central banker is not as good as Sir Alan, what makes the Chinese think they can do better? Remember that the United States went through a decade of high inflation that at times reached double-digit rates in the aftermath of the dismantling of Bretton Woods.

References

[1] The EMU countries are excluded because the data is not available for the complete sample period. One possibility, which we considered and did not pursue, was to construct a synthetic EMU using the countries' initial weights.
[2] Canto VA. A Blood Baht and the Tequila Effect: A tale of two regions. La Jolla Econ. 1997;. September 2.
[3] John Taylor, "What Comes After 'Bretton Woods II'?" The Wall St. Journal, August 15, 2005. A2.

17

The US Experience: An Interpretation

The trade balance is a commonly used macroeconomic indicator. There are different points of view regarding the information provided by changes in the trade balance of a country. For example, some textbooks view a trade balance deficit as a leakage of domestic aggregate demand. Such a leakage translates into increased demand for foreign goods with a supposedly corresponding multiplier effect. All else the same, had the demand for these foreign goods been channeled into the domestic economy, the overall output and employment levels would have been higher. Also, the trade deficit means that the country is financing its deficit by borrowing and thereby increasing its indebtedness. Viewed from this narrow perspective, a deteriorating trade balance is an undesirable outcome, as it means lower level of output, employment, and higher debt.

A domestic policymaker focused on the improved well-being of the overall economy would take steps to stem the tide and thus take measures to improve the trade balance and stop the leakage or export of jobs and economic activity to the rest of the world, as well as to reduce the country's ineptness. Some may argue that trade restriction may be what the doctor ordered, yet that is not a commonly followed course of action.

There are the memories of the Great Depression, which some attribute to the Smoot–Hawley tariffs. The use of across-the-board trade restrictions may invite retaliation from other countries. All of this suggests that even if the benefits of the across-the-board restrictions were as the mercantilist suggests, the cost imposed by the retaliatory actions of the other countries may negate any possible benefits. The threat of retaliation is a great deterrent to taking an across-the- board course of action. But tariffs are not the only tool available to those who wish to pursue across-the-board trade actions. There is one additional tool available to their disposal: currency manipulation or exchange rate management. The argument goes as follows: a decline in the exchange rate simultaneously makes the country's exports cheaper and the country's imports more expensive. Hence, exports will increase while imports will decline, thereby improving the country's trade balance.

The inferences derived by the negative relationship between the trade balance and the foreign exchange value of the dollar could easily lead people and policymakers down a bearish path. The obvious implication coming out of this analysis is that to improve the trade balance, the terms of trade (i.e., the dollar) will have to decline substantially. Another fear concerning the decline in the dollar is that if the improvement does not occur fast enough, the fall in the dollar needed to affect the improvement may degenerate into a financial crisis. And this is where many policymakers make a major mistake. Some may be tempted to accelerate the adjustment process by devaluing the currency. We contend that a deliberate devaluation is a major mistake. A monetary devaluation leads to higher inflation. Usually the accompanying economic measures associated with the devaluation lead to slower real GDP growth rate, which in turn leads to an outflow of capital.

The previously mentioned textbook trade balance theory only deals with half of the equation. Under a floating

Economic Disturbances and Equilibrium in an Integrated Global Economy. http://dx.doi.org/10.1016/B978-0-12-813993-6.00017-9

exchange rate, the balance of payments is always zero. The double entry bookkeeping tells us that the trade balance is the mirror image of the capital account. Thus, if a stronger dollar makes imports cheaper and results in a trade deficit, the stronger dollar has to produce a capital inflow. The only way this would make sense is if the stronger dollar is a reflection of higher real returns in the United States vis-a-vis the rest of the world. Hence, we must develop a theory that simultaneously explains both the trade balance and the capital account. We intend to outline such a view in the next few paragraphs.

Also, if the adjustment is costly, the new equilibrium will be reached gradually and market cycles will be observed both in the economy, as well as the price-clearing mechanisms. This is a very important insight. It means that there is an adjustment path as the exchange rate moves from one long-run equilibrium to another. At any point in time, exchange rate changes reflect adjustments to current actions, as well as the gradual adjustment to past shocks. The evidence presented in Fig. 17.1 clearly supports the theory that adjustment costs lead to persistent cycles. This is good news for investors who anticipate and correctly identify these cycles. They will be able to develop strategies to take advantage of the cycles. The implications for policymakers are that their actions may not have the immediate impact on the economy's international account. It also suggests that it would be a mistake to attribute the current level of exchange rates solely to current shocks.

TRADE BALANCE: VALUE OR GROWTH SIGNAL?

Although the trade balance reflects the net level of trade at a specific point in time, in the presence of adjustment costs, the trade balance may reflect the effects of past actions as well as future expectations. One simple way to explain our views of the trade balance is to draw a parallel between a country and a household and/or a publicly traded company. In all three cases, we have ongoing concerns that focus not only on the present, but also on the future.

In general, household expenditures will be based on their lifetime income or net worth. Early on in its life cycle, through education, the members of the household may increase their future earning power. If the net present value of the increase in future income exceeds the cost of educating, the household will invest in human capital. The household net worth increases relative to its current income. Since expenditures are a function of the net present value of future income, the household expenditures exceed their income during the early years. The households finance the excess consumption (i.e., its trade deficit in goods and services) through their borrowing (i.e., a capital inflow finances their investment in human capital). In the future, when their human capital and earnings power rises, the investment and borrowing used to finance past consumption will be repaid. Late in the life cycle, as the household is at or near retirement, its earned income declines. During these years, the household will spend well above its earned income. The household will be depleting its net worth during those years.

Similarly, if a company faces great future opportunities, it may choose some external financing to achieve its goals faster and maximize shareholder value. In this case, the "growth company" borrows money or sells new equities to finance its growth. On the other hand, if the company finds itself with a stash of cash and no great investment opportunities, returning its cash to its investors may be the proper policy. At this point, one may argue that the company has ceased to be a growth stock and has become a value stock. The lower growth prospect will also produce a lower Price Earnings (P/E) ratio.

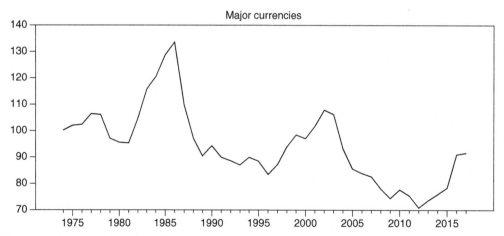

FIGURE 17.1   Foreign exchange value of the dollar.

The parallels between the household and a country or a business are straightforward. The gap between expenditures and production will be met through the trade balance, which is financed by capital inflows. Similarly, a growing country may find borrowing worthwhile. If the increase exceeds the cost, the investment is a worthwhile one and the country's net worth to income ratio (i.e. P/E ratio) will rise as the trade balance worsens. Finally, when the country matures past its peak, it will maintain its standard of living by selling assets. It will finance its excess consumption over its "earned income" through asset sales. During this time, the trade deficit will be accompanied by a declining P/E ratio.

Whether we use the household or company analogy, we have developed two distinct alternative explanations of why a trade balance deficit may occur. The question is which one of the two alternatives is the relevant one to the US situation. One simple way to distinguish between the growth and value stocks or the stage of life is to focus on the economy's P/E ratio. The household net worth to disposable income ratio will rise during growth stages and decline during value stages. Using the household borrowing analogy, if the money borrowed is invested and it earns a higher rate of return, household net worth will rise. The borrowed money finances investments that will result in a higher level of output and employment. Fig. 17.2 shows the household net worth as a percent of disposable personal income.

The data shows an uptrend that is not a smooth one, suggesting that there are periods of relative economic slowdown where the United States does not behave like a growth stock. The policymakers' quest is to find the appropriate policy mix that prevents or minimizes the "value"—like periods of the US economy. The data also points to an upward trend suggesting that, secularly, the economy is behaving like a growth company. If that is the case, the trade deficit is a good thing. It means that capital is flowing in because it can earn a higher risk adjusted rate of return in the United States. This evidence contradicts the mercantilist view of the world that equates the trade deficit with an undesirable and unprofitable increased ineptness. We argue here that the foreign capital has financed part of the US expansion and prosperity, a good thing and a desirable one.

THE TRADE BALANCE AND THE ECONOMY'S PRICE EARNINGS RATIO

The relationship between the inverse of the household net worth and the trade balance as a percent of disposable personal income is a tight one (Fig. 17.3). The approach outlined here provides some insight into the potential impact of different policy actions on the trade balance and, by inference, the terms of trade or real exchange rate. Our framework suggests two alternative ways of improving our trade balance. One is to reduce the US economy's P/E ratio, while the other is to increase the rest of the world's P/E ratio. The former approach, more likely than not, is a bearish one. In contrast, the latter is quite bullish. If the rest of the world adopts progrowth policies, capital will flow their way and their trade surpluses will decline and could even become trade deficits if they are successful enough. This would truly be a case of a rising tide lifting all boats. The world economy would soar.

Looking at Fig. 17.2, we notice a few inflection points in the economy's P/E ratio. It is apparent that once the Reagan tax policy was fully implemented, the P/E ratio rose and reached a new plateau and essentially remained there until 1995, when the Republicans took over Congress. Then in 2000, amidst the Y2K concern and the technology bubble bursting, the P/E ratio took a major hit. In time it recovered and got past its pre-1995 peak. The economy took another hit during the bursting of the housing bubble and the global financial meltdown, wherein again the data points to a complete recovery. The ratio of household net worth to income is once

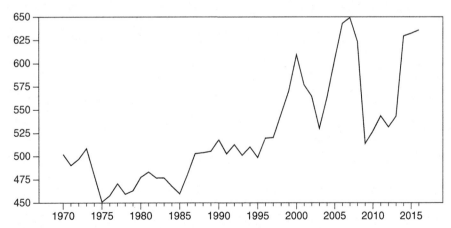

FIGURE 17.2 Household net worth as a percent of disposable personal income.

again at or near an all-time high. Notice the correlation of household net worth to income ratio and the policy inflection. We believe that the correlation is a causal one going from policy changes to the economy's P/E ratio, that is, the household net worth to GNP ratio. If that is the case and adjustment is costly, our framework can anticipate the future path of these variables as the federal government alters its policy mix, a useful insight for top-down global macroinvestors.

Our explanation requires two distinct assumptions. One is that in the long run (by this we mean that the economy will approach its long-run equilibrium) PPP will be restored. Shocks will give rise to temporary disturbances that push the economy away from its old equilibrium and into a new one. If the world we live in were frictionless, all adjustment would be instantaneous. Unfortunately, that is not the case. Adjustment costs mean that it may take some time for the economy to reach a new equilibrium. The path the economy takes to reach the new equilibrium depends on numerous factors. Nevertheless, at any point in time, the value of the exchange rate may reflect adjustments to previous and current market conditions. If one believes our interpretation of major inflection points, it is easy to see two cycles of appreciation. One begins around 1983–84 when the Reagan tax rates were being implemented, and the other during 1995 when the Republicans took over Congress. As the economy recovers from the financial crisis and wealth traces hold ground, is it possible that a third cycle may be in the offing? The big question is what are the policies that will take us there?

Getting back to the previous two peaks, there are two different explanations that tell the same story. Early on, the US economy behaved like a growth stock. Investors, both domestic and international, flocked to the United States; the capital inflow produced a higher stock market. Early on, as net worth increased relative to disposable income, we saw the US trade balance worsen (Fig. 17.3).

The United States outperformed the rest of the world. As investors tried to acquire dollars to invest in the United States, the dollar appreciated above its purchasing power parity value. Over time, as investment continued, the rate of return in new investments declined and eventually the rates of return returned to their long-run equilibrium. PPP was once again restored. Since the price rule essentially eliminates monetary disturbances as the source of exchange rate fluctuations, it follows that the bulk of the fluctuations in the dollar will reflect the US terms of trade or relative rates of return. Thus, early on as the rate of return increases, the dollar appreciates. However, if PPP is to be restored, the dollar will have to experience a round trip. More important, the price rule insures that the fluctuations in the dollar will not alter in any significant way the underlying inflation rate. In both cases we see the exchange rate behaves like an inverted "V" (Fig. 17.1).

TRADE, EMPLOYMENT, AND GROWTH

Double entry bookkeeping requires that a country's net exports equal the difference between its savings and investment rate. That is, a country whose savings rate exceeds its investment rate will be a net exporter. Countries with a trade deficit finance the net imports of goods and services by borrowing from abroad. However, the fact that a country is a net borrower or a net lender does not provide any information about the level of its savings and/or investment.

For example, a country may have a double-digit savings rate, say the highest in the world, and yet be a net borrower. All that this situation requires is that the investment rates exceed the country's savings rate. One simple explanation for this scenario is that the economy is full of opportunities. Income and wealth may be rising. If the former rises faster, then the savings rate

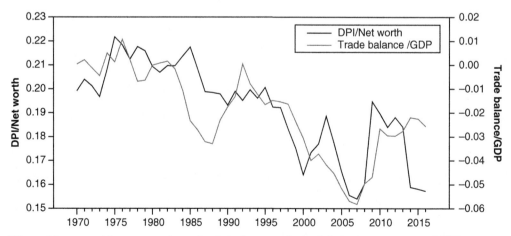

FIGURE 17.3 Disposable personal income as a share of net worth versus the trade balance as a percent of GDP.

will rise. However, since wealth is rising, consumption also rises. Hence if the income does not rise fast enough to keep up with the increase in wealth and consumption, the savings rate will decline, and the trade balance will worsen. This is the scenario that we have in mind for the United States during the 1980s and 1990s. Fig. 17.3 shows a negative relationship between the trade balance and the ratio of net worth to GDP. China's scenario, as we have discussed elsewhere, is a bit different, with income rising faster than wealth, and it leads to an increase in savings. The higher wealth leads to higher consumption. Finally, if the increase in savings exceeds the investment opportunities, the country will be a net saver, that is, exporter.

Now in a forward-looking world with well-developed capital markets, wealth is related to discounted value of income. Hence we expect to see a positive relationship between rising wealth and income growth. More importantly, there is another implication for the relationship between the trade balance and economic growth and/or employment. Unanticipated increases in economic growth that lead to an increase in the net worth to GDP ratio should result in a deterioration of the trade balance and thus produce a negative relationship between the trade balance and economic growth and employment. Fig. 17.4 shows the relationship between the trade balance and employment growth, while Fig. 17.5 shows the relationship between employment growth and real GDP growth. Figure 17.5 shows that the two variables are closely correlated as expected. Higher real GDP growth is closely correlated with a higher employment growth and vice versa. In contrast, Fig. 17.4 identifies an interesting relationship between the trade balance and employment growth. Notice the clear negative relationship between the spikes in the trade balance and employment growth, results that are counterintuitive in the context of the textbook traditional view. However, we have a simple explanation: an increase in output and employment also points to increased opportunities in the US economy, hence a capital inflow and that, in turn, means a deterioration of the trade balance. The relationships are not causal, but identified as correlations. However, it raises a

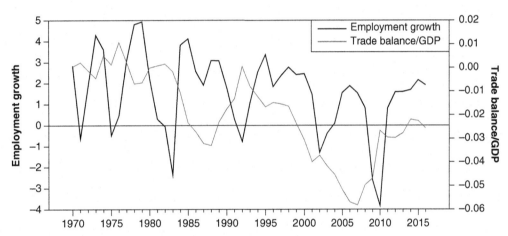

FIGURE 17.4 Trade balance as a percent of GDP versus employment growth.

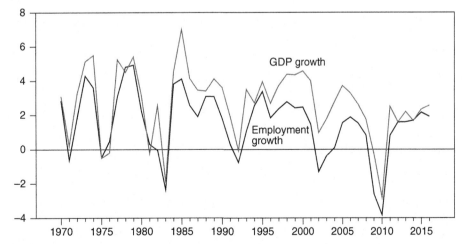

FIGURE 17.5 Real GDP and employment growth.

warning flag. Protectionist attempts to improve the trade balance may lead to a lower GDP and lower employment. The best example of this type of policy mistake is none other than the Smoot–Hawley tariffs and their impact during the 1930s.

DO EXPORTS CREATE JOBS? WHAT ABOUT IMPORTS?

Fig. 17.4 shows a negative correlation between employment growth and trade deficits. Put another way, the data does not support the mercantilist view that trade deficits mean a net export of jobs. That is a very narrow and static view of the world that is not supported by the empirical evidence.

Mercantilists argue that exports create jobs and that imports cost jobs. While the statement may be true in a *ceteris paribus* world, not everything else is constant, in a *mutatis mutandis* world that need not be the case. As we have already shown, the data suggests that an accelerating US economy leads to higher employment and a deterioration of the US trade balance.

We know from the lifecycle consumption theory that, on average, all wealth will be consumed. Hence, all income will be spent. This means that the lifecycle budget constraint requires that the value of exports and imports over the lifecycle be equal. In addition, since the world is a closed economy, the sum of all imports has to add up to the sum of all exports. The world trade balance is zero. There is no intergalactic trade. Put another way, the lifecycle trade balance has to be zero. The net savings over the lifecycle has to be zero. A policy that promotes exports has to automatically promote imports, and no net jobs are created by promoting exports (Fig. 17.6). Both imports and exports tend to move together as the lifecycle theory predicts. Thus, job creation should not focus on the trade balance. In fact, policies aimed at promoting

jobs and growth will, in the short run, lead to a deterioration of the trade balance. Attempts to improve the trade balance, promote exports, and/or restrict imports would only distort the economy and thereby retard economic growth.

ECONOMIC GROWTH, THE TRADE BALANCE, AND THE STOCK MARKET PERFORMANCE

Up to this point enough relationships between the US household net worth versus the trade balance as a percent of GDP (Fig. 17.3), employment growth, and the trade balance (Fig. 17.4) have been accumulated. We also showed the close relationship between employment growth and real GDP growth (Fig. 17.5). Given the high correlation between the employment and real GDP growth rate and the relationship between the employment growth and the trade balance, we can surmise a similar relationship between real GDP growth and the trade balance as a percent of GDP.

Next we explore the relationship between the trade balance and the US share of the world real GDP and the stock market Morgan Stanley Capital Index (MSCI) index. The relationships reported in Figs. 17.7 and 17.8 are consistent with the previous relationships reported. The common element between the two figures is the negative correlation between the spikes in the two variables included in the figures. This suggests that an increase in the US share of the world income is correlated with a deterioration of the trade balance. However, the US share of the world income can only rise if the United States grows faster than the rest of the world. The result for Fig. 17.8 is also similar. An increase in the US share of the world equity market is associated with a deterioration of the trade balance. Since the US share of the world's equity markets can only result when the US market valuation

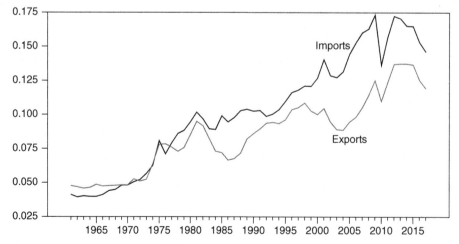

FIGURE 17.6   US imports and exports as a percent of GDP.

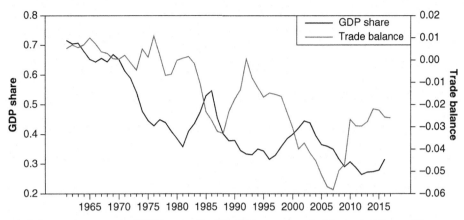

FIGURE 17.7   US trade balance as a percent of GDP versus the US GDP as a percent of the rest of the world.

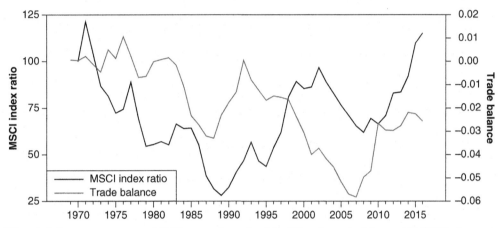

FIGURE 17.8   US trade balance as a percent of GDP versus the ratio of the US to the rest of the world MSCI index.

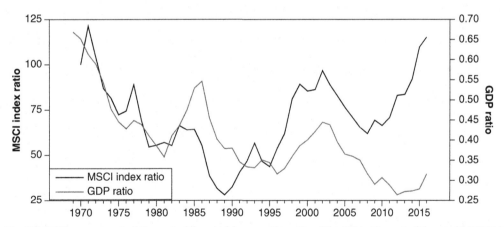

FIGURE 17.9   The US GDP as a percent of the rest of the world versus the ratio of the US to the rest of the world MSCI index.

rises faster than the rest of the world, we can say that the an improvement in the US relative growth rate and relative stock market returns are associated with a deterioration of the trade balance. The correlations reported in Figs. 17.7 and 17.8 say more than that. They suggest that there is a positive correlation between the real GDP growth rate and the stock returns. It suggests that there is a positive correlation between the United States outperforming the World real GDP growth rate and the United States outperforming the world stock market returns. Fig. 17.9 confirms what Figs. 17.7 and 17.8 implied.

A trade deficit means that we have a capital inflow; we are borrowing from our trading partners. Pundits worry that we are living beyond our means and that our best days are behind us or that we are eating our way into the poorhouse. If that was the case, we would expect to see the market anticipate this and decline relative to the rest of the world whenever the trade balance worsens. The implication here is clear. It predicts a negative relationship between trade deficits and the US stock market relative to the rest of the world. Yet that is not what the data says.

There is another, alternative interpretation: the reason for borrowing is that there are great investment opportunities, and, by borrowing, we take advantage of these opportunities. Put another way, better days are ahead of us. The higher future return allows us to pay for the amount borrowed without sacrificing current consumption. The higher investment returns attract capital, and as the market anticipates the higher returns, valuations will rise and the United States will outperform the rest of the world. Hence, not only US investors, but also foreign investors will want to take advantage of the opportunities in the United States. Advocates of the "better days ahead" alternative theory predict a negative relationship between the trade balance, stock markets, real GDP, and employment growth relative performances. Figs. 17.4 17.7 and 17.8 clearly support our views and contradict the alternative interpretation. As we argued, there is a distinctive and clear negative relationship between the trade balance as a percent of GDP and the relative stock market performance measured by the ratio of the United States versus the MSCI Rest of the World Indices. That is not all. As capital flows in, the demand for dollars will rise and a dollar appreciation is to be expected.

THE EXCHANGE RATE AND TERMS OF TRADE

To close the circle, we need to discuss the relationship between real GDP growth and the different variables. We have already established the negative relationship between real GDP and the trade balance as a percent of GDP. We also argued that as economic opportunity improves, capital will flow into the country and that, in turn, leads to a net increase in the demand for the US dollar. As a result, we expect to observe a positive relationship between real GDP growth and the foreign exchange value of the dollar, due to capital inflow, and to the relative stock market returns, due to the improving investment opportunities. Fig. 17.9 presents some clear evidence of a positive correlation between an improving relative stock market performance and the US real GDP growth rate. One striking result is reported in Fig. 17.10. Notice the close correlation between the US share of the world's GDP and the foreign exchange value of the dollar. At first one may be surprised by the results, but there is a simple monetarist explanation for this. If the demand for money is relatively stable, and the income elasticity of the demand for money is one, i.e. the demand for real balance is proportional to the income level in the country, then it follows that the price level will be proportional to the inverse of the income level. Therefore the nominal exchange rate, being the ratio of two price levels, will reflect the ratio of the two regions' output, that is the United States and rest of the world income levels. Fig. 17.11 shows the US share of the world GDP and the terms of trade. Notice that the relationship is not as close as the one reported in Fig. 17.10. The conclusion being that the terms of trade contain different information set than the nominal exchange rate, that is, the US dollar index.

Next, we move to the relationships between the trade balance and the foreign exchange value of the dollar and terms of trade. We also examined the relationship between the US stock market as a share of the world market and the dollar index as well as the terms of trade. Unfortunately as Fig. 17.12 shows, if there is a negative correlations between the US dollar and the trade balance as a percent of GDP It is a fairly weak one. A much stronger

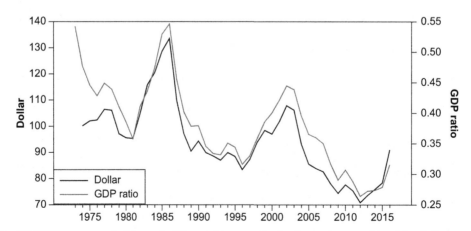

FIGURE 17.10   The US GDP as a percent of the rest of the world versus the foreign exchange value of the dollar.

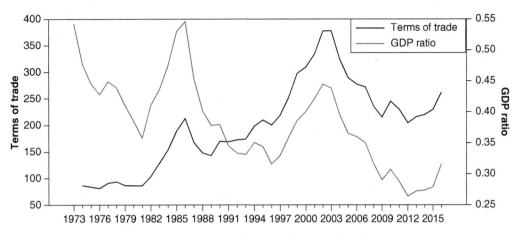

FIGURE 17.11   The US GDP as a percent of the rest of the world versus the terms of trade.

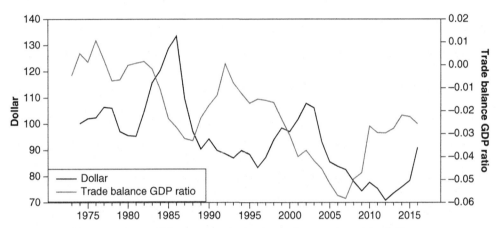

FIGURE 17.12   The trade balance as a percent of GDP versus the foreign exchange value of the dollar.

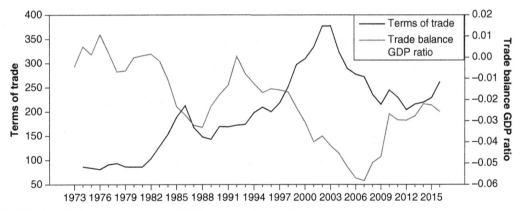

FIGURE 17.13   The trade balance as a percent of GDP versus the terms of trade.

correlation can be found between the terms of trade and the trade balance (Fig. 17.13). These results lend support to the view that it is real factors that determine the changes in the trade balance. As we have already mentioned, sometimes the exchange rate reflects changes in the terms of trade, and at other times, it reflects changes in the relative rates of inflation, or put another way, it reflects monetary shocks. This may explain the weak

negative relationship. The monetary shocks are noise that obfuscate the true relationship. The negative relationship is not anything new or an unexpected result in the context of the traditional view. Where we part company is with the interpretation. While it may be true that a "cheaper dollar" may improve the trade balance, that may not be a desirable outcome if all of the relationships identified in this section hold up. The "cheaper dollar"

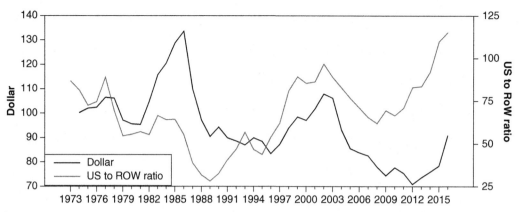

FIGURE 17.14   The ratio of the US to rest of the world MSCI index versus the foreign exchange value of the dollar.

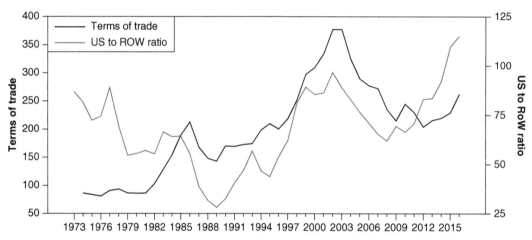

FIGURE 17.15   The ratio of the US to rest of the world MSCI index versus the terms of trade.

may be reflecting a deterioration of the terms of trade in which case an improvement in the trade balance due to a weaker dollar may signal an economic slowdown, higher unemployment, a capital outflow, or a lower relative stock market. We do not think these are desirable changes in these variables. In turn, if our interpretation is correct, the rising dollar and a deteriorating trade balance is a bullish sign. It is a sign of an improving stock market relative to the rest of the world. Fig. 17.14 shows that, as expected, there is a positive correlation between the US dollar and the US relative stock performance. However Fig. 17.15 shows that the relationship is much stronger when the terms of trade replace the foreign exchange value of the dollar.

So far, we have provided a parsimonious explanation for the various relationships, and that is good for it sug-

gests that our theory, at the very least, has a great deal of explanatory power. The exchange rate-based investment implication of this view of the world is straightforward: follow the money. Underweigh the economies whose exchange rate is expected to depreciate. More specifically, follow those whose terms for trade are expected to deteriorate and overweigh those whose economy is expected to appreciate. An obvious question is how can one tell which economy is going to do what? Our answer is that a top-down approach that pays attention to the policy changes, weather changes, and innovations may point the investors in the right direction. Also if adjustments are costly, returns cycles will be generated. So even if one misses the intimal turning point, there will be plenty of time for the astute and studious investor to take advantage of these cycles.

18

Relative Price Changes, Income Redistribution, and the Politics of Envy

Free market economists believe that relative prices play a very important role in the economy. They provide the economic signal that helps economic agents deploy resources at their disposal in a way that maximizes the returns generated by these resources.

The profit maximization process can be told either from the producer's or the consumer's perspective. On the producer's side, relative prices provide a signal to investors as to where the highest rates or returns are being earned and, as such, helps investors make decisions as to where to deploy their capital. In other words, high rates of return attract investments and that leads to an increase in the productive capacity or supply of goods and services. The higher supply in turn leads to lower long-run prices and thus a lower rate of return. Returns decline to their long-run equilibrium effectively signaling to the economy that perhaps resources may earn a higher rate of return elsewhere.

When the process is complete, excess profits opportunities will be exhausted and the rates of return will be equalized across activities. The same story can also be told from the consumer's perspective. The higher

relative price induces substitution away from the higher price activity to the lower price activity. That, in turn, brings about a readjustment of production, the relative prices, and the redeployment of the capital allocated to the different activities.

Over time, relative prices return to their long-run equilibrium and rates of return are equalized across activities. This is what we mean when we argue that market forces are self-correcting and have a tendency to maximize the utilization of an economy's factors of production. The market, absent externalities and other distortions, has a tendency to reach a stable, long-run equilibrium when left to its own devices. However, sometimes the electorate is impatient and not willing to wait for markets to run their course, and these groups apply political pressure to the government to take action and deal with the real or perceived problem.

If all the government did was accelerating the equilibrating process, everything would be fine. No mischief would take place and everyone involved would be grateful that the government accelerated the adjustment to the new equilibrium. Unfortunately, quite often spe-

Economic Disturbances and Equilibrium in an Integrated Global Economy. http://dx.doi.org/10.1016/B978-0-12-813993-6.00018-0

cial interest groups are myopic and create pressure that forces the government to adopt politically expedient solutions that appear to solve the problem in the short run at the expense of the long run. If the benefited groups do not care about the rest of the economy and they have political clout, they will force the government to affect the policy changes even if they are damaging to the long run well-being of the overall economy. That is the politics of special interest groups, to improve their own well-being even if it is at the expense of other groups in society [1]. They do not care how their well-being comes about, whether it is a result of an expanding economic pie or the redistribution of the existing pie. They will take whichever action is least costly to them, even if it is very expensive for the economy as a whole. That is why we call this the politics of envy. Selfishness is a bad thing.

NECESSARY CONDITIONS

There is a strong connection between the politics of special interest groups and relative price changes. The basic intent behind the politics of special interest groups is to alter the relative price of some commodities or groups of commodities to affect a net income transfer through an improvement in their terms of trade.

An increase in the relative price of oil, say an increase over and above inflation, means that a barrel of oil now buys more of other goods and services. Net oil producers will be able to acquire more goods and services than before and as a result are likely to experience an increase in economic well-being. In contrast, net oil consumers would tend to experience a decline in real income. All else the same, the consumers will be worse off and they will have an incentive to attempt to reverse the adverse terms of trade change. How do they do that? They do so by creating political pressure, forcing the government to take action to reverse the adverse terms of trade change or net income transfer. A clear example of this was during the 1970s when in response to oil price increases, consumers pressured the government into enacting a series of measures intended to reverse the income transfer resulting from high energy prices. The United States enacted oil and gas price controls as well as instituting a windfall profits tax.

Early in the new millennium, we saw the price of oil increase. While there was some noise regarding a windfall profits tax, nothing happened. No action was been taken by the government. We ask why? Our own answer is that the adverse change in the terms of trade is a necessary but not sufficient condition for the politics of envy. We need to look at the totality of the change. We also need to determine whether the economic pie is expanding or not. If it is, then we must determine whether the pie expansion offsets the adverse terms of trade. If that

is the case, the politics of envy will not pay out and political pressure will not be successful in bringing about policy changes. When people are clearly better off, they have no incentive to risk their well-being. A bird in the hand is worth two in the bushes.

We can easily explain why many of the new redistribution efforts during the last two or three decades have failed. The economy has been expanding at a fairly decent pace, thus the pie expansion overwhelmed the income redistribution brought about by relative price changes. However, as the economy slows down, political pressure groups become more active, the benefits of redistribution increase relative to the pie expansion, and the likelihood of change increases. If the next few years are ones of subpar economic performance, as some are forecasting, we need to brace for a sustained increase in the politics of envy. We should be quite worried about this possibility. Evidence is already surfacing regarding this possible bearish outcome.

AGRICULTURAL COMMODITIES, THE NEW OIL?

The oil price increase of the 1970s is customarily described as the poster child for the politics of relative price change where Organization of Petroleum Exporting Countries (OPEC) exploited its monopoly power to its benefit. The abruptness of the price hike and the immediate impact on the world economy that the higher oil prices brought about make the impact of the relative price changes on the income redistribution easily noticeable to the naked and/or untrained eye. But oil is not the only commodity where special interest groups have steadily tried to curry the favor of the government. The politics of relative price change has a long history in the United States and European agricultural sectors. Former farm bill legislations document the many successes of special interest groups in altering the terms of trade or relative price change in their favor.

The evolution of the agricultural price support programs is very complicated to describe. But it is clear to all that the net effect of the policies is to increase the income level of the favored agricultural groups. There is no denying that in the United States and Europe, agricultural price support and related programs are a testimony of the ability of the agricultural lobby to turn the terms of trade in their favor. These farm bills are a testament to the power of the politics of the special interest groups and its income redistribution power. While the politics of special interest groups may in the short run benefit the favored interest group, overall the economy loses. Even worse, the distortion generated by the politics of the special interest groups has unintended consequences that in some cases are quite negative for the rest of the economy.

In past writings, we have focused on the oil price hike during the 1970s. But an equaling compelling and perhaps even more damaging effect is that of the politics of the relative price change in agricultural goods.

IMPACT OF AGRICULTURAL PRICE SUPPORT PROGRAMS

Although we take some liberty in describing some of the actual policies, our story captures the essence of the impact of the policies and allows us to draw conclusions regarding the effect and success of the politics of relative price change. While United States and European countries pursue very convoluted farm policies, it is fair to say that the net effect of these policies is to produce a price higher than would prevail in an unfettered market, for this reason we characterize them as a price support system. Now in the textbook versions of a price support system, the government sets the price above the market-clearing price. The higher price produces a movement along the supply curve. Domestic production increases until the marginal cost of producing an additional bushel of grain matches the supported price. On the consumption side, if the prevailing domestic price is the support price, there will be a movement along the demand curve. The quantity demanded declines. Since the producers receive a higher price for their product, it follows that the price support system effectively alters the terms in favor of the producers. The farmers are clearly better off. The measure redistributes income from consumers to producers in the home country. The impact on the rest of the world is much different than at home.

UNINTENDED CONSEQUENCES: ECONOMIC DEPENDENCY

The agricultural price support programs of developed nations have had some devastating and unintended consequences to the economic well-being of the emerging world. Developed nations subsidize their domestic production by keeping domestic prices artificially high which results in excess domestic production. The surplus is sold in the world market to countries with little or no price support. Increased supply to the world markets results in lower prices and that, in turn, has several income effects on the rest of the world.

Consumers in the rest of the world now have access to a greater variety of agricultural goods at lower prices. The immediate thought is that the lower price of worldwide agricultural products makes the rest of the world consumers better off.

That may be true for consumers that do not depend on the agricultural sector. A good example would be those consumers who work in the maquiladora or manufacturing sectors. But what about those who work in the agricultural sector? If they are net sellers of agricultural products, the depressed world prices will clearly reduce their income level and as a result they will be worse off. The reason for this is that they produce more than they consume and sell the excess production. So for these people the decline in income would be greater than the consumption gains. If they have any clout, they will lobby for protectionist policies aimed at stopping the import of "cheap" grain. In other words, they will retaliate and as we all know, retaliation makes everyone worse off. If they do not have the political clout, the imported grain will come in and the impact on their income will be devastating.

In the extreme case that it is no longer profitable for them to produce these grains, these farmers, if they were in subsistence level economies, will now be below subsistence. Absent outside help, these people would suffer greatly. Starvation is a likely outcome. We can lay some of the blame for starvation in frontier countries on the agricultural policies of developed nations. That in turn elicits an additional response by the developed world. A likely remedy is to have international agencies buy part of the surplus production generated by distorting agricultural policies and distribute them free or sell them at below market prices in the frontier markets. The non-market mechanism is usually fraught with corruption and inefficiencies. In the end, the developed countries' actions create dependent economies with no hope of getting ahead by using the resources that they had historically used to improve their standard of living.

Viewed this way, the farmer's well-being is being bought at the expense of not only domestic consumers but the rest of the world farmers and economic development in these frontier countries. Even worse, if the developed countries' production declines unexpectedly, the end result is starvation if foreign aid is not forthcoming. But even in the case where aid is forthcoming and the developed countries' excess grain is used to feed poor people, the damage is already done.

The agricultural policies of developed countries destroy whatever little private initiative the frontier countries had. Now the politics of special interest groups and redistributionist policies will reign supreme in midst a declining economic pie and international agencies become extremely important as part of the distribution of goods. Replacing the market mechanism is not a good thing. While the developed countries may feel good, the policies of redistribution and aid engender corruption, patronage and destroy incentives to save, invest and produce. In the long run, they create a dependent class incapable of taking care of itself. To the extent that those resources are wasted or used inefficiently, society as a whole is worse off. As this example shows, a bad policy often leads to more bad policies. The unintended consequences of price support are pretty bad.

ECONOMIC GROWTH AND PRICE SUPPORT PROGRAMS

Now let's move forward and see what happens as the world economy expands? Stronger growth in the world economy means that world aggregate demand will rise. The increase in demand will be satisfied in a couple of ways. Companies with flexible production plans (i.e., elastic companies) meet the increase in demand by increasing production. On the other hand, companies with little or no flexibility (inelastic companies) cannot change their production plans and thus have to raise price to meet demand. In short, faster economic growth brings about different type of equilibrating outcomes. Inelastically supplied products experience an increase in price well above the average price increase with little or no change in production. The inelasticity can be natural or man-made. In some cases, it may be difficult to extract a mineral or the production or cultivation process may be complicated thereby resulting in high production costs. In other cases, government restrictions prevent the production process from accommodating to meet the increases in demand. How the inelasticity comes about is irrelevant. The outcome is the same, higher prices and higher income for the factors intensive in the production of the inelastic products.

The source of the inelasticity may be due to natural or economic reasons and that we cannot do much about. Another possible source of inelasticity is government regulation and price distortions. Here is where we can lay the blame on the politics of special interest groups. The distortions generated by the response to the political pressure are usually intended to favor a particular group at the expense of others. Yet as we already argued, there are unintended consequences.

UNINTENDED CONSEQUENCES: OIL AND AGRICULTURAL PRODUCTS

We have argued that the commodity prices have been kept artificially high in the United States and the rest of the developed world as a result of price support and other related agricultural policies. Now let's see how the economic growth has interacted with these policies to create some unexpected problems. First, the growth in the world economy has led to an increase in the demand for oil and other fuels. Government regulations about drilling and restrictions on the use of certain fuels reduced the market elasticity. The increase in demand due to higher global growth led to a rise in the price of fuels over and above the inflation rate. In short, the relative price of fuel increased.

We contend that the higher prices would have created incentives for drilling and building additional plants as well as developing new technologies. But the government chose to meddle in the energy market. Eliminating regulations on drilling and allowing the building of nuclear plants, etc. would have alleviated upward price pressures but the developed world governments chose not to do that. Instead, in the United States and elsewhere, governments chose to subsidize alternative energy, biofuels, etc. The unintended consequence here was high prices due to faster world growth combined with subsidies to biofuels. This created an incentive to plant land for the growing of biofuel inputs. There are two sources of land: new planting or diverting the use of existing land to the production of the biofuels. The latter means that the supply of agricultural land for foodstuff could decline. Substitution effects work in a very simple and clear way. The price of other agricultural goods will also rise in tandem with biofuels. But that is not all. The world demand for grain for consumption purposes also increases.

So we now have a net increase in the demand for agricultural products. If the supply is not forthcoming or matching the increase in demand, the end result is an increase in the domestic price of agricultural products. Given our argument that government regulations reduce the supply elasticities, the increase in prices is even higher then under normal conditions.

A WARNING

Now let's focus on the politics of agricultural goods. Our basic theory is that different groups try to alter terms of trade in their favor and thereby affect income redistribution in their favor. Conversely, an adverse change in relative prices elicits a political response as long as the relative price change has a negative impact on the income of the affected groups. Under a static or shrinking economy, the change in relative price and the income effect moves in the same direction. Higher relative prices mean a lower overall real income. In a growing economy, if sufficiently strong, the income effect generated by the higher growth will overwhelm the negative effect of an adverse relative price increase. In that case, the groups will be better off with the change and as a result, no political pressure will be forthcoming.

This, in part, explains why there has been little pressure on the government to do something about the high price of oil and other commodities during the first few years of the new millennium. Strong growth cures many ills, including increases in relative prices. Similarly, there has been little or no pressure to tax the "windfall" or excess profit of these commodities suppliers. Yet as the economy begins to slow down, the drumbeats of the special interest groups begin to sound. We can see farmers being blamed for the rising cost of food just as the oil companies are demonized for high oil prices. No one blames the consumer or government regulation. There is plenty of blame to go around. What we fear is that as the economy slows down, we embark in a new round of the politics of special interests. In such an environment, redistribution and higher regulations will be the order of the day and that will further distort the economy and lead to slower growth and more regulations. If we are not careful, we could very well fall into a vicious cycle of slow growth, income redistribution and catering to special interest groups.

MORE UNINTENDED CONSEQUENCES: STARVATION

One implication that is ignored in the market-clearing process is that as prices go up, less elastic consumers and those who cannot afford the commodity will drop out. We do not worry about elastic consumers dropping out. It means they have alternatives and can now purchase other goods. The worrisome case is that of consumers whose income is too low. As price increases, they are forced to reduce their consumption of goods inversely with the price increase. For these groups, the price increase translates into a reduction in their well-being.

The sad part of all this is that as the world economy grows and poorer countries are crowded out of the market, starvation becomes a real possibility. Poor farmers go bankrupt as prices decline. Domestic production also declines and yet these countries need to feed their own population. As their domestic production declines, these countries become even more dependent on foreign grain. Since they cannot afford to purchase the grain, they become more dependent on international organizations to provide them with grain to avoid starvation. But even there we have a problem. As the price of the grain increases, the international organizations budget does not go as far as it used to. This adverse cyclicality is ironic. International agencies can afford to feed the poor of the world the least during good times for the world economy. Also during these good times in the developed economies, in subsistence economies the problem is now worse. Since they abandoned production and have become dependent on hand outs, scarcity leads to shortages, and quite possibly starvation. And in time of desperation, riot, lawlessness, revolution, and even civil war are possible where the rule of law is completely ignored. This shows the perverse impact of misguided government policies that interfere with the functioning of the market. Price supports prevent the markets from responding to changing conditions and the incidence falls in poor unsuspecting countries far away from the subsidized countries.

MORE UNINTENDED CONSEQUENCES: TRADE RESTRICTIONS

Price supports in developed countries also affect producers in other parts of the world. As world demand increases and prices rise, the income of farmer's increases substantially and that creates additional political problems in economies producing these goods and services. Under a free trade regime, local consumers would now have to pay the higher world price for the commodity in question. The reduction in income experienced by consumers combined with the income gains for the producers creates resentment and political pressure for the government to alleviate the decline in the standard of living especially at a time when the producers are making a "killing." The politics of envy set in, especially in countries with populist governments.

There are many examples of these governments getting involved based on political pressure. In an effort to slow down domestic price increases, Argentina set up export taxes approaching confiscatory levels. Other countries took less revenue rising measures, more than likely an even more damaging approach to the problem. Instead of an export tax, these countries adopted an outright ban on the export of certain grains. India banned the export of rice other than basmati. The curbing of agricultural commodities was not confined to India. Vietnam also enacted export restrictions. And in many of these countries the effort went beyond export restraints. For example, Vietnam also banned rice speculation, whatever that means. Malaysia and the Philippines made moves to ensure that their citizens could afford grain as soaring prices triggered unease. The point is that price increases resulted in additional government intervention. Malaysia subsidized locally grown rice while the Philippine government issued special cards for the poor allowing them to buy rice at roughly half the world market price.

The effort to curb exports goes beyond agricultural commodities. In India, the ministries of steel and commerce proposed some export bans in the steel sector. That is why we believe that the issue was more than oil and agricultural commodities. Finally, we need to point out that as these countries enact trade restrictions to lower the price of commodities at home, in the rest of the developing world, the price of these commodities will increase, making the survival issues even worse for frontier markets.

Protectionism is not the domain of emerging economies; the same concerns are also evident in developed economies. The fear of import competitions, fair or unfair, taking away jobs and lowering income of domestic producers of income competing goods are quite real. According to the popular press, many politicians and economists, the biggest offender on this front is none other than China. Whether these fears are justified or not is a matter of great political debate and one can cite academic studies supporting the different points of views.

In a series of academic papers, David Autor and others have analyzed the economic impact of China's coming out party on the world stage [2]. While acknowledging that there are great benefits to trade, they also focus on some of the costs that the trade competition may have produced. In particular, their research finds that there are substantial adjustment costs and distributional consequences. The abstract of their *American Economic Review* paper written by the authors is quite unequivocal:

> Adjustment in local labor markets is remarkably slow, with wages and labor force participation rates remaining elevated for at least a full decade after the China trade shock commences. Exposed workers experience greater churning and reduced lifetime income. At the national level, employment has fallen in the US industries more exposed to import competition, as expected, but offsetting employment gains in other industries have yet to materialize.

These results are quite interesting and the first part documents something that we have argued and believe, that there are significant adjustment costs and thus it may take a while for the economy to reach a new equilibrium. However, the authors suggest that it may take longer than we thought to reach the new long-run equilibrium. The authors go on to conclude that:

> *Import shocks trigger a decline in wages that is primarily observed outside the manufacturing sector … These changes contribute to rising transfer payments through multiple federal and state programs, revealing an important margin of adjustment that the literature has largely overlooked.*
>
> ….The largest transfer increases are for federal disability, retirement, and in-kind medical payments. Unemployment insurance and income assistance play a significant but secondary role. By contrast, Trade Adjustment Assistance (TAA), which specifically provides benefits to workers who have been displaced by trade shocks, accounts for a negligible part of the trade induced increases.

As discussed, earlier statements raise a couple of interesting issues, the first being an obvious one being TAA negligible part and why federal disability and retirement play such an important part. Is it possible that the interaction between the shock and the social safety net may have delayed the recovery? We know that the higher the social safety net benefits, the higher the reservation wage will be. We also know that the mean testing of the social safety net programs also tends to reduce the incentives to return to the labor force. Finally, the longer the person

stays out of the labor force, the more their skills deteriorate. If the qualification requirements are loosened, the higher the participation in these programs will be. The US data show that the number of persons out of the labor force who have a disability has been steadily rising. The average increase has been about 1.9% year-over-year. All of this raises the question as to whether some of the adjustment costs are caused or driven by the interaction between the displacement and the social safety net? Then there is a rebuttal research by Jonathan Rothwell [3], who analyzed their data and concludes that … *their results are biased by the weaker macroeconomic performance of the 2000–07 relative to the 1990s.* Another interesting result is reported by Columbia University PhD candidate Ildiko Magyari [4], who examined the net effect of Chinese imports on firm level employment as opposed to local labor markets. The argument being that Chinese competition may reduce the employment at individual establishments, they may simultaneously lower the cost of production and allow firms to increase employment in industry in which the United States has a comparative advantage. She concludes that …. *although Chinese imports may have reduced employment within some establishments, these losses were more than offset by gains in employment within the same firms.*

Whether trade competition lowers or increases overall employment is, as we have shown, a matter of debate. What is not for debate is that those directly affected will suffer economic losses and given their close proximity, that is, employment in the same firm or sector, they could easily become a special interest group that will lobby for government action. That will unambiguously lead to an increase in protectionist pressures. Whether these groups succeed depends on many factors, but one thing is fairly clear: the loss of jobs increases the likelihood of trade actions, even if the costs exceed the economy's gains from trade.

A GENERALIZATION

A stagnant world or a slow growing world economy is an environment that propitiates the politics of special interest groups. The reason for this is that as the economy slows down, income redistribution may be the only option that certain groups will have to increase their standard of living. If these people do not care about other groups, we could fall into a vicious cycle where the politics of envy lead to redistribution policies and these, in turn, destroy incentives and produce slower growth. The slower growth further propitiates the politics of the special interest groups and redistribution that leads to a second round of lower growth, hence the vicious cycle.

The justification for redistribution is quite easy. All the special interest groups have to do is demonize the groups targeted to transfer some of their income to the special interest groups pressuring the governments. So the "problems" come in a variety of packages. One is the need for high domestic prices to protect an industry or group. In the United States, agricultural policies are sometimes justified as attempting to protect the family farm, although many of the beneficiaries are not family farms nor are they really in need of protection as they are profitable enough.

Other types of political pressures are quite obvious, such as consumers complaining about the high price of goods and services and riling against the "excessive" profits of the greedy suppliers. Yet we never hear them talking about the excessive losses of the poor producers during cycles of low prices. The policies pushed by these groups include the windfall profit taxes on domestic producers. In case of exporters, we see domestic consumer complaining about the excessive profits of the exporters and they pressure the government to enact export restraint aiming to keep goods and services in the domestic market rather than being exported to the high price world market. These measures are commonly applied in most of the agricultural exporting countries in the emerging market and even is some developed economies. These problems and the weak dollar have pushed aside from the top of the list what a few months ago was the cat's meow of the politics of special interest groups when we heard complaints about "unfair" competition because of the changing fortunes of the exchange rate.

As an economy slows down, the politics of greed, of expanding the economic pie will be replaced by the politics of envy focused on the redistribution of the existing economic pie. As governments and special interest groups attempt to redistribute income, incentives to increase the economic pie will decline. The end result could very well be a smaller pie for all involved and given that some interest groups improve their share of the pie means that those adversely affected will suffer both in absolute and relative terms. Beggar thy neighbor mercantilist polices based on a static view of the world as opposed to an expanding pie dynamic view of the world is quite a different scenario than what we have been used to since the Reagan Revolution.

MERCANTILISM DOES NOT MAKE FOR GOOD ECONOMICS

The call for protectionist trade policies is tempered by the experiences of the Great Depression. In 1930, congress passed the Smoot–Hawley tariffs, the largest tax increase on traded products in the history of the United States. The trade balance, which at the time had been deteriorating during the prior 10 years of rapid growth, improved. But the nation and the rest of the world were

impoverished. That experience, more than any other, stands in the way of wholesale effort to limit foreign trade.

This may go a long way to explain why the majority of economists agree that, in the extreme, trade restrictions are self-defeating, impoverishing foreign countries, and US citizens alike. The policy issue this centers on whether judiciously applied protectionist measures can contribute to domestic stability and growth. The investment issue is the magnitude of movement in equity values associated with the imposition of such trade restrictions.

In spite of the devastating legacy of the Smoot–Hawley tariffs, creeping protectionism has become a reality, not only in the United States, but among most of the industrial countries. "Judicious" use of across-the-board trade restrictions are frequently proposed as a way of narrowing the trade deficit and saving jobs. And, more and more, selected trade restrictions, such as countervailing duties, designating countries as currency manipulators, and so-called "voluntary restraints" have been advocated as a way of protecting American industry and jobs form "unfair" foreign competition. Whether or not protectionist policies actually enhance the performance of the economy or selected industries is an empirical question [5].

The logic in favor of the protectionist policies is very seductive, and is a factor that may explain its popularity at different points in time in the US history. This is not surprising that from time to time the United States has experienced bouts of protectionism. In the past, the increases in protectionist policies have been associated with rising and high trade deficits, rising and high unemployment, as well as a strong and rising dollar. The argument for the protectionist policies is based on the hope of creating a more favorable trade balance. The special interest groups and lobbyist advocating for the across-the-board protectionist policies commonly cite foreign competition, both fair and unfair. They attribute the surge in imports as the source of the problems of the weakest sectors in the economy.

PROTECTIONISTS VERSUS FREE TRADE ARGUMENTS

The debate on trade policy is much the same as it was 200 years ago. Arguments today that favor increased protectionism incorporate several mercantilists' concepts, including the importance of a positive trade balance to a nation prosperity. A trade surplus supposedly creates a cascading series of increased expenditures, that is, the foreign trade multiplier, while a trade deficit supposedly represents a leakage of demand from domestic to foreign goods and products, reducing with a multiplier income, profits, and employment.

Import tariffs and export subsidies are advocated as a set of polices capable of improving the trade balance of trade. Supporters of these policies observe that tariffs raise domestic price of imported goods and subsidies reduce the price of goods exported to foreigners. This reduction in imports and thus the stimulus to exports are believed to improve the domestic economic conditions. If the advocates of trade restrictions were correct, then across-the-board protectionist policies would be associated with the increased profitability (i.e., stock returns) and employment.

On the other hand, free trade advocates harken back to the principles propounded by Adam Smith and his predecessors. They argue that imports and exports are two sides of the same transaction. Goods are exported to ultimately be able to import and consume the goods produced by foreigners. Free traders argue that a restriction on imports is equivalent to a restriction on exports and can be expected to have little or no effect on the trade balance. Similarly, a subsidy on exports is equivalent to a subsidy on imports. This proposition is nothing more than Lerner's famous Symmetry Theorem [6]. Free trade advocates conclude that trade restrictions do not improve the trade balance, but do impair the efficient of the economy. To the extent that restrictions are effective, the benefits of free access to foreign goods and markets are lost to the economy. That is the case called gains of trade are reduced. Production incentives shift away from those goods produced more efficient domestically. If the advocates of free trade are correct, then protectionist policies would be associated with decreased profitability and employment. The assumption that protectionist policies will save jobs in America is static thinking that will take the administration down the wrong policy path.

Redistributionist policies may be justified in a zero-sum world. However, in an interdependent world of expanding opportunities, protectionism will bring everyone down. Conversely, a pro-growth, pro-free trade agenda will make us all better off. If market forces are operating, the production of lower value added items will be exported to us at much lower prices than if they were produced here. The gains to the United States come in two forms: the lower prices paid by consumers and the freeing up of resources that can now be invested in higher value added activities.

In real life, the adjustment process is not costless. However, the long-run benefits are obvious. One only needs to look at the Midwest. During the early Reagan years, we referred to it as the rustbelt. The smokestacks in the industrial Midwest were having a tough time. Yet looking back, one can see that the region retooled and recovered. In Cleveland, the river does not catch fire anymore and the Midwest became a thriving dynamic region. The technological revolution taking place in the world today is forcing similar adjustments. Add to that

the adoption of market-oriented tendencies in the rest of the world and we have the makings of another major readjustment in trade and production patterns. The sad part is that rather than accelerating the transition, the government actions retarding the adjustment to a new world order.

THE FACTS

Policy intervention in international trade appears to be systematically related to economic events. Across-the-board trade restrictions are not prompted by a slowdown in employment growth. Rather, the most important determinant of major trade-reducing policies since 1960 has been a deteriorating trade balance. At the industry level, the story is quite different. A decline in an industry's employment growth or in its stock returns relative to the average for the economy, however, results in a significant increase in industry-specific protectionist policies.

The empirical evidence suggests that trade restriction more often than not, does not achieve their stated objectives. Around the time across-the-board restrictions are imposed, equity values and employment decline, rather than improve [7]. Even policies aimed at protecting specific industries tend to fail to achieve their stated goal. Equity values fell in the leader shoe, color TV, automobile, and other industries following the implementation of protectionist policies. The employment performance around the announcement of trade restrictions also deteriorated. The steel industry experience with trade restrictions was associated with a deterioration in the industry stock price index [8].

The implications for policymakers, money managers, and financial analysts are clear: a protected economy or a protected industry will tend to underperform relative to economies and industries that are forced to meet the rigors of intentional competition. Worse yet, the protectionist policies only delay the inevitable. These protected sectors will have to retool to be a viable and compete in the market place. In the meantime, the economy's resources are being either wasted or used inefficiently.

References

[1] Canto Victor A. The Determinants and Consequences of Trade Restrictions in the U.S. Economy. New York: Praeger Publishing; 1986.
[2] Acemoglu Daron, Autor David, Dorn David, Gordon H Hanson, Price Brendan. Import competition and the great US employment Sag of the 2000s. J Labor Econ 2016;34(S1 (part 2)):S141–98. Autor David H, Dorn David, Hanson Gordon H. The China shock: learning from labor-market adjustment to large changes in trade. Ann Rev Econ 2016;8:205–40. Autor David H, Dorn David, Hanson Gordon H. The China syndrome: local labor market effects of import competition in the United States. Am Econ Rev 2013;103(6):2121–68.

[3] Jonathan Rothwell. Cutting the losses: reassessing the costs of import competition to workers and communities. Gallup Inc; 2017.

[4] Ildiko Magyari. Firm Reorganization, Chinese Imports, and US Manufacturing Employment. Available from: http://www.columbia.edu/~im2348/JMP_Magyari.pdf.

[5] Lerner Abba P. The symmetry between import and export taxes. Economica 1936;3(11):306–13.

[6] Canto Victor A, Dietrich J Kimball, Jain Adish, Mudaliar Vishwa. The determinants and consequences of across-the-board trade restrictions in the U.S. economy. Int Trade J 1986;1(1 Fall):65–78. Canto Victor A, Dietrich J Kimball, Jain Adish, Mudaliar Vishwa. Protectionism and the stock market: the determinants and consequences of trade restrictions on the U.S. economy. Financial Anal J 1986;42(5):32–42.

[7] Canto Victor, Laffer Arthur, Eastin Richard. Failure of protectionism: a study of the steel industry. Columbia J World Bus 1982;XVII(4 Winter). Canto, Dietrich, Jain, Mudaliar (1986 a,b).

[8] There is an extensive literature on the politics of special interest groups and rent seeking behavior.Becker Gary S. A theory of competition among pressure groups for political influence. Q J Econ 1983;98(3):371–400. Buchanan James M. Public Finance in Democratic Process: Fiscal Institutions and Individual Choice. UNC Press; 1967. Buchanan James M. The Demand and Supply of Public Goods. Rand McNally; 1968. Buchanan James, Tullock Gordon. The Calculus of Consent: Logical Foundations of a Constitutional Democracy. Ann Arbor: University of Michigan Press; 1962.

III. EXCHANGE RATE AND THE TERMS OF TRADE

19

Self-Sufficiency, Nationalism, and Protectionism: The Common Elements

Whenever a country has a trade deficit in a particular commodity or service, politicians are quite fond of arguing that we need to become self-sufficient in the commodity or service in question. Usually the proponents of this viewpoint argue that by becoming self-sufficient, employment in that commodity will improve. So far, we have no complaints about this argument. Then, more often than not, the policymakers and politicians extend the conclusion to the general economy. Unfortunately, while politically appealing, these self-sufficiency, nationalist, and sometimes protectionist arguments do not always deliver the goods. In fact, a strong argument can be made that nonmarket actions taken to induce the self-sufficiency will make the economy worse off in addition to being ineffective.

SELF-SUFFICIENCY POLICIES: POTENTIAL PITFALLS

One potential pitfall to the protectionist policies disguised as self-sufficiency policies is when a particular country gets singled out and there are other countries in the world producing the commodity in question (Chinese textiles for example). Presumably, the country being singled out is the low cost producer, otherwise it would not be penetrating the foreign markets. Whether the cost

advantage is the result of unfair competition, cheaper labor, or lower overall costs, the economic impact on the country imposing the import levy or restriction, say the United States, is the same.

In this example, if the country implementing the levy is not the second lowest cost producer, the levy on Chinese textile imports may only result in a shuffling of the deck or a change in the patterns of trade. If Vietnam is a lower cost producer than the United States, then Vietnam will now fill the void and people who used to buy from China will now buy from Vietnam and nothing changes in the world economy. Only a minor inconvenience of reshuffling the trade flows. Therefore if the self-sufficiency/protectionist policy is to be effective, it has to restrict all textile imports, not the textile imports from a single country. Otherwise what the policy will accomplish is a change in the patterns of trade among the nations of the world.

THE NARROW VIEW

The road to self-sufficiency requires that the local government takes steps to either stimulate the domestic production or restrict the domestic consumption of imported products. The inducement toward self-sufficiency can be done thorough import taxes, production subsidies,

Economic Disturbances and Equilibrium in an Integrated Global Economy. http://dx.doi.org/10.1016/B978-0-12-813993-6.00019-2

tariffs, and other tools available to the government. Yet as we now show, not all of these actions have the same effect on the economy.

A consumption tax increases the price paid by the local consumers. The domestic demand declines and so will imports. In theory, if the consumption tax is high enough, the consumption tax could wipeout the imports thereby making the economy self-sufficient.

Critics of this policy argue that although the self-sufficiency objective may be achieved through a consumption tax, the government actions distort the private sector's choices and increase the price of the import competing or import substitute. This will clearly make the domestic consumers worse off by this action, the exception being the presence of external effects, such as pollution damage to the environment. Hence, unless one is willing to argue that there is an externality that the consumption restriction is reducing, the principle of revealed preferences suggests that the current outcome is a second best solution, not the consumers' first choice. The obvious conclusion is that as the dependency on imports is reduced, the economy is worse off without any positive effect on the domestic employment in that sector.

A production subsidy leads to a higher level of domestic production and quite likely a higher level of employment in the protected, favored, or subsidized sector. But this does not necessarily mean that the economy's employment level unambiguously increases. It matters a great deal where the increased labor comes from. If the higher employment in the sector reduces the economy's overall employment, then one can conclude that the economy's overall employment level increased. But if the increased employment is at the expense of employment in other sectors of the economy, the economy's employment level remains unchanged.

Under a competitive outcome, the marginal cost of producing the commodity inclusive of the subsidy will be equal to the marginal costs of the imported good. While domestic consumers pay the same price for the domestically produced good as the foreign produced good, the fact that the domestic produced good includes a subsidy means that the costs, inclusive of the subsidy, exceed the price of the imported product. In the absence of an externality, the domestic economy is wasting resources producing a good that could be acquired cheaper through imports.

An import tax increases the price of the imported product. The higher imported price increases the price paid by the domestic consumer. The higher domestic prevailing price inclusive of the import tax is equivalent to a domestic production subsidy. The effects of the import tax can be replicated by the following two domestic components: a consumption tax and a production subsidy.

These tools are readily available to the government and while they tend to have a qualitatevely similar effect on self-sufficiency, they have different impacts on consumption, production, and the level of distortion in the economy. For example, a consumption tax reduces imports without significantly impacting domestic production or employment level. In contrast, a production subsidy increases domestic production and the subsidized sector employment level without significantly impacting domestic consumption. The magnitude of the consumption tax or the production subsidy depends on the domestic demand and supply elasticities, respectively. Now, since the import tax is a combination of the two taxes, its effects will be felt on both the domestic consumption and production of the taxed commodity. Since the sum of the magnitude of the demand and supply elasticities is larger than the individual demand or supply elasticity, one can safely conclude that the import tax rate that produces self-sufficiency is much lower than the stand-alone consumption tax or the production subsidy that achieves the same objective. This also means that the impact on the employment level in the sector in question will be larger than a self-sufficiency producing stand-alone domestic consumption tax but smaller than a stand-alone domestic production subsidy.

BUDGET CONSTRAINTS AND SELF-SUFFICIENCY POLICIES

The previous section showed that, if the self-sufficiency policies are to be effective, they have to apply to the rest of the world (ROW). If that is the case, it is appropriate to simplify the analysis by assuming that there are only two countries in the world. The United States and the ROW. Worldwide equilibrium requires that world demand, the sum of the two countries' demand, equals world supply, the sum of the two countries' supply. The implications derived from this simple framework show that when the global equilibrium conditions are satisfied, we can show the following: one country's import is the other country's export. That is, US imports equal ROW exports and the ROW imports equal the US exports.

In addition to the global equilibrium conditions, each of the countries is also subject to a budget constraint. On a global basis, there is no net borrowing or lending, a condition that applies to the world economy. Each country's income will equal each country's expenditures. This means that any excess production of one commodity in one of the countries, that is, exports, has to be matched by an excess demand for the other commodity, that is, imports. In short, if there is no net borrowing or lending, each of the country's trade balances has to add to zero. Therefore the value of one country's imports equals the value of that country's exports. The value of the US imports equal the value of the US exports and the value of the ROW imports equal the value of the ROW exports.

The conclusion derived from the budget constraint and global equilibrium is simple and straightforward: once one of the following variables—US imports, US exports, the ROW exports, and the ROW imports—is known, so are the other three variables.

SELF-SUFFICIENCY OR TRADE RESTRICTION POLICY EQUIVALENCES

It is true that the self-sufficiency policies could lead to an increase in the output and employment in the "protected" sector of the economy, the one that policymakers want to make self-sufficient. The implications derived from the previous conclusion are quite devastating to the protectionists who believe that by increasing the domestic self-sufficiency, the domestic output and employment will also increase. Policies intended to reduce imports will also reduce the same country's exports. Now if the country imports and exports less, so will the ROW. In short, the self-sufficiency policies result in a reduction in the volume of trade in the world economy. This is a very insightful result and it points to some potential pitfalls in the design of economic policy and the quest for self-sufficiency. It illustrates the potential for redundant and contradictory policies. Before we trace the effect of a US import tax, it may worthwhile to establish some equivalences.

A US import tax is analogous to a transportation cost tax. Whenever price differences fall within the import tax or "transportation costs," arbitrage of the price differences is not worthwhile. It is only differences above the "transportation costs" that are worth arbitraging. Hence, the domestic producer is free to increase the price above the world price as long as the price differential is below the broadly defined import tax or trade barrier. The import tax introduces a protective price band within which the foreigners will not find it worthwhile to arbitrage these differences in prices. The higher the import tax, the greater the degree of protection for the import industry.

Profit maximization leads to the conclusion that the domestic producers will charge a domestic price equal to the world price plus the import tariff. As the degree of protection increases, so will the price of the import substitute relative to all other commodities including the country's exported product. Therefore the import tax produces a terms of trade effect that reduces the relative price of the exported product. That, in turn, leads to the following conclusion: the US import tax is equivalent to a US export tax. The US import tax reduces the take of the foreign exporter, and the US import tax is equivalent to the ROW export tax.

Finally, the US import tax increases the relative price of US exports in the ROW. Hence, the US import tax is equivalent to a tax increase on the ROW's imported goods.

These equivalences are important and insightful, and they allow us to ascertain the consistency of the domestic policies as far as protecting domestic industries and promoting exports. An import substitution policy is nothing more than another variant of the self-sufficiency or protectionist argument. As such, it leads to an increase in the relative price of the protected good and if successful, it will reduce the imports. But if our equivalences are correct, then the import substitution policies will reduce the relative price of the exported goods, and that results in a reduction in the net exports. Our equivalences suggest that import substitution policies, in effect, are equivalent to a policy that reduces export promotion.

In contrast, an export promotion policy will result in higher exports if successful. But it will also alter the terms of trade. As the relative prices change, imports will increase. In effect, the export promotion policy also results in an increase in imports.

One obvious insight produced by the equivalences is that, policies aimed at self-sufficiency are inconsistent with policies aimed at promoting exports. They will tend to cancel each other and the end result will be a highly distorted economy. The poster child for this was Latin America, in particular Brazil, Argentina, and Chile during the 1950s and 1960s with its famous import substitution and export promotion policies. It was not until the southern countries embraced free trade and free market economics that their economic fortunes turned for the better. Chile is the best example. It abandoned the import substitution and export promotion policies and adopted market-oriented policies. In the process, it has transformed itself into a major exporting power house. The equivalences identified in previous paragraphs help us to understand why import substitution policies combined with export promotion policies failed the Southern Cone.

A point of clarification is that, the equivalences are based on the impact of these measures on the terms of trade. However, it does matter who imposes the tax, as they get to collect the revenues. Hence, when it comes to revenues collected, the equivalences breaks down. But that is not our focus here. The focus in on the impact on output, employment, and economic well-being, which we now turn to.

WINNERS AND LOSERS AND THE POLITICS OF SPECIAL INTEREST GROUPS

So far, our analysis agrees with that of the self-sufficiency proponents that as the US import tax increases, the volume of imports decline and at some point the volume of trade declines to zero as the tax increases. We also contend that the self-sufficiency proponents quite often take too narrow a view and focus only on the direct impact of the import tax increases on the level of imports and the domestic production and consumption of the import competing good. Yet we contend that the impact of the import tax is broader than that and the impact of the export sector of the domestic economy should also be taken into consideration. Here we go beyond this, we also examine the impact on the ROW. Now let's examine what happens to the economy's output employment and profits of the different sectors.

As the domestic import tax rate increases, domestic prices rise, and at the margin it will be equal to the foreign price plus the import tax. The higher domestic price increases the profitability of the import-competing domestic sector. Profit maximization induces the domestic producer to increase production and employment in the import-competing sector of the domestic economy. The producers and employees of the import-competing goods are clearly better off. Any short-term rigidity that prevents the domestic import-competing sector from adjusting means that the short-run supply elasticity is smaller than that of the longer run. Hence, in the short run, the profitability exceeds that of the long run and the long run profitability will in turn be higher than the profitability prior to the import tax increase. On the consumer side, the price increase induces a downward movement along the demand curve thereby reducing the overall consumption of the import competing goods. As the domestic consumer reduces the consumption level and pays a higher price for the import-competing good, it becomes apparent that the domestic consumers of the import-competing goods are not as well off as they were before the import tax increase.

The global equilibrium condition resulting from an import tax increase leads to a number of other results. If the tax increase extinguishes the local imports, the budget constraint leads to the conclusion that the country will have no exports either. As we have two countries—the United States and the ROW—the absence of imports and exports in one country means that the ROW exports and imports will also fall to zero. In this case, both the United States and the ROW will return to its autarkic condition. The ROW exports are nothing more than our imports. As our imports decline, so will the ROW exports. The explanation for this result is straightforward.

The difference between the prices in the two countries is nothing more than the import tax. The domestic import tax increases the price of the imports in the domestic economy. However, as the tax is deducted, the price received by the exporting country declines, which leads to an increase in the demand for the exportable goods in the ROW. As a result, the ROW's consumers of their exported goods are better-off. The relative price decline

also induces a movement along the supply curve. Production, employment, and the profitability in the export sector in the ROW unambiguously declines. Again, if there are adjustment costs, this industry's unemployment rate will increase in the ROW in the short run. Notice also that the discussion also illustrates how the domestic import tax is equivalent to, that is, has similar effects, as a ROW export tax.

The story with US exports is quite similar to that of the ROW exports. The import tax increase alters the terms of trade, that is, the price of the imports relative to the country's exports, and this results in a decline in the relative price of our exports. The relative price decline increases the domestic demand for the US exportable goods. The higher consumption and lower price make the domestic consumer of the export good better-off. The relative price decline also induces a movement along the supply curve. Our production, employment, and the profitability in the export sector unambiguously decline. If there are adjustment costs in the short run, then the adjustment in this industry's unemployment rate will also increase. Again, notice that a domestic import tax has similar effects as the domestic export tax.

The results reported in the previous paragraphs show that the relative price of the US exported product for the ROW declined unambiguously. As the relative price of the imported product is the inverse of the exported product, the relative price of the imported product in the ROW unambiguously increases as a result of our, that is, the domestic import tax. The higher relative price increases the profitability, production, and employment in the import-competing domestic sector. The producers and employees of the import-competing goods in the ROW are clearly better-off. On the consumer side, the terms of trade or price increase induces a downward movement along the demand curve thereby reducing the overall consumption of the import-competing goods. The ROW domestic consumer reduces the consumption level and pay a higher price for the import-competing goods. The conclusion being that in the ROW, the consumers of the import-competing goods are not as well-off as they were before the import tax increase. The discussion here shows that the effects of the domestic import tax has the same effect as the ROW import tax.

INTERTEMPORAL CONSIDERATIONS

So far, our analysis has assumed that the countries trade balance has been zero at all points in time. It is now time to relax this assumption. Under a two country global economy, a non-zero trade balance means that one country will experience a trade deficit while the other experiences and equal size trade surplus. Hence, whatever theory one advances about the trade balance should take into account the effect on both economies. A narrow focus on only one of the two economies could lead to the wrong policies.

Self-sufficiency advocates and protectionists view a trade imbalance, that is, a trade deficit, as a leakage or export of domestic jobs. The logic is very seductive. All else the same, if these goods were produced at home, these goods would generate additional jobs in the local economy. Unfortunately, under most general conditions, not everything else stays the same. A reduction in net imports will not necessarily increase the level of employment, as suggested by the nativist's analysis that holds everything else the same. In fact, it is quite possible that the overall level of employment will decline.

NIPA Accounting and Global Equilibrium: To show how this may be the case, we need to go back to the National Income and Product Accounts (NIPA). Before we get into the individual countries account, it is worthwhile to review some global equilibrium relationships.

Under double-entry bookkeeping, global equilibrium requires that the global demand, the sum of the two countries' demand, for one good equals the global supply at all times. The NIPA and global equilibrium also require that the sum of all expenditures equal the sum of all income. The equilibrium relationship means that for the world as a whole, the sum of all the countries trade balances are zero and that in equilibrium global savings will equal global investment at all times. The equilibrium relationship is means that one country' surplus will mirror the other country's shortage. Hence, each country's international account will be the mirror image of the ROW's international account.

Next, as we consider the individual countries' budget constraints, we find additional equilibrium relationships. If one country's expenditures exceed its income, the country will experience a trade deficit. Double-entry bookkeeping requires that the trade deficit must be financed somehow. Here is where the intertemporal considerations come into play. The country has to borrow from the ROW to finance the trade deficit, which yields the following result: a trade deficit is financed by a capital inflow that reflects the country's net borrowing, that is, the excess of domestic savings over investments. The global equilibrium requires that the ROW's corresponding accounts are the mirror image of our country's international accounts.

Policy Consistency: Armed with the equilibrium relationships derived in the previous section, we can now evaluate the consistency of the different trade policies advanced by the nativist, self-sufficiency, and protectionist advocates. Many politicians view a trade deficit as a leakage of jobs and as a source of indebtedness. The question is whether that is always the case? If not, when can we tell that is not the case? What are the necessary conditions to determine whether a trade deficit makes the economy better-off or worse-off?

Let's begin by focusing on the trade balance as a source of national indebtedness. There are several arguments made by nativists that foreigners are buying our country and as they own so much of our debt and resources, at some point in time they are going to use their clout. Another argument is that a trade deficit is a sign that we are mortgaging our future, and that we are consuming too much. If the self-sufficiency advocates and protectionists have their way, they will increase the pressure on the government to act to counter these presumed adverse relationships. The tools available to the government and suggested by the protectionists are many and may lead to in different policy responses. One may be restricting foreign ownership of certain business, or restricting capital flows and trade in goods.

The question one must ask is whether these policies will make the economy better- or worse-off? We assume that the politicians have the best intentions for the country, but that alone is not enough to insure that they adopt the best policies. In the case at hand, the policies adopted are the direct result of an assumption made regarding the trade deficit and or increased indebtedness. There is an implicit assumption that the borrowing is for nonproductive uses and that will hurt the economy in the long run. The analogy is that a person borrows money throws a big party and then wakes up with a hangover and in debt, not a good thing. In that case, an argument can be made for intervention. But that is not the only reason to borrow. What if the person borrows to invest and over time it is able to increase is earning capacity, service the debt, pay it off, and increase its income and standard of living? Clearly, the latter case produces a good outcome and should be encouraged. Given the two alternatives, then we can conclude that there will be desirable and undesirable deficits, the question is how can the government tell, to be able to take appropriate action and insure that it is not making a policy mistake?

We have argued many times that there is a simple way to determine whether the trade deficit is enhancing the economy's potential or not. If the country can earn a higher rate of return than in the ROW, then capital will flow in and the country will experience a net capital inflow and see an increase in foreign borrowings. As the capital flows are invested, the economy's productive capacity increases, as will output, employment, and profits. All of this suggests a series of relationships and correlations among the different variables. The capital inflows will be positively correlated to the trade deficit, higher output, higher employment, and higher profits. This correlation allows us to distinguish between the nativist, self-sufficient protectionist views and the pro-growth, free trade views of the world. Under the pro-growth scenario, we should observe a deterioration of the trade balance as a percent of GDP to be associated with an improving real GDP growth rate, improving stock market, and declining unemployment rate relative to the ROW.

Looking back, for most of the last three decades that is the prevailing relationship. So the question is, if instead of pursuing free trade, had the United States followed a protectionist strategy aimed at improving the trade balance and reducing its indebtedness, where would the United States be? We believe that the US economy's output, employment, and stock market would be much lower than they are today and the world would be worse-off.

IS SELF-SUFFICIENCY AND PROTECTIONISM THE ANSWER?

The road to economic disaster is paved with good intentions and great sound-bites. What we strongly disagree with are the generalizations that politicians and some economists make regarding the self-sufficiency. They conclude that by becoming self-sufficient, the economy's employment and well-being will unambiguously increase. That may be true for specific or protected industries, yet this conclusion is commonly the result of an incomplete economic analysis that ignores the downstream and upstream implications of policies adopted to produce the intended results (in this case, self-sufficiency). Yet as we argue here, this conclusion is quite often a *nonsequitur*. A common mistake in economic analysis is to use a particular situation and generalize it to make blanket statements about the overall economic well-being. While in many cases, the generalization is quite appropriate, that is not necessarily the case in all situations or circumstances.

One interesting case study that illustrates and validates many of the insights developed here is the case against Chinese steel, as documented John W. Miller in several articles in the *Wall Street Journal* where he chronicles the case against China, the trade action, and the initial impact of the trade restriction on various sectors of the economy.

The case against China is as follows: the Chinese government supports its industries through cash assistance, subsidized electricity, and other benefits. The grievance is that Chinese overproduction of steel and other products has driven down world prices and hurt its competitors resulting in the loss of jobs in the steel industry of these other countries. Not surprisingly, we have witnessed workers protest against Chinese imports in Europe, Australia, and the United States. The latter launched seven new investigations into alleged dumping during the first 3 months of 2016. During 2015, US Steel Corporation lost $1.5 billion, closed plants and laid off thousands of workers, actions which the company

mostly blamed on Chinese imports. In response, the US Commerce Department imposed a 266% preliminary import duty on Chinese cold-rolled steel. In 2016, US Steel filed a complaint against China at the International Trade Commission (ITC). The injury allegations include price fixing, transshipment via third countries to avoid duties, and cyber espionage to steal technology from US Steel computers.

The new tariffs on the steel imports produced higher prices in the United States. Steel producers were quick to take advantage of the new environment. Major US producers of steel sent letters announcing nonnegotiable price increases. The steel producers were also quite pleased with the government. According to a *Wall Street Journal* article, Stuart Barnett, owner of Chicago-based Barsteel Corporation was been quoted as saying, "our government has done a pretty good job of boxing out the guys who were importing the most-cheap steel."

The tariffs offered some protection to the local steel industry and it is apparent that they took advantage of the situation. Consistent with the analysis presented here, the import restriction resulted in an increase in the profitability and employment levels in the industry, while the ROW's production declined. By this account, the measure was quite successful.

Yet the press failed to identify the losers of the protectionist measures. One group of losers from the protectionist measures are consumers, who now had to pay higher prices. Another potential sector that may be negatively affected would be the rest of the economy. As long as resources migrate away from the rest of the economy into the steel sector, the production of the other goods or their costs will increase. One reason why these costs are usually not mentioned is that they are quite diffused and spread over large segments of the economy. The protectionist policy in effect creates a special interest group that will engage in politics aimed at continuing and extending the benefits are concentrated in the sector and the costs are spread over the economy. It will be hard for the people paying the costs to get together, while that is not the case for the industry and employment in the sector. To the extent that the politics of special interest groups is successful, the likelihood of the protective measures enduring increase significantly.

Not everyone is in agreement or in favor of trade restrictions and, not surprisingly, special interest groups emerged against the tariff. Car companies lobbied against steel tariffs. On a brief filed with the ITC, lawyers for Ford Motor Co. wrote "innovation and product quality are best served by a cutting-edge, competitive US steel industry; not one walled off from competition."

Although, initially the tariffs appeared to be effective, the question is whether they will remain so over the longer term and whether people will be able to circumvent them. Profit maximization gives the market an incentive to find a way around the restrictions. In a letter to the Department of Commerce requesting an exemption, Steelcase Inc. said a tariff on a special kind of Japanese steel could cost its subsidiary, Polyvision, $4–$5 million a year and may even result in the closing of one of its plants that employs about 50 people. The letter states that schools cannot afford to pay more for the whiteboard that Polyvision makes. They argue that if they raise their price, their customers may substitute their product for cheaper ones of lower quality and not made in the United States This argument suggests an obvious circumvention mechanism that Mr. Barnett is worried about. In his own words, he makes this point clearly: "but now the greatest fear we have is that China keeps the cheap steel for itself and makes products that undercut other industries."

Will the protectionists argue that the tariffs should be extended to these products too? If they do and are successful, the United States may be sliding down the slippery protectionist path.

III. EXCHANGE RATE AND THE TERMS OF TRADE

20

Immigration and Protectionism

When politicians talk about immigration reform, they usually mean the following: amnesty, open borders, and lower wages.

Immigration reform should mean something else entirely: it should mean improvements to our laws and policies to make life better for American citizens.

But if we are going to make our immigration system work, then we have to be prepared to talk honestly and without fear about these important and sensitive issues.

For instance, we have to listen to the concerns that working people have over the record pace of immigration and its impact on their jobs, wages, housing, schools, tax bills, and living conditions. These are valid concerns, expressed by decent and patriotic citizens from all backgrounds.

We also have to be honest about the fact that not everyone who seeks to join our country will be able to successfully assimilate. It is our right as a sovereign nation to choose immigrants that we think are the likeliest to thrive and flourish here.

Then there is the issue of security. Countless innocent American lives have been stolen because our politicians have failed in their duty to secure our borders and enforce our laws…

Right now, however, we are in the middle of a jobs crisis, a border crisis, and a terrorism crisis. All energies of the federal government and the legislative process must now be focused on immigration security. That is the only conversation we should be having at this time.

Whether it's dangerous materials being smuggled across the border, terrorists entering on visas, or Americans losing their jobs to foreign workers, these are the problems we must now focus on fixing … —*Candidate Donald Trump, Immigration Speech in Arizona, August 20, 2016*

The earlier quote nicely summarizes many of the President's view on immigration. While the President has strong views that one may or may not agree with, he makes a distinction between legal and illegal immigration. Within each of these two categories, he then focuses on the effects of immigration on economic issues, crime, and national security. It is in the context of these criteria that we must analyze and evaluate the views and policies espoused by the President.

ILLEGAL IMMIGRATION

The President's view on illegal immigration is unambiguous:

Under my Administration, anyone who illegally crosses the border will be detained until they are removed out of our country.

This denotes a significant change in policy from the previous "catch and release" policy where some illegal immigrants were given a summons to appear in court and then were released into the general population. The new policy combined with increased enforcement will unambiguously reduce the net inflow of illegal or undocumented immigrants into the country. But that is not all the President had to say:

For those here today illegally who are seeking legal status, they will have one route and only one route: to return home and apply for re-entry under the rules of the new legal immigration system that I have outlined above. Those who have left to seek entry under this new system will not be awarded surplus visas, but will have to enter under the immigration caps or limits that will be established.

Economic Disturbances and Equilibrium in an Integrated Global Economy. http://dx.doi.org/10.1016/B978-0-12-813993-6.00020-9

We will break the cycle of amnesty and illegal immigration. There will be no amnesty.

Our message to the world will be this: you cannot obtain legal status, or become a citizen of the United States, by illegally entering our country.

The President's statement sends a clear signal. If he means what he says, the benefits to immigrating illegally to the United States will be significantly reduced.

The abolishment of the catch and release policy combined with a firm promise of no path to citizenship, if believed by the illegal immigrants, should result in a significant decline in the illegal immigration flows. However, the situation is very different for the illegal residents already in the country. Even for them, President Trump had something to say:

In several years, when we have accomplished all of our enforcement goals – and truly ended illegal immigration for good, including the construction of a great wall, and the establishment of our new lawful immigration system – then and only then will we be in a position to consider the appropriate disposition of those who remain. That discussion can only take place in an atmosphere in which illegal immigration is a memory of the past, allowing us to weigh the different options available based on the new circumstances at the time…

So there is a promise that there may be a potential solution to those who are currently in the United States. The question is whether there will be a differential enforcement regarding the illegal immigrants who are here, as opposed to those who are trying to get into the country.

SECURITY

President Trump has made security a big part of his immigration enforcement campaign. On the security issue, candidate Trump's Arizona speech also expressed some clear and unambiguous views on illegal immigration:

On day one, we will begin working on an impenetrable physical wall on the southern border. We will use the best technology, including above-and below-ground sensors, towers, aerial surveillance and manpower to supplement the wall, find and dislocate tunnels, and keep out the criminal cartels, and Mexico will pay for the wall.

Security issues also weigh on the President's views on legal immigration:

We want people to come into our country, but they have to come in legally and properly-vetted, and in a manner that serves the national interest.

A March 12, 2016 editorial in the *Wall Street Journal* addresses the issue of crime and immigration [1]:

The anecdotes Mr. Trump cites result mainly from failures in federal and local law enforcement as well as overreaching court rulings. Between 2013 and 2015, about 8,000 convicted criminals were released as a result of the Supreme Court's Zadvydas v. Davis in 2001 that prohibited Immigration and Customs Enforcement (ICE) from indefinitely detaining immigrants.

Federal courts have also ruled that detention orders are not mandatory, and local governments can refuse to enforce them. Municipalities have even been sued for not releasing immigrants on bond. Foreign governments are often uncooperative, and the State Department could stop issuing visas to countries that don't repatriate their criminals.

Local governments have also resisted cooperation when they believe ICE is indiscriminately rounding up undocumented immigrants. Notably, local cooperation increased when the Obama Administration prioritized removing criminal immigrants. Former ICE director Sarah Saldana told Congress last year that "more than half of previously uncooperative jurisdictions are now cooperating."

Taking the President at face value, it is apparent that he is not opposed to immigration. He just wants a legal immigration that does not put the security of the country in jeopardy. On this issue the President has a point. If we are nation of laws, the laws should be enforced. If the people do not like the laws, there is a procedure for changing them in our democracy. The legislative process is the mechanism. If the legislators do not abide by the wish of the voters, the latter can go to the polls and elect legislators who will.

CRIME

Candidate Trump in his Arizona speech also chimed in on the issue of crime committed by immigrants:

A 2011 report from the Government Accountability Office found that illegal immigrants and other non-citizens in our prisons and jails together had around 25,000 homicide arrests to their names.

When the issue of immigration is addressed by President Trump, quite often he mentions names of murder victims of undocumented immigrants. He usually goes on to say that the government has failed these victims. On this issue he has a point. It is terrible that foreign criminals are caught and released only to perpetrate more violence. While these crimes could have been avoided if the laws had been enforced, it is a big jump to go from there to argue that immigrants commit more crimes than native-born citizens. The previously mentioned *Wall Street Journal* editorial addresses the issue:

In a newly published paper, researchers at the University at Buffalo and University of Alabama examined 200 metropolitan areas between 1970 and 2010. They found that murder, robbery, burglary and larceny rates decreased as immigration increased. A recent meta-analysis of 50 studies published between 1994 and 2014 concluded that cities with larger immigrant populations have lower crime rates.

Again, the distinction between legal and illegal immigration is very important. These results do not support the view that immigrants commit more crimes. While we would concede that strong enforcement of immigration laws would have eliminated many of the crimes committed by illegal immigrants, the aforementioned fact dispel the myth that immigrants, legal and illegal, commit crimes at a higher rate than the general population. The editorial goes on to say that:

> Copious research also indicates that immigrants are less crime-prone than native-born Americans. A 2012 study observed that "foreign-born individuals exhibit remarkably low levels of involvement in crime across their lifetime," though the second generation "caught up" to their native-born counterparts.
>
> A 2005 analysis of 180 Chicago neighborhoods between 1995 and 2002 found that first-generation immigrants demonstrated significantly lower rates of violence than blacks and whites and that their "odds of violence are almost half those of third-generation immigrants." At least on crime, immigrant families are assimilating too much.
>
> The Chicago study (and some others) discovered a robust link between "concentrated immigration" and lower crime. So whites and blacks who live in communities with more immigrants are less likely to experience crime. Researchers suggest that immigrants may be less criminal because they have strong family bonds and work ethic, which is underscored by their higher labor participation rate. Immigrants washing dishes probably aren't committing crimes in their down time.

The results reported in the editorial are very intriguing, such as a lower crime in the immigrant communities and why other ethnic groups are less likely to experience crime. The editorial points out to the researcher's conclusion that strong family bonds and work ethic contributes to lower crime and a higher labor force participation. The study also goes on to say by the second or third generations, the immigrants appear to catch up with the general population. The editorial poses the question as to whether the immigrants are assimilating too much. One possibility not considered is that the social safety net, as it is currently structured, may have a negative impact on the strong family bond. Is the social safety net replacing the family structure? If the answer is in the affirmative, the issue is not immigration. Perhaps we should reexamine the way the social safety net benefits are structured.

LEGAL IMMIGRATION: ECONOMIC ISSUES

Immigration has become a political hot potato in many parts of the world and it is in the front burner of any political or economic discussion. The different positions on the immigration issue range from people advocating for open borders to advocating for strict immigration controls. Since these positions have an economic and

political component, it is worthwhile to review some of the arguments used by the advocates of opposing points of views to make sense of the different points of views.

President Trump's position on immigration is quite clear:

> We will reform legal immigration to serve the best interests of America and its workers. We've admitted 59 million immigrants to the United States between 1965 and 2015.
>
> Many of these arrivals have greatly enriched our country. But we now have an obligation to them, and to their children, to control future immigration–as we have following previous immigration waves–to ensure assimilation, integration and upward mobility.

Those are laudable goals and we believe that most people will agree with the President, though some may have issue with the last sentence's reference to assimilation and integration. But more on this later. For now, let's focus on the economic issues.

The Implicit Assumptions and Their Implications

One major component of the immigration debate is whether the immigrants displace American workers and whether they benefit the nation economically. One possible answer to this question comes down to whether migrants (illegal or not) "substitute" for workers or "complement" them. If migrants compete for a job that a US worker could reasonably do, that substitution essentially increases the supply of workers, drives up unemployment, and drives down wages for natives. On the other hand, cheaper construction workers complement higher-paid managers by lowering company costs. That makes the firm better positioned to win new bids and, in theory, hire more workers, both immigrants and natives alike.

In the extreme, the substitute hypothesis as described earlier assumes that all labor units are perfect substitutes for each other, all units of capital are perfect substitutes for each other, and that the economy produces a single product. Under these conditions, an inflow of labor reduces the economy's capital to labor ratio and that, in turn, results in a lower wage rate and higher return to capital. Assuming that the different groups look out for their own self-interest, capital owners would be pro-immigration, while domestic labor groups would be anti-immigration.

Unfortunately, the results in the previous paragraph are highly dependent on the assumption that the economy produces a single composite good. What happens if we assume that the economy produces two distinct goods with different technology, such that the capital intensity differs across the two products? Obviously one good will be relatively more intensive in the use of capital, let's call it the capital-intensive good, while the other will be more intensive in the use of labor, which we call the labor-intensive good.

Profit maximization on the part of the producers, perfect mobility of the factors of production across industries, and utility maximization on the part of the consumer result in a market-clearing equilibrium. Once the market-clearing goods' prices are determined, one can also determine the market-clearing wage rate, the rental rate of capital, employment in the different industries, as well as their output.

The wage rental ratio and the technology will allow us to determine the optimal or profit maximizing capital labor ratio for each of the industries, the rays $(K/L)_1$ and $(K/L)_2$ in Fig. 20.1A. That, combined with the assumption of factor mobility, allows us to insure full employment. The distribution of labor and capital between the two industries that satisfy the profit maximization and full employment conditions is illustrated graphically in Fig. 20.1A.

The profit maximization determines the capital labor ratios, the (K/L) rays in Fig. 20.1A. L_1 denotes the amount of labor employed in the capital-intensive industry while L_2 denotes the amount of labor employed in the labor-intensive industry. The sum of the two adds to the total amount of labor in the economy, hence the full employment condition is satisfied. The profit maximization determines the capital labor ratios, the (K/L) rays in Fig. 20.1A. Hence Fig. 20.1A illustrates graphically the distribution of labor and capital that satisfies the profit maximization and full employment conditions.

Now let's determine the effect of an inflow of labor into this economy. The first thing to notice is that the endowment shifts to the right in Fig. 20.1B, with the same amount of capital and more labor. If the prices of the product do not change, neither will the wage rental ratio. As a result, the individual industries' capital labor ratio, $(K/L)_1$ and $(K/L)_2$, will remain unchanged. Again, we can solve graphically for the full employment conditions. Notice that to absorb the inflow of labor, equilibrium requires an increase in the employment of both capital and labor in the labor-intensive product. Since the capital labor ratio does not change, by assumption, the reduction in the amount of capital employed in the capital-intensive industry means that less labor will also be employed in the capital-intensive industry. The result of this process is that all the immigrants will be absorbed into the labor-intensive product and then some. Production of the labor-intensive product will increase, while production of the capital-intensive product will decline.

These results are diametrically opposed to the conclusion reached by some anti-immigrant advocates who argue that immigrants will lower the native-born population's wages. Here we have a case where all labor are perfect substitutes and yet we have described a full employment equilibrium without a wage decline. How is that possible? The answer is that our analysis implicitly assumes an open economy. In a closed economy, as the initial analysis assumed, the higher production of labor-intensive goods results in a price decline of the price of the labor-intensive goods, as well as a decline in the return to the factor-intensive in the production of the goods in question, that is labor. The increased production in the labor-intensive goods will be exported to the rest of the world, and the shortage of the domestically produced capital-intensive goods will be imported from the rest of the world. International trade dampens or completely

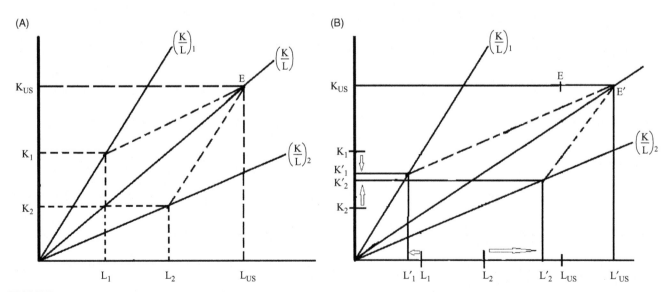

FIGURE 20.1   (A) Distribution of labor and capital in a two good, two factors of production economy. (B) The effect of immigration on the distribution of labor and capital.

offsets the price pressure that would be experienced in a closed economy.

Whether the immigration results in a lower wage rate depends on a multitude of issues such as whether one has an open or closed economy, the degree of mobility from one industry to another, the ease of capital flows, and the differences in capital intensities among industries. The point of all this analysis is that the assumptions about these variables determine the conclusions reached. So, it is important to pay attention to the implicit assumptions made by the proponents of the different immigration points of views. As one gives more weightage to certain factors, then the conclusions will tilt one way or the other.

Quotas and preference immigration systems and their implementation issues, and other criteria shape people's opinion about the topic. Recently the President added to the debate:

> Within just a few years immigration as a share of national population is set to break all historical records. The time has come for a new immigration commission to develop a new set of reforms to our legal immigration system in order to achieve the following goals:

- To keep immigration levels, measured by population share, within historical norms
- To select immigrants based on their likelihood of success in U.S. society, and their ability to be financially self-sufficient. We need a system that serves our needs – remember, it's America First.
- To choose immigrants based on merit, skill and proficiency
- And to establish new immigration controls to boost wages and to ensure that open jobs are offered to American workers first.

The statement by the President is a bit confusing. Is he advocating for racial quotas when he suggests to maintain the shares of the different ethnic groups? At the same time, is he advocating for a change in immigration that focuses on merit, skill, proficiency, and the likelihood of success in the US society. Those two ideas are clearly inconsistent.

Briefly we should mention that the United States has experimented with many variants of immigration policies. There is the US lottery, where people participate in a green card lottery program. Clearly this process does not take into consideration the skill level or the potential self-sufficiency of the applicant. If people look to improve their lot, the applicant pool will consist of those who stand to gain the most either in economic terms or political freedom or both. Keep in mind that for people living at the subsistence level, even the social safety net income levels will be a great improvement in their economic well-being. Also, those with income or skill levels high enough have other programs that they can use to gain access to

the United States. Just to cite a couple of examples, there are the H-1b for skilled workers and the EB-5 for wealthy investors. The point of all this is that a random lottery will attract those who do not have other avenues to come into this country. More than likely, they will be lower-skilled workers. Also, the random lottery will tend to attract people from the poorer countries and these are not the likely to be a large component of the current population. Hence the random lottery will alter the makeup of the population that the President aims to preserve. The random lottery does not meet the President's requirement.

The preference system also has a systematic bias. First, those with close relatives in the United States will get the higher preferences and thus go to the front of the queue. While one may argue that the reason why the relatives want to migrate to the United States is to be with family, they will also be leaving family behind. The economic argument is simple: those who have the most to gain will try to take advantage of the program. Again, the wealthy and skilled may have other avenues, but the less skilled may not. The conclusion is that the preference system will be biased toward those with a lower skill set, a fact that may be reinforced if their US relatives are also lower skilled.

The quota system is also easily gamed. During the 1980s, the US visas were based in part on hemispheric quotas, which then made it quite difficult for people in some areas to obtain their visas and legal papers to come to the United States. The example we have in mind is that of Taiwan and Hong Kong. They were subject to the Asian hemisphere and the quotes filled quickly and, as a result, waiting time was long. However, the western hemisphere had a surplus of visas and it was much more easy to gain entry into the United States through a western hemisphere application. Some countries sold privileged citizenships to the tune of $25,000 to $50,000 to the Taiwanese and Hong Kong residents. With these citizenships, they obtained US visas without ever setting foot in their "country of citizenship." Obviously the market-provided solution had two effects. One was to circumvent the quota and thus violating the tenet of maintaining the share of the population constant. The second effect would be the bias in the selection process. Only those wealthy enough were able to afford the citizenship. The second effect would be in line with the administration's self-sufficiency view.

Needless to say, the discussion presented earlier suggests that any non-market related immigration scheme would create opportunities for circumvention resulting in some cases with undesired or unintended effects. The discussion in the previous section also leads to some interesting unintended consequences. Let's assume a quota that, as the President puts it, maintains the population shares within historical norms. What happens if one group has a higher birthrate than another? Over time, that group will increase its share of the population. If it also turns out that this is the group that has the largest number of applicants trying to gain access to the United States, while the groups of declining population have the smallest applicants and their quotas go unfilled, then it is possible that the slow growing group becomes a binding constraint on immigration. To prevent the fast growing population from increasing its market share, the immigration policy could be forced to stop immigration from that ethnic group. It would not matter whether these people are skilled and self-sufficient. That is one of the downsides of a quota.

THE CASE FOR A SKILLS-BASED IMMIGRATION SYSTEM

Whether the President was aware of this or not, it was a pleasant surprise that during his recent speech to a joint session of Congress, the President expanded on his views on the issue of legal immigration reform and his preference for a skills-based system:

> I am going to bring back millions of jobs. Protecting our workers also means reforming our system of legal immigration. The current, outdated system depresses wages for our poorest workers, and puts great pressure on taxpayers. Nations around the world, like Canada, Australia and many others, have a merit-based immigration system. It's a basic principle that those seeking to enter a country ought to be able to support themselves financially. Yet, in America, we do not enforce this rule, straining the very public resources that our poorest citizens rely upon. According to the National Academy of Sciences, our current immigration system costs American taxpayers many billions of dollars a year.
> Switching away from this current system of lower-skilled immigration, and instead adopting a merit-based system, we will have so many more benefits. It will save countless dollars, raise workers' wages, and help struggling families—including immigrant families—enter the middle class. And they will do it quickly, and they will be very, very happy, indeed.

The President's talks about replacing the current "low-skilled" immigration system with a merit-based system needs some clarification. The current system is not necessarily a low-skilled system. It is a preference-based system aimed at keeping families together. In that sense, the current system is blind to the skill level and does not discriminate based on skill. If it ends up being a low-skilled immigration program, it is a legacy issue that is determined by the original immigrants that are now bringing their relatives into the country. The merits or demerits of such a system are discussed later. For now, let's focus on a merit system as the President suggests.

In lieu of the current system, the President prefers a merit-based immigration system which, if based on the Canadian and Australian systems, will require the immigrant to know the language and to be able to support themselves financially. From an economic point of view, this is a good thing. What this aspect of the proposal effectively insures is that those migrating are net contributors from an economic point of view. If implemented, the immigration system would more than save billions of dollars; it may even add significant revenues to the government coffers.

The President claims that the merit system will help families enter the middle class and raise wages. We agree that the merit system will help the immigrants' families enter the middle class. That is almost a tautology, since that is how they are selected. They must be self-supporting, English speaking, and skilled. Regarding the issue of raising wages, we may take some issues with that. Before we get into the discussion, let's consider an issue that we discussed earlier: the substitutability of the different types of labor. For example, are IT specialists perfect substitutes for agricultural workers? If one cannot perform the other's duties, they will not be substitutes. In this case, the two markets will be segmented and a disturbance in one market will not directly impact the other. If the program incorporates market conditions, immigration will give priority to what the economy needs. For example, if the issue is agriculture, that is picking crops, then what is needed is crop pickers, not IT specialists. In contrast, if what is needed are IT specialists, we need to let in IT specialists. Allowing immigration of IT specialists will increase their supply to the market place. The increased supply will result in a lower market-clearing salary for the IT specialists in the United States. Similarly, if what is needed is agricultural workers, as their supply increases, the equilibrium market wages in the agricultural sector will also lower without significantly affecting IT specialists' wages. Now let's discuss the average wage rate in the United States. Although the wages for the IT worker declines as IT workers immigrate, as long as their wages are above the national average, the average wage will increase.

THE UNINTENDED CONSEQUENCES OF AN IMMIGRATION SYSTEM

Even if the immigrants are skilled and are net contributors, that does not mean they will not create pressures at the local level. If there is some affinity among the immigrants, it is quite possible that they will choose to move to areas where other migrants have a similar culture, background, or nationality. A rapid inflow could have some effects that may strain community resources. For example, class sizes will increase in the local school, thereby diluting the resources devoted to education in these communities. If the immigrants are of the lower-income category and lack insurance coverage, their use of emergency facilities will increase. Even if they have government-provided insurance, waiting time in those communities will unambiguously increase. Then there is the social transformation of the neighborhoods. Businesses catering to the new immigrants will be created, the local "way of life" will change, and that may create resentment among the locals, thereby fueling anti-immigrant feelings. The social safety net programs could also add fuel to the fire. If the immigrants participate in the social safety net, they will not be viewed as net contributors. If some of the immigrant community is found to take advantage of these social safety net programs, the anti-immigrant sentiment will increase. The welfare "fraud" may, in many cases, be legal.

A good example to illustrate some of the potential issues with the open border view of immigration is that of the United Kingdom. Great Britain experienced many of the issues mentioned in the previous paragraph. And to add insult to injury, because of the open border there was not much they could do about welfare tourism either. Thus, people from some of the new European countries would move to England to take advantage of the higher welfare benefits. Worse yet, they collected for their children who remained at home and sent remittances to their families and there was nothing the United Kingdom could do. These rules were determined by the EU. Given that the EU would not alter the open border rules for goods and people and allow the United Kingdom to control its immigration borders, the United Kingdom chose to leave the EU. The political calculus of the people was that the control of their border and the makeup of their society was worth more than the economic gains of the truly open borders. Our analysis suggests that economic reasons and differences in social norms contributed to the BREXIT vote.

The more flexible labor markets, salary differential, and even welfare benefit differentials attracted migrants from the rest of the EU into the UK. The rapid inflow overwhelmed the system and created social pressures in many parts of the country and that contributed to the BREXIT vote.

There are several other examples of whether immigration has some unintended consequences both at the economic and social levels. Japan, the poster child for insularity and strong limitations on immigration, is one such example. Several decades ago, there was a massive migration of Japanese citizens from Japan to Brazil. Since the massive emigration, Japan has experienced a low population growth rate that has dipped below the population replacement rate. Given Japan's historical attitudes toward immigration, the "Japanese ex-pats" living in Brazil became a target of opportunity to solve the slow population growth in Japan. A few years back, the Japanese government developed a plan to attract the descendants of original Japanese emigrants to Brazil. They were ethnically Japanese and as such they would not alter the racial mix in Japan. The experiment was a failure. The Brazilian-Japanese moved in communities near

each other and the Japanese people felt that the Brazilian Japanese were too loud and noisy and that they were more Brazilians than Japanese. In contrast the Brazilian-Japanese had trouble adjusting to their new country.

Assimilation is a big issue that has long-term consequences. First, let's talk about some of the changes and political events taking place in continental Europe. One example that comes to mind is the recent surge in nativists in the continent and the effect that immigration may have had on the voters' opinion. In a recent op-ed in the *Wall Street Journal*, Leon de Winter writes [2]:

> The Netherlands has changed, but it has been a decade's long process. In the 1960s and '70s, the Dutch invited guest laborers from Morocco and Turkey to work temporarily in the wildly expanding economy. The boom ended, but the workers stayed, creating an underclass of low-skilled Muslim immigrants.
>
> Photos of the original laborers show young men in suits and dress shirts—completely Westernized, it seems. Now retired, they often dress as if they had moved back to rural Morocco or Turkey. Their children and grandchildren drop out of school and commit crimes at much higher rates than the original Dutch population. Many become more religious than their grandparents; some even move to the Islamic State caliphate in Syria. Non-Western immigrants and their descendants also depend on welfare to a much greater extent than the native Dutch. They are half of all welfare recipients but only 11% of the total population. Among recent Somali refugees granted asylum, 80% are on welfare.

Our interpretation of his statement suggests that the low skills of the immigrants with the generous welfare system explains the above-average participation on the Dutch welfare program by the immigrants, which combined with their religious beliefs may have also contributed to the dissatisfaction of the immigrant population. He goes on to explain that Holland is a nonreligious welfare state:

> Holland is truly a welfare state, and the Dutch are proud of it. Over 50% of their total earnings are collected by the state, the goal being to redistribute wealth and equalize chances for everyone. It works amazingly well, producing highways, railroads, dikes and bridges, world-class schools and health care, and a cradle-to-grave social-security system. Most political discussions in today's campaign are about the pressing question of how to preserve and expand the welfare state without going broke.
>
> The Dutch are disciplined, hardworking, well-educated, and at the same time open-minded, tolerant and antiauthoritarian—all of this because of our Calvinist heritage. We are also the most secular people in the world. Lots of Dutch say they believe only in "something." We even have a name for this postreligious religion: "Somethingism."

Mr. De Winter goes on to develop his hypothesis as to why Holland may be facing immigrant problems.

> This type of open and yet highly regulated society can function only if it is carried by a disciplined and well-educated citizenry with a reasonable degree of cultural homogeneity. But

because of political correctness and cultural relativism, Dutch elites agreed to absorb low-educated, even illiterate, mostly Muslim migrants from collectivistic rural areas. Significant numbers of them refuse to embrace the radical, secular tolerance of their new home.

Then he asks the key question:

> Can a welfare state become an immigration state? You know the answer: A welfare state with open borders will one day run out of money. But what moral justification is there for limiting migration in a globalized and unjust world? That's a tough question for the politically correct mind. (Interestingly, the American Democrats' main project is the reverse: turning an immigration state into a welfare state.)

He also addresses the issue of the xenophobia and provides a rebuttal to those who want to stigmatize and those who want to limit the open borders and free immigration policy.

> Did the Dutch really turn into xenophobes and racists? No, they are as open-minded as ever. But they have started to demand what most of their politicians (except people like Fortuyn and Mr. Wilders) until recently didn't dare mention because it was politically incorrect: that immigrants practice tolerance, work and study hard, and teach their children to be proud and contributing members of this society. That is the least you can ask when the fruits of your labor are taxed at 50%.

Mr. De Winter provides a possible solution to the problem. Taking his logic to the extreme leads some to argue that these problems do not necessarily occur in a homogeneous society. A follow-up argument is one that the immigrants' failure to assimilate and their high welfare participation leads to an increase in spending that combined with the low birthrate of the native population suggests that the differential growth rate of the two populations will ultimately result in welfare rising faster than revenues needed to pay for the program. That is unsustainable in the long run. The implication is that immigration should be restricted in such a way to maintain and/or improve the homogeneity of a nation's makeup.

Jason Riley, in a recent *Wall Street Journal* article [3], argues that "America Doesn't Have Europe's Immigration Problems." He presents a succinct and quite bullish argument in favor of immigration.

> …the immigrant populations with higher fertility rates don't feel particularly welcome in Europe also is demographically troubling. Countries like France, Italy and the Netherlands may pay lip service to inclusion, but the ethos in those places is that immigrants can never really become French, Italian or Dutch, no matter what their passports say. The emphasis is on tolerance and respect, but there's no real expectation that foreign nationals fit in.
>
> America doesn't have that problem because it has done things differently. Here, the emphasis is on shared ideals rather than shared cultural artifacts. The U.S. model for assimilation has been more successful because of the country's value frame-

work, which is the real immigrant magnet. Longitudinal studies, which measure the progress of the same individuals over time, show that U.S. immigrants today continue to assimilate despite the best efforts of bilingual education advocates and anti-American Chicano Studies professors. As with previous immigrant waves, different groups progress at different rates, but over time English usage, educational attainment and incomes do rise.

Miami and its Cuban population may be taken as one great example about immigration, assimilation, and economic prosperity. The United States accepted the Cuban refugees after the fall of Fulgencio Batista's government and Fidel Castro's rise to power. The United States also accepted the refugees from the Mariel boatlift. Over the years, Cuban exiles were given preference and to some extent the "wet foot, dry foot" policy was the equivalent of an open border. Once you get here, you are in. The Cuban immigrants have had a tremendous influence on Florida's economic performance over the last few decades. It is truly a bilingual city by choice. The immigrants have assimilated and are truly US citizens and their children speak English without an accent and are steeped in US customs. At the same time, they are also steeped in their parents' heritage, are truly bilingual, and bicultural where they switch from one culture to the other seamlessly. In the process, the Cuban and other immigrants have transformed Miami into a metropolis that many consider the capital of Latin America. Something that makes Miami different than other cities is that it is a prosperous metropolis where people are just as likely to vote for an Anglo-American, Spanish-American, or African-American candidate for office. It is also a city where minorities have won office and yet the continuity in policies remains, irrespective of who gets elected. Looking at the data in Fig. 20.2, one can see the correlation between Florida's economic performance and the Cuban inflow. Notice the increase in personal income relative to the US personal income during the years when the migration was taking effect. Notice also that the state has been able to maintain the level of income throughout the years, suggesting that substantial immigration and ethnic minority governance are not an obstacle to growth or good governance. All of this suggests that assimilation is one key to a successful integration.

THE EFFECT OF ALTERNATIVE IMMIGRATION SCHEMES

One important result derived from the experiences of alternative immigration schemes is that the interaction between the social safety net or welfare programs and the assimilation has an important effect that largely determines the success or failure of alternative immigration

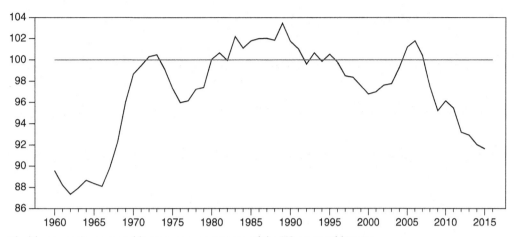

FIGURE 20.2   Florida per capita personal income as a percentage of the US personal income.

schemes. Success is being defined here in terms of the criteria outlined by President Trump regarding the impact of immigration on jobs, wages, housing, schools, tax bills, social safety net expenditures, and the likelihood of assimilation. The United States and European experiences of alternative immigration schemes uncovers some empirical regularities and insights that can be used to identify the key features of a successful immigration policy.

One of the potential vehicles for immigration to the United States is the immigration lottery, where people register and a limited number of people are selected at random and granted entry into the United States. Another component of the current immigration program is also the preference system, where the immigration law is based on keeping families together. Although in theory there is no reason why these programs would be biased in favor of lower-income people, we argue that the current implementation of these features is biased toward lower-income individuals. These are the people that are most likely to become early participants of the social safety net. To the extent that a large fraction of these people as a result of their skill level or for other reason are trapped in the social safety net and its implicit disincentive to work, that is the loss of benefits as earned income rises, these people will not be able to become financially self-sufficient. A problem that becomes worse as time goes by is that those who stay out of the labor force will experience a skill deterioration that makes them less employable further compounding the problem. One possible solution to this problem is a reform of the social safety net to include a workfare component where the participants acquire a skill and the immigrants learn the English language. These steps will force them out of their shells, their neighborhood, and force them to interact with the rest of the population, thereby exposing them to the opportunities variable to them and thus facilitating their integration.

An effective quota system as well as visa programs such as H1-B and EB-5 will reduce the immigration level relative to the one that would have prevailed in absence of the quota. Our own research shows that a quota will increase the effective cost of migrating to the United States. To the extent that these costs are fixed, the higher the cost, only the wealthy or higher earning income people will be able to afford the expenses associated with the immigration. Thus, these people are more likely to be self-sufficient and thus less likely to participate in the social safety net program. On the downside, the immigrant inflow is likely to be less diverse in terms of skills and quite possibly geography. Whether the immigrants are more likely to integrate is hard to tell without additional information.

The effects of the skill-based program depend on its implementation. The fact that they are fluent in English and have the skills that the economy needs makes it less likely that they will fall into the social safety net trap. Obviously the likelihood of falling into the social safety net trap will be lower the higher the income levels of the skill in question. The English fluency also suggests a knowledge of the United States and a higher likelihood of integration.

The previous paragraphs outline some key differences and likely effect of alternative immigration programs considered. So far, we have ignored one element all these programs have in common. They all will admit more people in the United States, and to the extent that these people become US citizens, they will all have voting rights. Now to the extent that the immigrants have different tastes, values, and opinions regarding different issues, depending on the issue they may be able to affect changes and seek accommodations to their views. Let's call this reverse assimilation or accommodation. This raises the question of whether a country has the right to limit immigration to prevent a reverse assimilation. The United Kingdom gave us a clear answer with the

BREXIT vote. The British people believe that a nation should have control of its borders.

Until now, we have avoided the discussion of free and unfettered labor mobility across national borders. Under these conditions, in absence of any transportation costs, factor mobility will insure the arbitrage of differences in factor returns across national borders. Mobility insures the equalization of factor returns. The downside of the open border is that such a country will have no control over what we have called reverse assimilation. If citizens do not share this view, they may enact polices to limit immigration and choose an immigration policy to align with their views and values.

Let's consider the opposite and extreme policy: closed borders. Obviously under this condition, there is no immigration and thus no chance that immigrants would cause a reverse assimilation. So we now have a policy that prevents the reverse assimilation, but what about the benefits of free mobility? Is there any way to enjoy them without migration? The answer is a big yes. Again, in absence of transportation costs, free trade under some general conditions will result in the equalization of factors returns and product prices across national borders. Viewed from this perspective, free trade in goods and services and no immigration produces all the benefits of a world in which factors of production are free to move without having any reverse assimilation through migration.

The previous paragraph highlights some interesting interaction between a country's trade and migration policy. The analysis suggests that an inflow of immigrants could alter the ethnic composition of a country with the potential of resulting in some reverse assimilation and increased spending that is not welcomed by the nonimmigrant citizens. That could be a powerful motivator in favor of restricting immigration flows. The question is whether countries have the right to restrict immigration? Or should they be forced by other nations to open their borders to immigration? The argument for forcing the countries to open their borders is very seductive. We see religious figures arguing that the North should allow migrants from the South. International countries pressure even emerging nations like Dominican Republic to accept some of the neighboring country citizens. In both cases, they argue that these actions are the appropriate humanitarian response. In many countries, the host countries are demonized when they do not acquiesce. But there is another view. We have argued that free trade and free mobility of factors of production combined with the absence of transportation costs and profit maximization insures the equalization of factor returns and product prices across national borders. People will migrate to arbitrage differences in income. In some cases, it is because the destination has much higher incomes and opportunities. In other cases, the differential is a result of the terrible economic policies pursued by the local authorities. Yet we don't see many of these people criticizing the authorities of the countries with underperforming economies. Improving economic conditions will keep the migrants at home. We believe that, all else the same, people prefer to stay at home. The critics of the host countries should be criticizing the country of origin for its failure to produce opportunities for its citizens.

References

[1] "Crime and immigration." Wall St J, March 12, 2017.
[2] de Winter L. The Dutch find welfare and immigration make an uneasy mix. Wall St J 2017;. March 13.
[3] Riley J. America doesn't have Europe's immigration problems. Wall St J 2017;. March 14.

21

Trade Policy, Protectionism, and Currency Manipulation

Over the years, China's currency practices have been a source of controversy. Twice a year, the US Treasury issues a report examining whether countries pursue policies that keep their currency undervalued. The assumption is that an undervaluation is a tool used by different countries to boost their exports. During his presidential campaign, Donald Trump threatened to label China a currency manipulator and promised to impose a 45% tariff to undo its unfair competition. As with other policies, his position has evolved and the press is now reporting that the Trump administration is considering designating "currency manipulation" as an unfair subsidy when employed by any country. Such a move would allow US companies to seek remedies by bringing antisubsidy suits to the US Commerce Department against countries or imports deemed to cause harm due to improper or unfair subsidies by the foreign governments. We believe that by pursuing such a policy, the United States is going down the wrong economic path and it reaffirms our views regarding President Trump's mercantilist trade views. There are several reasons for our disappointment with the policy, which we will now proceed to review.

GLOBAL IMPLICATIONS OF AN ANTICURRENCY MANIPULATION POLICY

The arguments against currency manipulation rests on the assumption that an exchange rate depreciation makes the exports of the country with the depreciating currency cheaper and makes their imports more expensive, thereby improving its trade balance. According to this view, the improvement in the trade balance results in a net job creation in the country with the depreciating currency. The argument is very seductive. However, it is not believed universally. There is also the pesky issue of whether or not it holds water empirically.

In this section, we focus solely on the likely global response to a US-initiated, anticurrency manipulation policy. While the US policy discussed in the press assumes that the rest of the world will stand pat and do nothing, there is no reason to expect that to be the case. If there are benefits to a weaker currency and costs to an appreciating currency as the anticurrency manipulation view argues, then it is to be expected that all countries will join and participate.

There is no question that most of the countries in the world will participate in an anticurrency manipulation game, but if they do, no one will gain an advantage and the game will easily degenerate into a negative-sum game where everyone loses. However, before we establish the end result, it may be worthwhile to review what drives a country's exchange rate.

The nominal exchange rate is nothing more than the price of one country's currency in terms of another. In turn, the value of each of the countries' currencies is determined by their purchasing power or how many goods will the local currency buy. That is the inverse of the country's price level. Assuming a textbook monetary view of inflation, the price level in each country is determined by the demand for and supply of money. If one is willing to assume that the local central bank controls

Economic Disturbances and Equilibrium in an Integrated Global Economy. http://dx.doi.org/10.1016/B978-0-12-813993-6.00021-0

the quantity of money and the real GDP growth rate is a good proxy for the money demand, then the excess of the money supply growth over the real GDP determines the excess money supply and thus the local inflation rate.

As the nominal exchange rate is the price of one currency in terms of another, it reflects relative purchasing power of the two currencies. Therefore the changes in the exchange rate reflect each of the countries' relative excess money supply. The country with the greatest excess money supply will experience a currency depreciation.

A country's relative excess money supply can be decomposed into a monetary component and a real component. If one country's money supply grows faster than the other, all else the same, that country will experience a larger excess money supply resulting in higher inflation and a currency depreciation. On the other hand, if a country grows faster than the other, all else the same, it will experience an excess demand for money and thus a lower inflation as well as a currency appreciation. The relative excess demand is determined by the sum of the two effects, the excess money growth and the excess real GDP growth.

The discussion in the previous paragraph suggests that the anticurrency manipulation may be implemented in one of two ways:

- Through a monetary policy/exchange rate policy
- Through a tariff or other trade restrictions policy

Each of the options would have its own alternative and undesirable effect on the global economy. The simplest way to make our point is examine what would happen if the United States adopts such a policy.

The monetary policy solution to the currency manipulation issue is a simple one. Each country will take actions to prevent its currency appreciation relative to other currencies. According to the theory behind currency manipulation, the appreciation will make the country's exports more expensive and the imports less expensive, which results in a deterioration of the trade balance and a reduction in employment. This is clearly an undesirable scenario, but there is an easy fix: increase the money supply to create an excess money supply and a currency depreciation.

Again, if one country gains an advantage pursuing this strategy, all other countries will adopt the strategy. The end result of this process is that no country will experience a currency appreciation. In effect, the world will return to a fixed exchange rate where every central bank policy is to prevent its currency from appreciating. Under these conditions, we know that arbitrage will insure a convergence of the inflation rates across national borders. What we have not determined is, what the inflation rate will be and who will determine it. The answer is straightforward. The country with the loosest monetary policy will be the one experiencing the currency depreciation. That country will force all other countries to react and prevent their currency from depreciating. Put another way, the country with the loosest monetary policy will force the rest of the world to adopt its loose monetary policy as they attempt to defend their exchange rate. The end game here is that the country with the loosest monetary policy will determine the world inflation rate and will effectively become the world's central banker.

Our analysis suggests that the monetary solution to the currency manipulation issue will result in a higher global inflation rate. Under this scenario, there is only one currency that will not depreciate and has historically retained its value during uncertain and inflationary times: gold. If the world goes down this path, gold should be a great investment.

The fiscal policy solution is also quite troublesome. It could easily deteriorate into a tit-for-tax enactment of tariffs and other trade barriers across national borders. The tariffs will clearly have a negative impact on the volume of trade and to the extent that they distort the various economy, the real GDP growth rate and profits will decline. This is a bearish scenario where the end game is not a pretty one. The world experienced a global depression in the aftermath of the Smoot–Hawley tariffs. Although there were many other policy mistakes—it would be hard to attribute the Great Depression solely to the imposition of tariffs—one cannot deny that they were a major contributing factor. Jude Wanniski's account of the effect of the Smoot–Hawley Act and its effect on the stock market/economy both in his book, *The Way the World Works*, and his *Wall Street Journal* piece on the subject have become classics. The investment implications of such policies are quite bearish. Exposure to stocks should be reduced under such scenario.

The End Game: The attempts to deal with currency manipulation will result in a world-collective response that has been characterized as the beggar-thy-neighbor policies. If governments attempt to deal with the perceived problem through tariffs and trade restrictions, the end game will be slower global growth and lower asset values, a bearish scenario that if unchecked could degenerate into a global depression. On the other hand, if governments attempt to deal with currency manipulation through monetary policy, the end game will be higher world inflation, which is another bearish scenario.

WILL CURRENCY MANIPULATION DELIVER THE GOODS?

The key assumption driving the currency manipulation hypothesis is that governments can control their currency and in doing so they will also impact their import and export prices. The theory expects that a falling exchange rate will make that country's imports more expensive and its exports relatively less expensive. Put another way:

- A depreciating currency would produce a decline in the country's terms of trade, that is, the price of exports relative to imports.
- An appreciating currency would produce an increase in the country's terms of trade.

These are testable implications. One way to answer the question as to whether the currency manipulation is an effective policy that delivers the goods is to look at the data and see what the evidence is. The Federal Reserve Bank of Saint Louis' database publishes alternative versions of trade-weighted index of the foreign exchange value of the dollar that measures how many units of the foreign currency are needed to acquire one dollar (Fig. 21.1A). We believe that for the purposes at hand, a trade-weighted index is appropriate. The broadest version includes the emerging and frontier markets and as such this is the version of the index that is most likely to show a dollar appreciation thereby bolstering the case of those who believe that a dollar appreciation results in an adverse terms of trade effect.

The data presented shows a secular uptrend beginning in 1981 and peaking around 2002. Within the time period in question, there are a couple of short periods where the dollar secular rise is arrested. The first one was during the 1985–87 time period, when the second Reagan tax rate cuts were being phased in, the Plaza Accord, and the Treasury secretary was threatening trade restriction while talking down the dollar. The second-time period surrounds the tech bubble and the Maestro's Y2K concerns. A clear dollar downtrend is also visible in Fig. 21.1A. It spans the 2002–07 time period, all during the George W. Bush administration. The downtrend is interrupted by the Great Recession. One possible

FIGURE 21.1   (A) Trade-weighted foreign exchange value of the dollar. (B) The US terms of trade. (C) The US terms of trade versus the trade-weighted dollar.

explanation is that the latter generated a flight to capital that resulted in a dollar appreciation. Once the financial crisis stabilized, the dollar either moved sideways or trended up, with the uptrend accelerating during the last couple of years.

The Fed also publishes a price index for US imports, as well as the price index for US exports. We define the ratio of the two as the US terms of trade (Fig. 21.1B). The information presented suggests that the terms of trade moved sideways during much of the 1981–2006 time period. The two exceptions being the short Bush recession during the early 1990s and the subperiod surrounding the Y2K turn of the century and the subsequent recession. The data also suggests a gradual transition toward a lower level, that is, a lower mean, beginning around 2004. Again, the exception to the sideways movement visible in the data is nothing more than the time period surrounding the Great Recession. Finally, the data suggests a return to the long-run terms of trade beginning in 2014. This discussion of the data suggests a couple of things. The first one is that the economic recession will impact the terms of trade in a predictable direction. The second one is that the terms of trade appear to be mean reverting over the longer term.

Armed with the information presented in Fig. 21.1A and B, we can now examine the underlying hypothesis regarding the exchange rate and the terms of trade (Fig. 21.1C). The information presented suggests five different time periods regarding the relationship between the dollar and the terms of trade.

- During the 1988–98 time period, the dollar showed an upward or secular appreciation trend, while the terms of trade moved sideways. Even worse, the dollar appreciation coincides with the push toward globalization and the adoption of freer trade along the North America Free Trade Agreement (NAFTA) lines. The data during the period contradicts the underlying hypothesis that a rising dollar would make imports cheaper relative to exports, that is, the terms of trade would decline or that globalization would have a negative impact on the US terms of trade. Equally interesting is the fact that the dollar rise coincides with a strong economic performance as measured by US real GDP growth rate.
- The second time period overlaps the tech bubble, the Maestro's concern over Y2K, and the shallow recession that ensued. Notice that in spite of all these difficulties, the dollar did not decline while the terms of trade did decline around the time of the recession. Again, the data shows that the dollar did not have a significant effect on the terms of trade and that perhaps the real factors leading to the recession were more important variables temporarily affecting the terms of trade. This suggests a link between the underlying real GDP growth rate and the terms of trade.
- If one is charitable to the hypothesis that the dollar affects the terms of trade, the 2002–07 time period is the one to use as evidence. A downward trend in the exchange value of the dollar is clearly evident. If one tortures the data, one can argue that the terms of trade also trended downwards. However, the big picture suggests something else: a lower mean for the terms of trade. If that is the case, then what caused the lower mean? Perhaps economic policies that resulted in a slower real GDP growth rate?
- The Great Recession is one time period where both the dollar and terms of trade move in the same direction. The correlation is clear and quite strong. The only question is which way the causal direction is going. Are the terms of trade causing the dollar to change or vice versa? Either causal direction is consistent with the data.
- For the last time period, notice that when the dollar exhibits a pronounced upward trend, the terms of trade continues to move sideways at a higher mean as the rate of GDP growth improved. This suggests that the terms of trade returned to its long-run mean and that the latter may not be invariant to the real GDP growth rate.

The information presented in Fig. 21.1C does not seem to support the view that the foreign exchange value of the dollar drives the terms of trade or real exchange rate. On the other hand, knowledge of the economic performance during the time period suggests a different interpretation of what drives the terms of trade. Notice that the terms of trade seem to be above its trend value during periods of above-average real GDP growth and below its trend value during periods of below-average real GDP growth. The relationship between the two is easily explained. A rising or higher terms of trade means that a unit of the US exports can now buy more of the imports, which is a good thing. In terms of returns, a rising terms of trade means that the rate of return of producing a US good is rising relative to the rate of return generated by the production of the foreign/imported goods. Again, this is a good thing. This suggests that rising terms of trade is a bullish sign indicating faster growth and higher rates of returns.

Now, if we are correct in our interpretation of the data and if money is only a veil, attempts to improve the trade balance through deliberate monetary devaluation will not have any lasting effect on the terms of trade. The only effect will be to increase the underlying inflation rate in the devaluing country. For those who do not subscribe to our interpretation of the data, we suggest they review the experiences of the Southern Cone countries during the 1970s when devaluation was the order of the day. The currency depreciation did not improve these countries' trade balance. However, several did experience hyperinflation.

Attempts to improve the trade balance through tariffs will reduce the after-tax rates of returns of the taxed activities. Retaliation will lead the other countries to impose countervailing duties, with the end result being a slower growth rate for all the countries, as well as collectively for the world as a whole. The Smoot–Hawley experience is a reminder of what protectionist policies can do, not only to a country, but also to the world economy.

CHINA

In recent years, China has become the country that politicians and economists love to single out as a currency manipulator. Even if China is in fact a currency manipulator, the question is whether China has been a successful one?

The first step in addressing the issue is to review China's exchange rate experiences (Fig. 21.2A). No one disputes that the Chinese central bank controlled the financial system with an iron fist during the early days. As the economy progressed and was gradually opened, the Chinese monetary authorities reduced some of the controls. However, the fate of an inferior currency is that as the restrictions are removed, the demand for the controlled economy declines and its exchange rate depreciates. By fixing to the dollar, as long as the fixed exchange rate regime was in effect, everyone knew what a yuan or renminbi would buy in the future. In the past, we have argued that fixing the exchange rate during the mid-1990s was a stroke of genius that increased the transparency and property rights of the Chinese economy. One of the additional benefits of the fixed exchange rate was that the increased confidence attracted foreign capital inflows and increased incentives to domestic production. Perhaps under pressure from the anti-currency manipulation forces, the Chinese partially floated the currency. Initially and during most of the 2005–15 time period, the managed currency appreciated. This is inconsistent with the view that the Chinese were manipulating their currency to improve their competitive advantage. Since 2015, the yuan has begun to gradually and steadily deteriorate, fueling the anti-currency manipulation forces.

To lend further support or refute the currency manipulation views, additional information was required. We needed to obtain an estimate of the Chinese terms of trade and with that information we can then examine whether the currency manipulation is an effective policy that affects the terms of trade in the way the currency manipulators argue. The Federal Reserve Bank of Saint Louis publishes a price index for Chinese imports. The calculation of the index is not based on data provided

by the Chinese. This index is relatively easy to calculate using data provided by the countries exporting to China. Thus, the Chinese import price index is quite reliable and consistent with other data published by the Fed. Unfortunately, the same cannot be said of the export index. For that, we needed to rely on Chinese data. Instead of relying on Chinese data, we take the US import price index as a proxy for the Chinese export price index. Dividing the US import price index by the Chinese export price index, we obtain a proxy for the Chinese terms of trade.

Fig. 21.2B shows the United States and China's terms of trade as we have calculated them using the data published by the Saint Louis Fed. The correlation between the variables is not the same over different subperiods. Notice that while the two series move in opposite directions as expected, the two series are not perfect mirror images of each other. To us, this means that the two series are not identical and the Chinese terms of trade variable contains information that is different than that contained in the US terms of trade.

Prior to moving on to examine the correlation between the Chinese exchange rate and terms of trade, it is useful to review the correlation implied by the currency manipulation thesis that a depreciating currency will cheapen the price of the country's exports, while simultaneously increasing the price of imports. The net of this is a decline in the terms of trade. Under these conditions, the correlation between the currency and the terms of trade will be a positive one. Any other correlations is *prima facia* evidence of the failure of the currency manipulation hypothesis. The different subperiods identify different set of correlations.

The data presented in Fig. 21.2C shows the tail end of the Chinese fixed exchange rate experiment. Notice that while the exchange rate was fixed—according to the currency manipulation view that we have developed here—we would expect the terms of trade to remain unchanged. But that was not the case. While the exchange rate was fixed, the terms of trade increased. The subperiod is not consistent with the currency manipulation view. Eventually the Chinese either succumbed to international pressure or maybe for their own internal reasons, the Chinese abandoned the fixed exchange rate regime and allowed a managed float of their currency. The Chinese monetary authorities allowed Chinese currency to appreciate. During that time, the terms of trade also appreciated, as predicted by the currency manipulation view.

The third period to examine is around the Great Recession. China also suffered and the recession hit its terms of trade quite hard. The recovery was quite slow. Given the terms of trade effect and the positive correlation posited by the currency manipulation hypothesis, we would have expected the movement in the currency to move in the same direction as the terms of trade. However, that

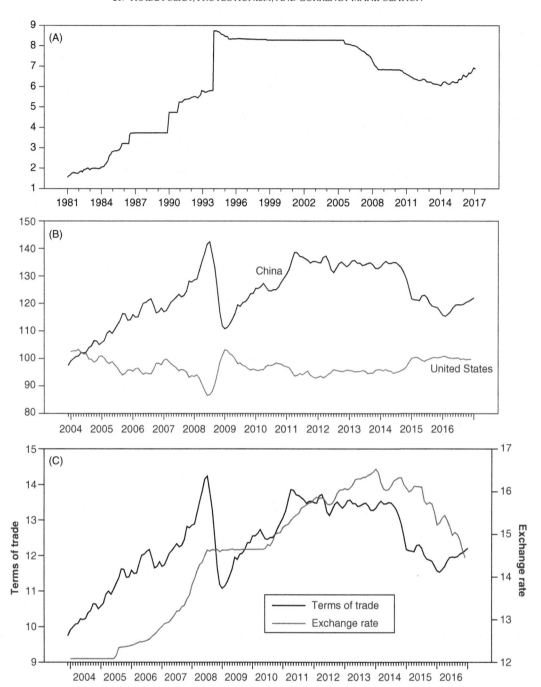

FIGURE 21.2 (A) China's exchange rate. How many yuans it takes to get a dollar? (B) United States and China terms of trade. (C) China exchange rate versus China terms of trade. How many dollars it takes to get a yuan?

was not the case. The exchange rate did not appreciate during this time, and the exchange rate remained steady. This shows that there was currency manipulation, and the Chinese managed to maintain a fixed exchange rate. What the data shows is that there was little or no correlation with the terms of trade. This result is inconsistent with the currency manipulation view. The latter would have forecast an unchanged terms of trade as a result of the quasi-fixed exchange rate during the crisis (Fig. 21.3).

The fourth episode spans the 2011–14 time period. The yuan appreciated, while the terms of trade moved sideways. Again, the correlation is not what the basic currency manipulation predicted. Then, around 2015, the yuan trended down and so did the terms of trade until sometimes during 2016 when the positive correlation reversed.

Looking at the correlation between the different subperiods, it is hard to argue that China is a currency manipulator in the sense meant by the administration

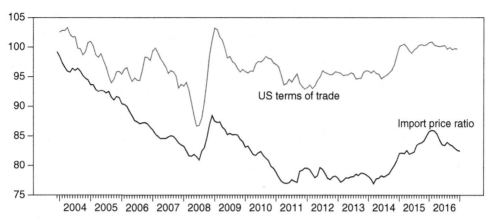

FIGURE 21.3 China import prices divided by the US import prices versus US export prices divided by US import prices.

and other protectionist or anti-China advocates. The data does not support the view that through currency manipulation the Chinese authorities have managed to control the country's terms of trade. If the administration goes after China for currency manipulation, it will be a policy mistake. Depending on the policy response, these actions could/will eventually reduce the level of economic activity and the well-being of both nations, and the world as a whole. A monetary response would only affect the underlying inflation rate; however a response that includes trade restrictions such as countervailing duties will at best alter the patterns of trade and at worst have a negative effect on the global economy level of economic activity.

22

Protectionism and Trade Policy

We've lost more than one-fourth of our manufacturing jobs since NAFTA was approved, and we've lost 60,000 factories since China joined the World Trade Organization in 2001. Our trade deficit in goods with the world last year was nearly $800 billion dollars. And overseas we have inherited a series of tragic foreign policy disasters.

President Trump, Speech to the Joint Session of Congress

It is clear from the quote above that President Trump believes that US job losses are related to trade. A much better picture of his views and in his own words can be found in his jobs speech delivered by then-candidate Trump on June 27, 2016 in Pittsburg, Pennsylvania.

I have visited cities and towns across this country where a third or even half of manufacturing jobs have been wiped out in the last 20 years. Today, we import nearly $800 billion more in goods than we export. This is not some natural disaster. It is politician-made disaster.....

America has lost nearly one-third of its manufacturing jobs since 1997 - even as the country has increased its population by 50 million people.

...The city of Pittsburgh, and the State of Pennsylvania, have lost one-third of their manufacturing jobs since the Clintons put China into the WTO. Fifty thousand factories across America have shut their doors in that time. Almost half of our entire manufacturing trade deficit in goods with the world is the result of trade with China.

.....As reported by the Economic Policy Institute in May, this deal doubled our trade deficit with South Korea and destroyed nearly 100,000 American jobs.

In what follows, we examine the theoretical framework upon which President Trump's conclusions are reached. We then examine whether the narrative derived from his framework is supported by the data. Let's begin with the statement the president made:

Trade reform, and the negotiation of great trade deals, is the quickest way to bring our jobs back.

To understand why trade reform creates jobs, we need to understand how all nations grow and prosper.

Massive trade deficits subtract directly from our Gross Domestic Product.

The president seems to believe that the US trade imbalance is, in large part, the result of poorly negotiated trade deals that allow the counter parties to cheat and take advantage of the United States. In turn, our poor negotiating skills have resulted in a worsening of the trade balance that has reduced employment and real GDP growth. Presumably the solution to that problem is to negotiate better deals or impose trade restrictions to eliminate the unfair advantage gained by the cheating trading partners. This line of reasoning leaves us with the following two insights:

- Poorly negotiated free trade agreements and/or trade actions lead to a deterioration of the US trade balance. A corollary is that under these conditions, trade restrictions improve the US trade balance.
- A trade deficit results in a loss of jobs, lower wages, and as a result, lower real GDP growth and a lower standard of living.

In support of his views, the president goes on to say:

From 1947 to 2001-a span of over five decades-our inflation-adjusted gross domestic product grew at a rate of 3.5%.

Economic Disturbances and Equilibrium in an Integrated Global Economy. http://dx.doi.org/10.1016/B978-0-12-813993-6.00022-2

However, since 2002 – the year after we fully opened our markets to Chinese imports – that GDP growth rate has been cut almost in half.

What does this mean for Americans? For every one percent of GDP growth we fail to generate in any given year, we also fail to create over one million jobs.

The implication is that the opening of trade with China reduced real GDP growth. A literal interpretation of the previous statement leads us to conclude that the president believes that the trade deficit with China cuts the US growth rate in half. But using the president's logic and keeping his assumption that the rest of the world has taken advantage of the United States, are we to believe that absent all the trade opening actions taken in the post-WWII period would have resulted in a faster growth rate? What does the data says? Is there any evidence to support or contradict his views?

THE TRADE BALANCE AND REAL GDP GROWTH

Looking at the information presented in Fig. 22.1, one can see two large trade deficit cycles. The first one began under President Reagan. It peaked during the Reagan administration and was erased during the George H. W. Bush administration. The second cycle began in earnest during the Clinton administration and continued throughout the George W. Bush administration, peaking just before the financial crisis. From that point on and during the Obama administration years, the trade deficit steadily improved, but we have not completely erased it.

If we take at face value that the trade balance deficit results in lower real GDP growth, the information presented earlier would suggest that the US real GDP growth rate would be below average or declining during the periods when the US experienced a trade deficit. The

situation would be even worse during periods of a growing trade deficit. Such a view would suggest that during the Reagan, Clinton, and W years, the US real GDP growth rate would be a weak one with the US economy performing well below average. Conversely, during the George H. W. Bush and Obama years, we would experience a robust, above-average economic performance. Yet we know from that this is not what the data says (Fig. 22.2). To ease the visual presentation, the deteriorating trade balance periods as a percent of GDP (i.e., growing deficits as a percent of GDP) have been shaded. Notice also that the shaded periods during which the trade balance was deteriorating include the only years during which the United States has grown at better than 3.5% since 1980.

So far, the information presented suggests that an accelerating and high real GDP growth is associated with a deterioration of the trade balance or a larger trade deficit as a percent of GDP. Additional evidence in support of our interpretation of the data is the fact that Japan, considered a protectionist country, ran trade surpluses when its economy barely grew in the 1990s and 2000s. In contrast, during the Reagan and Clinton administrations the US grew robustly with large trade deficits. These results and our interpretation raise several issues. The first one is whether the president has the proper framework. The second issue is even if his administration is successful in reducing the trade deficit, will it be able to increase the growth rate in the process of improving the trade deficit?

Table 22.1 provides us with a summary of the major trade actions that have taken place during the post-WWII time period. The information presented in Table 22.1 in combination with the historical trade balance as a percent of GDP (Fig. 22.1) and the real GDP growth (Fig. 22.2) shows that the timing of the most significant trade opening actions in the immediate postwar period, GATT and the Kennedy Round of tariff reductions, occurred

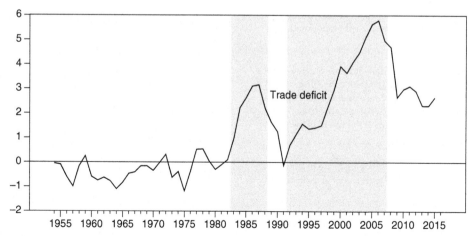

FIGURE 22.1   Trade deficit as a percent of GDP.

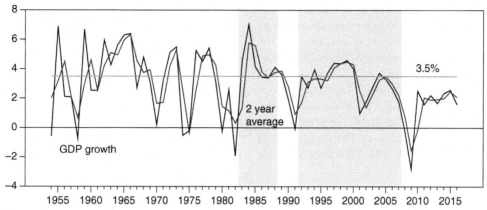

FIGURE 22.2 Annual real GDP growth rate and its 2-year moving average.

during a time when the US experienced a trade surplus and the United States was experiencing a strong and robust strong real GDP growth (Fig. 22.3A). One possible way to interpret this result in the context of the president's arguments is that the US negotiated great deals prior to NAFTA and prior to allowing China to ascent into the WTO, and that the way those latter deals were structured was disadvantageous for the United States.

Unfortunately, there are a couple of anomalies this interpretation does not explain. The first anomaly would be the Reagan years. There were no major trade deals negotiated and yet the trade balance deteriorated. The second issue to point out is that if the deterioration of the trade balance is a result of bad deals or foreigners taking advantage of the United States, does this mean that after the trade deficit peaked around 1989 and 2007

TABLE 22.1 Major Changes in US Trade Policy, 1930–81

Free trade	Protectionism
Trade Agreement Act of 1934	Smoot–Hawley Tariff Act of 1930
Bilateral trade agreement with 20 nations reduced average tariffs to half their 1934 levels	
General Agreement on Tariffs and Trade (GATT) I Geneva 1947 II Annecy France 1949 III Torquay England 1950–51	
Trade Agreement Acts extended (1995) for 3 years; Eisenhower authorized to reduce tariffs 5% a year and duties in excess of 50%	
Trade Expansion Act of 1962 (president given authority to reduce tariffs of July 1, 1962 by 50% in 5 years: allowed elimination of duties on specific commodities)	
The Kennedy Round (1962) (Authorized 50% tariff reductions on most industrial products and 30% to 50% on others)	
President Johnson calls for the abolition of American Selling Price (1968)	
	Trade Act of 1970 passed by the House and defeated in the Senate President Nixon closes Gold Window; 10% increase in tariffs (1971)
Implementation of Kennedy Round tariff reductions completed (1972)	
	OPEC Oil Embargo (1973)
Trade Act of 1974 (to maintain and enlarge foreign markets)	Trade Act of 1974 (provided safeguard and "adjustment assistance")
Tokyo Round—1975 (attempted to constrain non-tariff barriers)	Tokyo Round—1975 (implementation of safeguards and protection from international trade)
Trade Act of 1979 (domestic industries required to show injury by subsidized exports before offsetting duty would be imposed)	

that the US toughened up its enforcement and became better at identifying and correcting unfair advantages? Even if the answer to the previous question is in the affirmative, then another issue surfaces. Why didn't the improvement in the trade balance as a percent of GDP improve the real GDP growth rate? One may argue that there is a response lag, but if that was the case, the two-year moving average of the real GDP growth rate reported in Fig. 22.3A should pick up the lagged effect unless one is the willing to argue that the lags are long and variable.

The previous discussion suggests that every time there is an anomaly, a new layer of complexity must be added to justify the president's conclusions. Perhaps there is a simpler alternative explanation. Fig. 22.3B and C suggest an interesting relationship between economic activity and the real GDP growth rate. Notice that during periods in which the US economy growth rate accelerates, the trade balance worsens (see the shading in Fig. 22.3B). Similarly, Fig. 22.3C shows that recessions precede improvements in the trade balance. In short, Fig. 22.3B and C suggest a negative correlation between

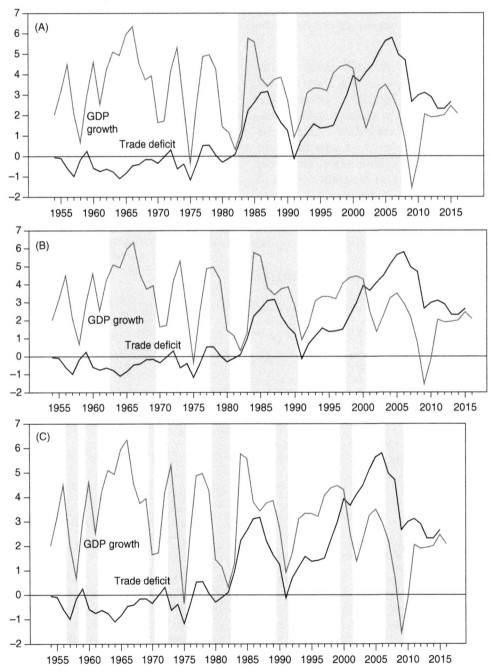

FIGURE 22.3 (A–C) Trade deficit as a percent of GDP versus the 2-year real GDP growth moving average.

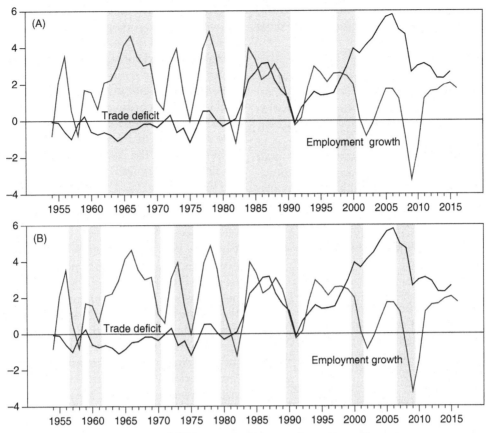

FIGURE 22.4 (A and B) Trade deficit as a percent of GDP versus the 2-year employment growth moving average.

the trade balance and faster economic growth and thus the simple explanation.

The trade balance and employment growth is another important component of the component of the president's view on trade policy. He seems to argue that a deteriorating trade balance lowers employment and the real GDP growth rates. This hypothesis is not consistent with the experience during the post-WWII period. The correlation between the trade balance and the real GDP growth rate is not what one would expect under the Trump hypothesis. Notice that the periods of strong and accelerating employment growth rates are associated with a rising trade deficit in Fig. 22.4A. More importantly, the large improvements in the trade deficit seem to occur around periods when the US experienced a recession and employment growth decelerated (Fig. 22.4B).

The question that we need to resolve is what causes what? One can argue that President Nixon's actions and the OPEC oil embargo are two trade-related events associated with US recessions, not the other way around. Also, it is difficult to argue that the other recessions were caused by trade-related policies when there was no major trade action surrounding these events. We come away with some interesting and possible generalizations. The improvements in the trade balance are all

associated with the real GDP and employment growth slowdown, even though not all the slowdowns were associated with trade issues. This leads us to believe or conclude that there is a strong evidence of a causal relationship that goes from the real GDP growth rate to the trade balance. While the data also supports the view that the trade actions impact the real GDP growth rate, the most extreme case being the Smoot–Hawley tariffs, even if this relationship exists, it is not what the president would like. The increased trade restriction actions are associated with a slower, not faster, growth rate. A final issue to raise regarding the president's views on the trade deficit and real GDP growth rate is if he means to imply that the United States would have grown even faster had the trade opening measures not been undertaken? That is not what our interpretation of the data says.

In an article in the *Wall Street Journal* editorial pages, Peter Navarro, the director of the White House National Trade Council asked and answered the earlier mentioned question. Here is what Mr. Navarro had to say:

> The economic argument that trade deficits matter begins with the observation that growth in real GDP depends on only four factors: consumption, government spending, business investment and net exports (the difference between exports and imports).

So far, so good. This is nothing more than an accounting identity in the national income and products accounts (NIPA). That is:

$$C + G + I + X - M = GDP \qquad (22.1)$$

where C denotes aggregate consumption, G government spending, I investment spending, X exports, and M imports.

As an identity, the previous equation must hold at all times. There is no economic theory here, only accounting theory. However, the next statement by Mr. Navarro begins to outline his theory:

> Reducing a trade deficit through tough, smart negotiations is a way to increase net exports—and boost the rate of economic growth.

The previous sentence contains two important assumptions critical to the official views on trade.

The first one is that smart negotiations are a way to improve or reduce the trade deficit. The second assumption being that an improvement in the trade deficit will boost real GDP, or the rate of economic growth.

Sound familiar? These are basically the same two insights we derived from the president at the beginning of this missive. While the first assumption is difficult to test as it depends on what we define as "smart," the second is easily testable using NIPA data, which is readily available in places like the Federal Reserve Bank of Saint Louis Economic DataBase (FRED). FRED is our go to website for US economic data. For those who doubt our interpretation of these assumptions, here is Mr. Navarro's explanation:

> Suppose America successfully negotiates a bilateral trade deal this year with Mexico in which Mexico agrees to buy more products from the United States that it now purchases from the rest of the world. This would show up in government data as an increase in US exports, a lower trade deficit, and an increase in the growth of America's GDP.

> Similarly, if the United States uses its leverage as the world's largest market to persuade India to reduce its notoriously high tariffs and Japan to lower its formidable nontariff barriers, America will surely sell more Washington apples, Florida oranges, California wine, Wisconsin cheese and Harley-Davidson motorcycles. Just as surely, the US trade deficit would fall, economic growth would increase, and real wages would rise from Seattle and Orlando to Sonoma and Milwaukee.

He also addresses offshore production:

> ...if such offshored production then generates products for export back into the U.S.—say, an American consumer buys a Ford Focus imported from Mexico rather than assembled in Detroit—the trade deficit rises, further reducing growth.

Everything Mr. Navarro says is true in a NIPA sense. However, his argument is best explained in the context of a *ceteris paribus* world. That is, a world where everything else is held constant. In such a world, an increase in exports, holding everything else (imports, government expenditures, and investments) constant, results in a higher GDP according to the NIPA accounting. See Eq. (22.1) above. In this context, a trade deficit reduces GDP. The equation also shows why traditional Keynesian books consider the trade balance as a leakage of domestic aggregate demand.

However, Eq. (22.1) does not tell us the whole story. What if these variables are interrelated and change in response to a disturbance in say the trade balance or vice versa. A change in one variable will affect the other variables and so on. In such a world, one cannot hold everything else the same. One has to move to the *mutatis mutandis* realm. A world where not everything else is held constant. Most general equilibrium models specify the interactions among these variables, as well as the magnitude of the interaction coefficients. In doing so, the specification limits the feedback and interactions among the different variables. The estimation and magnitude of these models is an empirical issue. Hence, there are two critical issues regarding these macroeconomic models. The first one is the specification of the different equations that determine the interaction among the variables. The second issue is the coefficients attached to the different variables, as they determine the magnitude of the interaction among the variables. As, we are not privy to the administration's models, it is hard to analyze the specification of its components. However, we can focus on the empirical validity of the insights and implications of the model as described by the president and his advisor.

Just the facts, like Sgt. Joe Friday used to say. Information on the US imports and exports as a percent of GDP can be found in Fig. 22.5A and B. The data shows a close correlation between the two variables. In general, imports and exports as a percent of GDP tend to rise and fall together, which raises the question as what causes the correlation between the two? A follow-up question that immediately comes to mind is if the correlation holds, will policies aimed at reducing imports also reduce exports and vice versa?

The data also shows that during the fast growth periods when the economy's trailing two year real GDP growth averages better than 3.5% (the shaded areas in Fig. 22.5A), the imports increase as a percent of GDP, while the exports show a flat to downward trend early in the cycle. The combination of rising imports and a flat to declining exports as a share of GDP leads to unambiguous deterioration of the trade balance. Fig. 22.5B shows that imports as a percent of GDP fall in the aftermath of economic recession while the exports either fall by a smaller amount as a percent of GDP or not at all.

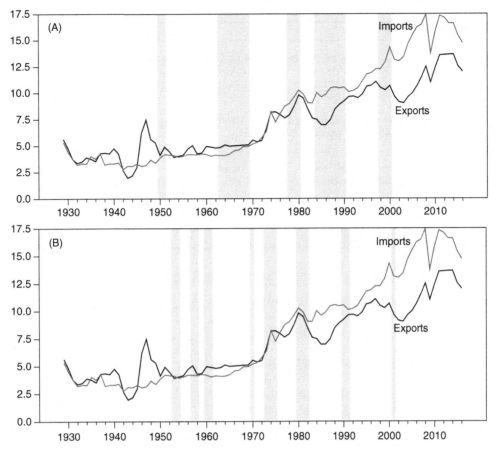

FIGURE 22.5 (A and B) Imports and exports as a percent of GDP.

The combination leads to an improvement in the trade balance as a percent of GDP. Combining the results presented in Fig. 22.5A and B with those of Fig. 22.3C and D, we now know that faster growth leads to an increase in the imports as a percent of GDP in absolute terms, as well as relative to exports as a percent of GDP, the net result being a deterioration of the trade balance. A recession or deceleration of real GDP growth produces the opposite result.

The relationship between the trade balance as a percent of GDP and the employment growth reinforces the relationship between the trade balance and the real GDP growth already reported in Fig. 22.3C and D. The data reported in Fig. 22.4A and B show that employment growth is associated with a rising trade deficit, while a recession results in reduced employment growth and is associated with an improving trade balance.

Who comes first? The temporal precedence of the GDP growth rate over the trade balance changes suggest a causal relationship going from real GDP growth rates to the trade balance. One also wonders about the possibility of the causal relationship going the other way. The information presented in Table 22.2 is very suggestive of different linkages. Notice that the major free trade

actions are associated with the high real GDP growth rate periods, while the major protectionist actions are associated with US recessions.

Our interpretation of this correlation is that the data suggests that protectionist trade actions have a negative impact on the pace of economic activity, while the implementation of free trade initiatives are associated with periods of faster growth. And for those who doubt this correlation, they only need to be reminded about the Smoot–Hawley tariffs preceding the Great Depression. Again, the data shows that major free trade initiatives are associated with the high US growth periods. This correlation is quite damaging to the underlying hypothesis of the Trump administration regarding international trade and US growth.

The information presented in Table 22.2 also shows that trade is not everything. There are high growth periods and recessions not associated with major trade actions. All of this suggests that other factors may also affect both the trade balance and the rate of GDP growth. For example, we believe that the phase-in of the Reagan tax rate cuts contributed to the Reagan recession, while the George H. W. Bush tax increase also contributed to the recession during his term in office. Then there are

TABLE 22.2   Trade Actions, US Recessions, and High Growth Periods

Real GDP growth		Trade actions	
High growth	Recessions	Free trade	Protectionist
1950–51	July 1953–May 1954 August 1957–April 1958 April 1960–February 1961	General Agreement on Tariffs and Trade (GATT)	
1963–69	December 1969–November 1970 November 1973–march 1975	The Kennedy Round (1962)	President Nixon closes Gold Window OPEC Oil Embargo (1973)
1977–80	January 1980–July 1980 July 1981–November 1982	Trade Act of 1979	
1984–90	July 1990–March 1991	NAFTA	
1998–2000	March 2001–November 2001 December 2007–June 2009		

financial events, such as the bursting of the tech and housing bubbles. These events suggest that the tax policy and the bubble bursting impacted both the pace of economic activity and the trade balance and quite possibly other interactions among the variables.

All of these results combined point to an interrelationship between imports, exports, the trade balance, and real GDP. Our analysis also suggests that there are many other variables that come into play. The one thing that the data points to is that while possibly improving the trade balance, protectionist policies will unambiguously slow down the rate of GDP growth and that is not what the administration believes.

THE TRADE BALANCE AND THE CAPITAL ACCOUNT

The national-security argument that trade deficits matter begins with this accounting identity: Any deficit in the current account caused by imbalanced trade must be offset by a surplus in the capital account, meaning foreign investment in the U.S.

Technically this statement is only true under a floating exchange rate where foreigners do not hold our currency. But unfortunately, the United States is a reserve currency country and there may be net money flows. That is, the balance of payments may not be zero and thus the capital account will not necessarily be a mirror image of the trade balance. But for the sake of argument, in what follows, we assume that is the case. The important implication here is that the earlier mentioned budget constraint requires that any theory explains the trade balance must also simultaneously explain the capital follows. As we show, while we disagree with his analysis, Mr. Navarro does precisely that.

In the short term, this balance-of-payments equilibrium may be benign, as foreigners return our trade-deficit dollars to American shores by investing in U.S. bonds and stocks and perhaps by building new production facilities. The extra capital keeps mortgage rates lower, the stock market abundantly capitalized, and Americans more fully employed.

But running large and persistent trade deficits also facilitates a pattern of wealth transfers offshore. Warren Buffett refers to this as "conquest by purchase" and warns that foreigners will eventually own so much of the U.S. that Americans will wind up working longer hours just to eat and to service the debt.

The earlier argument is not a new one. That was the prevailing view during the 1980s when the Japanese were supposedly going to buy the United States. They bought trophy properties like Pebble Beach Country Club. The protectionists worried, but their depressive forecast never came to pass. But before a formal rebuttal of the argument, it may be worthwhile to clarify the implicit argument behind the previous statement.

There is other anecdotal evidence that contradicts the Trump administration's views. For example, Japan was a net lender and had lower interest rates than the United States during the 1980s. In contrast, the United States was a net borrower and had a high nominal and real interest rates during the periods of rapid deterioration of the trade balance under President Reagan's administration.

Think of a person going to a bank and applying for a loan and getting it. There are two possibilities:

- One possibility—and it seems that this is the one implicit in Mr. Navarro's and Mr. Buffet's views—is the one where the borrower takes the money, goes to Vegas, has a good time, and then returns home with a hangover, no money, and in debt. Now that person must work to repay the debt and, to do so, the person has to reduce its consumption level and be beholden to the bank. But that is not the only ending to this story.
- The second possibility is more interesting to us. Suppose the person judiciously invests the money

and earns a rate of return high enough that allows them to repay the loan and have some money left over. Clearly that person is better off. Their income and quite possibly their wealth will also increase. The higher income and wealth allows that person to increase their consumption levels, while continuing to invest if the rate of return is high enough.

These are two very different stories. One is a success story that makes the borrower much better off, while the other is a sad story of squandered opportunities that in the long run makes the borrower worse off. Both stories are logically consistent. The question is how we can discriminate between the two alternatives.

The common element of the two stories is that both borrowers spend more in relation to their income. Extending that to the national economy, the increase expenditure relative to income means a trade deficit. But from here on, the two hypotheses diverge. In one case, the borrower invests and expands their productive capacity, income, and net worth. The other does not. This suggests a very simple way to discriminate between the two alternatives: if the borrower "squanders" the borrowing, his net worth will decline as he spends the borrowing. The result is an increase in the trade deficit and a decline in the borrowers' net worth relative to the rest of the world, that is, the lender. In contract, if the borrower is judicious with the proceeds of the increased indebtedness, the net worth should increase, while simultaneously the trade balance worsens.

The information presented in Fig. 22.6 allows one to discriminate between the two alternatives. Notice that increases in the trade deficit are associated with increases in the US stock market relative to the rest of the world ex-US, our wealth proxy. More importantly, the stock market data appears to lead the trade balance. Taken together, the data suggests that, on average, borrowing is a good thing. It allows the economy to take advantages of higher rates of returns above the

borrowing rate. This allows the borrower to service the debt and have some profits left over which increase the country's net worth as reflected by the stock markets' relative performance. The trade deficit is also explained in the context of the higher opportunities. The prospect of higher wealth makes the borrower credit worthy. In a forward-looking market and under the traditional consumptions theories, the prospect of a higher future net worth leads to an increase in current consumption and investment relative to income, and thus the deterioration in the trade balance. The trade deficit will increase as the relative stock market performance increases.

Viewing the situation from the foreigners' perspective, the increase in aggregate demand will result in a higher global real interest rates than would have prevailed. The higher interest rate induces the foreigners to delay part of their consumption and/or investment. The excess production can now be exported. Also, given that investment opportunities have increased in the borrowing country, the rest of the world would be willing to invest to participate in the higher rates of returns, capital will flow into the country whose future prospects have brightened. The inflow will finance the economic expansion and wealth creation.

The argument in the last two paragraphs provides a simultaneous explanation for the trade balance and capital flows from the perspective of both the borrowing and lending country. In this regard, we have satisfied one of the requirements specified by the budget constraints imposed by the NIPA accounting. Next, it is clear from Fig. 22.6 that the data supports the good borrower, not the borrower that uses the borrowing to finance its current consumption in excess of its income and in doing so squanders future opportunities and reduces its wealth. Also, as the exchange is voluntary, it is easy to conclude that all parties are happy with the deal and that both countries expect to be better off. All of this leads one to question the hypothesis that a trade deficit is bad and

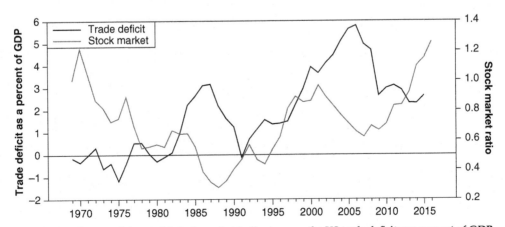

FIGURE 22.6 Ratio of US to the rest of the world stock market indices versus the US trade deficit as a percent of GDP.

reduces net worth, output, and employment. The data clearly shows that is not necessarily true.

THE CONQUEST BY PURCHASE

Dark though it is, Mr. Buffett's scenario may still be too rosy. Suppose the purchaser is a rapidly militarizing strategic rival intent on world hegemony. It buys up America's companies, technologies, farmland, food-supply chain—and ultimately controls much of the U.S. defense-industrial base. How might that alternative version of conquest by purchase end for our sons and daughters? Might we lose a broader cold war for America's freedom and prosperity, not by shots fired but by cash registers ringing? Might we lose a broader hot war because America has sent its defense-industrial base abroad on the wings of a persistent trade deficit?

Today, after decades of trade deficits and a mass migration of factories offshore, there is only one American company that can repair Navy submarine propellers—and not a single company that can make flat-panel displays for military aircraft or night-vision goggles. Meanwhile, America's steel industry is on the ropes, its aluminum industry is flat on its back, and its shipbuilding industry is gathering barnacles. The U.S. has begun to lose control of its food-supply chain, and foreign firms are eager to purchase large swaths of Silicon Valley's treasures.

Our interpretation of the data does not lend support to the "conquest by purchase theory" attributed to Mr. Buffett. Our story suggests that people borrow or invest to make themselves better off in the long run. That is the essence of investing in a free market. Just like individuals invest in the stock market to earn a rate of return without having control of the management of the operation, there is no reason to believe that all foreign investment is intended to control US corporations. However, that is not to say that there aren't activist funds that aim to do so. The same can be said of some national economies. But we believe that we have laws that protect the investors and the economy from the predatory behavior based on insider trading and other illegal methods. We contend that there is no need for additional laws. What we need is better and more resolved enforcement.

The United States has laws that regulate the transfer of technology. We have the legal mechanism in place to stop transactions that would grant access to foreign governments of our secret and sensitive technologies. There is no reason why the government could not devise an efficient way to insure the domestic production of products vital to our national defense. The key is to keep it simple. Take our domestic agriculture rules for example. Although bloated, the price support mechanism combined with acreage restrictions insures the domestic production of agricultural supplies. A simpler solution would be to guarantee the purchase of a certain amount and allow domestic producers to compete. The same is true for our defense. If the United States needs flat panel displays for military needs, the government rather than providing a complicated solution, should guarantee the purchase of the amount needed for national security and let the domestic suppliers compete for that market through an option system. This would minimize the cost to the government and insure the national defense supplies. By eliminating the unlimited price support, we could then initiate a program that guarantees the purchase of the minimum quantities needed to insure the security of the United States and the viability of the domestic producers.

Finally, the administration should not discount the possibility that people's behavior will change in response to its actions. For example, agricultural producers in the United States for whom a large portion of their income comes from foreign sales, worry that the US trade actions may affect their sales? Also, the TPP countries are not standing still. They have met to see how they can maintain alive the TPP and plan to proceed with the so-called "TPP minus one." There will be a domestic and foreign reaction to any Trump administration, whether United States wins remains to be seen.

THE BALANCE OF PAYMENTS

23

Global Investing: The Balance of Payments

In Part I, we explored the implications of a world in which economic agents maximized profits and their economic well-being where goods and services and factors of production were free to move across national borders without facing any impediment or "transportation costs."

The analysis focused on the market-clearing process, which, in turn, led to the identification of global and national equilibrium prices. The process yielded several insights, which we use to examine the impact of alternative policies on the economy and whether these policies in fact produce the results that the pundits and/or

Economic Disturbances and Equilibrium in an Integrated Global Economy. http://dx.doi.org/10.1016/B978-0-12-813993-6.00023-4

policymakers expect or promise. The analysis also allows us to identify the policies that, in the context of our framework, would deliver the desired objectives and those that would not. This is a very important result. In the context of an investment strategy, it allows us to anticipate effects that differ from the ones promised by the policymakers.

Part II focuses on the market-clearing process in the global and national goods markets. In particular, we focused on the national and global production, which gave us insights into the sources of changes in the global and national GDP. For example, a bumper crop produces a global imbalance and to restore global equilibrium, a decline in the global market-clearing prices must take place. To the extent that the countries in this world have normal demand and supply curves, the declining prices induce a common output response across all countries in the world. The declining price induces a reduction in the quantity supplied, a downward movement along each country supply curve. In an integrated economy, a rising tide lifts all boats or, as in the case of the previous example, an ebb tide lowers them. That is, the joy and the curse of an integrated economy. Price changes induce common trends that affect all of the nations in the world in a similar way. The difference in the magnitude of response of the national economies due to the price change is largely determined by the countries' supply elasticities with respect to the price change.

In addition to the market-clearing prices, we also paid a great deal of attention to the equilibrium quantities of the different goods and services produced and consumed in the different localities. For the world as a whole, the budget constraint at a point in time is inescapable. Global equilibrium requires that world income equal world expenditures. That is, the world trade balance has to be zero at all times. Profit and well-being maximization means that global production of each and every commodity will match global consumption. However, trade in goods introduces an important degree of freedom. The consumption of a particular good in a country does not have to match its local production level. The country is only bound by its budget constraint. So, if production exceeds the consumption of a particular good, the surpluses in that commodity can be used to finance additional consumption of other commodities, be it in the present or at some future time.

The budget constraint leads us to focus on the net trade of each individual commodity. Collectively, they make up the countries' trade balance. If all current income is spent on current goods and services, there is no net saving, and the value of goods imported by the country equals the value of exports. However, if the country is a net saver, the country's trade balance will be in surplus and the country will accumulate. I owe you (IOU)s. The country is a net saver and thus a lender.

In Part IV, we move away from the goods' markets and into the money markets. We examine how the profit maximization and mobility affect global prices of goods in terms of money, how the alternative organizations of the monetary system impact the world, and how individual countries underlie inflation rates, as well as how the net flows of money are across national borders. These determine the nominal exchange rate and balance of payments (BOP) of the different economies. However, before we get into the discussion, it may be worthwhile to review the basic monetary assumptions made in developing our framework.

THE MONETARY SYSTEM

Initially, we assume that there is a single closed economy using a single currency. We also assume that money is strictly a veil, and that inflation is and will always be a monetary phenomenon, too much money chasing too few goods. The demand for money is assumed to be the traditional transaction demand for money. As such, the demand for real balances is directly proportional to the economy's production level. The proportionality factor is nothing more than the inverse of the velocity of money or turnover rate. The demand for money is described by the following equation:

$$Md / P = Y / v \qquad (23.1)$$

where Md denotes the demand for nominal balances, P price level, Y real GDP, and v the velocity of money.

In log linear form, the percent changes in the variables can be written as:

$$\Psi d - \pi = \eta - \upsilon \qquad (23.2)$$

where Ψd denotes the logarithm of the demand for money, π the inflation rate, η the income elasticity of the demand for money, and υ the elasticity of the demand for money with respect to changes in the velocity of money. The latter is interpreted by us as a demand shifter.

We assume that the velocity of money is a function of the opportunity cost of holding that money. Hence there are two sources for money demand shifts: one is the real GDP changes, and the other is changes in the velocity of money. Thus according to this view, once the real GDP has been accounted for, all other shifts in the real demand for money are attributable to shifts in the velocity of money. Notice that the demand for real balances is nothing more than the quantity of money divided by the price level, that is, the real purchasing power of the quantity of money. Hence holding the velocity of money constant, the nominal demand for money will be proportional to the price level. That is, the quantity of money needs to keep pace with the price level if it is to maintain its purchasing power.

We also assume that in this economy the printing of notes and or bills is under complete control of the monetary authorities, that is, the central bank. This leads to a narrow definition of money, monetary base, B. The latter consists of the greenbacks printed by the Fed. It has two alternative uses, one is as currency in circulation, C, and the other is as bank reserves, R. That is:

$$B = C + R \qquad (23.3)$$

However that is not the only monetary aggregate. Much broader aggregates are used to denote the quantity of money in circulation in an economy. As already mentioned, under a fractional reserve banking system, high-powered money is strictly controlled by the Fed. The high-powered money consists of the circulating currency and all private bank deposits at the Fed. The broader monetary supply Ms (money stock) is nothing more than the product of the monetary base and the money multiplier, m.

Under a fractional reserve banking system, the money stock is larger than the monetary base because banks need only keep a fraction, say 10%, of the money deposited by a customer in his/her bank account as a reserve backing the deposit and this way insure that the bank is able to meet the customer's normal withdrawals. The bank then proceeds to lend out the remaining money not used as reserves. The money loaned is successively redeposited and reloaned by the same and or different banks. The net effects of these transactions is an expansion of the loan portfolios as well as the total deposits of the banking system. The maximum or potential net deposit creation is nothing more than the inverse of the reserve requirement. For example, a 10% reserve can support $10 worth of deposits for every dollar worth of reserves. This means that every dollar worth of reserves can now support $9 worth of loans. The latter two make up the bank's assets, which by the magic of double entry bookkeeping must also match the liabilities, the bank deposits in this case. The overall expansion determines the multiplier, or the amount by which the monetary base must be multiplied to produce the actual quantity of money circulating the economy. The previous discussion suggests that the money multiplier is not fully under the control of the Fed, something to keep in mind.

The economy's money supply is easily characterized by the following equation:

$$Ms = B * m \qquad (23.4)$$

where B denotes the monetary base circulating in the economy and m is the money multiplier.

Again in log linear form, the percentage changes in the monetary aggregates and its components can be written as:

$$\Psi s = \omega + \mu \qquad (23.5)$$

where ψs denotes the percentage change in money supply, ω the percent change of the monetary base, and μ the percent change of the money multiplier. We interpret the latter as a money supply shifter.

Monetary equilibrium requires the intersection of the demand for and supply of money that is:

$$Md = Ms \qquad (23.6)$$

Substituting Eqs. (23.1) and (23.4) into the previous equation yields a more detailed version of the market-clearing conditions in the money market.

$$(B * m) * v = P * Y \qquad (23.7)$$

Again, the dynamic version being

$$\omega + \mu = \pi + \eta - \upsilon \qquad (23.8)$$

The information in the previous equations can be rearranged to solve for equilibrium price level as well as the underlying inflation rate.

$$P = ((B * m) * v) / Y \qquad (23.8')$$

and

$$\pi = \omega + \mu - \eta + \upsilon \qquad (23.9)$$

The equations are fairly general and can accommodate different points of views and versions:

- For example, Eq. (23.8) shows that the product of the monetary base, B, times the money multiplier, m, denotes the quantity of money circulating in the economy, MZM.
- All else the same, increases in the quantity of money lead to a higher price level. Increases in real GDP, Y, lead to a decline in the price level.
- Also, as already mentioned, we do not necessarily assume that the velocity of money is constant, we have to allow for shifts in the demand for money or alternatively stated changes in the velocity of money.
- Nor do we assume that the money multiplier is under the strict control of the monetary authorities, but more on these two issues later on.

The dynamic version, Eq. (23.9), is fairly intuitive. The inflation rate is positively related to the growth rate of the monetary base and supply shifter. In turn the inflation rate is negatively related to the growth of real GDP and positively to changes in the velocity of money. The equation accommodates the view that inflation is a monetary phenomenon, too much money chasing too few goods. It also allows for shifts in the demand for and supply of money to affect the overall equilibrium inflation rate.

EXTENDING THE FRAMEWORK TO ACCOUNT FOR MULTIPLE ECONOMIES AND CURRENCIES

Our next step is to expand the model by incorporating more than one country and more than one currency. Let's consider the two countries introduced in the earlier section, Lakeland and Westland. In addition to the assumptions already made about these two countries, we will add that each country has its own currency, Lakeland uses the peso while Westland uses a currency called notes.

Earlier we showed that the assumption of free trade and perfect mobility of goods and services across national borders would yield the result that the peso price of each and every trade commodity would be the same across national borders. If it is not, then a profit opportunity would exist and it would be quickly arbitraged away. The same would hold for the notes price of each and every commodity.

We also showed that assuming that the two countries have similar tastes, the consumer baskets will be fairly similar if not identical across countries. If that is the case, the ratio of the price of Lakeland's consumer basket in pesos divided by Westland consumer basket in notes will give us the value of the exchange rate between pesos and notes. That is:

$$E = P_p / P_n \qquad (23.10)$$

where E denotes Westland' exchange rate, in terms of Lakeland's currency, that is, notes in terms pesos. P_p denotes the price of Lakeland's Consumer Price Index (CPI) in pesos and P_n is the price of Westland CPI in notes.

Again, differentiating logarithmically the previous equation, we obtain an expression for the exchange rate of Westland currency in terms of Lakeland's. That is the foreign exchange rate value of the notes in terms of pesos.

$$\epsilon = \pi_p - \pi_n \qquad (23.11)$$

The previous equation shows that everything else the same, increases in the inflation rate in Lakeland, that is, the inflation rate measured in notes, π_n, will result in an exchange rate depreciation of the notes relative to pesos. In contrast the higher the peso inflation rate in Lakeland, π_p, the greater the rate of appreciation of the exchange rate.

THE GLOBAL AND INDIVIDUAL COUNTRIES' MONETARY EQUILIBRIUM UNDER A FLOATING EXCHANGE RATE

The exchange rate is nothing more than the relative price of a currency. That is, the price of a currency in terms of another. Eq. (23.10) shows that the value of the exchange rate is easily calculated as the ratio of the

two countries' CPI. Eq. (23.11) then shows that the rate of exchange rate depreciation or appreciation is determined by the inflation rate differential. Eqs. (23.10) and (23.11) show that to determine the exchange rate levels and rate of appreciation all we need is information on each country's CPI and nothing else.

But there is more to this story. The question is: what determines the price level and or the inflation rate of a country? Looking back at Eq. (23.6) we find that world monetary equilibrium for a particular currency requires that the world demand for that money equals the world supply of the currency in question. Once the demand for and supply of that money is specified, it is possible to solve for the price of the goods in consumer basket in terms of the currency in question, that is, the CPI. The equilibrium conditions allow us to determine the market-clearing price of money in terms of the goods and services produced in the economy.

Given the fact that there are two currencies, it follows that global equilibrium requires the equality of the world demand for and supply of each of the two currencies. Once the two equilibrium conditions are determined, one can solve for the two price levels and thus determine the price of one currency in terms of the other, that is, the exchange rate.

This is in theory a simple problem. However, in practice it is a bit more complicated. The complications arise from the possible alternative specifications for the demand and supply conditions. Different variations give rise to different equilibrium conditions, which in turn have profound policy and investment implications. That is why we are fond of saying that the organization of the monetary system determines the inflation potential of an economy.

The next few paragraphs explore how the different assumptions affect the equilibrium inflation rate in each of the countries as well as the rate of appreciation or depreciation of the exchange rate.

VARIATIONS ON A THEME: ALTERNATIVE ASSUMPTION REGARDING THE MONEY DEMAND FUNCTIONS

The determination of the equilibrium exchange rate can be broken into a two-part process. The first one involves the determination of each of the countries' price levels. This requires two pieces of information for each country currency. Specifically, we need information on the global demand for and global supply of money for each of the country.

We do not need any additional information for as Eqs. (23.10) and (23.11) show, the exchange rate is the price of one currency in terms of another or the ratio of the two countries' CPI. Hence once the price level or inflation rate is known, then the exchange rate and its rate of appreciation or depreciation may be determined. We also know that the global equilibrium conditions for each country's currency, which determines the price level and its rate of change, are greatly affected by the elasticity of demand for and supply of each currency.

One issue that is extremely important and would like to explicitly consider in this section is the possibility of substitution effects across currencies [1]. This effect is commonly ignored in textbooks, but it is quite common in the real world and has some interesting implications for global equilibrium, the individual country inflation rates as well as their exchange rate. One clear example of the problem we have in mind is evident in the numerous definition of money. We have the monetary base, M1, M1a, M2, MZM, and even M3. We know that, in principle, the Fed controls the monetary base to the decimal point. However as already mentioned, the monetary base has two uses: one as bank reserves, and the other as currency in circulation. The bank reserves are used to support the bank deposits. The sum of bank deposits and currency in circulation make up the M's. On the supply side and for legal tender purposes, the components of the M's are perfect substitutes. You can pay with cash or a check, and so on. However on the demand side, they are not perfect; cash and checks have different attributes as far the users are concerned. The different aggregates have different characteristics that under certain circumstances would make one of the components more attractive than the other. In economic parlance, the different components are substitutes for each other, but not necessarily perfect substitutes. It is clear that the degree of substitutability will impact the makeup of the M's and as such the domestic price level.

The argument presented here could be easily extended to the use of foreign currencies as part of a broadly defined M. So the question is how relevant would that be in some of the economies of the world? For some economies, the use of a foreign currency as a transaction is very important while for others it is not. If that is the case, we then need to consider the possible ranges of substitutability between the domestic and foreign currency to get a sense of the possible impact this effect could have on an economy's inflation rate and equilibrium exchange rate. To do so, we will consider three different scenarios regarding the substitution effects across national currencies.

SCENARIO 1: THE TEXTBOOK SCENARIO WHERE EACH COUNTRY EXCLUSIVELY USES ITS OWN CURRENCY IN ALL DOMESTIC TRANSACTIONS

In this scenario, we assume that each country only uses its own currency within its borders. That is the peso is only used in Lakeland and the notes are only used in

Westland. This assumption greatly simplifies the analysis and yields some alluring and testable insights.

If the peso is only used on transactions effected in Lakeland, then it follows there is no reason for the people of Westland to hold pesos and vice versa there is no reason for the people of Lakeland to hold notes. Therefore the global demand for pesos consists solely of Lakeland's demand for pesos while the global demand for notes consists solely of Westland's demand for notes. The respective changes in global demand for pesos and notes are described by the following equations:

$$\Psi d_p = \pi_p + \eta l - \upsilon l \tag{23.12}$$

and

$$\Psi d_n = \pi w + \eta w - \upsilon w \tag{23.13}$$

where ψd_p and ψd_n denote the percent change in the global demand for pesos and notes respectively, π_p and π_n the peso inflation rate, that is, Lakeland's inflation rate and the notes inflation rates respectively. Also, ηl and ηw denote the income elasticity of demand for money in Lakeland and Westland respectively while υl and υw denote the percentage change in the velocity of money in each of the two economies. The latter is intended to capture shifts in the demand for money.

We also assume that the respective countries central banks are the only ones allowed to print the local currency. That is the Lakeland Central Bank is the only printer of pesos while Westland Central Bank is the only issuer of notes. Therefore the world supply of pesos is solely determined by Lakeland's Central Bank while the world supply of notes is solely determined by Westland's Central Bank. Again, the percentage change in the quantities of pesos and notes supplied by the respective central banks can be expressed as:

$$\Psi s_p = \omega l + \mu l \tag{23.14}$$

$$\Psi s_n = \omega w + \mu w \tag{23.15}$$

where ψs_p and ψs_n denote the percent change in the world supply of pesos and notes respectively and ωl and ωw the growth in the peso and notes monetary bases while μl and μw denote the percent change in the money multiplier in Lakeland and Westland respectively (see Eq. (23.7)).

Equilibrium requires that the changes in demand, Eq. (23.12), match the changes in supply, Eq. (23.14). Hence the equilibrium conditions provide us with enough information to solve for an expression regarding the underlying peso inflation rate.

$$\pi_p = \omega l - \eta l + \upsilon l + \mu l \tag{23.16}$$

Similarly Eqs. (23.13) and (23.15) allow us to solve for the equilibrium inflation rate in Westland's currency.

$$\pi_n = \omega w - \eta w + \upsilon w + \mu w \qquad (23.17)$$

We have already established that the nominal exchange rate is the price of the two currencies measured as the ratio of the two countries' CPI. The rate of exchange rate appreciation/depreciation can be expressed as:

$$\epsilon = \pi_p - \pi_n \qquad (23.11)$$

Implications: The assumption that each country uses its own currency means that the world demand for pesos is solely determined by Lakeland demand for pesos. Put another way the world demand for pesos and Lakeland demand for pesos are one and the same. Similarly the world demand for notes is nothing more than Westland demand for notes and the world supply of notes is nothing more than Westland supply of notes.

An important result, which is clearly dependent on these assumptions is that for this scenario the price level and or inflation rate for each locality, Eqs. (23.16) and (23.17), is determined solely by local demand and supply conditions. Lakeland's inflation rate is positively related to Lakeland's Central Bank peso printing, ωl, and Lakeland's real GDP growth rate, ηl. Notice that in Eq. (23.16), there is no term relating to Westland.

The allure of this analysis is the conclusion that according to these assumptions as we have shown, that the adoption of a floating exchange rate system can isolate an economy from external monetary shocks. The domestic central bank can pursue a monetary policy solely based on meeting domestic objectives without having to worry about the impact of other countries' monetary policies on the underlying inflation rate.

Taking a Lakeland perspective, it is clear that under these conditions, the exchange rate would absorb the impact of any external monetary shock. If the rest of the world increased its inflation rate, say Lakeland in this case, Eq. (23.11) shows that the notes/peso exchange rate would appreciate and no impact would be felt on Westland's domestic inflation rate. Eq. (23.17) for Westland's inflation rate has no term relating to Lakeland. Hence if the conditions assumed for this scenario hold, Westland's exchange rate would appreciate and would not be adversely impacted by a Lakeland monetary mismanagement. The other side of this argument is that Westland would get no benefit from a superior Lakeland monetary policy either. In that case, Westland's exchange rate would depreciate and prevent any of the benefits of the foreign monetary policy from filtering through.

Counterarguments: The insights developed with the assumption that each country only uses its own currency are very seductive. They hold the promise of isolating the domestic economy from other central bank mistakes.

A large number of economists who advocate free markets make the case in favor of a flexible exchange rate [2]. These economists pose an interesting argument that nothing could be better than a market-determined exchange rate. The alternative being a controlled or government-determined fixed exchange rate system. Presumably the market would provide a better signal and better policy design under the freely floating system.

While persuasive, the implications however have not quite borne out by the facts. The argument for a floating exchange rate system was made during the late 1960s and early 1970s. The floating exchange rate movement gained steam during the 1970s when the Bretton Woods gold exchange standard was dismantled. Yet the results were not as expected. Most of the economies of the world experienced a sharp increase in their underlying inflation rate and the global economy slowed down. This leads one to ask what happened to the promise of no contagion. Were all the central banks printing too much money? Clearly the unhinging of the gold standard and adoption of floating exchange rates did not turn out as auspicious as promised. The fact that, qualitatively, most countries had similar experiences suggests that either independently they all made similar policy mistakes or that the floating exchange rate did not isolate the economies as promised, or maybe both. Either way, the floating exchange rate experience of the 1970s was a disappointing one. Many countries experienced a bout of stagflation, which is not what they had signed up for when they adopted the floating exchange rate system.

Let us next examine the possible reasons for each country to exclusively use its own currency. How can that be possible in a global economy with free trade in goods and services? One possibility is that the government uses its powers and imposes legal tender requirements that force the local transactions to be effected in local currencies.

To prevent the use of foreign currencies, transaction costs related to the use of foreign currencies have to be truly prohibitive. If that is the case, then the transaction costs effectively reduce the volume of trade of monies across national borders to zero. Hence forcing the use of only local currencies is tantamount to a prohibitive tariff that eliminates trade in money and forces each economy into monetary autarky. If that is the case, it is ironic that the economists who promote free markets and free trade are the ones who promote floating exchange rates and implicitly the use of legal tender provision that force local people to use the domestic currency. In effect, they are money protectionists. A floating exchange rate that prevents the use of foreign money in domestic transaction is analogous to a tax on the use of foreign money. To the extent that choices are reduced, society will be worse off and the economic efficiency thereby reduced.

SCENARIO 2: EACH COUNTRY USES BOTH CURRENCIES IN DOMESTIC TRANSACTIONS

We now change the assumptions regarding the uses of foreign currencies in domestic transactions. The best example that comes to mind would be the use of the British pound and the euro in the UK and continental Europe [3].

The United Kingdom is a member of the EU but is not part of the euro. Yet the euro is widely accepted in Great Britain. The reverse is also true. We will assume in what follows that the choice of currency is influenced by the opportunity costs of holding either of the two currencies. On the basis of opportunity cost, it follows that if the UK inflation rate was higher than that of the EU, then a substitution effect away from the pound sterling into the euro should take place both in the UK as well as in the continent [4].

Returning to our two countries' example, we specify the percent change in the demand for money in Lakeland as:

$$\psi dl_p = \pi_p + \eta l - \upsilon l - \alpha * (\sigma l) * (\pi_n - \pi_p), \quad (23.18)$$

and

$$\psi dl_n = \pi_n + \eta l - \upsilon l + (1 - \alpha) * (\sigma l) * (\pi_p - \pi_n), \quad (23.19)$$

where the Lakeland's demand for pesos inclusive of the substitution effects, Eq. (23.18), has one more term than the demand function assumed when residents of Lakeland only use local currency. σl denotes the elasticity of substitution among the two currencies. The term that includes σl captures that the substitution effect is positively related to the inflation rate of Westland, that is, the other country inflation rate or π_n. If there is no substitution effect, then the third term of Eq. (23.18) is zero and the equation simplifies to tadeonal money demand assumed under the previous floating exchange rate scenario. Eq. (23.19) describes Lakeland's percent change in the demand for the foreign currency, notes.

The substitution effect, the third term in Eq. (23.18) is given as the product of:

1. The ratio of the real balances held in local currency α,
2. The product of the magnitude of Lakeland resident's elasticity of substitution between the two currencies, σl
3. The inflation rate differential among the two countries, $\pi_p - \pi_n$.

The inflation rate differential measures the relative loss of purchasing power of the two monies. The equation shows that people will move away for the currency experiencing the largest depreciation. The magnitude of the effects depends on these three effects.

Westland's percent change in the demand for the notes and pesos are given by the following two equations:

$$\psi dw_n = \pi_n + \eta w - \upsilon w - \beta * \sigma w * (\pi_p - \pi_n) \quad (23.20)$$

and

$$\psi dw_p = \pi_p + \eta w - \upsilon w - (1 - \beta) * \sigma w * (\pi_n - \pi_p)$$

$$(23.21)$$

Since people in Westland also use the peso, it follows that the world demand for pesos is the sum of the two countries demand for pesos. The percent change in the demand for pesos is nothing more than the weighted average of the individual changes in each country:

$$\psi d_p = \varepsilon * \psi dl_p + (1 - \varepsilon) * \psi dw_p \quad (23.22)$$

where ψdp denotes the percent change in the world demand for pesos and ε denotes Lakeland's share of the peso holdings. Substituting Eqs. (23.18) and (23.21) into the previous equation yields:

$$\psi d_p = \pi_p + [\varepsilon * \eta l + (1 - \varepsilon) * \eta w] - [\varepsilon * \upsilon l + (1 - \varepsilon) * \upsilon w]$$
$$- [(\varepsilon * \alpha * \sigma l) + (1 - \varepsilon) * (1 - \beta) * \sigma w)] * (\pi_n - \pi_p)$$

$$(23.23)$$

The world demand for notes can be expressed as:

$$\psi d_p = \pi_n + [\theta * \eta w + (1 - \theta) * \eta l] - [\theta * \upsilon w + (1 - \theta) * \upsilon l]$$
$$- [(\theta * \beta * \sigma w) + (1 - \theta) * (1 - \alpha) * \sigma l)] * (\pi_p - \pi_n)$$

$$(23.24)$$

where θ denotes Westland's share of notes circulating around the world.

The supply assumptions have not changed. We still assume that each country's central bank is the sole issuer of the local currency. The percent change in the supply of each currency is still characterized by Eqs. (23.14) and (23.15). Equilibrium requires that the world demand for each currency equal the world supply. We now have two equations characterizing each of the markets. However, unlike the case where people only use the local currency, the equations describing the equilibrium conditions will now have two unknowns, the two inflation rates. Therefore, the equations have to be solved simultaneously to obtain the equilibrium inflation rates.

After a few manipulations we find the equilibriums market clearing inflations to be:

$$\pi_p = \{(S_p - D_p) * [1 + [\theta * \beta * \sigma w \\
+ (1 - \theta) * (1 - \alpha) * \sigma l]] + (S_n - D_n) * [\varepsilon * \alpha * \sigma l \\
+ (1 - \varepsilon) * (1 - \beta) * \sigma w]\} / \{1 + [(\alpha * \varepsilon \\
+ (1 - \theta) * (1 - \alpha)) * \sigma l \\
+ ((\theta * \beta + (1 - \varepsilon) * (1 - \beta)) * \sigma w]\}$$

$$(23.25)$$

and

$$\pi_n = \{(S_n - D_n)*[1 + [\varepsilon*\alpha*\sigma l \\
+ (1-\varepsilon)*(1-\beta)*\sigma w]] + (S_p - D_p)*[\theta*\beta*\sigma w \\
+ (1-\theta)*(1-)*\sigma l]\} / \{1 + [(\alpha*\varepsilon \\
+ (1-\theta)*(1-\alpha))*\sigma l + ((\theta*\beta) + (1-\varepsilon)*(1-\beta))*\sigma w]\}$$

(23.26)

where

$$D_p = [\varepsilon*\eta l + (1-\varepsilon)*\eta w] - [\varepsilon*\upsilon l + (1-\varepsilon)*\upsilon w]$$

(23.27)

and

$$D_n = [\theta*\eta w + (1-\theta)*\eta l] - [\theta*\upsilon w + (1-\theta)*\upsilon l]$$

(23.28)

denote the components of the demand for money shifts.

Also,

$$S_p = \omega l + \mu l$$

(23.27)

and

$$S_n = \omega w + \mu w$$

(23.28)

denote the components of the money supply shifts.

IMPLICATIONS AND INSIGHTS

Eqs. (23.25) and (23.26) show that an excess supply of money growth, $(S_p - D_p)$, in Lakeland will have an impact on the inflation rate in each of the two countries. Similarly, excess money growth in Westland, $(S_n - D_n)$, will also have an impact on both countries' inflation rates. This is a different result from the results in the previous scenario.

The results in this section show that if there is a currency substitution on the demand side, the exchange rate will not insulate an economy from external monetary shocks. The transmission mechanism is as follows: if one of the two countries' inflation rate accelerates, people will attempt to reduce the inflation tax by switching to the other currency. The magnitude of the switch will depend on the inflation rate differential and the ease of substitution, that is, the convenience and acceptability of the other currency. The increase in demand for the other currency will, all else the same, reduce the inflation rate in that currency and the currency flight for the currency whose inflations rate has accelerated creates additional excess supply of money and as a result the inflation rate will rise even more, even if no additional money is being printed.

In conclusion, currency substitution effects will magnify the inflationary impact in the country where the excess money supply originates, while creating an incipient excess demand for money in the other currency and thus reducing the inflationary pressures in that currency [5].

One important point that we make here is that in these examples it is the private sector which imports and exports the other countries' monies as needed. These transactions need not be affected through the government traditional international accounts such as the BOP, but more on this later on.

The model developed in this second scenario is quite versatile and sufficiently general. It encompasses as a special case the conditions outlined in the previous scenario. All that we require is that it should not be convenient to use the other country's currency in domestic transaction. The inconvenience could be the result of government policies such as legal tender policies that significantly increase the costs of using the foreign currency or there may be other reasons. In technical terms, all that we require is that the elasticity of substitution between the two currencies is zero that is when:

$$\sigma w = \sigma l = 0$$

(23.29)

Substituting a value of zero in place of σw and σl greatly simplifies Eqs. (23.25) and (23.26). But that is not all. If the transaction costs are positive and the elasticity of substitution zero, then one can show that local residents will not hold the foreign currency and each country money supply will represent the world supply of that currency. That is:

$$\alpha = \varepsilon = \beta = \theta = 1$$

(23.30)

Eqs. (23.29) and (23.30) describe the precise conditions under which the general model developed here becomes the special case outlined in the previous section.

SCENARIO 3: ONE COUNTRY'S CURRENCY CIRCULATES BOTH AT HOME AND ABROAD, BUT THE SECOND COUNTRY'S CURRENCY ONLY CIRCULATES AT HOME

So far we have considered the case where either the two currencies circulate in each economy or only the local currency circulates. However, an intermediate case deserves attention. It is the case where the currency of one of the two countries circulates in the other economy, but the reverse is not true. The immediate example that comes to mind is the US dollar, which circulates with varying degrees of ease all over the world while the same is not true for many of the world currencies. Most of these currencies only circulate at home. Hence in this scenario what we have is a case of a one-way substitution and, as we shall argue later on, the country whose currency circulates all over the world may rightfully be called a reserve currency country (RCC) [6].

In the two-world country of Lakeland and Westland, we will assume that Lakeland uses both currencies, the local currency (pesos) and the foreign currency (notes). In turn, Westland only uses its own currency (notes). These assumptions can be formally expressed to mean that Lakeland will hold all the pesos in the world and a 100% of Westland money will be held in the form of notes. In the context of our model, these two conditions can be expressed as:

$$\varepsilon = \beta = 1 \qquad (23.31)$$

Also the fact that there is no substitutability between pesos and notes in Westland means:

$$\sigma w = 0 \qquad (23.32)$$

Substituting these conditions in Eqs. (23.25) and (23.26) the expressions simplify to:

$$\pi_p = \{(S_p - D_p) * [1 + [(1-\theta) * (1-\alpha) * \sigma l]] \\ + (S_n - D_n) * \alpha * \sigma l\} / \{1 + [(\alpha + (1-\theta) * (1-\alpha)) * \sigma l]\}$$

$$(23.33)$$

and

$$\pi_n = \{(S_n - D_n) * [1 + [(\alpha - \sigma l]] \\ + (S_p - D_p) * \alpha * \sigma l\} / \{1 + [(\alpha + (1-\theta) * (1-\alpha)) * \sigma l]\}$$

$$(23.34)$$

Although much simpler than Eqs. (23.25) and (23.26), the previous two equations still show that a one-way substitution can impact the reserve currency countries' (RCC) inflation rate.

Even under a floating exchange rate, currency substitution may induce countries in the rest of the world to increase the holdings of the RCC currency; this increase in demand leads to an excess demand, and thus lower prices/inflation in the RCC, Westland in this example.

Before we move on, there is one more issue that we would like to discuss. And that is what happens as the non-RCC country, in this case Lakeland, is small in relation to the RCC. By small we mean a price taker. In that case, we can argue that $(1-\theta)$ the non-RCC country share of the RCC country's money will be negligible or approach zero. All that this condition requires is that Lakeland's holding of notes is very small in relation to the stock of notes circulating in Westland. If that is the case, the two previous equations simplify to:

$$\pi_p = \{(S_p - D_p) + (S_n - D_n) * \alpha * \sigma l\} / [1 + \alpha * \sigma l]$$

$$(23.35)$$

and

$$\pi_n = \{(S_n - D_n) * [1 + \alpha * \sigma l]\} / [1 + \alpha * \sigma l] \qquad (23.36)$$

Eq. (23.36) shows that the inflation rate in the RCC depends solely on the RCC excess money supply conditions. While the non-RCC inflation rate depends on the domestic excess money supply as well as the excess money supply conditions of the RCC. In other words, the monetary mistakes of the RCC can be exported to the non-RCC while in the case of small non-RCC countries the reverse is not true. This means that the US inflation rate, the RCC, can have an impact on the inflation rate of a small non-RCC such as Dominican Republic while the reverse is not true. Yet while individual countries are small, collectively they could be treated as large. Collectively, all the non-RCC countries combined could have an impact on the RCC inflation rate.

EXTENDING THE FRAMEWORK: ACCOUNTING FOR ALTERNATIVE OPERATING PROCEDURES BY THE MONETARY AUTHORITIES

Over the years, we have argued that the organization of the monetary system determines the rules by which the monetary authorities increase the quantity of money and therefore an economy's inflation potential. And since the exchange rate denotes the price of one currency in terms of another, that is, the ratio of the two countries' CPIs, this means that the rate of appreciation or depreciation of an exchange rate is driven by the inflation rate differential between two economies. Therefore, managing a country's exchange rate requires the ability of that country to manage or affect the differential inflation rate between the two economies. Alternatively, managing the exchange rate is equivalent to managing the inflation rate differential between the two countries. The next few paragraphs will focus on the effect of alternative exchange rate mechanisms on the inflation rate differential among two economies.

Although there are several different rationales as to why a central bank may be interested in managing its exchange rate, we do not share many of these views of the world. According to street lore, currency devaluations, even if caused by monetary policy, result in a reduction in the price of a country's exports relative to its imports [7]. Under this assumption, it follows that concerns about the effect of the exchange rate may give rise to currency manipulations to improve a country's trade balance. Given the bilateral nature of trade, this concern if not managed could easily lead to a bout of competitive devaluations and trade wars. But we are not going to go that far in the current analysis, we will only focus on alternative polices that do not necessarily lead to currency wars.

SCENARIO 1: EACH COUNTRY'S CENTRAL BANK IS COMMITTED TO NOT ALLOWING ITS CURRENCY TO APPRECIATE AND THEREBY LOSE WHAT THEY PERCEIVE TO BE A COMPARATIVE ADVANTAGE DUE TO AN EXCHANGE RATE APPRECIATION

The stringiest version of this scenario is one where each central bank will not let its currency to appreciate. As we know that the exchange rate is the value of two different currencies, under the assumption that there are no relative price changes, the exchange rate between Lakeland and Westland can be expressed as the ratio of the two countries' CPI expressed in local currencies. That is, Lakeland's CPI expressed in pesos and Westland's CPI expressed in notes. In that case as we have previously specified, the peso exchange rate in terms of notes can be expressed as:

$$E = P_p / P_n \qquad (23.10)$$

and the percent change in exchange rate can be expressed in terms of the two economies' inflation rate:

$$\epsilon = \pi_p - \pi_n \qquad (23.11)$$

If the two central banks are successful, then the exchange rate will remain unchanged. That is:

$$\epsilon = 0 = \pi_p - \pi_n \qquad (23.37)$$

The previous equation shows that if the exchange rate is unchanged, then the inflation rate will have to be the same in the two countries. That is:

$$\pi_p = \pi_n \qquad (23.38)$$

Now that we have established that in equilibrium the inflation rate has to be the same in the two economies, all we have to determine next is what will be the level of the inflation rate. The answer is that the most expansive central bank, the one in the country with the higher inflation rate, say Lakeland, will determine Westland's and thus the world's inflation rate. The reason for this is quite simple. If Westland has a relatively restrictive monetary policy, it experiences a lower inflation rate and its currency appreciates.

However, as we have already mentioned, since the Westland Central Bank is committed to preventing the exchange rate from appreciating, it will take steps to increase the domestic money supply resulting in a higher inflation rate in Westland. The process continues until Westland's inflation rate matches that of Lakeland. At that point, the exchange rate neither appreciates nor depreciates. The equilibrium condition is one where no country

gains a perceived depreciation advantage. The outcries reach an impasse; no appreciation or depreciation.

The process described shows that to prevent their inflation rate from appreciating, the lower inflation rates' central bank has to expand their monetary creation to increase its domestic inflation rate and match that of the higher inflation rate or match the monetary policy of the most expansive central bank. This is easily accomplished since all the domestic central bank has to do is print more domestic money.

SCENARIO 2: EACH COUNTRY CENTRAL BANK IS COMMITTED TO NOT ALLOWING THE OTHER COUNTRY'S CURRENCY TO DEPRECIATE AND THEREBY PREVENT THE OTHER COUNTRY FROM GAINING WHAT THEY PERCEIVE TO BE A COMPARATIVE ADVANTAGE DUE TO AN EXCHANGE RATE DEPRECIATION

Let's assume that Westland and Lakeland both attempt to prevent each other's currency from depreciating. Again, equilibrium requires that all countries experience the same inflation rate. If one country, say Lakeland, experiences a currency depreciation it may be perceived as gaining a competitive advantage and Westland will be forced to buy pesos and take them out of circulation. The lower amount of pesos circulating means that Lakeland's inflation rate declines and the rate of depreciation slows down. The process continues until the depreciation is completely eliminated. Notice that the intervention requires that Westland's central bank accumulates pesos as international reserves as it withdraws them from circulation. This suggests a couple of things. The first one being that the country with the most conservative monetary policy determines the world inflation rate. The second point is that the country with the most conservative monetary (Westland) policy ends up accumulating Lakeland's currency, that is international reserves.

SCENARIO 3: ONE OF THE COUNTRY'S CENTRAL BANK DECIDES TO FIX ITS EXCHANGE RATE TO THE CURRENCY OF ANOTHER COUNTRY

If Lakeland decides to fix its exchange rate to the Westland's currency, then it effectively will attempt to prevent any appreciation or depreciation of the exchange rate. This exchange rate mechanism would be the equivalent of the two scenarios already discussed. For the two previous scenarios, the inflation rate is the same in both countries. The only difference is that when the country prevents the exchange rate from appreciating, the country with the most inflationary policy will determine the global inflation rate. When the country attempts to prevent the currency from depreciating, the country with the lowest inflation rate determines the world inflation. Since Lakeland fixes the exchange rate, Lakeland takes both sides of the adjustment. When Westland is too loose by pursuing a higher-than-expected inflation rate, Lakeland's central bank prevents its exchange rate from appreciating and adopts the looseness of Westland. When Westland pursues a lower inflation rate than expected, Lakeland Central Bank prevents its exchange rate form depreciating by adopting a less inflationary policy. The fixed exchange rate mechanism, where Lakeland guarantees the exchange rate, forces Lakeland to adopt Westland's monetary policy and as a result imports Westland's inflation rate.

If the foreign exchange value of the peso appreciates, it is up to Lakeland's central bank to restore the exchange rate back to its target level. This could be achieved in one of several ways. An obvious one would be for Lakeland's central bank to print more pesos thereby increasing the supply of pesos and increasing inflationary pressure on the peso, thereby reducing the foreign exchange value of the peso, that is depreciating the peso.

An equivalent way of insuring the process is to allow the private sector to arbitrage the price differences between the actual and target exchange rate. If Lakeland's central bank is willing to buy and sell Westland's currency (notes) at the target or official exchange rate, then whenever the exchange rate appreciates (whenever the peso fetches more notes in the open market than the official exchange rate), the private sector will have a profitable arbitrage opportunity. Arbitrageurs would bring notes into Lakeland's central bank and demand that Lakeland's central bank give them pesos at the official exchange rate. If that is lower than the market rate, which it would be if the peso appreciates, the arbitrageurs will make a profit equivalent to the difference between the open market and the official rate.

The guarantee of a fixed exchange rate by Lakeland's central bank introduces a potential arbitrage opportunity for the private sector. This arbitrage insures that the exchange rate will not deviate from the official rate. During the appreciating rate, Lakeland's central bank will accumulate international reserves, that is, Westland's notes. This discussion shows that it is very easy to be a central banker when the exchange rate is appreciating. All the central bank has to do is print pesos, a relatively inexpensive process, and receive notes in exchange. The question is whether this is a free lunch for Lakeland's central bank. Can it spend this money? The international reserves? Our answer is a rotund no. If the integrity of the system is to be maintained, the central bank should hold the reserves for a rainy day. If it does not, it will be susceptible to a successful speculative attack when the process reverses. Our position is that the bank does not own the reserves, all it has rights to is the interest earned by the reserves.

Now let's follow the process and see what happens when the exchange rate depreciates. If as we assume here, it is up to Lakeland's central bank to restore the target exchange rate, then Lakeland's central bank has to take action. A declining exchange rate means that the peso is losing value, that there are too many pesos relative to notes around the world. To restore the price back all Lakeland's central bank can do is either reduce the quantity of pesos or increase the quantity of notes. However to do the latter, it would have to have an inventory of notes, or inventory of international reserves. If we stick to the fixed exchange rate convertibility, then the private sector arbitrages the difference between the market and official exchange rates. That is when the foreign exchange value of the notes goes above the official exchange rate, the value of the peso goes below the official exchange rate. Hence arbitrageurs bring pesos and demand that the central bank give them the equivalent amount of notes at the official exchange rate, which is more notes than what they would get in the open market thereby making a profit.

As the process goes on, pesos are retired from circulation and Lakeland's central bank depletes its reserves of notes, which now enter the market economy. More notes and less pesos mean a lower foreign exchange value of the notes. The process continues until the parity between the official and the market-determined exchange rates is restored.

Notice that when the foreign exchange value of the notes exceeds the official exchange rate, the central bank will lose international reserves. This brings an important issue. Can the central bank run out of reserves? The answer depends on the central bank's behavior. If the central bank never spends the international reserves, it will have enough to meet any demand due to increases in the foreign exchange value of the notes over and above the official exchange rate. In this case, there is a guarantee of a 100% coverage of any convertibility attempt. It is when it spends some of these reserves that it will not be able to guarantee the integrity of the exchange rate system. Since there is no guarantee of a 100% guarantee of coverage, there is possibility of a successful speculative attack against the currency. The likelihood of a speculative attack increases as the reserve coverage declines.

We have already established that if the nonreserve currency country (NRCC) central bank strictly adheres to the fixed exchange rate intervention mechanism, the exchange rate will be fixed at all times. If that is the case, the Purchasing Power Parity relationship yields the following results:

$$\epsilon = 0 \tag{23.39}$$

and

$$\pi_p = \pi_n \tag{23.40}$$

This is not rocket science, if the countries have fixed exchange rates, and there is free trade and mobility across the economies and there are no terms of trade changes; then the two countries inflation rates will converge. More importantly, since Lakeland is the country fixing its exchange rate, in doing so the NRCC central bank is forced to alter its monetary policy to ensure that the two countries inflation rates are the same.

The domestic private sector can force the NRCC to print more money. All they have to do is bring in foreign currency to the central bank and exchange it for local currency and the country experiences a BOP surplus. On the other hand, if they have too much money, all they do is bring the pesos back to the NRCC central bank and trade the pesos for foreign currency and the country will experience a BOP deficit.

THE MECHANICS OF OPERATION OF A STRICT FIXED EXCHANGE RATE MECHANISM AND ITS IMPACT ON THE DOMESTIC MONETARY BASE

We have assumed that the people of Lakeland like the way the country of Westland runs its monetary policy and they have decided that its central bank should follow Westland's monetary policy by fixing Lakeland's exchange rate to that of Westland. This is accomplished by the following intervention mechanism: whenever Lakeland's exchange rate appreciates relative to Westland's currency, Lakeland's central bank is forced to intervene in the open market. It will buy Westland's currency and sell or print Lakeland's currency. In the process, it increases the supply of pesos in the economy, that is, Lakeland's currency. The increase in the monetary base is registered as an improvement in the BOP. Notice that if the rule is strictly adhered to, the monetary base will include the international reserves of the country and the sum of all current and previous BOP flows.

That is:

$$BOP = \Delta IR \tag{23.41}$$

and

$$IR = \Sigma BOP \tag{23.42}$$

where BOP denotes the Balance of Payments, ΔIR denotes the change in the international reserves of the central bank, IR the total of international reserves held by the central bank, and ΣBOP the sum of all past BOP

flows. As Lakeland is the country fixing its exchange rate and the country holding the other country's currency as reserves, we call Lakeland the NRCC and Westland the Reserve Currency Country or RCC.

The monetary base will therefore be defined as:

$$B = D + IR \tag{23.43}$$

where B denotes the monetary base and D denotes the domestic component of the monetary base. By this we mean that D is the number of pesos not backed by International Reserves. Thus if the central bank has a policy of 100% backing, then D will be zero at all times and the base will consist solely of international reserves.

The growth rate of the monetary base can be expressed as:

$$\omega = \delta * \kappa + (1 - \delta) * \Omega \tag{23.44}$$

where κ denotes the growth rate of the domestic component of the monetary base. Ω is the growth rate of the international reserves, that is the BOP divided by the stock of international reserves held by the central bank and δ denotes the domestic component of the monetary base as a percent of the monetary base. The discussion in the previous section suggests that δ is a critical variable, it may denote the viability of a speculative attack against a currency. The larger its value, the higher the viability and thus the higher the likelihood of a speculative attack. Again if the central bank adheres to a policy of 100% coverage of the monetary base, then the domestic component of the monetary base will be zero:

$$\delta = 0 \tag{23.45}$$

And Eq. (23.44) simplifies to

$$\omega = \Omega \tag{23.44'}$$

The equation shows that under this assumption, the growth of the monetary base will consists solely of the growth of international reserves.

The equilibrium conditions in the NRCC are determined by the equality of the demand for and supply of money:

$$Md = Ms \tag{23.6}$$

Substituting for the percentage changes in money demand and money supply, we obtain the following equilibrium condition:

$$\pi 1 + \eta 1 - \upsilon 1 = \omega 1 + \mu 1 \tag{23.46}$$

However as we know that under a fixed exchange rate system, the NRCC inflation rate, $\pi 1$, is the same as that of the RCC, πw, and that the growth in the monetary base is a weighted average of the domestic money creation and the growth of the international reserves, Eq. (23.46), the equilibrium condition can be written as:

$$\pi w + \eta l - \upsilon l = \delta * \kappa + (1-\delta) * \Omega + \mu l \qquad (23.46')$$

Finally, we know that,

$$\Omega = BOP / IR \qquad (23.46)$$

These two equations can be combined to yield an expression for the country's BOP:

$$BOP = (\pi w + \eta l - \upsilon l - \delta * \kappa - \mu l) * IR(1-\delta) \qquad (23.47)$$

Notice that the higher the world inflation, πw, and the higher the real GDP growth, ηl, all else the same, the larger will be the BOP inflow. The larger the increase in money velocity, that is, a decline in domestic money demand, and the larger the increase in the money multiplier, an increase in domestic money supply and the larger the domestic money creation the smaller the money inflow, the smaller the BOP.

The previous sets of equations provide us with insights regarding the NRCC BOP, Eq. (23.47):

- The higher the global inflation rate, the larger will be the BOP surplus and the larger the money growth in the NRCC. The reason for this is that as the inflation rate erodes the purchasing power of money, people need to replenish their cash balances to replace the loss of purchasing power. If the NRCC is unhappy with the RCC monetary policy, the NRCC can unhinge its currency or delink its currency *from* that of the RCC. One issue that we may discuss later is whether there is a mechanism that forces some discipline on the RCC central bank.
- The larger the real GDP growth rate in the NRCC country, the larger is the demand for money. The excess demand for money is satisfied in the NRCC country by importing money, thus the BOP surplus.
- The third term captures the shifts in the velocity of money and the banking system money multiplier, that is, the ability to leverage the banking system in the creation of loans and deposits. We summarize these effects as variables that impact the "moneyness" of money, the attractiveness of the local currency, and domestic financial system.
- The last term measures changes in the money multiplier, the ability of the banking system to generate endogenous domestic money. The greater the domestic money creation ability, the lower the need to import money to satisfy a rising domestic demand.

The fourth term in the equation captures the domestic money creation, and as we have already mentioned, the larger the amount of domestic money creation, the lower will be the net excess demand for money that has to be satisfied by importing money, that is, a BOP surplus. The

equation also gives us the precise conditions beyond which additional growth in the domestic component of the money supply results in a BOP deficit. That turns out to be:

$$\kappa = (\pi w + \eta l - \upsilon l - \mu l) / \delta \qquad (23.48)$$

Hence the higher the world inflation, the faster the economy grows, and combined with any decline in the velocity of money and banking sector money creation ability, the larger the amount of high-powered money that the domestic or NRCC central bank can print without causing a BOP deficit.

THE NONRESERVE CURRENCY COUNTRY EQUILIBRIUM RELATIONSHIPS

The NRCC by fixing its exchange rate causes the inflation rate to be the same in both localities, the RCC and NRCC. Since the inflation rate differential is nonexistent, there are no substitution effects either. Hence we do not have to be concerned with substitution effects. However the legal tender provisions induce each country's citizens to use the local currency. Also through convertibility combined with the fixing of the exchange rate, the NRCC effectively makes the two currencies a perfect substitute on the supply side [8,9].

The situation from the RCC perspective is a bit different. Since its central bank is not bound or compelled to maintain the fixed exchange rate, it is free to pursue its own monetary policy, which in turn will determine the underlying inflation rate. Since the only country that can print the reserve currency is the RCC central bank, the NRCC inflation rate will be at the mercy of the RCC monetary policy.

The inflation rate in the RCC currency is determined by the intersection of the global demand for and supply curves. Since the RCC is the sole issuer of the currency, it follows that the world supply of notes, the RCC currency, is nothing more than Westland's money supply function. In contrast, the world demand for the notes consists of the sum of two components. One is the NRCC stock of international reserves, IR, and the other is the RCC money demand function. In turn the percent change in the world demand for the RCC currency is nothing more than a weighted average of the two components. Equilibrium requires that the percent change in world demand for the reserve currency equals the percent change in world supply that is:

$$\lambda * (\pi w + \eta w - \upsilon w) + (1-\lambda) * (BOP / IR) = \omega w + \mu w$$
$$(23.49)$$

where λ denotes the share of the RCC currency circulating in the RCC.

Solving for the inflation rate we obtain:

$$\pi w = -\eta w + \upsilon w + [(\omega w + \mu w)/\lambda]$$
$$-[(1-\lambda)/\lambda]*(BOP/IR) \qquad (23.50)$$

The limiting conditions of the previous equation are quite interesting. As the size of the NRCC country in relation to the RCC declines so will $(1-\lambda)$. In the limit as λ approaches 1, the NRCC component gets smaller and smaller. In the limit, the inflation rate of the RCC is solely determined by the RCC demand and supply conditions. This approximation may be relevant when making a comparison between a large RCC in relation to a small NRCC, let's say a country such as the Dominican Republic, DR, using the US dollar as its international reserve. It is more than likely its international reserves will be relatively minute compared to the stock of money circulating in the United States. The approximation that the DR has no impact on the US inflation rate may be a reasonable one to make. However if it is much larger than DR, let's say that it is the rest of the world as was the case during much of the Bretton Woods years, then it seems reasonable to assume that collectively the rest of the world's international reserves will be a large and significant portion of the US money supply. In which case, one cannot assume that the rest of the world will have no impact on the money market equilibrium. Hence we need to figure out a way to incorporate the impact of the rest of the world. This is easily done by substituting equation (23.47) into (23.50):

$$BOP = (\pi\omega + \eta l - \upsilon l - \delta*\kappa - \mu 1)*IR/(1-\delta \qquad (23.47)$$

$$\pi w = -\eta w + \upsilon w + [(\omega w + \mu w)/\lambda]$$
$$-[(1-\lambda)/\lambda]*(BOP/IR) \qquad (23.50)$$

$$\pi w = -\eta w + \upsilon w + [(\omega w + \mu w)/\lambda]$$
$$-[(1-\lambda)/\lambda*(1-\delta)]*(\eta l - \upsilon l - \delta*\kappa 1 - \mu)$$
$$(23.50')$$

where the last term in Eq. (23.50′) captures the impact of the rest of the world demand for international reserves on the equilibrium inflation rate. Faster growth in the rest of the world reduces the global inflation rate while an increase in the velocity of money, the money multiplier, and an increase in domestic money creation in the rest of the world, all lead to a higher inflation rate.

REINING IN THE RESERVE CURRENCY COUNTRY

So far we have not imposed any restriction on the RCC central bank. There are some clear advantages to being a RCC. The fact that the rest of the world holds a stock of its currency means that the RCC will collect seigniorage on the international reserve stock held by the rest of the world. Second and more importantly, the RCC has the power to set the global inflation rate and thereby impose an inflation tax on the rest of the world. In this regard the RCC faces a choice to maximize seigniorage by increasing the demand for international reserves or to maximize the revenue from inflation or perhaps a third alternative combining both.

If the RCC central bank chooses to maximize the seigniorage it may do so by assuring the rest of the world that it will provide price stability. That will ensure that the rest of the world countries increase their real balances and thereby the demand for international reserves. How can the RCC accomplish that? It may accomplish that through a price rule where the central bank guarantees the purchasing power of the RCC currency.

There are several ways through which the RCC can achieve the desired objective. Interestingly these different RCC alternatives have a NRCC counterpart. We will discuss three alternative systems in the next few paragraphs.

There are several possible targets that the central bank can pursue. In the case of the NRCC, it targets the RCC exchange rate. There are also other options, which RCC have followed in the past. One option is the one we believe the United States pursued during much of the last three decades: by targeting he price level, that is, the domestic price rule.

The dynamic version of the domestic price rule would be inflation targeting. However such a system does not provide a mechanism where the rest of the world would force the central bank to adhere to the price rule discipline. Hence the system is one of self-enforcement. Another variant of the price rule is nothing more than the gold exchange standard. This system holds the promise of a market-enforced discipline on the central bank's actions.

The price rule without holding inventory of the targeted commodity works as follows: whenever the inflation rate is above the commodity target price and or inflation rate target, the central bank is forced to sell bonds and thereby reduce the quantity of high-powered money, that is, monetary base, circulating in the economy. If inflation is a monetary phenomenon, then the reduction in the quantity of money results in a lower price level and or inflation rate. If the inflation rate is below the target rate, the central bank buys bonds in the open market thereby increasing the quantity of money in circulation and thereby increasing the price level and or inflation rate.

One assumption that we implicitly made in the previous discussion is that the central bank does not hold the commodity in question when conducting its open market operations. The increase and reduction in the monetary base is effected through the purchase and sale of bonds. That is, the bonds are the mechanism by which the central bank alters the quantity of base money. The central bank only uses the commodity price and/

or target —inflation rate as a signal to issue more high-powered money, that is, monetary base, or to reduce the quantity of high-powered money circulating in the economy. This is a key point that many policymakers and pundits ignore. The central bank does not need to hold an inventory of gold to follow a gold exchange standard. Similarly it does not need to hold an inventory of the consumer basket when it adopts a monetary policy based on targeting the CPI, that is, a price rule, as witnessed in the last three decades.

The price rule system as we have described it is a voluntary one. All the changes are initiated by the central bank, and the private sector has no signaling or enforcement mechanism. The story is quite a bit different with a gold exchange standard. If the authorities are willing to buy or sell at a set price, then whenever the price in the open market is above the target level it signals that there is too much money in the system. Arbitrageurs will bring dollars to the central bank and ask for some gold bullions. Since the Fed has no inventory, it has to sell bonds in the open market and with the proceeds buy the bullion. The net of all this is that the private sector bond holding goes up and money holdings decline. The Fed is forced to perform an open market operation that extinguishes the excess money.

If in contrast, the price of gold in the open market falls below the target level, that would signal the Fed that there is too little money in the system. The private sector would also notice and arbitrageurs would buy gold in the open market and sell it to the central bank as the target price, thereby making a profit. The gold exchange standard, as we have described, has two alternative mechanisms by which the price level is restored back to its target price. One is the government watching the price directly and taking action, while the other is the private sector arbitraging the price difference and forcing the central bank to act. This is one case where greed is truly good. It forces the authorities to do the right thing.

THAT RELATIVE PRICE THING

So far in many of the topics discussed, we have initially made the simplifying assumption that there are no relative price changes. Once the framework is developed, we have relaxed this assumption and examined the effects of relative price changes. The exchange rate discussion is no different.

Before we get into the relative price discussion, it is worthwhile to review some of the arguments in favor of gold as a currency. It has many of the attributes of money: it is a store of value, unit of account, and medium of exchange. Another convenience is that it is durable.

Now let's move on to the relative price. Since gold is a commodity whose supply can only be increased

by mining, extraction costs determine how much gold is mined and minted. If the relative costs are constant, so will the price of gold relative to other commodities. However if the price changes, gold advocates argue that the relative costs are relatively constant over the long run. Hence any disturbance regarding the relative price of gold in terms of other currencies is temporary and mean reverting. These arguments make gold a good target for conducting monetary policy. For if, things are as we have described, keeping the price of gold in terms of the currency constant will keep the price level constant at least over the long run and quite possibly over the short run if there are no major disturbances.

While we concede that disturbances in the relative price of gold may be rare and short lived, the possibility for a longer-term disturbance is not out of the question as they indeed have occurred in the oil industry. For example, a technological breakthrough that allows us to produce more goods and services will clearly alter the relative price of gold in terms of those goods. On the other hand, the disturbance may occur in the gold market. One real example that comes to mind is the discovery of the new world. The Spanish conquistadores shipped so much gold and silver to Spain resulting in a tremendous increase in the Spanish gold backed money supply. The large increase in gold without having any technological impact on production of other goods meant that the price of the other commodities in terms of gold would rise. Spain suffered almost 200 years of double digit inflation. Hence it is possible for the relative price change in gold to last for quite a while.

Other relative price changes unrelated to the relative price of gold can also have significant impact on the system. What we have in mind here is the terms of trade or real exchange rate changes. Under a floating exchange rate system, a favorable terms of trade change will result in an exchange rate appreciation over and above the inflation rate differential.

The difference between the exchange rate appreciation and the differential inflation rate measures the terms of trade effect or relative price change. In effect this differential reflects the real rate of return differential across the two economies. However under a fixed exchange rate system, the exchange rate remains unchanged. This, in turn, raises the issue of how to measure the terms of trade effect. Here is where the real exchange rate concept earns its pay. It is calculated as an exchange rate adjusted by the ratio of the two countries' CPI. Therefore under a fixed exchange rate system, the real exchange rate is reflected as a change in the relative price of the two localities. The region experiencing the favorable terms of trade registers a faster increase in the price of the immobile factors of production, a higher inflation rate. A simple example illustrates our point. Prosperous areas tend to experience above-average increase in real estate prices.

People within the locality always complain of the high price of real estate. On the other hand, dilapidated areas tend to have low and falling prices. Two broad examples are Silicon Valley and Detroit. The price levels and rate of appreciation have been quite different over the last two decades. That is a terms of trade effect in practice.

The favorable terms of trade changes result in an increase in valuation and the relative rates of return of the factors intensive in the goods and services experiencing the favorable terms of trade. Capital flows into the area and the capital account experiences an improvement. Under a floating exchange rate system without currency substitution, the BOP will always be zero. Hence the capital inflow will be matched by a trade balance deterioration.

Under a fixed exchange rate there is no reason to expect anything different. The capital inflow at the margin lowers the rate of return in the area with the favorable terms of trade effect. The capital outflow in the region experiencing the adverse terms of trade effect leads to a marginal increase in the real rate of return, the net effect being a reduction in the differential real rate of return. As the process continues, eventually the differential begins declining. The process continues until the differential rate of return is completely eliminated, that is, arbitraged. At that point, the economies return to their long-run equilibrium and the real exchange rate fluctuation is completely erased. However during this process the country experiencing the capital inflow expands, and under a fixed exchange rate system where the central bank strictly adheres to the fixed exchange rate regime, there will be a shortage of money that has to be satisfied through a BOP surplus. The inflow will swell the international reserves of the central bank, which in exchange for these reserves will print local currency.

During favorable terms of trade, it is a great time to be a central banker. Reserves increase, the money supply expands, and the economy grows. Times are good. If the government is going to adhere to the fixed exchange rate system, they do not own the international reserves and the government is only entitled to the seigniorage or interest earned by these reserves. There is the temptation to use some of these reserves to finance domestic spending programs, be it infrastructure or social programs. The reason for this is that when the adverse terms of trade effect come, the capital flows will reverse and the central bank will lose reserves. If the local government has spent some of these reserves, then the currency will not have a 100% backing, and at some point people begin to doubt whether it has enough reserves to defend and maintain the fixed exchange rate system; at that point, the country is susceptible to a successful speculative attack. The —central bank will face some difficult choices; the list includes devaluation and/or capital flight. If on the other hand the central bank keeps all

of the reserves, it will have enough reserves to reverse any outflow. That is why we contend that under a fixed exchange rate with convertibility, the central bank does not own the international reserves. All it can lay claim to is the interest earned by these reserves, the seigniorage.

WHAT IF THE CENTRAL BANK CHOOSES TO HOLD A 100% INVENTORY OF THE COMMODITY USED AS RESERVE? HOW SAFE IS IT AGAINST A SPECULATIVE ATTACK?

There are several variants of the use of reserves. One case of particular interest both academic and practical is the case of a currency board, whose effects are similar or identical to a true gold standard. In that case the local currency is backed a 100% by the reserves. Alternatively, it is when a country uses another country's currency as its reserves and it holds a 100% reserve, as in the case of the Hong Kong currency board, where the HK monetary authorities have a 100% of the HK$ reserve in US dollars. The open market operations work as follows: when the HK$ appreciates, the HK monetary authorities print HK$ and buy US dollars. Again the mechanism could be the result of actions initiated by the HK monetary authorities or by the private sector. Either way, equilibrium is restored and the HK monetary authorities keep the US dollars received and hold them as reserves backing the HK$. When the HK$ falls, the HK monetary authorities sell US dollars and take HK$ out of circulation. Since there is a 100% backing of the currency, the monetary authorities always have enough reserves to affect the transaction.

How will such a system fare during a speculative attack? Fortunately, we have a real-time experiment to document. During the 1990's Asian crisis, speculators were betting against the HK$. They figured that if the HK$ devalued, they could make money by shorting the HK$. The speculators' actions caused an outflow of money and a reduction in the HK monetary base. The reduction in the quantity of base money also resulted in a contraction in the bank credit in Hong Kong. The credit squeeze produced higher interest rate and a decline in market valuation. In addition to shorting the HK dollar, they also shorted the HK stock market. The speculators figured they had a one-sided bet or free lunch: if HK devalued, they would win. If it did not, they would make money shorting the market. Either way they would win.

However the speculators did not count on one course of action available to the HK monetary authorities. The HK monetary authorities used the reserves to buy stocks and support the market. In effect, they took the other side of the speculators' trade. As the speculators' carrying costs began to mount, they eventually caved and unwound their positions. The HK monetary authorities successfully defended the HK$ and the Hong Kong stock market.

A true gold standard would work very much like the currency board and the central bank would hold a 100% reserves backing the amount of high-powered money, that is, monetary base, in circulation and should be well equipped to fend off any speculative attack against the currency.

Would a fractional backing of the currency work just as well? The likely answer is that under some general conditions, a fractional reserve backing of the currency issued would work. The argument here is similar to that of a fractional reserve banking system. In general, one would not expect everyone to attempt to exchange all the currency in circulation at once, just like one would not expect the depositors to go to a regular bank all at once and demand their cash.

Under a fractional reserve banking system, we know that the amount of deposits held is much larger than the reserves held by the banks. Thus if all depositors attempted to withdraw their funds at once, the banks would not be able to pay them off. Yet in spite of this, the banking system works fairly well. Although exceptions do occur and runs on the banks have been documented. The runs on the banks can be caused by speculative attacks against the banks or by a loss of confidence in the ability of the bank to meet its obligations. When that happens no one wants to be the last one to go and withdraw money. The same holds for a country that uses a fractional reserve backing of its currency, whether it is a commodity such as gold and/or another country's currency as international reserves.

A case can be made that this is precisely what happened during the dismantling of the Breton Woods fixed exchange rate system. The United States came out of WWII with a very large stock of gold held at Fort Knox. The large amount of gold may have tempted the authorities not to follow the discipline of the gold exchange standard. Instead, the US Fed pursued a monetary policy focused on domestic objectives. The loose monetary policy led to a rise in the price of gold in the open market. Under the gold standard operating procedures, that was a signal that there was too much money in the economy. The operating procedures would dictate that the central bank conduct open market operations to reduce the quantity of money. A reduction in the amount of circulating dollars would have reduced the ratio of dollars to ounces of gold circulating, and thereby reduce the relative price of gold as well as the price of other commodities in terms of gold.

The central bank did *not* respond to the rise in gold price by reducing the amount of dollars circulating in the open economy. The United States chose another alternative instead; it chose to sell gold in the open market. This way it restored the ratio of money to gold while pursuing its domestic objectives. As a result, the price of gold fell back within the target. However this action did not reduce the ratio of the quantity of dollars to other goods. All it did was to increase the ratio of the quantity of gold to other goods. The net effect was an increase in the price of goods in terms of both dollars and gold.

Seeing the purchasing power of the dollar decline, other countries attempted to enforce the discipline of the gold exchange standard. They brought their dollars in and demanded gold. The leader of this group was France under Charles De Gaulle, who vehemently disagreed with many of the policies the United States was pursuing around the world. The United States continued its policies and the loss of gold accelerated. Rather than change course, the United States chose to close the Gold Window and the dismantling of the gold exchange standard began. As the dollar inflation rate began to creep in as a result of the excess dollar creation, the United States began to dismantle the gold exchange standard. Simultaneously, many free market economists began to advocate for a floating exchange rate system, arguing that it would insulate the economies from the other countries monetary policy mistakes. Eventually the world moved to the floating exchange rate system. The dollar was devalued and the OPEC cartel shock added fuel to the fire. The US inflation rate and most of the developed world's inflation rates accelerated and reached double digits. Looking back, the floating exchange rate did not insulate the individual economies from the monetary policy mistakes of other countries. We attribute this to currency substitution effects as well as other policy mistakes.

Putting together the experiences of the Bretton Woods gold exchange rate standard, and other countries' experiences with a fractional reserve backing as opposed to a 100% reserve backing as the HK currency board, the conclusion is an easy one. The international reserves fractional backing of a fixed exchange rate system is susceptible to a successful speculative attack.

References

[1] (a)The currency substitution is nothing more than a special case of the near monies literature. See Chetty VK. On measuring the nearness of near-money. *Am Econ Rev* June 1969;59:270–81. (b) For the specific issue of currency substitution, see Calvo GA, Rodriguez CA. A model of exchange rate determination under currency substitution and rational expectations. *J Pol Econ* 1977;85:617–24.

[2] (a) Friedman M. The case for flexible exchange rates. Essays in Positive Economics Chicago: University of Chicago Press, 1953. (b) Johnson Harry G. The case for flexible exchange rates, 1969. In: Baldwin RE, Richardson JD, editor. International Trade and Finance: Readings, Boston, Little Brown, 1974.

[3] Miles MA. Currency substitution: perspective, implications and empirical evidence. In: Putnam B, Wilford DS, editors. The Monetary Approach to International Adjustment. New York, Praeger, 1978.

[4] The basis of the equations and the modelling can be found in Canto V, Miles MA. Exchange rates in a global monetary model with currency substitutions and rational expectations. Economic Interdependence and Flexible Exchange Rates, MIT Press, Cambridge, Mass.; 1983, pp. 157–76.

[5] Currency substitution on demand and the exchange rate mechanism, substitution on the supply side, lead to an integrated market where the inflation rate is determined on a global scale. Laffer AB. The phenomenon of worldwide inflation; a study in international market integration. In: Meiselman D, Laffer AB, editors. The Phenomenon of Worldwide Inflation, American Enterprise Institute; 1975, pp. 27–52.

[6] (a)Victor CA. Exotic currencies. In: Eatwell J, Milgate M, Newman P. The New Palgrave Dictionary of Money and Finance, London: Macmillan Press Limited, New York: The Stockton Press, 1992; Vol. 1, pp. 843–5. (b) On this issue and the case of the Dominican Republic and other exotic currencies, see Canto VA. Monetary policy "dollarization" and parallel market exchange rates: the case of the Dominican Republic. J Int Money Fin December 1985;4(4):

507–22 and Canto VA, Nickelsburg G. Currency Substitution: Theory and Evidence from Latin America, Kluwer Academic Publishing, Boston, Massachusetts, 1987.

[7] Dornbusch R. Devaluation, money and non-traded goods. Am Econ Rev December 1973;63:871–80.

[8] The analogy here is between coins, bills, and check; they are all prefect substitutes on the supply side. The can be exchanged at their face value. However they do face different legal tender and other transaction costs that make them imperfect substitutes for each other on the demand side.

[9] (a) For arguments for a fixed exchange rate and or a common currency, see: Laffer AB. Two arguments for fixed exchange rates. In: Johnson HG, Swoboda A, editors. The Economics of Common Currencies. London: George Allen and Unwin, 1973. (b) Mundell RA. Uncommon arguments for a common currency. In: Johnson HG, Swoboda A, editors. The Economics of Common Currencies. London: George Allen and Unwin, 1973.(c)Wanniski J., The Mundel-Laffer Hypothesis – a new view of the world economy. Public Interest, no. 39, spring 1975.

24

Monetary Views: Part I

The 2007 financial crisis led to a renewed focus on the role of money and the monetary authorities. This was precipitated largely by the tremendous expansion of the Fed's balance sheet in response to the crisis. At the time, the issue was whether the Fed's balance sheet expansion would result in an economic recovery or an inflation surge down the road. The results are in, the economy did not experience an inflationary bout nor did it experience a strong recovery.

While there is considerable disagreement as to the role of monetary policy in the United States and other economies of the world, these differences arise as a result of the differences of opinion regarding the impact of money on prices and the real economy. Traditionally, most US monetary analysis assumes either implicitly or explicitly that the domestic monetary equilibrium is determined by the US demand for and supply of money. For example, most flexible exchange rate models assume that the locals only use the local currency as a medium of exchange. It is only then that these models can conclude that the flexible or floating exchange rate will isolate the local economy from external monetary shocks. Much has been written on this and other topics regarding the proper role of monetary policy. It is hard to keep track of all the arguments without a reference point or scorecard. Hence, we are in need of a framework that could help us keep track of the issues and make sense of the situation. To accomplish these goals, we have settled on a simple textbook version of the equation of exchange to organize the different points of view and to see whether the implications derived from these views conform to the current economic realities. In mathematical form, the equation of exchange is expressed as:

$$MV = PY$$

where M is the quantity of money, V the velocity of money or turnover rate, P the price level, and Y real GDP.

As written, the previous equation is an identity. It holds true at all times. Hence, it represents a nice way to organize and partition the various theories used to describe the evolution of the economy, a solid starting point. It follows that when you have four variables (M, V, P, and Y) in an equation, once the values of three of the four variables are known, one can solve for the remaining variable. In other words, there are only three degrees of freedom. That is, we can have independent theories regarding the behavior of three of the four variables and with that information we can then solve for the fourth one.

Next, we review how the textbook representations of the different economic theories to use the available degrees of freedom to solve for the different variables. In this chapter, we will focus on the right side of the equation of exchange and how to partition the impact of changes in the monetary aggregates on the nominal GDP and price level components. Looking at the previous equation, one can surmise that there are three distinct possibilities:

1. The monetary aggregates only affect the nominal variables, that is, the price level.
2. The monetary aggregates affect only the real variables, that is, real GDP.
3. The monetary aggregates affect both the price and real variables, that is, both the price level and real GDP.

The theoretical underpinnings for each of these possibilities are well known and thoroughly discussed in macroeconomics textbooks. The first proposition assumes

Economic Disturbances and Equilibrium in an Integrated Global Economy. http://dx.doi.org/10.1016/B978-0-12-813993-6.00024-6

that money is only a veil and it has no real effect on the economy. Within this framework, inflation is too much money chasing too few goods. And since money is a veil, the Fed has no impact on the real GDP and all it can do is to affect the inflation rate.

The textbook representation of the second alternative is that the economy is underemployed and that rigidities prevent the prices from clearing. Under these assumptions, the economy's aggregate demand will be perfectly elastic, that is, horizontal, and as a result any increases in aggregate demand will lead to a higher level of output without significantly affecting the price level. The textbook representation of this view advocates easy money as a way to stimulate the economy. In contrast, monetarists warn that easy money policies lead to inflation. Sound familiar?

Textbook monetarists argue that money is only a veil and that it has no impact on the real economy in the long run. If that is the case, the only long-run effect of monetary policy will be on the price level. An alternative view, related to the textbook Keynesian view, is that as the economy approaches full capacity, bottlenecks give rise to price increases of certain products. The closer the economy is to full employment, the higher the prices. The implication is that rising employment or a decline in unemployment signals an increase in capacity utilization and thus results in rising prices. This line of reasoning posits a trade-off between output/unemployment and inflation. This relationship was immortalized in what has become known as the Philips Curve [1].

The textbook version of the Phillips Curve offers a third way. It offers a sort of blend of the Keynesian and monetarist split of the right side of the equation of exchange. Easy money will initially produce a lower interest rate and thereby stimulate the economy. However, over time, the easy money will result in higher prices. Thus from a policy perspective, the Phillips Curve poses quite a

challenge for monetary policy: using monetary policy to stimulate the economy is the policymakers' version of fly now, pay later. Even worse, if monetary policy is the sole policy lever, over time, to be effective, monetary policy has to be applied in ever more expansive doses and that could result in ever increasing and accelerating inflation.

The Phillips Curve also introduces another dimension to the policy analysis. According to this view, the policy implication is that through its impact on the underlying inflation rate, it can also influence the capacity utilization and/or unemployment rate in the economy. The view suggests the Fed should have a dual mandate, targeting the inflation rate and the unemployment rate.

The dual mandate also creates the need for an indicator that captures both of the policy objectives of the Fed: the unemployment rate and the inflation rate. Some may be included to develop a complicated way of weighting the two instruments depending on the economy's performance. If the weighting scheme became known, one can anticipate or predict the Fed's reaction to changing market conditions. This explains in part why people spend a great deal of time and resources trying to understand the Fed's behavior and decision-making process. Absent that, one has to start somewhere, and the market has developed a very simple way to evaluate the dual objectives. It is called the Misery Index. It consists of the sum of the unemployment rate and inflation rates.

The Misery Index became quite popular during the high inflation high unemployment years of the decade of the 1970s. In fact, it was used quite effectively in 1980 by the then-candidate Ronald Reagan to defeat the Jimmy Carter, the incumbent President. Candidate Reagan asked rhetorically if you were better off than you were 4 years earlier. The answer according to the Misery Index was a rotund no. Fig. 24.1 shows that leading to the 1980 election, the Misery Index was rising and approaching its 1974 all-time high.

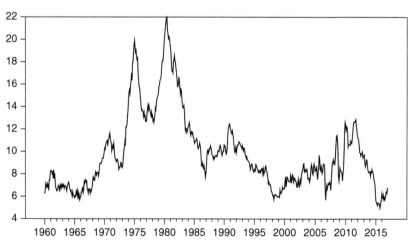

FIGURE 24.1 The Misery Index.

IS THERE AN INFLATION/OUTPUT TRADE-OFF?

Milton Friedman American Economic Association Presidential Address was a rebuttal of the Phillips Curve [2]. He argued quite persuasively that there is no output inflation trade-off; hence there is no permanent Phillips Curve. His argument was succinct and elegant; the pricing system was flexible enough to bring the economy to its natural rate of unemployment. Borrowing a page from the efficient markets and rational expectations developments that were taking place around the time of Friedman's presidential address, some economists including many of Friedman's disciples began to question the existence of a lagged effect of monetary policy [3]. The argument was as follows: if you know there is a 6 month lag, and you see the money supply going up today, you know that exactly 6 months from now prices will go up. A smart person would at 5 months and 29 days buy goods, hold them for a day and make big profits by selling them when prices go up. A smarter person would anticipate that move and would buy at 5 months and 28 days. The logic of the efficient market is clear and brings us to the first modification of the textbook monetarism. If people know that higher money growth causes higher prices, the lag has to disappear or else some profit opportunities are going unexploited. Hence, if there is any real effect, it has to come from unanticipated money changes. Any attempt to use monetary policy to push the economy beyond the natural unemployment or real interest rates leads to an ever-accelerating inflation rate. Early on the monetary authorities may be able to fool the economy by increasing the money supply unexpectedly. However, over time, the extra money would lead to higher prices and rising inflation expectations. In order for the monetary policy to continue having a real effect requires an ever-higher dose of monetary action/surprises. Ultimately the economy will figure out the game and prices will rise without the output effect. Friedman argued that the long-run Phillips curve is vertical; there is no long run or permanent trade-off.

The American Economic Association (AEA) Presidential Address made clear in no uncertain terms that there was no permanent inflation/output trade-off. Money is only a veil in Friedman's world. While the supply-siders agree with much of Milton's address, there is one modification. If the tax system is un-indexed, inflation would push people into a higher tax bracket and thus raise the economy's marginal tax rate. The higher tax rate leads to lower output and thus a lower demand for money. That, in turn, leads to a higher excess supply of money and thus a higher inflation rate. The process continues until all taxpayers are pushed into the highest tax bracket, at which point the progressive tax system becomes a proportional tax system and bracket creep ceases. The level of output would be permanently lowered as a result of the higher tax rate. From that point on anticipated inflation would not have any effect on the real economy (i.e., there would be no inflation/output trade-off). However, during the bracket creep period as inflation rises so will the unemployment rate. In other words, a perverse Phillips Curve or stagflation will be observed.

The interaction between inflation and the tax rate system offers a simple explanation of the stagflation phenomena that plagued the United States during the decade of the 1970s. That experience fueled an argument that gained much currency in favor of the monetarist view, and it is that price stability reduces uncertainty and promotes long-term economic growth. Therefore the monetarist view leads to a simple conclusion: The Fed should have a single mandate of price stability.

THE PHILLIPS CURVE AND THE DUAL MANDATE

Although Milton Friedman's 1967 criticism of the Phillips Curve was devastating, it was not enough to crush the rising popularity of the Phillips Curve in the popular press and some academic/policy circles. While Friedman's logic was impeccable, his views were not universally accepted. In 1972, the Phillips Curve was the topic of James Tobin AEA Presidential Address [4].

The Phillips Curve construct gained adherents and acceptance and in response to the rising Misery Index (Fig. 24.1), Representative Augustus Hawkins and Senator Hubert Humphrey created the Full Employment and Balanced Growth Act. It was signed into law by President Jimmy Carter on October 27, 1978. The Act explicitly instructs the nation to strive toward four ultimate goals: full employment, growth in production, price stability, and balance of trade and budget. Moreover, since the Fed has no direct impact on two of the objectives, that is, the balance of trade and the budget, the legislation mandates the Board of Governors of the Federal Reserve to establish a monetary policy that maintains long-run growth, minimizes inflation, and promotes price stability. The dual mandate was memorialized in this legislation which also instructed the Board of Governors of the Federal Reserve to transmit a *Monetary Policy Report* to the Congress twice a year outlining its monetary policy, as well as requiring the Chairman of the Federal Reserve to connect the monetary policy with the Presidential economic policy.

RULES VERSUS DISCRETION

Under the monetarist assumption the "optimal quantity of money" is easily derived [5]. Assuming a unit elastic income demand for money in the long run, a quantity of money that grows at the same rate as the real GDP will deliver a stable price level. The Fed's problem simplifies to forecasting real GDP and matching the changes with a corresponding percent change in the money supply. In technical terms the Fed's job is to match the demand shifts with a corresponding supply shift. Monetarists argue that the short-run forecasts are difficult to predict and trying to accommodate them may destabilize the inflation rate. Under a mean reversion hypothesis, a sensible solution to this problem is to focus on the long-run stability and ignore the short-term fluctuations in real GDP growth. The assumption is that the fluctuations around the trend will, in the long run, cancel each other out. The policy implication is obvious: constant money growth is the optimal monetary policy. It is superior to an active rule that tries to match every short-term fluctuation in real GDP growth. From the monetarist point of view, the rule-based monetary policy will protect the economy from the vagaries of policymakers that attempt to affect real changes in the economy through the pursuit of an active monetary policy.

As the monetarist believe that money is only a veil, the monetarists argue that the only long-run effect will be a less stable price level and quite likely a higher inflation. In contrast, the textbook Keynesian view believes that monetary policy can have real effects on the economy and, as such, it argues that the monetary policy is a policy tool needed to reach the dual mandate. Depending on the economic conditions, it should be sometimes used to control inflation and other times used to stimulate output. Who has the correct view is a topic that has occupied many great minds for years and we are not likely to resolve either. The important point that we need to make is that the different views lead to different policy initiatives. Therefore by knowing the background and inclinations of the policymakers, one may be able to anticipate the likely policy responses of the different administrations. With that in mind, one can then begin to formulate a strategy to identify the winners and losers of the alternative policy options. Investors can then position their portfolios accordingly to take advantage of the changes to come.

References

[1] Phillips AW. The relationship between unemployment and the rate of change of money and wages in the United Kingdom 1861–1957. Economica 1958;25(200):283–99.

[2] Friedman Milton. The role of monetary policy. Am Econ Rev 1967;68(1):1–17.

[3] Muth John F. Rational expectations and the theory of price movements. Econometrica 1961;29(3):315–35. A summary of the efficient markets and rational expectations literature can be found in Fama, Eugene, The efficient capital markets: a review of theory and empirical work, J Finance 1970; 25(2), 383–417 and Sargent, Thomas J., Rational expectations. In: The New Palgrave: A dictionary of economics Vol 4, 1987, p. 76–79.

[4] James Tobin. Inflation and unemployment. Am Econ Rev 1972;62(1):1–18.

[5] Friedman Milton. The Optimum Quantity of Money and Other Essays. Chicago: Aldine Publishing Co.; 1969.

25

Monetary Views: Part II

Our earlier chapter, Monetary Views Part I, focused on the right side of the equation of exchange. Now it is time to explore the left side of the equation of exchange to see what insights can be derived as we consider different assumptions regarding the control of the quantity of money and behavior of the monetary aggregates and velocity of money.

An assumption explicitly made in the textbook representation of the monetarist views is that the Fed controls the quantity of money, say M2 or Money of Zero Maturity (MZM). In doing so, the monetarists use one of the three degrees of freedom afforded by the equation of exchange. A second assumption or degree of freedom used by the monetarist is that demand for money is "stable." In the old days, when we were in grad school, the narrowest definition of stability was assumed. The textbooks assumed a constant velocity. The assumptions that the Fed controls the quantity of money and of a constant velocity of money, leaves the left side of the equation determined and completely controlled by the Fed. An implication of these two assumptions is that increases in the quantity of money will result in increases in nominal GDP (i.e., real GDP times the price level or $P*Y$). Hence the one degree of freedom left can now be used to determine the split between price increases and real GDP increases associated with increases in the quantity of money. This issue was explored in the earlier chapter, Monetary Views Part I.

THE MONETARIST VIEWS

The strict monetarist view assumes that money is only a veil and has no effect on the real economy. Increases in the quantity of money will have no effect on the real economy. Hence increases in the quantity of money will, everything else the same, translate into higher price levels. The policy implications for the monetarist framework are straightforward: Inflation is a monetary phenomenon, too much money chasing too few goods. The Fed, through its control of the aggregates, controls the price level and, thus, the inflation rate.

The monetarist view makes a series of simplifying assumptions that taken at face value appear to be quite reasonable. However, as the positive methodology taught by Milton Friedman tells us, you don't judge a model by its assumptions. Rather you judge it by its predictive or explanatory power. Before we evaluate the monetarist model, it is worthwhile to review the textbook assumptions associated with the monetarist model:

- Through open market operations the Fed controls the monetary base.
- Through the discount window and reserve requirements, the Fed controls the money multiplier.
- The demand for money is stable (i.e., in the simpler models the velocity is assumed to be constant).
- A floating exchange rate isolates the domestic economy form the rest of the world monetary shocks.

Economic Disturbances and Equilibrium in an Integrated Global Economy. http://dx.doi.org/10.1016/B978-0-12-813993-6.00025-8

As discussed, these assumptions are necessary and sufficient conditions to justify the conclusion that the Fed controls the quantity of money. These are very important assumptions for if the Fed controls the quantity of money; changes in the quantity of money reflect only supply shifts allowed by the Fed. That is why the monetarists are in the habit of calling the market clearing quantity of money the money supply.

An obvious question to ask is which aggregate is the one that the Fed is most likely to control? When the Fed buys bonds, it increases the amount of high powered or base money in circulation. When the Fed sells bonds, it reduces the amount of base money in circulation. It is clear that, under the current structure, the Fed controls the monetary base to the decimal point. A clear exception to this would be the specification of a mechanism such as a domestic price rule or an exchange rate rule that forces the Fed to conduct open market operations depending on market conditions. In that case, it would be the private sector who would have complete control of the monetary base. Hence, short of a formal price or exchange rate rule, it seems reasonable to assume that the monetary base is the aggregate most likely to be controlled by the Fed.

Given the assumption that the Fed controls the monetary base, we move on to ask whether the Fed controls the higher monetary aggregates. The answer to the question is that it depends on whether the Fed controls the money multiplier. Thus, to address the issue, we need to expand the expression describing the quantity of money and replaced it with the base and the money multiplier. We now specify the monetary aggregate as:

$$M = Bm$$

where B denotes the monetary base and m the money multiplier.

Replacing the expanded definition of the monetary aggregates into the left side of the equation, the expanded equation of exchange now becomes:

$$BmV = PY$$

CAN THE FED CONTROL THE QUANTITY OF MONEY?

The monetarist position is the starting point of the monetary views of the supply-side group of which we were active participants. The evolution of the monetary views is easily explained as one questions the basic assumptions of the monetarist models. Let's review each one of them.

Supply-siders agree that the monetary base is under the control of the Fed. Through open market operations (i.e., purchase and sale of government bonds), the Fed can control the base to the penny. Control of the money multiplier marks the first source of disagreement between the monetarists and supply-siders. Banks hold excess reserves and changes in the cash/deposit, demand deposit/time deposit ratios all affect the money multiplier whether these changes offset or magnify the changes in the monetary base is outside the control of the Fed. Differential rates of returns, shifts in expectations etc. alter the relative attractiveness of narrowly defined money. In technical economic parlance, the expected rates of returns differential will generate a shift in the demand for money.

The argument for a floating exchange rate assumes that local residents transact only in their country's currency. That is US residents transact only in US dollars etc. The assumption means that domestic money will never leave your country and foreigners will never hold it. Alternatively stated, there is no foreign transaction demand for our currency. Thus, demand shifts emanating from abroad will only affect the exchange rate and have no impact on the domestic money supply. While the assumption that local residents transact only in local dollars may be a good approximation for the United States, the same cannot be said for the rest of the world. We know that the dollar is used as a medium of exchange all over the world. Hence it is reasonable to assume that changing economic conditions in the rest of the world will alter the demand for US dollars. Dollars will flow in and out of the United States, hence the rest of the world could generate a shift in US money demand.

To truly control the quantity of money circulating in the economy, the Fed would have to account and offset undesired changes in the multiplier changes in expected rates of returns, as well as changes in the economic conditions outside the United States. Each and every one of these sources can generate a shift in the demand for US money. While the Fed may be able to offset any undesired changes over the long run, in the short run, the task is not that easy. The monetarists already concede this when they argue in favor of rules over discretion. However, we are saying more than that. Attempts by the Fed to control a variable that it does not truly control only leads to undesirable and or sub-optimal results.

EXPLORING THE LEFT SIDE OF THE EQUATION

The next step is for us to articulate different theories that use up the three degrees of freedom on the left side of the equation of exchange to determine the left side of the equation and solve for the unknown variables in the right side of the equation (i.e., nominal GDP). This discussion also helps us understand the conditions needed

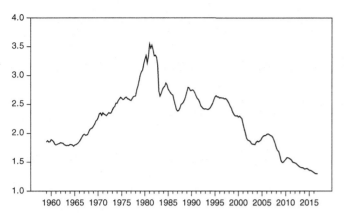

FIGURE 25.1 **MZM velocity of money.**

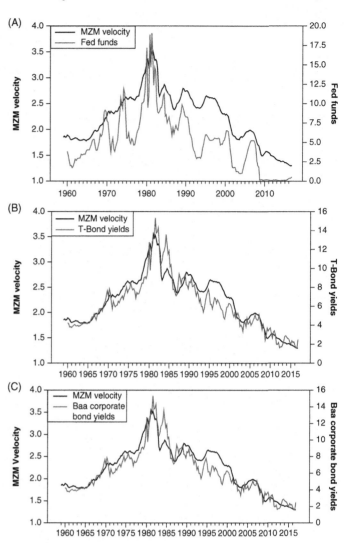

FIGURE 25.2 (A) MZM velocity and the Fed funds rate, (B) MZM velocity and the 10 year government bond yields, (C) MZM velocity and the Baa corporate bond yields.

in order for the monetary authorities to be able to control the quantity of money.

The Monetary Base: We already used one degree of freedom when we argued that the monetary base is the one aggregate most likely to be under the complete control of the Fed. So all we have left are two degrees of freedom and they relate to the money/credit multiplier and the velocity of money.

The Velocity of Money: Most money demand models assume a stable money demand or velocity of money. A special case of stable money demand is that of a constant velocity as commonly assumed in textbook representations. Unfortunately, the constant velocity assumption does not hold water empirically (Fig. 25.1). However, the fact that velocity varies over time does not necessarily rule out a stable money demand or stable velocity. A changing cost of holding money balances and the availability of less convenient substitutes is capable of generating substitution effects or movements along the money demand curve that result in predictable changes in the velocity of money.

Take the case of interest bearing deposits. Its rates adjust to market conditions and as a consequence these deposits will offer some protection against inflation. That is, when the inflation rate increases, so do the interest rates paid on these deposits thereby protecting the money against inflation. Hence the competitive interest payment is a mechanism by which the banking system indexes these deposits against inflation. At the other end of the spectrum, we have noninterest bearing money, such as currency, which offers little or no protection against inflation. So, when inflation increases, the purchasing power of noninterest bearing money will decline more than that of the interest bearing money. To protect themselves against the deterioration of purchasing power, money holders will attempt to switch to interest bearing money. An increase in the opportunity cost of holding transaction money would induce a movement along the "stable" demand curve. Given the variety of possible substitutes, we considered three different measures of

the opportunity costs, the Fed funds rate (Fig. 25.2A), the 10 year government bond yields (Fig. 25.2B), and Baa corporate bond yields (Fig. 25.2C). While the fit between the velocity of MZM and the various measures of the opportunity costs of holding MZM vary, the data clearly shows the predicted correlation between the two. So, it appears that we are on the right track. Inspection of the different relationships suggests that the 10 year government bond yields offer the tightest fit to the MZM money velocity (Fig. 25.2B).

The magnitude of the change in velocity or money demand depends on two factors: The magnitude of the change in opportunity cost and the elasticity of the demand function. All of this leads to an interesting sidebar: A constant velocity is only a special case of a stable demand function where there is no substitution effect. This can come about in one of two ways. The first one being that interest is paid on money and the opportunity cost of holding is zero (i.e., the money is effectively indexed). The second option is that it is very expensive to substitute out of money (i.e., there are no substitutes). These two conditions can generate what some may define as an "inelastic" money demand function. As we know that the velocity of money has changed in the past, we can safely rule out inelastic demand and argue that a period of stable demand for money and relatively constant velocity of money is the result of a monetary policy that keeps the opportunity cost of holding interest bearing money relatively constant.

The Money Multiplier: Now, on to new and related insights. The ability to use other countries' currencies and the creation of "near money" substitutes by financial institutions has increased the ability to replace the narrowly defined domestic monetary aggregates. In turn, these switches produce unintended consequences in the credit markets. Let's consider the case of an increase in the underlying inflation rate. As the inflation rate increases, people will move out of noninterest paying money into interest paying deposits and that, in turn, will affect the credit creation ability of the banks. In other words, the money creation and credit creation ability of the banks are intertwined and one affects the other. Some simple money and banking calculations will illustrate our point.

Let's assume that the Fed prints out $10 worth of money. Let's also assume a 10% reserve requirement for bank deposits. This means that the banking system can support $100 worth of deposits if $10 worth of base money is used as bank reserves. Looking at the financial institution's assets and liabilities, we find $100 worth of deposits on the liability side and $10 worth of reserves and $90 worth of loans on the asset side. So the $10 worth of base money could support a maximum of $100 worth of deposits and $90 worth of loans. If the $10 is used as reserve, then there is no currency in circulation and the quantity of money will be exactly equal to the deposits created or $100 and the money multiplier will be 10 and the credit multiplier 9.

At the other end of the spectrum, we have the possibility that the $10 worth of base money is used solely as currency in circulation. If that is the case, then no deposits will be created, nor will any loans be created by the banking system. Hence the credit multiplier will be zero. The only money in the economy will be the $10 worth of currency in circulation and the money multiplier will be 1.

These two extreme cases describe the boundaries for money and bank credit creation in the economy. Any combination of the two is possible. The $10 could support anywhere from $10 worth of money and no loans to $100 worth of money and $90 worth of loans. Which combination is chosen depends a great deal on the demand for money and for bank credit. The opportunity cost of holding the money and the price of credit changes to insure money and credit market clearing. Getting back

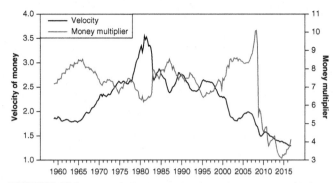

FIGURE 25.3   **MZM velocity versus the MZM money multiplier.**

to basics, we have argued that changes in the opportunity cost of holding money elicit substitution effects that alter the demand for money (i.e., velocity of money) and the credit creation ability of the banks in a clear and predictable direction.

Fig. 25.3 shows the MZM money multiplier and velocity of money. The figure shows a few things that we already knew. The first one is that the MZM velocity exhibited a secular uptrend leading up to the early 1980s and since then it has been on a secular downward trend. The secular trend for the MZM velocity is easily explained by the 10 year bond yields which during the 1960s and 1970s was on a secular uptrend and since Paul Volcker changed the Fed's operating procedures the bond yield have been on a secular downtrend (Fig. 25.2B).

Another interesting feature is the negative correlation between the cyclical fluctuations in the two variables. When the velocity of money abruptly changes relative to trend, the money multiplier abruptly changes in the opposite direction. This is consistent with the view that unanticipated shocks to the money multiplier will have an impact on the quantity of money and in the short term, to make due and carry the same amount of transaction, the MZM velocity has to increase. This interpretation of the data suggests that the deviation from trend by the money multiplier and velocity of money are related, that they are not random events and are reacting to changing economic conditions. In short, the Fed does not have complete control over either of these two variables.

THE CASE FOR A QUANTITY RULE

Monetarists then argue that given the economy's tendency to approach its natural growth rate over the long run, a constant growth in the monetary aggregates results in a stable long-run inflation rate. Hence they advocate constant money growth to achieve a desired target inflation rate. The policy implications of the monetarist view are simple and straightforward. The question is whether they hold water empirically.

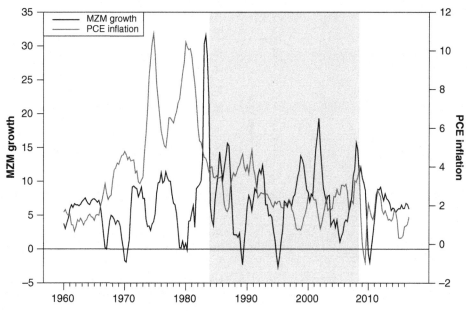

FIGURE 25.4   MZM growth versus the PCE inflation rate.

In Fig. 25.4 we show the trailing four-quarters MZM growth and US inflation rate. During the nonprice rule period when the Fed targeted the quantity of money, notice the secular uptrend in the US inflation rate. The data also illustrates a negative correlation between spikes in the inflation rate and MZM growth. Assuming that the monetary authorities controlled the quantity of money, MZM, the correlation is the opposite of what a strict monetarist interpretation of the data would produce. Another disturbing result is that during the 1980s MZM growth seems to be as high as or higher than the MZM growth during the 1970s, yet the inflation rate was much lower. Changes in the velocity of money or demand for money easily explain these correlations however, we still need to come up with an explanation or the causes for the changes in the velocity of MZM. All of this leads one to the obvious conclusion, that the monetary authorities do not fully control the quantity of money. Therefore, we need to look beyond the monetarist view.

THE CASE FOR A PRICE RULE

The domestic price rule provides the monetary authorities a mechanism that automatically accommodates shifts in the demand for money irrespective of their origins. The argument is very simple: following the monetarists, we believe that inflation is too much money chasing too few goods. Increases in money demand are associated with lower inflation and vice versa. Hence whenever the inflation rate rises, it is *prima facie* evidence of too much money. All the Fed has to do is sell bonds in the open market. Doing so

retires currency out of circulation and hence reduces the inflationary pressure. Similarly, when the inflation rate falls below the desired level all the Fed has to do is buy bonds in the open market. Doing so increases the quantity of base money circulating the economy and that relieves the deflationary pressures. The beauty of this approach is that it automatically adjusts for shifts in the demand for money. The mechanism does not care for the origin of the disturbance; it takes care of it no matter the origin. The *dirigistes* have a problem with this; they need to control and micromanage the process and under such a rule the base is no longer under the control of the monetary authorities. In a way, our analysis shows that our monetary views emanate from the Friedman views with one major modification. We acknowledged the existence of demand shifts and modified the analysis accordingly. Through the domestic price rule, we found a simple way to accommodate for the demand shifts and in theory.

The price rule yields some interesting implications regarding the relationship between money growth and inflation. First, since the price rule automatically adjusts for changes in money demand while keeping the inflation rate within the target range, it follows that under a price rule, fluctuations in money growth will be uncorrelated with the underlying inflation rate and positively correlated with real GDP growth. Another implication is that as the inflation rate converges to the price rule target rate and the volatility of the inflation rate declines, the moneyness of money increases and so does the demand for money. In plain language, the velocity of money will decline during the price rule period and will be related to the underlying inflation rate during the nonprice rule

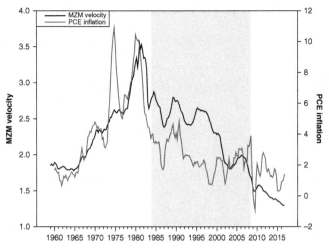

FIGURE 25.5   US inflation and MZM velocity.

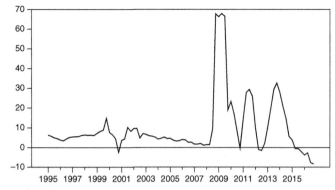

FIGURE 25.6   Monetary base growth rate.

period. Looking at Fig. 25.5, we find some support for the price rule arguments. During the price rule period the velocity declined as expected, a major blow to the textbook strict monetarist view that assumes a constant velocity. Here, we argue that the organization of the monetary system is capable of explaining why we have high money growth during both the high inflation rate period (the quantity rule period) and the price rule period. In the latter, we have an increase in the demand for money (i.e., a decline in the velocity), while in the former, fast money growth is associated with rising inflation and a decline in velocity that further accelerated the inflation rate.

THE FINANCIAL CRISIS

The previous paragraphs have outlined a simple framework that can be used to analyze and interpret monetary policy. In the process, we outlined the differences between our framework and traditional textbook representations of the monetarist, Keynesian, and Phillips Curve. While we showed that each of these frameworks produces a partial explanation of the 2007 financial crisis, we believe that our framework provides a much better and more complete explanation.

One common criticism of the Fed's behavior leading to the financial meltdown is that the Fed was too easy as it expanded its balance sheet which lead to an explosion in the growth of the monetary base, see Fig. 25.6. Recall that some of the Fed's critics used to argue that inflation would be coming down the pike. Our view then and now is that the critics focused solely on the expansion of the monetary base. Given this information, the critics inferred that there was too much money in the system. While we agree that inflation is a monetary phenomenon, we are not willing to concede that the money growth was excessive. Here is why. If the Fed was, in

effect, following a price rule, the money growth would simply reflect increases in money demand. If that is the case, the inflation rate should remain within the Fed's target range. In fact, as shown in Figs. 25.7 and 25.8, that was the case. MZM growth accelerated prior to the recession, yet its growth rate did not explode as the monetary base and neither did the PCE inflation rate. The latter dipped briefly and quickly rebounded to remain within the price rule range.

Other important relationships can be found in the different figures. For example, the relationship identified in Fig. 25.9 shows that. The money multiplier declined, yet the velocity of money does not show an abrupt change. It merely continued its downward trend. Fig. 25.10 shows

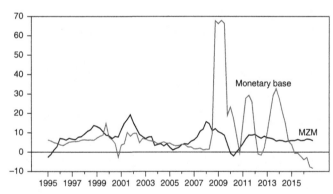

FIGURE 25.7   Growth in the monetary base and MZM.

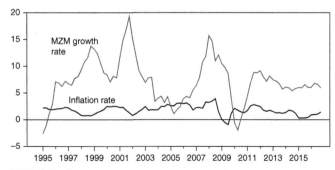

FIGURE 25.8   US inflation rate and MZM growth rate.

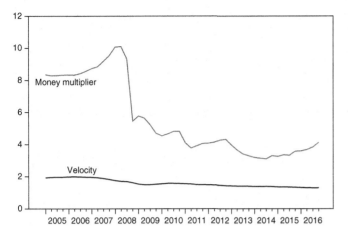

FIGURE 25.9   MZM velocity and the money multiplier.

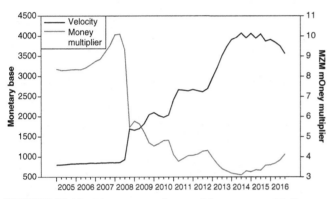

FIGURE 25.10   The monetary base and the money multiplier.

that the expansion of the monetary base eliminated the negative impact of the decline in the money multiplier, leaving the MZM essentially unchanged. The Fed did a great job in providing liquidity, that is, transaction money to the economy. In fact, we can say more than that the fact that the inflation rate did not creep up with the expansion of the base, if anything it did decline, see Fig. 25.9, this means that if anything the Fed was a bit cautious or tight.

More often than not the expansion of the money multiplier is associated with declines in velocity or increases in the demand for money. This suggests that the money and credit supply and their prices do adjust to bring about a new equilibrium in response to the changing market conditions. The fact that the Fed was able to offset the negative impact of the decline in the money multiplier on MZM does not mean that the Fed took care of everything in the financial markets. Yet, it did provide transaction money, but what about the credit markets. The decline in the money multiplier would significantly reduce the credit creation by the banking system and that would have a negative impact on the credit markets. Fig. 25.5 shows how, as expected, the yield on the lower quality credit increased and perhaps in a flight to quality the yield on the higher quaintly corporate declined. As

a result, the spread between the Baa and the Aaa bonds widened during the crisis.

Based on the framework outlined here and the previous chapter, we can make inferences regarding the possible impact of different shocks to the economy on the supply of credit and MZM as well as on the opportunity cost of holding MZM. More importantly, we can also show that the inference process is reversible. From the changes in the opportunity costs and the total amount of credit and money, we can clearly identify the nature of the shock. A few comments illustrate these points and put the monetary situation in perspective.

Let's say that for some reason the banks stopped lending. In that case, the credit creation will collapse to zero. The credit contraction will have an unintended effect; it will lead to a decline in the money and credit multiplier and, as a result the quantity of money will decline too (Figs. 25.7 and 25.10). That is exactly what happened during the financial crisis. If left to the market clearing mechanism, prices change to bring about a new equilibrium. The excess demand for money leads to a decline in the inflation rate (Fig. 25.8). That is exactly what happened in 2008. The question is whether the Fed overdid it? Our answer is simple. Some people would look at MZM growth. We would look at the inflation rate. Looking at Fig. 25.8, we can see that in the aftermath of the crisis MZM grew in the mid-teens on a year over year basis while the inflation rate declined. All of this suggests that the expansion of the monetary base barely offset the collapse in the money multiplier.

The credit market is another story. While the increase in the base added the needed transaction balances, it did not address the credit issue. A shortage of credit will lead to an increase in the price of credit and the spread between corporate and government bonds. That is exactly what happened in 2008 (Fig. 25.11).

An attempt by the government to fill in the credit void was not as successful. However, this was not for lack of trying. The Fed intervened at the long and short end of the yield curve. The Fed went back to its low Feds funds

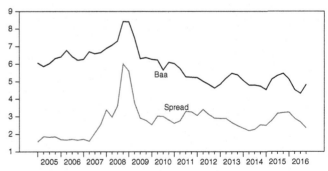

FIGURE 25.11   Baa corporate bond yields and Baa government bond yield spread.

rate and even though the flight to quality led to lower bond yields, the slope of the yield curve increased.

The point we want to make is that the money and credit markets interact with each other. If the Fed is to control the left side of the equation of exchange, it has to simultaneously manage the credit markets and the demand for money. These two objectives require at least two policy instruments on the part of the policy makers. The monetary base and the credit restraints (i.e., reserve requirements, etc.) should suffice. The velocity of money is also affected by inflation expectations and the opportunity cost of holding money. As long as we assume that the demand for money is stable, we can describe a systematic relationship between the multiplier, velocity, and the inflation rate. If inflation is to flare up, we expect to see an increase in the velocity of money and the money and credit multipliers. Those are the markers that we need to watch.

26

The Greenspan Monetary Rule

The remarks of Alan Greenspan at the 2005 Jackson Hole conference sponsored by the Kansas City Fed were quite enlightening [1]. The Maestro touched on what he considered were the most important developments on the way monetary policy had been approached and implemented under his tenure. The presentation is important for another reason. It documents how the quantity rule and price rule have had an impact on the design and implementation of monetary policy. His short presentation embarked on recounting what he considered important developments in central banking and the implementation of monetary policy.

He described the basic framework for Open Market Operations during the 1950s as follows:

> Credit was eased when the economy weakened and tightened when inflation threatened, but largely in an ad hoc manner. As a consequence, the Federal Reserve was perceived by some as often accentuating, rather than damping, cycles in prices and activity.

Moving along in time, his views of the 1970s are quite clear:

> Subsequently, however, the experience of stagflation in the 1970s and intellectual advances in understanding the importance of expectations--which built on the earlier work of Friedman and Phelps--undermined the notion of a long-run tradeoff. Inflation again became widely viewed as being detrimental to financial stability and macroeconomic performance. And as the decade progressed, a keener appreciation for the monetary roots of inflation emerged both in the profession at large and at central banks.

One possible implication of these experiences is to suggest a simple passive rule for monetary policy. However, the Maestro clearly shuts this option down:

At various points in time, some analysts have held out hope that a single indicator variable--such as commodity prices, the yield curve, nominal income, and of course, the monetary aggregates--could be used to reliably guide the conduct of monetary policy. If it were the case that an indicator variable or a relatively simple equation could extract the essence of key economic relationships from an exceedingly complex and dynamic real world, then broader issues of economic causality could be set aside, and the tools of policy could be directed at fostering a path for this variable consistent with the attainment of the ultimate policy objective.

He then goes on to explain why a quantity rule may not work out:

> M1 was the focus of policy for a brief period in the late 1970s and early 1980s. That episode proved key to breaking the inflation spiral that had developed over the 1970s, but policymakers soon came to question the viability over the longer haul of targeting the monetary aggregates. The relationships of the monetary aggregates to income and prices were eroded significantly over the course of the 1980s and into the early 1990s by financial deregulation, innovation, and globalization. For example, the previously stable relationship of M2 to nominal gross domestic product and the opportunity cost of holding M2 deposits underwent a major structural shift in the early 1990s because of the increasing prevalence of competing forms of intermediation and financial instruments.

At the time, we were hoping that Chairman Greenspan would endorse the price rule, whereby the Fed would automatically accommodate shifts in the economy's money demand. Declining prices would signal a shortage of money; through open market policies (i.e., the sale of bonds), the Fed would increase the quantity of money. Instead of the price rule, in his speech he articulated his "risk management" approach. In his own words, he describes the process as follows:

Economic Disturbances and Equilibrium in an Integrated Global Economy. http://dx.doi.org/10.1016/B978-0-12-813993-6.00026-X

In effect, we strive to construct a spectrum of forecasts from which, at least conceptually, specific policy action is determined through the tradeoffs implied by a loss-function. In the summer of 2003, for example, the Federal Open Market Committee viewed as very small the probability that the then-gradual decline in inflation would accelerate into a more consequential deflation. But because the implications for the economy were so dire should that scenario play out, we chose to counter it with unusually low interest rates.

The product of a low-probability event and a potentially severe outcome was judged a more serious threat to economic performance than the higher inflation that might ensue in the more probable scenario. Moreover, the risk of a sizable jump in inflation seemed limited at the time, largely because increased productivity growth was resulting in only modest advances in unit labor costs and because heightened competition, driven by globalization, was limiting employers' ability to pass through those cost increases into prices. Given the potentially severe consequences of deflation, the expected benefits of the unusual policy action were judged to outweigh its expected costs.

The essence of his approach was to anticipate and accommodate possible shocks to the economy. The one common element with the price rule is that both accommodate money demand shifts, the one difference being that the price rule reacts to it automatically while the risk management launches preemptive accommodations. Unlike the price rule approach that automatically accommodates the demand shifts, the preemptive approach requires that the Fed be vigilant about potential demand shocks. In particular, Greenspan stressed the ability to adjust to events without the comfort of relevant history to guide the central bank. He then focuses on the household net worth to disposable income ratio (Fig. 26.1).

The Maestro makes an insightful argument:

The determination of global economic activity in recent years has been influenced importantly by capital gains on various types of assets, and the liabilities that finance them. Our forecasts and hence policy are becoming increasingly driven by asset price changes.

FIGURE 26.1   Household net worth as a percent of disposable personal income.

He goes on to articulate his concern:

The steep rise in the ratio of household net worth to disposable income in the mid-1990s, after a half-century of stability, is a case in point. Although the ratio fell with the collapse of equity prices in 2000, it has rebounded noticeably over the past couple of years, reflecting the rise in the prices of equities and houses.

Whether the currently elevated level of the wealth-to-income ratio will be sustained in the longer run remains to be seen. But arguably, the growing stability of the world economy over the past decade may have encouraged investors to accept increasingly lower levels of compensation for risk. They are exhibiting a seeming willingness to project stability and commit over an ever more extended time horizon.

Before we go on, let's consider the determinants of the wealth-to-income ratio. In a forward-looking model, wealth is determined by the discounted future value of the after tax income. There are several drivers for the wealth variable: the discount rate (which generally is related to the long-term government bond plus a risk premium), the income growth rate, and the tax rate applied to the income earned as well as to any reinvestment of the income. He warns all of us about the dangers of the higher wealth-to-income ratio:

Thus, this vast increase in the market value of asset claims is in part the indirect result of investors accepting lower compensation for risk. Such an increase in market value is too often viewed by market participants as structural and permanent. To some extent, those higher values may be reflecting the increased flexibility and resilience of our economy. But what they perceive as newly abundant liquidity can readily disappear. Any onset of increased investor caution elevates risk premiums and, as a consequence, lowers asset values and promotes the liquidation of the debt that supported higher asset prices. This is the reason that history has not dealt kindly with the aftermath of protracted periods of low risk premiums.

In the previous paragraph, the Maestro outlines a very specific mean reversion path through which the net worth to disposable income ratio will adjust to the long-run equilibrium. First, he assumes that there is going to be an increase in risk premium and a disappearance of liquidity in the economy. In fact, he had the perfect example in his speech. When the Fed funds rate was lowered in the aftermath of the recession, the Fed flooded the credit market. In light of the abundance of credit, the risk premium declined. As the Fed now reduces the liquidity, it follows that the market will once again begin to pay attention to the risk characteristic of the different assets. His logic is impeccable if everything else holds the same. He seems to believe that the bulk of the increase in the household net worth to disposable income ratio was due to a reduction in risk premium.

The Greenspan story argued for a decline in risk premium going back to the mid 1990s. While it is true that the data points to an acceleration of the net worth to income ratio (Fig. 26.1), the same data points to a secular increase in the ratio dating back to the late 1970s. As we will show in the next few paragraphs, our interpretation of the data suggests that there is more than risk in this story. Some of it is due to monetary policy as the Maestro correctly pointed out in his speech:

> I acknowledge that monetary policy itself has been an important contributor to the decline in inflation and inflation expectations over the past quarter-century. Indeed, the Federal Reserve under Paul Volcker's leadership starting in 1979 did the very heavy lifting against inflation. The major contribution of the Federal Reserve to fashioning the events of the past decade or so, I believe, was to recognize that the U.S. and global economies were evolving in profound ways and to calibrate inflation-containing policies to gain most effectively from those changes.

The reduction in the inflation rate and the corresponding decline in yields have lengthened investors' horizons. As the inverse of the bond yields is a proxy for the value of a dollar in perpetuity, the inverse of the bond yield may be interpreted in several ways. One is as a measure of the investor's horizon and the other is as the minimum P/E ratio for a profitable ongoing concern. From the 1960s to 1985, the 10-year bond yield experienced a secular decline and a corresponding shortening of the investors' horizons. Since then, partially as a result of the Volcker operating procedures, bond yields have been on a secular downtrend and that has increased investors horizons. There have been cyclical fluctuations in the yields, which we attribute to the policy mix being implemented at that time, a topic that we now focus.

The data reported in Fig. 26.2 shows that the inverse of the bond yield and the net worth to disposable income ratio both trend together and the relationship is much stronger during the 1970s when the data fits like a glove. Beyond the 1980s, the data suggests that the increase in the wealth to disposable income ratio is higher than the inverse of the bond yields would suggest. What causes this disparity at or around 1980? And who can explain it?

We believe that we can. The Greenspan and the inverse of the bond yield story focuses solely on the discount factor of a valuation model (i.e., the denominator). It says nothing about the growth of after-tax earnings (i.e., the numerator). The latter is the clue to the disparity in the two series.

Our explanation for the various inflection points in the series is quite simple. Let's begin with the Nixon years. He took the US off gold and devalued the dollar; therefore, the inflation rate began a steady ascent. Tax rates, regulations, and bracket creep also increased during this time. Worse yet, US energy policies inadvertently made it the most important member of the cartel. It steered all the incremental demand for energy to sweet crude and there was one producer of sweet oil. The regulations reduced the US economy's ability to substitute out of these fuels, and as the demand increased and became more inelastic, the Organization of Petroleum Exporting Countries (OPEC) monopoly power increased and they exploited it [2]. The oil shock had adverse effects on the US economy. Valuation declined relative to disposable income. The inflection point for the US economy began in late 1979 when Paul Volcker changed the Fed's operating procedures. Shortly after, Ronald Reagan was elected president and he followed through on his promise to lower marginal tax rates and reduce regulations. Unfortunately, the tax rate cuts were phased in and that introduced incentives to delay income recognition and production. The US economy experienced a recession. But once the tax rates and Volcker's operating procedures were fully in place, the US economy took off. Real GDP grew at better than 3% every year up to the millennium, with the exception being the Bush read my lips episode (Fig. 26.3). Reagan's tax rate cuts increased after-tax income.

Once both tax rate cuts took effect, two things happened. There was a surge in earnings and the lower tax rate further increased the keep rate. Notice that in the early 1990s the United States experienced two tax rate increases. However, during the same time the Fed was lowering the inflation rate which, in effect, reduced the

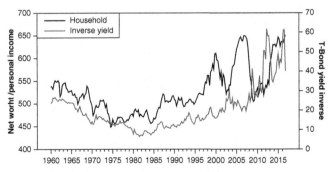

FIGURE 26.2 Household net worth as a percent of disposable income versus the inverse of the 10-year government bond yield.

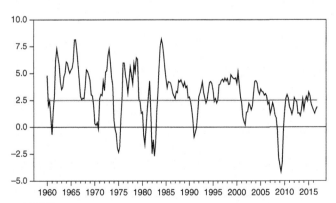

FIGURE 26.3 Real GDP growth rate (trailing 4 quarters).

effective tax rate on capital gains and minimized the impact of bracket creep. The net worth to income ratio moved sideways (Fig. 26.2). Once the Republicans took over Congress, gridlock and the Greenspan monetary policy were the elixir that the economy and financial markets needed. These are the so-called bubble years and low risk premium that the Maestro was talking about.

The game abruptly came to an end with the bubble bursting. Did the Fed have a hand in the bubble bursting? While it is true that the Enrons and other companies cheated and misstated their earnings, the Fed also provided excess liquidity in anticipation of Y2K and then rapidly withdrew the liquidity early in 2000. That is why some people argue that the Fed had a hand in the bubble bursting. Maybe Sir Alan learned a lesson and has now become an advocate of "measured responses" which allows the Fed to telegraph its intentions.

The election of George W. Bush initiated another cycle. The US economy began to recover, but the recovery was a weak one. The economy did not pick up its swagger until the Bush administration proposed the unification and reduction of the capital gains and dividend tax rates. The pickup in economic activity, higher earnings, and a lower discount rate, plus the administration's push for increased home ownership all contributed to the turbo-charging of the markets. Eventually the bubble burst and the economy went into recession.

The Fed acted admirably and prevented a full-blown deflation. Newly elected President Obama pushed and got a stimulus package. During his administration, taxes and regulations have steadily increased at the margin, yet the impact on the dividend and capital gains has been less than on ordinary income. As with the previous downturns, the net worth to disposable income ratio eventually recovered and reached the previous high. Unfortunately, the pace of economic activity had not hit its previous stride. It had not surpassed the 3% mark that was easily surpassed during the previous 25 years. One implication of this result is that all of the efforts by the monetary authority to stimulate the economy have coincided with the strong recovery of the financial markets, yet the real economy or real GDP recovery was been a sub-par one. Does this suggest that monetary policy does not have a real meaningful impact on real variables? Does it mean that the increased regularity burden, the higher taxes, and the expansion of the social safety net have all had a negative effect on incentives to work and produce? The conclusion is that the assignment of policy instruments to the different policy objectives matters a great deal. Looking at previous experiences, assigning monetary policy to the price stability objective and fiscal policy to the real economy was the winning assignment. The choice of the price rule, lower taxes, and regulations was a winning formula for Republicans and Democrats.

References

[1] https://www.federalreserve.gov/boarddocs/speeches/2005/20050826/default.htm
[2] Canto Victor A, Bollman Gerald, Melich Kevin. Oil decontrol: the power of incentives could reduce OPEC's power to boost oil prices. Oil Gas J 1982;80(2):92–101.

CHAPTER

27

Transparency and Rule-Based Monetary Policy

In spite of the dual mandate, the Fed has stated its opposition to a rule-based monetary policy on numerous occasions. It clearly favors discretion over a strict rule. Their argument is that they can adjust and take into account changing economic conditions and react before the actual economic data is reported in the press. The advantage of this approach is that the Fed may be able to react much more quickly. The downside is that they may make a forecasting mistake. Recall the joke that economists have forecast 9 out of the last 4 recessions.

The success of the discretionary approach will depend greatly on the ability of the central bank to anticipate shifts in the economy. We have our reservations. These are the same people who missed the onset of the financial crisis. Another potential mistake is to anticipate and attempt to deal with problems that do not actually materialize. Y2K is one such example. Greenspan was concerned that Y2K would result in a shortage of cash and as a result the Maestro flooded the market with cash to meet a potential need caused by a problem that never materialized. In the aftermath, to correct the forecast error, the Fed proceeded to quickly withdraw the excess cash and that may have contributed to the shallow recession at the century date change as the Maestro called Y2K.

Transparency issues also interact with the active/passive monetary policy debate. Under a passive rule, the mechanism for intervening and adjusting monetary policy to real economic shocks is outlined in advance. Hence, in this case, the system is fully transparent. However, under an active rule, being obtuse can increase the short-term impact of monetary disturbances. The reason for this is that investors and other economic agents have a more difficult time separating the impact of real and monetary disturbances. The secrecy of the Federal Open Market Committee (FOMC) meeting and other actions were clearly intended to obfuscate. This was clearly the intent during the Maestro's leadership. Here is what he said in response to a question:

> I know you believe you understand what you think I said, but I'm not sure you realise that what you heard is not what I meant. [1]

The obfuscation was intentional. The absence of transparency may be desirable to effectively reverse the effects of underside shifts in the demand for money that were not anticipated by the monetary authorities. Any action by the Fed that is not anticipated by the markets would have a larger short-run impact on the economy. But this does not necessarily mean that unanticipated is the way to go; there are benefits to being transparent. A fully anticipated monetary action may lead to a much faster market-clearing process and thereby a faster impact on the nominal variables, such as interest rates and the price level.

Economic Disturbances and Equilibrium in an Integrated Global Economy. http://dx.doi.org/10.1016/B978-0-12-813993-6.00027-1

DECONSTRUCTING MONETARY POLICY

Looking back, the Greenspan monetary policy can be deconstructed into several components. The Maestro believed that he could anticipate and accommodate most of the shifts in the demand for money, thereby maintaining price stability, that is, keeping the US inflation rate around the Fed's stated target rate. He also believed in obfuscation, which would allow the Fed to quickly reverse adverse shocks that he had not accounted for, hopefully before the market took note of his actions. As already mentioned, his record was not perfect. He correctly identified the productivity surge, but he also overstated the effect of Y2K on the demand for money. Overall, the Greenspan era was one of price stability and strong growth. If one uses the Humphrey–Hawkins mandate to judge his tenure at the Fed, one has to conclude that he did a great job.

ANTICIPATING MONETARY RESPONSES

The financial press is quite fond of reporting before every meeting that some members of the FOMC believe that the economy may be ready for a rate increase while others do not. These insinuations and the Fed deliberations always lead us to ask the following question: What does the Fed know that the markets do not know? The markets and private sector have an interesting signal extraction problem. How does the market extract the relevant information? To do so, we need information on several variables. The first step is identifying economic disturbances and their impact on the Fed objectives. Once the objectives, disturbances, and the framework used by the Fed are identified, it is relatively easy to forecast the Fed's monetary response.

The Disturbance: Previous press reports had raised several interesting questions. Considering the economic data at the time of the report, the economy was expanding at a 2.3% annual rate of growth during the second quarter of the year and a year-over-year inflation rate well below the 2% target rate. The economic performance of the economy had some people wondering as to why the Fed would choose to act.

The Objectives: When pressed on why the Fed was likely to raise interest rates in spite of the below target inflation and underwhelming real GDP growth rate in an interview by the *Wall Street Journal*, Atlanta Fed President Dennis Lockhart pointed to the so-called dual mandate [2]. The mandate, which has its origin in the 1978 legislation known as the Humphrey–Hawkins Full Employment Act, was based on the economic principles found in the Keynesian framework. The act explicitly mandates the Board of Governors of the Federal Reserve to establish a monetary policy that maintains long-run growth, minimizes inflation, and promotes price stability. It also requires the president to set numerical goals for the economy for the next fiscal year in the *Economic Report of the President* and to suggest policies that will achieve these goals. In addition, it requires the Chairman of the Federal Reserve to connect the monetary policy with the presidential economic policy. Hence the dual mandate. Finally, the act also instructs the Board of Governors of the Federal Reserve to transmit a *Monetary Policy Report to Congress* twice a year, outlining its monetary policy. Mr. Lockhart left no doubt as to what the Fed objectives were:

> Grounded in the dual mandate, the employment picture I would say continues to improve satisfactorily and the inflation picture obviously remains below target and affected at a headline level by continuing change in oil prices that play through to gasoline prices.

The Monetary Policy Framework: Regarding the issue as to whether the Fed should act, here is what Mr. Lockhart had to say:

> We are in a fuzzy middle if you want to use that term, because there has not been a clear breakout of wage acceleration; there has not been a lot of clarity around the inflation forecast; and growth is in the moderate range of 2% to 2.5% or 2.75%, but not right up against the 3% we were hoping would be the case in 2015.

The basis for the suggestion that the Fed should act are grounded in the Keynesian economic framework upon which many of the policymakers at the Fed make their policy decisions and recommendations, which assumes that price pressures will increase as the economy approaches full employment. Mr. Lockhart invoked the work of A.W. Phillips on the relationship between inflation and unemployment, known as the Phillips Curve [3]. Soon after the publication of Phillips' paper, the idea that there was a trade-off between a strong economy and low inflation caught the imagination of academic economists and policymakers alike. Milton Friedman, in his presidential address to the American Economic Association, argued that there is no long-run trade-off [4].

Some economists have also questioned the empirical validity of this relationship, whether this relationship has held over time or not. Yet in spite of this, Mr. Lockhart was openly advocating the Phillips Curve. When one looks at the data mentioned in the previous quote, it is evident that in the context of the Phillips Curve and the target inflation and real GDP growth rate, the data was not compelling enough in favor of taking monetary action. Mr. Lockhart's response was as follows:

> One of the key points I think is that in the absence of direct evidence that inflation is in fact converging to the target and in the absence of compelling or convincing direct evidence, I think

a policy maker has to act on the view that the basic relationship in the Phillips Curve between inflation and employment will assert itself in a reasonable period of time as the economy tightens up, as the resource picture in the economy tightens.

When asked how comfortable he was doing that, here is his response:

> I am quite confident that that basic expectation will materialize.

The quote expresses a firm belief in the Phillips Curve, even if the data does not support it. The response is interesting as it suggests that when the data fits the model, the Phillips Curve will dominate the Fed's response.

The issue of rules versus discretion is also implicit in Mr. Lockhart's response. His response is quite explicit when he stated that as long as he believed that the economy would eventually move to Phillips Curve relationship, which he does, then he would respond according to the Phillips Curve even if the current data did not support the relationship nor warrant it. This response puts him squarely in the active or discretion camp.

A CONCERN: CAN THE FED REPLICATE ITS PRECRISIS SUCCESS?

The relationship between the inflation rate and the pace of economic activity is not independent of monetary policy. If, as we believe, inflation is a monetary phenomenon, then the Fed controls the monetary emission. In principle, it can control the underlying inflation rate. More importantly, how the Fed specifies the rule for printing money will determine the economy's inflation rate and its relation to the economy's growth rate.

For example, if the Fed followed a price rule prior to the millennium financial crisis/Y2K (as we claim), one would expect to see an inflation rate around the target rate irrespective of the real GDP growth rate and/or unemployment rate. We would expect to see a mean reverting inflation rate around the target inflation rate. If that is the case, there would little or no correlation to the real GDP growth rate. Fig. 27.1A shows that this appears to be the case during the 1982–99 period. Perhaps the exception being the surge in productivity and bubble-related years at the end of the period. This is the time period we believe that the Maestro began to deviate from the rules and instead believed more in himself than the rules and chose discretion over a rule-oriented process. However, this lack of correlation does not disprove either the Keynesian Phillips Curve or monetarist propositions. Instead, it only shows that by adopting a price-rule policy (i.e., inflation rate targeting), the Fed can alter the correlation between the inflation rate and real GDP growth rate.

We contend that Y2K took the Greenspan Fed off the price rule and the economy gradually moved to a Phillips Curve type of rule during the last few years of the Greenspan Fed and the bulk of the Bernanke Fed. The rule for money printing under a Phillips Curve is simple: if the economy slows down, so will the prices, and the downward pressure is reversed by printing money. The increase in money, according to the Phillips Curve, results in higher inflation and higher output. According to the Phillips Curve, one should observe a positive correlation between inflation and the real GDP growth rate. Fig. 27.1B shows a positive correlation, suggesting that the relevant framework during the 2001–07 time period was the Phillips Curve, hence the positive correlation.

The financial crisis changed the monetary game. The integrity of the monetary and financial system became a major concern. The crisis reduced the credit worthiness of the borrowers, as well as the capital adequacy of the banks. All of this resulted in a collapse of the money multiplier. Bank credit collapsed and absent an injection

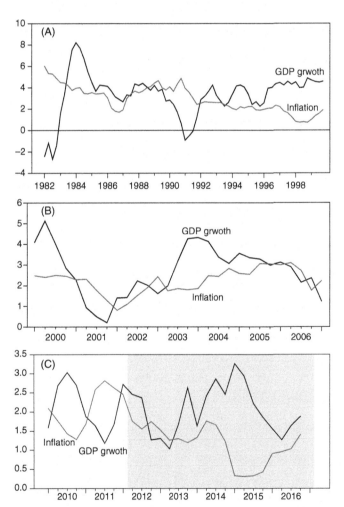

FIGURE 27.1 **Real GDP growth versus inflation.** (A) The price rule period: 1982–99. (B) The Phillips Curve period: 2000–07. (C) The postcrisis monetary policy: 2010–16.

of cash into the economy, the financial system could have easily collapsed. The name of the game became to generate an increase in the nominal price of financial assets to increase the net worth and capital adequacy of the banks, while at the same time implementing a delevering of the banking system. In this regard, the Fed departed from both the price rule and the Philips Curve. Helicopter Ben knew that inflation was a monetary phenomenon and by flooding the market with cash, he prevented a deflationary spiral. Immediately after the crash the monetarist view reigned supreme. As the economy recovered, given the flood of money, the demand for money would increase and the inflation rate would decline. An economic slowdown would produce the opposite effect. The data in Fig. 27.1C shows that in the years immediately after the crisis, say 2010–12, the correlation between inflation and real GDP is a negative one, as expected. However, as the economy recovered, Helicopter Ben remorphed into a Phillips Curve Keynesian. The Yellen Fed, as suggested by Mr. Lockhart's interview, lends support to the view that the Fed was operating on a Phillips Curve basis.

All of this brings us back to the quote in Mr. Lockhart's statement, which we repeat here:

We are in a fuzzy middle if you want to use that term, because there has not been a clear breakout of wage acceleration; there has not been a lot of clarity around the inflation forecast; and growth is in the moderate range of 2% to 2.5% or 2.75%, but not right up against the 3% we were hoping would be the case in 2015.

In spite of this, he believes in the relationship and he believes that it will materialize. The irony of all this is that, if our analysis is correct, the relationship need not materialize, if the Fed does its job and simply target the inflation rate. Monetary policy can insure price stability, even in an expanding economy. The 1982–99 time periods proves it (Fig. 27.1A). This leads us to question whether the Fed can or will return back to these golden years.

References

[1] Rupert C. Alan Greenspan: the buck starts here. Independent April 26, 2003;.
[2] Wall St J August 4, 2015.
[3] Phillips AW. The relationship between unemployment and the rate of change of money and wages in the United Kingdom 1861–1957. Economica 1958;25(200):283–99.
[4] Friedman M. The role of monetary policy. Am Econ Rev 1967;68(1):1–17.

28

A Single or Dual Mandate

There is always talk and speculation in the financial press regarding how the Fed will act at the next FOMC meeting. The pundits and analysts discuss whether or not the economy is ready for an increase in short-term interest rates, etc. Although, we have no direct knowledge as to how the Fed will act, we can safely say that the answer to the previous question depends in part on the basic framework adopted by the Fed members, in particular, the chairperson. The adopted framework will largely determine how the Fed reacts to the economic shocks and overall performance of the US economy.

The monetarists argue that inflation is too much money chasing too few goods. Hence, the recipe for price stability is a simple one: make sure that there is not too much or too little money chasing the goods and services. In a dynamic context, this can be achieved in one of two ways. If one knows the economy's long-term growth rate, then by setting or controlling money growth, one can control the long-term domestic inflation rate. Under this scenario, which we call the quantity rule, the central bank targets the growth of the monetary aggregates.

An alternative to monetary targeting is what has become known as the price rule. It would work as follows: when the inflation rate exceeds the monetary authority upper target range, the Fed withdraws money from the economy through open market operations. As the quantity of money decreases, so will the underlying inflation rate. The Fed keeps doing so until the inflation rate returns to its target range. When the inflation rate falls below the target range, the Fed adds to the quantity of money by buying bonds in the open market.

The dual mandate, that is, targeting the unemployment and inflation rates, presents a potential problem for the monetary authorities. If money is only a veil, the dual mandate is doomed to fail. Attempts to affect the long-run growth rate will be unsuccessful. The only effect of the monetary actions will be on the price level. But that is not all. Under these conditions, the additional objective, that is, the unemployment rate, only adds noise to the monetary policy resulting in a more variable and volatile inflation rate. The higher uncertainty will have a negative impact on market valuation and quite possibly the economy.

If, on the other hand, monetary policy can affect the real economy, the dual mandate poses a different set of problems than the one raised in the previous paragraph. The new problem is that the Fed is one instrument short. The policymakers, that is, the monetary authorities, need at least two different policy instruments, money and something else, if they are to target and successfully achieve two independent policy objectives—the inflation rate and real GDP growth. The Phillips Curve produces a nice and elegant solution that ameliorates the problem. By postulating a relationship or trade-off between the unemployment and inflation rates, the Phillips Curve suggests that the monetary authorities can pick a point along the trade-off relationship. Hence, we get back to one instrument picking the most desirable combination. However, this solution is still subject to the criticism that the combination of the fastest real GDP growth rate and price stability may not be feasible or available according to the Phillips Curve trade-off function. This does not even mention the fact that the monetarists feel that there is no trade-off; in which case, we need to find a policy objective to be assigned to the real GDP growth rate. One potential instrument is none other than fiscal policy.

Economic Disturbances and Equilibrium in an Integrated Global Economy. http://dx.doi.org/10.1016/B978-0-12-813993-6.00028-3

THE INTERACTION BETWEEN THE MANDATES AND THE ORGANIZATION OF THE MONETARY SYSTEM

Let's begin by looking at some of the underlying variables and building blocks related to the textbook Keynesian Phillips Curve framework. Fig. 28.1 shows the relationship between the economy's capacity utilization and unemployment rates. One can see that, in general, the two variables are mirror images of each other, as expected. As they provide similar information, in what follows, the variable we will use will depend on which variable simplifies the visual presentation.

Fig. 28.2 shows the relationship between the inflation rate and the economy's capacity utilization rate. The data show a strong and positive relationship between the two variables as predicted by the Phillips Curve prior to 1980. One possible explanation for the differences in the closeness of the relationship may be the organization of the monetary system. For example, under a strict price rule, fluctuations in economic activity and other shifts in money demand will be automatically accommodated, and no long-term effects on the inflation rate will be observed. Notice that from 1985 to the millennium, the inflation rate oscillated around the Fed's 2% target rate, while the capacity utilization rate oscillated quite a bit

without a discernable correlation pattern between the two variables during the period. This clearly suggests that the organization of the monetary system affects the relationship between real economic shocks and the inflation rate. However, during the other periods, there is a clear and positive correlation between capacity utilization and the underlying inflation rate.

Fig. 28.3A presents graphical information on the inflation rate and average unemployment rate, while Table 28.1 presents the average unemployment rate, inflation rate, and Misery Index for different periods during which the operating procedures of the Fed have varied. The first one spans the tail end of the Bretton Woods system, which was from 1960 to 1970. The second one begins with the Nixon devaluation and unhinging of the gold exchange standard and adoption of a monetary rule that targeted the monetary aggregate rule. Then late in 1979, Paul Volcker changed the operating procedures of the Fed, but it was not until the early 1980s that his version of the price rule became operational. The last period begins with the financial crisis. In theory, if the Phillips Curve holds, one would expect to see a negative relationship between the two variables. The lower the unemployment rate, the higher the inflation rate should be. The one interesting result from the data is that the average annual unemployment

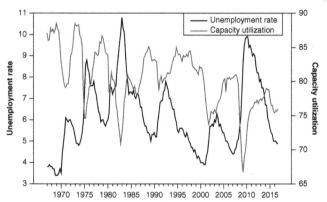

FIGURE 28.1　Capacity utilization and the unemployment rate.

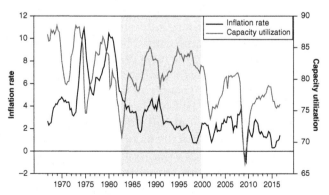

FIGURE 28.2　Capacity utilization and the inflation rate.

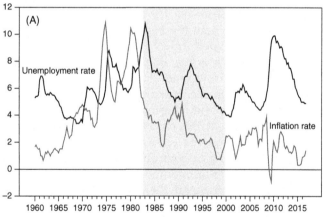

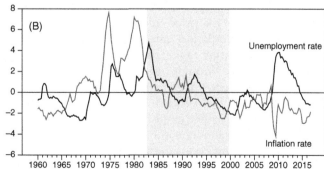

FIGURE 28.3　(A) Unemployment and inflation rates and (B) excess unemployment and inflation rates.

TABLE 28.1 Misery Index and its Components

	Misery Index	Unemployment Rate	Inflation
1960–70	7.13	4.79	2.34
1971–79	12.7	6.36	6.34
1980–81	16.52	7.13	9.39
1982–99	9.39	6.46	2.93
2000–07	7.27	5.02	2.25
2008–09	8.6	7.13	1.47
2010–16	8.75	7.3	1.45
1960–2016	9.33	6.07	3.26

and inflation rates both increase during the quantity rule period, 1970–79, as opposed to the price rule period, 1982–99, when both decline. This pattern points to a positive correlation between the two variables. A rising unemployment rate is associated with a rising inflation rate. The changes in period's averages are the opposite of what the Phillips Curve posits. More importantly, one can notice that during the price rule, the inflation rates and unemployment rates fluctuate in a trading range. In contrast, during the quantity rule periods (i.e., 1970–79), when the Fed targeted the monetary aggregates, the inflation rate and the unemployment rate were both well above-average. The last time period is the one that fits the Phillips Curve; notice that the average unemployment rate increased while the average inflation rate declined. Hence, the period averages support the hypothesis that the Fed is operating on a dual mandate and that its basic framework is none other than the Phillips Curve.

Fig. 28.3B presents the unemployment and inflation rates net of their sample averages. Now the relationship becomes much clearer. During the 1970–79 time period, the peaks and through of the two series move in the opposite direction, that is, they are negatively correlated, as posited by the Phillips Curve. However, as variants of the price rule were adopted, in 1960–69 and 1982–99, the two series tend to move together, the amplitude of their fluctuations declines, and the correlation between the peaks and troughs is not as discernible. What is clearly evident is that the inflation rate leads the unemployment rate. Fig. 28.3B also shows that in the aftermath of the financial crisis, the 2007–15 period, that while the correlation between the two variables is positive, the inflation rate no longer led the unemployment rate. This information points to the importance of understanding the monetary arrangements.

Fig. 28.4A through D shows scatter plots describing the combination of excess unemployment and inflation rates calculated by subtracting the sample averages from

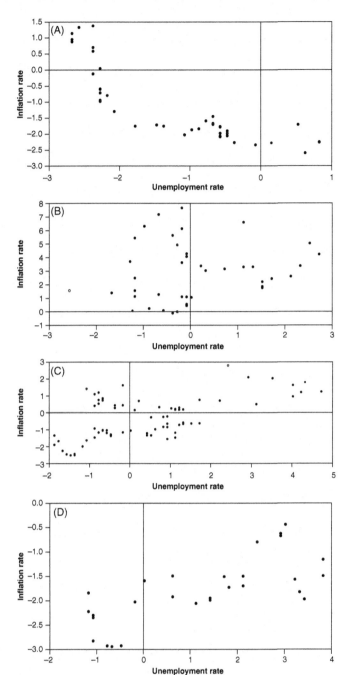

FIGURE 28.4 Excess unemployment and inflation rates. (A) Bretton Woods: 1960–69, (B) quantity rule period: 1970–79, (C) domestic price rule period: 1982–99, and (D) post-financial crisis period: 2010–16.

the quarterly unemployment and inflation rates during the four different time periods considered.

Although the sample is small, the period signaling the end of the Bretton Woods gold exchange standard, Fig. 28.4A, does not identify any systematic relationship between the variables. This is disappointing to the advocates of the Phillips Curve, but it is not difficult to explain once the organization of the monetary system is taken into account. Under a gold exchange standard, the private sector has the ability to offset monetary action of the central bank. Under these conditions, the unemployment rate will be uncorrelated to the steady inflation rate, which is exactly what happened during most of the period. On the other hand, if the central bank does not heed, the private sector loses international reserves, and eventually it will either reverse course or abandon the gold exchange system. That is precisely what happened to the United States, it experienced a massive loss of reserves, and President Nixon closed the gold window and moved to a fiat standard and declared that we were all Keynesians. The 1970s were not kind to the US inflation rate; the decade average annual inflation rate rose to 6.34% from 2.34% during the 1960s. During the same time, the unemployment rate rose to an annual average of 6.36% from an annual average of 4.79% during the 1960s. Fig. 28.4B shows that during the 1970s the relationship between the inflation rate and the unemployment rate is as predicted by the Phillips Curve.

Notice that the majority of the unemployment rate and inflation combinations consist of the following: a combination of high unemployment rate and low inflation rate, that is, clockwise the top left quadrant in Fig. 28.4B. It is also worth noting that during this time period, the Fed had adopted a fiat standard and targeted the monetary aggregates, something that proved to be a daunting task. The return to a price rule environment produced positive results. The average annual inflation rate declined to 2.93% from 6.34% during the prior decade. Also as with the gold exchange standard, the domestic price rule period produced no systematic relationship between the unemployment rate and the inflation rates. This result is not unexpected to the advocates of the price rule. Successfully targeting the inflation rate means that real fluctuations in the economy will have no impact on the underlying inflation rate, and, hence, there will be no systematic correlation. That is precisely what happened.

In contrast, the combinations of high unemployment rate/high inflation rate (second quadrant), as well as low inflation/low unemployment rates (fourth quadrant), are not contemplated in the textbook Phillips Curve relationship. Put another way, the Phillips Curve cannot explain stagflation or a deflationary expansion. More importantly, the same information presented in Fig. 28.4D does not show a downward sloping trend, that is, lower unemployment and higher inflation.

EVALUATING THE POST-CRISIS MONETARY POLICY

The evidence presented here suggests that the relationship between the unemployment rate and the inflation rate is not invariant to the organization of the monetary system. This suggests that the choice of operating procedures is of paramount importance to the economy's inflation rate and quite possibly the unemployment rate. Once the Fed adopts some version of a price rule, be it a domestic price rule that targets the inflation rate or a gold exchange rate standard, the inflation rate tends to be uncorrelated with the unemployment rate. However, the adoption of a price rule or any of its variant also means that the Fed is focusing solely on one mandate, the inflation rate. Once this is evident, then investors will have a better chance of anticipating or deciphering the Fed signals regarding its prospective actions.

Under the arguments and evidence presented here, the possibility of a Phillips Curve relationship being observed empirically requires that the Fed pursues a dual mandate. Unfortunately, while this is a necessary condition, it is not a sufficient condition for the Phillips Curve to be observed empirically. The relationship of the unemployment and inflation rate does not fit the Phillips Curve inflation unemployment relationship. This is true whether one focuses on the relationships between the sample average inflation and unemployment rates (Fig. 28.3A) or the deviations from the sample averages (Fig. 28.3B) or the scatter plot (Fig. 28.4D).

In conclusion, the data presented suggest that the post-financial crisis Fed operating procedures are not based on a true price rule, and more likely than not, the behavior of the Fed resembles one mandated by the Phillips Curve dual mandate framework. The Fed behavior in the aftermath of the crisis has been quite different than its crisis response. One possible explanation for this anomaly is that the Fed flooded the market with money to prevent a deflationary spiral; if that is the case, then kudos to the Fed. It prevented a deflationary spiral and brought the inflation rate to a level slightly below the average inflation rate for the period. Once the deflation stopped, the economy began recovering and the unemployment rate declined; with the inflation rate holding steady, Fig. 28.3B would show a leftward movement along a near horizontal line, which between 2009 and 2014 it does. This interpretation of the data suggests that if there is a Phillips Curve, the discretionary Fed policies overwhelmed the Phillips Curve effect in the period immediately following the financial crisis.

29

The Demise of the Global Price Rule

The 2009 G-7 meeting was an extraordinary meeting. The United States persuaded the world's industrial powers to endorse flexible currency exchange rates. The move was clearly a jab at Japan and China, as well as a signal to the world that the G-7 countries were willing to engage in mercantilists beggar-thy-neighbor policies that could lead to the ratcheting up of the worldwide inflation rate. Some of these issues continue to this day. Then there are the central banks with inflation target mandates facing criticism that they are not doing enough to stimulate the local economy when nothing could be further from the truth. Keeping the inflation rate within the mandated target is the central bankers' goal for the countries whose central banks have an inflation target or single mandate.

The experience of the 1970s showed us that an unhinged monetary policy accompanied by deliberate monetary devaluations only lead to inflation and does not have a long-term effect on a country's trade balance. It was sad to see nations going down the wrong path. In the case of many developed economies, and in particular the European ones, the failure of the continent's economies to reach a real GDP growth rate in the 2%–3% range cannot be attributed to monetary policy. Rather it was attributable to the euroesclerosis produced by a dirigiste economic policy with a Keynesian bent.

If the United States and other countries abandon inflation targeting, their inflation will become more volatile and perhaps slightly higher. The implication for the rest of the world could be very damaging especially for the smaller economies who fix their currencies to larger economies. By fixing to the US dollar and/or the Euro,

other countries are effectively importing the monetary policies of the United States and the European Economic and Monetary Union (EMU). Hong Kong is a prime example of what we are talking about. Our concerns for the rest of the world are twofold. First, we see the inflation rate rising and becoming more erratic in both the United States and the EMU, if the two regions' central banks abandon their inflation targeting. Second, by forcing the rest of the world to float their currencies, the G-7 was in effect forcing the countries to decouple themselves from the stable inflation rate that both the United States and the EMU have enjoyed. The experience of the 1970s taught us that countries with depreciating currencies tend to have a higher inflation than the countries with the appreciating currencies. We are not calling for double-digit inflation, we are just making the point that a higher inflation rate is not good for long-term fixed income securities.

THE ELEMENTS OF THE GLOBAL PRICE RULE

The global price rule has two distinct components. One or more countries will in general adopt a domestic price rule. Operationally, the domestic price rule is quite simple. Whenever the domestic prices exceed those of a target range, the central bank will, through open market operations, remove domestic money from circulation. The central bank will sell bonds in the open market and receive cash in exchange. As we believe that inflation is too much money chasing too few goods, the reduction

Economic Disturbances and Equilibrium in an Integrated Global Economy. http://dx.doi.org/10.1016/B978-0-12-813993-6.00029-5

in the high-powered money circulating the economy should lower the domestic price level. During periods in which the price level falls below the target range, the central bank increases the amount of money circulating in the economy by buying bonds in the open market. As the government pays for the bonds by printing money, the higher quantity of money leads to an increase in the domestic price level.

The price rule adjustment mechanism is general enough to accommodate several variants. The one favored by us is based on the domestic Consumer Price Index (CPI), while another version focuses on the price of gold. Either way, the price rule provides for an automatic adjustment mechanism for increasing and reducing the money supply.

Other countries, if they choose to, could adopt the price rule of another country by simply fixing their exchange rate to that of the country whose price rule they want to adopt. To see this, consider the operating mechanism. Whenever the exchange rate depreciates, the satellite country's central bank, that is, the nonreserve currency country, would have to reduce the quantity of domestic currency circulating. The lower quantity of domestic money will lead to an appreciation of the currency and eventually the currency would reach its target range.

Next, let's assume an absence of transportation costs and/or trade restrictions in the economy. Under these idealized conditions, arbitrage insures that the dollar price of a given commodity is the same in the two localities. If the exchange rate remains fixed, it follows that the rate of price increases of the traded commodities has to be the same in the two economies. Alternatively stated, the inflation rate will be the same in the two economies.

The exchange rate is a simple way for a country to adopt another country's monetary policy. In doing so, the country is importing the reserve currency country's inflation rate. In the case of the reserve currency country, there are several choices for conducting its own monetary. The one we prefer, the domestic price rule, provides an automatic adjustment mechanism that keeps the underlying inflation rate within a specified target range.

WHAT COULD GO WRONG?

The domestic price rule is not immune to misinterpretations and misapplications. One particular case that concerns us is when the central bank accumulates a large reserve of the commodity used to implement the price rule. To show our concerns, let us consider the case where the central bank has no accumulated inventory of the commodity in question. Let's also assume that all the central bank has is a printing press and a furnace. Then every time the prices get out of line, the central bank has

to fire up the printing press or the furnace to bring the prices in line. In this case, the adjustment is automatic and instantaneous.

Next consider the case where the central bank has an accumulated inventory of the commodity in question. If we also assume that the central bank's inventory is large enough to affect the market price, the question then is what happens when the currency value falls below the target price? We know that equilibrium is restored when the currency value is brought back in line with the target range. There are two ways this can be accomplished. The proper and sustainable way is to withdraw money from the system through an open market operation, like the one described earlier. However such a procedure may be interpreted as contractionary as the central bank would be withdrawing money from the system. For this reason, some politicians may prefer an alternative way to bring temporary equilibrium: selling part of the inventory of the commodity held by the central bank. Doing so will increase the supply of the commodity and thus lower its market price, thereby bringing the money price of the commodity back into the target range.

The problem with the second approach is that eventually the central bank will run out of reserves and as soon as it becomes clear that this is the case there may be a problem, a speculative attack will be mounted against the intervention mechanism. That is exactly what happened to the United States under Bretton Woods. The United States did not adjust its money supply to bring the price of gold back into equilibrium. Instead it chose to adjust the supply of gold in the market by selling gold. When it became clear that the United States did not have enough gold, other countries (like France under the leadership of Charles de Gaulle) began demanding payment in gold rather than in dollars. As the United States began depleting its reserves, instead of adjusting its monetary policy and reducing the money supply, the Fed ultimately refused to exchange the dollars for gold. The gold window was closed and there was no anchor or restraint to the US monetary policy. As the unhinging of the system progressed, so did the US inflation rate and interest rates. The rest of the world did not fare much better, especially the countries who embarked in a truly floating exchange rate. The inflation experience was, on average, worse than that of the United States. The spiraling inflation did not come to an end until the operating procedures of the Fed changed.

Under the leadership of Paul Volcker, the United States abandoned targeting the quantity of money and focused instead on a domestic price rule. Inflation began to decline and so did interest rates. The secular decline in inflation fueled a bull market in bonds that lasted over 20 years. Many of the emerging countries in the world also changed their operating procedures and targeted some of the major currencies in the world. In doing so, they adopted those countries' inflation rates. Worldwide inflation declined as the price rule propagated among the world central banks.

NONRESERVE CURRENCY ISSUES

Monetary problems are not unique to the reserve currency countries. In many respects, the countries adopting an exchange rate rule also face similar issues. If they accumulate foreign exchange, they have to be careful of how they intervene in the foreign exchange market. If they use the reserves to maintain some independence within their domestic monetary policy, eventually the country will be subject to a speculative attack. If the central bank breaks, devaluation will ensue and domestic inflation will rise matching the amount of the devaluation. Examples of this abound. During the 1990s, the world experienced the Tequila Effect, the Asian Contagion, and the Russian crisis among others. All of these countries' experiences showed that whenever the domestic central banks began tinkering with the domestic price rule, by spending the inflow of foreign exchange during the good times, they did not have enough to finance the outflow during the bad times. Eventually the speculative attacks on the currency broke the bank and the currencies were devalued, the inflation surged, and the countries experienced a significant setback.

30

The US Inflation Rate

The strict monetarist view assumes that money is only a veil and has no effect on the real economy. The textbook assumptions associated with the monetarist model help us identify the relevant aggregates. The monetarists also assume that the Fed controls the monetary base through open market operations. Through the discount window and reserve requirements, the Fed controls the money multiplier. Another assumption is that the demand for money is stable. (i.e., in the simpler models, velocity is assumed to be constant). A Fourth assumption is that a floating exchange rate isolates the domestic economy from the rest of the world's monetary shocks. The relaxation of these different assumptions gives rise to alternative specifications regarding the appropriate monetary aggregates, as well as the proxies for money demand.

THE DIFFERENT SPECIFICATIONS

The policy implications for the monetarist framework are straightforward: Inflation is a monetary phenomenon, or too much money chasing too few goods. Therefore, according to the strict monetarist view, in order to forecast or explain the US inflation rate, we only need two pieces of information. One is the US real GDP growth, which, holding the money velocity constant, is our proxy for the demand. The other piece of information is the quantity of money, and it is the proxy for the money supply. Since according to this view, the Fed controls all the aggregates, it does not matter which one we use. In what follows, we will use two proxies: a narrow aggregate, the monetary base, and a broader aggregate, M3.

As the monetarist assumptions are relaxed, the proxies for the demand for US dollars and supply of US dollars changes. For example, the Fed controls the monetary base to the decimal point. In turn, the monetary base has two uses. The dollars can be used as either currency or reserves. In formal terms, the two are perfect substitutes in supply. This also means that the Fed does not control how the private sector allocates the base between bank reserves and currency in circulation. This also means that the Fed does not completely control the money multiplier and that, in turn, means that the multiplier can change and potentially offset undesired changes in the monetary base or amplify desired changes in the base. In principle, this makes the narrower aggregate a better proxy for money controlled by the Fed. However, that ignores the organization of the monetary system. Under a price rule, the open market operations are determined by the underlying inflation rate relative to the target rate. The point of all of this is that, if the broader aggregate is endogenous (as we are arguing here), they cannot cause inflation. In fact, the reverse is true. Another insight produced by this analysis is that the broader the aggregate the greater the explanatory power.

One point that we need to make here is that for many of the countries in the world, the financial system and the banking system are not as developed and deep as in the United States; therefore in these countries, the flexibility of the money multiplier may be limited. In simple terms, the central banks may have a better control of the domestic monetary aggregates. But this does not mean that foreign central banks have complete control of the quantity of money circulating in these economies.

Economic Disturbances and Equilibrium in an Integrated Global Economy. http://dx.doi.org/10.1016/B978-0-12-813993-6.00030-1

The traditional models assume that under a floating exchange rate system only local residents use the local money. Implicitly, this assumption assumes that there are legal tender provisions that prevent the use of foreign monies in the local economy. This means that the currencies are not substitutes of each other in the domestic transaction. In technical terms, the monetarist assumes the elasticity of substitution across currencies to be zero. However, we know that foreign currencies circulate and are accepted in many economies of the world, and if the holding of these currencies respond to changes in the relative inflation, we can interpret that as evidence of currency substitution. Viewed from this perspective, it is clear that the case where local residents only hold the local currency is one where the elasticity of substitution is zero.

At the other end of the spectrum, we have the perfect substitutability case. This would be the case under a fixed exchange rate system. The convertibility assures that one country's currency is a good as another. The more general case is when the currencies are imperfect substitutes for each other. In that case, the changes in the income in the rest of the world and the rest of the world's money supply will affect the global demand for US dollars. The parallel here is that of the broader monetary aggregates, currency in circulation and demand deposits are not perfect substitutes in demand. They have slightly different characteristics and or transaction costs associated with their use.

Once the substitution effects among currencies are considered, it is obvious that the local central bank does not control the quantity of money circulating in the economy. This means that the rest of the world's demand for dollars depends on how stable a monetary policy the local central bank runs. Changes in expectations and the actual domestic inflation rate induce the foreign economies to alter their demand for dollars to use in domestic transactions. While each individual country's change may be insignificant relative to the US economy, collectively they may not be. Hence the rest of the world's demand for US dollars to be used in local transactions could have an impact on the US monetary equilibrium, and thus the US inflation rate.

This line of reasoning produces alternative specifications for the estimation of the US inflation rate. They depend critically on the degree of substitutability, at one end of the spectrum if the different currencies are perfect or high substitutes. One specification is based on the world demand for dollars, as opposed to the US demand for dollars. The former assumes a high degree of substitutability among the currencies, be it demand and or supply through a fixed exchange rate system. The narrower aggregate based solely on local money assumes that there is no substitutability among the currencies. This gives rise to three possible specifications for the

demand for dollars. One is to calculate the world income in US dollars, another possibility is to break down the world aggregates into their United States and rest of the world components and the third and final one is to consider only the US aggregates.

THE RESULTS

Using annual data going back to 1980, we estimated the relationship between the US inflation rate and various monetary aggregates and real income measures. Table 30.1 presents the results for the various relationships using different variants of M3, our broader measure of money. The first column is the traditional monetarist inflation equation. The explanatory variables consist of a constant, the growth in the US M3 aggregate and the growth of the US real GDP. There is no evidence of autocorrelation of residuals and the signs of the M3 growth rate and the real GDP growth are consistent with the monetarist view of inflation that a faster M3 growth rate leads to a higher inflation rate, while a faster real GDP growth to a lower inflation rate. Unfortunately, the coefficients are not statistically significant.

The second column of Table 30.1 estimates a different specification that considers the possibility of some substitution effects on the demand for various currencies. If that is the case, the growth in the rest of the world's monetary aggregates and real GDP should have an impact on the U.S. equilibrium. The signs for the domestic M3 growth rate are the opposite of what we expected. However, the signs for the domestic real GDP growth and the foreign real GDP growth are negative. The results are consistent with the view that the higher real GDP growth rate here and abroad increases the demand for money and thereby produces a lower inflation rate. While our interpretation is interesting, the results are not statistically significant at the usual confidence levels.

The third column is the most ambitious one. It assumes that there is one world money market and that the US inflation rate is determined by the world money supply measured in dollars and the world real GDP growth. Here we get some incremental good news. The world real GDP growth has a negative and statistically significant impact on the US inflation rate. The coefficient for M3 is positive as expected. However, as before, the coefficient for M3 is not statistically significant.

Are these results disappointing? Not to us. They are consistent with the view that M3 is mostly endogenously determined and as a result of interest rate paid at the margin on M3, the aggregate is indexed against inflation and unaffected by it. If that is the case there is no reason to expect that M3 would have any significant relationship to the inflation rate. This discussion suggests that we need to focus on an aggregate under the

TABLE 30.1 US Inflation Rate and M3

R-squared	0.026	0.1	0.1
P-value	0.00025	0.01	
Constant	**2.79**	**3.26**	**3.02**
t-stat	**3.2**	**3.52**	**6.97**
US M3 growth	0.087	−0.002	
t-stat	0.69	−0.01	
US real GDP growth	−0.091	−0.09	
t-stat	−0.57	−0.57	
Rest of the world M3 growth		0.03	
t-stat		0.88	
Rest of the world GDP growth		−0.08	
t-stat		−1.54	
World real GDP growth			**−0.12**
t-stat			**−1.82**
World M3 growth			0.06
t-stat			1.03

The values in bold are statistically significant at the usual confidence levels.

potential control of the monetary authorities, such as the monetary base. Although not reported, the results using the monetary base instead of M3 are even less significant.

A FINAL THOUGHT

It is interesting to note that the monetary aggregates do not appear to have a significant effect on the underlying inflation rate. We have already presented a partial explanation as to why the M3 aggregates may not have a significant impact on the inflation rate. But what about the monetary base? Our answer is that the organization of the monetary system matters a great deal. As Chairman Greenspan said in his 2005 Jackson Hole speech, the Fed had been on a price rule or some variant. The Greenspan variant was to anticipate the shifts in money demand and accommodate them. Let's presume that he was as good as he thinks he was and that prior to him the Fed followed a price rule. This means that whenever the US economy grew, the Fed would know that the demand for money would increase and thus would accommodate the demand increase. If the Fed was successful, then the inflation rate would be completely uncorrelated to the money growth.

Yet to the extent that the Fed's knowledge is not perfect, unanticipated increases in real GDP would lead to too little money chasing too many goods, which means a decline in the underlying inflation rate. Eventually the price rule would accommodate. But that is not all that the Fed has to anticipate. The rest of the world's real GDP growth rate will affect the worldwide demand for money and to some extent the US dollar. Easy monetary policy in the rest of the world would also lead to a higher worldwide inflation rate if there is currency substitution. A floating exchange rate system does not insulate the economy from external monetary shocks. Especially if locals use the foreign currency in domestic transactions. The changing inflation rate differentials will alter the demand for the different currencies and that in turn will affect the inflation rates. This we define as currency substitution on the demand side. Also, if the rest of the world central banks watch the foreign exchange value of their currency, the substitution effects will be reduced and the broad global monetary aggregates would then be a very good proxy for the relevant monetary aggregate to focus on. In the extreme case of a fixed exchange rate, the central bank will make the currencies perfect substitutes on the supply side. Either way, the substitutability argument suggests that the global money supply may be an important indicator and or explanatory variable.

31

The Exchange Rate and the Rest of the World Inflation

In this chapter, we continue our quest by focusing on determining the relevant proxies for the money and goods variables that best explain the underlying inflation rate and exchange rate of a particular country or area. The second part of the chapter provides some estimates that allow us to indirectly test our hypothesis by focusing on the explanatory power and goodness of fit of the different specifications.

The purchasing power, the value of a currency, is nothing more than the inverse of the CPI. That is, how many goods one unit of the currency will buy. Alternatively, it is how many units of the currency one has to give up in order to acquire the consumer basket. As we believe that inflation is too much money chasing too few goods, it follows that the purchasing power of the money, that is, the inverse of the CPI, will be determined by the relative abundance of goods, GDP, money, and the monetary aggregates.

THE PERFECT SUBSTITUTABILITY OR FIXED EXCHANGE RATE

Under a fixed exchange rate, the price of one currency in terms of another is fixed. In principle, as a result of the fixed exchange rate, people can exchange as many units of one country's currency into the other country's currency. They are interchangeable and as long the exchange rate remains fixed, one is as good as the other; this is what we mean by perfect substitutability.

To test our hypothesis, all that remains to be determined is the relevant proxy for the quantity of money and the quantity of goods. Since the money is interchangeable, it follows that the demand for money encompasses at least all the countries in the fixed exchange rate area, which is the real GDP of the whole monetary union area. In this case, the relevant quantity of money is nothing more than the combined money supply of the monetary union. Obviously, the limiting case on the upside being the whole world. All of this means that there is a single market for the money, the world, and that the purchasing power of that money is determined by global demand and supply conditions. Assuming perfect mobility of goods across national borders, the prices of goods will be determined in the global economy and so will the purchasing power of the currency. Hence, the inflation rate, while still a monetary phenomenon, will be determined by the global money supply growth and the global real GDP growth.

THE TEXTBOOK FLEXIBLE EXCHANGE RATE

At the other end of the substitutability spectrum is the textbook case for a flexible exchange rate. It assumes that locals only use the local currency and no other. There is no substitutability among currencies or that the elasticity of substitution is zero. Under these conditions, the global demand for a currency is nothing more than the local demand. Hence, to characterize the equilibrium conditions and determine the price level or local inflation rate, all one has to do is substitute the local real GDP and local money supply in the global equilibrium described in the previous paragraphs. Money is still too much money chasing too few goods, the difference being that now only local money and local goods are part of the equation determining the inflation rate. Notice that what happens in other countries does not matter. That is the promise made in the case for the flexible exchange rates, that it would isolate a local economy from the monetary shocks of another countries, that the exchange rate would absorb the shocks.

The zero substitution assumption makes the empirical job significantly easier. All one need is the local money and local GDP to determine the local inflation rate. But there is a bonus. As the locals only use the local currency, that is, the zero substitutability assumption, the exchange rate reflects the price of one currency in terms of another and the inverse of the CPI denotes the price of a currency in terms of goods, its purchasing power. It follows that the exchange rate will reflect the ratio of the two countries' CPI. The exchange rate changes reflect changes in the CPI, which in turn are determined by too much money chasing too few goods in each of the localities. The percent changes in the exchange rate will be determined by the growth in the quantity of money and real GDP growth rates in each of the economies.

The next issue to discuss is what is the relevant quantity of money? As we have already mentioned in many parts of the world, the capital markets are not as developed as in the United States. Also in these economies, financial institutions are highly regulated. To the extent that these regulations are effective and or expensive to evade, the money multiplier will not be as flexible, and as such it will not be able to offset a significant fraction of a change in the domestic monetary base. This means that the local central bank controls both the monetary base and to a great extent the broader monetary aggregates. Hence, all of the monetary aggregates are potential proxies of the quantity of money chasing goods. The area with the relative too much money chasing relative too few goods will experience a depreciating currency. In this case, we only need four pieces of information, the two countries' money growth and real GDP growth.

THE PARTIAL SUBSTITUTABILITY CASE

Some may question the relevancy of this scenario. They may point out that not too many people use the peso or the Thai baht when transacting it into the US dollar. Our reply is that while this is correct, that does not rule out the currency substitution effect. We would point out that people in the peso areas or Thailand and many other economies of the world readily accept the US dollar in local transactions. In effect, we would characterize this as a one-way substitution effect. It is the foreigners that are going in and out of the dollar as the conditions change in their local economies [1].

The one-way substitution effect produces an interesting insight. As individuals in different countries substitute in and out of the dollar, the amounts of dollars circulating in the rest of the world changes. Some currency will enter those countries legally and be recorded in the respective countries' balance of payments. Alternatively, the dollars could enter in an unregistered manner, in which case they will not be recorded in the balance of payments. They will be recorded in the errors and omissions entry of the balance of payment accounts. The recorded and unrecorded inflow of US dollars may be meaningful in many of these countries. This gives us an interesting insight. Even though the local monetary authorities control the domestic money circulation in the economy, they will not have complete control of the dollars circulating and as a result they will not have full control of the quantity of money circulating in its economy, that is, the pesos plus dollars. Also to the extent that the dollar displaces the pesos, the demand for pesos declines and that leads to an inflation rate much higher than that predicted by the flexible exchange rate model that assumes no currency substitution.

From the US perspective, most people will argue that countries such as Thailand are too small compared to the US economy. Hence a shift in the demand for dollars for transaction purposes will have little or no impact on the US economy. The policy implication being that the US monetary authorities should not be concerned about the impact of these one-way substitution effects on the economy. But that could be a mistake. The sum of little effects can add up to a significant and large effect on the US inflation rate. It will depend on the rest of the world real GDP growth as well as the rest of the world money supply growth relative to that of the United States.

Depending on the organization of the US monetary system, the foreign fluctuations in the demand for money will impact the US inflation rate. In fact, we argue that keeping track of the rest of the world's use of dollars may be an arduous task for individual investors and analysts. There is one short cut they can take. One can argue that the US inflation rate captures the changes in the US money market equilibrium. As such, it captures the impact of the changes in the US and rest of the world growth in real GDP and monetary aggregates. More importantly, the shortcut is invariant to the organization of the monetary system.

Take the case of a domestic price rule as an example. In this scenario, the US central bank accommodates the domestic and foreign demand for US dollar to insure that it meets the target inflation rate. If that is the case, and the currency of the country in question is only used in that country, all one needs to worry about is the US inflation rate and the individual countries money supply and real GDP growth. However, to the extent that the United States is not following a domestic price rule, the potential world demand for dollars has to be taken into consideration. A way to pick up the effect on the overall equilibrium condition is simply to use the US inflation rate.

EMPIRICAL RELATIONSHIPS: THE EXCHANGE RATE CHANGES

Using IMF data going back to 1980, we examined the relationship between each of the countries in our sample and the monetary base and real GDP growth of the individual countries, as well as the US data. The estimated equation closely matches the relationship implied by the textbook version of the exchange rate where local residents only use the local currency. As our dependent variable is the dollar exchange rate or how many units of the foreign exchange are needed to buy one dollar, under the assumption that inflation is too much money chasing too few goods, we would expect that a rise in the US real GDP and an increase in the foreign quantity of money leads to an appreciation of the dollar. That should result in a positive estimated coefficients for these two variables. In contrast, a higher growth rate in the non-US countries and an increase in the quantity of money in the United States will, all else the same, result in a depreciation of the US dollar. Hence, we expect the estimated regression to produce a negative coefficient for these two variables.

The results of the estimation are reported in Table 31.1. A summary of the results is quite interesting:

- Only five of the coefficients for the individual countries' monetary base growth were positive and statistically significant.
- Twenty-six of the 32 estimated equations produce a negative and significant coefficient for the domestic real GDP growth.
- In only 1 of the 32 equations is the coefficient for the US Monetary Base growth negative and statistically significant.
- In only 7 of the 32 estimated equations is the coefficient for the US real GDP growth positive and statistically significant.

Collectively, the results suggest that local conditions, in particular local real GDP growth, are a major driver of the fluctuations in the exchange rate. The data also suggests that the growth in the US monetary aggregates and real GDP has little or no impact on the exchange rate movements. One possible explanation for this result points to the organization of the monetary system. If the Fed was in fact operating under a domestic price rule and it effectively ceded the open market operations to the private sector, by targeting the inflation rate, it fixed the rate of change of the purchasing power of money, it effectively made the money perfect substitutes to the consumer basket. They are interchangeable at the underlying inflation rate. The Fed would accommodate shifts in the demand for money in such a way that the target inflation would be met. We have already argued that under these conditions the quantity of money and the real GDP would not have a significant effect on the underlying inflation rate.

The logic also extends to the foreign countries. If they fix their domestic price or exchange rate system, there should be little or no correlation between the domestic money growth, real GDP growth, and the underlying inflation. The fixed exchange rate country will be importing its inflation rate from the country to which it fixes its exchange rate. There is one special case in the sample that allows us to explicitly test this interpretation: Hong Kong. With its currency board and fixed exchange rate to the US dollar, Hong Kong meets all the requirements that we have outlined. The Hong Kong equation estimated coefficients are not statistically significant as predicted by this argument.

Table 31.2 reports the results for the exchange rate equation using M3 as the relevant monetary aggregate. The results are not much different than those produced when the monetary base is used as the relevant

TABLE 31.1 Selected Countries' Dollar Exchange Rates, Monetary Base, and Real GDP Growth

Country	R2	P-value	Constant	MB	GDP	US MB	US GDP	Constant t-stat	MB t-stat	GDP t-stat	US MB t-stat	US GDP t-stat
Australia	0.49	0.00	-4.68	0.09	-0.77	0.39	1.61	-1.24	-0.70	-4.33	-2.52	1.60
Brazil	0.89	0.11	-28.47	0.91	-0.73	1.30	8.34	-1.34	13.00	-1.44	1.74	1.34
Canada	0.88	0.07	-1.56	-0.24	-0.83	0.36	0.82	-1.26	-4.19	-8.27	7.14	2.52
Chile	0.41	0.07	-4.03	0.15	-0.27	0.35	1.83	-0.88	2.52	-1.45	2.24	1.41
China	0.66	0.00	9.02	0.01	-0.78	-0.01	0.33	3.07	0.08	-6.29	-0.09	0.38
Colombia	0.53	0.45	4.30	0.20	-0.88	0.23	1.71	1.01	2.25	-4.76	1.40	1.59
Czech Republic	0.55	0.20	-11.71	-0.04	-0.46	0.43	3.24	-2.09	-0.64	-1.90	2.21	1.48
Denmark	0.61	0.00	-2.30	-0.03	-0.95	0.19	0.94	-0.78	-0.53	-6.27	1.45	1.13
Egypt	0.71	0.66	11.63	-0.49	-0.29	-0.17	-0.40	2.92	-5.05	-2.56	-1.04	-0.31
Hong Kong	0.21	0.01	0.08	0.00	0.03	0.00	-0.05	0.16	-0.35	0.79	-0.33	-0.33
Hungary	0.48	0.09	-3.81	0.39	-0.70	0.29	2.36	-0.72	2.61	-3.00	1.55	1.41
India	0.97	0.14	6.43	-1.53	0.64	0.58	3.72	1.05	-1.33	0.68	2.76	2.36
Indonesia	0.76	0.22	1.66	-0.11	-0.74	0.39	4.30	0.26	-0.38	-5.38	2.04	2.04
Israel	0.56	0.18	12.32	-0.95	0.59	-0.53	-4.02	0.73	-0.75	0.45	-0.73	-0.70
Japan	0.68	0.02	1.16	0.09	-0.76	-0.20	-0.41	0.47	0.82	-7.02	-1.74	-0.58
Korea	0.47	0.01	-0.13	-0.11	-0.33	0.38	0.45	-0.04	-0.98	-1.97	2.56	0.50
Malaysia	0.31	0.34	-1.77	0.07	-0.36	0.17	1.03	-0.74	1.49	-3.00	1.68	1.59
Mexico	0.66	0.05	4.14	0.57	-1.03	0.00	-3.01	0.56	3.38	-5.02	-0.01	-0.01
New Zealand	0.51	0.01	-5.44	-0.08	-0.73	0.40	2.53	-1.29	-1.01	-4.38	2.06	2.19
Norway	0.53	0.11	-0.04	0.02	-0.77	-1.02	3.13	0.00	0.22	-2.07	-1.37	1.37
Peru	0.38	0.00	103.69	-1.06	-2.58	-1.50	-9.72	2.66	-1.41	-2.42	-1.02	-0.94
Philippines	0.50	0.02	-0.25	0.13	-0.84	0.24	1.65	-0.07	0.92	-4.32	1.59	1.38
Poland	0.47	0.45	-9.91	-0.07	-0.56	0.54	3.77	-1.64	-0.32	-2.14	2.83	2.06
Russia	0.65	0.11	9.05	-0.34	-0.86	0.30	6.63	0.63	-0.96	-3.86	0.76	1.77
Singapore	0.45	0.28	-3.95	0.01	-0.31	0.13	1.44	-1.53	0.13	-2.52	1.47	1.92
South Africa	0.71	0.00	-0.36	0.29	-1.05	0.30	1.48	-0.08	1.25	-7.44	1.80	1.30
Sweden	0.61	0.03	-0.45	0.05	-0.78	0.14	0.52	-0.13	0.78	-6.22	0.80	0.57
Switzerland	0.63	0.00	-3.54	0.03	-0.84	0.14	0.71	-1.06	0.34	-6.29	1.00	0.70
Thailand	0.49	0.02	1.71	-0.21	-0.40	0.10	0.76	0.58	-3.52	-3.06	0.82	0.96
Turkey	0.48	0.00	14.91	0.13	-1.20	0.30	5.87	0.93	0.49	-3.46	0.72	1.65
United Kingdom	0.69	0.00	-1.53	-0.30	-0.37	0.47	0.74	-0.61	-4.17	-2.21	3.73	1.02

TABLE 31.2 Selected Countries Dollar Exchange Rates, M3, and Real GDP Growth

Country	R^2	P-value	Constant	M3	GDP	US M3	US GDP	Constant t-stat	M3 t-stat	GDP t-stat	US M3 t-stat	US GDP t-stat
Australia	0.41	0.00	−0.14	0.80	−0.91	−0.72	0.28	−0.02	1.55	−4.35	−0.85	0.29
Brazil	0.97	0.05	−56.60	1.09	−0.24	6.96	2.12	−2.20	19.11	−0.72	1.97	0.76
Canada	0.25	0.00	−2.72	0.56	−0.72	−0.18	0.72	−0.53	1.05	−3.03	−0.36	1.00
Chile	0.26	0.21	7.88	0.23	−0.53	−0.61	−0.71	0.91	1.82	−2.04	−0.52	−0.58
China	0.86	0.28	21.40	−0.07	−0.80	−1.98	−0.26	7.93	−1.02	−10.22	−5.29	−0.54
Colombia	0.60	0.01	2.01	0.64	−1.02	−0.30	0.63	0.26	3.42	−4.96	−0.35	0.71
Czech Republic	0.22	0.46	9.44	−0.15	−0.23	−1.53	−1.39	0.63	−0.16	−0.57	−0.72	−0.74
Denmark	0.58	0.01	1.79	−0.02	−0.91	−0.20	0.34	0.43	−0.07	−6.16	−0.31	0.43
Egypt	0.92	0.42	12.09	−0.95	−0.08	0.06	−0.64	3.82	−12.40	−1.21	0.12	−1.07
Hong Kong	0.24	0.01	0.17	0.01	0.02	−0.05	−0.01	0.34	0.33	0.45	−0.66	−0.22
Hungary	0.55	0.20	11.09	0.61	−0.64	−2.11	0.01	1.33	2.07	−2.99	−2.10	0.01
India	0.94	0.20	14.04	0.95	−1.37	−2.23	0.34	0.53	0.72	−4.00	−1.39	0.16
Indonesia	0.70	0.18	6.33	0.16	−0.67	−0.05	1.62	0.40	0.28	−3.06	−0.04	1.03
Israel	0.67	0.07	−3.67	6.08	−0.63	−6.28	3.74	−0.29	1.02	−1.12	−0.91	0.96
Japan	0.71	0.03	−0.12	0.76	−0.89	−0.70	0.16	−0.04	2.35	−8.16	−1.48	0.27
Korea	0.37	0.03	4.28	0.24	−0.55	−0.42	−0.32	0.74	1.08	−3.83	−0.58	−0.36
Malaysia	0.26	0.16	−2.93	0.39	−0.32	0.03	0.41	−0.56	1.58	−2.68	0.06	0.70
Mexico	0.92	0.03	1.46	0.90	−1.00	−1.28	0.34	0.29	11.14	−9.82	−1.74	0.35
New Zealand	0.41	0.00	−0.62	0.18	−0.74	−0.13	1.16	−0.10	0.50	−4.24	−0.14	1.08
Norway	0.04	0.38	1.14	−0.64	0.08	0.09	0.68	0.09	−0.75	0.21	0.06	0.38
Peru	0.37	0.00	126.95	−0.96	−2.73	−8.80	−4.68	2.59	−1.22	−2.36	−1.25	−0.52
Philippines	0.51	0.01	−3.17	0.54	−0.84	0.28	0.46	−0.43	2.32	−4.54	0.33	0.47
Poland	0.41	0.15	0.90	0.95	−0.53	−1.09	−0.99	0.06	2.36	−1.87	−0.56	−0.64
Russia	0.61	0.05	19.00	−0.20	−0.92	−0.53	3.74	0.61	−0.36	−3.17	−0.12	1.00
Singapore	0.43	0.15	5.31	−0.33	−0.35	−0.45	0.23	1.01	−1.35	−2.39	−0.75	0.35
South Africa	0.69	0.00	4.93	0.60	−1.09	−0.80	0.59	0.70	1.61	−7.54	−0.99	0.59
Sweden	0.64	0.03	0.99	0.69	−0.84	−0.45	−0.19	0.23	2.23	−6.82	−0.74	−0.24
Switzerland	0.62	0.01	4.17	−0.25	−0.78	−0.62	−0.18	0.91	−0.48	−5.79	−0.94	−0.21
Thailand	0.78	0.03	6.57	−0.56	−0.23	−0.20	0.50	2.32	−8.06	−2.37	−0.51	1.11
Turkey	0.73	0.19	26.45	0.63	−1.17	−3.00	−0.82	1.79	3.38	−5.08	−1.65	−0.34
United Kingdom	0.64	0.00	1.42	−0.29	−0.46	0.25	0.40	0.39	−3.87	−2.59	0.46	0.58

IV. THE BALANCE OF PAYMENTS

monetary aggregate. This fits the monetarist view that the monetary authorities exercise control over the monetary base and M3. We attribute this to the fact that the financial system in the rest of the world countries in our sample is much less developed and that allows the local central banks greater control over the broader aggregates.

One common element of the results reported in Tables 31.1 and 31.2 is the lack of statistical significance of the US monetary aggregates and the US real GDP growth. Possible reasons for these results may be the fact that the United States was pursuing a domestic price rule as we already explained. Another reason may be that the specification is not taking into account the rest of the world demand for US dollars, that is, the currency substitution effect. There are two ways to correct or account for this. One is to calculate the world demand for and supply of US dollars. We already did this in an earlier chapter and found support for this view as it improved the explanatory power of the US inflation equation. But this is a tedious process, as it requires that one convert all of the countries' money supply into US dollars to arrive at a world money supply figure. Fortunately, there is a short cut. According to our framework, the US inflation rate is nothing more than the rate of change of the market clearing equilibrium conditions. Therefore, one can use the US inflation rate to replace the world money demand and money supply conditions in estimating the nominal exchange rate changes.

Estimates of the changes in the nominal exchange rate using the local monetary base and real GDP growth rates, as well as the US inflation rate are reported in Table 31.3. While the results for the local variables are essentially unchanged when compared to the results reported in Table 31.1, the US inflation is statistically significant in 22 of the 32 countries. Replacing the monetary base with M3 yields similar results (Table 31.4). In both cases, there is a marked improvement over the significance level of the US monetary aggregates and real GDP growth rate reported in Tables 31.1 and 31.2.

A summary of the statistically significant coefficients produced by the different variables in the different equations is reported in Table 31.5. The results are consistent with the view that domestic excess money creation leads to a currency depreciation, while the US inflation leads to a currency appreciation in the foreign countries.

The results also point to the weakness of the explanatory power of the monetary aggregates. Very few of the domestic monetary aggregates are statistically significant. There may be several possible explanations for this result. Our favorite has to do with the conduct of monetary policy. The belief that the exchange rate manipulation can affect a country's terms of trade is a fairly strong one. Many governments manage the exchange rate and as a result take steps to prevent the domestic currency from appreciating beyond a target level. In effect, this is nothing more than a fixed exchange rate band.

EMPIRICAL RELATIONSHIPS: THE INFLATION RATE

In this section, we continue utilizing the same functional forms to estimate the relationship between the inflation rate and dependent variables utilized to explain the countries' exchange rates relative to the US. Table 31.6 provides a summary of the number of significant coefficients for the different variables yielded by the different equations. For example, the inflation equations using only the growth in the monetary base and the real GDP growth produces only seven statistically significant coefficients for the monetary base and only three for the real GDP growth rate in the countries in question. Table 31.7 presents the individual equations for the 32 countries in the sample. Table 31.6 shows that replacing the monetary base with M3 yields much better results regarding the ability of the variables to explain the countries individual inflation rates. The significant coefficients for the monetary aggregates increase to 15, while the real GDP coefficient rises to 6. The data suggests that the M3 version of the equation has a much higher explanatory power and a greater degree of significance. A summary of the individual country equations using M3 can be found in Table 31.8.

Adding the US Monetary aggregates and real GDP growth to the previous equations, see Table 31.6, shows only marginal improvements in the number of significant coefficients. Only four of the US monetary aggregates are statistically significant and either three and or four of the US real GDP growth rate are statistically significant. A summary of the individual equations can be found in Tables 31.9 and 31.10.

Now including the US inflation rate in lieu of the US monetary aggregates and real GDP leaves the number of statistically significant coefficients for the individual countries monetary aggregates and real GDP unaffected. What the equations show is that the US inflation has a statistically significant coefficient in 20 countries when the monetary base is explanatory monetary variable for the countries in question, see column 5 in Table 31.6. In contrast when M3 is used, the number of countries for whom the US inflation rate produces a statistically significant coefficient drops to 16. A summary of the individual countries estimated equation suing the US inflation rates and individual countries monetary aggregates can be found in Table 31.11, for the Monetary Base and Table 31.12 for the equation using M3.

TABLE 31.3 Selected Countries Dollar Exchange Rates, Monetary Base, Real GDP Growth, and US Inflation Rate

Country	R^2	P-value	Constant	MB	GDP	US inflation	Constant t-stat	MB t-stat	GDP t-stat	US inflation t-stat
Australia	0.45	0.00	−3.86	0.03	−0.77	2.24	−1.03	0.25	−4.26	2.10
Brazil	0.89	0.32	−34.11	0.82	−0.92	16.06	−1.56	10.59	−1.83	1.92
Canada	0.63	0.00	6.42	−0.30	−0.88	−0.68	2.38	−2.81	−5.24	−1.06
Chile	0.64	0.02	−10.75	0.13	−0.55	5.95	−3.09	2.80	−3.77	4.90
China	0.66	0.00	7.22	−0.04	−0.75	0.89	1.88	−0.34	−5.97	0.70
Colombia	0.53	0.35	4.85	0.16	−0.87	1.97	1.24	1.74	−4.82	1.81
Czech Republic	0.49	0.26	−16.85	0.04	−0.86	7.43	−2.31	0.51	−2.40	2.15
Denmark	0.65	0.02	−5.76	−0.02	−0.90	2.45	−1.66	−0.41	−6.42	2.26
Egypt	0.70	0.66	6.28	−0.47	−0.31	0.92	1.69	−5.11	−2.81	0.89
Hong Kong	0.27	0.02	0.11	0.00	0.03	−0.08	0.42	−0.56	1.25	−0.87
Hungary	0.55	0.06	−9.82	0.23	−0.75	6.20	−1.71	1.52	−3.55	2.57
India	0.87	0.14	3.62	0.62	−1.33	1.25	0.35	0.42	−1.30	0.47
Indonesia	0.74	0.23	−3.54	0.16	−0.73	5.04	−0.44	0.71	−5.50	2.04
Israel	0.97	0.04	−6.19	0.34	−0.81	4.20	−4.59	2.88	−7.40	6.14
Japan	0.67	0.02	−4.78	0.04	−0.77	1.07	−1.79	0.42	−7.32	1.53
Korea	0.43	0.09	−1.22	−0.04	−0.51	1.95	−0.36	−0.33	−3.39	2.10
Malaysia	0.22	0.31	1.41	0.06	−0.34	0.25	0.58	1.11	−2.78	0.35
Mexico	0.78	0.02	−18.48	0.55	−1.30	8.73	−2.66	4.73	−7.51	3.76
New Zealand	0.48	0.01	−4.93	−0.07	−0.66	2.58	−1.09	−0.87	−3.89	2.16
Norway	0.55	0.17	−17.15	−0.03	−0.91	8.32	−1.77	−0.31	−2.77	2.18
Peru	0.63	0.01	−84.52	−0.69	−2.09	51.29	−2.41	−1.20	−2.58	4.56
Philippines	0.50	0.01	−1.83	0.18	−0.86	2.48	−0.44	1.35	−4.59	1.82
Poland	0.31	0.02	−10.27	−0.13	−0.84	6.89	−1.31	−0.54	−2.25	1.89
Russia	0.68	0.09	−4.01	−0.31	−1.32	13.75	−0.29	−1.04	−4.98	2.24
Singapore	0.48	0.41	−4.54	0.04	−0.42	2.29	−1.81	0.53	−3.80	2.25
South Africa	0.74	0.00	−2.94	0.29	−1.03	2.80	−0.71	1.39	−7.82	2.72
Sweden	0.69	0.02	−5.24	0.05	−0.70	2.28	−1.78	1.11	−6.27	2.74
Switzerland	0.65	0.00	−6.24	0.05	−0.85	1.94	−1.78	0.85	−6.67	1.68
Thailand	0.50	0.01	1.35	−0.21	−0.42	0.98	0.48	−3.63	−3.32	1.29
Turkey	0.60	0.00	−9.01	0.26	−1.33	11.97	−0.57	1.16	−4.39	3.20
United Kingdom	0.58	0.00	−1.10	−0.15	−0.59	1.48	−0.35	−2.20	−3.63	1.77

TABLE 31.4 Selected Countries Dollar Exchange Rates, M3, Real GDP Growth, and US Infation Rate

Country	R²	P-value	Constant	M3	GDP	US inflation	Constant t-stat	M3 t-stat	GDP t-stat	US inflation t-stat
Australia	0.46	0.00	-6.38	0.37	-0.80	2.03	-1.29	0.78	-4.36	1.87
Brazil	0.97	0.51	-30.26	0.96	-0.75	9.96	-2.66	21.74	-2.87	2.25
Canada	0.26	0.00	-1.84	0.01	-0.57	0.93	-0.55	0.02	-2.69	1.10
Chile	0.55	0.01	-9.90	0.12	-0.63	5.79	-2.54	1.18	-3.89	4.10
China	0.68	0.00	7.53	-0.14	-0.75	1.15	2.21	-1.22	-6.46	1.07
Colombia	0.60	0.01	0.15	0.62	-0.98	0.52	0.04	2.92	-5.70	0.44
Czech Republic	0.58	0.23	-12.96	-0.89	-0.60	8.06	-2.26	-1.34	-1.99	2.73
Denmark	0.64	0.02	-5.68	-0.04	-0.88	2.43	-1.58	-0.22	-6.62	2.24
Egypt	0.93	0.28	6.51	-0.96	-0.07	1.49	3.75	-14.69	-1.25	3.11
Hong Kong	0.24	0.02	0.00	0.00	0.04	-0.06	-0.01	0.10	1.15	-0.70
Hungary	0.56	0.43	-12.62	0.49	-0.75	5.80	-2.24	1.62	-3.62	2.33
India	0.87	0.16	0.34	0.56	-1.02	1.53	0.02	0.51	-3.22	0.71
Indonesia	0.73	0.41	-1.10	0.06	-0.76	4.93	-0.12	0.14	-4.28	1.91
Israel	0.83	0.03	-2.55	-0.13	-0.71	3.12	-0.62	-0.25	-2.82	2.35
Japan	0.68	0.02	-4.02	0.58	-0.85	0.24	-1.66	1.38	-7.40	0.27
Korea	0.42	0.10	-1.20	-0.03	-0.54	2.00	-0.32	-0.11	-4.26	1.76
Malaysia	0.24	0.24	-1.93	0.37	-0.33	0.09	-0.63	1.48	-2.96	0.13
Mexico	0.91	0.12	-10.18	0.84	-1.05	2.57	-2.44	9.63	-9.21	1.58
New Zealand	0.47	0.01	-4.84	-0.18	-0.63	2.85	-1.14	-0.49	-3.88	2.13
Norway	0.47	0.16	-15.61	-1.11	-0.62	10.63	-2.36	-1.79	-1.86	3.62
Peru	0.62	0.00	-87.08	-0.53	-2.11	51.89	-2.47	-0.90	-2.39	4.57
Philippines	0.55	0.01	-4.55	0.44	-0.87	1.93	-1.05	2.05	-5.06	1.44
Poland	0.47	0.09	-15.83	0.77	-0.81	4.88	-2.22	2.13	-2.48	1.49
Russia	0.68	0.10	-2.74	-0.48	-1.35	15.69	-0.19	-1.00	-5.02	2.27
Singapore	0.54	0.32	-2.18	-0.34	-0.34	2.32	-0.81	-1.68	-3.36	2.43
South Africa	0.73	0.00	-2.98	0.31	-0.99	2.60	-0.60	0.84	-7.58	2.27
Sweden	0.69	0.01	-6.61	0.36	-0.75	2.05	-2.21	1.20	-6.45	2.32
Switzerland	0.64	0.00	-4.69	-0.22	-0.81	1.82	-1.05	-0.43	-6.28	1.53
Thailand	0.80	0.05	3.03	-0.56	-0.23	1.11	1.72	-8.86	-2.74	2.34
Turkey	0.77	0.05	-12.11	0.62	-1.29	7.99	-1.35	4.45	-6.13	2.74
United Kingdom	0.70	0.00	-1.72	-0.28	-0.39	1.69	-0.68	-4.30	-2.62	2.44

TABLE 31.5 Summary of Statistically Significant Coefficients in the Different Estimated Exchange Rate Equations

Constant	4	6	13	13
GROWTH IN				
Rest of the world				
Monetary base	5		5	
M3		10		7
Real GDP	26	25	29	28
US				
Monetary base	1			
M3		3		
Real GDP	7	0		
Inflation rate			22	20

TABLE 31.6 Summary of the Statistically Significant Coefficients in the Different Estimated Exchange Rate Equations

Constant	27	13	21	13	9	6
GROWTH IN						
Monetary base	7		7		5	
M3		15		15		13
GDP	3	6	3	7	5	7
US monetary base			4			
US M3				4		
US GDP			3	4		
US inflation rate					20	16

The results reported in Tables 31.11 and 31.12 show that the coefficient for the United States is more often than not positive and statistically significant. The question is why that is the case? We can come with two different interpretations as to why the US inflation would impact the monetary equilibrium in the rest of the world. One possibility has to do with currency substitutions on the demand for the different currencies. Under this scenario, the changes in relative inflation across the individual countries and the United States will alter the relative attractiveness of the dollar vis-a-vis the local currency. When the local inflation rises relative to the United States, the demand for dollars increases and as the people substitute out of the local currency, the local excess money supply increases, leading to a higher domestic inflation rate. But that is not the only way. There are also some supply side effects. As we have already mentioned, there is the predominant view that a currency appreciation leads to a deterioration of the terms of trade. This has led to countries focusing on the management of their currencies and limiting its appreciation. Hence, if the United States experiences a rising inflation rate that would lead to an appreciation of the local currency, the local central bank may be prompted to increase its money supply to prevent the local currency appreciation. The local monetary authorities have a shield, they can collect an additional inflation tax as the inflation rate increases.

TABLE 31.7 Inflation Rates, Growth in the Monetary Base, and Real GDP

Country	R^2	P-value	Constant	MB	GDP	Constant t-stat	MB t-stat	GDP t-stat
Australia	0.11	0.00	3.78	0.07	−0.04	6.67	1.82	−0.84
Brazil	0.90	0.01	1.32	0.90	0.16	0.17	16.53	0.47
Canada	0.12	0.00	3.87	−0.09	0.00	6.79	−1.86	0.03
Chile	0.02	0.00	7.20	0.01	0.10	4.05	0.29	0.71
China	0.13	0.00	3.67	0.19	0.00	2.02	1.84	0.03
Colombia	0.21	0.00	11.88	0.15	−0.23	6.58	2.33	−1.71
Czech Republic	0.39	0.30	2.30	−0.02	0.06	4.65	−1.99	1.51
Denmark	0.03	0.00	3.00	0.00	−0.03	8.15	−0.06	−0.87
Egypt	0.15	0.00	10.54	−0.11	0.06	11.40	−2.29	1.06
Hong Kong	0.67	0.11	−0.52	0.06	0.68	−0.66	2.19	4.28
Hungary	0.08	0.00	9.86	0.13	−0.12	4.66	1.14	−0.69
India	0.41	0.23	13.30	−0.47	0.29	5.09	−1.67	1.55
Indonesia	0.59	0.00	7.16	0.20	−0.22	2.57	1.66	−3.08
Israel	0.13	0.06	2.54	−0.01	0.05	3.05	−0.06	0.65
Japan	0.01	0.00	0.87	−0.01	0.00	2.98	−0.57	−0.05
Korea	0.03	0.00	4.82	−0.01	−0.04	6.92	−0.16	−0.68
Malaysia	0.00	0.00	2.92	0.00	−0.01	8.16	−0.13	−0.15
Mexico	0.61	0.00	0.39	0.81	−0.16	0.10	6.15	−0.89
New Zealand	0.00	0.00	4.86	−0.01	0.01	5.04	−0.19	0.19
Norway	0.34	0.55	2.28	−0.01	−0.04	9.23	−1.68	−1.25
Peru	0.14	0.00	64.19	−0.33	−1.88	3.72	−0.41	−1.63
Philippines	0.04	0.01	6.42	0.04	−0.08	6.60	0.71	−0.91
Poland	0.17	0.01	4.21	0.11	−0.13	3.45	1.28	−1.35
Russia	0.72	0.08	4.88	0.54	−0.40	1.43	4.47	−4.73
Singapore	0.21	0.01	1.33	0.04	0.05	3.12	1.39	1.11
South Africa	0.04	0.00	8.87	0.02	−0.06	7.00	0.18	−1.12
Sweden	0.07	0.00	3.44	0.02	−0.04	5.96	1.20	−0.85
Switzerland	0.05	0.00	1.57	−0.02	0.01	4.83	−1.17	0.29
Thailand	0.04	0.03	3.92	−0.01	−0.04	8.26	−0.34	−1.04
Turkey	0.13	0.00	20.86	0.33	−0.16	1.71	1.38	−0.51
United Kingdom	0.00	0.00	2.78	0.00	0.00	6.98	−0.16	−0.07

TABLE 31.8 Inflation Rates, Growth in M3, and Real GDP

Country	R^2	P-value	Constant	M3	GDP	Constant t-stat	M3 t-stat	GDP t-stat
Australia	0.24	0.00	0.97	0.35	-0.07	0.83	3.05	-1.45
Brazil	0.94	0.13	-8.90	1.01	0.19	-1.42	21.63	0.70
Canada	0.12	0.00	0.94	0.34	-0.05	0.81	2.01	-0.64
Chile	0.06	0.00	6.13	0.08	0.06	3.02	0.99	0.47
China	0.10	0.00	3.01	0.19	0.04	1.45	1.60	0.29
Colombia	0.76	0.00	0.24	0.73	-0.34	0.14	9.25	-4.50
Czech Republic	0.33	0.33	0.83	0.23	-0.03	0.94	1.69	-0.55
Denmark	0.15	0.00	2.43	0.09	-0.03	5.79	2.06	-1.02
Egypt	0.02	0.00	10.66	-0.06	0.03	10.50	-0.72	0.43
Hong Kong	0.50	0.02	0.87	-0.02	0.53	0.68	-0.15	2.35
Hungary	0.60	0.02	1.19	0.82	-0.18	0.55	5.44	-1.52
India	0.21	0.36	13.75	-0.31	0.05	3.04	-1.04	0.56
Indonesia	0.58	0.00	4.78	0.36	-0.18	1.12	1.59	-1.95
Israel	0.42	0.03	0.72	0.23	0.07	0.46	1.23	1.09
Japan	0.43	0.01	-0.17	0.26	-0.03	-0.62	4.73	-1.56
Korea	0.37	0.02	1.05	0.26	-0.08	0.99	4.04	-1.95
Malaysia	0.23	0.26	0.95	0.18	-0.04	1.30	2.97	-1.26
Mexico	0.78	0.00	-5.48	0.99	-0.10	-1.68	9.37	-0.74
New Zealand	0.47	0.00	-0.08	0.50	0.01	-0.07	5.14	0.27
Norway	0.05	0.28	2.23	-0.03	-0.02	5.11	-0.44	-0.57
Peru	0.14	0.00	62.72	0.19	-2.30	3.62	0.23	-1.85
Philippines	0.21	0.01	3.82	0.23	-0.12	2.67	2.42	-1.52
Poland	0.66	0.11	0.21	0.45	-0.15	0.17	4.87	-2.38
Russia	0.88	0.05	-6.48	0.91	-0.45	-2.02	8.14	-8.10
Singapore	0.18	0.03	0.85	0.09	0.06	1.16	1.00	1.29
South Africa	0.07	0.00	7.33	0.13	-0.06	3.73	0.94	-1.09
Sweden	0.06	0.00	2.82	0.11	-0.05	2.96	0.93	-1.13
Switzerland	0.10	0.00	2.27	-0.19	0.01	4.04	-1.69	0.42
Thailand	0.06	0.00	3.72	0.03	-0.06	7.50	0.94	-1.34
Turkey	0.60	0.00	5.73	0.73	-0.22	0.91	5.63	-1.14
United Kingdom	0.08	0.00	2.85	-0.03	0.02	8.20	-1.39	0.45

IV. THE BALANCE OF PAYMENTS

TABLE 31.9 Inflation Rates, Growth in M3, Real GDP, US Monetary Base, and Real GDP Growth

Country	R^2	P-value	Constant	MB	GDP	US MB	US GDP	Constant t-stat	MB t-stat	GDP t-stat	US MB t-stat	US GDP t-stat
Australia	0.12	0.00	4.36	0.07	−0.04	−0.02	−0.17	3.99	1.79	−0.81	−0.50	−0.57
Brazil	0.91	0.01	−12.44	0.91	0.18	0.61	3.13	−0.87	16.28	0.51	1.10	0.88
Canada	0.28	0.00	5.76	−0.10	0.03	−0.05	−0.61	5.63	−2.19	0.41	−1.26	−2.25
Chile	0.03	0.00	7.52	0.02	0.08	−0.04	0.07	2.11	0.33	0.54	−0.31	0.07
China	0.16	0.00	3.62	0.19	0.02	−0.05	0.27	1.17	1.77	0.18	−0.58	0.29
Colombia	0.24	0.00	13.13	0.15	−0.22	−0.11	−0.03	4.10	2.22	−1.62	−0.90	−0.04
Czech Republic	0.68	0.08	1.79	−0.02	0.05	0.04	−0.02	2.01	−2.34	1.27	1.29	−0.06
Denmark	0.03	0.00	2.84	0.00	−0.03	0.00	0.06	3.89	−0.12	−0.87	0.12	0.30
Egypt	0.17	0.00	9.38	−0.11	0.05	0.08	0.19	4.68	−2.08	0.81	0.92	0.33
Hong Kong	0.85	0.20	−0.77	0.02	0.63	0.06	−0.03	−0.37	0.53	4.72	1.94	−0.04
Hungary	0.12	0.00	11.84	0.13	−0.10	−0.12	−0.33	2.79	1.05	−0.55	−0.82	−0.24
India	0.90	0.13	14.74	−1.28	1.01	0.18	1.03	9.25	−4.27	4.06	3.21	2.51
Indonesia	0.61	0.00	5.21	0.18	−0.22	0.10	0.61	1.46	1.12	−2.86	0.92	0.51
Israel	0.93	0.61	4.69	−0.11	0.21	−0.09	−1.22	2.76	−0.89	1.56	−1.25	−2.08
Japan	0.02	0.00	0.74	−0.02	0.00	0.01	0.02	1.32	−0.68	−0.09	0.43	0.12
Korea	0.11	0.02	6.59	−0.01	−0.04	−0.06	−0.52	5.02	−0.12	−0.66	−1.14	−1.47
Malaysia	0.04	0.00	2.90	0.00	−0.01	0.02	−0.08	3.92	−0.22	−0.15	0.69	−0.40
Mexico	0.65	0.00	8.61	0.90	−0.13	−0.39	−3.13	1.33	6.06	−0.75	−1.54	−1.36
New Zealand	0.01	0.00	5.37	−0.01	0.02	−0.02	−0.18	2.82	−0.14	0.21	−0.17	−0.34
Norway	0.50	0.24	2.99	−0.01	−0.04	0.03	−0.29	4.17	−1.63	−1.34	0.44	−1.53
Peru	0.17	0.00	96.00	−0.37	−1.92	−1.40	−8.03	2.58	−0.45	−1.63	−0.90	−0.79
Philippines	0.05	0.01	7.17	0.05	−0.08	−0.02	−0.28	3.87	0.66	−0.83	−0.34	−0.48
Poland	0.39	0.04	0.75	0.12	−0.18	0.08	1.35	0.35	1.54	−1.86	1.16	2.05
Russia	0.85	0.35	−5.79	0.60	−0.37	0.37	2.30	−1.31	5.49	−5.42	3.11	2.01
Singapore	0.57	0.28	0.68	−0.02	0.11	0.08	−0.08	0.89	−0.69	2.87	2.83	−0.34
South Africa	0.05	0.00	9.12	0.03	−0.06	0.00	−0.19	5.09	0.31	−1.08	−0.01	−0.39
Sweden	0.13	0.00	4.84	0.04	−0.03	−0.09	−0.27	3.68	1.75	−0.62	−1.36	−0.76
Switzerland	0.16	0.00	2.35	−0.03	0.01	0.00	−0.34	3.23	−1.73	0.26	0.12	−1.54
Thailand	0.06	0.16	4.59	−0.01	−0.05	−0.02	−0.21	4.62	−0.42	−1.09	−0.45	−0.81
Turkey	0.28	0.00	18.16	0.27	−0.26	−0.21	4.12	1.29	1.16	−0.86	−0.57	1.32
United Kingdom	0.35	0.00	4.16	−0.03	0.07	0.01	−0.70	6.01	−1.32	1.57	0.20	−2.97

TABLE 31.10 Inflation Rates, Growth in M3, Real GDP, US M3, and Real GDP Growth

Country	R^2	P-value	Constant	M3	GDP	US M3	US GDP	Constant t-stat	M3 t-stat	GDP t-stat	US M3 t-stat	US GDP t-stat
Australia	0.34	0.00	-0.30	0.28	-0.03	0.38	-0.17	-0.21	2.31	-0.64	1.91	-0.75
Brazil	0.94	0.12	-13.06	1.02	0.24	0.90	-1.09	-0.69	18.67	0.78	0.37	-0.43
Canada	0.29	0.00	-1.14	0.31	-0.02	0.42	-0.09	-0.68	1.80	-0.32	2.54	-0.40
Chile	0.06	0.00	6.90	0.08	0.04	-0.13	0.06	1.17	0.88	0.25	-0.16	0.08
China	0.48	0.13	13.10	0.20	0.02	-1.87	-0.16	3.81	2.17	0.22	-3.93	-0.27
Colombia	0.79	0.01	6.09	0.70	-0.44	-0.74	-0.21	1.81	8.66	-4.98	-1.96	-0.54
Czech Republic	0.52	0.05	1.78	0.23	-0.02	-0.07	-0.41	0.79	1.67	-0.30	-0.21	-1.47
Denmark	0.30	0.00	0.89	0.05	-0.03	0.31	-0.02	1.05	1.13	-0.95	2.34	-0.10
Egypt	0.03	0.00	11.90	-0.05	0.04	-0.10	-0.33	4.05	-0.56	0.50	-0.24	-0.60
Hong Kong	0.80	0.09	-0.57	-0.01	0.66	0.35	-0.67	-0.24	-0.10	3.47	0.94	-2.17
Hungary	0.74	0.08	11.69	0.66	-0.16	-1.48	-0.46	3.00	4.79	-1.59	-3.15	-0.78
India	0.84	0.42	28.33	-0.84	0.10	-0.94	-1.00	4.70	-2.80	1.22	-2.57	-2.13
Indonesia	0.65	0.03	-5.69	0.53	-0.09	1.05	0.86	-0.74	2.02	-0.87	1.57	1.14
Israel	0.92	0.07	3.77	0.85	-0.03	-1.08	-0.04	2.40	1.15	-0.41	-1.28	-0.08
Japan	0.43	0.01	0.12	0.27	-0.03	-0.04	-0.03	0.20	4.59	-1.52	-0.49	-0.31
Korea	0.42	0.10	2.64	0.26	-0.08	-0.16	-0.31	1.57	4.08	-1.80	-0.78	-1.21
Malaysia	0.25	0.33	0.84	0.19	-0.03	0.05	-0.13	0.62	2.92	-1.06	0.38	-0.86
Mexico	0.79	0.00	-5.73	0.97	-0.12	-0.21	0.87	-0.81	8.67	-0.83	-0.20	0.65
New Zealand	0.56	0.00	-1.46	0.47	0.04	0.43	-0.46	-0.88	4.65	0.90	1.71	-1.53
Norway	0.13	0.17	2.76	-0.01	-0.02	-0.05	-0.16	3.00	-0.20	-0.60	-0.43	-1.21
Peru	0.17	0.00	119.97	-0.02	-2.42	-7.83	-4.32	2.24	-0.03	-1.91	-1.05	-0.48
Philippines	0.37	0.11	9.97	0.16	-0.15	-0.78	-0.45	3.35	1.68	-2.05	-2.28	-1.13
Poland	0.70	0.24	-2.54	0.42	-0.13	0.33	0.47	-0.71	4.40	-1.92	0.70	1.25
Russia	0.89	0.08	-2.54	0.95	-0.48	-0.61	-0.56	-0.33	6.96	-6.65	-0.57	-0.61
Singapore	0.38	0.41	1.75	0.06	0.07	0.04	-0.46	0.95	0.67	1.41	0.17	-2.01
South Africa	0.09	0.00	6.55	0.16	-0.05	0.17	-0.24	2.34	1.04	-0.84	0.53	-0.61
Sweden	0.11	0.00	1.41	0.10	-0.04	0.30	-0.12	0.79	0.80	-0.86	1.20	-0.39
Switzerland	0.28	0.00	4.14	-0.14	0.01	-0.28	-0.26	4.51	-1.36	0.45	-2.13	-1.53
Thailand	0.15	0.05	5.87	0.04	-0.09	-0.29	-0.15	4.29	1.08	-1.88	-1.57	-0.67
Turkey	0.62	0.00	17.75	0.63	-0.28	-1.74	0.54	1.35	3.86	-1.35	-1.07	0.26
United Kingdom	0.51	0.00	5.73	-0.02	0.08	-0.31	-0.74	6.64	-1.17	2.06	-2.40	-3.99

TABLE 31.11 Inflation Rates, Growth in the Monetary Base, Real GDP, and US Inflation Rate

Country	R^2	P-value	Constant	MB	GDP	US inflation	Constant t-stat	MB t-stat	GDP t-stat	US inflation t-stat
Australia	0.43	0.00	0.93	0.04	−0.03	0.97	1.10	1.24	−0.80	4.02
Brazil	0.90	0.01	−3.95	0.89	0.15	1.94	−0.31	15.39	0.43	0.51
Canada	0.74	0.00	−1.40	0.01	0.00	1.39	−1.83	0.34	−0.05	7.57
Chile	0.17	0.00	1.51	0.00	0.01	2.32	0.47	0.10	0.11	2.08
China	0.13	0.00	3.24	0.18	0.01	0.16	0.78	1.38	0.07	0.11
Colombia	0.41	0.00	5.49	0.11	−0.20	2.26	2.11	1.78	−1.64	3.11
Czech Republic	0.46	0.37	0.97	−0.02	0.00	0.67	0.68	−1.22	0.03	1.00
Denmark	0.42	0.00	0.25	0.00	−0.03	0.94	0.37	−0.42	−1.01	4.37
Egypt	0.22	0.00	7.87	−0.10	0.07	0.83	4.08	−2.16	1.18	1.57
Hong Kong	0.71	0.15	−1.78	0.07	0.65	0.50	−1.17	2.39	4.05	0.97
Hungary	0.20	0.00	2.39	0.04	−0.20	3.46	0.50	0.29	−1.12	1.73
India	0.53	0.03	12.58	−0.22	0.11	−0.64	4.47	−0.55	0.41	−0.88
Indonesia	0.59	0.00	6.80	0.20	−0.22	0.14	1.53	1.62	−2.98	0.11
Israel	0.19	0.08	1.99	0.03	0.01	0.34	1.20	0.21	0.09	0.41
Japan	0.63	0.00	−1.32	0.00	0.01	0.66	−3.63	0.16	0.35	6.94
Korea	0.67	0.10	0.04	−0.02	−0.06	1.58	0.06	−0.63	−1.66	7.48
Malaysia	0.52	0.02	0.48	−0.02	0.01	0.81	0.95	−1.80	0.26	5.56
Mexico	0.72	0.00	−17.79	0.79	−0.38	7.03	−2.60	6.91	−2.21	3.08
New Zealand	0.37	0.00	−0.46	−0.01	0.06	1.62	−0.29	−0.43	0.97	3.86
Norway	0.37	0.41	1.76	−0.01	−0.04	0.21	1.89	−1.49	−1.33	0.58
Peru	0.28	0.00	−9.17	0.01	−1.87	22.66	−0.26	0.02	−1.74	2.38
Philippines	0.42	0.01	1.07	0.03	−0.11	2.01	0.68	0.67	−1.54	3.86
Poland	0.23	0.00	1.62	0.10	−0.23	1.34	0.59	1.17	−1.70	1.04
Russia	0.85	0.10	−6.69	0.46	−0.57	6.32	−1.50	4.83	−6.72	3.21
Singapore	0.28	0.02	0.13	0.04	0.03	0.54	0.13	1.44	0.66	1.34
South Africa	0.26	0.00	5.53	−0.02	−0.03	1.17	3.44	−0.20	−0.62	2.92
Sweden	0.62	0.00	−1.34	0.00	0.00	1.52	−1.61	0.34	0.09	6.47
Switzerland	0.60	0.00	−1.36	−0.02	0.00	1.06	−2.51	−1.60	0.08	5.88
Thailand	0.50	0.03	0.86	0.00	−0.05	0.97	1.26	−0.04	−1.68	5.19
Turkey	0.28	0.00	−2.76	0.38	−0.30	7.95	−0.17	1.68	−0.98	2.13
United Kingdom	0.40	0.00	0.21	0.00	−0.03	0.95	0.28	0.13	−0.86	3.72

TABLE 31.12 Inflation Rates, Growth in M3, Real GDP, and the US Inflation Rate

Country	R²	P-value	Constant	M3	GDP	US inflation	Constant t-stat	M3 t-stat	GDP t-stat	US inflation t-stat
Australia	0.49	0.00	-0.64	0.23	-0.05	0.87	-0.60	2.26	-1.30	3.71
Brazil	0.94	0.13	-9.16	1.01	0.19	0.10	-0.90	20.08	0.69	0.03
Canada	0.77	0.00	-0.18	-0.18	0.01	1.41	-0.30	-1.67	0.35	9.06
Chile	0.18	0.00	1.36	0.04	0.01	2.18	0.43	0.44	0.04	1.89
China	0.11	0.00	1.16	0.16	0.05	0.70	0.30	1.23	0.42	0.58
Colombia	0.76	0.00	-0.28	0.69	-0.33	0.43	-0.15	7.17	-4.21	0.80
Czech Republic	0.45	0.63	-0.32	0.16	-0.07	0.80	-0.25	1.13	-1.11	1.26
Denmark	0.51	0.00	-0.17	0.08	-0.03	0.90	-0.26	2.34	-1.08	4.56
Egypt	0.11	0.00	7.57	-0.06	0.04	0.97	3.68	-0.76	0.63	1.71
Hong Kong	0.50	0.02	0.76	-0.02	0.53	0.05	0.40	-0.14	2.10	0.08
Hungary	0.61	0.01	0.44	0.79	-0.18	0.45	0.13	4.42	-1.51	0.31
India	0.51	0.03	12.70	-0.12	-0.01	-0.82	3.02	-0.37	-0.12	-1.34
Indonesia	0.59	0.00	5.56	0.38	-0.17	-0.47	1.12	1.59	-1.69	-0.33
Israel	0.42	0.03	0.72	0.23	0.07	0.00	0.37	0.91	0.61	0.00
Japan	0.66	0.00	-1.24	0.10	-0.01	0.53	-3.84	1.72	-0.44	4.49
Korea	0.69	0.08	-0.56	0.08	-0.08	1.36	-0.69	1.46	-2.73	5.42
Malaysia	0.52	0.13	-0.11	0.10	-0.03	0.63	-0.17	1.90	-1.35	4.23
Mexico	0.78	0.00	-5.35	0.99	-0.10	-0.06	-0.93	8.27	-0.62	-0.03
New Zealand	0.55	0.00	-1.80	0.36	0.04	0.93	-1.44	3.34	0.84	2.35
Norway	0.17	0.29	1.47	-0.05	-0.04	0.44	2.26	-0.81	-1.37	1.53
Peru	0.29	0.00	-11.80	0.39	-2.21	23.14	-0.35	0.50	-1.92	2.47
Philippines	0.49	0.00	-0.13	0.16	-0.13	1.79	-0.08	2.02	-2.05	3.58
Poland	0.66	0.09	-0.59	0.43	-0.18	0.48	-0.31	4.44	-2.06	0.55
Russia	0.90	0.17	-9.68	0.81	-0.52	2.72	-2.61	6.59	-7.47	1.53
Singapore	0.24	0.02	-0.28	0.09	0.04	0.52	-0.24	0.99	0.88	1.25
Svouth Africa	0.26	0.00	5.61	-0.03	-0.03	1.19	2.97	-0.19	-0.67	2.74
Sweden	0.65	0.00	-1.08	-0.12	0.02	1.68	-1.32	-1.45	0.47	6.93
Switzerland	0.59	0.00	-0.88	-0.11	0.00	1.02	-1.28	-1.38	0.06	5.49
Thailand	0.54	0.00	0.65	0.03	-0.07	0.98	0.98	1.43	-2.13	5.42
Turkey	0.62	0.00	-1.57	0.68	-0.30	3.41	-0.18	5.13	-1.49	1.22
United Kingdom	0.42	0.00	0.43	-0.02	-0.02	0.89	0.58	-0.96	-0.41	3.53

Reference

[1] Canto VA, Nickelsburg G. Currency substitution: theory and evidence from Latin America. Boston, Massachusetts: Kluwer Academic Publishing; 1987. Miles Marc A. Currency substitution: perspective, implications and empirical evidence. In: Putnam B, Wilford DS, editors. The monetary approach to international adjustment. New York: Praeger; 1978.

SECTION V

THE FINANCIAL CRISIS—A CASE STUDY

32

The Financial Crisis: Inflection Point or Black Swan?

In 2009 amid the financial crisis and its aftermath, a good friend and client suggested that the United States had developed a false sense of security over the prior 25 years. His argument went something like this: tax rate reductions, deregulation, globalization, freer trade, as well as the fall of the Evil Empire were the growth elixir that the world needed. The United States lifted the rest of the world out of the doldrums. But the fiscal side was only half of the story. The decline in the underlying inflation rate to the low single digits and an easy credit policy at different points in time led to a significant and dangerous increase in leverage across the world's economies, including the United States.

The increased leverage was in part explained by developments in finance in the form of securitization, which led people to believe that they were no longer constrained by income. The only relevant constraint was wealth, which allowed people to borrow a high percent of their net worth. From an individual perspective, it created a sense of security. The results of the government policies combined with the financial innovations were a bull market since 1982, which convinced everyone, including many academics like Jeremy Siegel [1], that equity markets were the place to be. In addition, the sustained market expansion led to the belief that policymakers had found a magic wand and business cycles were a thing of the past. All of this led to the expectations of an ever-expanding pie.

The developments in financial economics allowed individuals to trade away all sorts of specific risks by giving them a false sense of security. As we know now and should have known then, some of the risks that people insured for could not be fully diversified away. Individual diversification of risk is sometimes nothing more than a game of musical chairs. Ultimately, someone is holding the risk and when the music stops they were eliminated from the game through bankruptcy or some other hardship. Collectively, society remained at risk.

From an individual perspective, the question commonly asked was how much risk were the individual players taking and what did the investors use to gauge their risk levels? The value at risk (VAR) proved to be the most popular method used to answer the question. In theory, VAR measures the likelihood of a mark-to-market loss on a fixed portfolio over a fixed time horizon. The underlying assumption in these calculations is that of normal functioning markets. This assumption means that VAR is nothing more than a sophisticated trend analysis. During the trend, or so-called normal market conditions, the model can measure the variation around the mean of the different variables and from that calculate the likelihood of gains and losses around the trend values. However, the model breaks down whenever there is an inflection point and a new trend is established. Around the inflection point, the VAR will become useless. At this point, the occurrences and/or losses may be deemed hard-to-predict as otherwise rare events beyond the realm of "normal expectations." What we have described so far gives rise to two alternative interpretations of the events. One is that the financial and

Economic Disturbances and Equilibrium in an Integrated Global Economy. http://dx.doi.org/10.1016/B978-0-12-813993-6.00032-5

economic developments of the years prior to the financial crisis collectively combined to form a predictable perfect storm. Then there is the concept of a Black Swan, a theory popularized by Nassim Nicholas Taleb, which gained currency among those in the financial community who believed that the financial crisis could not have been predicted [2]. We contend that there is a rational and logical explanation for the perfect storm conditions that led to the financial crisis.

DID WE FIND A BLACK SWAN?

The Black Swan concept is very fatalistic. The criteria commonly used to identify a Black Swan event is that the event has a major impact, appears as a complete surprise, and that after it has appeared, it is explained by human hindsight. There is not much we can do to forecast and/or anticipate events that are rare and beyond the realm of normal expectations. But the question we ask ourselves is whether these events are truly random? If they are not, there is hope. Perhaps by using a different modeling approach, we may be able to anticipate or at the very least identify earlier changes in the processes driving the economic system.

Looking back, we might be able to understand how we got there. Only then, we can truly answer the question of whether the financial crisis and the ensuing economic crash was a Black Swan. This is an important issue that we need to consider. We must determine whether the volatility was truly random. If we conclude that the volatility was not random, the next step is to figure out what caused the volatility and whether we could have anticipated it.

Needless to say, we do not believe that the financial markets and economic volatility was random. In fact, we believe that it was forecastable. In line with one of the conditions of the Black Swan, we will use hindsight to attempt to understand the market volatility and uncertainty surrounding the crisis. In our defense, we believe that we can say something even stronger. We wrote about the negative impact of the delevering of the United States and world economy. Unfortunately, we anticipated a swifter and more adequate policy response. The point here being that some of what happened leading to the crisis was a forecastable event [3].

AN INFLECTION POINT?

As we believe in incentives, we must be willing to argue that policy changes alter people's behavior in the short- and long-run, and that policy changes can alter an economy's risk return profile. If the application of the policy persists, people will begin to understand these changes and will react to them. The individual responses then leads to changes in the economy's return process, as well as the perceived risk return profile. In short, we are arguing that the trend and the fluctuations around the trend are in part policy driven, while simultaneously being affected by the individual market participants' reaction to these policy changes.

A final possibility to consider is that the policy changes, in addition to affecting the risk returns of the economy, they also resulted in some changes and innovations that proved to be quite beneficial in the long run, even though some short run excess may have been created. To illustrate the impact of the policies on the incentive structure, let's focus on the retention rates reported in Table 32.1. They represent the amount an investor would keep after paying the top rates applicable.

HINDSIGHT OR FORESIGHT?

The US Treasury's intervention of Fannie Mae and Freddie Mac during the financial crisis brought back memories of the S&L debacle and the Resolution Trust Corporation (RTC) [4]. A review of the S&L debacle provides several important lessons for financial institution regulators and investors in general. Moreover, the legislation enacted in response to the crisis substantially reformed the industry and dramatically altered Federal Deposit Insurance Corporation operations. The possibility of parallels between the two episodes and the differences in responses to the crisis provides some insight into the differences in performance of the economy in the aftermath of the government intervention as a result of the S&L crisis and the financial crisis that resulted in the Great Recession.

Looking back, one can argue that the election of Ronald Reagan marked an inflection point. Some may say that hindsight is 20/20, but in our defense, we can say that much of what we are now writing, we did anticipate and forecast at the time [5]. We also did forecast other things that did not come to pass, but we do believe that our calls were roughly consistent with what has transpired over the last three decades. So, we do not quite believe that it is all hindsight. Rather than review all of the policies, let's focus on the economic policy adopted by Reagan. In 1979, corporate debt yielded $30 worth of after-tax income; capital gains resulted in a net of $38.90, while dividends netted only $16.20 (Table 32.1). Clearly in 1979, capital gains were the preferred vehicle, as it resulted in the highest after-tax return. Capital gains had a $22.70 advantage over dividends. Think of it this way, if one could convert dividends into capital gains, the investor could receive an additional $22.70. In other

TABLE 32.1 Impact of the Constellation of Tax Rates on the Incentive Structure

	1979	1982	1983	1988	1990	1993	1998	2002	2012
Top tax rates (%)									
Corporate	46	46	46	35	35	35	35	35	35
Capital gains	28	20	20	28	28	28	20	15	25
Personal	50	50	50	28	31.90	40.80	40.80	36.10	44.60
Dividend taxes	70	50	50	28	31.90	40.80	40.80	15	25
SS	10.20	10.80	11.40	12.10	12.40	12.40	12.40	12.40	12.40
Medicare	2.10	2.60	2.60	2.90	2.90	2.90	2.90	2.90	2.90
Retention rate per $100									
Labor income	$44.00	$43.40	$43.10	$61.40	$57.90	$50.40	$50.40	$54.40	$47.10
Debt	$50.00	$50.00	$50.00	$72.00	$68.10	$59.20	$59.20	$63.90	$55.40
Dividends	$16.20	$27.00	$27.00	$46.80	$44.27	$38.48	$38.48	$55.25	$48.75
Capital gains	$38.88	$43.20	$43.20	$46.80	$46.80	$46.80	$52.00	$55.25	$48.75
Advantage per $100 of Pretax corporate profits									
Debts over dividends	$33.80	$23.00	$23.00	$25.20	$23.84	$20.72	$20.72	$8.65	$6.65
Debts over capital gains	$11.12	$6.80	$6.80	$25.20	$21.30	$12.40	$7.20	$8.65	$6.65
Capital gains over dividends	$22.68	$16.20	$16.20	–	$2.54	$8.32	$13.52	–	–

V. THE FINANCIAL CRISIS—A CASE STUDY

words, corporations had a strong incentive to deliver returns in the form of capital gains. No wonder capital gain-intensive vehicles like small-caps outperformed during the 1970s.

The Reagan tax rate reduction also altered the relative attractiveness of the return delivery mechanisms available to corporations. The tax rate reduction increased the after-tax returns of corporate debt, dividends, and capital gains (Table 32.1, column 2, and rows 4–6). The first Reagan rate cut increased the after-tax return of interest dividend income by 67%. The second Reagan tax rate cut had an equally impressive increase in the after-tax return of these two vehicles. It should not surprise people that the market valuation attracted capital and resulted in a market increase that was a multiple of the increase in after-tax return.

The Reagan tax rate had other effects on the economy and the markets. It significantly altered the relative attractiveness of the different vehicles. Corporate debt became top dog. By 1982, debt had a $23 and $6.8 advantage over dividends and capital gains, respectively. The debt advantage over dividends and capital gains grew to $24.5 by the time the second Reagan tax rate cut had taken effect. Viewed this way, it is easy to see why corporations and investors had a strong incentive to convert corporate profits into interest or corporate debt payments. Two basic strategies emerged: one was to capture accumulated capital gains of companies that were carrying their assets at historical costs. The other was to reduce the tax liability of profitable corporations by altering their structure and the way they delivered returns to investors. The basic idea of the second strategy is to load up the company with debt, such that the interest payments erase the corporate profits. Doing so effectively eliminates the corporate tax payments and the income is taxed only once at the individual level.

A financier named Michael Milken understood that many corporations were carrying assets at historical costs and that the market value of these assets was significantly higher. He also understood that many profitable corporations were delivering their returns in the form of dividend payments to their investors. Debt was the vehicle that allowed for the reduction of the tax payments associated with capital gains and/or dividends. The structure used by Milken required some equity, some bank financing and the bulk of the financing in the form of his high yield instruments. Milken, then a successful bond salesman for the firm Drexel Burnham Lambert, accurately gauged the markets appetite for leverage buyouts (LBOs) and popularized the perfect LBO financing instrument: junk bonds. As investors would buy junk bonds, which promised high returns based on future company cash flows, the LBO itself would be financed and everyone concerned would

come out a winner. Indeed, for several years the process worked splendidly. LBOs went through and rather than being just high risk, junk bonds delivered high returns, and at favorable tax rates to boot.

As the LBO/junk-bond marriages went off without a hitch, junk bonds were set on a high pedestal by the financial media. Not only were they high yield, but also their default rates were not much greater than higher-quality, lower-risk bonds. Junk, for a time, wasn't so shabby, in particular because LBO operations, *rather* than paying dividends, were converting existing cash flows into debt. In other words, early on there was real money behind these transactions, and the over-focus on debt was sustainable. Soon enough, however, the merit of the LBO mattered much less than the financing instrument.

Everyone wanted in on junk bonds, and regulators in their infinite wisdom allowed savings and loans (S&Ls) into the game. The S&Ls either held or issued high yield bonds. Unfortunately, as competition increased, standards were relaxed and the leverage factor increased. For many S&L borrowers the projects were close to 100% financed. Even worse, the loans were secured by the project themselves. So in many ways these investments became a one sided bet. If they worked, the project owner got a big payoff and realized huge capital gains. If the project failed, the owner walked away and the lending institution, the S&L, was left holding the bag. It is easy to see that with such an incentive structure, projects became increasingly riskier and the end game was easy to forecast. This is one clear example where government policies altered the risk characteristics of the overall economy. With the repeated applications, that is, loans, the outcome could not be in doubt. We all know how a game of Russian roulette ends. This was the case with the famous S&L debacle.

This is the first part of the story. But at this point, it is worthwhile to draw the parallel with the financial crisis. The story is the same, all one has to do is change the name of the players. The government increased the tax advantage of home ownership, which led to a surge in the real estate prices. But it did more than that. It also relaxed the qualification requirements for financing. The rising home prices and easier financing increased not only the demand for real estate and real estate financing, but it also increased the leverage factor. Much like the S&L crisis, the increase in financing and leverage was facilitated by new financing instruments. Securitizations became the financing mechanism that facilitated the leverage factor much like the junk bonds had done earlier. The rising prices also leads to an increase in the supply of real estate and eventually as the demand is satisfied, the prices will stop rising. But that is not all. If at that price there are excess returns and there are little or no restrictions to entry, new supply will continue coming online until the excess profits are eliminated and the prices and rates of returns converge to their long run average. This is a simple explanation that does not assume a Black Swan event.

Once the crisis hit, the government had to intervene and that gets us to the second part of the problem. It took over and closed many S&Ls, credit became tight, and the economy slowed down. To deal with troubled assets, the RTC was created. Over time the RTC disposed of these assets. However, in the meantime, the asset overhang had a significant negative impact on the real estate market for a few years. But the aftermath of the S&L crisis was nowhere near that of the effect of the financial crisis that led to the Great Recession. Taking the failure of the Lincoln Savings and Loans as the epicenter of the S&L crisis and the subsequent and unrelated events, such as the invasion of Iraq in 1991 and the George H.W. Bush tax rate increase, it is easy to see why these events would have a negative and adverse effect on the US economy. The S&L debacle, the credit crunch, and the tax increase culminated in a recession. Fortunately, the fundamental policy changes put in place by the Reagan administration remained in place even during the Clinton administration. While it is true that President Clinton raised personal income tax rates, at the same time, the United States inflation rate declined. More importantly, in 1994 the Republicans took over Congress and gridlock was the key word for the remainder of the Clinton administration. Clinton was unable or unwilling to reverse the Reagan policy mix. During the gridlock years, President Clinton lowered the capital gains tax rates and a different set of issues came to the forefront. The point here is that there was no Black Swan.

THE PARALLELS

There is a clear parallel between the events leading to the S&L debacle and recent events. We believe that in both cases cycles began with a change in the tax rate. In the S&L case, it was the Reagan tax rate cuts. In the Great Recession case, it was the 1997 treatment of residential real estate. In both cases, the tax rate change created an increase in the derived demand for credit and when credit became available, it resulted in a higher degree of leverage prior to both the S&L and the financial crisis.

Additionally, government policies and regulations in the quest to increase home ownership—a goal of both Democratic and Republican administrations—pushed leverage to excessive levels. It is widely accepted that much of the current market malaise began with the housing market debacle. We also believe that the 1997 legislation that changed the tax treatment of owner occupied houses marked the beginning of the housing boom. Let's look at a housing investment from a tax perspective. We know that the imputed income of an owner occupied house is not taxed. Similarly, the cost of carry, that is, the mortgage payment, is tax deductible to the homeowner. Finally, the homeowner gets to enjoy up to $500,000 worth of tax-free capital gains every 2 years. Assuming a normal down payment, a 4–1 leverage factor would not be uncommon. This means that a house that appreciated at the inflation rate would generate a return on equity well above those of the stock market's historical returns. The 1997 legislation induced homeowners to increase the size of their homes and to turn them over more frequently. The increase in demand due to the favorable tax treatment may very well explain why home prices did not experience a decline during the 2000 recession. However, it does not explain the explosion that occurred after the new millennium. For that, we need at least two additional factors and more than that will make our case even stronger.

One of the needed factors was the Fed's easy money policy that lowered interest rates for a considerable period. The so-called "Greenspan Put," which reduced the cost of carry significantly and encouraged a carry trade, resulted in an increased leverage for the economy as a whole. Then there is the tax rate structure. Recall that in 2002 under President Bush the top income tax rates were reduced and the capital gains and dividends began to be taxed at the same rate (Table 32.1). The personal income tax rate reduction increased the after-tax return of the corporate debt interest payments to $63.9 from $59.2. More importantly, debt still retained an advantage over capital gains of $8.7 per $100 worth of pretax income. Hence, debt was the preferred financing vehicle during the Bush administration. But to complete the parallel, we need to identify the equivalent of high yield bonds of the 1980s. The securitization of mortgage-backed securities filled that void. The logic of the mortgage-backed financing early on was right on the money. But as with high yield bonds, eventually everyone wanted in. Fannie and Freddie wanted in and, in time, they would purchase them. We know what happened next: a replay of the S&L crisis except that this time the crisis was deeper and wider than the S&L crisis. Also, unlike the S&L crisis, the government did not step in to create an RTC-like vehicle to take over the failed real estate that mortgage-backed issuers were financing. This interpretation of the events leads to the conclusion that there was no Black Swan, just bad policy and some excesses. The RTC during the S&L crisis accomplished its mission and the economic expansion continued. The US economy had a couple of economic slowdowns in between before the financial crisis hit.

References

[1] Siegel J. Stocks for the long run. McGraw Hill; 1984.
[2] Taleb N. The Black Swan: the impact of the highly improbable. Random House; 2007.
[3] See Canto, "Delivering and the Financial Markets," www.lajollaeconomics.com, December 15 2008.
[4] A primer on the S&L crisis can be found in the appendix.
[5] Canto Victor A, Bollman Gerald, Melich Kevin. Oil decontrol: the power of incentives could reduce OPEC's power to boost oil prices. Oil Gas J 1982;80(2):92–101.

33

The Financial Crisis: Could We Have Avoided It or At Least Minimize Its Impact?

A few years back we wrote a report that focused on the possible impact of the credit market's innovation that allowed the private sector to reduce the impact of their current income as a constraint on their spending shift toward a wealth constraint. The credit market's innovations facilitated a credit expansion and that, in part, fueled a prosperous economy. The decline in long-term interest rates combined with a rising net worth fueled an increase in the leverage and debt service of the economy. The increased debt made the economy vulnerable to an asset decline. That, in turn, would reduce the credit worthiness of the borrowers and capital adequacy of the lending institutions. We argued that the rising asset prices would lead to an increase in the housing supply and eventually the prices would stop rising and even a decline that if unchecked would create a vicious cycle.

At the time, we argued that whether a vicious cycle developed or not, and the strength of such a cycle would depend on the policy action enacted as the asset downturn began. This line of reasoning suggested that the financial crisis would not be a Black Swan event. In fact, we believed that the beginnings of the crisis could have been anticipated and some people did. Below, we present an analysis published by us in 2004. At the time it correctly identified the relevant issues. When discussing whether an incipient crisis would deteriorate into a full-blown crisis depended on the actions undertaken by the monetary authorities and the federal government. We pointed to examples such as Japan, where monetary policy was ineffective in restoring economic growth, as well as to the Resolution Trust Corporation (RTC) and Long-Term Capital Management (LTCM) financial crisis, where the authorities were successful in averting a major contagion to the rest of the economy.

The concluding remarks also illustrate something that investors face every day. They have no choice and thus must make decisions regarding their portfolios and their views of the economy. In this case, we believed that past performance would be a good indicator of future performance. We expected the authorities to look back at incidents like the LTCM and RTC and act accordingly. Based on this, we did not anticipate a downdraft as large as that of the financial crisis. However, an unexpected policy outcome does not invalidate the analysis. We still believe that had the authorities followed the blue print of previous crisis, the down draft would have been milder and less painful. We also believe that the recovery would have been faster and stronger.

Economic Disturbances and Equilibrium in an Integrated Global Economy. http://dx.doi.org/10.1016/B978-0-12-813993-6.00033-7

THE CREDIT AND LEVERAGE ECONOMY (OCTOBER 21, 2004)

In the absence of the credit markets, expenditures of individual consumers are constrained by their income flows, and thus, consumption has to match income each period. The consumption pattern will be one of famine during the low-income years and feast during the high-income years. This is opposed to a more steady consumption over their lifetime that could be achieved in a world where borrowing and lending are allowed. Another implication of the absence of capital markets is that individuals will be forced to delay or slow down their investment in human capital. That, in turn, reduces the future benefits of any investment. Thus, we can safely say that without the capital markets, the stock of human capital and the well-being of the individuals would be lower than it otherwise would be. In contrast, in a perfect capital markets world, individuals face a single constraint that the net present value of their income must not exceed the net present value of their expenditures over their lifetime. Consumption will be smoothed out and because of the financing opportunities, more investments will be undertaken earlier in time.

It is easy to see why that as the credit markets' development has taken us from the no credit world to fully functioning capital markets, economic well-being has increased. Another implication of the development of the capital markets is that the importance of the income constraint in any one year has diminished and given way to that of the net wealth constraint. To see this, look at the perspective of the lenders. All they want is to insure that they get repaid and as such, develop some decision rules that incorporate the vagaries of life. For example, they will never lend an amount higher than the borrower's net worth. Again, they want to make sure that the borrower has enough cash flow to make periodic interest payments. The loan-to-net worth and debt service-to-income ratios are two of the key variables used by the lenders to determine the ability of the borrowers to service and repay their debt. It is easy to see that to protect against the risk of default, lenders have developed rules that take into account uncertainty and the borrower's ability to repay and service the debt among other things.

In recent years some analysts have begun to raise a red flag regarding the use of credit by households. Many people believe that we are approaching a danger zone and that some adverse shock could create a major disaster in the credit market, which could propagate to the rest of the economy. The argument goes like this: while most economists are optimistic that the economic expansion can continue, the economy faces serious challenges. US citizens have taken on enormous amounts of debts in recent years, much of it tied to real estate.

That leaves them highly exposed to increased interest rates or a weakening housing market. The fear is that a decline in net worth or the ability to service the debt would reduce private sector spending. Another fear is that if the loan-to-value ratio increases above one, and the lending institutions are forced to mark to market, a major credit market crisis could ensue. Depending on the nature of the response, the regulatory agencies could either improve or worsen the situation. The potential for a meltdown of the credit system is a real one.

THE ANATOMY OF A CRISIS

A decline in housing prices could lead to a decline in household net worth and net capital of lending institutions, which leads to a secondary round of loan contraction and reduced spending. This would create the preconditions for a vicious cycle.

A reduction in the real estate prices below their loan-to-value ratio will effectively wipe out much of the net worth of many families, which in turn will reduce the household creditworthiness and borrowing ability. In fact, the decline in net worth may trigger the calling of other personal loans by the banks. In addition, households may be reluctant to walk away from the loan by turning the house back to the lending institution. Walking away means that the lending institution will send them a 1099 for the difference between the loan and the resale value of the house. Also if the resale of the house is higher than the cost basis, the homeowner may be also liable for capital gains taxes. So in addition to getting an IRS tax bill and having their credit ruined, households will have to pay rent on their new place. When all these factors are taken into consideration, the solution is to hunker down, make the mortgage payments, and cut everything else. History has shown that real estate trends up secularly, thus waiting it out is a viable option. In due course, the value of the house will increase to the point that the homeowners are above water and they can get out. The alternative to waiting is bankruptcy, which will wipe out the debt but it will also ruin the household's credit. A large enough decline in home prices could paralyze household spending for quite a long time.

A decrease in the value-to-loan ratio below one will reduce the net capital of the lending institutions. In Appendix A, we have some numerical examples illustrating the potential effects on a financial institution such as a bank. The analysis is fairly general and is easily extended to other types of lending institutions. The major point of the examples developed in Appendix A is that as net capital declines, even if the institution keeps the same capital adequacy ratio, their credit creation ability is reduced. To add insult to injury, in many cases prudence and/or the regulatory bodies force an increase in the capital adequacy ratio that in turn further reduces the credit creation of the institution.

JAPAN IS A PERFECT EXAMPLE

The funk of the Japanese economy during the 1990s is easily explained this way. Banks did not lend because of capital adequacy issues, while borrowers could not borrow because of net worth issues, as they did not qualify for the loans. The only way to get out of the funk is to take steps to increase the capital adequacy of the lending institutions, as well as increase the net worth of the borrowers. The steps taken by Japanese government's did not accelerate the solution to the overhang created by the bad loans and their impact on the banks' capital adequacy ratio. Hence, the banks did not extend credit even in the face of easy money and reserves. The Japanese central bank failed to understand that additional reserves would not be lent; they would all be held as excess reserves. That is why some people were saying that Japan was a modern example of a liquidity trap (nominal interest rates fell both at the long and short end of the curve and reached historic or near zero interest rates).

A GENERALIZATION OF THE CRISIS PRECONDITIONS

A decline in real estate prices that leaves financial or lending institutions with a great exposure to these loans in weakened conditions could under certain conditions develop into a financial crisis. Presumably, the adverse shock would simultaneously have a negative impact on the credit worthiness of borrowers and a decline in the net capital and capital adequacy ratio of the lending institution and that, in turn, would trigger a deleveraging of the credit system.

This type of analysis also applies to businesses as well as individuals. One immediate parallel is that of hedge funds. Both use borrowed money, as well as capital from homeowners and/or investors to acquire their assets. It is not uncommon for either one to borrow 2 to 4 times their initial equity investment (i.e., down payments). Therefore, both hedge funds and residential real estate investments are leveraged investments and, as such, they are critically dependent on the well-functioning of the US credit system. If one takes the parallels between the hedge funds and homeownership seriously, the concerns about excessive borrowing is potentially a more general problem than people realize.

We know that in recent times there has been a proliferation of hedge funds. We also know that during the last few months, many hedge funds have been underwater.

Until they make up for these losses, the hedge funds will not be able to collect their carry. This is especially important for the newer funds. They may not have the wherewithal to withstand the tough times. The incentives for the newer underwater hedge funds are to close shop and start again with a clean slate somewhere else. Individually, most of the funds we have in mind are small. However, as there are many of them collectively they may be as large in their holdings as were those of LTCM. A flurry of closings of many of the newer hedge funds could have a big impact on financial institutions holding some of the underwater hedge funds' papers. If the lending institutions rush to close out the position of the troubled hedge funds, they may have to write off or mark to market the paper. The institution holding the paper could experience a shortfall of capital, as well as an increase in the capital adequacy ratio, triggering a delevering and regulatory action. Will these adverse turns of events create a "run on the bank" or a major financial crisis? Our answer is that it depends on how the relevant regulatory authorities react to the initial shock to the financial system.

One can easily see the concerns of the markets regarding Fannie and Freddie and how they could create a major financial crisis similar to that of the S&L's during the late 1980s. First, both Fannie and Freddie have an equity exposure to the real estate market. Second, the recent accounting problems suggest that these institutions' net worth may be lower than previously thought, in turn requiring an increase in capital or a reduction loan issuance. Given the magnitude of the financing provided by these two institutions, it is clear to see why an adverse shock may trigger a potential crisis in the financial system. More recently, people have added a couple of other concerns. Fannie Mae and Freddie Mac have both run into trouble for the way they keep their books. Fannie and Freddie, through their intermediation function, have added a great deal of liquidity to the credit markets. A disruption in their operations would affect both home financing and the buyers of the Fannie and Freddie securities, such as hedge and mutual funds. Thus, it is easy to see how the regulators' response to the actions of Fannie and Freddie could affect the credit markets and the overall economy. A recent article in *The Wall Street Journal* said it best [1]:

> …There are banks and others that originate mortgage loans, but don't want to tie up their money. There are investors, such as giant institutions and mutual fund shareholders, who want the income from making mortgages without the hassle.
>
> So the middlemen buy mortgages and sell them in bundles to investors. Fannie and Freddie guarantee that homeowners will make monthly payments. Investors take the risk that plunging interest rates will prompt homeowners to pay loans early.

So far so good. These are laudable objectives and illustrate how financial intermediation can make society better off. The problem is that Fannie and Freddie did not stop here. As the same *Wall Street Journal* article eloquently put it:

> Over the past decade, Fannie and Freddie have gone a step further and held on to more mortgages instead of selling them. As of the end of August, the two held a total of $1.56 trillion in mortgages.
>
> This is a lucrative business because the companies borrow so inexpensively, thanks to widespread market perceptions that the U.S. government will bail them out if they get in trouble... Holding mortgages, particularly 30-year fixed rate mortgages, in a world in which interest rates gyrate is a volatile business. To damp that, Fannie and Freddie hedge in financial markets. The proper accounting for such hedges is now at issue at Fannie.

HOW TO DEAL WITH A POTENTIAL CRISIS

Financial crises begin with an adverse shock that reduce the net worth of borrowers and the net capital of lending institutions. We have shown how a decline in net capital could reduce the supply of credit while the decline in net worth reduces the borrowing ability of the private sector. The two combined are a recipe for disaster. Thus, any attempt to prevent an adverse shock requires that the relevant authorities take steps to minimize the impact of the adverse shocks. Looking back at the last two decades, steps have been taken to isolate the capital adequacy issues from the lending issues. The imminent insolvency of LTCM had the potential to degenerate into a major crisis. The counterparty to the LTCM position was at risk; they would not be able to collect if LTCM went under. The financial institutions backing many of these loans would have to mark the market and take a hit to their capital and even if there was no change in their capital adequacy ratio, the lower capital would force the financial institution to abruptly delever the economy. The Fed, by stepping in quickly, arranged to isolate the LTCM portfolio in a way that minimized the impact on the financial institutions' capital and liquidity provision.

The Fed was quick to act to insure the liquidity of the system. Steps were taken to carve out the impact of the LTCM portfolio on the net capital of the financial system and a major crisis was averted. The focus was on the impact the crisis would have on the credit market and the economy. We know that if the crisis were allowed to develop, the solvency of these institutions would be called into question. The decline in the net capital of these institutions would impose an additional constraint on the loan creation ability of these institutions (see Appendix A).

The United States was able to weather the storm in short order and the recovery was much faster. In the case of the S&L crisis, the vehicle used by the regulatory authorities to isolate the decline in net worth of the S&L industry was the RTC, which allowed the system to clean up the balance sheet of surviving S&L's. Bankruptcies and return of the properties also helped to clean up the private sector balance sheet. However, to an extent the credit history stayed with them and the overhang of the RTC portfolio of properties may have slowed down the equilibrating process.

The common denominator to the crises we have in mind has been Alan Greenspan. We must give him credit for the superior performance of the US financial system during these crises. The Fed has been quick to insure enough liquidity in the system. It has also increased the monetary base and, in some cases, effectively reduced the capital adequacy ratio by encouraging the banks to lend.

One point that needs to be made is that sometimes the regulatory/monetary authorities are the cause of the shock. Our example here is the Maestro's concern with Y2K. In mid-1999 the Fed accelerated its money creation (i.e., monetary base) but through regulation and threats of regulation, it cajoled the financial institutions to increase their lending rate. In effect, the Fed regulatory action increased the capital adequacy ratio because what the Fed wanted to insure was that there would be enough cash to meet any problems with Y2K. However, as the "century date change" took effect and nothing happened to the financial system, the Fed quickly pulled the cash out of the system but insofar as it did not remove the regulatory burden, credit also declined. Overlay on that the impact of a declining net worth due to the stock market decline on the borrowing ability of the private sector and we had the makings of an economic slowdown, a vicious cycle where declining net worth results in lower credit and vice versa. In effect, the Fed facilitated an already declining economy and stock market decline.

HOW RESILIENT IS THE US FINANCIAL SYSTEM?

Some worry about the response by the relevant authorities while others express doubts as to the ability of the system to withstand certain types of shocks. Yet the US experience with incidents such as the savings and loan crisis of the late 1980s in many ways may parallel any potential problems with Fannie and Freddie. The incident with LTCM, a hedge fund, highlights potential problems with the hedge fund industry. Y2K on the other hand points to other possible disturbances with the credit markets. The resilience of the US economy and the robustness of the financial markets to withstand these economic shocks are reassuring. There is no reason to believe that financial markets will not be able to withstand another credit/financial shock. Looking back at these three episodes, it becomes clear that the response of the relevant authorities, such as the Fed or any pertinent regulatory agency can either accelerate the recovery and/or exacerbate the crisis. It behooves investors and analysts to consider the range of policy responses and looking back at these three episodes is one way to do so.

APPENDIX A: CREDIT CREATION CONSTRAINTS

The banking system credit and money creation abilities are linked and limited by two distinct factors: reserve requirements and capital adequacy ratios. Let us consider each one of them individually.

Reserve requirement: At a 10% reserve requirement, $10 worth of reserves can support $100 worth of deposits. In turn, the $100 are recorded as liabilities of the banks. On the asset side of the ledger, the banks will record the $10 worth of reserves backing the deposits plus $90 worth of loans. The lower the reserve requirement the higher the deposit and credit creation ability of financial institutions. A reduction of the reserve requirements to 5% will increase the banks' deposit creation to $200 and the loans creation to $190.

Capital Adequacy Ratios: So far our analysis has assumed that the capital adequacy ratio, the other constraint on domestic credit creation, is not binding. An example illustrates our point. A bank with a 3% capital adequacy ratio and $5 worth of capital is only willing to extend $166.5 worth of credit. Thus even if we assume no reserve requirement, the maximum credit creation potential of a bank is limited by the capital adequacy ratio and domestic credit creation limits imposed by the reserve requirement on bank deposits. During economic slowdowns, increases in the monetary base will only lead to excess reserve holding which means that the interest rates paid on deposits will decline. The slope of the yield curve will flatten.

The Credit Market Equilibrium: In the previous example, the credit creation ability of the banks is limited by two distinct constraints: the reserve requirement and the capital adequacy ratio. In the previous example, a 3% capital adequacy ratio and $5 worth of capital will support $166.5 worth of credit, while the $10 worth of reserves and the 5% reserve requirement support $190 worth of loan. In this example, the limiting factor is the capital adequacy ratio. If the bank capital increases to $10, a different scenario occurs. Now the capital adequacy ratio will support twice as many loans or $333 while the reserve requirement constraint on deposit creation remains the same at $190. As now the binding constraint is the reserve requirement and not the capital adequacy ratio, the credit creation will now be $190. Equilibrium will require an increase in the spread between the short and the long end during economic expansions and a decline in the slope during the recession.

Reference

[1] Wessel D, Fannie, Freddie won't do big harm. Wall St J, October 7, 2004.

34

The Roadmap to a Backcast

We believe that there is a strong parallel between the Savings and Loans (S&L) crisis and the Great Recession and financial crisis. Yet despite the parallels, the post-crisis economic performance was quite different. This immediately leads one to wonder that the differences in performance was mostly attributable to the differences in policy response during the two crises. This is a topic suggested by a comparison of the parallel and differences between the two crises that we will pursue in this section. However, prior to doing so, we must establish the parallels between the policies that led to both crises. In the process of describing some of the innovations and policy initiatives, we also discuss some implications and derive some insights regarding these policies, which will prove quite useful for a subsequent analysis.

A PRIMER ON THE S&L CRISIS

The causes for the S&L crisis have been documented by academics for more than a decade. The list includes among others the following:

- Thrifts were exposed to interest risks (caused by a mismatch in duration and by the interest rate sensitivity of assets and liabilities).
- The elimination of regulation Q which caused increasing costs of thrift liabilities relative to many fixed rate assets.
- State and Federal regulations allowed thrifts to enter new but riskier markets.

- A reduction in capital requirements, which allowed the thrifts to use alternative accounting procedures to increase reported capital levels.
- The repeal of the safe harbor leasing provision in 1986, originally enacted in 1981, which had greatly benefited commercial real estate investments.
- The development during the 1980s of the brokered deposit market.

Our Interpretation: Rather than provide a broad history of events, our focus is narrower. We want to provide a stylized version of the events leading up to the crisis, as well as the remedies taken after the crisis. Our approach is very simple. We assume that, initially and broadly speaking, the S&L market was in equilibrium and something new had to happen to disturb the market. The thrifts' exposure to interest risks and/or duration mismatch was not new to the thrifts. They borrowed short and lent long. We find it difficult to believe that the duration mismatch was the source of the equilibrium disturbance. If the elimination of the regulation Q reduced the relative profitability of the thrifts, expansion of their loan portfolio would only increase the magnitude of the losses. The elimination of regulation Q could not have been the source of the expansion of S&Ls during the 1980s.

Perhaps to counter the negative effects of regulation Q, the Federal Home Loan Bank Board attempted to attract new capital by liberalizing ownership restrictions for stock-held institutions. Federally chartered stock associations were required to have a minimum of

Economic Disturbances and Equilibrium in an Integrated Global Economy. http://dx.doi.org/10.1016/B978-0-12-813993-6.00034-9

400 stockholders; no individual could own more than 10% of an institution's outstanding stock, and no controlling group more than 25%. Also 75% of the owners had to reside or do business in the S&L market area. The elimination of these restrictions coupled with the Garn-St Germain Depository Institutions Act of 1982, as well as the Depository Institutions Deregulation and Monetary Control Act of 1980 (DIDMCA) reduced and relaxed the capital requirements as well as the ability to acquire an institution by contributing "in kind capital" (i.e., stocks, land, real estate, etc.). These changes attracted new owners into the industry.

Unfortunately the two laws made a number of other significant changes that impacted thrift institutions, particularly the expanded authority of federally chartered thrifts to make acquisitions, development, and construction (ADC) loans enacted in DIDMCA. Add to this the Garn-St Germain elimination of the previous statutory limit on loan to value ratios and S&Ls were able to make high-risk loans to developers for 100% of a project's appraised value. Sounds familiar? It is clear from this summary that the regulations reduced the capital requirements and gave these institutions a greater flexibility in terms of expanding and the nature of their portfolios.

The "moral hazard" problem was exacerbated by these legislations. On the depositor's side, DIDMCA increased the federal deposit insurance to $100,000 per account, more than doubling the previous $40,000 limit. Clearly the increase in Federal Deposit Insurance Corporation (FDIC) exacerbated the moral hazard problem. As long as investors had less than $100,000, their money was safe. So investors put their money in the institutions that paid higher interest rates. These were often the institutions in weaker financial situations that were about to fail. Depositors did not mind or care as their money was safe.

A large percentage of S&L assets were devoted to ADC loans; these were very attractive because of their favorable accounting treatment and the potential for future profits if the projects were successful. In many cases, prudent underwriting standards were ignored. Necessary controls were not put in place and lending on construction projects were based on the overly optimistic assumption that property values would continue to increase. Often the S&L lent 100% of the investment amount upfront. More important to our story, ADC loans were frequently nonrecourse loans meaning the borrower was not required to sign a legally binding personal guarantee.

The One-Sided Bet: So far, as we have described the situation, we have the making of a one-sided bet. Borrowers had quite an incentive to borrow and make risky investments. If the investment panned out they would stand to make quite a bit of money as did the bank with

their equity position. If the investment did not pan out, the investor with 100% of the investment amount lent would not be worried. They had no skin in the game. If the S&L went under, the depositors with less than $100,000 were not worried either. They were covered by the FDIC. In short, everyone was encouraged to take risk. The cumulative effect of the risk taking would be failure, but all parties had their downside covered by the government.

THE IMPACT OF THE REGULATORY CHANGES ON THE S&Ls

We are fond of saying that people respond to incentives. The S&L debacle is a perfect textbook example that illustrates this point even when the incentives are of the perverse kind. Looking back, with the benefit of hindsight, we can identify some of the effects of the changes enacted at the time. The legislative changes and the safe harbor leasing provisions of the Reagan tax rate cuts encouraged a swift and rapid change in the S&L industry. The demand for loans increased dramatically, a demand in part fueled by an influx of deposits, often via money brokers into institutions willing to pay above-market rate interest rates. From the end of 1982 to the end of 1985, total S&L assets increased to $1,068 billion from $686 billion, or 56% more than twice the growth rate at commercial banks. Another major change resulting from the deregulation was that beginning in 1982, S&L investment portfolios changed from traditional home mortgage financing to investments in everything from casinos, ski resorts, and even windmill farms. On the financial engineering front, the S&L invested in junk bonds, arbitrage schemes, and derivate instruments.

SPILLOVER EFFECTS

The S&Ls' changes had a profound impact on the profitability of the banks. On the liability side of the balance sheet, the S&Ls were willing to pay above-market interest rates to attract money to invest in new activities. S&Ls would advertise their rates and use in-house "money desks" or get in touch with brokerage houses to gain access to funds. In doing so they increased the cost of funds not only for the thrifts, but also for the banks. The higher cost of funds clearly reduced their profitability. Unfortunately banks also got hit on the asset side of the balance sheet. The S&Ls were moving into the bank's lending turf.

Second, as a result of the disturbance, excesses were committed and at some point in time either the economy (i.e., the market) or the government attempted to restore equilibrium. An issue that comes to mind is whether the government actions accelerated the adjustment process or whether it had an additional impact on the economy. The final issue we will try to deal with is to identify the winners and losers of the government-imposed solution. However our first step is to highlight some background information leading to what experts consider to be the sources or contributions to the S&L crisis.

The Catalyst: We have already argued that the excess of the S&Ls would eventually lead to a crisis. However, the inevitable was accelerated by a change in tax laws. The elimination of the safe harbor leasing provision of the Reagan tax rate cuts altered the economics of some real estate investments. Once appreciation decelerated and asset prices even declined, loan losses were being recorded by S&Ls. Their capital began to deteriorate and to stay in business they would have to increase deposits and raise additional capital. Reckoning day was coming and the change in the tax laws accelerated it.

The Government Solution: Through the decade, losses in the S&L industry continued to mount as the decline in real estate values deepened. From 1986 to 1989 the Federal Savings and Loan Insurance Corporation closed or resolved 296 institutions with a combined asset base of $125 billion. But that was not enough. Congress enacted the Financial Institutions Reform, Recovery and Enforcement Act of 1989 (FIRREA). FIRREA created the Resolution Trust Corporation (RTC). It marked the beginning of taxpayer involvement in the cleanup of the savings and loan industry. The RTC was slated to resolve the thrifts placed into conservatorship or receivership between January 1989 and August 8, 1992. It was to cease operations by December 31, 1996. By 1995 the agency had resolved 747 additional thrifts with total assets of $394 billion. By the end, the number of thrifts had declined by approximately 50%. The decline forced a major restructuring of the industry.

THE FANNIE AND FREDDIE CRISIS

We want to emphasize five factors that we believe contributed to the Government Sponsored Enterprise (GSE) crisis.

1. The GSE twins were exposed to interest risks.
2. Federal regulations allowed thrifts to enter new but riskier markets.
3. A reduction in capital requirement, which allowed the GSE to use alternative accounting procedures to increase reported capital levels.
4. The development of the securitization subprime MBS.
5. The GSEs thought they could go beyond their original mandate and by using derivatives to hedge

their position and replicate the original intent while at the same time expanding the amount of business and profitability.

Our Interpretation: As with the S&L section, our first step is to provide a stylized description of what we consider to be the key features of the "market equilibrium." In the process, we highlight some key similarities and differences with the S&L industry. The key similarity is that much like the S&Ls of yesteryear, Fannie and Freddie were in the business of financing residential real estate. However, there are some clear differences between S&Ls and the GSEs:

- The mandate for S&Ls was a bit broader, while initially Fannie and Freddie were restricted by law to purchasing single-family homes with unpaid balances below a specific amount (i.e., the conforming loan limit). The limits are adjusted each year to reflect changes in the national average of single home prices. As of 2006, the conforming loan limit is $417,000.
- Fannie and Freddie had no depositors and as a result there was no danger of them suffering a run as Northern Rock did in the United Kingdom.
- Another difference between S&Ls and Fannie and Freddie was the capital requirements. The statutory minimum capital level for the GSE was 2.5% of the aggregate balance sheet assets and 0.45% of the off-balance sheet assets. These capital requirements afford the GSE a higher degree of leverage than S&Ls. For example, the twins had core capital of $83.2 billion at the end of 2007 supporting $5.2 trillion of debts and guarantees, producing a 65 to 1 leverage ratio. There is no way a private bank would be allowed to have such a highly leveraged balance sheet, nor would it qualify for an AAA rating.

S&Ls are exposed naturally to interest rate risks caused by a mismatch in duration and by interest rate sensitivity of assets and liabilities. That was not necessarily the original intent for GSEs. Fannie and Freddie guaranteed investors who bought Fannie and Freddie bonds a reasonable amount of protection. Since the group focused on mortgages to borrowers with good credit scores and a down payment, the investors would have quite a bit of protection against a housing downturn. So far, the story is a good one. The GSE facilitated and improved home financing.

However, as the securitization of prime and subprime loans took off, new competitors entered the market and the twins saw their market share decline. The GSEs understood the desire of political class to have "affordable housing" and took advantage of this and effectively and successfully lobbied to relax some of the restrictions they faced and the began to buy MBS issued by others. Again, this was nothing more than a version of the carry trade, as they used their cost advantage or cheap financing to buy higher yielding assets.

With their funding advantage, lower capital requirements than other regulated financial institutions and banks, combined with the increased demand for residential real estate, Fannie Mae and Freddie Mac were right there. Given their profit margin and their credit guarantee, there was a simple way to increase their profits: they purchased and invested in huge amounts of mortgages and MBS. In some years, the twins were buying 50% of all "private label" MBS, which left them exposed to the very subprime assets they were supposed to avoid. But that is not all; the regulators allowed the twins to operate with very little capital. According to Office of Federal Housing Enterprise Oversight (OFHEO), the two had a core capital of $83.2 billion at the end of 2007 supporting $5.2 trillion of debt and guarantees and were counterparties in $2.3 trillion worth of derivative transactions related to their hedging activities. Because of the GSE's relatively small equity in relation to their portfolio, an adverse downdraft would have a large negative impact. With so little equity cushion, an adverse shock could easily wipe out their equity. Leverage works both ways. When someone does not have too much capital, things only have to go a little wrong to wipe you them out. During 2006 and 2007, the GSEs were losing something like $5 billion a year. At the time, if the assets and liabilities were realized immediately, both had negative net worth.

Other landmines were the insurance protective measures undertaken by the GSE. One concern was the issue of delinquent loans. When borrowers failed to keep up payments on mortgages in the pool that support asset backed loans, Fannie and Freddie had to buy back the loans. But that forced the twins to take a write-off at times when the market price of asset-backed loans was depressed. Instead the twins sometimes paid the interest into the pool to keep the loans afloat. A second issue was that the GSE took steps to insure their portfolios against interest rate risk. One major concern was whether the borrowers would pay back their loans early leaving them with cash to invest at a lower rate. Then there is the insurance that the GSE bought against borrowers' default when the homeowner put a down payment less than 20%. The insurance and hedging associated with these activities induced them to take huge positions in the derivatives markets that later were at the center of the GSEs' accounting scandal earlier in the decade.

The "moral hazard" problem can be traced to the legislation creating the GSE. The implicit government guarantee allowed the GSE to borrow more cheaply than what they could get on the securitized mortgages they bought. Hence, the GSE made the spread afforded by the implicit government guarantee. It was a license to create profits. The GSEs did not have to be exposed to interest rate risk. However, the implicit guarantee became a one-sided bet and pushed them in that direction. The GSE obtained regulatory relief that allowed them to buy and hold subprime mortgage backed securities. They did so as a result of a simple carry trade strategy aimed at increasing their profits.

The experiences of the GSE suggest that in some cases the private and public purpose combination is a lethal mix. On the one side, the private purpose suggests that the shareholders get to keep all the gains, while the implicit government guarantee means that ultimately the government gets to keep the losses. In other words, the combination skews the risk reward distribution in favor of taking additional risks, hence the moral hazard issues. One way to deal with the moral hazard issue is through regulations and that brings us to another issue. A direct solution is better than an indirect one. A direct solution links the shareholder's positive and negative incentives by allowing them to keep the good (i.e. profits) and also make them responsible for the bad (i.e. losses). Looking back, it is apparent that had the GSE not deviated from their original mandate and intent of the legislation creating them, things may have worked out for the better. In fact, that seemed to be the case while the regulations worked. Unfortunately GSEs had an incentive to circumvent or modify the original regulations, hence their army of lobbyists and largesse in their political contributions they were successful in altering the way they were regulated. Only in that way could they insure their franchise and profitability.

Two Wrongs Don't Make a Right: The desire to maximize profits through the exploitation of the government-guarantee-cost advantage created a perverse incentive whereby the GSEs lobbied the government in order to be able to expand their loan portfolios. Unfortunately, the expansion of the portfolio increased the risk of ruin and the potential liabilities of the federal government. The incentive structure created by the guarantee led the GSE to deviate from the original intent of their creation and as they expanded their activities the overall risk of their portfolios was increased in an excessive manner. That forced the GSEs to buy insurance against some of their risk exposures which in turn added to the complexity of their portfolios. For example, they bought insurance against borrower default when the homebuyer lacked the 20% down payment. Another factor adding to the complexity of the twins' financial situation was the need for both GSEs to insure their portfolios against interest risk - in particular, the danger that borrowers would pay their loans early if interest rates fell forcing them to invest at a lower rate. This risk caused the GSE to take huge positions in the derivate markets. In fact, this led to some accounting scandals among the GSEs.

Viewed in the best possible light, they thought they could replicate the same results by going beyond their original mandate and they would use derivatives to hedge their position and replicate the original intent while at the same time expanding the amount of business and thus making the spread or comparative advantage granted to them by the GSE. By expanding their volume of loans, they made the potential downside even worse.

The expansion of the GSE portfolio by itself would not have made matters worse. What led to the downfall is the end to the housing price appreciations. Once that occurred the math did not work for sub-prime borrowers, and those with a non-recourse loan could walk away from the deal leaving the lender to face the music. Given the structure of the market for mortgage backed securities, the slicing and repackaging of the risk tranches was hailed as a major innovation in financial economics that made the market vastly more efficient. However, the proponents overlooked one thing: the repackaging of the mortgages meant that once repackaged it would be very difficult to surgically remove a bad loan from the portfolio. More importantly, it would be very difficult to track the health of the individual loans in the portfolios. It would be also virtually impossible to determine the impact on individually packaged mortgages. In short, as the popular saying goes, you cannot unscramble the omelet. The transaction could not be undone if there was a problem with one of the loans used in the tranches. So, the whole market suffered and if leverage worked as expected, it multiplied the profits of the GSEs during the good times as well as multiplying the losses during the bad times. The latter led to a decline in GSE capital and when it reached the "critical capital" and the regulators in accordance with the law were forced to appoint a conservator.

Members of the Congress were strong supporters of Fannie Mae and Freddie Mac. Despite warnings and red flags raised by some, they continued to allow the companies to increase in size and risk, and encouraged them to purchase an increasing number of lower credit quality loans. So, per our interpretation, it was the deviation from the original intent that caused the problems for the GSEs. They should have never been allowed to purchase MBS.

The Response to the Crisis: The newly elected President Obama inherited a financial crisis that was not of his making. Even prior to taking office, the incoming demonstration coordinated with the outgoing Bush administration policies aimed at easing the effects of the crisis. Once in office the Obama administration took steps aimed at correcting the financial crisis affecting financial institutions and the overall economy. The centerpiece of the reforms are embodied in the Dodd-Frank Legislation and the Consumer Financial Protection Bureau. A brief chronology of these two legislations follows:

- The Dodd–Frank Wall Street Reform and Consumer Protection Act, commonly referred to as Dodd–Frank, was initially proposed by the Obama administration in June 2009, when the White House sent as a response to the financial crisis sent a series of proposed bills to Congress. The Dodd–Frank legislation constituted the most significant changes to the regulatory apparatus of the financial industry since the great depression.
- The institutions affected by the legislation changes include most of the regulatory agencies that up to that time were involved in monitoring the financial system such as the FDIC, US Securities and Exchange Commission (SEC), Office of the Comptroller of the Currency (OCC), Federal Reserve (the "Fed"), the Securities Investor Protection Corporation (SIPC), and so on, and the elimination of the Office of Thrift Supervision.
- In addition to eliminating an agency, the Office of Thrift Supervision, Dodd–Frank created new institutions, the Financial Stability Oversight Council and the Office of Financial Research in addition to the Bureau of Consumer Financial Protection.
- The legislation aims to provide rigorous standards and supervision to protect the economy and American consumers, investors, and businesses; end taxpayer-funded bailouts of financial institutions; provide for an advanced warning system on the stability of the economy; create new rules on executive compensation and corporate governance; and eliminate certain loopholes that according to the Obama administration led to the 2008 economic recession.

The Dodd–Frank legislation changes the existing regulatory structure and in many ways represents a change in the way America's financial markets will operate in the future. As a practical matter, it expanded the reach of the regulatory apparatus. For example, prior to the passage of Dodd–Frank, investment advisers were not required to register with the SEC if the investment adviser had fewer than 15 clients during the previous 12 months and did not hold itself out generally to the public as an investment adviser. The act eliminated that exemption, thereby rendering numerous additional investment advisers, hedge funds, and private equity firms subject to new registration requirements. And that leads us to what we believe will be the vehicle of change:

- The Consumer Financial Protection Bureau (CFPB) is established as an independent agency located inside and funded by the United States Federal Reserve. The agency was designed to consolidate employees and responsibilities from a number of other federal regulatory bodies, including the Federal Reserve, the Federal Trade Commission, the Federal Deposit

Insurance Corporation, the National Credit Union Administration, and even the Department of Housing and Urban Development.

- The bureau writes and enforces rules for financial institutions, examines both bank and nonbank financial institutions, monitors markets, and collects and tracks consumer complaints.
- The CFPB jurisdiction includes banks, credit unions, securities firms, payday lenders, mortgage-servicing operations, foreclosure relief services, debt collectors, and other financial companies operating in the United States.

A PRIMER ON THE FINANCIAL CRISIS

Structured investment vehicles (SIV) are an example of the credit creation innovations that preceded the financial crisis. The SIVs were invented by Citigroup in 1988, and SIVs were large investors in asset securitizations.

- The rationale for the SIVs is nothing more than a variation of the "carry trade," the same as traditional credit spread banking. They raised capital and then levered that capital by issuing short-term securities, such as commercial paper and medium-term notes and public bonds, at lower rates and then use that money to buy longer-term securities at higher margins, earning the net credit spread for their investors.
- These instruments did not expose themselves to either interest rate or currency risk and typically held asset to maturity.
- Due to their structure, the assets and liabilities of the SIV was more transparent than traditional banks for investors.
- The long-term assets invested by these carry trade vehicles could include, among other things, residential mortgage-backed security (RMBS) collateralized bond obligation, auto loans, student loans, credit cards securitizations, and bank and corporate bonds.
- They were generally established as offshore companies and in doing so avoid paying tax and escaped the regulation that banks and finance companies were normally subjected to.

Until changes in regulations around the financial crisis, the SIVs could often be kept off the balance sheet of the banks that set them up. This way the SIV escaped even indirect restraints through regulation. They were considered part of the shadow-banking system as they operated in the shadows of the bank sponsors' balance sheets. As such, they were not considered to be part of the bank financial system. After a slow start, the SIV sector tripled in assets between 2004 and 2007 and at their peak just before the financial crisis in mid-2007. However, the financial crisis brought the SIV financing to an end. By October 2008, there were no active SIVs.

Our Interpretation: Again, rather than provide a broad history of events, we want to provide a stylized version of the events leading up to the financial crisis, as well as the remedies taken after the crisis. As before we assume that, initially and broadly speaking, the real estate and credit markets were in equilibrium a disturbance occurred and the economy adjusted to reach a new equilibrium.

President Clinton, President Bush, and the Republicans and Democrats in Congress were very proud of the expansion of home ownership in America. A catalyst that created an increased demand for residential real estate was the 1997 legislation that allowed married couples to keep up to $500,000 worth of capital gains every two years. The GSEs understood the political class's desire to have "affordable housing" and took advantage of this and effectively and successfully lobbied to relax some of the restrictions they faced. The successful lobbying created a dual objective for Fannie and Freddie. The politicians were aware and in some sense complicit of their higher profits, but allowed them to continue because of the increase in "affordable financing." The exposure to interest risks and/or duration mismatch was not new to the GSEs. We believe that the tax treatment and the relaxation of financing regulation fielded the housing and credit expansion that would down the road contribute to the crash.

With their funding advantage, lower capital requirements than other regulated financial institutions and banks, combined with the increased demand for residential real estate, Fannie Mae and Freddie Mac were right there. Given their profits margin and their credit guarantee, there was a simple way to increase their profits; they purchased and invested in huge amounts of mortgages and MBS. In the process of doing so, the companies and their investment portfolios became very large.

Subprime Lending: It should not be surprising that the large profits being generated by the twins attracted new entrants or competitors. These competitors found a way to get into the securitization business and they did so through financial innovation that took advantage of the lower interest rates and the positive slope of the yield curve. Wall Street developed mortgage products tied to one-year interest rates based on different indices such as the constant maturity treasury (CMT), the monthly treasury average (MTA), the London Inter Bank Overnight Rate (LIBOR), Cost of Funds Index (COFI), or Cost of Savings Index (COSI). These different indices and instruments had different characteristics and the securities based on them included what then were considered exotic features like interest rates only, while others allowed for negative amortization.

The adjustable rate mortgages were sold to borrowers as loans that the borrowers could refinance their loans before rates adjusted upward. The low teaser rates were very attractive to some borrowers who believed they could refinance before rates went up. Add to the mix lax underwriting guidelines such as stated income or liar's loans and it is easy to see how subprime lending would take off. "Private Label" MBS provided a lot of the necessary capital for the subprime mortgages. The lending fueled a dramatic increase in available mortgage credit and it allowed people who previously had difficulty obtaining mortgages due to low credit scores to have access to loans. Private lenders made a lot of money by pooling and selling the subprime mortgages. The pooled securitized subprime mortgages often received high ratings from the credit agencies. The securitization of these mortgages into MBS and Collateralized Debt Obligations (CDO) were attractive to investors due to the fact that they offered higher interest rates than assets backed by prime mortgages. Tranches of these securities were sold to investors. Lower quality tranches were offered with higher interest rates in return for absorbing the first losses associated with defaulting mortgages before the senior tranches. In 2006 around 80% of the subprime loans were private label MBS. By 2007 the value of the subprime mortgages had grown to around $1.3 trillion.

The "moral hazard" problem was exacerbated by innovations in securitization. The business model of the securitizers was simple: make the subprime loans, repackage them or securitize them, and sell them to willing and ready buyers like pension funds, hedge funds, insurance companies, and even foreign governments.

Since the securitizers did not keep these loans, presumably they faced little or no risk. Also as they did not keep the loans, their source of profits was the yield spread between their cost of funds and the yield paid by the institutions. The way for them to increase their profits was simple: make more loans. They had every incentive to increase their securitization activities even if that meant that the riskiness of the securitized securities would increase significantly thereby exacerbating the moral hazard issue faced by these institutions.

The adjustable rate mortgages created by Wall Street were quite popular. The lenders suggested to the borrowers that they could refinance well before the rate and/or payments adjusted upward. The advantage of the adjustable rates and/or teaser rates was that they allowed the borrower to qualify for a larger loan and that meant higher securitization profits. Once the borrower accepted the terms of the adjustable loans, it became a race against time as to whether his or her income would rise faster than the rate adjustment. If that did not occur, the borrower would be faced with some unpleasant choices: to default on the loan if there was little or no equity or, if there was enough equity on the house, the borrower could sell it or else refinance. Another way to increase the loan's origination was to lower the qualification standards such as the stated income of the borrower instead of the verified income figure used for qualification.

Necessary controls were not put in place and lending was often based on the overly optimistic assumption that property values would continue to increase. The government favored increased home ownership, so the regulators either looked the other way or tolerated the deterioration of the standards. In short, everyone was encouraged to take risk. Often the lender lent 100% of the investment amount upfront. More important to our story, the residential real estate loans were frequently nonrecourse loans meaning the borrower was not required to sign a legally binding personal guarantee.

The One-Sided Bet: So far, as we have described the situation, we have the making of a one-sided bet. Borrowers had quite an incentive to borrow and make risky investments. If the investment panned out, they would stand to make quite a bit of money with their equity position. If the investment did not pan out, the investor with 100% of the investment amount lent would not be worried. They had no skin in the game. If securitization agents were not worried either, they did not hold, at least early in the cycle, the packaged securities, they only made a spread. As they only made a spread and did not hold the securities, they had no skin in the game either. The cumulative effect of the risk taking would be failure, but all parties had their downside covered by the government.

SPILLOVER EFFECTS

The SIVs were the precursors of many of the leveraged products that became popular in the years after their invention. The SIVs differ from asset-backed securities and CDOs in that they were permanently capitalized and had an active management team. The SIVs did not wind-down at the end of their financing term, but rolled liabilities in the same way that traditional banks did. Cheap credit and the expected asset appreciation was the common element of the spread products. In turn, the diversity of long products led to many variations of the carry trade. Borrow short (i.e., at cheap rates) and invest long to capture the expected appreciation. To further increase profits given the abundance and cheapness of credit, many investors engaged in significant leverage.

While as we believe that MBS were a true innovation, it is also clear that some troubles associated with MBS were due to a breakdown in the different risk tranches. As some of the investments that made up the different

MBS went sour, they impacted the lower risk tranches the most. Unfortunately the way the MBS had been put together made it very difficult to unwind or take out of the instruments the loan that had gone sour. As a result, the whole package of the different tranches making the original MBS was impacted and so were the various institutions that held these securities. This is truly a case where financial solvency broke down because of the weakest link. Neither the financial engineers nor the buyers of the instruments spent time thinking about this possibility. The solution to the problem would have been some self-regulations in the construction of the MBS and the tranches, such that a bad loan could have been extricated from the package. Limiting the number of loans in a package may have gone a long way to do so. This is not a very difficult issue to solve and going forward, it is likely to be solved. Credit default swaps (CDS) are another innovation that gained popularity during recent times. It is also another instrument that suffered from the weakest link syndrome. If someone defaulted, then all the downstream deals associated with that CDS got into trouble. Again, while serious, this is not a difficult problem to solve. Chicago has solved this issue. The exchanges there solve it by creating a clearing house for contracts that way one can figure out the leverage of the counterparty. Unfortunately, with the opaque instruments it was quite difficult for the buyers of the subprime securitized instruments to figure the leverage of the counterparty.

The SIVs and the associated increase in securitization had a profound impact on the profitability of financial institutions, the subprime borrowers in particular, and the economy in general. Excesses were committed and at some point in time either the economy (i.e., the market) or the government attempted to restore equilibrium. An issue that comes to mind is whether the government actions accelerated or slowed down the adjustment process or whether it amplified or dampened the recovery process. The final issue we will try to deal with is to identify the winners and losers of the government-imposed solution. However, our first step is to highlight some background information leading to what experts consider to be the sources or contributions to the financial crisis.

The Catalyst: We have already argued that the excess of the securitizations would eventually lead to a crisis. However, the inevitable was accelerated by a change in tax laws. Federal legislation in 1997 increased the tax advantage significantly. Since 1997, married couples can keep up to $500,000 worth of capital gains tax-free every two years. This makes the owner-occupied housing gains tax-free for most investors.

A potential advantage is that for most people, a residential investment is a leveraged investment. Given the historical uptrend in residential real estate and its buy and hold nature, the leverage is a definitive advantage. The greater the leverage the greater the potential returns in an upmarket. Hence potential home owners have an incentive to increase the leverage factor as much as possible. This can be done in one of two ways, reducing the down payment or buying a bigger house or both. Now to the extent that the home loans are nonrecourse, all the home owners have at stake is the down payment. Profit maximization would push the home owners to minimize his or her down payment, thereby increasing the borrower's upside and reducing their downside and increasing the risk of default.

The government's tax treatment of home ownership and other policies that encouraged home ownership resulted in a tremendous increase in the derived demand for credit. Worse yet, to the extent that borrowers faced little downside potential risk, they faced a one-sided bet that encouraged leveraging and indebtedness. The securitization of subprime loans and the relaxation of lending standard combined with some new financial instruments fueled an explosion of packaged or securitized loans.

The Government Solution: Once appreciation decelerated and asset prices even declined, the ripple effects of these adverse developments propagated through the economy with devastating effects. The losses related to subprime lending, the securitization industry, and so-called shadow banking system continued to mount as the decline in real estate values deepened. The first visible institution to run into trouble was IndyMac, a Southern California-based savings and loan and a Countrywide Financial spin-off. After a string of failures such as New Century Financial Corporation, Bear Sterns, Lehman Brothers, and others, this helped fuel the crisis.

Here is a summary of some of the Fed's and Federal government's key actions that followed:

- In August 2007 the Federal Reserve announced that it would provide reserves as necessary.
- In October US Treasury Secretary Paulson announced the HOPE NOW initiative, an alliance of investors, servicers, mortgage market participants, and credit and homeowners' counselors encouraged by the Treasury Department, and the Department of Housing and Urban Development.
- In December, The Federal Reserve Board announced the creation of a Term Auction Facility (TAF) in which fixed amounts of term funds will be auctioned to depository institutions against a wide variety of collateral.
- In February 2008, President Bush signed the Economic Stimulus Act of 2008 into law.
- In March, the Federal Reserve Board announced the creation of the Term Securities Lending Facility (TSLF), which will lend up to $200 billion of Treasury

securities for 28-day terms against federal agency debt, federal agency residential mortgage-backed securities (MBS), nonagency AAA/Aaa private label residential MBS, and other securities.

- In June, the Federal Reserve Board announced approval of the notice of Bank of America to acquire Countrywide Financial Corporation. In July the Fed closed IndyMac. In September the Federal Housing Finance Agency (FHFA) placed Fannie Mae and Freddie Mac in government conservatorship.
- The US Treasury Department announced three additional measures to complement the FHFA's decision: (1) preferred stock purchase agreements between the Treasury/FHFA and Fannie Mae and Freddie Mac to ensure the GSEs positive net worth; (2) a new secured lending facility, which will be available to Fannie Mae, Freddie Mac, and the Federal Home Loan Banks; and (3) a temporary program to purchase GSE MBS.
- The Federal Reserve Board announced the creation of the Asset-Backed Commercial Paper Money Market Mutual Fund Liquidity Facility (AMLF) to extend nonrecourse loans at the primary credit rate to US depository institutions and bank holding companies to finance their purchase of high-quality asset-backed commercial paper from money market mutual funds. The Federal Reserve Board also announced plans to purchase federal agency discount notes (short-term debt obligations issued by Fannie Mae, Freddie Mac, and Federal Home Loan Banks) from primary dealers.
- The US Treasury Department announced a temporary guaranty program that would make available up to $50 billion from the Exchange Stabilization Fund to guarantee investments in participating money market mutual funds.
- The Office of Thrift Supervision closes Washington Mutual Bank. JPMorgan Chase acquires the banking operations of Washington Mutual in a transaction facilitated by the FDIC.
- The US Treasury Department opens its Temporary Guarantee Program for Money Market Funds. The temporary guarantee program provides coverage to shareholders for amounts that they held in participating money market funds as of the close of business on September 19, 2008.
- In October, Congress passed and President Bush signed into law the Emergency Economic Stabilization Act of 2008 (Public Law 110-343), which establishes the $700 billion Troubled Asset Relief Program (TARP).
- The FDIC announced an increase in deposit insurance coverage to $250,000 per depositor as authorized by the Emergency Economic Stabilization Act of 2008.
- US Treasury Department announces the TARP would purchase capital in financial institutions under the authority of the Emergency Economic Stabilization Act of 2008. The US Treasury made available $250 billion of capital to US financial institutions. This facility allowed banking organizations to apply for a preferred stock investment by the US Treasury. Nine large financial organizations announced their intention to subscribe to the facility in an aggregate amount of $125 billion.

The previous chronology shows that the government's focus during the financial crisis was to guarantee or try to make whole most depositors. The government's solutions tried to treat the crisis as a banking crisis and insure that the depositors were made whole, to minimize the depositors losses. This approach was intended to stem the run on the banking and financial system. However the government never addressed the real estate issue directly by creating a facility like the RTC during the earlier S&L crisis. Instead the Obama administration chose the regulatory path, through the Dodd-Frank Legislation, combined with a good dosage of Keynesian stimulus through its TARP program.

WERE THE RTC LESSONS USEFUL?

Looking back at the RTC experience and the behavior of the GSE, it is apparent to us that the solution is straightforward. All the government needed to do is remove the one-sided bet or moral hazard. One such step entailed removing the government guarantee. That would force Fannie and Freddie to balance risk and rewards when making new loans. The removal of the guarantee reduces the rewards and increases the risk to the institutions; it is safe to argue that the volume of loans would decline. Also, we can argue that the nature of their loans will also change. Safer loans would have been made. But that is not the only solution to the problem. More regulations may also accomplish a risk reduction. Unfortunately, this alternative requires continuous monitoring and quite possible an increased bureaucracy.

The reason we mention an increased bureaucracy is that in the past, there was a regulatory structure and yet it did not prevent the S&L and or financial crisis. The answer from a regulator perspective is that we did not have enough regulations and/or strong enforcement, hence what is needed is more regulations and stronger enforcement. That is the path the Obama Administration took: more regulation. The alternative would have been an RTC-type solution. Whether the regulatory structure built and enacted by the Obama Administration prevented a worst debacle and delivered the best economic performance feasible is something we disagree with. Whether the new regulations will deliver lower systemic risk remains to be seen. What is unambiguous is that the regulations increased the regulatory burden on the economy and that raises the possibility that the increased regulatory burden may have slowed down rather than accelerate the economic recovery. In conclusion, the analysis presented here leads one to wonder whether had the Bush and then the Obama administration had applied the RTC playbook, could the depth of the recession and the slow recovery had been avoided? One also wonders whether the policies of the Obama administration contributed to the slow recovery.

CHAPTER

35

Credit, the Carry Trade, Tax Rates, and the Residential Real Estate Market: A Retrospective

In early 2005, a front page *Wall Street Journal* article caught our attention [1]. The headline posed an interesting theory: while lagging behind the wealthy, many used debt to catch up. The argument was succinctly summarized in the following quote from the article:

> .....More and more Americans are turning to debt to pay for lifestyles their current incomes can't support. They are determined to live better than their parents, seduced by TV shows like "The O.C." and "Desperate Housewives," which take upper-class life for granted, and bombarded with advertisements for expensive automobiles and big-screen TVs. Financial firms have turned credit for the masses into a huge business, aided by better technology for analyzing credit risks. For Americans who aren't getting a big boost from workplace raises, easy credit offers a way to get ahead, at least for the moment......

This interpretation led to some uncomfortable implications:

> ....Yet many fear credit has spread so widely that many Americans are overextending themselves, leaving a growing number anxiously in debt and, increasingly, bankrupt. Outstanding household debt doubled to more than $10 trillion

between 1992 and 2004, after accounting for inflation. Because of low interest rates, consumers' monthly debt burden didn't increase nearly as rapidly.

> Economists disagree whether this relatively benign situation can continue. Interest rates are rising -- although long-term rates remain low -- and wage growth is sluggish. One danger: Housing prices could stall or decline, upending calculations ......

How prescient. One of the concerns raised by the above quote is how hard would the economy's landing be? In the same article, the author suggested an alternative interpretation of the situation that did not produce such dire conclusions:

> Despite the dicta of old sages, many economists -- led by Federal Reserve Chairman Alan Greenspan -- see the expansion of credit to lower-income families as a sign of progress. Some speak of the "democratization" of credit. In an April speech, Mr. Greenspan said that in colonial times through the late 19th century, only the affluent had access to credit and rates were high. In the early 20th century gasoline companies and retail stores started issuing credit cards, but cards didn't

spread widely until the late 1960s when banks piled into the business. Now, Mr. Greenspan says, "innovation and deregulation have vastly expanded credit availability to virtually all income classes."

Those who celebrate credit's new reach, such as University of Chicago economist Erik Hurst, talk about income "smoothing" -- the idea that debt enables people to borrow from their future earnings. In an earlier era, many people had no choice but to save first and spend later. Now, with credit, they can spend right away. For many young people, it's realistic to expect their earnings to rise. Their spending isn't just on baubles -- they may buy a house in a neighborhood with good schools, helping their children get ahead over the long term.

The previous quotes point to two different views of the world. In one, the current situation was inevitable. The second, while not ruling out the economic mishap, suggested that a necessary precondition for an unpleasant economic correction would require either a policy mistake or some unexpected shock to trigger a financial crisis.

THE DEMOCRATIZATION OF CREDIT AND INCOME SMOOTHING

According to street lore, the increase in consumer debt is mostly due to a secular decline in debt service ratio due to the interest rates charged on the loans. It allows consumers to support a higher level of debt. There is no question about that. However, as one looks at Fig. 35.1, one can see that from 1989 to 1992, the debt service figure steadily declined, while from 1994 to 2010 it appears to be on an upward secular trend. Yet throughout the period, bond yields were steadily declining (Fig. 35.2). The secular decline in bond yields took place during periods of both rising and falling debt service-to-disposable personal income ratios. This appears to contradict the view that the secular decline in bond yields drives the debt service. There is more to the debt service story than the decline in yields.

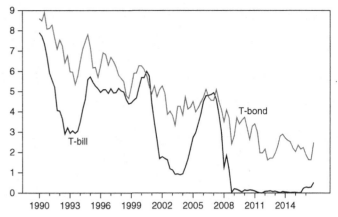

FIGURE 35.2   T-bill and T-bond yields.

While we complain that the crisis was in part due to the excessive credit creation and lax standards, this does not mean that the financial innovations introduced always had a negative effect on the economy. We contend that the negative aspect was the excessive use of credit and the lack of standards. But for a large fraction of the population, the innovations made them much better-off.

The democratization of credit allowed access to the credit market to many "subprime" people that had to rely on alternative methods of financing, some which were not legal and others significantly affected the timing of the consumption patterns. One simple example to illustrate this point is to recall the layaway plans of yesteryears. In the layaway program one had to make payments, be it weekly or monthly, and could not take the item until it had been fully paid for. The introduction of credit cards allowed people to enjoy their consumption earlier and the pay for the item at a speed equal to or faster than the minimum payment installments. Similarly the financial developments of the last couple of decades allowed for the securitization of items that no one thought could be securitized. The securitization allowed people to expand their constraint beyond their current income to other assets and eventually to their net worth. The credit allowed people to smooth their consumption and not be constrained by the vagaries of the timing of their income.

The "consumption smoothing" is easily explained in terms of the current prevailing consumption theories, be it Milton Friedman or Franco Modigliani. As already mentioned, absent the credit markets, expenditures of individual consumers are constrained by their income flows and, thus, individual consumption has to match income each period. The consumption pattern will be one of famine during the low-income years and feast during the high-income years. This is opposed to steadier consumption over their lifetime that could be achieved in a world where borrowing

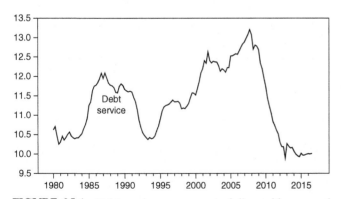

FIGURE 35.1   Debt service as a percent of disposable personal income.

and lending are allowed. Another implication of the absence of capital markets is that individuals will be forced to delay or slow down their investment in human capital. That, in turn, reduces the future benefits of any investment. Thus we can safely say that without the capital markets, the stock of human capital and the well-being of individuals would be lower than it otherwise would be. In contrast, in a perfect capital markets world, individuals face a single constraint: the net present value of their income must not exceed the net present value of their expenditures over their lifetime. Consumption will be smoothed out and, because of the availability of financing opportunities, more investments will be undertaken earlier in their lifecycle.

One final issue that needs to be discussed is that under an unregulated credit market, what is going to prevent the individual from borrowing in excess of their net worth or borrow an amount they cannot service? In asking the previous question, we have identified two potential sources of risks faced by the lending institutions that could lead to a borrowers default. For lack of a better term, we call them "balance sheet" or "net worth" risk, or the ability to obtain credit (i.e., credit crunch) which we call "income statement" or "cash flow" risk. To see the two types of risks, look at the perspective of the lenders. Then and now, all lenders want to insure that they get repaid and as such, they develop some decision rules that incorporate the vagaries of life. For example, they will never lend an amount higher than the borrower's net worth thereby minimizing the balance sheet risk. Also they want to make sure that the borrower has enough cash flow to make periodic interest payments. The democratization of credit introduced an additional risk consideration into the system: the possibility that the expected income would not materialize in the future. In this case, the consumer will not be able to meet its financial obligations. Again, here the institutions have taken steps to attempt to minimize the income statement or cash flows risks. The loan to net worth and debt service to income ratios are two of the key variables used by the lenders to determine the ability of the borrowers to service and repay their debt. It is easy to see that to protect against the risk of default, lenders have developed rules that consider uncertainty related to the two types of risk previously outlined here.

The previous discussion leads us to a couple of very simple questions. Was the balance sheet risk and income risk out of line prior to the crisis? Were they deteriorating too fast? One way to answer these questions is to look at the data. Information on the debt service as a percent of household disposable income is presented in Fig. 35.1. It is interesting to note that the debt service increased around the time of the century

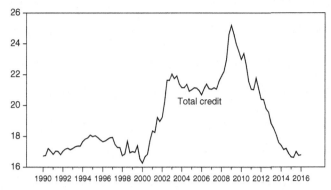

FIGURE 35.3   Total credit as a percent of household net worth.

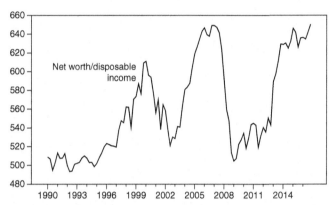

FIGURE 35.4   Household net worth as a percent of disposable income.

date change, that is, Y2K, and during the Greenspan Put, a time when interest rates were low or declining. This information and the rising wealth at the time indicates that the debt service increase per household net worth was due to an increase in the household debt. This inference is corroborated by the data on the household credit as a percent of household net worth during the same time period reported in Fig. 35.3. The data also shows that the debt-to-net worth ratio doubled during this time, while the debt service only increased about 10%. Hence if there was any increase in risk, it came from the increase in total debt not form the debt service. It was a balance sheet risk, not an income statement risk.

Other interesting points to note is that during the crisis, the debt-to-household net worth increased dramatically, but the increase was driven mostly by the denominator declining. It was mostly due to a decline in net worth. In the aftermath of the crisis, the household net worth recovered (Fig. 35.4), yet the debt-to-net worth ratio has declined significantly, suggesting that either the credit has become less scarce or that borrowers have become more income centric as far as their expenditures go. The traditional consumption theories point to the former.

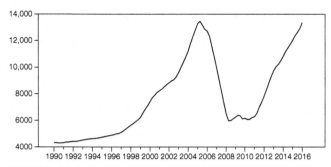

FIGURE 35.5 Real estate equity as a percent of household net worth.

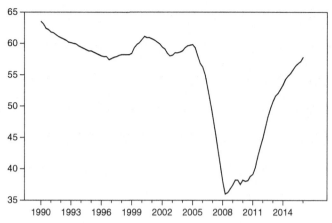

FIGURE 35.6 Real estate equity as a percent of the real estate value.

THE ROLE OF REAL ESTATE IN THE CREDIT EQUATION

Next, we argue that the tax treatment of residential real estate induced people to alter their behavior in significant ways. First, the advantageous tax treatment of owner-occupied houses induced individuals to forgo other investments at the expense of real estate. In retrospect, one can argue that the tax advantage made for an excessive investment in the sector. That, combined with the reduction in the regulatory burden and the ease of financing, fueled an increase in the demand and the valuation of real estate. The data presented in Fig. 35.5 shows the dramatic acceleration of real estate as a percent of household net worth, an acceleration that coincides with Y2K and the Greenspan Put and the modification of the loan qualification standards such as stated income or liar's loans.

Another key point in our analysis is the fact that the tax treatment of residential real estate made the deductibility of interest the preferential vehicle for homeowners to finance their personal expenditures. This would suggest that homeowners would use their equity as piggy bank. They did do that, but the data also shows that homeowners as a group were mindful of their loan-to-value ratio and kept it at what was then considered a prudent ratio or approximately 40% (Fig. 35.6). This information suggests that the homeowners with equity were not reckless spendthrifts which, in turn, suggests that some of the excesses of real estate were the result of not only easy credit but also the tax treatment of residential real estate and its financing.

THE ADVANTAGES OF OWNER-OCCUPIED RESIDENTIAL REAL ESTATE

The first advantage of owner-occupied real estate is that the imputed income from owning and living in one's home is not taxed. Thus the greater the effective tax rates on personal income, the greater the advantage to owning a home. A second advantage that existed prior

to 1997 was that the homeowner could rollover the gains on a house into the next one. This in effect allowed the home to compound the gains tax-free. More importantly, in the end, the gains would be taxed at the capital gains tax rate. Compare this to the IRA and 401k programs. They both allow for the compounding of the rate tax-free, but withdrawals at retirement are taxed at the ordinary income tax rate. Given that the tax advantage has been in place prior to the enactment of the IRA and 401k programs, one can safely conclude that that, in effect, owner-occupied housing enjoyed many of the tax advantage currently enjoyed by retirement plans. But over time the advantage has gotten better. Since 1997, married couples can keep up to $500,000 worth of capital gains tax-free every 2 years. This makes the owner-occupied housing gains tax-free for most investors. A third advantage is that for most people the investment is a leveraged investment. Given the historical uptrend in residential real estate and its buy and hold nature, the leverage is a definitive advantage. For example, considering the historically normal down payment, homeowners will initially have a leverage factor on the order of 4 to 1. Thus if the stock market historical return is in the order of 8%, the homeowner only needs a 2% appreciation to match the historical stock market gains. Put another way, just by having the house appreciate at the inflation rate, the homeowner will match the long-run average stock market return. Unfortunately, as people found out during the financial crash, leverage works both ways. A fourth advantage is that the interest payments on the mortgage are tax deductible. This is a big deal. Recall that other interest payments are only deductible against interest income, while mortgages, now with certain limits, are deductible against ordinary income. Thus residential real estate is the way that ordinary people make interest payments on their personal debts tax deductible. In other words, investors had a strong incentive to make residential real estate debt their preferred financing vehicle. Again, one can argue that the tax treatment of residential real estate pushed people into a higher debt-to-net worth ratio and a higher debt service ratio, thus increasing the risks associated with the democratization of the credit markets. A generalized decline in residential real estate values and the reset of some of the mortgages significantly increased the two risks of defaults associated with real estate.

FINANCIAL INNOVATIONS AND THE LOSS OF TRANSPARENCY

The previous sections provide a very simple rationale for the credit explosion observed during the 15 years leading up to the financial crisis. A domestic price rule, an expanding economy, and a deepening of the financial markets all led to the democratization of the credit market. So far, we have a simple explanation for the increased supply in credit paper, as well as the real estate debt. Unfortunately the story does not end here.

During the three decades prior to the financial crisis, we learned the benefits of diversification, the concept of diversifiable risk, and so forth. The progress in financial economics led to the development of new instruments or "derivatives." For example, individual loans that were considered illiquid or risky could now be packaged together and using the tools of modern finance one could show that collectively the bundle of loans was safer than the individual loans. From a risk perspective, the whole was more than the sum of the parts. Diversification was a wonderful concept that greatly enhanced the collective attractiveness of the individual loans.

A second innovation was to use the tools of modern finance to split the pooled funds into tranches of different risk reward combination and related derivatives. The application of modern financial developments led to the creation of the collateralized market. However, this proved to be the Trojan horse that contributed to the amplification of the financial crisis.

Once the various risk/return tranches were constructed, it was virtually impossible to disentangle a portion of the tranches and thus reconstruct the original loans. It became an all or nothing proposition. The price paid for the latter developments was a loss of transparency. To see the potential impact of the loss of transparency, let's consider the following hypothetical example. Let's say that you are given a portfolio of 20 stocks. Let's also assume that you do not know the names of the companies and you are also told that for one of the stocks its value will go down to zero. What should we do? Given the information available, the way to minimize the impact of the demise of the stock is to equal weight the stocks in the portfolio. When asked about to estimate the possible loss to the portfolio, one is tempted to say 1/20

or 5%. However, that is not necessarily true. If there is any positive correlation between the stocks, the loss will exceed the 5%, the higher the correlation the higher the losses. That is the downside of the opaqueness produced by the collateralization.

Another misconception is the assumption related to the hedging of risk. This reminds of the 1980s when portfolio insurance was the rage. While it is true that through a swap arrangement one may shift the risk to another individual or institution, collectively society cannot hedge the risk. The question then is when the events that we tried to protect happens, how will the system respond? Is it able to absorb the shock? We know the answers to these questions. The financial crisis provided them for us.

We attribute some of the market troubles to misapplications of some of the instruments developed during the first few years of the new millennium. Yet looking back, we believe that these instruments were true innovations. We are not saying that these instruments were perfect. In fact, there were some design flaws and some misuse that could be easily corrected with some minor modifications and/or government regulation. What seems clear after the fact is that most people focused only on the potential benefits of the new instruments and no one focused on their downside or possible misapplications. It is clear now that many of the instruments were sold assuming a perfect environment where nothing would go wrong. In doing so, we created a very rigid system susceptible to contagion. The examples of this are obvious.

Securitization was one of the great financial innovations of the time. The logic was compelling. Using the basic principles of modern portfolio theory, it made sense that by pooling different instruments, a much safer pool could be created. The idea being that in this way some risk can be diversified away. So far, so good. The financial engineers then took the next step. They reasoned that they could break the overall instrument and separate it into tranches of different risks. This was done to satisfy some of the needs of different clients who could not invest in the riskier instruments. In separating the bundled instrument into the various tranches, the financial engineers would be able to collect higher fees. Doing so introduced some additional issues. The separation into tranches depends on the methodology used to evaluate risk and the assumptions made regarding the stability of the variance–covariance matrix. Here is where we believe that financial analysts failed to consider the downside of these instruments. All we need to do is go back and look at the Long Term Capital Management experience. They had two Nobel Prize winners but still could not get their statistical arbitrage right. Correlations broke down and the leverage worked in a way they did not expect.

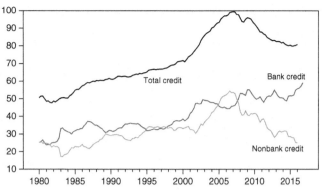

FIGURE 35.7   Total credit and bank credit as a percent of GDP.

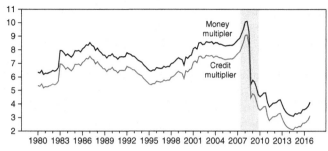

FIGURE 35.8   Money multiplier and credit multiplier.

THE CREDIT EXPLOSION

The first step in identifying the possible relationship between bank credit and the economy is to develop an estimate of the credit creation in the US economy. The broadest measure we could find is the household liabilities and it shows that the amount of credit per GDP was higher during the 1990s than the 1980s (Fig. 35.7). The data also shows that around the millennium, the total credit variable begins a steep secular ascent after peaking at the end of 2008. Why the sudden credit explosion during the time prior to 2008? Elsewhere we have argued that the surge in credit was largely due to a confluence of factors. The treatment of the housing markets and the deregulation of the financial system combined with a series of innovative products fueled the explosion of credit. We contend that the famous Greenspan Put contributed significantly to the credit explosion and increased leverage of the period. The Put removed the risks that the short end of the yield curve would rise and erase any profits made by arbitrating the spread between the short and long rates. Fig. 35.2 shows a time series for the 3-month T-bill yields and the 10-year T-bond yields. Notice the drop in interest rates shortly after the millennium and lasting until 2004, that is, the time period of the Greenspan Put was in effect before he gradually removed it. To the extent that Mr. Greenspan kept his word, and he did, the carry trade would be one-sided bet that the financial institutions and other borrowers would partake with gusto. Furthermore, if they knew the timing of the put, the speculators would know exactly when to get out. Notice also that it was not until 2007 when the carry trade benefits were completely erased. This raises another issue, if one knows the schedule for the wiping out of the put, the way to maintain the profits of the strategy is to increase the leverage factor and to bail out just as the put is fully removed. Something to ponder.

Looking at Fig. 35.7, it is visually clear that the banks accelerated their lending during the Greenspan Put. The expansion peaked around the time the removal of the Greenspan Put began. The bank credit per unit of GDP

slowed down and even declined. Fig. 35.7 also shows that this was not the case for nonbank credit, it continued unimpeded and it peaked around the time of the financial crisis.

Additional information regarding the banking system leverage factor is presented in Fig. 35.8 which shows the bank and credit multipliers. That is the amount of Money of Zero Maturity (MZM) money, and bank loans created per greenback in circulation. The multipliers confirm what we already inferred form the information in Fig. 35.2, that the banks' credit creation peaked around 2004, and between then and 2007, the multiple declined slightly. But that was not the case for the nonbank credit. Fig. 35.7 shows that the increase in nonbank credit continued past the Greenspan Put period in an uninterrupted trend that did not end until the financial crisis in 2007. Taken together, these results suggest that the Greenspan Put contributed to the expansion of credit. However, the fact that the nonbank credit expansion continues suggests that there is much more than the Greenspan Put to the increased leverage in the economy and that the culprit was the nonbank sector.

EXCESSIVE CREDIT CREATION AND THE ECONOMY

Excessive credit creation is considered by many as one of the main causes of the financial crisis of 2008. The information presented in Figs. 35.2, 35.7, and 35.8 are consistent with this interpretation. More importantly, the evidence presented suggests the increased demand for credit generated by the tax changes combined with the deregulation that took effect around this time of credit attracted many new entrants into the market. Add to this the developments in financial economics and one can anticipate the creation of many new instruments that promised to liquefy and reduce the risk of many heretofore illiquid or risky investments. Add to the mix the rising asset prices and the expectation of a continuation of price appreciation, and it is easy to see why all of this led many financial institutions, especially the less-regulated ones, to extend credit based on the prospects of capital gains realizations, thereby ignoring the net worth of the borrower at the borrowing time.

In many cases, the new investors were approaching infinite leverage as they put little or no money down. The math was perfect as long as everything went according to plan. Unfortunately leverage works both ways. However, once the rate of appreciation slowed, many of the leveraged investments became unprofitable. As there was little or no capital at risk on the part of borrowers, many walked away or had their properties repossessed. The lenders suffered many of the losses which, in turn, reduced their capital adequacy and the amount of loans they could create. A vicious cycle ensued and the markets and the economy went on a downward tailspin.

THE FED'S ROLE AND THE CARRY TRADE

Our view is that the principal role of the Fed is to provide price stability, and that the price rule does just that. However, that is not all the Fed does. It can also affect the credit creation of the banking system. According to the street lore in the wake of September 11th, the collapse of the dot-com bubble, and the economy's confidence imploding, the Fed made a bet on the consumer to keep the economy afloat. The Maestro drove short-term rates down to 1% and that gave rise to the famous Greenspan Put. For those who had any doubt, the following quote from the Federal Open Market Committee (FOMC) at the time will clear any of the doubt [2]:

> However, with inflation quite low and resource use slack, the Committee believes that policy accommodation can be maintained for a considerable period.

The previous quote and other companion statements by the FOMC were interpreted as evidence that the Fed was committed to keeping short rates low. True to its word, since 2001 the Fed kept short rates low for a considerable time. It could be seen at the end of 2000, when the slope of the yield curve bottomed and then rose throughout 2001 and remained fairly high for a considerable period (see Fig. 35.2). The data on the T-bills and T-bonds combined show that the bulk of the interest rate action was at the short end of the curve. It is this interpretation that gave rise to the prevalence of the carry trade.

If you know that the Fed will keep rates low, then we know precisely the effect the carry trade will have on the fixed-income market as the carry trade equilibrating process induces a flattening of the slope of the yield curve. The long-end yields will decline. Another way to say the same thing is that the price of the long bonds will rise and that means that the people who put the carry trade on will make money. The downside of the carry trade is

the risk of rising short-term rates. However the Fed took care of that in the previous announcement. More than that, it also gave investors ample warnings as to when it intended to raise the short-term rates. In effect, the Fed eliminated the downside risk of the carry trade, and it became a one-sided bet. It was all upside until the Fed changed its stance. If people knew that the Fed would be raising rates in an orderly fashion, in theory they would know when the carry trade would cease to work and thus they may be able to unwind it ahead of the Fed.

Investors devised several variations of the carry trade. In some cases they sold a low-interest rate instrument, say yen denominated short-term securities, and invested the proceeds in a higher-yielding instrument such as US T-bills and T-bonds. Another variant sold short-term dollar denominated securities, such as commercial paper, and bought longer maturities securities. Some of these were fixed-income securities or in other cases they chose assets with an expected return in excess of the short-term fixed-income securities. The necessary condition to implement these variations of the carry trade was the difference in yields or returns. However these variations introduced additional risks. In the case of the yen carry trade, the risk was the exchange rate. An adverse move in the exchange rate, (i.e., a yen appreciation) could wipe out the interest rate differential. Similarly, those who borrowed short at fixed rates to invest in appreciating assets with nonguaranteed nominal returns, the risk was that the return would fall below the short-term rate. Investors who speculated implicitly assumed that while the position was held, the exchange rate or asset values would not move against them.

DID THE CARRY TRADE FUEL THE MARKET?

Despite the terrorism risk and slow growth in employment, the 2001 recession was one of the mildest on record. By all accounts the consensus was that the Maestro's strategy worked. However critics contend that easy credit created a housing/asset bubble, which was bound to break as the Fed corrected its easy money/ credit mistake.

Low interest rates tend to lengthen investors' horizons and abundant credit makes it easy to acquire durable assets. Thus the abundance of credit leads to an increase in the demand for durable assets resulting in what some may call asset inflation. Ultimately profit maximization and competition lead to a reduction in the yield or price to earnings ratio of the durable asset. In an expanding economy, the reduction in the yield is accomplished through asset appreciation. Viewed this way, we have a very simple explanation for the asset inflation during the 15 years leading up to the bubble bursting. The implication being that businesses would go on a borrowing binge and individuals too; however the tax treatment of residential real estate would channel a large portion of the personal borrowings to the home equity market.

In the end, any excessive borrowing against real estate can be blamed on Fed's easy credit policy and the tax code. Homeowners would be able to say, and many did, that the tax code and the Maestro made them do it.

THE MAKING OF A STORM

The Fed's public announcement of an orderly dismantling of the Greenspan Put would give the market participants ample time to unwind their carry trade position. Hence from this vantage point, the financial institutions would have been well equipped to handle the gradual increase in short-term rates and ultimately the delevering required by the unwinding of the carry trade. Any unwinding problem would not be directly related to the Fed's publicly announced policy. This brings us to the issue if not the Fed, then what? Our answer is that one has to go back to the elements of the broadly defined carry trade. We argued in the previous section that in the broad definition of the carry trade, some investors were taking exchange rate risk while others were taking equity returns risk. It is the latter that we want to focus now.

Remember that we have argued that the tax code forced people to borrow on the equity on their homes if they wanted to make interest on their debt deductible. We also argued that real estate was significantly tax advantaged. Looking back, we can then argue that the tax treatment would lead to an increase in the net after tax income generated by the home. Thus the demand for residential real estate would increase. The value of the tax shield would be worth more the greater the income of the taxpayer and thus the higher the marginal tax rate they faced. This suggests a virtuous cycle for residential real estate. As the demand increased, home prices rose, and that had several effects on the economy. First, the higher return would make a home trade strategy more attractive. Second, the increase in home prices would also lead to an increase in homeowners' net worth. That in turn results in higher consumption and very likely an increase in the use of the home equity lines of credit. This way the interest in the consumer discretionary expenditures were made tax deductible. All of these positive developments attracted new investors, which fueled the cycle. However these developments also attracted additional investments, and housing construction and condo conversion also increased. In an unfettered market, increases in demand are initially rationed through price increases if the supply is inelastic. However, over time, the supply will adjust and prices will converge to a

new equilibrium. We know that at the new equilibrium the underlying factors of production will be earning normal rates of return. At that point, the benefits of the carry trade disappear, assuming that the Fed had in fact raised the interest rates as they projected. The point we want to make here is that if people underestimated the speed of adjustment, equilibrium would be reached faster than they expected and the profitability of the carry trade would turn into a loss. The question is whether a vicious cycle would now ensue? If so, how long would it last? The final question being whether economic policy could shorten the cycle and whether a wrong policy mix would lengthen the cycle and slow the recovery?

THE ANATOMY OF A CRISIS

The interaction between the credit markets and the carry trade has clear and important implications for the economy. Let's illustrate it in the context of a decline in housing prices (however, as one can see, the phenomena is much more general than this). We have argued in the previous paragraphs that the housing market would be at the center of any storm for two distinct reasons. One being that home mortgages are one of the few interest deductions available to many borrowers, thus the deductibility resulted in a higher loan-to-value ratio than we would have seen otherwise. The carry trade, tax advantages, and economic prosperity all funneled into a higher demand for housing. The 1997 change in tax treatment of residential real estate led to an increase in the demand for owner-occupied housing. The low interest rate policy of the Fed reduced the carrying costs, not surprisingly the demand for and the price of owner-occupied housing surged. The price increase would be a signal for suppliers to supply, over time equilibrium would be reached, and the price appreciation would slow down to the long-run average. The return to normalcy would eliminate the speculative elements and that means that the price of residential real estate would decline. We have seen all that and we contend that the beginning of the financial crisis was the beginning of the adjustment stage. The question then was how bad the adjustment process was going to be and whether the government and monetary authority's action would accelerate the recovery or exacerbate the crisis. The right policy mix would put out the economic fire, while the wrong policy could fuel it and or prolong it.

A decline in housing prices leads to a decline in household net worth and the net capital of lending institutions, which in turn leads to a secondary round of loan contractions and reduced spending. This could potentially create the preconditions for a vicious cycle that would spread to the rest of the economy. A reduction in real estate prices below their loan-to-value ratio will effectively wipe out much of the net worth of many families. A reset of the interest rate on the residential real estate loans effectively reduces the disposable income of the homeowners who kept their homes. The combination of lower net worth and higher payments has devastating effects on the finances of these homeowners. One clear implication here is that consumer discretionary spending would significantly decline. Looking back at the financial crisis, that appeared to have been the case. The sector returns posted large declines.

The combination of higher mortgage payments and lower home prices, in turn, reduced household credit worthiness and borrowing ability for the homeowners who stayed in their homes. In fact, the combination of these two destroyed any hope of refinancing at a lower rate and in some cases triggered the calling of other personal loans by banks. That put many homeowners in the position of considering whether to walk away from the loan by turning the house back to the lending institution. In the old days, walking away meant that the lending institution will send them a 1099 for the difference between the loan and the resale value of the house. Also if the resale of the house is higher than the cost basis, the homeowner may be also liable for capital gains taxes. In addition to getting an Internal Revenue Service (IRS) tax bill and having their credit ruined, households will have to pay rent on their new place. When all these factors are taken into consideration, for those who decide to stay, the solution is to hunker down, make the mortgage payments, and cut everything else. History has shown that real estate trends up secularly, thus waiting it out is a viable option. In due course, the value of the house will increase to the point that the homeowners are above water and they can get out. The alternative to waiting is bankruptcy, which will wipe out the debt but it will also ruin the household's credit. A large enough decline in home prices could paralyze household spending for quite a long time. That is when the contagion in the housing market spreads to the overall expenditures of the consumer.

Recall that President Bush went on national TV to announce that the IRS would not do what we just outlined. This meant that people could walk away without fearing getting a bill from the IRS. The president significantly increased the attractiveness of short sales. People could walk away from their homes without having the IRS on their case and depending on how the short-sale negotiations are conducted, the damage to their credit would be much less than if they walked away or choose bankruptcy protection. The President's action facilitated walking away from the homes and starting again with a clean slate and without the drag of the excessive mortgage payments in relation to the homeowners' income. This has two clear effects on the economy. One is that the impact on consumer discretionary income is positive. The second is that the housing price decline would be much deeper. That, in turn, will effectively lower the rent for those who walk away [3].

The effect on the financial institutions was a bit different. If, as we have already argued, the changes in the economic environment facilitated walking away from the homes and that in turn resulted in an overshooting of the decline in home prices, the financial institutions would take it on the chin. They would have to shoulder the brunt of the decline and the downward revaluation. It impacts their capital and thus the capital adequacy ratio and their ability to extend loans. If these institutions did not replenish their capital, then their loan creation ability would be impaired and that would have a negative impact on the level of economic activity as it did. A decrease in the value-to-loan ratio below one reduced the net capital of the lending institutions. The major point is that as net capital declined, even if the institution kept the same capital adequacy ratio, their credit creation ability was reduced. To add insult to injury, in many cases prudence and/or the regulatory bodies forced an increase in the capital adequacy ratio that further reduced the credit creation of the institution. Finally, at the time we argued that there was the possibility that the capital adequacy becomes a binding constraint and even when the Fed eases, the increased availability of reserves would not be put to work. In other words, the banks would not increase their loans. Be it because the lack of capital adequacy ratio or the lack of credit worthy clients. The bottom line is that under these conditions, the increased reserves will be held as excess reserves and the interest rates will then decline. For those who doubted this scenario, we argued that Japan is the poster child for this scenario. So if the banks' capital is not adequate, the banking system credit creation will be greatly diminished and that could lead to an economic slowdown. We believe that the regulations enacted have reduced the banking sector's credit creation ability and that contributed to the subpar economic recovery.

References

[1] Davis B. Lagging behind the wealthy, many use debt to catch up. Wall St J May 17, 2005.
[2] https://www.federalreserve.gov/boarddocs/press/monetary/2003/20031209/.
[3] In parts of Europe the effects were a bit different, the loans were full recourse. People who walked away or lost their home were still responsible for loan payments. That had a devastating effect on their income and thus their spending.

36

The Fed's Crisis Response

Around the time of the crisis, a *Wall Street Journal* editorial reported on Treasury Secretary Timothy Geithner's interview with Charlie Rose on PBS, in which Geithner admitted that the Federal Reserve may have had a hand in the financial meltdown. While he may be new to that point of view, others have held it for quite a while. According to the article [1]:

> The Fed's loose policy from 2003 to 2005 created the commodity and credit bubbles that made these countries flush with dollars. Given their low domestic propensity to consume, these countries then recycled those dollars back into dollar-denominated assets, such as Treasurys and real-estate-related assets such as Fannie Mae securities. The Fed itself had created the surplus dollars that kept long rates low and undermined for a substantial period its belated attempts to tighten.

Leading up to the financial crisis, we believe the data supports the *Journal's* assertion. Fig. 36.1 shows the relationship between the trailing 12 months US inflation rate compared to the excess of the base growth over the money of zero maturity (MZM) growth (i.e., MZM is the Fed monetary aggregate that most closely resembles a true medium of exchange or transaction money). Notice the close correlation between the two. The inflation rate appears to follow the pattern of our monetary aggregate. This is reassuring to those of us who believe that inflation is a monetary phenomenon, or too much money chasing too few goods. Some may disagree with our proxy for excess money. Yet there is no denying the relationship and its consistency with the monetary view of inflation.

THE GREENSPAN FED'S PREEMPTIVE STRIKE

Fig. 36.2 presents additional evidence supporting the view that the Fed made some monetary mistakes. It also denotes a prelude of likely monetary mistakes to come. Notice the huge spike in the growth of the monetary base during the latter part of 1999. At the time the Fed was worried about Y2K, and whether the century date change would create havoc on financial institutions' computers. The Fed reasoned that disruptions would lead to a temporary collapse in the bank-created component of credit and money supply. The Fed preempted the potential problem by creating enough cash to sustain the economy in case things went wrong. Once the century date change occurred and nothing happened, the Fed pulled all the base money back from the economy.

The Y2K incident showed in a compressed time the impact of the excesses of the Fed. The monetary expansion shown in Fig. 36.1 leads the surge in the US inflation rate and the overall economy and financial markets around the century date change. The withdrawal of the excess base the Fed had provided leading up to Y2K resulted not only in a decline in the US inflation rate, but also a bursting of the tech bubble and a recession. This interpretation suggests that the Greenspan Fed overdid it on the way up and the way down. It also shows that changes in the Fed balance sheet of this magnitude are very hard to "fine tune," leaving the real economy at risk of either a significant slowdown or an inflationary event depending on the direction of the policy miss.

Economic Disturbances and Equilibrium in an Integrated Global Economy. http://dx.doi.org/10.1016/B978-0-12-813993-6.00036-2

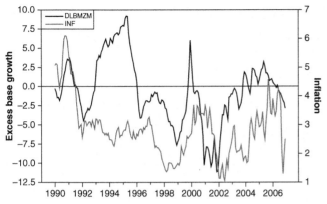

FIGURE 36.1 Excess of the monetary base growth over MZM growth versus the inflation rate. *MZM, Money of zero maturity.*

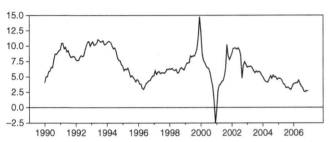

FIGURE 36.2 The growth in the monetary base (trailing 12 months).

TWO WRONGS DO NOT MAKE A RIGHT

Perhaps as a result of the Greenspan Fed's previous success when it anticipated the productivity surge of the 1990s and accommodated it with the double digit growth rate in the monetary base (Fig. 36.2), the Greenspan Fed believed it could anticipate and accommodate shifts in money demand. That may explain why the Fed's behavior was not affected by the Y2K fiasco. The incident made the fed even more determined to prevent an economic slowdown. The result was the famous "Greenspan Put," which kept short rates low for a considerable time. The events also made the Fed more cautious and it assumed a more gradualist posture. As the economy recovered under the leadership of Greenspan, the Fed increased the fed funds rate gradually by slowly reducing the growth of the monetary base. Unfortunately, the monetary base measures only the part of the money supply controlled by the Fed, and the supply side alone is not sufficient for anyone to obtain enough information to determine whether there is a monetary equilibrium, an excess demand for money, or an excess supply of money. To determine the overall market condition, one also needs information about the demand side of the money market. Fig. 36.2 shows that

around the century date change, the growth of the monetary base was declining, and those who focus solely on the supply side of the monetary equation would erroneously conclude that there was a tightening by the Fed. Yet, they would be wrong. Fig. 36.3 shows the decline in the growth rate of the monetary base was less than the decline in the demand for the monetary base. As a result, during the first 5 years of the new millennium, there was excess base growth (see the shaded area of Fig. 36.3). The true tightening, as indicated by the yields at the short end of the curve (Fig. 36.4), did not begin until 2005. During that time, the inflation rate was rising (Fig. 36.1), and it was not until after the tightening began that the US inflation rate subsided.

So far, we have a monetary explanation for the events leading to Y2K and the subsequent Greenspan Put. The logical conclusion of our analysis is that the Fed had a major hand in the inflation outcome, as well as the performance of the real economy and financial markets. The simplicity of the explanation makes one wonder whether this approach is robust enough to be applied to other situations, such as the financial and credit meltdown. Does our approach offer any insight that help choose between the two competing views debated at the time? One was an impending inflation spiral, the other was a deflationary trap in a prolonged recession with fears of a depression?

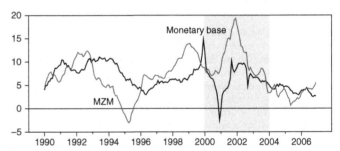

FIGURE 36.3 Monetary base and MZM growth (trailing 12 months). *MZM, Money of zero maturity.*

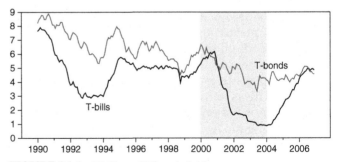

FIGURE 36.4 T-bills and T-bond yields.

SOME MONEY AND BANKING MECHANICS

To address the Fed's response to the economic conditions at the time, we need a frame of reference, and as such, we need to review the mechanism by which the Fed affects the economy's monetary equilibrium. For example, under a gold standard or a fixed exchange rate system, there will be an explicit intervention mechanism that forces the central bank to maintain the convertibility or exchange rate. However, under our fiat standard there is no such mechanism. All we know is that the Fed can conduct open market operations. Buying the bonds in the open markets leads to an increase in the amount of currency circulating in the economy (i.e., monetary base). When the Fed wants to reduce the amount of currency circulating in the economy, it simply sells bonds in the open market. It does this through the New York Federal Reserve Bank, either through the outright buying or selling of bonds, or by lending reserves through repurchase agreements. The counterparties are the sixteen Fed-approved dealers.

Viewed this way, we conclude that in principle the Fed can control to the penny the monetary base or the amount of high-powered money circulating in the economy. However, the level of MZM is not determined by supply alone. We need to focus on demand conditions too.

One way to analyze the demand side of the money market is to focus on the uses of the monetary base. There are two possible uses for high-powered money. One is as cash circulating in the economy and the other is as a reserve requirement in the banking system. The latter use interconnects the money market (i.e., the demand for transaction money) to the credit markets. To see this, let's assume that the banks have a 10% reserve requirement. It follows that $10 worth of reserves could support a maximum $100 worth of demand deposits. Now the $90 difference between total deposits and the reserve requirement denotes the amount of credit created by the banking system. The money and banking mechanisms are straightforward. The total quantity of money and credit created by the banking system would range from a low of $10 in cash—no bank reserves, no deposits, and no credit—to a high of $100 worth of deposits with $90 worth of credit, $10 worth of reserves, and zero cash. Finally, any combination of the two extremes is also possible. It is determined in large part by the interactions of the demand for credit and transaction balances which we discuss in the next chapter. It also illustrates the government's perception of the problem. In fact, TARP-based ownership of the financial institutions is an outgrowth of the attempt to address the credit concerns.

The point of the previous exercise was to show the mechanics of the deposit and credit creation. Depending on the combination of deposits and cash held by individuals, the total amount of money (cash plus demand deposit) and "banking" credit would then be determined. Banking is in quotations because much of the US credit growth has been through nonbank bank institutions, the so-called shadow banking, which include asset backed security trusts (ABS), investment banks, real estate investment trusts (REITs), and mutual funds. These entities funded credit demand directly, disintermediating the banks. The issue here is that the Fed did not directly regulate the nonbank banks and it did not control the demand side. People determine the amount of money and credit they desire, and the risk they want to take with their deposits. It is the interaction between these demand and supply conditions that simultaneously determines the overall equilibrium in the money and credit markets.

Thus, to analyze the money and credit markets, we need to focus on four key variables: the demand for money and demand for credit, which are determined by the private sector, and the supply of money and supply of bank credit, which are determined by the monetary authorities (i.e., the monetary base and the credit regulators).

HELICOPTER BEN'S CRISIS RESPONSE

Armed with this framework, we can begin to evaluate the Fed's actions, and we can surmise the impact that possible Fed actions will have on the economy's future inflation rate. Let's start with the supply of credit. Fig. 36.5 shows the decline in the money and credit multiplier around 2007. Holding the monetary base constant, the amount of MZM and bank credit would decline in the same proportion that the multipliers were declining. This was a true deflationary pressure combined with a tremendous downdraft in the bank credit creation. Fig. 36.6 illustrates the Fed's response to the liquidity events that began in late 2007 and exploded in

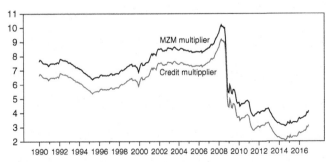

FIGURE 36.5 **The money and credit multipliers.**

September, 2008. Fig. 36.6 shows the vertical ascent of the monetary base at the time the money multiplier was declining.

In the aftermath of the Lehman failure, and the "breaking of the buck" of the Reserve Fund leading to its inability to honor withdrawals, the financial system experienced a run on nonbank banks and money market funds. The nonbank banks could not obtain funding as overnight or deposit funding stopped. They had to deliver. Money market funds were overwhelmed with withdrawals and became net sellers of commercial paper, the key source of funding for many businesses. In addition, financial institutions recognized large losses, resulting in a lack of capital and a loss of confidence in the system. The panic that ensued led to the demand for money going through the roof while credit collapsed. Fig. 36.6 shows the explosion of the US monetary base and the collapse of the MZM money multiplier (Fig. 36.5). This collapse in credit was especially severe in the nonbank bank sector—asset backed securities, investment banks, REITs, and mutual funds. These events led to a stunningly large fall in nonbank lending (Table 36.1) in the fourth quarter of 2008. Our estimate

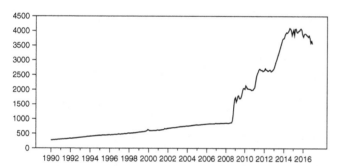

FIGURE 36.6 The monetary base.

shows that nonbank bank lending fell at an annualized rate of $1.6 trillion, or 11.2% of GDP. The credit collapse shock was too big for the real economy to absorb and growth stopped around the world.

The Fed responded rapidly to the financial shock. It expanded its balance sheet to replace this lending by initiating a wide range of lending facilities. The key facilities are the Asset-Backed Commercial Paper Money Market Fund Liquidity Facility (AMLF), the Commercial Paper Funding Facility (CPFF), the Term Asset Backed Securities Lending Facility (TALF), and the Term Auction Facility (TAF). These new facilities expanded the collateral the Fed would lend against, from T-bills and conforming Fannie and Freddie mortgage standard, to a wide range of assets and maturities. This is referred to as "quantitative easing." The result was the Fed expanded its balance sheet in an attempt to offset the sudden collapse of nonbank bank credit. This can be seen clearly in Table 36.2. The Fed's actions prevented a wave of bankruptcies and panic by allowing nonbank banks to fund and money market funds to honor withdrawals. The Fed did this by using its open market operations described above to be the lender of last resort to a wide range of financial intermediaries. This is also quite visible in Fig. 36.6. In fact, the Y2K response pales in comparison to the expansion of the monetary base during the financial crisis. But this is logical given that the size of the drop in non-bank bank lending was greater than 11% of GDP.

The information in Fig. 36.7 shows the impact of the explosion of the monetary base on MZM, a blip, insignificant in relation to the explosion of the monetary base, Fig. 36.6. More importantly the information presented in Fig. 36.8 shows that with the slight decline in the growth rate of MZM and the inflation rate, the deflation that some expected as a result of the collapse of the credit

TABLE 36.1 Lending Flows ($ Billions)

	10/17/2008	1/7/2009
Total lending flows (all sources)	**4179**	**2858**
Domestic nonfinancial sectors	75	−175
Financial sectors	2956	3016
Rest of the world	1148	17
Nonbank bank lending	**807**	**−1602**
Asset-backed securities	570	−599
Mutual funds	356	−241
Broker-dealers	−89	−439
REITs	−32	−94
Finance companies	2	−229

TABLE 36.2 Fed Balance Sheet Changes ($ Billions)

	10/17/2008	1/7/2009	Change
Total assets	996	2266	1270
Term asset credit	150	450	300
Commercial Paper Funding Facility	n/a	334	334
Asset-Backed Commercial Paper	n/a	24	24
Total Liabilities and Capital	996	2266	1270
Depository institutions	99	860	761

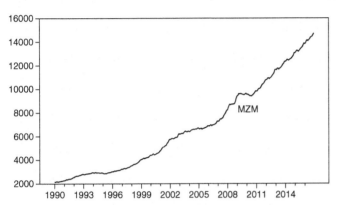

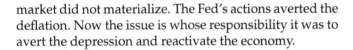

FIGURE 36.7   **Money of Zero Maturity.**

FIGURE 36.8   **MZM growth and the inflation rate.** *MZM, Money of zero maturity.*

market did not materialize. The Fed's actions averted the deflation. Now the issue is whose responsibility it was to avert the depression and reactivate the economy.

Reference

[1] Wall St. Journal Editorial Board. Geithner's Revelation. Wall St J May 12, 2009.

37

Monetary Policy and the Interaction Between the Money and Credit Markets

In the aftermath of the financial crisis, the Humphrey–Hawkins legislation forced the Fed's hand. It had to take steps to maintain maximum employment, production, and purchasing power as mandated by the legislation. The Fed adopted what some have called Keynesian Monetarism, a policy of low interest rates intended to stimulate aggregate demand and reactivate the economy. The Japanese central bank had done this before, but appears to have thrown in the towel regarding the ability of Keynesian Monetarism to stimulate the economy.

Unfortunately, monetary policy is not the Fed's only policy objective. When it comes to evaluating the job of central banks, there are too many moving parts, and we must isolate each one of them to come to a judgment as to what is going on in the world. We need some sort of scorecard or way to evaluate the totality of the central bank's actions and the impact of its policies on the financial system. We need to focus on price stability, the credit market, and the foreign exchange value of the dollar.

MONEY MARKET DISTURBANCES, UNCERTAINTY, AND THE DEMAND FOR CASH

Let's consider what happens when there is a disturbance in the money markets. One simple way to determine what happens to the demand for cash is to ask the following question: what would happen to the demand for cash if your ATM card, credit card, and checking account ceased to function? Obviously, the demand for cash would go through the roof. Under that scenario, an accommodative Fed would expand the monetary base to avoid any inconvenience or failure in the banking system. If the Fed were successful, the equilibrium quantity of money would remain unchanged. The increase in the base would offset one-for-one the shortage of cash. The point of all this is to show that when the Fed reacts to shocks, we have a way to determine whether the Fed completely or partially offset the shock. If it offsets it completely, the pre- and postcrisis quantities of the different aggregates, the inflation rate, and interest rates will remain unchanged. On the other hand, a partial offset would result in different levels of inflation, interest rates, and monetary aggregates. Hence, by looking at these variables of pre- and postcrisis, one can make inferences regarding the effect of the policy actions on the overall equilibrium.

Presumably once the crisis is over and/or confidence is restored, the Fed must pull out of the economy the excess base or else inflation will rise. Again, if the Fed is successful, after the ATM crash ends, the Fed will withdraw the cash, and the bank-created money will increase to its precrisis level. However, the Fed has to be wary of not pulling cash out too fast, as it could push the economy down the recessionary slippery slope. This is not a farfetched scenario. It happened under the Maestro's leadership leading to the century date change event.

Economic Disturbances and Equilibrium in an Integrated Global Economy. http://dx.doi.org/10.1016/B978-0-12-813993-6.00037-4

Recall that Greenspan was worried that as a result of the Y2K bug, computers would not function, and thus, he flooded the market with cash leading up to Y2K, to insure enough cash to realize transactions in the event that computers failed. The growth in the monetary base increased (Fig. 37.1) and so did the underlying inflation rate (Fig. 37.2). Well Y2K came and went and nothing happened. Sir Alan proceeded to withdraw the cash quickly. Notice the quick decline in the inflation rate (Fig. 37.2). In fact, some argue that the withdrawal was too quick and that it pushed the economy into a recession. It is clear from Fig. 37.3 that the cash withdrawal preceded the recession, as well as the steep decline in the industrial production index. A similar situation could

very well had been in the offing as the economy began to recover in the aftermath of the Great Recession when the Fed flooded the market with greenbacks and the monetary base exploded (Fig. 37.4). The danger was that if the Fed would withdraw the money too fast, it could really push the economy into a depression. Monetary policy was truly at the margin then. Luckily Ben Bernanke was a student of the Great Depression and he did not make that mistake.

The demand of money story goes a long way to explain the explosion of the monetary base and the lack of inflation (Fig. 37.5). The financial crisis leading up to the Great Recession resulted in an increase in the demand for money and the Fed accommodated the increase. We have to say that as far as the quantity of money goes, the Fed did a good job. The question is what will happen when confidence is restored and the process reversed. So far, the Fed has done a good job on the inflation front.

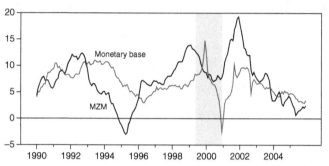

FIGURE 37.1　The monetary base and MZM growth (trailing 12 months). *MZM, Money of zero maturity.*

THE INTERACTION BETWEEN PRICE STABILITY AND THE CREDIT MARKETS

As different shocks have different impacts on the economy and the markets in question, identifying the shocks early on and understanding the adjustment process to a new equilibrium, dictated by the organization of the monetary system, may give an edge to an astute investor in developing investment strategies aimed at taking advantage to the economic environment created by

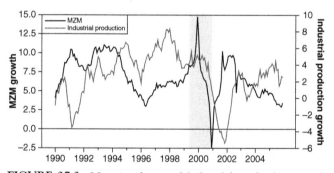

FIGURE 37.3　Monetary base and industrial production growth rate (trailing 12 months).

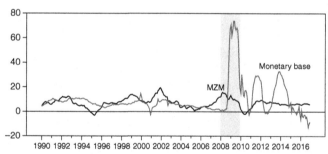

FIGURE 37.4　The monetary base and MZM growth (trailing 12 months). *MZM, Money of zero maturity.*

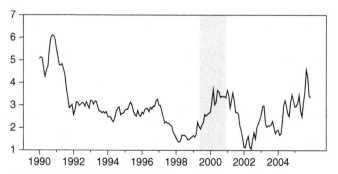

FIGURE 37.2　US (CPI) inflation rate (trailing 12 months).

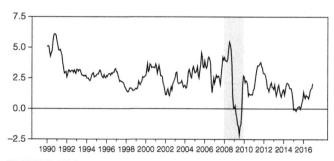

FIGURE 37.5　US (CPI) inflation rate (trailing 12 months).

the shocks and the response of the monetary authorities. Once we catalog the shocks and the different monetary arrangements, we can navigate the maze of possibilities and implement a successful strategy. Looking back, we can identify a few shocks and the empirical regularities associated with these shocks and policy changes. In fact, ideally we would like to develop a one-to-one mapping between the equilibrium quantities of the monetary and credit aggregates and the equilibrium or market-clearing prices, such as the underlying inflation rate, credit spread, and so forth.

Under a fractional reserve system, credit creation and the domestic money creation potential are inexorably linked. To see this, consider a simple example where the Fed prints $10 worth of monetary base. Under a fractional reserve system that requires banks to hold a 10% reserve requirement, the banks multiply that reserve 10 times (i.e., the inverse of the reserve requirement). Banks would create up to $100 worth of deposits.

Looking at the assets and liabilities of the banking system, we would find that it has liabilities worth $100 (the demand deposits) and assets worth $100 (the $10 worth of reserves and $90 worth of loans). However, for this combination to happen in equilibrium, the economy would have to want $100 worth of deposits and $90 worth of loans. But what if that is not the case? Let's say that the economy wanted $63 worth of loans and $73 worth of transaction money. Could the banking system do that? The answer is yes. All we need to do is have $7 worth of reserves and $3 worth of currency in circulation. The reserves would support $70 worth of deposits, which added to the $3 worth of cash that would generate $73 worth of money of zero maturity (MZM) or zero transaction money. On the asset side, the banks would hold $7 worth of reserves and $63 dollar's worth of deposits.

Now the interesting question is what happens if the combination of transaction money and credit that people want cannot be met by the banking system? Then something must give. Assuming that the different aggregates are imperfect substitutes for each other, we can then argue that either the price of the different variants of credit (i.e., interest rates and the quality spread) or the purchasing power of money (i.e., the price level/inflation rate) or opportunity cost of holding noninterest bearing money (i.e., short-term interest rates) must change to bring the market back into a market-clearing equilibrium. To outline the equilibrium process, we need to consider the possible shocks to the system.

MONEY DEMAND AND SUPPLY SHOCKS

The easiest money demand shock to consider is to assume that suddenly people decide to carry more cash in their pockets. Given the monetary base, an increase in currency holding leads to a one-for-one reduction in the reserves available to the banking system, resulting in a decline in bank loans. Double entry bookkeeping and the assumption of no excess reserves tell us that as loans decline, so will deposits. Under a fractional reserve system, the decline in the deposits will be larger than the increase in currency holding by the private sector, which means that the quantity of transaction money MZM will decline, and so will the money multiplier (MZM divided by the monetary base).

To clear the credit and money markets in response to the aforementioned disturbance, the prices of credit and money have to change. First, we know that in equilibrium the price of money has to increase. The opportunity cost of holding money, for noninterest bearing liquid assets, will increase. The price of money in terms of goods must increase too. This means that the price level and/or inflation rate will decline. In turn, higher interest payments on deposits will entice people to switch back to demand deposits. Under a competitive environment, the higher interest rates paid on deposits are the result of the higher interest rates charged on loans, and the increase will be greater the lower the quality of the borrower. In other words, the credit spread will also widen.

The changes in interest rates or market-clearing prices will result in a partial offset of the initial disturbance. To the extent that the initial disturbance is not completely offset, the new equilibrium will consist of a higher price of money or lower inflation rate, a higher price of credit, and a larger spread. These changes in turn will result in the new equilibrium quantities: a higher currency holding, a lower MZM and lower deposits and bank credit. This is the one-to-one mapping that we have in mind, linking the new equilibrium quantities of money and credit to the new market-clearing prices.

A shift in the demand for currency leads to a market-clearing equilibrium process that results in a negative relationship between the equilibrium quantity of currency and the inflation rate, as well as a negative relationship between the currency holding and the opportunity costs of holding noninterest bearing money. An increase in the supply of currency would result in the opposite correlation. This analysis suggests a simple way to determine the nature of the disturbances in the money and credit markets, examine the correlation between these aggregates and determine the relevant prices.

Data presented in Fig. 37.6 shows that MZM and its currency and credit components tend to move together most of the time. The data also shows some deviations from the trend where the correlation among the different variables also deviates from the long-term trend. These are the episodes that may be used to identify disturbances in the money and credit markets as well as these markets adjustments to a new equilibrium. Fig. 37.7 presents information on the fluctuations in the currency–bank credit ratio over time. Visually the information presented in Fig. 37.7 provides a much better way to identify the different Currency–Bank Credit cycles that we have defined as our financial/monetary market disturbances. This in turn allows to infer the market-clearing prices that a new equilibrium would require.

Our earlier analysis argued that when a disturbance occurred, the prices in the money and credit market would change to eliminate any excess demand and/or supply in any of the markets. We also showed that the correlation between the market-clearing prices and the equilibrium quantities would depend on the nature of the shock, that is, a demand shock or a supply shock. Fig. 37.8A–C illustrates the correlation between the currency–bank credit ratio and different asset prices.

The information presented in Fig. 37.8A shows that prior to approximately 1990, there was a close correlation between the two variables and little or no correlation afterwards. One possible explanation for this is the organization of the monetary system. If as we believe, the Fed was pursuing a successful domestic price rule, then one would expect the inflation rate to oscillate around the price rule target, which means there will be

little or no correlation between the currency–bank credit ratio and the underlying inflation rate. In effect, the Fed was fixing the price of money in terms of goods. Hence, we need to look at the other price variables as possible explanations for the market-clearing mechanisms. The information presented in Fig. 37.8A also shows that prior to the adoption of the price rule, the inflation rate leads the currency–bank credit ratio suggesting that it was the excess money creation that was "causing" the changes in the currency–bank credit ratio.

The positive correlation between the currency–bank credit ratio and the T-bill yields, the opportunity cost of holding interest bearing money, can be seen in Fig. 37.8B. The data shows a close fit during the nonprice rule period. Although the correlation appears to weaken during the price rule period, it is as expected. The T-bill mirrors the currency–bank credit cycles up

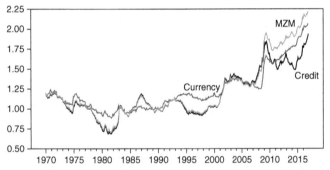

FIGURE 37.6   Indices of MZM and its currency and credit components (index base 1970). *MZM, Money of zero maturity.*

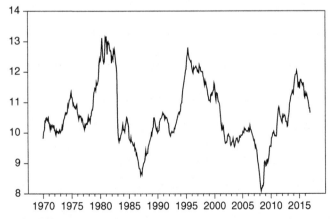

FIGURE 37.7   Money of zero maturity currency–bank credit ratio.

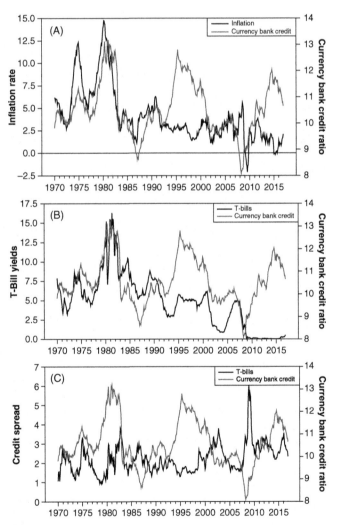

FIGURE 37.8   (A) The currency–bank credit ratio index versus the inflation rate. (B) The currency–bank credit ratio versus the T-bill yields. (C) The currency–bank credit ratio versus the spread of the BAA lessens the T-bond yields.

to the financial crisis. Even there as the Fed kept rates near zero, the currency–bank credit ratios increased and peaked around the time that the Fed began increasing short-term rates. The final correlation between the currency–bank credit ratio is shown in Fig. 37.8C. Notice the negative correlation between the spread of the Baa corporate bond yields and the 10-year T-bond yields. The fit tightens after financial crisis.

Taken together the three graphs suggest that at different points in time, the money and credit market are subjected to different disturbances. Thus comparing the new equilibrium quantities or the new market-clearing prices to the preshock equilibrium quantities and market-clearing prices, one can infer the impact of the different shocks and the effectiveness of the measures taken by the authorities to offset these shocks.

38

Is Central Banking an Art?

When trying to determine if central banking is an art or a science, the past few years have shown us one thing: central banking is a complicated issue. While there are many reasons why this is the case, we know some of these reasons. The first one being the issue of multiple policy objectives. For example, per the Humphrey–Hawkins legislation, the Fed's monetary objectives are price stability and economic growth. The dual objectives have gained currency during the past two decades when some of the major and most important central banks around the world began to appoint very smart and competent MIT-trained economists as their leaders. These central bankers faced different constraints in their respective institutions and economies, but there was a common thread. The theoretical foundations for these policies, which we call Keynesian Monetarism or more commonly quantitative easing (QE), were provided by the Phillips Curve.

In the United States, the dual mandate was the vehicle for the application of the Keynesian Monetarism. Strict Phillips Curve adherents argued that once the economy recovered, the unemployment rate or the natural rate of unemployment was too low and any further decline could result in rising inflationary pressures. Others argued that the unemployment rate did not account for the excessively low labor force participation rate. This gave rise to some debate as to the appropriate variables or indicators. Potentially, the most serious one being the theoretical arguments against the inflation-output trade-off posited by the Phillips Curve. Some monetarists,

most notably Milton Friedman, have argued that there is no such thing as a long-run inflation-unemployment trade-off. The conclusion is that by focusing solely on price stability, the Fed can achieve the one objective it can do something about. The benefits of such policy are easy to articulate. Think of it this way: if everyone knows what the value and/or purchasing power of the dollar is going to be 30 years from now, would people behave differently than if they were uncertain as to the value of the dollar? That is why we believe that price stability should be the Fed's main goal. The easiest way to achieve the objective is through the implementation of a domestic price rule. Despite these arguments and the empirical evidence about the inflation output trade-off, the construct of the Philips Curve is alive and well among central bankers, and even in different countries' executive and legislative branches.

LOW-INTEREST RATES AND KEYNESIAN MONETARISM

In the aftermath of the financial crisis, most of the major central banks in the developed world adopted similar monetary policies. As already mentioned, a common factor among many of the central bankers that adopted these policies is the fact that many of these bankers trained or taught at the same university. And that raises an interesting question: was their policy response the result of ideology or training? We will leave

Economic Disturbances and Equilibrium in an Integrated Global Economy. http://dx.doi.org/10.1016/B978-0-12-813993-6.00038-6

the answer and debates associated with the answer to the historians. The rationale for the adoption of the policies is water under the bridge; now we must contend and deal with the consequences of the policies adopted. That is our focus here.

The basic idea behind the lowering interest rates is readily found in Keynesian economics textbooks. The argument goes something like this: by lowering the interest rates, the Fed (who presumably controls the interest rates) will be able to stimulate aggregate demand, resulting in a higher level of output. We have dubbed the low-interest rate policy Keynesian Monetarism. The logic behind this argument contains two implicit assumptions that we will retain, at least for arguments sake. The first one is that the Fed controls short-term interest rates. The second one is that the decline in interest rates leads to an increase in aggregate demand. One argument behind the increase in aggregate demand used in textbooks is that the lower interest rates lead to higher investments. But we believe there is more; the lower interest rates also reduce the discounted price of future consumption, which in turn induces an intertemporal substitution away from future consumption into current consumption. The two effects combined point to a net increase in aggregate demand. Some critics argue that such an analysis is incomplete. In the context of the textbook Keynesian models, the decline in interest rates also reduces the income of the economy's savers and that could lead to a reduction in their expenditures. Whether there is a net increase in aggregate demand depends on whether the intertemporal substitution effects overwhelm the decline in income. *Ex-post* there is a way to determine which of the effect dominates, all we need to do is look at the data.

It has been several years since the financial crisis and the adoption of the so-called Keynesian Monetarism and the data needed to evaluate the effect of these policies is beginning to accumulate. Examining the data, the best that the proponents of the policy may claim is that the policies prevented a worldwide depression. The accumulated data points to a very tepid recovery in the developed world. Even if one attributes the increases in aggregate demand solely to the low-interest rate policy, the tepid recovery suggests that the QE or Keynesian Monetarism had a weak or small impact on the economy's aggregate demand.

Proponents and defenders of the US version of Keynesian Monetarism argued that the US recovery was the envy of the developed world. That may be, but the relative performance alone is not sufficient evidence that the Keynesian Monetarism delivered the desired or promised results. Even worse, the quest for greater stimulus has pushed many of these central banks into a continuous decline in interest rates that pushed some of these economies into negative interest rates territory.

YIELD: DOCUMENTING THE EFFECTS INDUCED BY LOW-INTEREST RATES

The decline in yields has had a devastating effect on people who live on a fixed income. Prior to the financial crisis, the 10-year bond yield hovered around 5%. So, a person with a $1,000,000 would generate $50,000 a year of interest income. Let's say that the person used that money to supplement their social security income. That same $1,000,000 generated only $18,000 shortly after the crisis. For these people to maintain the level of expenditures without increasing their risk exposure, they would have to dip into their capital to the tune of $32,000 a year. Another option available to the hypothetical persons was to search for higher yield, even if it meant increasing the person risk exposure. That is precisely what many people did.

Although, we do not have specific statistics, the evidence suggests that investors pursued both options. The risk averse savers/investors mostly reduced their standard of living and/or dipped into their capital. Others have chosen to pursue the higher yield strategy, even if it meant increasing their risk profile. Depending on the investor's risk tolerance and preference, the decline in yield would induce substitution effects and the magnitude of the substitution would be in direct proportion to the substitutability among the different assets. Let's begin at the short end of the curve, where the Fed, presumably, has more control over the yields of short-term securities. A decline in the short-term government securities induces a substitution effect, and the magnitude will be stronger for the closer substitutes than for the weaker substitutes. Hence we expect the impact to be stronger for the shorter duration government instruments, that is, close substitutes, and weaker for the longer maturity instruments, that is, near substitutes.

Based on the substitution effect alone, we would expect the substitution into the long end of the yield curve to result in an increase in the price of longer maturity instruments, which would produce a decline in the yields of government instruments. All else the same, given the substitution effects, the decline in yields will be smaller for the government bonds the longer the duration. Fig. 38.1 shows that this has been the case in the previous instances–Y2K, the Greenspan Put, and the Financial Crisis–when the Fed deliberately lowered the short end of the yield curve.

The substitution effects induced by the low-interest rates are not exclusive to the government fixed income instruments. Some investors' search for yield led them to corporate bonds, the high yield markets, and some even pursued high dividend stocks. Fig. 38.2 shows the effect of the policy initiatives. Early on, the yield differential between the Baa Corporate yields and the government 10-year bond yields widened, reflecting the differences

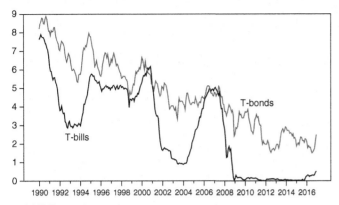

FIGURE 38.1   T-Bill and T-Bond yields.

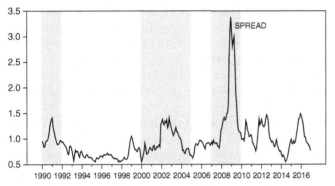

FIGURE 38.2   Baa less the 10 year government bond yields.

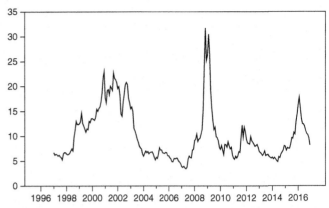

FIGURE 38.3   Merrill Lynch lower than BBB bond yields less (Moody's Baa bond yields).

in substitutability among the different instruments. Over time, the economy and markets adjusted to the Fed policy and the initial disturbance was partially accommodated. The initial shock was partially reversed and the yields approached their long-run averages. The lower the quality of the instruments and the lower the degree of substitutability, the greater the increase in spread. Fig. 38.3 shows that the spread between the Merrill Lynch High Yield Index and Moody's Baa spread widened. The data also shows the same pattern, initially the spread widened, but after some time the market seems to have returned to its long-run trend of long-run equilibrium.

Some of the more aggressive and sophisticated investors delved into exotic and riskier markets, such as catastrophe bonds or cat bonds. These bonds were invented in the early 1990s to help insurance companies mitigate the risk of disasters such as hurricanes and earthquakes. The cat bonds have been extended to cover events such as whether too many people die in a pandemic, whether people live beyond their expected lifetimes, cyber hacking, accounting fraud, and rogue traders among others. Some have argued that, because of the search for yield, bonds have turned the fixed income market into a giant insurance company wannabe. In short, collectively this is clear evidence that the low-interest rates pushed

investors to seek higher returns. In the process, they had to increase their risk profile.

WHAT DOES THE DATA TELL US?

Two years ago, the European Central Bank, ECB, cut interest rates below zero to encourage people to spend more. The Bank of Japan, BoJ, has used similar logic to justify its monetary policy too. Yet the economic data shows that after the adoption of the negative rates, consumers were saving more in Germany and Japan, as well as in Denmark, Switzerland, and Sweden, three countries with negative interest rates. This raises the issue as to what signals do negative interest rates send. One possibility is that the low-interest rates induces an increase in aggregate demand and is thus simulative. That is the orthodox view. But this is not the only possible signal. What if the low-interest or negative interest rates signal that the economy is not improving? If that is the case, why would anyone borrow money to invest, irrespective of the lower interest rates? In fact, some argue that the low or negative yield may be an indication of reduced expectations regarding the economy. Are the negative rates communicating a fear over the growth outlook and the central bankers' ability to deal with the situation? Not surprisingly, companies were also holding on to funds and foregoing cheap loans.

At the household level, the argument also has additional implications. If people expect their net worth to decline, they will reduce their current consumption and thus the economy's aggregate demand. Putting together the private sector (both household and corporate), the answer is that if their expectations for the future are bleak, their aggregate demand will decline and the savings rates will increase. The higher savings will, all else the same, result in lower interest rates in the banking sector and lower yields of the money instruments.

The increased savings is nothing more than the private sector rebuilding its wealth, which was adversely affected by the financial crisis. Fig. 38.4 presents some evidence in support of the view that the declines in wealth result in an effort to rebuild the wealth. Households can rebuild their wealth in one of two ways: capital gains and/or savings. Absent capital gains, we would expect the savings rate to increase. On the other hand, if the capital gains are large enough, there will be no need to take actions through the savings rate.

This view of the world explains much of the behavior before and after the financial crisis. Before the crisis, the rapid asset appreciation reduced the need to save to accumulate wealth. In fact, if sufficiently large, the households could borrow, increase their current consumption, and have a rising net worth. In effect, households were increasing their leverage during the good times. During a declining wealth period, households are forced to delever, reduce their consumption, and since there is no capital gains during a downdraft, the only way to replenish their net worth is through higher savings. Savings and net worth provide a simple explanation for savings behavior of the US economy. During the crisis, net worth declined and the savings rate rose. After the Fed implemented its low-interest rate policy, which some claim distorted the market and fueled a stock market rise, there was no need to increase savings to restore the household net worth.

KEYNESIAN MONETARISM'S TRACK RECORD

Japan is the country with the most experience on the Keynesian Monetarism or QE bandwagon. Yet in spite of the supposed benefits, the policy has not produced a significant economic expansion. Something else is needed to stimulate the economy and produce economic growth. Sadly, the Abe administration tried a failed policy when it fired the Keynesian stimulus gun a second time in his

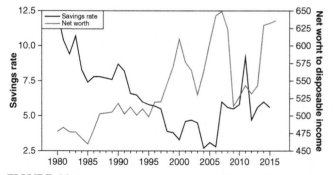

FIGURE 38.4 Savings rate as a percent of disposable personal income versus household Net worth as a percent of personal disposable income.

administration. The program consisted of a series of infrastructure projects like upgrading ports to accommodate foreign cruise ships, as well as interest-free loans for infrastructure projects building new hotels for foreign tourists and a magnetic levitation train connecting Tokyo and Osaka. The stimulus plan also included cash handouts to low-income people. The Prime Minister has called it "an investment in the future." Yet we fail to understand how a hand out to low-income families is an investment in the future. It is based on simple Keynesian theory that the recipients will spend the money? Who pays for the transfer? It points clearly to the taxpayers. To the extent that they anticipate the future taxes, they will reduce their spending. The Abe administration can argue that it is postponing the prior scheduled tax increase by 2½ years, underscoring the weakness in the economy. However, if postponing the tax is a good thing, why not take the argument to its logical conclusion and eliminate it completely?

The infrastructure building is something that deserves some attention. Whether it provides a stimulus or not depends on whether the net present value of the projects is positive or not. If the net present value is positive, wealth will be created and the increased wealth will result in an increase in aggregate demand for goods and services. The infrastructure would presumably result in a higher level of output and employment.

Selecting positive net present value projects is not a slam dunk. Government regulations and other restrictions, as well as the economics of the project come into play. In the aftermath of the financial crisis, most of the developed countries embarked on an infrastructure kick. It has not worked out for Japan, why would we expect that this time is different. Here in the United States, President Obama's stimulus package was supposed to target shovel ready projects. Even the president of the United States found out that it is not easy to find shovel ready projects, as regulatory reviews, legal challenges, and restrictions on the type of labor to be used in public projects all add to the costs and delay their construction. Perhaps if the federal government eased on the regulatory burden and other mandates, the private sector would undertake many of these projects or the federal government would be a bit more successful in delivering the infrastructure investment. Another concern regarding the infrastructure investment financed by public debt is that eventually the debt must be repaid.

MONETARY POLICY'S BURDEN

Looking at the experiences of the developed world with QE, on the real side, most economies have either complemented the Keynesian Monetarism or substituted it with a stimulus program and/or an expansion of public services and transfer programs. Looking at the Japanese experience, the European experience, and even our own experience, it is hard to argue that the policy packages have been a great success based on the data. Defenders of the US programs argue that the US economy is the envy of the world. That may be the case, but that is only a relative measure. What matters to some is the absolute performance and the fact is that the US recovery has been a sub-par one by historical standards. Hence, based on the data, we may rule out these policies as a mechanism for restoring the rate of economic growth. The process of elimination leaves lower regulation and lower tax rates as the likely catalysts for faster growth. To the extent that the fiscal component did not produce the stimulus that was initially promised, under the dual mandate, monetary policy must pick up the slack. That is a tall order. Absent the faster growth, it will be very difficult for the Fed to raise rates without negatively impacting stock market valuation. In a historical context, the results produced by the Keynesian stimulus and QE appear to be, at best, underwhelming. This reinforces the monetarist view that the focus of monetary policy should be on maintaining the purchasing power of the domestic currency.

V. THE FINANCIAL CRISIS—A CASE STUDY

39

After the Deluge?

The bursting of the real estate market bubble is considered by many as the ground zero for the meltdown experienced by the financial markets that led to the Great Recession. At the time, politicians and economists offered many possible solutions to the crisis. Different people advanced a variety of ideas on how to restore confidence in the system and avoid an economic slowdown. That is a moot point now. The Obama administration and the Fed made their choice and there is no way to go back in time. All we can do now is a postmortem analysis of the economic data to gain insights into which policies worked and which did not. In the process, we reach some conclusions regarding the effectiveness of what we call Keynesian Monetarism.

A BRIEF DESCRIPTION OF THE PROBLEM AND ECONOMIC CONDITIONS AS WE SAW IT

The decline in home prices had a devastating effect on the market valuation of subprime loans. In turn, the lower values affected securities based on the packaging of subprime loans called mortgage backed securities (MBS). The lower home prices and lower MBS valuation had additional effects on the economy. On the consumer side, the declining value lowered their net worth and their credit worthiness, prompting some financial institutions to reduce the credit extended to many of their clients. On the side of lending institutions, the decline in MBS and home prices reduced the capital adequacy of the lending institutions forcing them to reduce their lending.

In addition, individual investors as well as the lending institutions experienced the adverse impact of leverage. When things go well, leverage multiplies the profitability of an investment, and when things do not go so well it multiplies the losses of the investment. The combination of leverage and adverse conditions had a devastating impact on the net worth of borrowers. For subprime borrowers who had 100% financing, the effect was a negative net worth and a strong incentive to walk away from their investment. For the financial institutions, the impact was a tremendous reduction in capital. Given the opaqueness of MBS, investors had a tough time figuring out which institutions had adequate capital and which ones did not. The uncertainty and lack of information created the conditions which fostered speculative attacks, and, as we know, no institution can sustain a speculative attack or run on the bank where all depositors withdraw at once. Similarly, under such conditions, institutions would not want to trade with others perceived to be in weak financial positions. These crosscurrents combined into a perfect storm that resulted in a collapse of the bank credit, a full-fledged financial crisis and a subsequent recession. A timeline of some of the milestones of the financial crisis that tipped the hands

Economic Disturbances and Equilibrium in an Integrated Global Economy. http://dx.doi.org/10.1016/B978-0-12-813993-6.00039-8

of the government and the central bank can be found in the appendix.

The ripple effects of the housing crisis affected the world economy, shook the foundations of the world financial system and led many to question the virtues of free-market capitalism and chose instead to advocate for more government regulations and a greater degree of intervention in the economy. It was the source of the new regulations that emanated from legislation initially proposed by the Obama Administration in 2009, which later became the Dodd–Frank Wall Street Reform and Consumer Protection Act signed into law on July 21, 2010. While the effects of these policies are important and are discussed elsewhere, our focus here is going to be on the Fed's response to the crisis.

THE MONETARY BASE, BANK CREDIT, MONEY OF ZERO MATURITY, AND THE FINANCIAL CRISIS

At the time around the financial crisis, the Fed and government officials were quite worried that the US economy could spiral down into a deflationary economic depression. The federal government took measures to stimulate aggregate demand by adopting a fairly large "stimulus" spending program. Whether the program was as successful as the designers hoped is not relevant at this point. However, to the extent that it was not, it made the Fed's job a bit more difficult given the Fed's dual mandate.

The decline in banks' net capital and borrowers' credit worthiness associated with the housing crisis led to a collapse of the bank created credit. In turn, the credit collapse through the fractional reserve banking system had a negative impact on the quantity of money. To summarize, the market collapse led to an incipient decline in the supply of bank credit and transaction money which could have, in principle, produced a deflationary spiral, as well as a major economic recession or quite possibly a depression, if not arrested. Double-entry bookkeeping requires that the banking system's loan creation go hand-in-hand with deposit creation. Hence, as credit was extinguished during the crisis, so was the amount of deposits held by the banks. All else the same, the decline in deposits would produce a collapse of the amount of transaction money circulating in the economy. The banking system's money and credit creation ability per a dollar's worth of monetary base, that is, the money supply function, was significantly curtailed. The data suggests that the decline in asset prices and the capital adequacy of the banks and financial institutions had a negative impact on the credit creation of the banking system, and suggests a collapse of the money multiplier. Fig. 39.1 shows not only the collapse of the credit multiplier

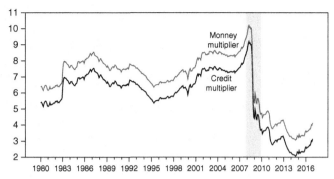

FIGURE 39.1 MZM money and credit multipliers.

during the crisis, but it also shows that the credit multiplier continued to decline even after the crisis downdraft. All else the same, one would expect that as asset values and the capital adequacy of the banks recovered, so would their credit creation ability. But that was not meant to be. While the credit multiplier began to recover subsequently, it has not reached its previous historical levels.

This outcome is consistent with the analysis presented in this section. The diminished credit creation ability of the banking system has negative consequences for the economy. The lack of bank credit will increase the demand for an alternative financing mechanism, that is, the substitution effect. Put another way, the void created must be filled somehow, and in a market economy the price mechanism is the signal that induces a greater supply of alternative financing. In general, the end result is one of a smaller overall credit creation and a higher price of credit. Both of these have a negative impact on the level of economic activity and limit the ability of the economy to expand rapidly. The weak economic recovery since the recession is consistent with this interpretation of the events discussed here. More importantly, if our analysis is correct, the data suggests that the banking system has yet to regain its flexibility or credit creation ability. In response to the crisis and in an attempt to prevent similar excesses in the financial system in future, the Dodd–Frank Legislation was passed in 2010. The new law also authorized the creation of the Consumer Financial Protection Bureau and a whole host of other regulations. The legislation was somewhat controversial and it had significant opponents and proponents.

If we attribute the inability of the banking system to reach previous levels of credit creation to a combination of the Fed's policy to maintain a low-interest rate as far as the eye can see in conjunction with the Dodd–Frank legislation, we can then argue that a return to normalcy will restore some of the banking sector's credit creation ability. Unfortunately, the impact of Dodd–Frank will remain. In conclusion, we believe that as the Fed returns to normalcy, bank credit creation will not return to its prerecession level. A return to the precrisis equilibrium requires a major modification of Dodd–Frank and associated regulations.

THE FED'S CRISIS RESPONSE

On the demand side, the financial crisis increased the demand for liquidity and produced a flight to quality, resulting in an increase in the demand for money and a decline in the demand for bank credit. A strong case can be made that as a result of the dual mandate, the Fed was obligated to react and to try to stabilize the economy and prevent both a deflation, as well as an economic depression. The Fed's response was quick and swift, as it expanded its balance sheet by an unprecedented amount. As the Fed purchased the government securities, its share of the ownership of the federal debt increased dramatically. The Fed's purchases of government securities were financed by an expansion of the monetary base, that is, the printing of money. The expansion of the monetary base was extraordinary and unprecedented, and the economy was flooded with greenbacks (Fig. 39.2).

The net effect of a smaller multiplier, a larger monetary base, a flight to quality, and a need for liquidity on the two aggregates MZM and bank credit can be found in Fig. 39.3. In the aftermath of the crisis, the equilibrium quantity of MZM per unit of output rose, suggesting that the Fed arrested the deflationary pressures brought about

by the crisis. In addition, the Fed's action returned the monetary aggregate Money of Zero Maturity (MZM) to a path of price stability. The data also shows that bank credit as a percent of GDP moved sideways or declined. All we can say is something we already knew: at best, the Fed's actions arrested the collapse of the credit market but it did not restore it to anywhere near its precrisis level.

The inference that we make from the data is that the joint outcomes suggest that the Fed's actions more than offset the initial decline in the supply of money created by the financial meltdown. The Fed's action is best described as an outward shift in the money supply function. We also surmise an outward shift in the demand for money produced by the increased demand for liquidity and a flight to quality. As both the demand for and supply of money experienced an outward shift, the equilibrium quantity of money unambiguously rose. An aggressive Fed would counter the deflationary pressures with an increase in the monetary base. As the credit creation was collapsing (Fig. 39.1), the Fed flooded the market and in the process expanded the monetary base quite a bit (Fig. 39.2). If lucky enough or smart enough to increase the base by the amount that deposits were extinguished, the quantity of money would remain unchanged and the underlying inflation rate would not change. The information presented in Fig. 39.4 suggests a slight increase in the rate of growth of MZM, however by all accounts the Fed was not excessively aggressive. The Fed's intervention and expansion of its balance sheet was just about right and for that the Fed deserves an A.

Now whether the price of money rises or falls as a result of the Fed's balance sheet depends on the relative magnitude of the demand for and supply of money shifts. As we know that the Fed was targeting a 2% inflation rate, we have a way to evaluate the Fed based on its success of keeping the inflation rate around its target rate. The fact that the inflation rate was below the 2% target range meant that the purchasing power of money was not declining as fast as the Fed wanted. In other words, if inflation is a monetary phenomenon, the below target inflation rate meant that the quantity of money was not growing fast enough to simultaneously

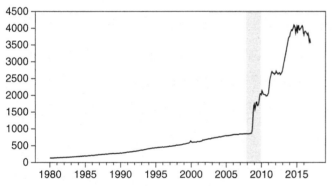

FIGURE 39.2 The monetary base.

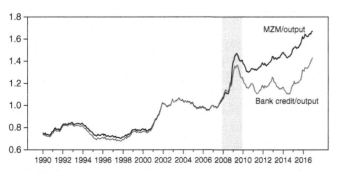

FIGURE 39.3 Index of MZM and bank credit per unit of industrial output.

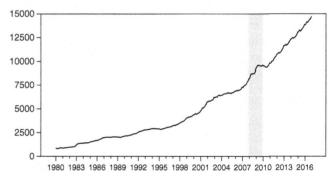

FIGURE 39.4 MZM: the quantity of money.

FIGURE 39.5   CPI inflation rate (trailing 12 months).

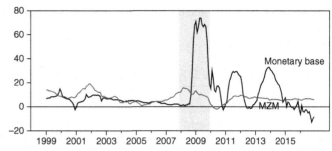

FIGURE 39.6   Monetary base and MZM growth rates (trailing 12 months).

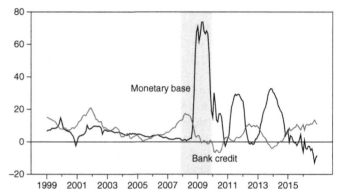

FIGURE 39.7   Monetary base and bank credit growth rates (trailing 12 months).

accommodate the increased demand for money and reach the inflation rate target level. Notice that despite the expansion of the monetary base and the slight surge in MZM (Fig. 39.4), the consumer price index (CPI) inflation rate surged a bit early during the development of the crisis and then declined below the Fed's 2% inflation rate (Fig. 39.5). From this vantage point, we believe the Fed acted responsibly and admirably during the crisis.

Looking at the bank credit market, Fig. 39.3 shows that in the aftermath of the crisis, the quantity of credit per unit of output declined. We also know that the price of credit, in particular that of the government securities, declined. A lower price and a lower equilibrium quantity are consistent with an inward shift in aggregate demand exceeding the outward shift in aggregate supply of credit. This result suggests that to restore equilibrium, an increase in the demand for credit relative to its supply is needed. The question then becomes what policy instrument or policy action is the most effective way to stimulate the aggregate demand for credit. We know that increased regulations will not do that. So, it is not surprising that the regulatory actions taken did not accomplish an increase in credit demand. Then there is the stimulus program. Judging it by the subpar economic recovery, its impact on the economy is nothing to write home about.

THE MONETARY AGGREGATES AFTER THE CRISIS

Fig. 39.6 provides us with what appears to be somewhat disturbing information. It shows large swings in the monetary base relative to MZM in the aftermath of the crisis. When compared to the precrisis levels, these swings in base growth seem excessive. However, Fig. 39.6 also provides positive information. Notice that despite the large swings the monetary base growth rate, the growth rate of the quantity of MZM money does not seem too affected in a significant way. Then there is an interesting detail that the growth in the monetary base and the credit creation of MZM move in the opposite direction since 2012 (approximately). The negative correlation is

consistent with the view that the reduction in the monetary base rate of growth is being offset by the increase in the bank credit and money multipliers (Fig. 39.1).

The results presented in Fig. 39.7 confirm the inference previously mentioned. It shows that since the financial crisis, the swings in the growth of the monetary base do mirror the swings in the banking system credit creation and thus cancel each other out as far as MZM growth rate is concerned. In turn, the MZM growth rate continues a steady trend line of a mid-single digit growth rate thought the postcrisis period. Next, if we interpret the downward trend in the growth rate of the monetary base as an activist Fed attempting to tighten, the data shows a resilient banking system undoing much of the undesired Fed action, the net result being no significant change in the MZM growth rate (Fig. 39.6).

INFLATION RATE, INTEREST RATES, THE SLOPE OF THE YIELD CURVE, AND THE CREDIT SPREAD

So far, we have focused on the effects of different shocks on the changes in the monetary and bank credit aggregates needed to restore a new equilibrium. We then focused on the impact of the Fed open market operations and the expansion of its balance sheet in response to the financial crisis. However, the equilibrium quantities are only one way to describe the overall equilibrium. The other way is to focus on the market clearing prices. Although equivalent, this analysis provides us with a slightly different perspective as it forces us to focus on the magnitude of the associated substitution effects among the fixed income instruments generated by the shocks and the corresponding the change in equilibrium prices/yields of the various fixed income instruments.

Again, the relationship among different variables is not invariant to the organization of the monetary system. It is the organization of the monetary system that determines not only the Fed response to economic disturbances, but also how it goes about doing so. Under normal conditions, we believe that the Fed controls the short end of the yield curve, it is subject to the dual mandate, and it targets a 2% inflation rate.

One implication of the inflation target is that the quantity of MZM money becomes endogenous. If the inflation rate exceeds the target, the Fed determines that there is too much money in the system. As a result, it will conduct open-market operations to reduce the quantity of greenbacks circulating the economy. An inflation rate below the inflation target reverses the process. In doing so, the Fed effectively fixes the price of money in terms of goods, that is, the purchasing power of money. That leaves the other price of money as the market clearing prices that adjust to bring about overall equilibrium. That price of money is the opportunity cost of holding noninterest bearing money, the short-term interest rates. Fig. 39.8 shows the MZM growth rate and the T-Bill yields time series. Notice that prior to the financial crisis, the spikes tend to be negatively related. A result consistent with the view that as the opportunity cost of holding money increases, the attractiveness of holding MZM money declines, hence the negative correlation.

If, as we have assumed, the Fed controls interest rates, to the extent that the prevailing short rates are not what would have prevailed in an unfettered market, it means that the Fed is distorting the short-term market. The distortion being the difference between the rates that would

have prevailed in an unfettered market and the Fed-controlled rates. As we do not know the rates that would have prevailed, we cannot measure the distortion with accuracy. Nevertheless, we can qualitatively establish the substitution effects generated by the distortion.

HOW DISTORTED IS THE FIXED INCOME MARKET?

As already mentioned, we assume that the Fed can control the short end of the yield curve. To the extent that the Fed induces a market clearing price that differs from what an unfettered market clearing price would be, the difference between the two prices will be the result of the distortion imposed by the Fed. Looking at Fig. 39.8, it is apparent that interest rates have remained quite low since the financial crisis. The fact that the Fed has been successful in maintaining the low T-Bill yields for so long lends support to the view that the Fed does in fact have a great deal of influence or control over the short end of the yield curve. Although we do not report data over a longer period, the current levels of T-Bill yields are well below the post-WWII average. That difference may be a good proxy for the degree of distortion on the yields of the short end of the financial markets.

The information presented in Fig. 39.9 also shows the yields of the 10-year T-Bonds. Notice that while the T-Bond yields trend downward, the disparity with its values over the preceding decade are not as pronounced. We have a possible explanation for the nonabrupt decline. As the Fed lowered the T-Bill yields, it induced a substitution effect away from the short end of the yield curve into longer duration instruments. As the demand for these instruments rose, all else the same, their prices were bid up and thus their yield declined. In turn, as the yield of T-Bonds declined and the spread with corporate bonds widened. This generated a substitution effect

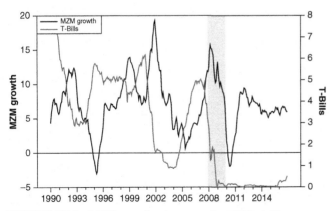

FIGURE 39.8   MZM growth rate versus the T-Bill yields.

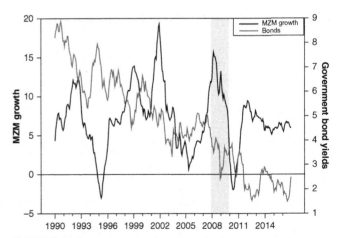

FIGURE 39.9   MZM growth rate versus the 10-year government bond yields.

away from government bonds into corporate bonds, such as high yields. All else the same, that resulted in an increase in the price of these instruments with a corresponding decline in yields and the spread between the high yield corporate and government bonds.

Although one can argue that the Treasury controls the composition and amount of the government bonds outstanding, one must keep in mind that there are readily available private substitutes, such as corporate bonds. While the US Treasury controls the supply of government bonds, it does not control the supply of private substitutes. Finally, the key point to take into consideration is that the changes in the yield differentials depend on several factors, including the available supplies of the different instruments and the degree of substitutability among these fixed income instruments.

The imperfect substitutability among the different financial instruments yields an interesting insight. As the Fed removes the distortion, the T-Bill yields will rise to their historical trend. That will induce a substitution effect into the shorter-term instruments. Hence the short end of the yield curve will unambiguously rise. As people substitute away from the long end of the yield curve to the short end, the demand for long-term government bonds will decline and so will their price. The end result is an increase in the yield of the long maturity government bonds. The lower the degree of substitutability among the different maturity instruments, the greater will be the yield differential needed to affect the switch. This suggests that the yield curve will move up across the board and its slope will steepen. The difference in substitution effects and their impact on the slope of the Baa-government spread are evident in the data (Fig. 39.10). The substitution effects combined with the relative supply go a long way in explaining the corporate high yields. The Fed is not the only source of disturbance that causes substitution effects. During a financial crisis, risk considerations may cause substitution effects away from the riskier yield-generating asset classes. This is what the popular press calls a flight to quality. It is

nothing more than a substitution effect away from the riskier yield producing assets into the perceived safer government instruments. Notice in Fig. 39.12, that the Baa corporate yields spread spiked during the financial crisis, as well as during the previous uncertainty produced by the recession associated with Y2K. Also notice that when the crisis and the economy stabilized, the yields declined and returned to their normal sample range.

The one common element between the growth of MZM and the slope of the yield curve (Fig. 39.11) and the Baa-government spread (Fig. 39.12) shows that spikes in the MZM growth rate, a proxy for disturbances, are also negatively correlated to the changes in the market-clearing yield variables. Both series tend to be highly correlated, hence we will provide a general interpretation that suits both proxies. The data is consistent with our substitution-effect theory provided that one is willing to contemplate alternative disturbances. We have already mentioned two. One is risk related or a flight to quality and the other is what we have characterized as the Fed's distortion of the yield market as characterized by low interest rates as far as the eye can see. The flight to quality explains the spike caused by Y2K-related recession and the financial crisis. The Fed's control of interest rates can explain the upward secular drift in the high yield spreads since the financial crisis, as well as the secular

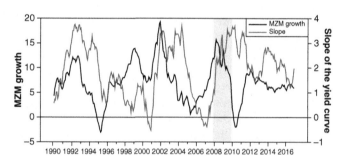

FIGURE 39.11   MZM growth rate versus the slope of the yield curve.

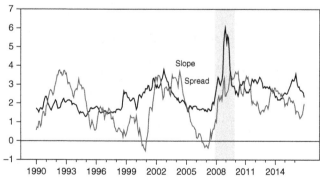

FIGURE 39.10   Slope of the yield curve versus the corporate spread.

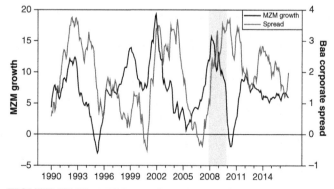

FIGURE 39.12   MZM growth rate versus the government—Baa corporate yield spread.

downward trend during the two spread spikes associated with the two recessions since the millennium.

The implications derived from this analysis are straightforward. Reducing the Fed's distortions and the risk of economic slowdowns will result in an increase in the slope of the yield curve and simultaneously reduce the spread of the high yield instruments relative to government bond yields. This suggests that a return to normalcy means that the long end of the yield curve will underperform the short end of the yield curve, as well as the high-yield market. If this analysis is correct, long bonds should be underweighted or avoided.

V. THE FINANCIAL CRISIS—A CASE STUDY

40

The Panic of 2008: Cause and Consequences

Macroeconomic policymaking and saving for retirement are activities that have a long horizon and, as such, they involve making multiple decisions across time. Each decision made at a point in time affects the opportunity set faced in the future. Therefore future choices are also impacted. All of this suggests that the optimization problem faced by investors and policymakers is a complicated one that must account for these time dependencies. The question faced by policymakers is how to induce savers/investors and various economic agents to behave in a way that maximizes the long-run well-being of the economy. To this end, governments hope to design rules that induce economic players to make choices that maximize the chances of achieving long-term objectives. In a world of certainty, the issue is simple. If the government knows exactly the choices the economy would face at every point in time, it could easily design the rules that lead to the desired objectives. Unfortunately we do not live in a perfect foresight world; randomness and uncertainty play a role too. Hence the government needs to incorporate the impact of randomness and uncertainty when it designs the rules that govern the behavior of different players.

Risk and uncertainty introduce some interesting possibilities regarding the realization of undesirable outcomes. One is simply to make bad choices. However, that is not the only way to have an undesirable outcome. It is possible that a government may have done everything possible by setting the proper environment, yet investors or other economic players can make choices that result in undesirable outcomes. The bad outcome could be due to random events producing undesirable results. In short, it is quite possible to make good choices and have an undesirable outcome. This is an important point. It suggests that an undesirable outcome is not necessarily an indictment of the people in charge or of a bad decision-making process. The policy implication here is quite simple. If the outcome is the result of random adverse effects, there is no need to alter the decision-making process. On the other hand, if the outcome is the result of poor choices,

Economic Disturbances and Equilibrium in an Integrated Global Economy. http://dx.doi.org/10.1016/B978-0-12-813993-6.00040-4

then a modification of the rules regulating behavior is in order. We need to keep this in mind when analyzing undesirable outcomes.

BAD LUCK OR BAD POLICIES

According to newspapers, the Panic of 2008 was the worst financial crisis since the Great Depression. In an attempt to deal with the crisis, the government proposed a $700 billion bailout plan that was in addition to lending as much as $85 billion to American International Group (AIG), the insurance giant. In the midst of all this, the Fed approved Goldman Sachs Group Inc. and Morgan Stanley to become bank-holding companies. In the process, the Fed provided them with liquidity support by extending credit to their US broker-dealer subsidiaries. If we add the Fannie and Freddie intervention, the liquidation of Bear Stearns, and the failure of Lehman Brothers, it is easy to see why people consider the Panic of 2008 the most severe crisis since the Great Depression. So the question facing us is whether the crisis was a bad outcome or the result of choices induced by bad policies? Clearly the answer does not need to be a binary one. It is possible that there is some bad luck involved as well as some bad choices. As analysts, we now need to pause and apportion the effect on the recent market fluctuations to each of these two possibilities. Only then can we come up with a long-term solution that increases the chance of economic success in the long run.

LACK OF REGULATION

At the time of the crisis, both presidential candidates called for more regulations, as did many legislators. In effect they were saying that lack of regulation led to the crisis. But as we argue below, that is not necessarily the case. This brings a warning regarding legislators. As the saying goes, legislators legislate. As one reviews many of the arguments in favor of more regulations, counterarguments emerge suggesting that people who argue for the lack of regulation and/or regulatory oversight may be overstating their case. Let's take the case of lack of regulation. As the *Wall Street Journal* pointed out at the time, the less-regulated entities did not get in as much trouble as the regulated ones. The hedge funds and private equity vehicles fared much better than the investment banks, but more on the regulations later.

SEARCHING FOR CAUSES AND CURES: THE CARRY TRADE

The central bank and "easy" monetary and credit policies were blamed as a major cause for the crisis. The origin of the easy policy goes back to the famous "Greenspan Put," when the Fed lowered short-term interest rates as low as 1% for a "considerable time." This created a one-sided bet. With long-term rates well above the 1% range, institutions had an incentive to borrow short and buy long, thereby making the spread. Levering the position would increase the profits from the spread. So an extension of this argument is that the Greenspan Put and the Fed's easy money policy fostered and condoned an increase in the leverage of the banking and financial system. So far, we agree with the argument.

Our reasoning does not necessarily mean that the riskiness of the financial system was increased by these actions. Let's point out a couple of facts arguing against the increased riskiness due to the famous put. First, we know that the carry trade is the banking system's business. They borrow short by taking deposits, and then they buy long by making long-term loans. The interest they pay in deposits is less than the interest they charge for their loans, hence the carry trade element. That brings us to another possible source of risk that may cause some adverse outcomes. Notice that these institutions had a "duration mismatch." Thus, the possibility existed that an adverse shift in interest rates, in this case an inversion of the yield curve, would eliminate the carry trade gains, bringing substantial losses as a result of the duration mismatch. To protect these institutions, measures to protect against interest rate risks would be needed. However, we do have a couple of counterarguments. First, we know that over the centuries banks have existed and survived many crises. Second, we know that Greenspan had announced and, in fact, did raise short-term interest rates in an orderly fashion. By essentially pronouncing the rate increases, the people implementing the carry trade would have time to unwind trades in an orderly fashion without major disruptions to the credit market and the economy. While we do not rule out mistakes due to excessive leverage, duration mismatch, etc., a carry trade argument does not carry the day.

SEARCHING FOR CAUSES AND CURES: THE GOVERNMENT-SPONSORED ENTERPRISES

In our opinion, a major and perhaps the main culprits of the current crisis were the Government-sponsored Enterprises (GSE), and Fannie Mae and Freddie Mac. Much like Savings and Loans (S&Ls), Fannie and Freddie were in the business of financing residential real estate. However there were some clear differences between S&Ls and the GSEs. Fannie and Freddie had no depositors and as a result there was no danger of them suffering a run on the bank. Another difference between S&Ls and Fannie and Freddie were the lower capital requirements on GSEs. The statutory minimum capital level for a GSE is 2.5% of the aggregate balance sheet assets and 0.45% of the off-balance sheet assets. These capital requirements afforded the GSE a higher degree of leverage than S&Ls, thereby increasing the GSEs sensitivity to interest rate risk.

There is more to this story. GSEs were viewed as government-backed buyers of financial instruments, a belief that has now become a reality with the takeover of the two institutions. However, here we need a sidebar. The GSE creation, per se, did not lead to an inevitable debacle. The evidence is clear. The conforming loans made by the GSE were not in trouble. On average, neither were the conforming borrowers. This suggests that the GSE's lending was not necessarily bad. Something else was at stake and we have a simple explanation: GSEs were able to borrow at lower market rates. Studies at the Fed and the CBO show that in spite of the "subsidized" rates at which the GSE borrowed, they did not significantly lower borrowing rates. The spread approximated profits per dollar worth of loans that the shareholders of the GSEs made. As the GSEs could not affect the spread, the only way to maximize or increase profits would be to increase the volume of loans generated by the GSEs. Unfortunately the conforming regulations got in the way. These regulations limited the amount of loans that the GSE would make. Removing or effectively circumventing the conforming loans would lead to an increase in the riskiness of the GSEs.

It is our opinion that the GSEs understood the political class's desire to have "affordable housing." The GSEs effectively lobbied to relax some of the restrictions they faced. President Clinton, President Bush, and the Republicans and Democrats in Congress were very proud of the expansion of home ownership in America. They were proud of all their actions aimed at increasing the affordability of housing. The GSEs succeeded in their lobbying effort. They were allowed to purchase mortgage-backed securities (MBS). Some years, GSEs bought better than 50% of all MBS. In this way they met two objectives. One objective was the affordable housing program needed to keep politicians happy and the other was to increase their profitability. The politicians were aware of their higher profits but allowed them to continue because of the increase in "affordable financing."

The GSEs bought MBS from conventional mortgage lenders which were loaded with subprime loans. The incentive structure created by the guarantee and their quest to maximize profits led the GSEs to deviate from the original intent of their creation and as they expanded their activities the overall risk of their portfolios was increased in an excessive manner. In the GSEs' defense, we have to say that they believed they could use the tools of modern finance to replicate the safety of their original "conforming" portfolio. To do so, the GSEs bought insurance against some of their risk exposures which, in turn, added to the complexity of their portfolios. For example, they bought insurance against borrower default when the homebuyer lacked the 20% down payment. Another factor that added to the complexity of the twins' financial situation was the need for both GSEs to insure their portfolios against interest risk—in particular, the danger that borrowers would pay their loans early if interest rates fell forcing them to invest at a lower rate. This risk caused the GSEs to take huge positions in the derivate markets. In fact, this led to some accounting scandals among the GSEs. Unfortunately the expansion of the portfolio increased the risk of ruin and the potential liabilities of the federal government.

This exercise illustrates a basic principle in economics: a direct solution is better than an indirect one. First, it is very difficult to avoid the market's discipline. Absent the government's implicit guarantee, the GSEs would not have had a cost advantage and there would have been no need to regulate them. Second, if the GSEs had stuck to their original intent, they would not have gotten into trouble. The policy implications are straightforward.

Viewed in the best possible light, the GSEs thought they could replicate the same results by going beyond their original mandate and using derivatives to hedge their position and replicate the original intent, while at the same time expanding the amount of business and making the spread or comparative advantage granted to them by the government. Expanding their volume of loans, given the higher leverage ratio of the GSEs relative to S&Ls and other banks, made the potential downside even worse. So according to our interpretation, it was the deviation from the original intent that caused the problems for the GSEs. They should have never been allowed to purchase MBS.

SEARCHING FOR CAUSES AND CURES: THE HOMEOWNERS

So far we have focused on the supply side of the equation, the provision of credit/loans. Now let's focus on the demand side, in particular the demand for residential real estate loans. It is commonly argued that the Fed's easy credit or Greenspan Put fueled the residential real estate market. However, that is not the only reason for the increase in the demand for real estate. Going back to 1997, a change in the treatment of real estate may have something to do with the housing boom. The new law exempted, for married couples, the first $500,000 worth of capital gains every two years. Excess capital gains would now be taxed at the lower 15% rate, while the imputed income from living in owner-occupied housing would not be subject to tax. Add to this the deductibility of interest income and one can see why real estate would become hugely tax advantaged. The tax story, while complementary to the credit story, adds to the explanation as to why real estate demand increased substantially. In turn, the higher real estate volume led to an increase in the demand for real estate loans.

So far we have a story of higher demand for loans. There is no reason why these loans could not have been financed by the conforming loans the GSEs offered. In which case we contend that the real estate related problems would have been greatly reduced. But that is not what the United States did. Instead, the political process, for reasons already mentioned, moved to relax the qualifications for acquiring and financing real estate. To make a long story short, the system allowed for 100% financing of real estate. In effect, the homeowners were granted a free option. In many cases 100% financing was rationalized by the fact that residential real estate prices were increasing and the homeowner would be able to build equity in little or no time. Another relaxation of the standard was teaser rates, which allowed the purchaser to qualify in the hope that as real estate prices increased they would be able to refinance at a lower rate. However this strategy was a race against time. The Greenspan Fed had announced that rates would be raised in an orderly fashion. That meant that the reset in mortgage rates would be going up, making the cost of carry even higher than originally stated. So the issues were whether a subprime borrower could refinance before the rates reset and whether they could get a low enough fixed rate. Obviously many did not.

Moving away from conforming loans was a major mistake. It artificially increased the demand for housing. The excess demand led to higher home prices which attracted additional investors. Ultimately supply would catch up with demand and as the reset took place, people could not afford their homes and had to walk away. Now we need to work out excess supply. In the interim, home prices decline and the residential real estate market will be in a slump. Eventually equilibrium will be reached and construction will begin anew. The government response to this shock could either accelerate or delay the adjustment process.

The politicians liked to say that people were losing their homes and that was a tragedy. In some sense it was true. However in another sense, it was not. First, these people did not put any money down, so by walking away from the homes they lost nothing. In fact, with the oversupply of housing they were be able to rent for a lower price. So it is not at all clear that the subprime homeowner was materially worse off. For the prime borrower, who put a substantial down payment, he or she may be down. But as long as they did not have to mark-to-market, they would be able to maintain their lifestyle if they have a fixed rate mortgage. In conclusion, we argue that the net disposable income would not decline in a significant way. The impact on the economy, if there was any, came on the financing side.

SEARCHING FOR CAUSES AND CURES: THE FINANCING MECHANISMS

The past couple of decade's development in finance led to what many called advances in financial economics. Some of the innovations were significant and led to many applications. On the positive side, we point to securitization. However, not all the innovations are without cost.

One example of financial innovation was the development of MBS. The idea to slice the different mortgages into risk-related tranches was brilliant. That way investors could sort themselves and buy the risk that matched their tolerance. Modern financial theories and the law of large numbers all worked to reassure the investors. Unfortunately, there was one feature that was not highlighted at the time, and it has come back to haunt the issuers. The splitting of the securities did not increase the transparency of the system, instead it increased its opaqueness. When a lender keeps the whole mortgage in a package, if a particular mortgage goes bad it is easily removed from a portfolio. However under the MBS system, as the bond has been split into tranches removing the bonds would affect several MBS. To remove the bond, one would have to tinker with all the tranches, and that may not be easy or feasible. In addition, it may be difficult for the buyer to track all the underlying securities and/or protect themselves against default from individual borrowers. During a crisis, investors may not know which of the MBS contain the troubled components and, as a result, they may punish all of them. The opaqueness reduces system liquidity during a crisis, and as such it increases the odds of a calamity.

Another development was that of the credit default swap (CDS). These new instruments allowed people to transfer their risk to other parties. In theory, it works very well for the individual investor. Nevertheless, collectively society cannot escape the risk. So the CDS is nothing more than a game of musical chairs that ends in chaos when everyone wants to bail out. But the problems do not end here. By buying a CDS and shorting the stock, speculators had a simple way to double down on a bet. Shorting a stock, if successful, would create downward pressure on the price while simultaneously increasing the CDS's value. Whether such a speculative attack succeeds in breaking the bank or not depends on how much capital the different players are willing to risk. And this brings us to the final point we want to make here. Speculators would then have a strong incentive to go after businesses that have low enough capital so that they could, in theory, break the business. The odds are in their favor. If they succeed they stand to make a lot of money. If they fail, they only lose their transaction costs fees. It is hard to imagine how the stock would rise in such an environment. Outside investors, those who do not own the company in question, have no skin in the game and no desire to get involved. This is one example where pure speculation could lead to a negative outcome even though the investment in question is a viable one. In theory, there is nothing wrong with speculating this way. The problem is the asymmetry of capital. Those with access to a very large pool of capital may overwhelm companies with significantly smaller capital. If the access to capital is asymmetrical, here is where leverage may come into play and have a destabilizing effect.

SEARCHING FOR CAUSES AND CURES: WEALTH VERSUS INCOME

Absent credit markets, people's spending is constrained by their current income. However, as markets expand, people may be able to smooth their consumption by borrowing during low-income years and repaying the loans during high-income years. A major benefit of the financial developments of the past three decades is our increasing understanding of risk considerations. The progress made has been phenomenal. People have been able to effectively securitize anything and as a result they no longer need to be constrained by their current income, instead they are constrained by their net worth. Income only matters in so far as the net present value of income is a key component of a borrower's net worth. As long as a borrower can service its debt, he or she will lend up to a high fraction of his or her net worth. In technical terms, the consumer instead of facing a series of one-year income constraints, now faces a lifetime wealth constraint. Since the need to borrow is higher during low-income years, one can easily show that the wealth constraint leads to higher debt levels (i.e., increased leverage ratio). This was a major development and it created a new set of issues as wealth is constantly changing. Lenders have to take steps to insure repayment. In addition to debt service ratios, lenders began to use more frequently measures such as loan to net worth ratios. The focus on net worth leads to higher loans and higher level of debts on the part of the consumer which, in turn, leads to a greater emphasis on measures designed to insure that there is enough equity backing the loans in addition to the traditional measures insuring that the borrower would have enough income to service the debt.

One side effect of the switch to loan to net worth and away from debt servicing is that during rising markets, as net worth increases so does the ability to borrow. The opposite happens during a down market. This means that the fluctuation in net worth will lead to additional fluctuations in the borrowing levels of individual households and investors.

SEARCHING FOR CAUSES AND CURES: CAPITAL ADEQUACY RATIOS

The impact of changes in wealth may not be symmetrical. It is possible that as wealth changes so will the lending standards and the loan to value ratio could very well change with the level of wealth. In short, fluctuations in wealth lead to exaggerated fluctuations in credit creation. But that is only half of the story. Lenders have rules and regulations regarding loan to value ratios which we call capital adequacy ratios. If you think of conforming loans by the GSEs as analogous to a bank reserve requirement (i.e., 20% down on any loan amount), we can argue then that the GSEs effectively circumvented their reserve requirement even though they deluded themselves into believing that they were replicating the same risk profile by buying insurance against default and implementing an interest risk management program. The results show that they failed. How can that be with so many rocket scientists around? Our answer is that they made the same mistake that other high-powered financial institutions like Long-Term Capital Management (LTCM) made in the past. It is a mistake to take as a God-given truth the correlations among different instruments. We have written in the past that these correlations are not invariant of the economic environment and when they change so does the risk profile. To be truly safe, these institutions would also have to forecast the variance covariance of all instruments. This is something that they either take for granted or are not very good at forecasting. Finally, it is the lack of understanding of these correlations that produces the opaqueness in the system. On the downside, this dynamic could be troublesome. The decline in values could trigger additional restrictions on credit creation and the well-functioning of the system. If you have doubts about the viability of the counterparty, why trade with them or why have your money there? The lack of confidence, in effect, generates a run on the bank so to speak. The past few weeks are a clear reminder of this situation.

We have used GSEs to argue that through their lobbying they effectively circumvented the 20% reserve requirements in their conforming loans. But that is not the only way that companies can circumvent their loan to value ratio. We argue that the GSEs were effectively increasing their leverage and reducing their capital adequacy ratio. In effect, the GSEs had two sets of regulations. One was the conforming loans and the other was the actual capital adequacy ratio. As long as the conforming loans kept them above the capital adequacy ratio, there was no trigger point for the regulators to intervene. As we have explained earlier, the GSEs had a strong incentive to lower their effective capital adequacy ratio. That would increase their loans and, given the implicit government guarantee, their profitability. The point here is that regulated entities have an incentive to circumvent the regulations, while the job of the regulators is to enforce the regulations.

Regulators have mandated different loans to value ratio for different industries. Banks are subject to reserve requirements as well as a capital adequacy ratio. Other regulated businesses face capital adequacy ratio requirements. One important issue during the crisis was how to value the assets used to calculate the capital adequacy ratio. This was the government's or regulators' way of attempting to insure that these businesses did not overextend themselves. We have the mark-to-market valuation. But there are problems with such measure. Many of these instruments were hard to price. And sometimes the values were based on models. So mark-to-market effectively became a mark to model. Making matters worse, as we have already mentioned, these valuation models were based on correlations that sometimes break down as the environment changes. As we have seen in the past few years, sometimes the government succeeds and sometimes it fails. It is clear that mark-to-market did not work out and contributed to the problems in the financial system. The reason is that these instruments were priced favorably during the good times and were difficult to price and thus are unfavorably priced during downswings. These problems and the financial crisis experience triggered a debate as to what to include in the computation of the capital adequacy ratio and how to value assets. Here we like to borrow a page from residential real estate. A homeowner with a conforming loan puts down 20% at the time of the purchase. As long as the homeowner is current with his loan, then the homeowner only worries about marking-to-market twice during the ownership. When they buy and when they sell. A hefty down payment goes a long way to eliminate frivolous walking away when the price declines in the short run. The insight here is that long duration assets need not be mark-to-market continuously.

SEARCHING FOR CAUSES AND CURES: THE FED AND OTHER GOVERNMENT AGENCIES

It is apparent that an increase in capital is needed to restore the confidence in the system, as well as the credit creation ability. The Fed had tried to do this in a variety of ways. Institutions under its jurisdiction are subject to capital adequacy ratios and reserve requirements. Shortages of capital and/or reserves as assets are marked-to-market and cause a credit contraction. During the crisis, the Fed in effect injected capital by allowing institutions to borrow at face value against assets whose market value is, in effect, lower. The difference between the face value and the market value represented the additional injections of reserves. However, as long as mark-to-market accounting was in effect, the value of the nonpledged assets would also affect the capital adequacy ratio and in a downdraft we know the direction of the impact on credit. That in turn triggers additional pledging until either all assets are pledged at which point the Fed would effectively control the banks or until the market recovers and asset prices begin to rise. But even in this case, the institutions are not out of the woods. As long as asset values are below the amount at which the Fed values them, these institutions will not be able to expand their activities unless they get additional capital.

SOME CONCLUSIONS

One way to restore confidence in the financial system during a financial crisis as that of 2007–08 is that regulators have to find a way to isolate these assets, to reassure the economic agents that a decline in the value of these assets will not trigger additional credit contraction or capital deficiencies. Here we can learn something from the hedge fund industry. In the parlance of the hedge fund industry, they need to create a side pocket. That is what the government did during the S&L crisis of the 1990s when it created the Resolution Trust Corporation or RTC.

Presumably that is what the $700 billion Congress authorized for the Troubled Asset Relief Programs, TARP, was intended to do, help stabilize the US financial system. Although Congress initially authorized $700 billion for TARP in October 2008, that authority was reduced to $475 billion by the Dodd–Frank Wall Street Reform and Consumer Protection Act (Dodd–Frank Act). However we contend that here the administration may have missed an opportunity. Rather than create an RTC-like organization, the administration chose a different route. The following amounts were committed through TARP's five program areas:

- $250 billion was committed in programs to stabilize banking institutions.
- $27 billion was committed through programs to restart credit markets.
- $82 billion was committed to stabilize the US auto industry.
- $70 billion was committed to stabilize AIG.
- $46 billion was committed for programs to help struggling families avoid foreclosure, with these expenditures being made over time.

The authority to make new financial commitments under TARP ended on October 3, 2010.

Looking back at the results obtained by the TARP, one can only wonder whether an RTC-like program would have yielded results similar to those produced by the RTC, a much better outcome than that of TARP.

In addition to TARP, there were other interesting options available to the government and regulators. In regard to Fannie and Freddie, the ideal thing was to remove Fannie and Freddie's implicit government guarantee and allow them to compete in the marketplace without any special advantage or *quid pro quo*. If that was not possible, then the two should have been forced to go back to the conforming model and should have been prohibited from buying MBS.

Leverage is one issue that people were concerned with. But we argue that some remedy in this area would automatically take place. By becoming banks, the investment banks reduced their leverage factor, held higher reserve requirements, and avoided some of the mark-to-market vagaries. In addition, the lower leverage factor and increased transparency would force these institutions reduce their holding of hard to price assets. All this is good.

Marking-to-market gained popularity in the past few years leading up to the financial crisis. However, as we have seen, many of the new instruments were difficult to price, and as a result, marking-to-market models increased in popularity. But that only makes matters worse during a crisis. We need to revise the pricing of the assets. Those with long holding periods should not be subject to mark-to-market rules.

Finally, much was talked about the homeowners. At the time, we felt that not much should be done in favor of subprime borrowers. They put no down payment and if they walked, they suffered no significant penalty. Their wealth was not be significantly affected if they lost their home. They should not get a windfall because of a crisis.

41

Realignment?

The election of Barack Obama as president of the United States is an event of major historical importance. It showed the world that a minority could be the freely elected president of the United States. To say that alone would be a disservice to the progress made by this country. As one recounts the progress made during the last few decades, it becomes clear to many that Barack Obama was not a black candidate running for president. Barack Obama was a presidential candidate that happened to be black. To a great many people, the color of his skin was irrelevant; they simply saw him as the best person in the field of candidates. His message resonated with the electorate. Given the size of his victory and his party's majority in both the House and Senate, there was no doubt that President Obama got a mandate, which brings us to an obvious question: did the Obama policies realign the political landscape? If so, how long will the realignment last? We cannot say with confidence whether the Obama policies resulted in a realignment of the political and economic landscape or not. However, we can confidently identify the issues that may or may not fuel the realignment mentioned in the press. A quick review of the policies enacted may also shed some light on the issue.

It seems clear to us that President Obama was confident in his agenda and that he genuinely believed that it would work both in the short and long run. As with most economic analysis, the logic of the Obama plan

was impeccable once you bought into its underlying assumptions. Unfortunately, these assumptions were not universally accepted. The question was whether the assumptions held water empirically, and whether they were a reasonable approximation of the economic reality.

Press reports during and after the campaign viewed the President as a transformational candidate along the lines of Franklin Delano Roosevelt (FDR). His public works/stimulus bill, the expansion of the social safety net and related entitlements such as ObamaCare, unemployment benefits, the housing and education relief programs are just some of the programs that drew the parallel. Whether or not President Obama viewed himself in this light, we cannot say. However, what we can say is that there is a distinct parallel between many of his economic views and the rationale behind his policies and those of FDR.

A GOVERNMENT THAT WORKS?

It is clear that the Obama administration saw government spending as a key catalyst to achieving its overall economic goals. In his inaugural speech, the President correctly argued that we should not be concerned about the size of the government per se, rather the focus should be on a government that works. We agree wholeheartedly

Economic Disturbances and Equilibrium in an Integrated Global Economy. http://dx.doi.org/10.1016/B978-0-12-813993-6.00041-6

with the statement. Unfortunately, the track record on government spending is not a good one.

Government enterprises are not usually run with a profit maximization motive in mind. The profit motive provides an automatic incentive to use resources efficiently. Since the government does not have these incentives, one must develop an alternative to the profit motive that insures the efficient use of resources. This is important in cases where the government competes with the private sector. If these entities are not run with a profit motive, the efficiency will not be there. The government operations will be more expensive and less beneficial than the private sector alternative. We contend that the larger the government, the more likely this problem will emerge. That is why we tend to be against government expansion. Milton Friedman used to say that if you put the government in charge of the Sahara, it would run out of sand in five years. We need to point out that a large government is not the domain of one political party. We have just witnessed a tremendous expansion of public spending in both domestic and defense spending by a Republican administration and a Republican Congress during part of the time. The one common thread among the large government programs of the different administrations is the inefficiency. This does not mean that the programs are bad. It is possible that the benefits of these programs far exceed their costs. What we are saying is that the services could have been delivered more efficiently and society would have been better off since the saved resources could have been deployed elsewhere. Then there is the issue of the substitution effects or behavioral changes induced by tax rates and increases in government regulations. These substitution effects tend to undermine the government actions.

We tend to have a healthy respect for these substitution effects and believe that they are much larger than Obama administration believed them to be. In fact, President Obama sees the issue as one that has been settled. Here is what the *Wall Street Journal* quoted him as saying [1]:

> Republican proposals are "rooted in the idea that tax cuts alone can solve all our problems, that government doesn't have a role to play, that half measures and tinkering are somehow enough, that we can afford to ignore our most fundamental economic challenges," the president said in an address at the Department of Energy. "Those ideas have been tested, and they have failed."

Some people may disagree that the Republican tax rate policies were tested and failed. They would argue that it is the big government idea, which we had during the administration preceding President Obama. Fortunately, some time has passed since President Obama made the above statement. His presidency is now over, and the data on the economy's performance during his administration is readily available. Comparing the economic performance during his administration and those

of the administration that tested the tax rate cut ideas and "failed," that is, the Reagan administration, may shed some light on the validity of the president statement.

FAILURE OR SUCCESS, WHAT DOES THE DATA SAY?

If one is willing to assume that the policies enacted by an administration are the main drivers of the economic performance during the administration tenure, a comparison of some of the key macroeconomics indicators provides information regarding the effectiveness of these policies. For example, Fig. 41.1 presents information on the cumulative change in the real GDP during both the Reagan and Obama administrations. For ease of visualization, we have superimposed the 8 years of the Reagan administration on the 8 years of the Obama administration. The data in Fig. 41.1 shows that the cumulative real GDP increase is greater during President Reagan than during President Obama. Advantage President Reagan. Fig. 41.2 shows the unemployment rate during both administrations. Notice that President Reagan experienced a higher unemployment rate than President Obama and while both administrations achieved significant reductions in

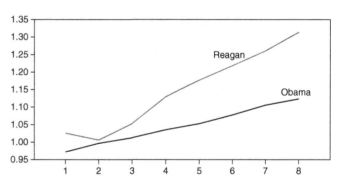

FIGURE 41.1   Cumulative increase in real GDP during the Reagan and Obama administration.

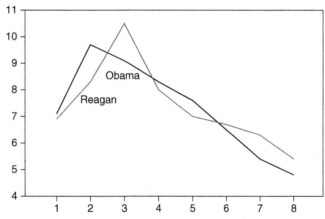

FIGURE 41.2   Unemployment rate.

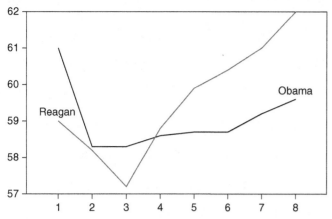

FIGURE 41.3   Civilian employment-population ratio.

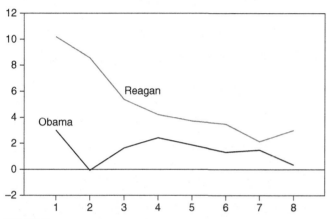

FIGURE 41.4   PCE inflation rate.

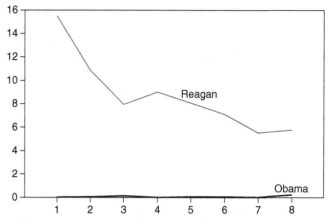

FIGURE 41.5   T-Bill yields.

the unemployment rate, at the end of their term in office, the unemployment rate was lower for the Obama administration. Advantage President Obama. Fig. 41.3 provides information for the civilian employment-population ratio. Notice that the Reagan administration began with a lower ratio than the Obama administration but by the end of their terms the Reagan administration showed a vast improvement in the employment-population ratio, well ahead of the Obama administration results.

If one is willing to assume that fiscal policy is the main driver for the real economy and monetary policy the main driver for the underlying inflation rate, then the successes of the real economy must be attributed to the fiscal policies of the various administrations while the inflation rate and short-term interest rates must be attributed to the Fed's actions. This is the underlying assumption maintained throughout this analysis. Taken together, the indicators reported in Fig. 41.1–41.3 do not point to a failure of the Reagan policies, if anything they suggest that Reaganomics produced better results than Obamanomics.

Figs. 41.4 and 41.5 provide information on the Personal Consumption Expenditures' (PCE) inflation rate and the 3-month T-bill yields, our proxy for monetary policy and its effects on the economy. The information

presented in Fig. 41.4 shows a steep decline in the inflation rate during the Reagan administration; this decline is attributable to the change in operation procedures enacted by then Fed Chairman Paul Volcker. In 1979, the Fed switched from targeting the monetary aggregates, that is the quantity rule, to targeting the domestic inflation rate, that is the price rule. The inflation rate gradually declined to the 2% target range. In contrast, in the aftermath of the financial crisis, the Fed switched by what some have called a Keynesian Monetarism. The Fed expanded its balance sheet and adopted a policy of keeping interest rates low as far as the eye can see, in an attempt to reactivate and stimulate the economy. Our view that the Fed controls the monetary variables, the inflation rate, and short-term instruments suggests that the results of the policy are not attributable to the Obama administration and as such the administration should not be saddled with them. The results are the results of the Fed's actions and they can be used to evaluate the different monetary policy initiatives. It is important to note that the Keynesian Monetarism policies failed to increase the inflation rate to the 2%–4% target range of the so-called "domestic price rule." Also the policy failed to stimulate an "average" economic recovery. Unless one is willing to argue that had the Fed and the administration not acted, the results would have been worse, the economy would have collapsed, the same can be said for the situation the Reagan administration confronted. Hence we return to our evaluation criteria and the policies will be judged by the economic performance during the time the administrations were in power. The results of the Fed's action suggests that monetary policy is ineffective as far as the real economy is concerned and it should be focused on maintaining price stability.

One final indicator of the effect of the policy mix adopted by the different administrations is the impact of their policies on asset prices such as the stock market. Fig. 41.6 shows that the average annual stock appreciation during the Obama administration was higher than that

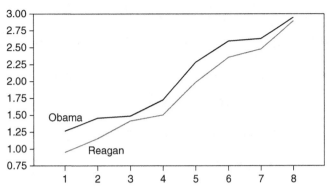

FIGURE 41.6 Cumulative increase in large-cap stocks during the Reagan and Obama administration.

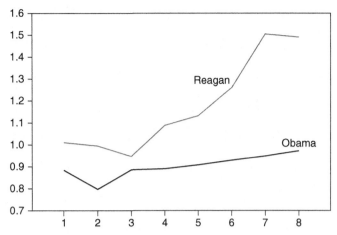

FIGURE 41.7 Cumulative stock size differential during the Reagan and Obama administration.

of the stock appreciation during the Reagan administration. While it is very difficult to disentangle the differential impact of the fiscal policy and monetary policy, the famous Greenspan and or Fed valuation model provides us with a simple way to do so. It approximates the value of an asset as the discounted value of an earnings stream. Fiscal policy has a dominant effect on the real economy; it will drive the economy's earnings, the numerator of the valuation model, and real rates of return. In turn, monetary policy affects the underlying inflation rate and nominal interest rates, the denominator of the valuation model. In this simple valuation model, the faster the rate of economic expansions, the higher the earnings and thus the higher the valuations; this is the fiscal policy effect. In contrast, all else the same, the higher the interest rates, the lower will be the discounted value of an income stream. The simple valuation model allows one to apportion the stock market appreciation to fiscal and monetary policy. Looking at the results reported so far, we know that the Reagan years produced a higher real GDP growth rate; this leads us to conclude that fiscal policy had a greater impact on the stock market valuation than the fiscal policies of the Obama administration. In contrast the Fed's monetary contribution during the two administrations were the reverse. The lower inflation rate and interest rates point to a lower discount rate that resulted in higher valuation. Hence monetary policy had a larger impact on the nominal stock appreciation during the Obama years than during the Reagan years. This partitioning of the returns suggests that the Obama fiscal policies played a smaller role than the Reagan fiscal policies in generation of the stock returns during their respective administrations.

Other writings have argued that in large part, the size effect is the result of the nimbleness of the smaller capitalization stocks. Sometimes we characterize the size effect as the ability of the small-cap stocks to circumvent, avoid, and evade taxes and regulations. With this in mind, we can make inferences regarding the impact of the tax and regulatory burden. Information on the annual rate of return differential between large and small capitalization stocks is presented in Fig. 41.7. The data

shows that the large-caps outperformed the smaller capitalization stocks by a larger margin during the Reagan administration than during the Obama administration. The results fit our views regarding the size effect. During the Reagan administration, tax rates and regulations declined while the same increased during the Obama administration. Not surprisingly, the large-caps outperformed the small-caps during the Reagan administration and underperformed during the Obama administration.

When all is said and put together, the economic data reported here suggest that the higher tax rates are associated with slower growth, lower earnings-driven stock appreciation, and a size effect that benefits the smaller capitalization stocks. These results contradict President Obama's statement regarding the "failed policies" that he was referring to. Next, we focus on the major policy differences for a possible explanation for these results.

POLICY-INDUCED MORAL HAZARD AND SUBSTITUTION EFFECTS

Proponents of the policy initiatives enacted by the Obama administration defend these policies and point to the benefits produced by these actions. While it is true that the beneficiaries of the actions may be better-off, the regulations and taxes associated with these actions may have negative effects on the economy. In general, the counterargument made is that these disincentive effects are relatively small. We do not necessarily agree with this assessment. But even if that were true, the combined effects of the many actions with small effects may collectively have a large impact on the economy. The sum of many small effects can add up to a very large one. Next, we review some of the possible substitution effects generated by several of the legislations and executive orders enacted during the Obama administration.

ObamaCare, as the Patient Protection and Affordable Health Care Act is commonly called, is the signature piece of legislation of the Obama administration. The case for health care from an economic point of view is simple. Proponents argue that the health care increases make the direct recipient better off, and that reduces the incidence of disease in the rest of the population. We can safely argue that there is an external benefit here. Even the taxed people may be better off once the benefit of the healthier population are balanced against the additional taxes. If this happened it would be an example of a government at its best. If, as we have argued, the benefits to the rest of the population are truly an external effect, the private sector would have never reached such an outcome. The government action eliminated the external effect.

Another justification for the increase in health spending in the previous example was that it will save money in the future and thus could also be sold as a fiscally responsible increase in spending. This is the argument used by Speaker Pelosi to justify the increase in spending in contraception and related measures. We believe that she misread or misapplied Steven Levitt's *Freakonomics* [2]. Continuing the argument, it would follow that as future health spending is reduced and additional tax revenues are collected from the healthier population, future government revenues could then be deployed to solving other problems. But what if we change one assumption in the analysis: let us add the impact of what economists call substitution effects as opposed to the income or external effects that we have been discussing up to this point. For the sake of argument, let us say that the tax rates enacted to finance the increase in health expenditures reduce people's incentives to save, work, and invest. If this is the case, higher tax rates will have a negative impact on both the demand for and supply of goods and services. The big question is whether these effects are sufficiently large to offset the aggregate demand effect outlined in the previous paragraph. Theory alone cannot settle the matter. It is an empirical issue whether the substitution effects are large enough to offset the aggregate demand/income effects. If the substitution effects dominate, output will decline in the long run. If the aggregate demand effects dominate, output will increase. Although there are several components that could generate substitution effects, we will only focus on two of them.

The first component is the definition of what constitutes a full-time employee. Originally the Affordable Care Act (ACA) designated anyone working 30 hours or more as a full-time employee. If ACA does in fact increase the relative costs of employing that labor, employees that do not alter their behavior will suffer a reduction in profitability equal to the increase in costs. A profit-maximizing employer will take steps to rearrange its labor force in a way that it maximizes their profits. An obvious substitution effect that people noted right away was to reduce the work hours of the employees to less than the 30 h in order to avoid paying the tax. That is what we call a substitution or dynamic effect. If the switch to less than 30 h and hiring more people to have the same number of hours worked does not alter output, the employer's profits are not impacted and the ACA produces no benefit to this portion of the labor force. In fact, these workers will be worse off to the extent that they will be working less than 30 h when they want to work more. Not all the businesses have the flexibility to alter the composition of their labor force at will. Those who cannot will experience incremental costs and lower profits.

Let us summarize what we believe was the impact of the ACA. Cleary those who got the benefit of the ACA and did not have previous insurance and remain working as much were clearly better off. If the government truly believes that society is better off as a result of the ACA, then the government must believe that the benefits accruing to the people receiving the coverage more than make up for the loss of profitability of the businesses and the costs associated with the people who now are working less than 30 h a week because the businesses are avoiding the costs associated with the ACA. That is a debatable issue and the answer is not an obvious one either way. What is clear to us is that as people make attempts to minimize the impact of the ACA, substitution effects will be generated. The use of resources spends avoiding the impact of the government actions denotes a dead weight loss for society as a whole. The result is lower output and a less-efficient economy.

The other significant and controversial provisions of the Affordable Care Act is the excise tax on high-cost health plans that provide workers the most generous level of health benefits, also known as "Cadillac plans." These high-end health plans' premiums are paid for mostly by employers. They also have low, if any, deductibles and little cost sharing for employees. It is somewhat ironic that the legislation goes after these plans because, to a large extent, they are the creation of the tax code. Fringe benefits are deductible to the corporation and not taxable to the individual. Therefore fringe benefits are the portion of income that is truly tax exempt. A utility maximizing consumer or worker will equate the benefits of 1$ worth of after-tax income to the benefits provided by a tax-free health care. A person on the 35% bracket will net 65 cents on the dollar per every pre-tax dollar worth of income. Hence as long as the health care delivers more than 65 cents, the consumer will be better off. If we are correct, we can then calculate the waste or inefficiency caused by the government tax policy at the margin. In this example, it is on the order of 35 cents on the dollar.

Proponents of the 40% excise tax on Cadillac plans argue that these benefit-rich plans insulate workers from the high cost of care and encourage the overuse of care (unnecessary tests and hospital visits) which raise health costs overall. In this they are correct, but they have the wrong solutions. A direct solution is always much better than an indirect one. As we already mentioned, the reason for this problem has to do with the nontaxation of fringe benefits. If these were taxed in a revenue-neutral way, the tax rate could be lowered for all workers and that would make the economy much more efficient. Yet the Obama administration chose to single out the Cadillac plan because they believed it benefited the higher-income groups (it does). Finally, the fact that the implementation of several components and enforcement mechanisms of the ACA, and the modification of several components by executive order, suggests the Obama administration was trying to plug the holes created by unanticipated behavior on the plan of the participants. Put another way, the substitution effects.

The final issue is that most of these programs, including the ACA, are mean tested and the subsidies decline as the income of the insured rises. The reduction in benefits is analogous to a tax, which combined with the income tax rates and social security contribution could result in very high marginal tax rates for the people affected by the mean testing. If the tax rates approach 100%, which in some cases it does, the beneficiary will opt not to work. The benefits and taxes will exceed the increased labor income. This is what we call the poverty trap. The dynamic effects of the poverty trap are even worse, for the longer the person stays out of the labor forces, the greater the skill deterioration and the less employable they become.

The minimum wage and other labor-related initiatives intended to address income inequality issues are other potential sources of substitution effects. Take the case of California, where state law provides 55% of workers' salary for 6 weeks of paid family leave. The San Francisco Board of Supervisors voted 11-0 in favor of a proposal that would require San Francisco employers with more than 20 workers to cover the remaining 45% of a worker's pay during that same period. The proponents argued that the parental leave mandate would help low-income earners. Our position is that parental leave should be left to the market place. Many of the technology companies in the area already offer generous paid parental leave. Hence these firms would not be impacted by the mandate. The effect will be felt by the smaller firms. Will the mandate increase their costs and put these firms at a regional disadvantage? If so, their employment levels will decline and will end up hurting the people it intended to help.

The arguments in favor of a higher minimum wage differ. A common one is the "moral" argument and it goes like this: due to the decline of trade unions and the spread of aggressive management techniques, low-paid workers now have little bargaining power and few legal protection. Only the government can ensure that they receive a living wage. President Obama chimed in on the moral argument by stating that "Even with the tax relief we've put in place, a family with two kids that earns the minimum wage still lives below the poverty line. That's wrong." The implication of the argument is simple and straightforward: legislate and it shall be done. If that is true, why $15 an hour? Why not $60 and that way the workers will get an even better standard of living? By not going so high, there is an implicit assumption that the market and the economy will not bear such a high minimum wage.

Another argument is based on cost of living adjustments. Proponents of this view argue that the wage rate has not kept up with inflation, which alone would justify a rate increase. However, that is not the actual impression we get from the data. Fig. 41.8 shows the nominal wage rate and the inflation adjusted or real wage rate, where the latter is obtained by deflating the nominal wage rate by the Personal Consumption Expenditure (PCE) price index. The inflation-adjusted minimum wage was the equivalent of $5.75 in 1969; it rises and peaks at around $8 in 1968 and then slides down to $5 by 1990, and remains in the $5.5–$6.75 range since then. Notice that Fig. 41.8 shows that the minimum wage increases have effectively marked-to-market. Put another way, the constant dollar wage rate has remained more stable in terms of purchasing power.

Then there is the argument in favor of raising the minimum wage because the US minimum wage is low compared to its counterparts in other advanced countries. In France and Ireland, for example, the minimum remuneration level is more than $11 an hour. Even in Great Britain, which is usually regarded as a country with a flexible, US-style labor market, it is close to $10 an hour. Yet proponents of this view fail to point out that these countries with higher minimum wage have experienced a slower growth rate than the United States. Is that a trade-off that we are willing to make?

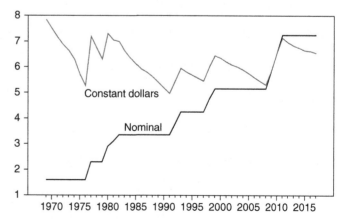

FIGURE 41.8   **Minimum wage in nominal and real terms.**

Some proponents of the higher minimum wage argue that there is no obvious link between the minimum wage and the unemployment rate. This argument has several variations. One group points out that during the 1960s, when the minimum wage was raised sharply, unemployment rates were sharply lower than they were in the 1980s, when the real value of the minimum wage fell dramatically. Another group says that if you look across the states, some of which set a minimum wage above the federal minimum, you cannot see any sign of higher rates leading to higher unemployment. The conclusion is that what these figures tell us is that other factors, such as the overall state of the economy and how local industries are doing, matter a lot more for employment than the level of the minimum wage does.

There are counterarguments to each of the aforementioned conclusions. The first one regards the states and that is an area that we are intimately familiar, as we have written extensively on the states' competitive environment. A statistical answer is required here. When one compares across state lines, one obtains what economists call a cross-section of data. This data can be treated as one sample only if it comes from the same distribution. That is, if we assume that the states respond equally to the different shocks. But we know that the states have different tax structures and different endowments. So there are reasons to suspect that a cross-sectional analysis may not be the appropriate approach. There are some statistical tests readily available where one can test whether the results across state lines are from the same distribution. Our own research shows that is not the case, and that it is inappropriate to mix the different samples [3]. The correct procedure is to look at the relationship between the unemployment rate and the state minimum wage across time for each state. That is, a time series model for each state is the appropriate way to examine the relationship. Once the cross-section data is eliminated and one focuses solely on the time series relationship for each of the states, a relationship is uncovered.

We should also illustrate the importance of identifying the causal relationship among the different variables and recall the important statement that correlation does not imply causality. During the Presidential campaign, we heard Democratic candidate Bernie Sanders simultaneously make an argument for a higher minimum wage while demonizing Walmart all in one shot. Paraphrasing the senator, he said that it was a shame that Walmart pays so little to their employees that they have to get food stamps to survive. We will grant the senator that there are Walmart employees that also collect food stamps. What we question is the causal direction. Is it possible that the Walmart employees do not have enough income, and to supplement their income they find part time or full time jobs at Walmart?

Our interpretation suggests that the causal direction is the opposite of what Senator Sanders said. If that is correct, then rather than demonizing Walmart, it should be commended for providing the opportunity to supplement their income. There is a simple test to the alternative hypothesis, and it is the elderly and/or retiree. What percent of the Walmart labor force consists of entry-level workers who are able to move up the ladder and what percent of the workers are elderly, supplementing their income? If the combined percentage is high, then one can argue that the senator was wrong in his assessment of the causal direction.

Now on to the substitution effects. An increase in the minimum wage to say $15 an hour within several of the "progressive states" in the union will increase the labor costs relative to other inputs in the production of goods and services. The cost increase will induce a substitution effect away from the now higher input. This may take many forms, but a simple example will make our point. When different states have announced a staggered minimum wage increase that in a few years will reach $15 an hour, some businesses began to prepare for this. For example, a coffee chain announced a change in its reward program and gives extra credit to customers who order ahead. We interpret this as a strategy to get the costumers used to ordering ahead and getting them ready for possible changes when the $15 an hour minimum wage takes effect. If everyone orders ahead there will be less need for cashiers, also the barista will be able to stagger the orders and fill them in a production line type of setting. All of this means less personnel. Restaurants and other services have introduced tablets, kiosks where the costumers order and pay through them. All of these are substitution effects that reduce the derived demand for labor services [4]. The substitution effect is the result of several factors: technological innovations, lower technology costs, as well as the increased labor costs. The result being a reduced demand for labor services. Under that scenario, the question is who gets left out and who will be hired. We contend that the effect will be to let go of the least skilled and to hire the more technologically savvy employees. Unfortunately, given the substitutability, that is the availability of technological alternatives, it is difficult to see how these entry jobs will offer much income upside in the short run. The reduction in entry-level employment also has dynamic effects, there are less people being offered the opportunity to move up the ladder.

Home ownership and education appear to be two unrelated topics; however there is a common thread that we want to examine. From a societal point of view, one can make a case that home ownership and more education are highly desirable. So it is not surprising that a well-intended government would try to encourage both. But sometimes good intentions are not enough and the policies adopted do not produce the desired result. There are parallel unintended consequences in the programs intended in promoting education and home ownership.

The government took actions to induce an increase in home ownership and college education. Among the measures taken was to facilitate the financing of both. In the homeownership case, Fannie and Freddie were the backstop financing, while on education it was Sallie. These agencies lowered the bar for the borrowers. In the case of home ownership, no down payments and stated income were not uncommon. For student loans, the bar was not too high either. The institutions they could attend and qualify for loans were numerous and the requirements quite lax. It seems that the design of these programs did not consider the downside. That the value of the homes could fall below the value of the loan or that the education would not improve the earnings potential of the students. If the loans were nonrecourse, the home owners could walk away from their obligations by simply giving the house back to the lender. For the students, if there was no income, there is no way to collect.

In stylized form, the programs offered no downside to the borrowers while offering some upside. That would increase the demand for the subsidized loans. The increased demand due to the subsidies would lead to a higher price for homes and education, inclusive of the subsidy. The relaxation of the lending standard, who qualified, and what would type of house or education the lending would be extended to would attract new students, as well as new entrants or suppliers. As the standards were relaxed, the percent of at-risk borrowers would rise, and even if there was no downturn, the failure rates would unambiguously increase. People made bad investments in both education and home purchases.

Now let us focus on the housing market. The downturn really impacted many of the subprime borrowers, as well as some regular borrowers. Without explaining the downturn, we know that household net worth and the lending institutions' capital adequacy declined and that contributed to the worsening of the recession and the slowness of the recovery. We contend that many of these failures would have been avoided had the borrowers been forced to have skin in the game and to prove their income, as well as lenders not having a ready place to dump their sketchy loans, that is Fannie and Freddie were run like a for profit, private institution. But that would have meant a lower home ownership, an outcome contrary to what the Clinton and Bush administrations wanted. In response to the crisis, the government demonized the lenders, and then Dodd-Frank and the Consumer Protection Act was passed in 2010. The irony in all this is that institutions such as Bank of America, whom the government asked to take over other failed lenders such as Lending Tree, were later forced to settle with the government for the bad loans made by Lending Tree prior to it being owned by Bank of America. The result of these policies was a big bill for the taxpayers, more regulations of financial institutions, and no lessons learned. Currently there are new programs that borrowers do not need to put down the customary 20%. The government has once again reduced the exposure of the borrowers, or the amount of skin in the game.

The question, and perhaps the suspicion, we have is that student loan debt could easily end up in a bad case scenario similar to the housing market borrower. The government has reacted to the potential crisis by going after some for-profit institutions and attempting to regulate the educational system by suggesting certain rating of the institutions. While those steps may help, public institutions should also be held to these same standard, and as the for-profit colleges, the lenders should also do more homework. Not everyone is credit worthy, and not everyone will be successful in college. If the lenders do not have standards, there will be no way to filter people who will flunk out and will never be able to repay their loans. There is no reason not to expect a student loan crisis in the near future, a crisis where the taxpayers foot the bill and dreams are shattered to borrowers that should have never qualified for the loans. All parties should be held accountable. The crisis, if it occurs, will result in new regulations of the educational institutions, as well as higher taxes. The higher regulatory burden and the taxes will also have a negative impact on the long-term level of economic activity.

Energy and the environment is another area where the Obama administration showed a heavy hand. Although the administration often boasted that US energy production increased under its watch, the increase was in spite of—not a result of—the administration's policies. The Obama administration took actions to reduce the supply of fossil fuels. Unfortunately these actions mostly and disproportionately affect the domestic fossil fuel economy. It reduced the areas where oil companies could drill. It increased the regulatory burden to the point where it made it unprofitable to operate certain energy-producing plants. The effect of the administration's energy policy on domestic fossil fuel supplies was twofold: it produced an inward shift in the domestic supply and it also reduced the elasticity of the domestic supply curve (the ability and responsiveness of the domestic production to change output as the price of the different fuels changes). These actions increased the cost of producing the fuels domestically, distorted the economy, and increased the vulnerability of the US economy to a global energy shock. Some may argue that we are crying wolf. They point to the abundance of energy and the low-energy prices. But that misses the point. The low-energy prices are the result of the commodity super cycle and China's slowdown. However, eventually the global economy will return to a long-run equilibrium, and unless there are significant innovation in other forms of energy, that is when the US energy vulnerability will be felt. The Obama administration's defense was that by taking these actions, it was inducing the US economy to move to clean energy at a faster clip and that will be good for both the United States and the world. Time will tell which view is the correct one. However it is unquestionable that the transition is such that in the near term it reduces the US economy's flexibility to adjust and adapt to adverse energy shocks.

Corporate inversions are a very good proxy to describe the taxation attitude of the administration. Before delving into the topic, let us outline some key features that lead to the corporate inversions. The first one is that, unlike other countries that only tax profits within their borders, the United States taxes corporations on their worldwide income. However the foreign profits are only taxed when they are repatriated to the United States. The US top corporate tax rate was 35% and most other countries have much lower tax rates. This creates an incentive to find a vehicle to have those foreign-earned profits at a lower tax rate. For example, $1 worth of pre-tax profits in the United States would net 65 cents after corporate taxes. In contrast, $1 worth of corporate profits in Ireland would net 85 cents in after-tax profits. That is a 30% increase in the after-tax keep rate per dollar worth of pre-tax corporate profits. Viewed this way, a corporate CEO whose mandate is to maximize shareholder value has a strong incentive, some may say a duty, to search for such a vehicle. Corporate inversions are one vehicle available to the corporate CEOs.

Dynamic scoring and the legislative process is another reason why the above quote of what the president said is important, that is, the view espoused by President Obama also spills over to some other interesting policy debates such as whether to use dynamic scoring or not. Static scoring assumes little or no change in behavior. In other words, there is no feedback or substitution effect and people's behavior is unchanged in the face of changing incentives to save and invest. According to this view, income effects dominate everything. However if people change their behavior in response to incentives, it follows that the tax base will shrink in response to the tax increase. Notice the equivalence between the income effect and aggregate demand, and the substation effect and the dynamic effect of tax rate changes.

So the issue is whether the reduction in the base is large enough to offset the increase in the tax rate. In other words, this is an empirical not a theoretical issue. In any event, the president's comments are very revealing and clearly the economic performance during his administration in comparison to that of the Reagan administration provides a test between his views and the alternative view, as well as a possible explanation for the slow recovery during the Obama years.

MULTIPLIER EFFECTS?

An important and key component of the Obama economic strategy was the administration's belief that increases in government spending result in a multiplied increase in aggregate demand. Some argue that this was the engine of growth for the Reagan and the FDR administration's economy recovery strategy. The data in Fig. 41.9 shows that the Obama administration spending as a percent of GDP was higher than that of the Reagan administration throughout most of their time in office. Yet as we have already shown in Fig. 41.1, the United States experienced a larger expansion during the Reagan years than the Obama years. The multiplier theory would have predicted the opposite results. What went wrong?

Since this is a controversial issue, taken as gospel by some and as heresy by others, it may be worthwhile to review the conditions under which increased spending does and does not lead to higher aggregate demand. This is best illustrated by an example. Let us say that the government decides to provide free school lunch identical to what the kids were bringing from home every day. Under these circumstances, it is obvious that parents will no longer buy lunch for their children. In that sense, there will be a one for one offset or a substitution effect. Now, the question is, how is the public-school lunch program paid for? If it is through a tax on families with school-aged kids, then the family is effectively paying for the lunch through its taxes. In this case, all we have is the government displacing the private sector. Now if the government is not as efficient and there are collection costs involved, the lunch program will be more expensive. Furthermore, if the government is not as responsive to the kids, the lunch will not be as appetizing. Overall, society will be worse off and there is no net increase in aggregate demand. Now if instead of lunch, the government provides a good that is totally unrelated to current expenditures, some will say public health care to the uninsured, the increase in spending will not be offset since these people do not have any insurance, hence in this case there the government actions

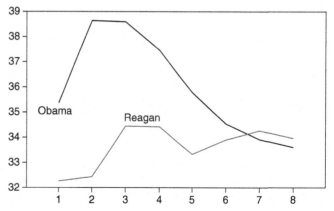

FIGURE 41.9 Government spending as a percent of GDP.

will not affect private sector purchases. However there is still the question of financing the expenditures. Clearly since these people did not purchase the good before, charging them for the cost of the goods will not make them feel better off. In any event, if they get taxed their expenditures will decline. If someone else is taxed, clearly the taxed group's aggregate demand will decline in part offsetting the increase in demand due to government expenditures. In this case the increase in aggregate demand will be less than the increase in government expenditures and the possibility exists that it will be completely offset one for one. Under these conditions the redistribution policies will not increase the economy's net aggregate demand, their only effect will be that of an income redistribution. We know that the Obama administration relaxed the qualification requirement for many of the social safety net programs. Assuming that the bulk of the income redistribution policies take the form of social safety net and nondefense domestic spending, the higher domestic spending as a percent of GDP during the Obama administration (see Fig. 41.10) reflects a higher income redistribution policy that has little or no impact on aggregate demand. This does not mean that the redistribution policy is not desirable or that there are no winners. The beneficiaries of the redistribution policy are clearly better off and that may be what the Obama administration intended.

Not all government spending is geared to income redistribution; one clear example is defense spending. Normally it is justified in the context of a public good and then there is the issue of how much spending is enough. Our answer is that we would rather have one lock too many in our house than one too few. This reasoning may lead to excessive spending. But also to the extent that it is truly a public good, it may also increase aggregate demand. The differences in defense spending across the administration may also explain some of the differences in economic performance. Fig 41.11 shows that the defense spending as a percent of GDP was much higher during the Reagan administration than during the Obama administration.

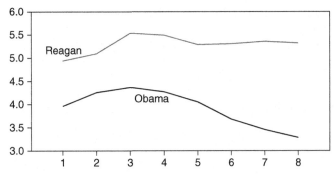

FIGURE 41.11   Defense spending as a percent of GDP.

THE POLITICS OF SPECIAL INTEREST GROUPS

The income and substitution effects or static versus dynamic issue goes beyond the forecast of tax revenues. It has significant implications for the possible effectiveness of spending programs in delivering benefits to the desired target groups, as well as the politics of special interest groups. Targeted spending can in theory be delivered to specific groups or sectors of the economy. In principle, the benefits can be surgically delivered benefiting those we want to help without affecting the rest of the economy. In such a world, government spending could in theory eliminate any undesirable inequality in the distribution of income. While this may very well be the case, it is a static view of the world. If benefits are doled out to a specific group, what makes us think that those who did not benefit would not try to alter the government allocation or that those receiving the benefits would not try to enlarge them. In any event, it is clear that the politics of special interest groups will set up a different dynamic than that implied by the simple static model. That is what political contributions and lobbying set out to do and there is no reason to expect that suddenly people will stop doing so, especially when the degree of government intervention as measured in terms of government spending as a percent of GDP, regulation, and outright nationalization has definitely increased and is poised to increase some more. The politics of special interest groups suggests that rather than diminish, the politicking will increase in the future. The pressure will push Congress and the government to provide what the special interest groups want. In fact, some critics of the stimulus package argued that this is precisely what the package did. It had something for every possible democratic constituency.

The politics of special interest groups also affects the political process in other ways. For example, the trend to remove people from the tax code has accelerated in recent years and we are rapidly approaching the point where there will be more people exempt from paying taxes than those subject to personal income taxes. The

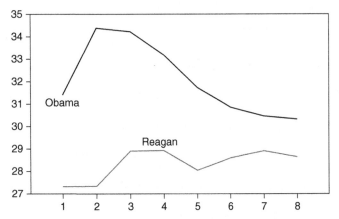

FIGURE 41.10   Non-defense spending as a percent of GDP.

potential dynamic is not pretty. If the static view prevails, the politics of special interest would clearly push for more redistribution of income. The people exempt from tax rolls have the numbers. Now whether they think in terms of static or dynamic terms, ultimately the process will be limited or constrained by dynamic effects. The reason being that the attempts to redistribute the income will reduce incentives for taxpayers to work, save, and invest and that will ultimately reduce the tax base and the take of those who want to redistribute income. In the end, all will be worse off. In conclusion, the politics of redistribution will ultimately end up hurting the whole economy. The question is whether the redistributionists see it that way early on and would be willing to limit their redistribution efforts, as some claim the Clinton administration did early on (i.e., in 1994). If they don't, in time we will all pay. In the short or medium run, they might do okay, but in the end, they will lose and the political process will adopt pro-growth policies.

The underlying analysis for the politics of income redistribution is based on a simple assumption: when an income group improves their well-being, that is increases their real income or net worth, they do not really care that other people make larger or smaller gains. What matters to the different groups is their gains and improvements in well-being. If that is the case, during periods where all groups make income gains, the distribution of income will be a political nonissue. If everyone is making gains, this means that the economic pie is expanding. Is the converse also true?

An expanding economic pie, in principle, allows everyone to get a larger slice and thereby improve their economic well-being. The pie expansion helps explain, in part, the popularity of the Reagan and Clinton administrations. In both cases, after the initial first two years, once the expansion set in and the economy began expanding at a rapid clip and jobs were plentiful, so were the economic opportunities. As a result, the popularity of the two administrations began to rise in spite of a deterioration of the distribution of income. During the Reagan and Clinton administrations, the expansion of the economic pie trumped (no pun intended) the deterioration of the income distribution; everyone was better off.

CLASS WARFARE, THE POLITICS OF REDISTRIBUTION, AND THE SLOW GROWTH TRAP

What happens if the growth is not fast enough to afford a pie expansion for everyone? The groups that are left behind, that is those whose income is not growing, will create pressure groups aimed at influencing policies and legislation to increase their well-being at the expense of another group.

The slower the pace of economic growth, the smaller the chances of the economic pie expanding for everyone, and the greater the likelihood of increased political pressures to adopt redistributionist measures to increase their economic pie. The slow or no growth scenario turns the different groups' income gains into a zero sum game. But that is only the beginning. Such a zero sum game has a dynamic component. To collect revenues to redistribute to the winning groups, regulations and tax rates have to increase to achieve some redistribution favoring the preferred or protected groups. This, in turn, leads to a vicious cycle. To avoid the higher taxes and regulations, the taxed or regulated groups will take actions to minimize the impact of the regulations. These actions require the use of resources that otherwise could have been deployed to increase the economy's output. As a result of the evasion and avoidance, output and the taxable base will be smaller than initially projected, resulting in a revenue shortfall. The zero sum game just turned into a negative sum game.

Then there are the secondary effects. Slower growth produces a shortfall in revenues between the actual and expected revenue collected. The slower growth and revenue shortfall increases the pressure for additional redistribution. If the government caves to these special interest groups, then additional taxes and regulations will be enacted. That will further slow the economy and the vicious cycle will be created.

As the cycle continues, the benefits of redistribution will eventually decline and leading to two possible outcomes. The first possibility more closely resembles the scenario that we foresee. It is one where initially the revenues of the redistribution policies exceed their costs. But as the tax base and the growth rate slow down, the benefits decline and produce a steady state of high taxes and regulations, as well as a slow growth. The slow growth scenario implies a state of constant political pressure to redistribute, tempered only by the lack of incremental revenues. This scenario traps the economy into a slow growth, high redistribution scheme very reminiscent of the European Euroesclerosis situation.

The steady state described in the previous paragraphs is one of repressed equilibrium. It requires constant intervention, or economic repression, depending on which side of the redistribution scheme the groups are. However one important point here is that this equilibrium is not stable without government taxation and regulations. More importantly, economic disturbances have an effect on the equilibrium in so far as they impact the revenue collection and the overall redistribution scheme. Also there is the fact that there is a tendency for revenue collections to erode.

The second possible outcome occurs as people attempt to minimize the impact of taxes and regulations, which induces avoidance and evasion, thereby producing a continuous revenue shortfall. That leads to an additional incremental pressure for higher taxes and regulations resulting in even slower growth. As the process continues, eventually the benefits of redistribution fall below their costs, and at that point there will be a political turning point away from these redistribution policies. A reversal of the taxes and regulations will, at the margin, make every one better off. And as Rick said in Casablanca, that could be the beginning of a beautiful relationship that will beget more reductions and deregulations. We contend that is exactly what happened during the Reagan administration.

At this point a sidebar is necessary. How long the redistribution cycle lasts depends on a number of factors, such as how easy it is to evade or avoid the regulatory and tax burden, the legal structure of the economy, and the protection afforded to the private sector. When the costs exceed the benefits, the cycle ends. It could end abruptly and lead to drastic change. One example is Venezuela, where the implosion is imminent and the cycle appears to have been much shorter. Then there is Cuba, where repression has helped the cycle endure a long time. We are not arguing that the United States is going to become a new Argentina, Venezuela, or Cuba. What we are arguing is that the United States could easily approach a European-style redistributionist state where democracy and the rule of law prevails and the social safety net is very expansive. The price to be paid for such a redistributionist state is nothing more than a strong bout of Euroesclerosis.

The slow growth environment is not unique to the United States. In many ways, it is a global phenomenon and as such it also will have nativist, protectionist, and redistributionist effects in the rest of the world. But the slow growth produced by the increased tax rates and regulations also has another side effect: corruption. The reason for this is simple. If people can convert high-tax income into lower-tax income, be it by moving tax jurisdictions or other means, they will do so as long as the cost of the avoidance is less than the taxes paid. That leaves ample room for corruption. The revelations produced by the "Panama papers" provides an example of the intertwining of the tax avoidance and corruption around the world, as well as the views of the tax collectors.

The Panama Papers provided a trove of information on the activities of individuals involved in tax evasion and money laundering. The uncovering of offshore accounts by officials and executives of different corporations has opened the door for further actions against corporate inversions here in the United States and corporate operations in "tax havens." The EU has been cracking down on companies trying to avoid taxes after the disclosures in 2014 that many multinationals struck deals with countries such as Luxembourg that allowed

them to pay little taxes to the EU bloc. The view of the tax bureaucrats is that the EU lost €50 billion a year in lost revenues. Their view is that the tax revenues were theirs. The EU seems to be intent in taking the next step. Large multinational corporations operating in the EU may have to publish details of profits and tax bills generated in countries considered tax havens. There is another option they have not considered: instead of increasing regulations, how about lowering their tax rates and regulations? That is a lesson that the United States also needs to learn.

A LASTING LEGACY?

Our argument for a transformational administration and a lasting legacy is not the bullish scenario that many people associate with a transformational administration. We believe the redistributionist cycle will continue for many years and it will end when one of two things happen. The natural one will be when the redistributionists run their course and there are no more incremental benefits to redistribute. With the distortions in place as the tax base shrinks, eventually the benefits of redistribution will fall below their economic costs. At that point society will be better off by abandoning the redistributionist policies. Another way the cycle ends is with the election of a charismatic figure, much like Mr. Obama, JFK, and Ronald Reagan, who through sheer force of their personality convinced the country to follow them in a different direction. Clearly the scenario where the redistributionist process runs its course will be longer than one where a disruptor or charismatic leader emerges from the political process.

Our argument for a long-lasting redistributionist cycle and a transformational Obama administration is straightforward. Many of the Obama administration's economic programs and regulations have multiyear implications, some of which have yet to be fully implemented. Once these components of Obamanomics take effect, they will further distort the economy. The increased distortions will reduce the incentives to invest, save, work, and produce and will thereby result in a lower level of GDP. The shrinking pie will increase the redistributionist pressures and the vicious cycle will continue. As the economy slows down, the states' economic pies will also shrink, increasing the pressure for state and local governments to implement redistributionist policies. But that is not all. As the world economy slows down, the redistributionist policies will also result in beggar thy neighbor policies. The point of all this is that we are looking for a vicious cycle where the redistributionist policies will rise and that will beget more redistributionist programs.

SUMMARY AND IMPLICATIONS

President Obama in defending his economic program argued that his opponents were stuck in the failed economic policies of the past that emphasized tax rate cuts, less regulation, and a smaller government with a strong defense. Instead he offered an alternative vision in his inaugural speech; President Obama correctly argued that we should not be concerned about the size of the government per se, rather the focus should be on a government that works. President Obama had a clear vision of what he wanted to accomplish. His policies and initiatives can be described as based on the expansion and enactment of social safety net and income redistribution programs as the potential drivers of an expansion of the public sector. Hence the parallel with FDR.

President Obama was quite successful in implementing his agenda, and now that his time in office has passed, one can compare the economic performance during his time in office with those of a "failed" Reagan administration. Two administrations with diametrically opposed views regarding the role of government, tax rates, and regulation. Equally important is the fact that both administrations faced terrible economic conditions at the beginning of their terms in office. Both overcame these obstacles with varying degree of success and speed of recovery. We contend that such an analysis may help identify the causes and/or drivers for the differential performance between the two administrations as well as provide an explanation for the slow economic recovery in the aftermath of the financial crisis. The lessons learned could be useful to future administrations in either preventing a crisis similar to what both the Reagan and Obama administration faced or suggesting policies that may speed up and or strengthen the economic recovery in case they experience a slow down or recession.

Our interpretation of the data suggests that the lower tax rates and regulations increase incentives to work, save, and invest, and may explain in large part the differential performance during the Reagan and Obama administration. The former lowered tax rates and regulations while the other altered or raised the tax rates. The differences in tax policies generated substitution effects that increased the level of economic activity for the Reagan administration while lowering the incentives for the Obama administration. The tax rate divergences

go a long way to explain the differential performance. We also contend that the defense spending could in fact generate multiplier like effects, given that the Reagan administration increased defense spending as a share of GDP and the Obama administration reduced it.

We found another potential source for the below average recovery during the Obama administration. If as we argue domestic spending is a good proxy for the income redistribution policies of the administration and/or for the provision of goods and services that could be provided by the private sector, no net aggregate demand is expected from this component. However this does not mean that there is no effect. First the beneficiaries of the public services are clearly better off. Second the greater the level of spending, ultimately the higher the marginal tax rates needed to finance the higher spending. No aggregate demand and higher tax rates and regulations is a recipe for slower growth. That is what we mean by the sclerotization of the US economy. While not desirable from a faster economic growth perspective, it is a desirable feature from an income redistribution perspective that may create a lasting legacy for some of the policies of the Obama administration. If in fact the ObamaCare, the student loan programs, and any other income redistribution program initiated by the Obama administration takes on the aspect of an entitlement program, the politics of special interest groups will not only keep the program alive, but also fuel its growth. If unchecked it would first lead to the sclerotization of the US economy, with slow growth and high government spending. As the economy slows, the income redistribution pressure will increase and if unchecked it could evolve into a vicious cycle that will end under two very different conditions. One would be when there is nothing more to redistribute. The other one would be when a candidate emerges that promises and delivers faster economic growth. An expanding pie has the potential to allow everyone to get a bigger slice of the economic pie.

References

[1] Weisman J, Bendavid N. Obama turns up heat, slams GOP ideas. Wall St J, February 6, 2009.
[2] Levitt S, Dubner S., Freakonomics, William Morrow and Co; 2005.
[3] Canto V, Webb R. The effect of state fiscal policy on state relative economic performance. South Econ J July 1987;54(1):120–86.
[4] Puzder A. The minimum wage should be called the Robot Employment Act. Wall St. J, April 4, 2017.

CHAPTER

42

Obamanomics: An Evaluation

The election of Barack Obama as President of the United States was a historic event. Many hoped that he would fulfill his campaign promise and become a transformational figure as opposed to a partisan politician. Yet not everyone shared this view of the president-elect. Some Obama opponents feared that the economic program advocated by then candidate Obama would lead to income redistribution that could degenerate in class warfare. The views and economic platform of candidate Obama had political implications regarding the menu of policy options that he would pursue. To put these views in perspective and the results produced by his economic program, we must contrast them with the economic views, policies enacted, and results produced by the policies of the different administrations during most of the last 8 decades.

Comparing the economic performances of the different administrations is potentially a controversial issue; one must choose a measuring rod by which to compare and measure the performance of the different administrations. Then one has to decide how much of the economic performance during an administration is due to the policies of the previous administrations. In what follows, we make the following simplifying assumption: we hold the administrations responsible for whatever happens under their watch. But we also allow for some of the possible effects of the previous administration policies may have on subsequent administrations by taking into account the initial conditions. We calculate and compare to other administrations, the improvements and/or deterioration of key economic variables that we

use to evaluate the absolute and relative performance of the Obama administration.

WAS PRESIDENT OBAMA DEALT A BAD HAND?

President Obama certainly thinks so. On this issue, here is what he said while campaigning for Senator Harry Reid's reelection.

And let me tell you, when we took office amid the worst economy since the Great Depression, we needed Harry's fighting spirit. We had lost nearly three million jobs during the last six months of 2008. Over 750,000 jobs in January 2009 alone – the consequence of a decade of misguided economic policies; a decade of stagnant wages; a decade of falling incomes.
President Barack H. Obama at UNLV on July 8th, 2010

In this speech, President Obama made the claim that he inherited the worst economy since the Great Depression. It was immensely popular with members of his administration and supporters. His speech suggested that he was dealt a terrible hand. Whether that is true or not depends on the indicator used to define the economy. The president indicated the loss of employment as evidence substantiating his statement. While the loss in employment may have been the largest since the Great Depression, so was the size of the economy at the time. Hence to make comparisons across time, we need to normalize the economic variables. One clear indicator that normalizes for the size of the economy while remaining true to the spirit

Economic Disturbances and Equilibrium in an Integrated Global Economy. http://dx.doi.org/10.1016/B978-0-12-813993-6.00042-8

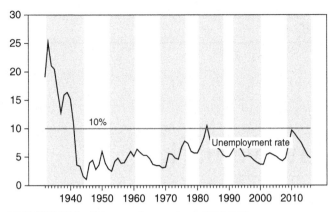

FIGURE 42.1   US unemployment rate 1926–2010.

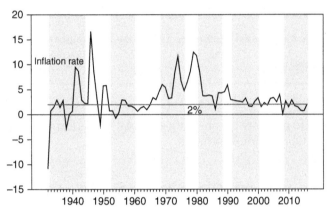

FIGURE 42.2   US inflation rate 1926–2010.

of the president's indicator is the unemployment rate. We are willing to give the president the benefit of the doubt, and his indicator suggests that he is not too far from the truth. Since the Great Depression, the United States has averaged a 10% unemployment rate for a whole year only twice. The unemployment rate averaged 10.8% in 1982 and 10% in 2009 (Fig. 42.1). Looking at the monthly rates, the unemployment rate hit the 10% mark during only three years: 1982, 1983, and 2009. Thus, a literal reading of the data suggests that as far as the unemployment rate is concerned, only President Reagan faced a situation just as bad as or even worse than President Obama. More importantly, the case for who faced the worst economic condition is not as clear cut as President Obama makes it out to be. President Reagan inherited a much higher inflation rate than President Obama (Fig. 42.2).

THE MISERY INDEX

The unemployment rate is too narrow an indicator; a broader and perhaps better measure is the so-called Misery Index, the sum of the unemployment rate and the inflation rate. The Misery Index has been part of the policy landscape for the last 40 years. It is an outgrowth of the Full Employment and Balanced Growth Act of 1978, also known as the Humphrey–Hawkins legislation, which directed the Fed to promote effectively the goals of maximum employment and stable prices. In passing this act, Congress declared that it would monitor the Federal Reserve Board's actions. The Fed chairman was commissioned to testify before Congress each February and July, first to the House Banking Committee, and then followed by the Senate Banking Committee. During the Congressional testimony, the chairman is to set target ranges for various economic variables that depicted growth/unemployment and inflation. The Humphrey–Hawkins legislation expired in the late 1990s. Even though the Fed is no longer required to testify, the semi-annual testimony continues. The Humphrey–Hawkins legislation provides a simple framework from which to evaluate policy initiatives and the economic environment.

During his run for the presidency, President Reagan kept asking the American people whether they were better off than they were four years earlier. The Misery Index was the key indicator cleverly used by his political campaign to answer his rhetorical question. When then-candidate Reagan asked the question, he knew the answer. The Misery Index had deteriorated during the Carter administration. The Reagan campaign successfully cemented the Misery Index as a key indicator for the working people to gage improvements in their well-being.

Now on to President Obama's claim. Viewed from the policy and historical perspective, the Misery Index may provide a better perspective of the economic well-being of the American economy at different points in time during the last century. This broader definition of the well-being of the economy further weakens the president Obama's argument. While the economic situation inherited by President Obama was bad in terms of the Misery Index, we have seen worse at least a couple of times during the post-war era, just look at Fig. 42.3. Again, the data in Fig. 42.3 shows that President Roosevelt, President Carter, and President Reagan confronted worse Misery Indices when they took office. However, as the Misery Index was also higher when President Carter left office, an argument can be made that the Carter administration's policies resulted in an economic deterioration. The index was lower in Roosevelt and Reagan's cases, suggesting that their policies improved economic well-being. The deterioration of the Misery Index disqualifies the Carter administration as a model of a successful economic policy to be compared to the Obama administration.

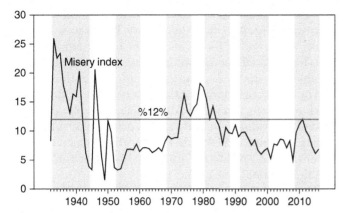

FIGURE 42.3   US Misery Index 1926–2010.

policy differences and how can we benefit from their experiences.

THE RANKING OF THE ECONOMIC PERFORMANCE

The Misery Index while popular as an indicator, is best interpreted as a measure of the economic well-being of labor income. As such it does not provide direct information regarding other factors of production in the economy, that is, the real rate of return on capital. Hence the Misery Index does not provide a complete picture of the changes in economic well-being thus a better indicator or a complement to the Misery Index is needed. One easily obtainable indicator that may be used as a proxy for the economy's rate of return on capital is the rate of change of the stock market. The combination of Misery Index and stock returns not only provides a picture of the economic well-being, it also provides information about the improvements in well-being of labor and capital separately. In turn, these two indicators will allow us to make inferences about the distribution of income between labor and capital, a topic that has become a hot political issue in recent years.

The average performance of the Misery Index, the stock returns during the different administrations as FDR is reported in Table 42.1. The last of the data shows

The Misery Index data suggests a couple of interesting issues. The first one is that President Obama may have overstated his case somewhat. The second one is how does the Obama administration's overall performance stack up against those of the administrations that preceded it, in particular FDR and Reagan's? The third and perhaps more interesting question is whether the divergence in economic performance among the different administration was the result of the policy mixes adopted by those administrations? If the answer is in the affirmative, then what were the

TABLE 42.1   The Misery Index, Stock Returns, and Size Effects During the Different Administrations

President	Term	Party affiliation	Misery Index	Large cap returns	Large cap average returns minus small cap average returns
Herbert C Hoover	1929–1932	Republican	12.5%	−21.2%	6.2%
Franklin D Roosevelt	1933–1944	Democrat	14.3%	14.5%	−13.7%
Harry S Truman	1945–1952	Democrat	8.9%	16.6%	4.9%
Dwight D Eisenhower	1953–1960	Republican	6.3%	16.9%	−0.2%
John F Kennedy	1961–1963	Democrat	6.8%	13.7%	3.8%
Lyndon B Johnson	1963–1968	Democrat	7.6%	10.8%	−18.4%
Richard M Nixon	1969–1974	Republican	11.8%	−2.1%	15.0%
Gerald R Ford	1974–1976	Republican	13.4%	30.5%	−11.3%
James E Carter Jr.	1977–1980	Democrat	17.0%	12.6%	−4.8%
Ronald W Reagan	1981–1988	Republican	10.9%	14.8%	5.0%
George H W Bush	1990–1992	Republican	10.0%	16.6%	4.9%
William J Clinton	1993–2000	Democrat	7.1%	18.2%	7.9%
George W Bush	2001–2008	Republican	7.8%	−0.7%	−5.2%
Barack H Obama	2009–2016	Democrat	8.4%	14.9%	−1.0%
Donald J Trump	2017–	Republican			

that during the Obama administration the Misery Index averaged 8.4% and the stock market gains averaged 14.9%. A respectable performance by any account and President Obama should be proud of the economic accomplishments during his administration.

The administration's performance by itself does not provide answers to a few interesting questions. The first one is how does the Obama economic performance compare to those of other administrations? The second question we find more interesting: Are the differences in performance policy-related? If so what have we learned and how can US policy improve?

One simple way to answer the first question is to look at the rankings of the Obama administration relative to the US administrations going back to FDR. That information is contained in Table 42.2. The data compiled shows that the Obama administration ranks 6 in terms of both categories, the Misery Index and stock returns. Based on these numbers alone, the Obama administration ranks slightly above average when compared to its peers. Not too shabby.

A follow up question of interest is to ask how did the other two administrations that faced a 10% unemployment rate or higher when they took office compares to the Obama administration performance? Earlier when we began our analysis and solely focused on the unemployment rate, we identified four different administrations that had confronted a 10% or worse unemployment

rate: FDR, Carter, Reagan, and Obama. We know from looking at Fig. 42.3 that the Misery Index was in fact higher at the end of the 4 years of the Carter administration. In terms of the overall ranking the data reported in Table 42.1 shows that the Carter administration ranks 14th or dead last in terms of the Misery Index and 10th in terms of the stock returns. All of this makes obvious the answer to the question that President Reagan was asking during his run for the White House. The voters were not better off and President Carter lost his reelection bid to Candidate Ronald Reagan.

The elimination of the Carter administration from the comparison leaves us with two competitors who faced a higher than 10% unemployment rate at the beginning of their terms: FDR and Ronald Reagan. At the time of President Obama's election, the press believed that President Obama could be a transformational president along the lines of FDR. That belief was partly fueled by the philosophical affinity of the policies of the two presidents, hence it is fitting to compare their performance. Notice that FDR ranks 13th in the Misery Index scale and 8th on the stock return scale. In the context of these two indicators, one may be tempted to give the nod to the Obama administration.

The final one-to-one comparison is that of an administration that had a very different perspective and economic orientation: the Reagan administration. In fact, presumably it was the administration that popularized

TABLE 42.2 Misery Index and Stock Returns Rankings

President	Term	Party affiliation	Misery Index	Stock returns	Improvement in Misery Index	Improvement in Stock returns
Herbert C Hoover	1929–1932	Republican	11	14		
Franklin D Roosevelt	1933–1944	Democrat	13	8	11	1
Harry S Truman	1945–1952	Democrat	7	5	2	5
Dwight D Eisenhower	1953–1960	Republican	1	3	4	8
John F Kennedy	1961–1963	Democrat	2	9	6	10
Lyndon B Johnson	1963–1968	Democrat	4	11	9	9
Richard M Nixon	1969–1974	Republican	10	13	13	11
Gerald R Ford	1974–1976	Republican	12	1	10	2
James E Carter Jr.	1977–1980	Democrat	14	10	12	12
Ronald W Reagan	1981–1988	Republican	9	7	1	4
George H W Bush	1990–1992	Republican	8	4	5	6
William J Clinton	1993–2000	Democrat	3	2	3	7
George W Bush	2001–2008	Republican	5	12	8	13
Barack H Obama	2009–2016	Democrat	6	6	7	3
Donald J Trump	2017–	Republican				

the so-called "failed policies" that President Obama railed against. Looking at the data reported in Table 42.1, the Reagan administration is ranked 9th and 7th in terms of the Misery Index and stock returns, respectively. They were slightly below average on the Misery Index and average in terms of the stock returns. Nothing to write home about. Therefore in the context of the average performance, the Obama administration easily beats the close competitors that we identified.

But there is more to this analysis. The average performance of the Misery Index and the stock returns during an administration is a good first step, yet it may not provide an accurate picture. While one may disagree as to whether President Obama was handed the worst economy since the Great Depression, there is a larger point in his statement. Initial conditions matter. In addition to just paying attention to the average performance during the term in office, one should also pay attention to the economic improvements in the average performance generated by the policies enacted by an administration.

IMPROVEMENT OVER THE INITIAL ECONOMIC CONDITIONS

We have calculated the average changes of these two variables during the different administrations and the rankings are also reported in Table 42.1. The data shows that with a 7th place, the gains in the Misery Index are slightly below average while the 3rd place ranking in stock returns gains put the Obama administration well above average. The Obama administration was slightly above average as far as the labor income is concerned and well above average as far as the rate of return on capital is concerned. The results are in line what other economic data, such as the deterioration of the distribution of income experienced during the Obama administration, a slow economic recovery, and a strong stock market.

When all is said and done, one can argue that the Obama policies were average at worst when compared to its peers since the FDR administration. Not only that, the performance compares quite favorably with some of the administrations that faced a higher than 10% unemployment rate. For example, the Carter administration ranks 12th in both the changes to the Misery Index and stocks returns. The combined score puts the Carter administration in a neck-to-neck or virtual tie with the Nixon administration as the worst performers.

The FDR administration ranks 11th as far as improvements in the Misery Index is concerned, suggesting a slow recovery and a slow decline in the unemployment rate. However, as far as the stock returns is concerned, the FDR administration ranks 1st. There is some commonality in these results. Both the FDR and Obama administrations experienced a slow unemployment recovery, suggesting a slow economic recovery and a strong stock returns recovery. The irony of this result should not go unnoticed. Both administrations expanded the social safety net, adopted income redistribution policies, as well as other social and economic policies aimed at improving the lot of the working man. Yet the result reported in Table 42.1 suggests that these policies ended up benefiting capital much more than labor. The result being a deterioration of the distribution of income.

In contrast to the FDR and Obama administrations' results, the Reagan administration ranks 1st as far as improvement in the Misery Index goes and 4th as far as improvement in the stock returns go. These results compare quite favorably with those of the Obama and FDR administrations. More importantly, viewed from the perspective of the two indicators, there is some irony in these results. The Reagan administration, which was supposed to be pro-capital, implemented a neutral policy that did not favor capital or labor. If anything, they tilt a bit toward labor rather than capital.

TRANSFORMATIONAL CHANGE OR TRICKLE UP ECONOMICS

Most people agree that Reaganomics meant low tax rates, strong defense, and a strong dollar. The defeat of the Evil Empire was another major plank of Reaganomics. On domestic spending, Reaganomics did not say much. The Gramm–Rudman–Hollings law defined that the Reagan administration limited spending and remained true to conservative principles. While critics derided the supply-side policies, the lower tax rates delivered the goods. In contrast, President Obama pretty much campaigned on a reversal of Reagan's economic principles. President Obama is quite fond of talking about the failed policies of the past. Perhaps incorrectly, former President Bush's economic policies are linked to those of President Reagan. Thus, it seems reasonable to conclude that a repudiation of the Bush administration led to a repudiation of the Reagan policies. This phenomenon is quite common during political turning points. The perfect example of this is the former Soviet Union satellites. Once they freed themselves, they made a 180 degree turn in economic policies moving away from collectivist, redistributionist, and *dirigiste* policies to free market economics. During the 2008 election cycle, the market debacle led many to question free market capitalism and endorse a greater degree of regulation and government control of the economy, an environment perfect for President Obama's economic views and philosophy.

But were proponents of the Obama administration correct when they attributed the financial crisis to the failures of low tax rates and free market capitalism? What if the administration was wrong in its linking of Bush policies to Reaganomics? In the process of repealing the Bush policies, were Reaganomics components also eliminated? Here we need to give credit and high marks to the Clinton administration, which started going down the path of more government intervention and when defeated at the midterm election, it changed paths and delivered the economic goods. Contrasting that behavior with that of President Bush, we get a much different perspective. Some say that President Bush was stubborn and a big spender. In many ways, the same and more can be said about President Obama. Not only was he a big spender, he was also a big redistributionist and regulator. The budget deficit and other budget considerations did limit the magnitude of the changes President Obama had in mind after suffering a defeat at the midterms. But unlike President Clinton, President Obama doubled down on his policies. The president intensified trickle up economic policies to achieve its objectives faster.

Put together, the different figures suggest that if one is to select an administration for comparison based on the level of the unemployment rate at the beginning of the term and the improvement in the index at the end of the years in office, then the Reagan administration should be the one to compare if one adheres to President Obama's view that they inherited the worst economy since the Great Depression. The Obama administration experienced a slower improvement in the real economy or Misery Index than the Reagan years, while both experienced significant improvements in the stock returns. The question is what accounts for the differences in Misery Index and the similarity in stock returns ranking? Can the fiscal and monetary policy mix explain these rankings? The next few paragraphs give it a try.

If President Obama was a transformational candidate, as some of his supporters believed that he was, his election this could be a turning point not seen since the election of FDR. Especially if the Trump administration turns out to be infective in reversing many of the Obama policies. It is quite possible that we have seen the end in low tax rates for decades to come. Table 42.3 lends support to this view. The crash of 1929 led to a reversal of many of the policies enacted earlier in the decade. We passed incredibly protectionist legislation such as Smoot-Hawley, as well as reversed the Mellon tax rate cuts as a new democratic administration initiated a secular trend of tax rate increases that continued under both Democratic and Republican administrations. Interestingly, it was a Democratic administration, that of JFK, who reversed the secular trend.

In spite of a prolonged economic downturn, the FDR administration remained popular and was able to implement its agenda and FDR became a transformational figure. We now know that some of the policies enacted at the time were responsible for prolonging the economic malaise. Amity Shlaes' book provides an interesting account of the period consistent with our interpretation [1]. Yet FDR's popularity remained very high. We attribute this in large part to FDR's ability of successfully, and perhaps unfairly, blaming the economic failures on the policies of his predecessor. The story here is that as President Bush's personal popularity was hurt, if Obama could shift the blame of any economic malaise to the Bush administration, then he could continue implementing his agenda even as the economy recovered slowly. Yet there is one important point that we need to make. While there is a great difference in the Misery Index performance of the various administrations, the Obama economic performance—as far as the Misery Index was concerned—was either above average or its improvement was slightly below average. On the stock return front, the performance was well above average. So, if people vote their pocket, there was really no compelling reason to change the top of the ticket. Viewed from this perspective, his reelection was consistent with the economic performance delivered by his administration.

An important issue to discuss is the explanation of the differences in results produced by the Reagan and Obama administrations in the context of the economic policy mix pursued by the two administrations. On the fiscal policy side, the differences could not be greater. Regulations and the top marginal tax rates declined during the Reagan administration, while the Obama administration increased the top marginal tax rates (Table 42.3), as well as significantly increasing the regulatory burden. Given our views that the economic agents respond to incentives, we would expect the lower tax rate and lower regulations to unleash the "animal spirits," hence an increase in economic activity is to be expected once the tax rate cuts take effect. The experience of the Reagan administration is consistent with this view. In contrast, even if one assumes that the economy has a tendency toward equilibrium in the aftermath of an adverse shock and thus it would tend to recover; higher tax rates and regulations would slow down the recovery process. Again, this interpretation is consistent with the Obama's slow recovery.

Next let's tackle the valuation and the stock market returns using a simple valuation model that capitalizes the earnings of the economy. The slow recovery implies also a slow rate of increase in corporate profits and, as such, it cannot account for the above average rate of stock market appreciation, which is the above average stock returns. This process of elimination leaves a declining discount factor as the one possible source for a higher valuation. So, the entity that controls the discount factor is in effect the dominant player in the increase in valuation and the higher rate of return and that player is none other than the Federal Reserve. If we are correct that the Fed—and not fiscal policy—is responsible in large part

TABLE 42.3 Top Tax Rates

President	Term	Party affiliation	Year	Personal income (Labor income)	Corporate income	Capital gains
Herbert C Hoover	1929–1932	Republican	1930	25	12	12.5
			1931	63	13.75	12.5
Franklin D Roosevelt	1933–1944	Democrat	1936	78	15	22.5
			1938	78	19	15
			1940	80	31	15
			1941	88	40	25
			1942	88	40	25
			1944	94	40	25
Harry S Truman	1945–1952	Democrat	1946	86.5	38	25
			1948	82.1	38	25
			1950	91	50.75	25
			1951	91	52	26
			1952	91	52	26
Dwight D Eisenhower	1953–1960	Republican	1954	91	52	25
John F Kennedy	1961–1963	Democrat	1963	91	50	25
Lyndon B Johnson	1963–1968	Democrat	1964	70	48	25
			1965	70	48	25
			1967	75.3	52.8	26.9
			1968	77	52.8	27.5
Richard M Nixon	1969–1974	Republican	1969	50	49.2	30.2
			1970	50	48	32.5
			1971	50	48	35
Ronald W Reagan	1981–1988	Republican	1981	50	46	20
			1987	28	34	28
			1988	28	35	28
George H W Bush	1990–1992	Republican	1990	31.9	35	28
William J Clinton	1993–2000	Democrat	1993	40.8	35	28
George W Bush	2001–2008	Republican	2004	36.1	35	15
			2009	35	35	15
Barack H Obama	2009–2016	Democrat	2012	44.6	35	25

for the above average stock returns during the Obama administration, then this result is quite different than during the Reagan period. The Fed, under the leadership of Paul Volcker, changed its operating procedure and switched to a price rule. As the inflation rate was declining, the nominal interest rate topped 15.84% and the real interest rate rose to double digit levels. The discount factor unambiguously increased during the early years of the Reagan administration, yet valuation increased. This means that the denominator of the valuation formula,

that is, earnings and its future earnings expectations, increased by an amount larger than the increase in the discount factor. This is a very different explanation for the increase in valuation than the case of the Obama administration, where we contend that the source was a decline in the discount factor.

Additional evidence in favor of our hypothesis is that for three of the four administrations that faced a better than 10% unemployment rate during their term in office, the small-caps outperformed the larger capitalization stocks. The exception being the Reagan administration. The common elements of the three administrations—FDR, Carter, and Obama—is either the top tax rates increased or the regulatory burden increased. In the past we have argued that the smaller-caps are more adept at inflation hedging, tax avoidance, and regulatory skirting than their large-cap counterparts. For that reason, we argue that in an environment of rising tax rates and an increased regulatory burden, the smaller-cap stocks would outperform. We also know that of the four administrations, only one reduced tax rates and the regulatory burden. It is during this administration that the large cap outperformed as expected (Table 42.1).

Our interpretation of the data suggests that the Obama administration owes a portion of its above average stock market performance to the Fed. But the data also shows that while the Fed may take credit for the valuation increase, its policy failed to generate a normal recovery. Given that we attribute the slow recovery to the fiscal policy side of the equation, we end up with the traditional monetarist conclusion regarding the assignment of policy instruments. Monetary policy should be focused on price stability, while fiscal policy should be focused on the real economy. Interjecting the Fed on the real economy does not add much. In fact, we believe that the expansion of the Fed portfolio has resulted in a policy that has reduced the bank credit creation and that, in turn, contributed to the slow recovery.

Reference

[1] Amity Shlaes. The Forgotten Man: A New History of the Great Depression. Harper Collins; 2007.

SECTION VI

CHINA—A CASE STUDY

43

China in a Global Economy: An Interpretation

In the next few chapters, we explore how the different transmission mechanisms and relationships outlined in the previous chapters facilitate our understanding of a nation's international accounts and some of its key macroeconomic variables. Though we use China as our example, the framework we have outlined should be useful to those who are focused and interested in analyzing, understanding, and anticipating global trends that impact the local economy and the financial markets. To understand where China may be heading monetarily, it is important to understand where it is coming from. For that reason, we focus on China's monetary policy over the last two or three decades.

WEEDING OUT THE WRONG THEORIES

In the process of examining recent monetary experiences, we also illustrate the applicability of the framework that we have developed in the chapters leading up to this point. We begin by making some generalized comments based on some simple macroeconomic relationships. This is a case where the double-entry bookkeeping used in accounting is truly useful.

The accounting relationships help in two different ways. The first one is to identify the possible scenarios and weed out the impossible ones. The second way the accounting relationship helps is that it allows us to weed out *inconsistent* theories. While the double-entry bookkeeping doesn't assure us that we will have the correct view of the world, at least it narrows the choices by

weeding out some of the possibilities leaving only the consistent stories to be considered. A couple of applications will illustrate our point.

THE POSSIBILITIES UNDER A FLOATING EXCHANGE RATE SYSTEM

The National Income and Product Accounts (NIPA) identifies the trade balance (TB) and the capital account (KA) as the two major components of the balance of payments (BOP). In equation form, the accounting identity can be written as:

$$BOP = TB + KA \qquad (43.1)$$

Under the textbook floating exchange rate system, each country uses its own currency in domestic transactions. Hence, there is no net currency flows across national borders and double-entry bookkeeping requires that the BOP be zero at all times. This means that the previous equation can be written as:

$$BOP = 0 = TB + KA \qquad (43.1')$$

Put another way, under a floating exchange rate, the BOP is always zero and that means that the TB and KA are mirror images of each other. This restricts the possible outcomes to two distinct scenarios:

- A trade deficit and a capital inflow
- A trade surplus and a capital outflow

Economic Disturbances and Equilibrium in an Integrated Global Economy. http://dx.doi.org/10.1016/B978-0-12-813993-6.00043-X

The accounting relationship rules out the scenarios where both accounts improve or deteriorate simultaneously. Any theory that posits such an outcome is clearly wrong.

This is a common mistake made in the financial press, where some writers develop a separate TB and capital flow theory. Yet as double-entry bookkeeping of the NIPA shows, only those that simultaneously explain both accounts are feasible theories. Hence, double-entry bookkeeping helps us rule out inconsistent theories, as well as eliminate unlikely scenarios. A second insight derived from the accounting relationship is that Eq.(43.1') allows for only one degree of freedom. Once you specify either the TB or the KA, the other one is determined. They are mirror images of each other. This is an important insight, as it suggests that any TB theory, to be considered a viable theory has to simultaneously explain the capital flows and vice versa. That is a pretty good first step in the development of a framework needed to analyze the global economy and China's journey to becoming a fully functioning reserve currency country (RCC) and not one in name alone.

THE FIXED EXCHANGE RATE SCENARIOS

In general, under a fixed exchange rate system, the non-reserve currency country (NRCC) is burdened with fixing their exchange rates to that of the RCC. That means that the NRCC central bank has to hold an inventory of the RCC currency to accommodate the net flows generated by the TB, capital flows, and liquidity needs of the local economy. One way to view the BOP is that the fixed exchange rate adds on an additional layer of capital flows to that of the floating exchange rate discussion. Under a fixed exchange rate system, domestic residents can bring foreign currency to the central bank and exchange them for local currency.

Essentially, the fixed exchange rate mechanism provides the private sector a way to either reverse (through a capital outflow) or enhance (with a capital inflow) the actions of the domestic central bank. If there is not enough money in the economy and prices begin to fall relative to the rest of the world and/or interest rates begin to rise because of a credit crunch, the private sector will import the foreign currency, bring it to the central bank, and convert it to local currency. Then it could be used either as a transaction medium or as reserves for the banking system. If the local central bank provides too much money, a capital outflow could, in theory, eliminate the excess domestic money creation.

The previous discussion presents a very simple framework to analyze the RCC and NRCC actions. All one needs to do is simply overlay the capital flows generated by the demand for the money needs of the different economies in the floating exchange rate model discussed in the previous section. That gives rise to four possible outcomes:

- One possible scenario includes a TB and a BOP surplus. Under a floating exchange rate, the capital flows would be a mirror image, hence they would net out. Now, as we overlay the demand for money, we can describe the BOP. If there is a shortage of money in the country in question, assuming it is a NRCC, there will be a capital inflow and a BOP surplus. For the RCC, the situation is different. If there is shortage of money and the RCC central bank does not accommodate it, what happens? There will be a worldwide shortage of that currency and that will lead to a change in the price level. Remember, we still believe that inflation is too much money chasing too few goods. Hence, under the RCC scenario, a shortage of money leads to a decline in the underlying inflation rate.

- If the RCC is printing too much money, it will export it to the rest of the world and if the excess persists, the purchasing power of the money will have to change. The RCC will experience a BOP deficit and the world will have a higher inflation rate. For the NRCC countries, the situation is straightforward. If, as the case before, the country has a trade deficit, then the capital inflow will be less than the trade deficit and the country experiences a BOP deficit smaller than before. The lesser amount or BOP deficit results in a reduction in domestic money that is exported as a result of the BOP deficit.

- The third scenario to consider is a BOP surplus combined with a trade surplus. The BOP surplus signals a net import of money. The trade surplus signals a capital outflow. Hence to produce a BOP surplus, there needs to be a capital inflow large enough to offset the TB-related capital outflow and yet leave some positive balances to expand the domestic money supply.

- The fourth scenario to consider is a BOP deficit combined with a trade surplus. The trade surplus signals a capital outflow. Hence the capital inflow cannot be large enough to fully offset the TB-related capital outflow, but small enough to still generate a negative BOP to contract the domestic money supply.

WHERE IS CHINA TODAY?

We know that during the last few years, China experienced a tremendous sustained economic expansion. They have been a net exporter of goods, experienced trade surpluses, and accumulated quite a large amount of international reserves. On the monetary side, China has experimented with a floating exchange rate, then it fixed its exchange rate to the US dollar from 1994–2005, and in 2005 it moved to what can best be described as a managed float.

So far, our discussion has focused on what has been. But things are changing in China. As the press reported, China's TB has been worsening. This may be explained in part for the rise in wealth and the desire by the Chinese to consume and enjoy their new-found wealth. But the increased clout associated with higher wealth does not stop there. As China's stature increases and the economy opens up, questions naturally begin to arise: is China important enough to run its own monetary policy? Is China an important enough player in the world stage? If the answers to these two questions are in the affirmative, then the next question is whether China's policy will be good enough to provide price stability and transparency in such a way that its currency becomes a unit of account and medium of exchange in the rest of the world? The loss of nearly a quarter of the international reserves in a short period of time during the financial turbulence caused the Chinese economy glide to a slower pace of economic expansion and suggests that China may face a few obstacles and difficult choices on its way to becoming the player it wants to be on the international financial scene. Simply put, can China become a true player in international finance by becoming a true and fully functioning RCC in the near future? Obviously, we do not have a definitive answer. However, we do know what is required and what it takes to become one. In the next few chapters, we will outline some of the key determinants, as well as developing a view that allows us to interpret the changes that are going on in China and the world economy in a simple, consistent, and integrated way.

44

China's Wealth, Income, and the Savings Rate: The Complete Markets Case

To develop some insights into the relationship between China's wealth, its savings rate, and its trade balance, we look to the Modigliani and Friedman consumption function theories [1]. In a world with complete markets and perfect mobility, where consumers can borrow and lend, the trade balance and savings rates are simple vehicles that allow households to smooth out their consumption over their lifecycle. Hence, a consumption theory combined with the timing of income realization patterns should be able to explain the behavior of a country's savings rate, trade balance, and real GDP growth. China is no exception. (See the Appendix for Chapter 2 for a summary of the insights developed from the two consumption theories.)

More to the point, the fact that a country, that is, China, is a net borrower or a net lender does not provide any information about that country's level of savings or investments in that country. For example, a country may have a double-digit savings rate, say the highest in the world, and yet be a net borrower. While this situation may seem paradoxical or impossible, it is quite real and common in the emerging markets. The necessary condition is easily met. All that is required is that the country's investment rates exceed the country's savings rate. During the past few decades, China certainly fits this bill. One simple explanation for the scenario we are describing is an economy full of opportunities where income and wealth are rising. If the former rises faster, then the savings rate rises.

Rising wealth relative to income leads to an increase in consumption relative to income level, and that is recorded as a decline in the savings rate. Put another way, when wealth rises relative to income, the capital gains are the key vehicle leading to the increase in wealth. To the extent that there are capital gains, the private sector does not need to save as much money out of current income to reach their long-run target wealth levels. The higher the capital gains, the lower the amount saved, defined here as income less expenditures, and the higher the proportion of current income consumed.

In fact, if the increase is large enough, it is possible that consumption rises and may even exceed the income level. At that point the economy experiences "negative savings" and thus we expect the trade balance to deteriorate. That is what happened in the United States during the 1980s and 1990s, when the housing and stock market rose by double-digit rates on average. The savings rate declined and the trade balance deteriorated. Conversely, a decline in wealth relative to income leads to an increase in the savings rate. Again, that is exactly what happened in the United States in the aftermath of the housing collapse and the tech bursting bubble. The savings rate rose and the trade balance improved.

The point of the discussion in this section is that savings depends on the timing of the changes in wealth and income. This suggests that increases in wealth relative to income lead to a deterioration of the trade balance and a decline in the savings rate.

Economic Disturbances and Equilibrium in an Integrated Global Economy. http://dx.doi.org/10.1016/B978-0-12-813993-6.00044-1

This interpretation works well for the developed markets. However, the theory does not seem to hold when applied to the emerging markets. For example, we know that China is a net exporter and a fast-growing economy. Under normal circumstances, we would expect a fast-growing economy with a rising stock market, that is, our proxy for wealth, to experience deterioration in the trade balance. Until recently, China had not. So the question is whether China is the exception or not. Is our theory wrong or incomplete?

In the next couple of sections, we provide a simple explanation that expands our views. We attribute the results to the lack of well-developed capital markets at the time. The implication is that as capital markets develop over time, the relationship among the different variables in China will approach those of the developed world.

WEALTH, INCOME, AND THE SAVINGS RATE: THE INCOMPLETE MARKETS CASE

The previous section's analysis assumes complete and perfect markets, where individuals are able to borrow and lend based on their lifetime incomes. However, if the individual economic agents cannot borrow, then to optimize consumption in later years, they will have to save and accumulate resources for a rainy day. Once the funds have been accumulated, then the "life cycle" optimization can take place and consumption can be smoothed out. But, before we get to that point, consumers are essentially constrained by their income, not their net worth or expectations of the future. Though their income is rising fast, to acquire consumer durables, these people will have to save. They need to save to put either a full payment or else a hefty down payment on a house, etc.

Over time, credit markets will develop, people will gain access to revolving credit and long-term financing which, in turn, will facilitate the intertemporal optimization that leads to a smoothing of their consumption. For example, if they lose their jobs, they may be able to borrow and keep their consumption levels until they find new work. Absent capital markets, they would be forced to drastically cut their consumption, only to resume it when they find new work. That would clearly be an inferior solution to the one where the consumer can borrow to tide them over. We can now provide a couple of simple explanations as to why, in countries like the United States, we are likely to observe a negative correlation between wealth and the savings rate, while in some of the emerging markets, that is, China, we observe a positive correlation (rapid increases in wealth as well as a high savings rate, well in excess of the domestic investment rates). The reason for the divergence in correlations is that in the emerging economies the ability to borrow against wealth is much lower than in the developed countries.

Given the high growth rate and the income gains made by China during the past few years, as well as the deepening of their capital markets, we expect the capital markets to close the gap. "Incomplete" capital markets, where borrowing and other forms of financing are very expensive and usurious, tend to discourage the development of capital markets and thus lower the discounted value of future income relative to those of the developed world, where better developed capital markets result in a lower discount rate. Hernando de Soto has made a career out of pointing out how poorly defined property rights, lack of title, etc., and creates an informal and cash economy [2]. The lack of proper title does not allow individuals to borrow to expand their business or improve their property. To do so, they have to save or be constrained to operate on a small scale. Once the title/property right issues are developed, capital markets form and growth rates increase.

IMPLICATIONS

Our hypothesis leads to several insights. The first one is that in spite of the high growth and investment rate, emerging nations may have a savings rate that will exceed their domestic investment rate. Put another way, the excess savings over investment will, according to the double-entry bookkeeping of the NIPA, result in a positive trade balance. This is a counter-intuitive result. China, in spite of being a fast-growing country in need of high investment, turns out to be a net lender.

The incomplete capital markets hypothesis suggests that during the early stages of development in the emerging markets, individuals will have much higher savings than in the developed countries. We may call that the incomplete markets savings premium. This leads us to our second insight: as the emerging countries grow and the capital markets develop, the correlation between the savings rate and the trade balance in China and other emerging countries will approach that of the developed countries. Hence, the incremental savings over and above perfect capital markets, that is, the incomplete markets savings premium, will disappear. As the component of the savings rate that was attributable to the incomplete markets disappears, we expect the emerging markets' relationship between the trade balance, savings rate, and real GDP growth to be similar to that of the developed countries. In conclusion, as the net savings rate declines and the capital markets deepen, we expect the trade balance to worsen in the emerging markets.

One important insight derived from this analysis is that as the savings rate declines, we expect the real rate to rise. The development of the capital markets in the emerging world signals the end of the savings glut and quite possibly the beginning of a bear market for US government securities. The emerging markets, in particular China, will be a net borrower. Put another way, China could become a net seller of their international reserves, that is, US government securities.

Unanticipated increases or expected and sustained increases in economic growth that lead to an increase in the net worth-to-GDP ratio should result in a deterioration of the trade balance. Though under the conditions outlined here, the deteriorating trade balance should be a cause for joy, but static thinkers will not see it that way. The deteriorating trade balance raises a warning flag, and protectionist pressures will unambiguously increase. Yet ironically, if successful, the protectionist attempts to improve the trade balance may lead to lower GDP and lower employment. The best example of this type of policy mistake is none other than the Smoot–Hawley tariffs and their impact during the 1930s. Jude Wanniski's book provides an interesting account [3].

If our analysis is correct, as China grows, its trade balance will worsen. Hence, we expect the protectionist pressures in the United States to subside. However, the protectionist pressure may emerge in an unlikely place: China. It will be tough to argue that China is a protectionist country when it is experiencing a trade deficit. In fact, it is the Chinese who will now be able to play the protectionist card. If they do, they will be just as wrong as the US protectionists.

The final point is that if China is successful and becomes a true well-functioning reserve currency country, then China will experience a balance of payments deficit. The reason is that if the rest of the world is going to use the renminbi as international reserves or as currency in circulation, then the rest of the world has to import the currency from China, hence the balance of payments deficit.

Under the scenario that we have been discussing, China will be experiencing a trade deficit as well as a balance of payment deficit. That will clearly change the political debate. It will unambiguously reduce the pressure to punish China for being uncompetitive and currency manipulators. The criticism may be that they are becoming a debtor nation. Another important issue is whether the Chinese officials will be able to stay the course as the balance of payments and trade balance turns to deficits. An Reserve Currency Country (RCC) is a steward of the world economy's monetary stability. Is China ready to play such a role, even if it could?

One final point is that as the net savings rate declines, the economy opens up, and China becomes more transparent, there may be a balance of payments settlement. The difference between the total capital flows and the trade balance-related capital flows is what some may call "hot capital" flows. As we will argue later, these hot flows are in part the net result of monetary policy in the host country relative to the rest of the world. Depending on the host country's central bank policy and/or reaction to the capital flows, the latter could cause large fluctuations in the domestic quantity of money and bank credit creation, thereby affecting local market credit conditions.

APPENDIX TO CHAPTER 2: CONSUMPTION, SAVINGS, AND NET WEALTH

We will begin by focusing on a blend of forward looking corporate finance combined with the traditional consumption theories. The two consumption theories we want to focus on are Franco Modigliani's lifecycle hypothesis and Milton Friedman's permanent income hypothesis. The essence of the Modigliani theory is that in a perfect foresight world, forward looking, rational consumers will match the present value of their consumption to the present value of their income.

Next, Modigliani shows that consumers will like to smooth out their consumption. Hence during the low-income years, that is, early in life and during retirement, they will borrow money, and during the high-income years, they will save money. If one allows for borrowing and lending, in a world with complete markets, the Modigliani theory suggests that people would not be constrained by their individual income in any single year. That is, their consumption does not have to match their income in any given year. The only constraint they need to obey is that of the lifetime expenditures matching lifetime consumption.

There are some general results that can be derived from both theories. For example, an increase in net wealth of $100 results in a permanent increase in consumption of $10 per year. That is, the increase in wealth times the interest rate. Whether the increase in wealth results in an increase in the savings rate depends on the timing of the increase in income. If the increase occurs the first year, the consumer will invest it and have $110 at the end of the year and $10 will be consumed and the rest saved. On the other hand if the $100 comes at the end of the lifespan, the consumer will borrow $10 every year and repay the debt when the $100 is realized.

References

[1] Friedman Milton. A Theory of the Consumption Function. Princeton University Press; 1957. Ando A, Modligliani F. The life-cycle hypothesis of saving: aggregate implications and tests. Am Econ Rev 1963;53:55–84. Modigliani F, Brumberg R. Utility analysis and the consumption function. In: Kurihara K, New Brunswick NJ, editors. In Post-Keynesian Economics. Rutgers University Press; 1954. p. 338–436. Modigliani F, Ando A. Tests of the life-cycle hypothesis of savings. Bull Oxford Univ Inst Econ Stat 1957;19:99–124.

[2] De Soto Hernando. The Other Path: The Invisible Revolution in the Third World. Harper Collins; 1989.

[3] Wanniski Jude. The Way the World Works. New York: Basic Books, Inc; 1978.

45

Examining China: Purchasing Power Parity, Terms of Trade, and Real Exchange Rates

The degree of mobility of goods, services, and the factors of production is a key element of our global framework. At one extreme, we have perfect mobility where the goods and services do not face any transportation costs or other barriers. Under these conditions, the world is a single, integrated economy and a particular commodity has the same dollar price irrespective of the locality where the commodity is transacted. If the price of the commodity, say an orange, in New York is higher than the price in Brazil, then a profit opportunity arises. Someone will have an incentive to buy the orange in Brazil and ship it to New York and arbitrage the difference in price. In the process of doing so, the supply of oranges in Brazil declines, creating upward pressure in the Brazilian market. In turn, the increased supply in New York will lead to a downward pressure. The process continues until the prices are equalized in all localities and the profit opportunities are eliminated. Under the conditions outlined, the world for oranges is a single market and it is determined by the world demand and supply for oranges (the sum of the individual countries' demand for and supply of oranges).

The differences between local demand and supply conditions relative to the other regions determine whether the localities import or export oranges. But

global equilibrium requires that world demand equals world supply, or put another way, equilibrium requires that the sum of the imported oranges adds up to the sum of the exported oranges.

A PURCHASING POWER PARITY WORLD

In a truly integrated world, there is only one world price for the particular commodity. That is, purchasing power parity (PPP) prevails. The dollar price of an orange will be the same irrespective of the locality where it is transacted. If the price of an orange is 50 cents and it costs 4 yuan in China, it then follows that the exchange rate between the dollar and the yuan should be 8 yuan to the dollar. Any other exchange rate would signal an arbitrage or profit opportunity.

One implication of this is that in a world where PPP holds, the law of one price means that the exchange rate appreciation/depreciation will reflect the countries' differential inflation. So, if the yuan depreciates at a 10% rate and the US inflation rate is 2%, it follows that the prevailing Chinese inflation will be 12%. That was roughly the situation in China prior to 1994. The currency depreciation reflected the inflation rate differential. But then, in

Economic Disturbances and Equilibrium in an Integrated Global Economy. http://dx.doi.org/10.1016/B978-0-12-813993-6.00045-3

1994, China pegged its currency to the US dollar and, lo and behold, Chinese inflation converged to that of the United States (Fig. 45.1) just as the PPP theory suggests. Notice the convergence of the inflation rates once the Chinese pegged to the US dollar.

Fixing the exchange rate was a brilliant move. It solved the inflation problem and introduced some transparency into the Chinese economy and, to a large extent, it enhanced property rights. As long as the peg was maintained, the Chinese people knew what the purchasing power of their currency would be. In fact, they knew more than that. They knew that the target decline in their purchasing power would be around 2%, the Fed's inflation rate. Outsourcing its monetary policy to the Fed was a stroke of genius.

NONTRADED GOODS: A VIOLATION OF PPP?

Perfect mobility is not the only possibility considered in our framework. At the other end of the spectrum, we have imperfect immobility across national borders. For the immobile factors or goods and services, the transportation costs across national borders are prohibitive. Hence, these services are never exported or imported, which means that the market clearing conditions are solely determined by local demand and supply conditions. The immobility does not necessarily mean that the goods and services are uncommon. In fact, it is possible that these goods are commonly available in the different economies. Good examples of these nontraded goods are haircuts and houses. They fit the definition of a nontraded good. Transportation costs make it prohibitive for individual consumers to arbitrage differences in haircuts across national borders.

All of this suggests that while haircuts are available in every country, the prices may differ across countries. More importantly, transportation costs may prevent consumers from arbitraging the differences in price. As we already mentioned, under these conditions, the price of

the haircut will be determined by local demand and supply conditions. In contrast, the fully traded commodities that face little or no transportation costs have prices that are determined in the global economy by global demand and supply conditions.

The range of transportation costs suggests that there are varying degrees of price integration across national economies. For the fully integrated commodities, the prices will move in unison, while for the nontraded commodities, the prices may be totally uncorrelated and dependent on local demand and supply conditions. The concept of PPP is the idea behind the Big Mac standard, popularized by *The Economist*. It converts the price in local currency to a dollar price to measure the deviations from PPP across national borders. Hence the closer the dollar prices, the greater the degree of integration, and vice versa.

RATES OF RETURNS AND RELATIVE PRICE DIFFERENTIALS ACROSS NATIONAL ECONOMIES

When world demand for traded commodities exceeds that of world supply, the price of the traded commodity rises relative to other commodities, that is, nontraded commodities. If the increase in demand leads to an excess demand relative to future consumption, the price of current consumption relative to future consumption rises, that is, the real interest rate increases.

Armed with these insights, we can now derive some implications regarding different relative prices across different localities. To begin, during the period in question China's exchange rate was mostly fixed to the US dollar, the PPP framework suggests that the traded goods' inflation rate would be determined by the Fed and the underlying traded goods' inflation should be the same for both countries at all times during the period.

The nontraded goods story is a bit different. Take for example, the episode during the global financial meltdown. At the time, the United States experienced a deep recession, while China's market continued its high and positive rate of growth. Based on the change in relative economic performance between the United States and China, we can argue that relative to the traded commodities, the price of nontraded goods and services declined in the United States, while at the same time the price for the nontraded relative to traded commodities rose in China.

The rate of change of the price of the traded goods will be somewhere in between the inflation rate of the two's (i.e., China and the United States) nontraded goods. That alone suggests that China should have experienced a higher "measured" inflation than the United States. Fig. 45.1 suggests that was the case. Notice that

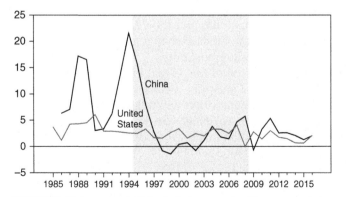

FIGURE 45.1   US and China inflation rates (trailing 12 months).

China's inflation rate steadily rose relative to the United States since the beginning of the millennium, and was higher than the US inflation rate in the aftermath of the US recession.

The differences in inflation rates are attributable to the change in nontraded goods (e.g., housing prices, haircuts, and other services) across the region and their relative weight in the national consumer price index (CPIs). As each national CPI has a domestic component of "nontraded" goods, the ratio of the two countries' CPIs (in a common currency, i.e., the US dollar) captures the changes in the nontraded goods' relative price across national borders. So, we can use the ratio of the two as a proxy for the traded versus nontraded goods arguments.

If we are right, we should see the CPI in the US decline relative to the Chinese CPI, measured in dollars, during recession periods when the housing market and other nontraded goods declined in the United States relative to the price of nontraded goods in China. The data reported in Fig. 45.1 is consistent with this interpretation. More importantly, the decline in nontraded goods will have a larger downward pressure on the CPI in the United States than the nontraded good prices in China will have on the Chinese CPI.

PURCHASING POWER PARITY VERSUS THE TERMS OF TRADE

The final point we want to make is that the ratio of the US CPI to the Chinese CPI in US dollars captures what we have called a change in the terms of trade. The latter measures how much of the traded good one unit of the local or nontraded goods acquire. Hence, the inflation rate differential diverges from the PPP relationship by the amount the relative price change. Put another way, in terms of the Big Mac standard, we expect the price of a Chinese Big Mac to rise relative to the US Big Mac. In fact, the Big Mac approach provides us with a way to separate the PPP effects from the terms of trade effects. Here is a summary of the two effects:

- Under a floating exchange rate system, the PPP effect tells us that any currency's appreciation will, all else the same, lead to a decline in the domestic inflation of the traded goods vis-a-vis the inflation rate of the traded goods in the rest of the world. That is, under PPP, exchange rate fluctuations reflect inflation rate differentials across regions. Under a fixed exchange rate system, the PPP effect tells us that the inflation rate for the traded commodities will converge across countries.
- Violations of PPP may also be reflected in the exchange rate. However, unlike the PPP framework, these changes in the exchange rate reflect terms of trade changes, not inflation differentials. Put

another way, they reflect a differential rate of return across national boundaries. The country with the appreciating real exchange rate will be able to acquire a larger quantity of the traded goods than the one with the depreciating terms of trade. The country with the appreciating terms of trade tends to experience a higher rate of return.

The two distinct effects suggest that investors and policymakers have a signal extraction problem. When they see exchange rate fluctuations, they will have to determine whether the exchange rate reflects a differential inflation rate, as the PPP framework suggests, or real return differentials across national boundaries, as the terms of trade effect suggests.

Fortunately, *The Economist*'s Big Mac standard provides us with an answer. If the exchange rate reflects an inflation differential, that is, a PPP world, the dollar price of the Big Mac in the foreign economy will be the same or move in unison with the price of the Big Mac in dollars. If there are changes in the dollar price of the Chinese Big Mac relative to the United States, then Big Mac prices would reflect a terms of trade change, that is, a change in relative rates of return. Generalizing the Big Mac standard to the overall price level, we get a measure of terms of trade between two economies. The results of such calculations are reported in Fig. 45.2. The data presented suggests a secular upward trend from the 1980s to the millennium. Obviously, there are some cyclical fluctuations around the secular trend, which also suggests that there were some hiccups along the way. Fig. 45.2 also points to a steady deterioration of the US terms of trade vis-a-vis China that began around 2005 and lasted until 2014. It is interesting and ironic, as that is when the pressure began to mount to designate China a currency manipulator. The irony is that during this time period the Chinese maintained a fixed exchange rate period. How could they haven manipulating the currency to gain a competitive advantage? The only way that would

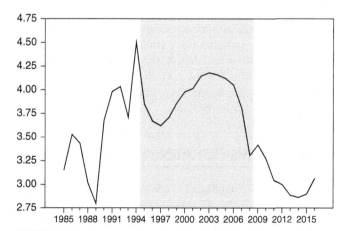

FIGURE 45.2 US–China terms of trade.

make sense if one had evidence that the exchange rate would have appreciated had it been free and reflected the terms of trade. However, as the data show, during that time the US–China terms of trade were deteriorating. That is, a unit of a Chinese goods was able to acquire a larger quantity of US goods. Even with a fixed exchange rate, the US–China terms of trade were adjusting and the adjustment was contrary to what the procurrency manipulators suggested. The US goods were becoming increasingly cheaper to the Chinese. Yet in spite of all this, every year US legislators have proposed some version of a currency manipulation bill. Fortunately, they have yet to be successful.

Nevertheless, there is legislation in place that allows the United States to pursue such actions. The process is a bit complicated. The US Treasury Department, in consultation with the International Monetary Fund (IMF) have to analyze the exchange rate policies of foreign countries on an annual basis. Treasury must decide by April 15 and October 15 whether to label countries like China a currency manipulator in its biannual report to Congress on the currency policies of its trading partners. The reports examine whether countries are manipulating their currency's exchange rate with the US dollar "for purposes of preventing effective balance of payments adjustments or gaining unfair competitive advantage in international trade." Such a designation would not necessarily result in the imposition of any penalties. Currently, the administration has discretion on how to respond to countries seen to be engaging in currency manipulation. However, if manipulation is found, the Treasury Secretary shall "initiate negotiations with such foreign countries on an expedited basis, in the IMF or bilaterally, for the purpose of ensuring that such countries regularly and promptly adjust the rate of exchange between their currencies and the United States dollar." The Secretary of the Treasury "shall not be required to initiate negotiations in cases where such negotiations would have a serious detrimental impact on vital national economic and security interests." In such cases, the secretary must notify leaders of the Senate Banking Committee and the House of Representatives' Financial Services Committee of his decision. Although the legislators have tried almost every year to modify the existing legislation, the modifications legislation has failed to reach the president's desk. During that time, the executive branch has chosen not to designate China a currency manipulator.

WAS CHINA'S CURRENCY OVERVALUED?

Under a fixed exchange rate system, the PPP effect tells us that the inflation rate for the traded commodities will converge across countries. In contrast, the adjustment for the PPP violations is a bit different. As the

exchange rate is fixed and the inflation rates tend to converge, the terms of trade effect, that is, the relative price change of nontraded relative to traded goods, leads to deviations in the domestic inflation rate from the PPP rate. As we already mentioned and showed in Fig. 45.1, the countries with the fastest growth rate will experience a higher increase in the relative price of nontraded goods and thus a deviation in an above trend increase in the inflation rate.

The slower growing country will experience a below trend increase in the inflation rate. The differential inflation rate then reflects the terms of trade changes. Applying the Big Mac standard, we expect the dollar price of China's consumer basket, that is, CPI, to rise relative to the US basket. Fig. 45.2 shows that how many units of the Chinese consumer basket that one unit of the US consumer basket bought over the years. The data show that the US terms of trade steadily improved and peaked around the 1990s. As then the trend has been a downward one. This means that one unit of a Chinese nontraded goods steadily bought an increasing larger amount of the traded goods relative to the US counterparts. Fig. 45.3 plots the terms of trade and nominal exchange rates. A close inspection of the two series shows the close parallel between the two as the fixed exchange rate period. Prior to that, the nominal exchange rate rose much faster than the terms of trade, which we attribute to the higher inflation rate differential between the two countries. Since 1995, Chinese monetary policy during the fixed exchange rate period induced a convergence to the US inflation rate and, to the credit of the Chinese central bank, they have maintained the low-inflation rate policy (see Fig. 45.1).

The terms of trade adjustment are not unique to China and the dollar adjusted CPI ratio is not the only way to measure it. Take the case of the euro. Member countries also have a fixed exchange rate system. Hence, terms of trade changes cannot be accommodated by changes in

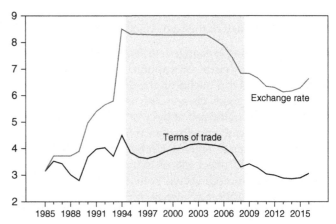

FIGURE 45.3 The nominal exchange rate and the US–China terms of trade.

the exchange rate. The terms of trade effects have to be accommodated by changes in domestic prices and/or production costs. This may be reflected in many different ways. For example, since the inception of the euro, up to 2015, unit labor costs in Germany have increased by single digits, somewhere around 6%. Yet during the same time, Greece's unit labor costs have risen by more than 40%. This means that during that time, Germany's competitive position has improved by 34%. Had the euro not existed, the mark would have appreciated 34% against the drachma. Put another way, with the same nominal production costs, German producers will have much higher profits and/or rate of return than Greek producers.

This example illustrates a simple point: markets have enough flexibility to accommodate relative price changes. Which prices change to accommodate or affect the relative price changes depends on the organization of the monetary system. Under a floating exchange rate combined with a domestic price rule, the exchange rate will reflect the relative price changes. Under a fixed exchange rate, domestic prices and unit labor costs have to change to reflect the relative price or terms of trade change.

Those politicians who argue that the Chinese or any other currencies fixed to the dollar are manipulating their currency to gain an unfair advantage are wrong. China's currency is not overvalued by some 27%, as the protectionists say. The domestic prices and unit labor costs have already accounted for the terms of trade effect and, in doing so, they restored and maintain the true market-driven relative price, not an artificial one, as the critics of the then-China fixed exchange rate argued. At the time we argued that it was possible that China's exchange rate would rise if its currency was floated, but we also argued that would be a reflection of a good monetary policy. Judging from the Chinese inflation, the answer must be that prior to the Chinese slowdown, the central bank did a pretty good job. We will discuss this topic further in a later chapter.

46

Examining China: Economic Growth, Exchange Rates, and Relative Stock Performance

Up to this point, enough relationships between the household net worth versus the trade balance as a percent of GDP and real GDP versus employment growth have been accumulated. So far, we have provided a parsimonious explanation for the various relationships, and that is good, as it suggests that our theory, at the very least, has a great deal of explanatory power. In this section, we will further test the explanatory power of our views, as we extend the analysis to the relationship between these variables and the foreign exchange value of the dollar, and stock market relative performance.

A TALE OF TWO COUNTRIES

Under a floating exchange rate system, a trade deficit means a capital inflow or borrowing from their trading partners in the rest of the world. For developed countries, pundits worry that a country with a trade deficit means the country is living beyond its means and that its best days are behind, or that the country is eating its way into the poorhouse. If that was the case, we would expect to see the market anticipate this and decline relative to the rest of the world whenever the trade balance worsens. The implication here is clear: it predicts a positive relationship

between trade deficits and the stock market and real GDP growth rate relative to the rest of the world. In other words, a deteriorating trade balance signals a slower future growth and a declining relative stock market valuation.

There is, however, another alternative interpretation: if the reason for the borrowing is that there are great investment opportunities and that investors can take advantage of these opportunities by borrowing. Put another way, better days are ahead of the country with the trade deficit. The higher future return allows the country to pay for the amount borrowed without sacrificing current consumption. The higher investment returns attract capital and, as the market anticipates the higher returns, valuations will rise. The country will outperform the rest of the world. Hence, not only local investors, but also foreign investors, will want to take advantage of the opportunities in the economy with the trade deficit. Advocates of the "better days ahead" alternative theory predict a negative relationship between the trade balance and the stock market's relative performance. A deteriorating trade balance means that the future looks brighter. The country is borrowing from abroad to invest at home, where it can earn a higher rate of return and increase the level of production.

Economic Disturbances and Equilibrium in an Integrated Global Economy. http://dx.doi.org/10.1016/B978-0-12-813993-6.00046-5

ARE THERE MORE THAN TWO TALES?

The previous scenarios are not the only ones. Implicitly, the two examples assume a shift in aggregate demand. In the first case, the country is borrowing to finance current consumption. In the second case, it is borrowing to finance additional investment that will result in a higher level of output and wealth. But these are not the only possibilities. So far, we have ignored impacts of supply shifts on the overall macroeconomic equilibrium conditions.

Let's consider the mirror image of the country living beyond its means. It would be the case of a country living below its means, or a thrifty country that is saving at a higher rate to provide for the future. In this case, we should also observe the mirror image of the profligate country that is consuming beyond its means. We should observe a positive trade balance associated with higher growth and a rising net worth and/or stock market.

Let's consider the case of an increase in the country's productivity, modeled as an outward shift in the economy's aggregate supply curve. If the country is large enough, the world aggregate supply of goods will increase relative to its supply. That will have several effects on the global economy. First, to restore equilibrium, the relative price of current goods and services relative to future goods will decline. This means the real interest rates have to decline. In addition to the lower world prices, the increased production will crowd out other producers with higher costs. The consumers of these goods will be better off, as they will be buying the same goods at a cheaper price. The losers here will be the higher cost producers. As the rest of the world produces less and consumes more, it follows that the country experiencing the productivity gains will become a net exporter.

The story does not end here. The country with the productivity gains is now a lower cost producer, it follows that the rest of the world's investors will attempt to move production to the lower cost producer to maximize its gains, and the country will experience a capital inflow. Depending on the organization of the monetary system, the central bank will accumulate foreign/international reserves.

Now let's see how the domestic consumers and producers fare. We have already established that the producers will increase their profits as a result of the productivity. Competition will induce them to pay higher wages, so workers' income will also increase. Higher profits and higher income means that the aggregate demand and domestic consumption will increase. But the increase will not be large enough to absorb the increase in production. The country becomes a net exporter, incomes rise, and the market valuation increases. In this case, the relationship between the trade balance and real GDP growth, as well as the relationship between the trade balance and the local stock market will be a positive one.

One question that immediately comes to mind is how realistic or possible is this alternative. The answer is that it is quite likely if the country is not too strict with intellectual property rights and has a large mostly agricultural labor force that worked at a subsistence level. By "borrowing" or importing the technology from abroad, and moving some of the workers to the city, large productivity gains could be generated in a short period of time. Furthermore, these gains can go on for a long period of time.

Think of it this way, a little over a century ago in the United States, over 90% of the population worked in the agricultural sector, while currently less 3% work in agriculture. The migration from the farms to the cities was largely to the result of an increase in productivity that allowed the United States to increase its production of agricultural goods, while freeing labor to migrate to the city and increase its manufacturing base. One way to think of it is that, on average, the migration amounted to 1% of the population moving from the countryside to the cities. Apply that to China and we can see why the Chinese miracle has gone on for so long. Furthermore, given the parallels with the United States, 1% of the Chinese population migrating to the cities means that China will have to build something on the order of one city like Chicago and New York City every year.

Now, returning to the initial question in this section, we conclude that there are two tales for the demand shocks and two tales for the supply shock. Consider the cases of a demand and supply shocks where the economy borrows because there are great investment opportunities. Another way to frame the tales is focusing on the nature of the shocks. Aggregate demand shocks and better investment opportunities will induce a negative relationship between the trade balance and the country's relative GDP growth and stock market returns relative to the rest of the world. In contrast, an aggregate supply shock with better investment opportunities will induce a positive relationship between the trade balance and the real GDP growth and stock returns relative to the rest of the world.

WHICH TALE IS THE RELEVANT ONE?

The relationship between the trade balance as a percent of GDP, a country's relative stock market performance and relative real GDP growth allows us to discriminate between the competing hypotheses. Fig. 46.1 shows that there is a distinct and clear positive relationship between the current account as a percent of GDP and the relative stock market performance measured by

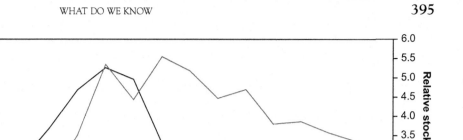

FIGURE 46.1   China current account as a percent of GDP (stock market as a percent of the world index).

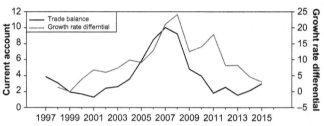

FIGURE 46.2   China current account as a percent of GDP versus China–US growth rate differential.

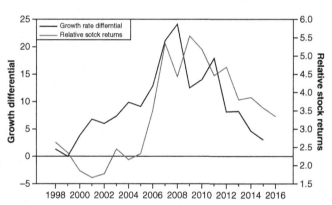

FIGURE 46.3   China US growth rate differential versus relative stock returns.

the MSCI returns of the Chinese stock index relative to the world index.

To close the circle, we need to discuss the relationship between real GDP growth and the different variables. We argued that as economic opportunities improve, capital will flow into the country and that, in turn, will result in a net increase in the demand for the yuan. As a result, we expect to observe a positive relationship between real GDP growth and the trade balance. As expected, that is the case (Fig. 46.2). Finally, due to the improving investment opportunities, the country will experience an increased capital inflow, a net accumulation of international reserves and an improving relative stock

market returns. Fig. 46.3 presents some clear evidence. An improving relative GDP growth rate in China's favor leads to an improvement in value of the Chinese stock market index relative to the world stock market index.

In China's case, this relationship among the macroeconomic variables lends support to the view that an aggregate supply shift due to a productivity increase is at the heart of the Chinese economic expansion.

CAN CURRENCY MANIPULATION AFFECT THE TRADE BALANCE?

One final relationship to be discussed in this section is that of the trade balance and the foreign exchange value of a country currency. While it may be true that a "cheaper dollar" may improve the trade balance, that may not be a desirable outcome if all of the relationships identified in this section hold-up. An improvement in the trade balance due to a weaker yuan may signal an economic slowdown, higher unemployment, a capital outflow, or a lower relative stock market. All of this suggests that attempts to manipulate the currency and lower its value, if successful, will end up hurting the economy. It would be a major mistake for the Chinese authorities to attempt to depreciate its currency.

In turn, if our interpretation is correct, then an appreciating currency is a bullish sign. It's a sign of an improving stock market relative to the rest of the world, of a higher relative growth rate, as well as an improvement in employment conditions, all good and bullish signs.

WHAT DO WE KNOW

Knowing the nature of the shocks allows one to determine whether governments are pursuing policies consistent with their objectives. For example, a deliberate devaluation will only result in an increase in the inflation rate differential and will not affect a country's terms of trade or trade balance. The analyses presented here points to the danger of using the trade balance as an indicator of competitiveness or economic well-being. The relationship between the trade balance and the real GDP growth rate and the trade balance and the stock market depends on the nature of the macroeconomic shock or disturbances affecting the economy. An aggregate demand increase and an aggregate supply increase both lead to a rising stock market and a rising output level. But their effects on the trade balances are mirror images of each other. That is the peril of using the trade balance as an economic indicator. We must also specify the nature of the shock. Our analysis shows that a trade deficit resulting from an aggregate demand shock is a bullish and welcome economic shock as is a trade surplus caused by an aggregate supply shift. In contrast, a trade improvement caused by an aggregate demand shift and a trade deficit during an aggregate supply shock are both bearish outcomes.

The evidence shows that these relationships are intertwined and depend, in part, on the nature of the shock. However, the point we wish to make here is that attempting to control one of the variables will also affect the equilibrium level of the other variables. This is useful to investors, for they can set up strategies to take advantages of the collateral impact of the direct policy responses. For the policymakers, knowing that there are collateral effects suggests that they need to take an approach that focuses on the overall economic environment.

Examining China: Monetary Policy, Inflation Potential, and the Organization of the Monetary System Under a Floating Exchange Rate System

When it comes to monetary policy and inflation, we are quite fond of making two complementary statements. The first one is that we believe that inflation is a monetary phenomenon—too much money chasing too few goods. Hence, to get a sense of the inflation rate outlook, all we need to determine is the growth rate of the monetary aggregates relative to the demand for these aggregates. The second statement that we are also fond of making when discussing monetary matters is that the organization of the monetary system determines the inflation potential of an economy. The reason for this is that the organization of the monetary system may impose some constraints and rules that can, under some circumstances, limit the rate of growth of the monetary aggregates. Hence, if we know these rules, we can determine the inflation potential of a monetary arrangement. These two simple concepts go a long way to explain a country's inflation rate, the behavior of its monetary aggregates, and international reserves.

China is no exception. In fact, during its floating exchange rate period, China was almost a perfect textbook example of a floating exchange rate. The analysis of a floating exchange rate traditionally assumes that the country in question only uses its domestic currency for transaction purposes and that the rest of the world does not use the local currency in their transactions.

That appears to be the case in China before the Chinese decided to fix their exchange rate to the US dollar. The lack of use of foreign currencies at home is easily attributable to legal tender requirements where the authorities made it difficult, and in some cases illegal, to use foreign currencies. The use abroad is much more pedestrian. Foreigners had no use for the Chinese currency—a currency that was very difficult to take out of the country—outside of China.

Given the regulatory apparatus, the Chinese had a great deal of control over the monetary aggregates. If one is willing to go that far, then it seems reasonable to assume that the Chinese central bank controlled these aggregates. At the very least, it controlled exactly the narrowest of the aggregates, the monetary base.

As we already mentioned, the textbook representation assumes that the central bank controls the quantity of money precisely and that the local currency is used only in the local economy. That is, the demand for the local currency is determined solely by local factors. If inflation is too much money chasing too few goods, inflation will be observed when the money growth/creation by the monetary authorities exceeds the growth in the demand for money. Viewed this way, one can see that there is no limit to the inflation potential of this economy. Fig. 47.1 presents evidence in support of the monetarist

Economic Disturbances and Equilibrium in an Integrated Global Economy. http://dx.doi.org/10.1016/B978-0-12-813993-6.00047-7

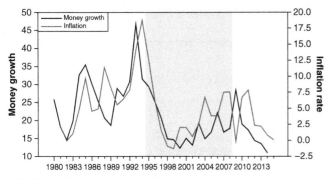

FIGURE 47.1   China's inflation and money growth rates.

proposition under the conditions outlined in this section. The money growth is closely correlated to the Chinese inflation rate.

We have not specified a mechanism that may limit the central bank money creation process, which could evolve into a hyperinflation if unchecked. Monetarists who advocate a floating exchange rate argue that central banks should keep the monetary growth rate at a constant rate that approximates the country's underlying growth rate. The assumption is that the growth rate is a proxy for the demand for money and that, over the long term, if the money grows at the real GDP growth, the money demand and supply will be in balance and there will be no excess inflation. The constant money growth at the rate of real GDP will, in the long run, produce price stability. The only problem will be in the short term, over the business cycle, when real GDP deviates from its long-run trend.

Political pressures may force the central bank to abandon the constant money growth. If the central bank sticks to the quantity rule, then the inflation rate will deviate from trend, and that may not be politically acceptable. But doing so leads to a countercyclical inflation rate. During periods of rapid growth, all else the same, the demand for money will rise and that would lead to a decline in the underlying inflation rate. In contrast, during periods of economic decline, the demand for money will fall relative to the constant growth in money supply and that will lead to a rise in the underlying inflation rate. Under an inflation targeting regime, the central bank would then reduce the quantity of money to keep the inflation rate constant.

Notice that this is the opposite of what Keynesians believe. The countercyclical response could get into trouble if unanticipated shifts in the demand for money occur. For example, during periods of rising inflation, people may switch to other currencies or other commodities, and that will reduce the demand for money and lead to an even higher inflation. Also, budgetary pressures may force the central bank to abandon the constant money growth rule. Once the central bank departs from the strict quantity rule, there is no real constraint that

may prevent the excess demand from steadily rising. Whether it is because the demand for money is less than forecast, or because of budgetary issues, the central bank is forced to print money in excess of the target rate due to budgetary and/or political reasons.

The bottom line here is that there is no constraint or limit on how high the inflation rate can go under a floating exchange rate system. At that point, only a crisis brings about an abrupt change in the organization of the monetary system. On the other hand, as we will argue later on, the adoption of a price rule or fixed exchange rate amounts to the Chinese central bank outsourcing its monetary policy. The results of these experiments were quite remarkable and in line with the purchasing power parity (PPP) view of the world. Once the fixed rate system was implemented, from 1995 on, China's inflation rate collapsed and converged to that of the United States (Fig. 47.1).

CHINA'S MONETARY POLICY AND THE FLOATING EXCHANGE RATE EXPERIENCE

In spite of the presumed control over the monetary aggregates, the outcome in China was not a pleasant one. As shown in Fig. 47.1, during the early 1990s, the inflation rate accelerated and peaked at around 25%. One is hard pressed to justify such a high inflation rate. Either the Chinese did not exert complete control over the demand for money, or budgetary pressures forced the central bank to print too much money. Either way, the inflation rate exploded. We can see that the year-over-year growth rate in the monetary aggregate also rose to better than 30% during most of the first half of the 1990s.

The monetary data certainly fits the view that inflation was too much money chasing too few goods. Under a floating exchange rate, when China's inflation rate was in the double-digit range and the rest of the world (i.e., most of China's trading partners) was experiencing single digit inflation rates, PPP theory would suggest that China's currency depreciated against the rest of the world. It did. In 1990, it took 4.96 yuan to get a dollar. By 1994, it took 8.51 yuan (Fig. 47.2). That is a 71.6%

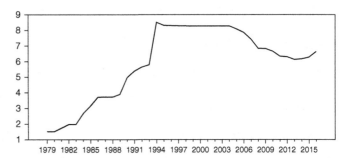

FIGURE 47.2   Yuan/dollar exchange rate.

depreciation over 4 years or approximately 17.6% per year. The yuan's annual depreciation roughly matches the growth in China's monetary aggregate.

THE CENTRAL BANK REACTION TO THE FLOATING EXCHANGE RATE EXPERIENCE

China experienced an annual double-digit excess money creation, inflation during the 1990–94 time periods. The Chinese experience also shows that under the floating exchange rate, the excess money growth less the US inflation rate does a pretty good job of explaining the yuan's fluctuations (Fig. 47.3). The close fit between the two variables in Fig. 47.3 during the floating exchange rate is consistent with the PPP view of the world.

If inflation is an undesirable outcome, it should not surprise anyone that the Chinese authorities reacted to

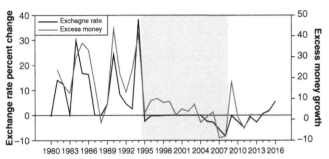

FIGURE 47.3   Yuan/dollar exchange rate fluctuations versus the Chinese money growth net of China GDP growth and US inflation.

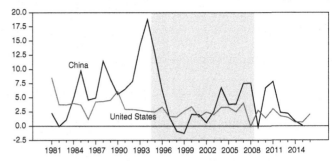

FIGURE 47.4   China and US inflation rates.

the deteriorating monetary situation and rising inflation rate. However, the big surprise was the action they took. They fixed China's exchange rate to the US dollar. The floating exchange rate experience shows that even in a command performance economy, the central bank has a tough time controlling the underlying inflation rate.

Under a fixed exchange rate system, in absence of transportation costs, the dollar price of freely traded goods and services will be the same across the world. Also, if the broadly defined transportation costs are constant, the rate of change of the dollar price of the traded commodities will be the same across localities. The implication is fairly clear: by fixing the exchange rate to the US dollar, the traded goods' inflation rate in China had to converge to that of the US dollar. If tradable goods make up the bulk of the price index, one would expect to see the Chinese inflation rate converge to that of the US inflation rate. The data reported in Fig. 47.4 shows that is the case. PPP is the proper framework to evaluate and analyze the Chinese inflation and exchange rates policies.

Examining China: Monetary Policy, Inflation Potential, and the Organization of the Monetary System Under a Fixed Exchange Rate System

When it comes to monetary policy and inflation, we are quite fond of making two complementary assertions, under a fixed exchange rate system, absent transportation costs, the dollar price of freely traded goods and services will be the same across the world. Also if the broadly defined transportation costs are constant, the rate of change of the dollar price of the traded commodities will be the same across localities. The implication is fairly clear: by fixing the exchange rate to the US dollar, the traded goods inflation rate in the two countries has to converge. Thus the convergence and inflation potential is determined by the organization of the monetary system. That is, the intervention mechanism specified by the way the countries fix their exchange rate determines the system's inflation potential. In the next few paragraphs, we discuss the two basic organizational forms from which most exchange rate mechanisms emanate:

- Countries erroneously worried that the nominal value of their exchange rate hurting their trade balance would try to prevent their exchange rate from appreciating vis-a-vis the rest of the world. If every country attempted to prevent their currency from appreciating, then every time they observe an incipient appreciation, the domestic central bank would increase the domestic money supply to prevent the currency from appreciating. As currency appreciation under purchasing power parity (PPP) measures relative inflation, it follows that the country with the highest inflation rate will have the weakest currency and, as such, it would set the world inflation rate. Preventing the currency from appreciating would cede the determination of the inflation rate to the most expansive central bank in the world economy. Under these circumstances, the most inflationary central bank would set the world inflation rate. Hence the weakest currency forces everyone to react.

- Countries worried about their inflation rate will try to prevent their currencies from depreciating relative to the currencies with stable inflation. If every country did this and prevented their currency from depreciating, it follows that the least expansionary central bank would set the tone for worldwide inflation. In this case, the strongest currency forces every country to react and adjust their inflation rate to prevent exchange rate depreciation.

THE RCC AND NRCC COUNTRIES

Combining the two previous intervention mechanisms gives rise to the reserve currency country (RCC) approach where one country, the nonreserve currency country (NRCC), fixes its exchange rate to that of the other country, the RCC. The NRCC has to intervene on both sides of the exchange rate fluctuations, to prevent an appreciation and depreciation of its currency relative to that of the RCC. The fixed exchange rate and PPP requires that the two countries' inflation rate of traded goods converge. More importantly, as the NRCC is the country doing the adjustment, by fixing its exchange rate, it is importing the RCC's inflation rate.

One question that immediately comes to mind as we discuss China during its period of a fixed exchange rate to the US dollar is why? An obvious answer is that it was more expedient, faster, and cheaper for China to outsource its monetary policy to a country with a better monetary policy. But what guarantee did China have that the United States would do the right thing? There was none, other than the fact that China was free to unhinge from the dollar whenever it suited China. Why the dollar? The answer was that, historically, reserve currency countries have provided an above-average monetary policy where the purchasing power of their currency has held up better than most countries in the world. In addition to being a store of value, the currency also becomes a unit of account and a medium of exchange.

Finally, how can the rest of the world tell or be assured that this was going to continue being the case? The answer lies in the organization of the monetary system. If the RCC is disciplined, it may also be subject to a price rule. While China and other NRCCs fix to the RCC's currency, the RCC may be forced to guarantee the value of its currency one way or another.

England did this when it fixed its currency to the price of gold. When gold rose above the price, it sent a signal to the central bank to reduce the quantity of money. It did so through open market operations. It sold gold and that reduced the quantity of money in circulation. The United Kingdom fixed its currency to the price of gold without a significant amount of gold. How did England do this? To acquire the gold, it sold bonds in the open market and with the proceeds it bought gold that was then sold. In the process, the amount of currency circulating in the economy was reduced. Gold was the instrument used to perform an open market operation.

In modern times, instead of the price of gold, some central banks, including the US Federal Reserve, have used the domestic price level as an indicator. When the price level rises above the target level or target inflation rate, the Fed reduces the quantity of money through open market operations. Similarly, when there is too little money and the price level falls below the target rate, the Fed increases the quantity of money circulating in the economy by buying bonds with newly minted cash. Fig. 48.1 shows that since Paul Volcker changed the Fed operating procedures in 1979, the inflation rate gradually converged to the target range and for the most part it

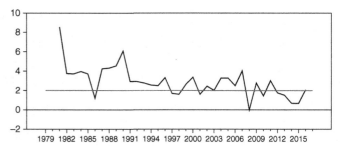

FIGURE 48.1   The US inflation rate.

appears that the United States has adhered to the domestic price rule that targets a 2% inflation rate.

In conclusion, in a world where most commodities are internationally traded, arbitrage ensures that the dollar price of each commodity will be the same in each and every locality. In such a world, when the NRCC fixes its exchange rate to that of the RCC, it will be outsourcing its monetary policy and importing the RCC inflation rate. In turn, if the RCC follows a domestic price rule or targets an inflation rate, the RCC can deliver price stability or low inflation for the local economy and the world as a whole.

CHINA'S MONETARY POLICY AND THE FIXED-RATE EXPERIENCE

In 1994, facing a double-digit inflation rate, China altered its exchange rate and monetary policy and switched from a floating exchange rate regime to a fixed exchange rate system. The fixed exchange rate regime ended in 2005, and since then the yuan has gradually appreciated. It now takes less yuan to acquire a dollar than it did during the fixed-rate period (Fig. 48.2).

In effect, the intervention mechanism that resulted in the fixing of the exchange rate assured China and the rest of the world that the Chinese inflation rate would not be different from that of the United States. Essentially, by fixing its exchange rate, China, the NRCC, outsourced its monetary policy to that of the United States, the RCC. As previously mentioned, the intervention mechanism

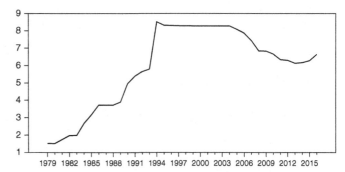

FIGURE 48.2   The yuan-dollar exchange rate.

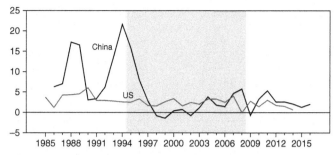

FIGURE 48.3   China and US inflation rates.

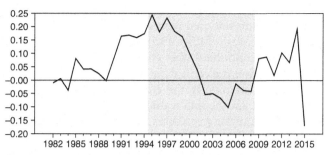

FIGURE 48.5   China balance of payments as a percent of GDP.

effectively resulted in the NRCC country, China, adopting the RCC country's inflation rate. The inflation rate collapsed and converged to that of the United States (Fig. 48.3).

The convertibility produced additional benefits to the Chinese economy. As long as the convertibility was maintained, the Chinese people and the rest of the world would know that the yuan would buy as much as a dollar. So as long as there was confidence in the stability of the purchasing power of the dollar, people would have confidence in the yuan.

The fixed exchange rate mechanism introduced a transparency to the Chinese economy. The decline in inflation expectations and other improvements in the economy led to a significant increase in the demand for money. The surge in money demand allowed the Chinese central bank to increase the domestic money supply without suffering any inflationary consequences and/or exchange rate depreciation pressures.

Fig. 48.4 shows the sustained double-digit growth of the domestic quantity of money even though the country experienced a decline in its inflation rate to the single digits. That was a win/win situation or what economists call a "free lunch." By fixing the exchange rate, inflation fell and the central bank transferred the power to conduct open market operations to the private sector. If there was not enough yuan circulating in the Chinese economy, the people could bring dollars to the

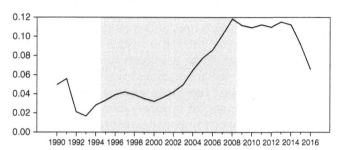

FIGURE 48.6   International reserves held by China central bank as a percent of the Chinese money supply.

Chinese central bank and exchange them for the legal tender. This is precisely what happened to China shortly after it fixed its exchange rate; the balance of payment surplus (Fig. 48.5) added to the central bank's international reserves (Fig. 48.6). In turn, the convertibility and increased reserves effectively forced the central bank to automatically accommodate the increased demand for money. In so far as the Chinese monetary authorities were timid or tight, the inflow of reserves would be the major mechanism effecting an increase in the money supply. This is precisely what happened early on during the fixed-rate period. As China grew and the demand for money increased, the balance of payment surpluses added to the international reserves and accommodated an increase in the domestic money supply.

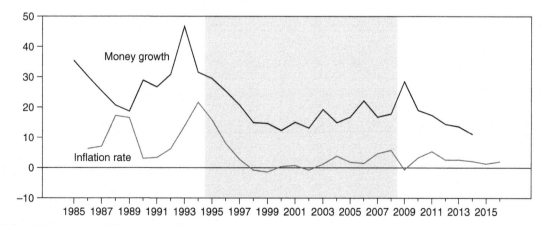

FIGURE 48.4   Inflation rate and the growth in the quantity of money.

Notice also that the backing of the domestic money in terms of international reserves also increased during the fixed-rate period (Fig. 48.6). As long as the Chinese central bank honored the convertibility, it must be pointed out that the central bank was not entitled to the reserves. It was merely the custodian, for if the situation changed and people wanted to reduce the quantity of money circulating in China, the balance of payment flows would reverse. This is precisely what happened during the 2015–16 stock market worries about the slowing Chinese economy. There was a significant outflow of capital, and China lost about a quarter of its reserves in the span of a few months.

If the central bank is not entitled to the reserves, then what are they entitled to? The answer is that all they are entitled is the seigniorage or interest gained from being the custodian of the international reserves. But there were other benefits: the increased certainty, transparency, and lengthening of investors' horizons produced by the fixed exchange rate made investments in China very attractive to not only the rest of the world, but also to domestic residents. The fixed exchange rate fueled a tremendous expansion of the Chinese economy. This is one scenario where monetary policy has a positive effect on the economy and market valuations. The Chinese were smart enough to seize the opportunity and thus reaped the benefits.

Looking forward, the data in Fig. 48.6 shows something quite interesting. In the period immediately following the unhinging of the fixed exchange rate system, the international reserves backing the Chinese money supply stopped rising and began to move sideways with a slight downward drift which may have accelerated during China's slowdown to a more modest real GDP growth rate. Fig. 48.4 also shows a deceleration of the growth in the quantity of M1. All of this suggests that the decline in the international reserves and the domestic money creation by the Chinese central bank have contributed to a slowdown of the growth in the quantity of

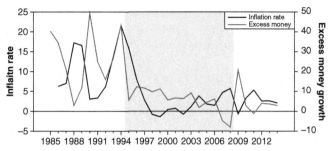

FIGURE 48.7 China's inflation rate versus the Chinese money growth net of China GDP growth.

M1 circulating in the Chinese economy. Yet this result combined with the yuan appreciation during the early part of the managed float (Fig. 48.2) appears to be at odds with the fact that the Chinese inflation was a bit higher than the United States (Fig. 48.3).

The international reserves and the Chinese central bank only account for the supply side of the monetary equilibrium. The demand side also has something to say about the overall equilibrium. Earlier we produced a crude estimate of the excess supply of money in China. It consisted of the growth in the quantity of M1 less the Chinese GDP growth rate. The estimate was quite useful in explaining the fluctuations in the nominal exchange rate. Fig. 48.7 shows that the excess money supply also does a reasonable job of explaining the Chinese inflation rate. The exception being the spikes in the two series, which we interpret as unanticipated shocks in the excess demand for money. The correlation was predicted by the monetarist view. Hence, we do have a simple explanation for China's monetary experience during the managed float period. The final issue to address is whether China will improve on the system they have or will the Chinese monetary authorities regress to the old days? The data does not reassure us that China is on the right path. Whether it becomes a true and effective RCC remains to be seen.

49

Examining China: China as a Nonreserve Currency Country

China's central bank has been accused of many things by its detractors. Some US senators and even presidential candidates have accused China, we think unfairly, of being a currency manipulator. Yet, as we look back in time and focus on the data, we find that during its fixed exchange rate period, China's central bank has shown a clear understanding of the role of a nonreserve currency country (NRCC). It is as if the Chinese central bankers had been at the University of Chicago when Nobel Laureate Robert Mundell and the late Harry G. Johnson were developing the "Monetary Approach to the Balance of Payments." If there ever was a textbook case, China is it [1]. Let's see why.

THE FIXED EXCHANGE RATE MECHANISM LINK TO THE DOMESTIC MONEY SUPPLY

Under a fixed exchange rate, the NRCC has to insure that its exchange rate is fixed to the reserve currency country (RCC) at all times. The NRRC stands ready to buy or sell any amount of the foreign exchange at the exchange rate price. This is an important component of the organization of the monetary arrangement, as it transfers the power to conduct open market operations to the private sector. A shortage of money in China will lead to

an appreciation of the yuan in the marketplace, say from 8 yuan to the dollar to 7 yuan to the dollar. This example creates an arbitrage opportunity. Chinese and non-Chinese investors will bring dollars to the central bank and get 8 yuan to the dollar and then go out and buy a dollar with 7 yuan's in the open market. The arbitrageurs will make a 1 yuan profit. However, in doing so, they have increased the Chinese money supply by $1, or at the official exchange rate, 8 yuan. As long as the free market is different than the official rate, investors will continue bringing the dollars to the central bank. In the process, they increase the domestic supply of yuan and the central bank increases its international reserve holdings, that is, its dollar reserves. The increased supply of yuan relative to the dollar leads to a depreciation of the dollar/yuan exchange rate. Put another way, the exchange rate approaches the 8 yuan to the dollar exchange rate. When it reaches 8, there is no more profit opportunity and equilibrium is restored.

The NRCC fixed exchange rate mechanism affords the private sector the opportunity to conduct open market operation. The private sector can affect a change in the domestic money supply as well as a corresponding change in the international reserve holdings of the central bank. An increase in international reserves is registered as a balance of payment (BOP) surplus and a reduction in the international reserves is registered as a BOP deficit.

Economic Disturbances and Equilibrium in an Integrated Global Economy. http://dx.doi.org/10.1016/B978-0-12-813993-6.00049-0

THE LIMITS TO THE CENTRAL BANK'S MONEY CREATION ABILITY

If the Chinese central bank does not print any local currency, then the only way that the monetary base increases is if the private sector brings dollars to the central bank and converts them to yuan. In this extreme case, increases to the monetary base consist solely of the BOP surplus that the country is experiencing. The stock of monetary base consists of the stock of international reserves.

The private sector is not the only source of money creation. The central bank can also create or print money. However, the money creation ability of the central bank is not unlimited. If the central bank prints too much money, the private sector can reverse it, by simply bringing the yuan to the central bank and demanding dollars. This will be registered as a BOPs deficit, a reduction in the bank international reserves, and a corresponding reduction in the monetary base. Again, in the extreme case that the central bank prints too much money, it is possible that the bank will have zero or little international reserves. In that extreme case, the monetary base will consist solely of domestically printed yuan or what we will term "domestic credit creation."

DOMESTIC CREDIT CREATION: TOO LOOSE OR TOO TIGHT

The key point of the previous section is that the domestic monetary base is endogenously determined. If the Chinese central bank prints too much money, that is, is too loose, China will experience a BOPs deficit and the fixed exchange rate mechanism will force it to reduce its monetary base. On the other hand, if it prints too little money, that is, too tight, it will experience a BOP surplus that will force it to print additional yuans.

As the monetary base is endogenously determined, the Chinese central bank has no control over the magnitude of the monetary base. All they have control over is the composition of the monetary base. If it prints too many yuans, the BOPs deficit will reduce the international reserve holdings of the central bank. If it prints too little, there will be capital inflows and an increase in the international reserve holdings that will force the central bank to print additional yuans. Hence, by looking at the proportion of the money backed by international reserves, we can get a sense as to whether the Chinese central bank has been too loose or too tight.

Fig. 49.1 shows the ratio of international reserves held by China's central bank to the Chinese M1. One can see that while it has slowed down and even declined in recent years, the ratio of reserves to the monetary base

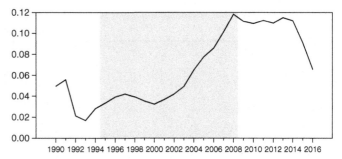

FIGURE 49.1 International reserves held by China central bank as a percent of the Chinese money supply.

has steadily increased during the first decade of the millennium. The NRCC fixed exchange rate mechanism, combined with the rising international reserves, means that over the time the reserves were rising, the Chinese monetary policy became increasingly tighter. The tight monetary policy has had several effects. One was the decline in the ratio of domestic, high-powered money creation. This is an important point because under a floating exchange rate system, a tight monetary policy would lead to a currency appreciation and lower domestic prices and/or inflation rate. If anything, this data suggests that the Chinese central bankers were quite hawkish on inflation during the fixed exchange rate period.

THE BALANCE OF PAYMENTS

The international reserves held by the central bank are nothing more than the cumulative sum of the BOPs. So, the fact that China's international reserves steadily increased in absolute terms and relative to the monetary base during the fixed exchange rate period means that the private sector had to take action and import money to provide what was considered the optimal amount of money given China's inflation rate and real GDP growth rates as a result of the tight-monetary policy during the period. Is there more explicit evidence? How did the equilibrating process work? Well there is some evidence that fits our interpretation of the data. Yet before we present it, we need to take care of some theoretical issues associated with the RCC and NRCC models.

In previous paragraphs, we have shown that the RCC sets the global inflation rate. It determines the purchasing power of its currency. Hence, that component of money demand is exogenous to the NRCC. We also know that the RCC determines the global amount of dollars in circulation. So, the question is how are the incremental dollars allocated across regions? The answer is simple. If everyone grew at an average rate, the dollars would be distributed proportionately to their size. Therefore those who grow above average will tend to accumulate international reserves, while those who grow at a

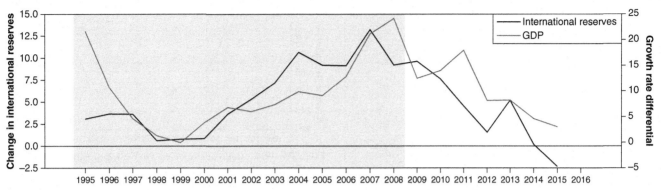

FIGURE 49.2 Change in international reserves as a percent of GDP versus the China–US GDP growth rate differential.

below average rate will experience a loss of international reserves. Furthermore, those with an improving growth rate will experience an improvement in their BOPs. This is a testable implication. Fig. 49.2 shows that as the adoption of the fixed exchange rate mechanism, the change in international reserves, that is, the BOPs, have behaved as expected. When China's relative growth rate improved, so did the change in international reserves or BOP. When China's relative growth rate deteriorated, so did the changes in international reserves or BOP.

DOMESTIC CREDIT CREATION AND HOT CAPITAL FLOWS

One issue of great importance in the NRCC economies is hot capital flows. According to street lore, these money flows that travel around the world looking for higher rates of returns are quite fickle and tend to come and go abruptly. Even worse, if unchecked under the NRCC exchange rate mechanism, the capital flows result in an expansion of the monetary base, which, all else the same, leads to an increase in the domestic money supply. All of this brings us to the issue of whether these capital flows can be destabilizing and create speculative bubbles in an NRCC economy. If they do, what can the central bank do to ameliorate or temper these effects?

We do not believe the central banks are without tools to combat the credit expansion induced by capital inflows or asset bubbles. While we do not distinguish between hot or normal capital flows (we do not know how), we all can agree that both types of flows result in changes in a NRCC's BOPs, and thus the stock of international reserves held by the central bank. We have already mentioned that the Chinese central bank was quite timid, if not tight, on the issuance of domestic high-powered money not backed up by international reserves during the fixed exchange rate period. In fact, Fig. 49.1 shows that, over time, the ratio of international reserves to the M1 base steadily increased. The increased ratio meant

that a larger component is due to the action of private agents who bring their dollars to the central bank and convert them into yuan.

The inflow of international reserves allowed the banks to expand the quantity of money through its creation of domestic deposits under a fractional reserve banking system. The logic is simple. Under a 10% reserve requirement, 1 yuan would create a maximum of 10 yuans worth deposits. As the deposits denote a liability to the banking system, under a double-entry bookkeeping, the asset side must also match. The bank's assets consist of 1 yuan worth of bank reserves and 9 yuans worth of loans. The credit creation is equivalent to the amounts of deposits less the reserves held by the banks.

The previous calculations illustrate an important point. The banking system creates the credit, but the supply of the credit is determined by the amount of reserves and the effective reserve requirement imposed on the deposits. Absent government regulations, one would expect the quantity of money and credit to grow at the same rate. One would not expect to find any changes to the money multiplier. However, to the extent that the ratio of the credit creation to the money creation changes, it reflects either a government regulation (i.e., tinkering with the reserve requirements) or differential growth in the demand for credit and money. The latter is the domain of the private sector and depends on a multitude of factors that we are not going to discuss at this time. The important point is that by paying attention to the credit to deposit ratio, we may identify any differential impact on the two markets and with a little luck, we may be able to discern the source of the differential performance.

Looking at Fig. 49.3, it is evident that the ratio of credit-to-deposits steadily decreased during the fixed exchange rate period. This result is quite interesting, especially for those who worry that capital flows could result in an excessive credit creation. First, if the reduction in credit-to-deposits is part of the private sector equilibrating process, this is a reassuring outcome. The market automatically

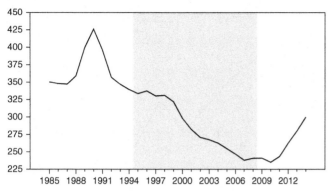

FIGURE 49.3   Ratio of bank credit to bank deposits.

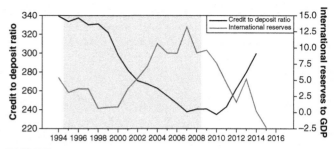

FIGURE 49.4   Ratio of bank credit to bank deposits versus change in international reserves as a percent of GDP.

adjusts to deliver the results desired by the private sector. This makes a lot of sense. If, as we have assumed, under a fixed exchange rate system the private sector initiates open market operations, it will increase or reduce the quantity of international reserves held by the central bank and all else the same, that expands the monetary base and quantity of money. The second explanation is that the Chinese monetary authorities marginally increased the reserve requirements of the banks, thereby reducing the credit creation ability relative to the deposit creation ability of the banks.

Other interesting details are also evident in Fig. 49.4. Notice a divergence between the two series around 2008. The data suggest that during that time the credit created by the banking system increased relative to the deposits created. Hence, from 2008 going forward, the money multiplier has risen in China. Put another way, China's domestic credit per yuan worth of reserves increased during this time. To the extent, that the ratio of international reserves to the monetary base also rose, it allows us to rule out hot capital flows as a source of the credit easing. Looking at Fig. 49.4, it is apparent that during the 2008–14 time period that the rate of increase in international reserves declined, it still remained positive even though the credit creation per yuan was declining. This means that the international reserves were growing throughout this time and thus we can rule out the hot capital outflows theory. However, this leads us to another question: if not hot capital flows, then what?

Our answer is simple and we have already hinted at it: central banks can also affect the domestic credit creation of the banks through moral suasion and reserve requirement increases. And we know that China's authorities have a great deal of moral suasion. Increases in the credit creation have to be allowed by the Chinese monetary authorities. During the bubble years, the Chinese monetary authorities reduced the credit creation ability of the financial institutions in China. The credit multiplier declined steadily throughout the period. This does not mean that credit declined. During that time, the monetary base was expanding. All it means is that the amount of credit produced by each yuan's worth of reserves was reduced as the central bank raised its reserve requirements.

It is evident to us that China's monetary authority has the tools to regulate the domestic credit creation ability of the banks and it does with gusto when it deems appropriate. Viewed this way, it is not the hot capital flows that caused China to change its banks credit creation ability. The surge in the credit multiplier may be attributable to Chinese concerns about the slowdown in the global economy and their desires to keep their economy expanding at a rapid pace. However, the possibility remains that China may overdo it. If it does, its inflation rate will begin to increase, the exchange rate will depreciate, and the international reserves may decline as a result of a capital outflow. The next few years will tell us if we were correct in believing that China made a mistake in abandoning its fixed exchange rate system.

GRADING CHINA'S PERFORMANCE AS A NRCC

The evidence presented here shows that China's monetary authorities have taken enough steps to perform as an above-average NRCC. First, during the fixed exchange rate period, by being relatively restrictive in the creation of domestic monetary base, the Chinese monetary authorities created a shortage of domestic money and that forced the private sector to import currencies and bring it to the central bank to exchange for yuans. The inflow of dollars was registered as a BOPs surplus. In the process, the central bank built up its holding of international reserves. The fact that China steadily increased its reserves and that the reserves as a proportion of the monetary base have steadily risen is our evidence that China pursued a "tight" domestic money creation policy during the fixed exchange rate period.

Given the imported inflation rate, determined by the RCC's central bank, China had the amount of money needed by the economy to function properly. More importantly, the money was created by the private sector through the BOPs. As we deem inflation to be too much money chasing too few goods, it follows that absent the international reserves inflow and under a floating exchange rate, the noninternational component of the monetary base would not have been enough to satisfy the economy's money demand. Under a floating exchange rate, the shortage of money would have, all else the same, resulted in a decline in the underlying inflation rate and an appreciation of the exchange rate. For those who equate the nominal exchange rate with the terms of trade, these would be the opposite of what a currency manipulator would do.

If one believes that the nominal exchange rate affects the terms of trade, China's action would have produced a rising currency and therefore a deterioration of its trade balance. The one point where the critics of China's exchange rate policy were correct was that if China allowed its currency to float, all else the same, it will appreciate. So far, that was the case under the early days of the managed float. What these critics missed was that the appreciation is due to the tight-monetary policy that the Chinese monetary authorities have pursued as fixing the exchange rate. The tight policy has resulted in a monumental accumulation of international reserves. That is precisely the mechanism by which the private sector forces the central bank to print more domestic currency. And the central bank is assured that any money creation is precisely what the private sector wants. If the central bank did not have the right money creation under a fixed exchange rate system, the private sector would take care of it. It had the power to reduce or increase the quantity of money through a BOP deficit. In turn, under a floating exchange rate system, all the private sector can do is alter the purchasing power of the money to achieve the desired level of real balances, that is, the inflation rate. In the process, as the purchasing power of the money adjusts, so will the exchange rate. Under a managed float, an excessive monetary policy would lead to a combination of the two. Higher inflation and a capital outflow translates into a loss of reserves. This is precisely what has been happening during the last couple of years. The yuan has depreciated and it now takes more yuans to get a dollar (Fig. 49.5). Additionally, China has lost some of its international reserves (Fig. 49.1).

During the fixed exchange rate period, the Chinese monetary authorities were also mindful of the credit market conditions. They were quite active in raising reserve requirements of financial institutions and, in so doing, they reduced the deposit and credit creation abilities of these institutions. China's monetary authorities have been quite active. Deciding whether or not allowing the recent expansion of credit was a wise policy decision is hard to argue against, given the central bank's track record. We feel the central bank made a mistake, but time will tell if they were right or wrong.

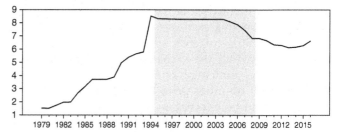

FIGURE 49.5 The yuan–dollar exchange rate.

Looking back in time, it seems to us that the Chinese monetary authorities have been very shrewd and quite active when they had to be. They have also been fairly conservatives and smart. They outsourced their monetary policy and gained instant credibility and transparency. That was the right move at the right time. They have also been quite active at regulating the financial institutions' credit creation ability. At a time when the Maestro was talking about irrational exuberance and did nothing, China's monetary authorities raised the reserve requirements of the banks and restricted banks' domestic credit creation as a percent of GDP. Greenspan could have learned a thing or two about monetary policy from the Chinese.

Contrary to the perception in the press, China ran a very conservative monetary policy. Its domestic credit creation was been minimal. That, in turn, forced to the private sector to import money to increase the domestic monetary base. As a result of these policies, China experienced consistent BOP surpluses and accumulated a huge amount of international reserves over time.

Under a floating exchange rate system, the "tight" domestic creation would have resulted in a decline in the inflation rate and, quite possibly, deflation, as well as an appreciation of its exchange rate. The fixed exchange rate appreciation provoked the ire of protectionists in the United States who confuse the nominal exchange rate with the terms of trade. These people correctly believed that if allowed to, the Chinese yuan would appreciate, as it did during the early stages of the managed float. Where they went wrong was that they also believe that the rising currency would lead to a decrease in the price of imports and an increase in the price of exports. Put another way, a change in the terms of trade. It is apparent to us that these people either do not subscribe to the *Economist* or if they do, they have forgotten about the *Economist's* Big Mac calculation where the price of a Big Mac in local currency is converted to dollars and compared to that of a Big Mac in the United States.

The Economist's calculation illustrates a simple point. If the dollar price is the same across borders, purchasing power parity holds. In that case, the domestic price changed to offset any change in the exchange rate. That is the point the protectionists are missing in the case of

China. While it is true that the Chinese monetary policies under a floating exchange rate system would have resulted in a 26% currency appreciation, as the critics argue, the fact that the exchange rate remained fixed eliminated the exchange rate as a price adjustment mechanism. If no other price changed, then the terms of trade would be affected as the protectionists argue. However, if other prices change, then the Big Mac standard may still hold. Since the beginning of 1994, around the time China fixed its exchange rate to 2005, China's domestic prices relative to the US's prices rose about 25%. The exchange rate adjustment that the protectionists were expecting had already been effected. Domestic prices, nontraded goods in China in particular, increased enough to result in an approximated cumulative excess inflation rate of approximately 25%. The floating of the exchange rate would have only changed which variable would have been affected—the exchange rate instead of domestic prices—yet the outcome would have been the same. While the Chinese may be unfair competitors, the fixing of the exchange rate does not prove that they are currency manipulators. In fact, the data presented here suggests that they behaved like a textbook NRCC. And if we had to give them a grade, it would have to be an A+.

Being a successful NRCC does not mean that they will be a successful RCC. However, the fact that they have mastered their domestic and international monetary aspects gives China a chance to become a successful reserve currency country if they do in fact become one.

Reference

[1] Johnson HG. The monetary theory of balance-of-payments policies. In: Frenkel JA, Johnson HG, editors. The monetary approach to the balance of payments; 1976. London: Allen and Unwin, Toronto: University of Toronto Press. Mundell RA. Monetary Theory: Inflation, Interest, and Growth in the World Economy. Goodyear; 1971.

Index

Printed in the United States
By Bookmasters